EDUCATIONAL EVALUATION: NEW ROLES, NEW MEANS

Officers of the Society
1968-69
(Term of office expires March 1 of the year indicated.)

JOHN I. GOODLAD
(1969)
University of California, Los Angeles, California

ROBERT J. HAVIGHURST
(1971)
University of Chicago, Chicago, Illinois

W. C. KVARACEUS
(1970)
Clark University, Worcester, Massachusetts

HERMAN G. RICHEY
(Ex-officio)
University of Chicago, Chicago, Illinois

RUTH M. STRANG
(1971)
Ontario Institute for Studies in Education
Toronto, Ontario, Canada

RALPH W. TYLER
(1970)
Director Emeritus
Center for Advanced Study in the Behavioral Sciences
Stanford, California

PAUL A. WITTY
(1969)
Northwestern University, Evanston, Illinois

Secretary-Treasurer

HERMAN G. RICHEY
5835 Kimbark Avenue, Chicago, Illinois 60637

ii

EDUCATIONAL EVALUATION: NEW ROLES, NEW MEANS

The Sixty-eighth Yearbook of the
National Society for the Study of Education

PART II

By
THE YEARBOOK COMMITTEE
and
ASSOCIATED CONTRIBUTORS

Edited by

RALPH W. TYLER

Editor for the Society

HERMAN G. RICHEY

19  69

Distributed by THE UNIVERSITY OF CHICAGO PRESS • CHICAGO, ILLINOIS 60637

The responsibilities of the Board of Directors of the National Society for the Study of Education in the case of yearbooks prepared by the Society's committees are (1) to select the subjects to be investigated, (2) to appoint committees calculated in their personnel to insure consideration of all significant points of view, (3) to provide appropriate subsidies for necessary expenses, (4) to publish and distribute the committees' reports, and (5) to arrange for their discussion at the annual meeting.

The responsibility of the Society's editor is to prepare the submitted manuscripts for publication in accordance with the principles and regulations approved by the Board of Directors.

Neither the Board of Directors, nor the Society's editor, nor the Society is responsible for the conclusions reached or the opinions expressed by the Society's yearbook committees.

Published 1969 by

THE NATIONAL SOCIETY FOR THE STUDY OF EDUCATION

5835 Kimbark Avenue, Chicago, Illinois 60637

Copyright, 1969, by HERMAN G. RICHEY, Secretary

The National Society for the Study of Education

First Printing, 10,000 Copies

Printed in the United States of America

The Society's Committee on Educational Evaluation

BENJAMIN S. BLOOM
Professor of Education
University of Chicago
Chicago, Illinois

MARION D. JENKINSON
Faculty of Education
University of Alberta
Edmonton, Alberta, Canada

JACK C. MERWIN
Assistant Dean and
Professor of Educational Psychology
University of Minnesota
Minneapolis, Minnesota

ROBERT E. STAKE
Associate Director
Center for Instructional Research and Curriculum Evaluation
University of Illinois
Urbana, Illinois

RALPH W. TYLER
(Chairman)
Director Emeritus
Center for Advanced Study in the Behavioral Sciences
Stanford, California

Associated Contributors

RALPH F. BERDIE
Professor of Psychology and
Director of Student Life Studies
University of Minnesota
Minneapolis, Minnesota

v

97874

ASSOCIATED CONTRIBUTORS

HENRY M. BRICKELL

*Professor of Education and
Associate Dean for Research and Development
Indiana University
Bloomington, Indiana*

RICHARD C. COX

*Associate Professor
University of Pittsburgh
Pittsburgh, Pennsylvania*

TERRY DENNY

*Director
Research Office of the Educational
Products Information Exchange Institute
University of Illinois
Urbana, Illinois*

JOHN C. FLANAGAN

*Director
American Institutes of Research
Palo Alto, California*

JOHN K. HEMPHILL

*Director
Far West Laboratory for Educational
Research and Development
Berkeley, California*

TORSTEN HUSÉN

*Professor of Education and
Head of Institute of Educational Research
University of Stockholm
Stockholm, Sweden*

E. F. LINDQUIST

*Professor of Education and
Director of Iowa Testing Programs
University of Iowa
Iowa City, Iowa*

C. M. LINDVALL

Professor of Education
University of Pittsburgh
Pittsburgh, Pennsylvania

MALCOLM PROVUS

Director of Research
Pittsburgh Public Schools
Pittsburgh, Pennsylvania

JOHN M. STALNAKER

President
National Merit Scholarship Corporation
Evanston, Illinois

HERBERT A. THELEN

Professor of Education
University of Chicago
Chicago, Illinois

DEAN K. WHITLA

Director
Office of Tests
Harvard University
Cambridge, Massachusetts

FRANK B. WOMER

Professor of Education
University of Michigan and
Staff Director
Committee on Assessing the Progress of Education
Ann Arbor, Michigan

Editor's Preface

Since the publication of its first yearbook in 1902, the National Society has brought out seven volumes directly related to the problems of measurement and evaluation, and a considerable number of its other yearbooks have dealt with such problems in relation to various aspects of education.

Beginning with its earlier volumes, *The Measurement of Educational Products* (1918) and *Intelligence Tests and Their Uses* (1922) and extending through *The Impact of School Testing Programs* (1963), the Society has been fortunate in numbering among its contributors such leaders in the field as Thorndike, Courtis, Trabue, Starch, Whipple, Terman, Pitner, Thurstone, Brownell, Gates, Tyler, and Findley.

During 1965, the Board of Directors examined the past publications of the Society that dealt with measurement and studied the feasibility of and the need for bringing out a yearbook which would deal in some detail with the developments in evaluation since the late thirties during which Tyler and his associates developed new models that for thirty years have remained the most powerful influences in shaping the development of evaluation and of the curriculum as well.

The Board decided to bring out such a yearbook providing Mr. Tyler could be persuaded to accept responsibility for its preparation. Mr. Tyler presented the proposal for this yearbook at the 1966 Annual Meeting of the Society. The Board approved the proposal and appointed a yearbook committee consisting of Ralph W. Tyler (Chairman), Benjamin S. Bloom, Marion D. Jenkinson, Jack C. Merwin, and Robert E. Stake.

The Committee and a group of most outstanding authors have produced a yearbook which will stand as a landmark in the development of evaluation. To paraphrase a passage in one of the chapters, the place of this yearbook in the literature of measurement is to be defined in terms of the impetus that it will give to a rethinking of the broader aims and purposes of evaluation, to the consideration of new and untried methods, and to the refinement of procedures that have been developed. The yearbook not only advances scholarship in the field but also provides direct assistance to teachers, curriculum specialists, administrators, and others who are seeking to provide a relevant quality education for the school's rapidly changing clientele.

Editor for the Society
HERMAN G. RICHEY

Table of Contents

CHAPTER I

Introduction

RALPH W. TYLER

Since World War II, and particularly during the past decade, profound changes have been taking place in educational evaluation. This yearbook reviews some of these developments and seeks to assess their significance for both educational theory and practice.

New concepts, new procedures, and new instruments of evaluation are emerging from the interaction among new needs for educational evaluation, new conditions that must be met, new knowledge about education, and new technologies that can be utilized. As an example of this interaction, most theories of testing and evaluation have been developed on the assumption that the primary uses for tests and other evaluative devices are to measure individual differences and to furnish reliable estimates of the mean scores for groups of persons. The theories formulated to guide practice under this assumption have emphasized homogeneity of test content and the concentration of item difficulties near the 50-per-cent point. Since Sputnik, massive financial support has been given to projects concerned with the development of new courses in science and mathematics. Those supporting the construction of the new courses and teachers and administrators who are considering the use of them in their schools are asking for an evaluation of the effectiveness of the courses in comparison with other courses in the same fields. Most tests on the market were not constructed to furnish relative appraisals of different courses, and they have been found inadequate for the task. This need for evaluation of courses and curriculums is stimulating the development of new procedures, instruments, and theories that are designed to meet the need.

Similarly, Title I of the Elementary and Secondary Education Act of 1965 authorizes nearly $1 billion to be allotted to schools with a high concentration of children from homes in poverty, and the Act requires each local district receiving such funds to evaluate the effectiveness of the educational efforts thus supported. Many schools and a majority of the states reported that they had no means readily available for conducting such evaluative studies. This led to the establishment of several centers that are developing new theories and procedures for evaluating Title I activities.

A third illustration of the influence of new needs is the demand being made by influential groups of citizens for appraisals that will furnish sound data to guide educational improvement. The statement of July, 1968, by the Research and Policy Committee of the Committee for Economic Development is a case in point. It reads:

> Innovation in education, whether it involves the use of new curriculum materials or new educational technology, has become essential if the schools are to be genuinely effective in achieving their aims and goals. Continuing assessment of the product of the schools also is necessary. This means the development of principles and techniques for critically judging the worth of whatever the schools teach and the effectiveness and efficiency of their methods of instruction.[1]

The recent rapid increase in the number and availability of technological devices in education, such as television, tape recorders, and computers, has brought to attention the need to evaluate the effectiveness of these devices for various kinds of educational tasks. Traditional test theory has not been sufficiently relevant to design evaluative studies of technological devices, nor have the available achievement tests been satisfactory for this purpose. The effort to appraise some of these devices has led to new developments in evaluation.

The changes in American society are creating new conditions for education that frequently require new types of evaluation in order to obtain valid appraisals appropriate to the new conditions. For example, the applications of science and technology in agriculture, industry, defense, commerce, and the health services have shifted the nature of human occupations from those based largely on physical strength and manual dexterity to those involving large components of intellectual activity and social sensitivity and skills. Very few young people who have not attained the functional lit-

1. *Innovation in Education: New Directions for the American School* (New York: Committee for Economic Development, 1968), p. 13.

eracy represented by the average achievement of students at the end of the fifth grade can find jobs.

At the other extreme, the great employment opportunities are in science, engineering, education, the health services, recreation services, social services, management, and accounting. In our time, the role of the school has shifted from that of selecting out a small per cent of the pupils for more advanced education (while the others dropped out and went to work) to that of effectively reaching every child to enable him to go on learning far beyond the expected level of twenty-five years ago. The task of the college is not to find a favored few but to identify a wide range of potential talents and to help each student realize this potential both for his own self-realization and in order to meet the ever increasing demands of a complex technological society. These changed conditions are stimulating the development of new instruments and new procedures of educational evaluation.

Another illustration of the changing conditions affecting the theory, procedures, and instruments of evaluation is afforded by the current stress upon improving the educational opportunities of disadvantaged children. Recent studies of achievement-testing of children in poverty have shown that the test items do not include a reliable sample of things being learned by most disadvantaged children. Furthermore, interviews with the children revealed that the language of most tests was such that many poor children and many from the disadvantaged minority groups did not understand what they were asked to do in responding to each test question. Efforts to meet the need for appraising the educational progress of disadvantaged children are producing new ideas and new means of educational evaluation.

New knowledge about education is also influencing evaluation. For example, the recent findings of many studies regarding the powerful effects of the student's home culture and community environment upon his learning have clarified the need for evaluating these factors in order to guide and improve education. New theories were necessary to rationalize procedures for appraising home and community environment and new instruments had to be developed.

As another illustration, a series of investigations like those of Newcomb and Coleman have shown the strong influence of peer-group attitudes, practices, and interests upon the learning of its members.[2] These investigations have also shown the need for evaluating the nature, direction, and amount of peer-group influences in developing effective school programs.

The emergence of new technologies has also strongly influenced developments in educational evaluation. The high-speed electronic computer is the most obvious illustration of an emerging technology that is, in many respects, revolutionizing evaluation. The computer has made possible the recording and storage of complex data of many types in a way that permits nearly instantaneous retrieval and processing. This capability has strengthened the interest of evaluators in large-scale studies of individual performance involving large numbers of variables, and new theories, procedures, and instruments are being developed.

The technology of high-fidelity recording and reproduction of sound has influenced the range of objectives appraised and the devices used in the fields of language and music, and it has aided the standardization of group-test administration by permitting the substitution of a tape recording for the directions given by a local proctor. These two examples represent only a fraction of the new technologies that are currently influencing developments in educational evaluation. A more extended discussion appears in chapter xv.

With these kinds of changes taking place in society at large and in educational institutions in particular, it is easy to see why the field of educational evaluation is in a state of great ferment. Already, the new perspectives, procedures, and instruments have made a sizable impact on practice in the schools. This yearbook seeks to describe and explain the developments taking place and to discuss critically their implications.

Chapter ii furnishes a brief historical review of changing conceptions of evaluation in order to furnish a background for the consideration of current developments.

2. See Theodore M. Newcomb, "The General Nature of Peer Group Influence," *College Peer Group*, ed. Theodore M. Newcomb and Everett K. Wilson (Chicago: Aldine Publishing Co., 1966), 2-16; see also, James S. Coleman, "Peer Cultures and Education in Modern Society," in the same volume, pp. 244-69.

Chapter iii discusses some of the major theoretical issues that are involved as old patterns of evaluation are broken and new ones formed. The issues treated in this chapter can serve to focus attention on questions arising in the rest of the volume.

In chapters iv through xiii new developments in evaluation are considered in terms of the uses for which educational appraisals are made. This constitutes the bulk of the book, since most of the changes that have occurred in evaluation have been, at least in part, responses to the kinds of uses to be made of the results of appraisals.

Chapter xiv provides a useful international background for better understanding and appreciation of developments in the United States. It also furnishes an interesting essay in comparative education.

In chapter xv illustrations are given of the potential that new technologies offer for improving the quality and adequacy of evaluation in many aspects of education.

In a sense, chapter xvi is a companion to xv for it discusses the gaps presently existing in available techniques and instruments of evaluation.

Finally, chapter xvii seeks to review the entire volume in terms of the present status of educational evaluation and where it seems likely to go.

CHAPTER II

Historical Review of
Changing Concepts of Evaluation

JACK C. MERWIN

The title of this chapter implies that there have been changes in concepts of educational evaluation over the years. Indeed this is true. And as one surveys the literature, it becomes obvious that these changes have evolved primarily through interactions of evaluation practices with three other aspects of education. In one such interaction, evaluation practices have affected and been affected by the acceptance of various learning theories and approaches to education. A second interaction has been that of evaluation practices with roles accepted for evaluation. The third interaction has been between evaluation practices and technical developments in measurement and evaluation itself.

Within this framework of interactions and development, concepts of evaluation have changed on and relating to such issues as (*a*) who (or what) should be evaluated, (*b*) who should evaluate, (*c*) how evaluations should be conducted, and, (*d*) how evaluation can best be integrated into the educational process.

Introduction

Since the publication of its first NSSE yearbook in 1902, the National Society for the Study of Education has brought out seven volumes directly related to the problems of measurement and evaluation, and many other of its yearbooks deal with the subject in relation to various other aspects of education. This emphasis on the subject suggests the importance of educational evaluation in the educational process.

In the introductory chapter of the Society's Seventeenth Yearbook, *The Measurement of Educational Products*, Ayres noted that a schoolmaster in England, the Reverend George Fisher, produced what he called a "Scale-Book" in 1864. While Ayres observed that Fisher's efforts seem to have produced no lasting results, he proposed that Fisher's work might be accepted as the starting point of measurement in education, making it a little more than fifty years old in 1918. Ayres went on to state that the work of Dr. J. M. Rice, some 25 years later, might also be considered the starting point. He called Rice the "pioneer and pathmaker among American scientific students of education." [1] DuBois, taking a somewhat broader point of view, pointed out that the emperor of China is said to have used a rudimentary form of proficiency-testing about 2200 B.C. to examine his officials every third year.[2] The exact content or methods of testing at that time are not a matter of record, but for 1115 B.C. (during the Chan dynasty), approximately a thousand years later, the nature of the testing employed is clear. At that time, job-sample tests requiring proficiency in music, archery, horsemanship, writing, and arithmetic were used. Just where and when concepts of educational evaluation can be first identified depends, perhaps, upon the interests of the investigator.

In concluding his chapter in the Seventeenth Yearbook a half century ago Ayres said:

The importance of the [educational measurement] movement lies not only in its past and present achievements, but in the hope of the future. Knowledge is replacing opinion, and evidence is supplanting guess-work in education as in every other field of human activity. This is the supreme fact to which this Yearbook bears witness. The future depends on the skill, the wisdom, and the sagacity of the school men and women of America. It is well that they should set about the task of enlarging, perfecting, and carrying forward the scientific movement in education, for the great war has marked the end of the age of haphazard, and the developments of coming years will show that this true in education as in every other organized field of human endeavor.[3]

1. Leonard P. Ayres, "History and Present Status of Educational Measurements," *The Measurement of Educational Products* (Seventeenth Yearbook of the National Society for the Study of Education, Part II [Bloomington, Ill., Public School Publishing Co., 1918]), p. 9.

2. Philip H. DuBois, "A Test-Dominated Society: China, 1115 B.C.—1905 A.D.," *Proceedings of the 1964 Invitational Conference on Testing Problems* (Princeton, N.J.: Educational Testing Service, 1965), pp. 3-11.

3. Ayres, *op. cit.*, p. 15.

In the final chapter of that Yearbook, Judd noted that:

The time is rapidly passing when the reformer can praise his new devices and offer as the reason for his satisfaction, his personal observation of what was accomplished. The superintendent who reports to his board on the basis of mere opinion is rapidly becoming a relic of an earlier and unscientific age. There are indications that even the principals of elementary schools are beginning to study their schools by exact methods and are basing their supervision on the results of their measurements of what teachers accomplish.[4]

At the time of the preparation of the Seventeenth Yearbook, Ayres and Judd had little basis for prophesying that the interaction of changing concepts of what education *can* and *should* be with new approaches to educational evaluation would lead us now, some fifty years later, to prepare this yearbook with somewhat less assuredness than formerly expressed that indeed the "scientific age" of education has arrived. Tyler identified the time of which Ayres and Judd wrote as roughly marking the "first flush of behavioral concepts" of the objectives of education which were to have such a tremendous effect on concepts of education in general and on concepts of evaluation in particular.[5]

As noted earlier, changing aspects of educational evaluation have evolved through interaction with (*a*) accepted theories and practices of education, (*b*) the role accepted for evaluation in the educational process, and (*c*) technical developments in educational evaluation. Let us then consider changing concepts of educational evaluation as they are found to intertwine with these other aspects of educational development.

Concepts of Evaluation and Theories of Education

The turn of the century is a reasonable starting point for a look at the effect of curriculum, educational philosophy, learning theory, and teaching methods on concepts of evaluation. Rice's comparative study was conducted in the 1890's and was proposed by Ayres

4. Charles H. Judd, "A Look Forward," *The Measurement of Educational Products, op. cit.,* pp. 159-60.

5. Ralph W. Tyler, "The Curriculum—Then and Now," *Proceedings, 1956 Invitational Conference on Testing Problems* (Princeton, N.J.: Educational Testing Service, 1957), p. 81.

as a meaningful event from which to consider the development of measurements in education.[6] Tyler reported that, "The dominant educational psychology in 1900 was based on the theory of formal discipline expressed in terms of 'faculty psychology'." [7] The educational picture at that time, and what it foretold for educational evaluation, was made clear in Thorndike's *Educational Psychology*. In this volume, Thorndike wrote, "The one thing that educational theorists of today seem to place as the foremost duty of the schools—the development of powers and capacities—is the one thing that the schools or any other educational forces can do least." He commented further, "We cannot create intellect, but we can prevent such lamentable waste of it as was caused by scholasticism." [8] In his 1956 address to the Invitational Conference on Testing Problems, Tyler commented on the earlier disenchantment with faculty psychology and the increasing concern with behavioral psychology. He noted that the years, 1918-1925, roughly marked a period in which educational objectives were perceived in highly specific terms—"a natural corollary to the prevailing associationists theory in the psychology of learning." [9] By 1925, the formulation of other theories of learning was evolving around more generalized behavior. Dobbin, commenting on measuring achievement in the changing curriculum, noted that not only fundamental changes in learning theory, but also sweeping changes in enrolment and school-organization patterns have led to changing concepts of assessing achievement since the early 1930's.[10]

Starch, in the Fifteenth Yearbook published in 1916, struck a note that was to be sounded anew many times in the half century that followed the publication of that volume. In essence, he suggested that educational evaluation should concern itself with the

6. Ayres, *op. cit.*, p. 9.

7. Tyler, *op. cit.*, p. 80.

8. Edward L. Thorndike, *Educational Psychology* (New York: Lenche and Buechner, 1903), p. 45.

9. Tyler, *op. cit.*, p. 81.

10. John E. Dobbin, "Measuring Achievement in a Changing Curriculum," *Proceedings, 1956 Invitational Conference on Testing Problems* (Princeton, N.J.: Educational Testing Service, 1957), p. 103.

identification of individual differences in what pupils have learned.[11] Concepts of evaluation that were to evolve from this general idea have been reflected in educational practices ranging from "homogeneous grouping" through individualized instruction.

Educational practice has set demands for evaluative information, and evaluation, in turn, has helped mold educational practice. Dressel reported that this influence on practice got to be a touchy matter within the profession during the forties. He said that, while test-makers had been attempting to show the value of scientific testing, they had been "leaning over backward to avoid the criticism of controlling or determining curriculum or teaching methods." He realistically pointed out that testing cannot avoid influencing instruction and proposed that "a qualified subject matter man who seriously turns his attention to evaluation attains a degree of insight into the student mind and into the significance and inter-relationships of the subject." [12]

The Role of Evaluation in Education

Conceptions of evaluation as they have evolved from the interaction of evaluation practices and the role accepted for evaluation in the educational process can be categorized as concepts of role in general educational planning, in instructional organization and operation, and, more recently, in student decision-making. Setting aside reference to what is measured, we can at this point consider evolving concepts of evaluation as they relate to these various roles.

THE ROLE IN GENERAL SCHOOL PLANNING

Haggerty conducted a survey on the role of evaluation in the solution of general school problems in 1917. In the Seventeenth Yearbook he reported that following circulation of a questionnaire,

11. Daniel Starch, "Standard Tests as Aids in the Classification and Promotion of Pupils," *Standards and Tests for the Measurement of the Efficiency of Schools and School Systems* (Fifteenth Yearbook of the National Society for the Study of Education, Part II [Chicago: Distributed by the University of Chicago Press, 1916]), p. 143.

12. Paul L. Dressel, "Information Which Should Be Provided by Test Publishers and Testing Agencies on the Validity and Use of Their Tests: Achievement Tests," *Proceedings, 1949 Invitational Conference on Testing Problems* (Princeton, N.J.: Educational Testing Service, 1950), p. 73.

he received 200 replies, "62 [of] which reported some conscious alteration in the work of the school following the use of a standardized scale or test." [13] The replies indicated that, as a result of testing, there were changes in (a) classification of pupils, (b) school organization, (c) courses of study, (d) methods of instruction, (e) time devoted to subject, and (f) methods of supervision. Twenty years later, Reavis commented: "The development of the measuring movement and the perfection of tests for the measurement of achievement and mental capacity have made possible great advances in educational administration." [14] He noted that during the period from 1900 to 1910 such problems of administration as classification of pupils, appraisal of pupil progress, diagnosis of learning disabilities, identification of special aptitude, promotion of pupils, and appraisal of relative effectiveness of teaching could not be studied objectively and scientifically. He reported that the contributions of research based on objective measurement increased rapidly after 1914.

From a broad point of view, evaluation has been very much a part of school surveys, first introduced shortly after the turn of the century and now conducted by various public and private research and service bureaus throughout the country. While such surveys have generally focused on the inputs of education, there appears to be a developing concern that outcomes be surveyed as well.

THE ROLE IN INSTRUCTION

It is of interest to note that in the 1930's there was considerable concern that the "scientific age" of education had not as yet arrived. In the 1938 *Review of Educational Research*, Frutchey stated:

The most important use of evidence concerning the mental, social, emotional, and physical behavior of boys and girls is to aid in developing an understanding of them. Teaching may be based upon valid

13. M. E. Haggerty, "Specific Uses of Measurement in the Solution of School Problems," *The Measurement of Educational Products, op. cit.,* p. 25.

14. William C. Reavis, "Contributions of Research to Educational Administration," *The Scientific Movement in Education* (Thirty-seventh Yearbook of the National Society for the Study of Education, Part II [Bloomington, Ill.: Public School Publishing Co., 1938]), p. 27.

evidence, carefully collected and wisely interpreted, or it may rest upon a series of untested assumptions, poor guesses, and wishful thinking— or some degree between the two.[15]

In the same volume, Scates wrote:

The improvement of classroom testing seems to lie in the following three directions: (*a*) a more carefully considered set of purposes for which testing is done; (*b*) a greatly broadened and enriched set of outcomes which must be measured; and (*c*) the development of instruments appropriate to the newly created needs.[16]

In this statement Scates basically summarized one of the most significant movements in educational evaluation. This movement was given its initial thrust by Tyler during the early 1930's. Tyler's position unfolded through a number of issues of the *Educational Research Bulletin* of the Ohio State University published between 1931 and 1933. These bulletins were later brought together in a book entitled *Constructing Achievement Tests*.[17] The turn to more generalized behaviors as goals of education was seemingly in response to the break from the associationist theory of the psychology of learning which had led to very specific objectives. It was also seemingly in response to the view of the general role of education in society held by those who fostered the Progressive education movement. Tyler called for a close tie between objectives as they serve as a basis for instruction and as a basis for evaluation. He proposed some rather specific guidelines for the formulation of those objectives.

Tyler said that objectives needed to be spelled out in statements of student behavior which should then serve as the objectives of teaching and as the basis for testing. He proposed that our very limited view of evaluation of specific elements of knowledge should be broadened to encompass all important outcomes of education. Techniques for evaluating "higher mental processes" were

15. Fred P. Frutchey, "Educational Prevention, Diagnosis, and Remediation," *Review of Educational Research*, VIII (December, 1938), 513.

16. Douglas E. Scates, "The Improvement of Classroom Testing," *Review of Educational Research*, VIII (December, 1938), 523.

17. Ralph W. Tyler, *Constructing Achievement Tests* (Columbus, Ohio: Ohio State University, 1934).

described in detail. He suggested that in addition to the cognitive outcomes, including knowledge and higher mental processes, we should teach for and evaluate affective outcomes of education. The principles and procedures advocated by Tyler more than a quarter of a century ago have served as the basis for most of the major efforts in evaluation since that time. Their most immediate application was to be found in the evaluation portion of the Eight Year Study for which Tyler was responsible. The study ran from 1933 through 1941 and the evaluation aspects of it are described in the Smith and Tyler volume, *Appraising and Recording Student Progress*.[18] The continuing emphasis on this approach is clearly evident in the chapter by Cook in *Educational Measurement*[19] and, more recently, in Wrightstone's chapter in the Sixty-second Yearbook.[20]

The whole approach of making evaluation a more rational and positive part of the instructional program led to a number of considerations for the preinstructional use of evaluation instruments. During the 1930's there were a number of proposals that school testing programs should be conducted in the fall of the year as a basis for teacher planning or instruction rather than in the spring as a basis for evaluating the level of achievement following instruction. Ebel proposed the development of achievement tests to aid instructional planning.[21] Troyer viewed pretesting on a somewhat broader base. He proposed that pretesting be used to evaluate the extent to which the students had achieved the prerequisites, i.e., the skills and knowledges on which the course of

18. Eugene R. Smith and Ralph W. Tyler, *Appraising and Recording Student Progress* (New York: Harper & Bros., 1942).

19. Walter W. Cook, "The Functions of Measurement in Improving Instruction," *Educational Measurement*, ed. E. F. Lindquist (Washington, D.C.: American Council on Education, 1951), pp. 3-46.

20. J. Wayne Wrightstone, "The Relation of Testing Programs to Teaching and Learning," *The Impact and Improvement of School Testing Programs* (Sixty-second Yearbook of the National Society for the Study of Education, Part II [Chicago: Distributed by the University of Chicago Press, 1963]), pp. 45-61.

21. Robert L. Ebel, "Obtaining and Reporting Evidence on Content Validity," *Educational and Psychological Measurement*, XVI (Autumn, 1956), 269-82.

instruction was to build, and the extent to which students had already learned what the teacher planned to teach.[22]

Preinstruction evaluation reduced to the individual level leads into diagnosis. While diagnosis had long been a matter of concern for educators,[23] it received renewed emphasis in the thirties and forties. The Society devoted an entire volume to educational diagnosis in 1935[24] and a chapter to it in 1938.[25] In the Forty-fifth Yearbook, Douglass and Spitzer wrote:

> For many years we have believed that good teaching begins where the child is, at the point to which his achievement has brought him. We realize that we must take into consideration what the pupil already knows if we are to guide his learning from then on in an effective manner.[26]

THE ROLE IN STUDENT DECISION-MAKING

Simpson called for attention to the need to help students develop evaluation skills. He cogently argued that most learning takes place outside of the classroom and that much more learning could take place if students developed skills for realistically planning and evaluating their own educational experiences.[27]

Changing Concepts and the Content of Evaluation

Changing concepts of evaluation as they relate to the various roles of evaluation in the educational process obviously call for

22. Maurice E. Troyer, *Accuracy and Validity in Evaluation Are Not Enough* (The J. Richard Street Lectures, 1947 [New York: Syracuse University, 1947]).

23. Walter Scott Monroe, *Measuring the Results of Teaching* (Boston: Houghton Mifflin Co., 1918).

24. *Educational Diagnosis* (Thirty-fourth Yearbook of the National Society for the Study of Education [Bloomington, Ill.: Public School Publishing Co., 1935]).

25. Leo J. Brueckner, "General Methods: Educational Diagnosis," *The Scientific Movement in Education, op. cit.*, pp. 333-40.

26. Harl R. Douglass and Herbert R. Spitzer, "The Importance of Teaching for Understanding," *The Measurement of Understanding* (Forty-fifth Yearbook of the National Society for the Study of Education, Part I [Chicago: University of Chicago Press, 1946]), p. 24.

27. Ray Hamill Simpson, *Improving Teaching-Learning Process* (New York: Longmans, Green & Co., 1953).

changes in who and what are to be evaluated. The content of evaluations seemingly has several general dimensions. One is the detail—general dimension of accomplishment. Another is breadth— going beyond the evaluation of cognitive outcomes to include affective outcomes and environmental inputs into the educational situation. A third is the concept of evaluating status as opposed to change. A fourth is the concept of evaluation of groups, rather than individuals. Related, but somewhat apart from these considerations, are new aspects of what is to be evaluated brought about by new educational efforts extending from the early nursery school to the graduate school and including those of the armed forces (discussed later, see pp. 20, 156 ff.). We may now consider in turn these dimensions as they have related to changing concepts of evaluation.

SPECIFIC VERSUS GENERAL ACHIEVEMENT

Regarding the dimension of specific-versus-general achievement to be evaluated, it would appear that we are in the process of completing a cycle approximately fifty years in length. As described in Monroe's book, *Measuring the Results of Teaching*, evaluation during the first part of the century focused on very detailed objectives related to skills.[28] The *Courtis Arithmetic Tests* were four timed tests with 24 examples of identical type in each (e.g. the addition test is composed of 24 examples, each containing three columns of nine figures). Graphs for individual pupils across time (based on such tests of detailed skills) are found in the Fifteenth Yearbook.[29] At the 1967 Invitational Conference on Testing Problems, Glaser presented graphical descriptions of the accomplishments of individual students over time on relatively minute units of learning.[30] Between the publication of these two reports, there

---

28. Monroe, *op. cit.*

29. D. C. Bliss, "The Application of Standard Measurements to School Administration," *Standards and Tests for the Measurement of the Efficiency of Schools and School Systems, op. cit.*, p. 75.

30. Robert Glaser, "Adapting the Elementary School Curriculum to Individual Performance," *Proceedings of the 1967 Invitational Conference on Testing Problems* (Princeton, N.J.: Educational Testing Service, 1968), pp. 3-36.

has been considerable emphasis on more general outcomes as reflected in the "in-basket" approach and the "tab-item" approaches to assessing the student's ability to apply his learning to practical situations.

STATUS VERSUS CHANGE

Most evaluation in education to date has been in terms of status with little systematic reference to prior measures. However, acceptance of the philosophical position that the teacher should take each child "where he is" and move him as far as possible toward his maximum potential development calls for a measure of status at two points in time as a basis for determining change, or "growth". A symposium on technical problems involved in the measurement of change was published under the editorship of Harris.[31] In recent years, many questions, inquiries, and concerns about the effectiveness of instructional methodology, approach, or "innovation" have prompted further concerns for evaluating change. Here, however, the emphasis has been on evaluating change in the performance of groups.

BREADTH

In discussing the dimension of breadth of characteristics to be measured, it must be noted that Tyler called attention some quarter of a century ago to the need to broaden our evaluation efforts to be more inclusive of the educational objectives to be attained. This broadening was given considerable impetus by the publishing of the *Taxonomy of Educational Objectives: Handbook I, Cognitive Domain*.[32] This volume pointed up the need for attention to the evaluation of more than simple knowledge, thus moving evaluation procedures into the realm of "higher mental processes" so often verbalized in abstract terms in our educational objectives. The more recent publication of *Handbook II: Affective Domain*[33] holds

31. *Problems in Measuring Change*, ed. Chester William Harris (Madison: University of Wisconsin Press, 1963).

32. Benjamin S. Bloom (ed.), *Taxonomy of Educational Objectives: The Classification of Educational Goals, Handbook I: Cognitive Domain* (New York: Longmans, Green & Co., 1956).

33. David R. Krathwohl, Benjamin S. Bloom, and Bertram B. Masia,

promise for similarly stimulating considerably more concrete efforts toward broadening our evaluation procedures to take into account very important educational objectives that fall in the affective area.

Environmental factors affecting learning have long been recognized,[34] but only in recent years have there been serious attempts to obtain measures of perceptions of environmental factors. Notable among these more recent efforts are the work of Pace and Stern,[35] (who developed instruments to obtain perceptions of various groups regarding the characteristics of university and high-school communities) and the research of Wolf [36] and Coleman.[37] The earlier approach to this type of evaluation in terms of community characteristics (e.g. median family income, size of city, etc.) as reflected in the work of Thorndike[38] did not involve the measurement of psychological perceptions used in more recent work.

INDIVIDUAL VERSUS GROUP

The fourth dimension around which concepts of evaluation have developed is the focus of evaluation on the individual or on the group. The whole concept of dealing with individual differences of learners—diagnosing individual difficulties, planning remedial programs, and the "taking-the-child-where-he-is" approach—focused evaluation on the individual.

Taxonomy of Educational Objectives: The Classification of Educational Goals, Handbook II: Affective Domain (New York: David McKay Company, Inc., 1964).

34. Paul T. Rankin, "Environmental Factors Contributing to Learning," *Educational Diagnosis, op. cit.*, pp. 79-92.

35. C. R. Pace and G. G. Stern, "An Approach to the Measurement of Psychological Characteristics of College Environments," *Journal of Educational Psychology*, XLIX (1959), 269-77.

36. Richard Wolf, "The Measurement of Environments," *Proceedings of the 1964 Invitational Conference on Testing Problems* (Princeton, N.J.: Educational Testing Service, 1965), pp. 93-106.

37. James S. Coleman *et al.*, *Equality of Educational Opportunity* (2 vols.: Publication of the National Center for Educational Statistics, OE38001 [Washington: Government Printing Office, 1966]), I.

38. Edward L. Thorndike, "American Cities and States: Variation and Correlation in Institutions, Activities and the Personal Qualities of the Residents," *Annals of the New York Academy of Sciences:* XXXIX, Art 4:2 (New York: The Academy of Sciences, 1939), pp. 13-98.

In recent years a good deal of attention has been given to the development of educational evaluation as it relates to teaching materials, instruction, and curriculum. While many have viewed these as new considerations, it is interesting to note the following titles of books published before 1920: *Standards and Tests for the Measurement of the Efficiency of Schools and School Systems*,[39] *Measurement of Teaching Efficiency*,[40] *Measuring the Results of Teaching*,[41] and *The Measurement of Educational Products*.[42]

Considerable attention was given in the early twentieth century to the evaluation of the performance of groups as a basis for evaluating school systems, school programs, and teaching. Rice systematically studied the outcomes of different attempts to produce learning.[43] His early testing across schools was aimed at questions not unlike those being raised by many in the latter part of the 1960's.

There is little question but what new curriculum programs such as those developed by the School Mathematics Study Group (SMSG), Madison School Project, the Physical Science Study Committee (PSSC) in physics, and the Biological Sciences Curriculum Study (BSCS) program in biology led teachers to raise questions regarding program evaluation. Evaluation received added impetus as computer technology was applied to instruction, resulting in curricular packaging which involved "hardware." These activities in recent years have called for evaluation in the development of the curriculum (for what Scriven has called "formative evaluation"), as well as for evaluation in selection among curriculums (labeled "summative evaluation").[44]

39. Fifteenth Yearbook of the National Society for the Study of Education, Part I, *op. cit.*

40. Felix Arnold, *The Measurement of Teaching Efficiency* (New York: Lloyd Adams Noble, 1916).

41. Monroe, *op. cit.*

42. Seventeenth Yearbook of the National Society, Part II, *op. cit.*

43. Joseph M. Rice, "The Futility of the Spelling Grind," *Forum*, XXIII (April, June, 1897), 163-72, 409-19.

44. Michael Scriven, "The Methodology of Evaluation," *Perspectives of Curriculum Evaluation: American Educational Research Association Monograph Series on Curriculum Evaluation* (Chicago: Rand McNally & Co., 1967), pp. 39-83.

Recognition of these needs led to the appointment of a joint committee to produce recommendations for reporting the effectiveness of programed instruction materials.[45] It also prompted appointment of an *ad hoc* committee on curriculum evaluation by the president of the American Educational Research Association in 1964 which became a standing committee in 1965. This committee initiated a monograph series on curriculum evaluation, the first issue of which was published in February, 1967.

As this chapter is being prepared, many efforts are being aimed at improving techniques for the evaluation of curriculums in the broad sense—of instructional materials, teaching methods, and the organization and presentation of instructional materials. One of these efforts has involved informal meetings of a group interested in the possibility of a consortium of institutions to deal with problems of curriculum evaluation.

This new (or renewed) trend of concern with curriculum evaluation was given considerable impetus by the requirement of evaluation for Title I and Title III projects under the 1966 extension of the National Defense Education Act. As this yearbook was being prepared, the lay public and their legislative representatives, were raising increasing numbers of questions about the value of various curricular approaches and instructional materials for which funds have been appropriated. These demands for evidence of quality in educational production have been instrumental in directing efforts in evaluation toward the evaluation of groups and educational programs.

Cronbach's paper [46] on the use of unmatched designs for gathering information on the educational achievement of groups directed a good deal of attention to practical means of assessing group outcomes without having every student take every item, as would be necessary in a testing program. Thus far, the largest effort along these lines has been the extensive work of the Exploratory Com-

45. Joint Committee on Programmed Instruction and Teaching Machines, *Recommendations for Reporting the Effectiveness of Programmed Instruction Materials* (Washington, D.C.: National Education Association, Division of Audiovisual Instructional Service, 1966).

46. Lee J. Cronbach, "Course Improvement through Evaluation," *Teachers College Record*, LXIV (May, 1963), 672-83.

mittee on Assessing the Progress of Education which is described in chapter xiii of this yearbook.

NEW EDUCATIONAL EFFORTS

As education and educational involvements have expanded, there has been an accompanying need for new evaluation concepts. Such programs have primarily centered on the military, colleges and professional schools, and early childhood education. The military, facing the need for efficient measures of general ability during World War I, prompted some of the most intensive testing activity to that time. During World War II, it found a need for proficiency-testing and aptitude-testing as a basis for selection and placement of specialists. During and following World War II, it set up an extensive testing system in connection with an educational program involving correspondence courses, class instruction, and independent study under the United States Armed Forces Institute.

Colleges and professional schools have increasingly faced problems of evaluation in dealing with admissions and placement. It should be noted that this fact reflects a change in the concept of evaluation to encompass the problems of selection and quotas neither of which had been serious problems in the past. The steps that have been taken to solve these problems are detailed in the later chapter on admissions, placement, and scholarship programs.

The third new area which has prompted a good deal of evaluation activity has been that of early childhood education. An increasing amount of research which points to the severe handicap of children who enter school without a prior stimulating environmental experience has centered much attention on the young child. In the past, designers of educational evaluation, as a rule, have paid little attention to children under the traditional school age. However, when such federal projects as Head Start and various programs sponsored by the Office of Economic Opportunity called for work with children of preschool ages, they prompted a flurry of activity in attempts to do the kind of evaluation that was needed as a basis for planning meaningful educational activities for youngsters in this age group.

Technical Developments and Changing Concepts

We can now turn to the changing concepts of evaluation which have grown out of technical development and the modes of interpretation which have been developed to go along with new testing techniques. In this connection there are three general areas of concern. The three major considerations are (*a*) intra-individual comparisons, (*b*) the normative-versus-standards approach to interpretation of scores, and (*c*) attempts to account for achievement in terms of potential or ability.

INTRA-INDIVIDUAL COMPARISONS

A new dimension was added to standardized testing in 1923 when Terman, Ruch, and Kelly published the *Stanford Achievement Tests*. These tests represented the first attempt to establish achievement norms for different subject areas on the same group, thus making the concept of a test battery operational. For the first time, there was a basis for intra-individual study of levels of achievement across different school subjects. The battery approach to standardized achievement testing has been a generally accepted source of achievement information for many years.

When standardized achievement batteries can be administered most profitably is an issue which has not been resolved over the years. Some have argued that they best serve as a measure of individual and group accomplishments and should be given at the end of the school year. Others have argued for fall administration to provide information to teachers as a basis for planning instruction. Increased fall administration indicates that in recent years the latter position has gained preference. However, there is little evidence to support the contention that teachers do, indeed, use the results for instructional planning.

THE NORMATIVE-VERSUS-STANDARDS APPROACH

Due to the problem of adequately sampling school accomplishments by essay tests, or even through efficiencies made possible by the use of objective tests, the use of absolute (percentage) scores for tests gave way to a normative approach. Thus, this general normative approach, attending to content coverage of achievement tests in evaluation but calling for the development of instruments which reliably differentiate between individuals, became the major focus of interpretation for several decades. These decades were bracketed by attempts at the turn of the century to develop school standards (commonly school medians) and in recent years by several projects which are establishing standards in terms of the requirements of the tasks rather than basing them on school medians. The "mastery" testing used in the Oak Leaf Project at Pittsburgh is an illustration.[47] As this yearbook goes to press, it appears that we are in for some serious attempts to achieve that which Ebel described as the "meaningfulness" of test results rather than validity as traditionally conceived.[48] While sharing some characteristics, the current concept of evaluation in terms of standards represents a significant departure from the concepts that prevailed during the early part of the century.

ACHIEVEMENT IN TERMS OF POTENTIAL

Interpretation in terms of achievement as related to potential has held an attraction for educators over many years. Many attempts have been made to use general ability measures as a basis for comparing achievement with potential. The quotient approach to the scoring of the Stanford version of the Binet Test using chronological age served as a model for such concepts as "achievement age." The "A.Q." (achievement quotient) approach to evaluation of individual students was relatively short-lived. One factor hastening its demise was the technical problem of interpretation. Another was the seeming "no contest" resolution of the "nature-nurture" controversy, the general acceptance that all learning is a function of both hereditary and environmental factors. Technical problems, however, constituted the more important factor in the dropping of the A.Q. as may be inferred from the fact that attempts to account for achievement in terms of measured "aptitude" persist, for better or worse, in other forms.

Nothing has stirred the statistically-naïve, professional educator

47. Glaser, *op. cit.*

48. Robert L. Ebel, "Must All Tests Be Valid?" *American Psychologist,* XVI (October, 1961), 640-47.

and laymen as much as aptitude-achievement relationships expressed as "expectancies" and the related concepts of "underachievers" and "overachievers." In recent years it has become common practice for a test-publisher to administer a measure of general academic ability while "norming" an achievement test battery. The use of aptitude scores has in some cases been the basis for identifying selected norm groups.[49] In other cases, they have been used to establish achievement scores regressed on the aptitude test scores and have been labeled "expectancies." Lack of understanding of the latter process has led, unfortunately, to much misinformed labeling. The belief of many that "underachievers" can come up to their predicted level of performance if they will just "apply themselves" is truly an oversimplification of a complex situation. The concept of a student's being an "overachiever"—in the eyes of the statistically naïve, doing better than he is capable of doing—has been a source of confusion. However, the person who is neither an underachiever nor an overachiever but is operating at his expected level also has produced some problems, especially when the expectancy has been low.

It has been proposed that students with measured low ability do not become overachievers. The teacher expects low performance from such students and that is what he gets. This has been labeled the "self-fulfilling prophecy."

Centralization

The last general area around which changing concepts of evaluation have developed is that of the degree of centralization of concern in evaluation. A major concern of educational evaluation over the years has been the provision of information for the teacher's use in working with students. While much has been written about the large number of standardized tests administered in schools, the number is small in comparison with the number of tests developed and administered by teachers. With the advent of standardized tests in the early part of the century, a new potential for considering results of different classes on a common examination

49. Eric F. Gardner *et al., Stanford Achievement Test: High School Battery* (New York: Harcourt, Brace and World, Inc., 1967).

became possible. Many schools moved in the direction of a systematic testing program. While standardized tests did not replace teacher examinations, they did place educational evaluation on a schoolwide basis.

Somewhat later, evaluation became a statewide consideration. Some of these statewide concerns led to statewide testing programs offered to high schools on a voluntary basis (as exemplified by the Minnesota program started in 1928). Others, operated by state departments of education, were in some cases voluntary and, in others, mandatory. In recent years, with federal financial support for their operation, the number of statewide testing programs in operation has significantly increased.

The U.S. Office of Education has for some time gathered information on public schools in the United States. However, this information has been almost exclusively in terms of inputs—teacher's salaries, teacher-pupil ratios, and the like. Only recently has the need for nationwide information in terms of outcomes been considered. The need for such information in dealing with significant educational problems on a nationwide scale is clearly reflected in the work of the Exploratory Committee on Assessing the Progress of Education. At the same time that the Exploratory Committee was devising means for the collection of national assessment information, the international assessment project described elsewhere in this volume was also in progress.[50] Thus, over the years there has been increasing concern for the expansion and centralization of the collection of educational evaluation information. This concern has not negated or replaced concern for local evaluation information. Rather, it has added to and supplemented classroom use of teacher-constructed evaluation instruments.

Summary

Concepts of evaluation have changed over the years. They have changed in relation to such issues as who is to be evaluated, what is to be evaluated, and how evaluations are to be made. These concepts have evolved along with changing concepts of who is to be

50. Torsten Husén (ed.), *International Study of Achievement in Mathematics: A Comparison of Twelve Countries* (New York: John Wiley & Sons, 1967).

educated and how people are to be educated, and along with technical developments within evaluation itself.

Concepts of evaluation have developed in response to needs for evaluation growing out of educational practice and have, in turn, helped mold educational practice. Concepts of evaluation will change in the future. There is every reason to believe that such change will come about through a continuing integrative development of evaluation and educational practice.

CHAPTER III

Some Theoretical Issues Relating to Educational Evaluation

BENJAMIN S. BLOOM

Nature and Use of Specifications

There has been some controversy recently about the need for specifications as to the desired outcomes of a course of instruction.[1] Much of this controversy has been engendered by investigators who have observed teachers in the process of teaching a group of young children. Teachers appear to respond to individual students during the instructional period, and they appear to alter procedures and interactions rapidly as they focus on the needs of individuals or subgroups in the class. When probed, the teachers have difficulty in stating their objectives or in relating what they do in class to a set of long-term objectives for the subject matter.

Other fuel has been added to the controversy by curriculum-makers who have great difficulty in getting subject matter experts to state their objectives in other than the most general and vague terms. In contrast, curriculum-makers find the subject matter experts more explicit in defining the subject matter content that should be learned and quite skilful in suggesting instructional procedures to make explicit the ways in which they would like the interaction among teacher, student, and learning material to take place.

Quite in contrast to this reluctance to state or use specifications is the great need for and rather avid use of specifications by per-

1. E. W. Eisner *et al.*, "Educational Objectives: Help or Hindrance?" *School Review*, LXXV (Winter, 1967), 250-82; Philip W. Jackson and Elizabeth Belford, "Educational Objectives and the Joys of Teaching," *School Review*, LXXIII (Autumn, 1965), 267-91; W. J. Popham, J. M. Atkin, and J. Raths, "The Instructional Objectives Controversy" (Symposium, Annual Meeting of the American Educational Research Association, Chicago, February, 1968).

sons working with instructional technology or evaluation. Workers on instructional materials find it difficult to determine what to include in programed instructional material, computer-aided instruction, educational films, or other learning materials unless they know precisely what is to be learned by the students. If specifications are not available from other sources, these workers find it difficult to start their work until they have constructed an appropriate set.

Persons constructing evaluation instruments to be used by more than a single teacher or a single school also find it difficult to begin their work until a set of specifications are provided. Here again, if specifications are not available, these workers find it necessary to construct them or to create a committee or other type of consensus mechanism to develop a set of specifications against which they can construct and validate an evaluation instrument.

If one takes these statements about teachers, curriculum-constructors, educational technologists, and evaluators at their face value, one finds real conflict between the first two and the latter two. Yet, if one probes to a deeper level, it is quite likely that all four groups have a set of specifications in mind which differ only in explicitness, detail, and form.

No teacher can work with a group of students for a term or more without some model or framework to guide him with respect to the learning desired or expected of his students. At the very minimum he must have a set of expectancies which guide his teaching in order that his students will be ready for the next grade or course in a sequence. Thus, the second-grade teacher is in part guided by what the third-grade teacher expects to do in reading, arithmetic, and the like. The sequence of expectations in our graded schools makes it impossible for any teacher to ignore what is required by the educational system and to do exactly as he pleases with his students. Minimal requirements for students with respect to various learning and developmental tasks are made very clear to all teachers, although the teachers may be more or less free with respect to the way in which they teach and to the timing of their instruction on particular topics or material during the term or year. Beyond these minimal requirements, teachers are quite free as to what they may expect or desire of their students. In some instances the teacher may wish to do unique things with individual students while in other instances the teacher may attempt to get all students to develop in similar ways.

It is possible that most experienced teachers have their minimal requirements so clearly in mind that they take them for granted and see little reason to state them as objectives or content to be learned.

The curriculum-makers who are reluctant to state their objectives are not reluctant to state the content or ideas they wish to have developed through the curriculum. Perhaps their resistance is to the formulation of educational objectives, a formulation which they believe represents meaningless "pedagese." In instances in which the curriculum-makers are scholars and experts in their own subject field, it is likely that they will place primary emphasis on the instructional treatment of the ideas and subject matter rather than on the learning processes that might and should take place in individual students. Some curriculum-makers regard curriculum-making as an artistic process which should not be specified in advance. Such curriculum-makers may be less opposed to an analysis of the objectives included, after the curriculum has been constructed.

For the educational technologists and evaluators, the clearer the specifications are in terms of both content and behaviors, the better. Such specifications define the problems they must solve in the construction of instructional materials or evaluation instruments, and such specifications provide the criteria against which the materials and instruments are validated.

It would seem to this writer that it is virtually impossible to engage in an educational enterprise of any duration without having some set of specifications to guide one—whether one is a student, teacher, administrator, curriculum-maker, educational technologist, evaluator, or guidance worker. What may be different from worker to worker is the explicitness of the specifications, the forms in which they are cast, the sources from which they are derived, and the extent to which they are used for various decisions.

EXPLICITNESS OF SPECIFICATIONS

It is quite possible for the specifications that guide a teacher or curriculum-worker to be implicit in his actions, processes used, or products developed rather than stated in precise and explicit form. One may work for many years as a teacher without making his purposes explicit in verbal form. Unfortunately, specifications which are implicit are difficult to communicate to others, they are rarely analyzed and clearly revised, and they do not serve as clear guides to particular decisions or actions. Implicit specifications may shift without the educational worker's being clearly aware of any change, and, because of poor communication, the attainment of the specifications may defy any attempt at systematic appraisal.

If education and educational materials are to be systematic in their effects and open to inquiry, the specifications for them must be put forth in some explicit form. One cannot determine whether two or more educative actions, experiences, or products are consistent or inconsistent with each other, whether they are additive or nullify each other, or whether they have positive or negative effects on the students unless they can be exposed to analysis and inquiry. If education is to be open, public, and examinable, the specifications for it must be explicit, and either the process of education or the outcomes of the process must be examinable in relation to such specifications. Trust in professionals is a highly desirable goal for any field, including education, but each profession must either police itself, if it is to merit the confidence of the public that supports or uses it, or expose itself to external scrutiny when the confidence of the public is impaired.

If the purposes and specifications for education are not explicit, then it is possible for them to be altered by social pressures, by new fads and fashions, and by new schemes and devices which may come and go with momentary shifts on the educational scene. Implicit purposes are difficult to defend, and the seeming vacuum in purpose invites attack and substitution of explicit purposes by a constant stream of pressures and pressure groups.

That *all* the purposes and specifications for education cannot be made explicit does not mean that *no* purposes or specifications should be made explicit.

Purposes and specifications which are explicit tend to be those which are relevant for groups of students. Such purposes and specifications may attempt to describe the ways in which students are to be altered by the educational activities. Although in actual fact the students may vary in the extent to which they are altered by the educational activities, all are expected to be modified to some degree in the ways specified.

It is possible to develop specifications for the changes to take place in an individual student, but this has rarely been done by teachers. Such specifications are more likely to be developed by tutors, guidance workers, or other professionals who work primarily with individuals on a one-to-one basis. Perhaps the current emphasis on individualization of learning may result in the development of such specifications.

In addition to change in relation to the purposes and specifications which were made explicit, it is possible for groups of students to change positively (or negatively) in ways not included in the specifications. Some of these changes are not intended by the teachers or curriculum-makers and may either be accidental, in that no one could have foreseen them, or occur as foreseeable effects of the educational activities if the teachers and curriculum-makers are fully cognizant of human behavior and the forces which produce change.

Finally, there may be other changes which take place in individual students as the result of specific activities of the teachers which are designed to affect these individuals. These may be implicit in the teacher's activities but, for a variety of reasons, are not made explicit. Such implicit purposes may not be made explicit because they are fulfilled only as the teacher senses a particular need of the student in the actual process of interacting with the student—that is, they cannot be or are not planned in advance. Other implicit purposes may be achieved unconsciously by the teacher's interactions with individual students or groups of students.

The point to be made is that not all purposes of education can or should be made explicit. However, it is the thesis of this chapter that, insofar as possible, the purposes of education and the specifications for educational changes should be made explicit if they are to be open to inquiry, if teaching and learning are to be modified as improvement or change is needed, and if each new group of students is to be subjected to a particular set of educative processes.

THE FORM OF SPECIFICATIONS

Education may be regarded as consisting of some content or subject matter to be learned (topics in science, areas of living, material to be studied, ideas, etc.) as well as processes to take place in individuals (retention of information, problem-solving, attitude formation, and the like). Thus, the explicit specifications may take the form of descriptions of the ways in which each group of students is to be altered by interaction with the material of instruction and the process of instruction. Most teachers and curriculum-makers have little difficulty in defining the content or subject to be included. They may have greater difficulty in defining the processes which they desire or expect to take place in individuals.

Various workers have differed as to the appropriate degree of specificity in defining these processes. Some would insist on great detail with each behavior defined and stated with considerable precision.[2]

To be able to solve linear equations

To be able to repair a television set

Given a list of thirty chemical elements, the learner must be able to recall and write the valences of at least twenty-five

To be able to write three examples of the logical fallacy of the undistributed middle

Others[3] make use of more generalized statements of objectives such as the following:

Familiarity with dependable sources of information in the biological sciences

Ability to analyze arguments and propaganda

Ability to recognize unstated assumptions

2. R. F. Mager, *Preparing Instructional Objectives* (Palo Alto, Calif.: Fearon Publishers, 1962); Popham, Atkin, and Raths, *op. cit.;* R. M. Gagné, "The Analysis of Instructional Objectives for the Design of Instruction," in *Teaching Machines and Programmed Instruction,* ed. Robert Glaser (Washington: Department of Audiovisual Instruction, National Education Association, 1965), pp. 21-65.

3. R. W. Tyler, *Basic Principles of Curriculum and Instruction* (Chicago: University of Chicago Press, 1951); B. S. Bloom (ed.), *Taxonomy of Educational Objectives, Handbook I: The Cognitive Domain* (New York: David McKay Co., 1956); D. R. Krathwohl *et al., Taxonomy of Educational Objectives, Handbook II: The Affective Domain* (New York: David McKay Co., 1964).

Ability to apply social science generalizations and conclusions to actual
  social problems
Ability to make mathematical discoveries and generalizations
Responds emotionally to a work of art or musical composition
Enjoys reading books on a variety of themes

The degree of specificity sought (as represented in these two
examples) is determined in part by the extent to which the curriculum-makers or teachers wish to anticipate and program the work
and activities of students and teachers. If the changes in students
are to take place primarily because of the interaction of a student
with specific learning material, the specifications must be most
detailed. If the changes are to take place through the interaction of
student, teacher, and material, the specifications are usually less detailed in order that the teacher may have greater freedom to use
those procedures and instructional processes which he may believe
to be most appropriate in a given set of circumstances and at a
given moment in time.

Another reason for the difference in specificity has to do with
the view of learning and education accepted by the curriculum-
maker, instructional-material producer, or teacher. If the worker
believes that each element to be learned must be included in the
instruction, he will be most detailed in his specifications. Thus
Thorndike,[4] in the teaching of arithmetic, specified several hundred
detailed objectives to be attained. Some would insist that this is
training rather than education. In contrast is the view that students
can learn to generalize from a small number of appropriate learning
experiences. For example, if there are about thirty major principles
in physics and literally several million possible applications of these
principles, this view of learning would attempt to determine how a
small number of illustrations and applications could generalize into
"the ability to apply principles of physics to new problems." The
main point to be made is not that the more precise and detailed the
specifications, the better. One level of detail may be better from one
point of view, while a more general set of specifications may be
better from another point of view.

Other specifications may be in the form of a series of tasks or

4. E. L. Thorndike, *The Psychology of Arithmetic* (New York: Mac-
millan Co., 1926).

problems to be solved. Such tasks or problems may be analyzed to determine the content and processes which are included in them, or they may be used as illustrations of the content and purposes already made explicit in a table of specifications. The value of such a set of tasks or problems is that they do make explicit what the student is to do, although they may not be very effective in defining the intent behind the materials to be used. As such, they are more effective in determining what is to be done by the student than as specifications for alternative sets of materials or as criteria for a range of evaluation procedures. The development of test-item banks is one way in which test items may be used to illustrate the specifications and to give operational definitions to them.

Finally, the specifications may be in the form of learning activities in which the student is to engage. Here again, the astute analyst may infer the content and behaviors which are implicit in the learning activities, but he is hard-pressed to determine what learning activities may be substituted for the stated ones or precisely what evaluation procedures are relevant for appraising the effectiveness of the learning activities.

The basic problem in developing a set of specifications is to make the desired outcomes of learning sufficiently explicit that they can be used to communicate what is desired to other teachers, curriculum-workers, educational technologists, and evaluators. If the specifications can be made explicit enough to communicate clearly to others, they can be used to furnish the criteria for many alternative learning tasks, a variety of evaluation procedures, and a variety of interactions among students, teachers, and materials. Furthermore, the specifications can be judged for their appropriateness for a given group of learners, for their relevance to students with particular characteristics, and for their relations to prior as well as to later educational specifications.

THE SOURCE OF SPECIFICATIONS

A set of specifications may, in part, be drawn from an analysis of the important ideas or subject matter available in a subject field. This requires some decisions about what in the subject field is most significant, what will contribute most to the student's development, and what aspects of the subject are likely to be most relevant and important for other learning the student is likely to do in this or in related subjects. Different conceptions of the subject field are likely to result in different priorities with regard to content and behavior. For example, if a subject is viewed as closed and likely to change very little in the future, the specifications may stress knowledge and comprehension of a systematic account of what has been learned by scholars in the field. However, if the subject is viewed as open and highly changeable in the future, the specifications may stress inquiry objectives, higher mental processes, and the processes used in developing the subject rather than the products of previous research and scholarship. Under this view, the content may be selected both because of some view about its importance and because of beliefs about its value in developing these more complex behaviors.

Different views about the relation of the subject to other learning (and to other subjects) may also result in different priorities with regard to content and behaviors. If a subject is seen as being clearly related to other subjects, the specifications must take this into consideration, and the learning of one subject will not be viewed as an end in itself. If learning is seen as developmental and sequential, the specifications should show how one set of learnings is to be related to previous and subsequent learning. If a subject is seen as related to ongoing processes in contemporary life as well as arising from historical processes, the specifications should take these views into consideration.

The subject matter of a field furnishes the content and processes to be considered in a curriculum. However, the subject matter to be included in a set of specifications, while guided by what a particular group of subject experts may suggest, must transcend the limitations of the subject specialists. However competent he is in his own subject, a subject expert may not be fully aware of what a group of students in the Freshman year of high school can learn and what is important to such students. A young person is to be educated and the specifications as to what he is to learn are dependent on his previous educational development, his abilities and skills, and his aspirations and motivations. A curriculum and a set of specifications for it should be the product of the best thinking of wise and expert men about what will best promote the fullest development of the individual as a man, as a citizen, and as a contributing member of a society. It is likely that no one set of specifications will suffice for all students, teachers, and schools.

The behavioral part of the specifications is likely to emerge from some views about the subject, but this also may arise in part from research as well as from views about the nature of the students, the nature of the society, a philosophy of education, and a conception about the nature of learning. Students differ in many ways, and the specifications must in part be based on selected characteristics of the students who are to be changed by the educative process. The educational objectives and the nature of the learning experiences must be partly determined by the kinds of students in the school and by the cultural conditions in which they develop.

Each nation and society has its own special problems, concerns, and interests. These special qualities of the nation and its subgroups must be reflected in the educational program. Implications for the specifications of a curriculum must be drawn from studies of contemporary society as well as from studies of trends for the future. Social scientists who are experts on the society, both as it is and as it is coming to be, should play a vital role in furnishing the raw data for curriculum-planning. Curriculum development is a type of social planning, since it is concerned with the kinds of learning students will need if they are to play a significant part in the society as it develops in the future. Educational planning and social planning must be interrelated at many points if they are to be mutually reinforcing. All too frequently there is a marked disjunction between the schools and the contemporary problems and changes taking place in society.

In a highly stable society, the basic values which the society prizes become an integral part of the educational philosophy, and the organization and activities of the schools reflect these values. In a society in rapid transition, there is usually confusion about values and the ways in which they can be implemented by the schools. An explicit educational philosophy can do much to give meaning and direction to the schools. It can help to determine the hierarchy of educational objectives, and it can serve to provide the organizing principles for the content and learning experiences. The specifications for a course as well as those for an entire curriculum should reflect the educational philosophy of the school and, if possible, the educational philosophy of the society.

A theory of learning can be one basis for ordering the possible objectives of education and for the determination of the objectives which should be given highest priority. Such a view of learning and evidence in support of it can be used to determine the likelihood that a particular objective can be achieved (or not) by a particular group of students. Finally, a psychology of learning is of value in determining the appropriateness of particular learning experiences as means for attaining particular objectives.

The point of all this is that specifications should not be the whims of particular teachers, subject experts, or curriculum-makers. The specifications properly result from a very complex analysis of the conditions and context in which the learning is to take place. The specifications for one place and time may not be appropriate for another place and time. It is unlikely that any single person has a comprehensive grasp of the entire situation. Only as a variety of resources are brought to bear can the specifications fully take into consideration the multitude of information and conceptions that are necessary.

USE OF SPECIFICATION FOR MAKING DECISIONS

One objection to the making of specifications and, especially to the stating of objectives is that it has no effect on the curriculum, the instruction, the evaluation, or even the learning of students. Some people view the stating of objectives as a meaningless charade advocated by educationists which, once done, can easily be forgotten. If educational objectives are regarded only as the introductory statements for a course, a set of instructional materials, or a dean's speech to a new group of students, then they are best forgotten, and to state them is a pointless exercise.

But educational specifications can and should have far-reaching consequences for all that follows in an educational enterprise. We can state a few of the educational decisions which require an explicit set of specifications with regard to content and objectives.

What is to be included or excluded in a particular subject, curriculum, or educational program? There is so much to be learned, so much to be understood, so many specifics in any field of learning that some set of considerations must guide the curriculum-maker or teacher. If the specifications are clear and understandable, they provide criteria for determining what in the subject matter is useful and what is not, what should be emphasized and what need not be emphasized, and which details can be omitted and which are absolutely essential.

Furthermore, the specifications can be utilized to determine how the materials should be treated. Is a particular item of information to be learned in its own right, or is it to be learned in order that some larger theory or concept can be understood? Is a principle to be learned in order to be remembered, is it to be learned in order to develop the ability to apply principles, or is it to be learned because it is part of a process of inquiry in the subject? Thus, decisions about how the subject matter is to be learned can follow from decisions about the specifications.

Decisions about the teaching-learning process in the classroom also are dependent upon a set of specifications. When to use a lecture or discussion; when to use secondary sources, primary sources, or firsthand experience; when to use independent learning, group processes, or discovery-learning strategies; when to use pro-gramed instruction, computer-assisted instruction, or workbooks and drill procedures, etc.—these are decisions which, in part, are dependent on the use of a set of specifications. It may be true that a teacher depends on feelings, hunches, and a quick grasp of a particular learning situation to determine what to do and how to do it. Without a set of specifications, however, these decisions are likely to be repetitions of what he has always done or expressions of what the teacher likes, believes he is good at, and gives him fewest problems. If the decisions are to promote the learning of students rather than to make the interests and attitudes of the teacher central, the teacher and teaching must be guided by some set of specifications which have been carefully developed and which are workable for the subject matter and the students involved.

Decisions about the evaluation process are also dependent on a set of specifications. What types of evaluation procedures are to be used: open book or closed book, essay or recognition form questions, products or processes, observation of the student or observation made by the student, cognitive tasks or affective responses of the students, frequent testing or comprehensive examinations, formative or summative evaluation—these are all possibilities for evaluation which may be used in various combinations depending on the specifications. Decisions about the particular objectives and content to be appraised, the weight and importance to be given to particular aspects of the evaluation, and even the standards to be used are largely dependent upon the specifications. Again, evaluation can be determined by the particular predilections of the evaluator, his skills, his habits, etc., or it can be determined by an explicit set of specifications which furnishes a blueprint for what should be evaluated and how it should be evaluated. The "state of the art" of evaluation is far more complex than the skills and habits of a particular examiner or evaluator. A set of specifications can, with proper technical facilities, provide for evaluation that transcends what can be evaluated by a particular teacher or evaluator.

Evaluation of Non-specified Outcomes of Instruction

One argument against the use of specifications is that there are differences between the outcomes of learning and instruction and the learnings which were specified in advance. This argument may be developed in two ways. First, not all of the outcomes that have been specified are achieved. This, of course, is one of the main reasons for evaluation. That is, if one attempts to evaluate for all the specified outcomes of instruction, it is possible to determine which ones have been achieved to a satisfactory degree and which have not. Thereafter, the problem becomes reduced to research and inquiries to determine why certain outcomes have not been attained and to the development of alternative procedures to attain them. It is quite possible, even after considerable time and effort has been expended, that certain outcomes are really impossible to attain with a given group of students and teachers under a given set of conditions. If this conclusion is finally reached, the specifications may have to be altered accordingly. One does hope that means can be developed to attain those outcomes which a group of teachers and curriculum-makers firmly believe to be desirable and important, but it is recognized that not all that one reaches for is attainable.

The second argument is that individuals vary, teachers vary, and the learning process is so complex that students learn far more than can be specified in advance. That this may be so should not be seen as an argument against specifying and evaluating the outcomes that are desired. It should be regarded as an argument for inquiry and research into the nature of the non-specified outcomes.

Some of the non-specified outcomes may be regarded as desirable from the viewpoint of curriculum-makers and teachers, and, if possible, they should be studied and evaluated. If the curriculum and the instruction stimulate some students to read and study far beyond the requirements of the course, this may be regarded as desirable. The extent to which this occurs may be appraised by relatively informal evaluation procedures. If the curriculum inspires some students to seek additional courses or other learning experiences in the subject, this may also be regarded as desirable, and it may be studied by appropriate methods. If the instruction results in some student's seeking interrelationships between what he has studied in one course and what he has studied in other courses, between the course and contemporary problems of the society, or between the course and his own personal problems, this may also be appraised. All of these "desirable" outcomes should be studied in an effort to understand the effects of instruction and perhaps to seek ways in which such effects may become more widespread. It is possible, on reflection, that some of these effects may become so predictable and widespread that they may be included in the specifications. The other desirable effects may be regarded as plusses which occur in an unpredictable way, and, one should be content when and if they occur.

However, there may be side effects of the instruction and curriculum which are clearly undesirable. These may be difficult to detect, but they need to be identified and corrected, if possible. If some students develop considerable cognitive competence in a subject but learn to dislike the subject with great intensity, this is clearly an undesirable consequence, and it should be appraised in order to determine why it occurs and how it can be altered. If the curriculum, the evaluation methods, and the standards that are used lead many students to regard themselves in a negative way or to develop a negative attitude toward school and learning, this is most unfortunate and should be investigated and, hopefully, corrected. If teacher attitudes are positive toward some students and negative toward others, the effects of this should be ascertained and corrected.

Increasingly there is evidence that middle-class children are encouraged while lower-class children may be discouraged by teachers and by particular aspects of the curriculum. Especially in a rapidly changing society, we must search to determine the intended as well as the unintended effects on children of particular practices, methods, curriculums, teachers, and organizational characteristics of education. Public education cannot be permitted to develop some children at the expense of others or to develop some desirable characteristics in children at the price of developing even more far-reaching negative characteristics in them.

It is quite likely that many of the unintended positive as well as negative outcomes of instruction can be detected by competent observers who approach the problem in a clinical way. An understanding of learning and of human development should enable competent observers of the process of learning and instruction in actual classrooms to predict many of these side effects. Once they have been detected and identified, it is possible to devise evaluation procedures to determine their frequency and their qualitative characteristics.

The point of all this is that there are undoubtedly many outcomes of instruction and curriculum that cannot be specified in advance. Such outcomes should be investigated by clinical and other techniques in the hope that the desirable outcomes can be strengthened and the undesirable outcomes corrected or eliminated. One need not limit evaluation to only the desired and specified outcomes of instruction if there is some reason to believe that certain additional outcomes are likely to take place. While the medical analogy is not entirely appropriate, it does suggest the importance of searching for the side effects of a particular treatment. All too frequently, the side effects of medical treatment are as important as the desired main effects.

Effects of Evaluation

It is possible to measure the length of a bar of metal in such a way that the measurement process does not appreciably alter the shape or size of the bar. Precautions must be taken to insure that the body heat of the measurer does not affect the expansion of the metal and that the weight of the measuring instrument does not alter the shape of the metal.

More complex processes of studying, testing, or measuring in the physical and biological sciences can have greater consequences on the phenomena being investigated, and more elaborate controls and precautions must be taken to insure that it is the phenomena which are being investigated rather than the "phenomena as influenced by the research procedures."

Whatever the case may be in the natural sciences, the effects of study, testing, or measurement in the social sciences are such that frequently the phenomena being investigated may be markedly altered, distorted, or affected in other ways by the process of investigation. Samoa being studied by Margaret Mead is altered in the very process by the presence of Dr. Mead and her methods of study. Human beings may rarely be studied without being affected by the study procedures. Especially in education, the process of studying or testing may have so much effect on students, teachers, and others that what we are investigating cannot be completely separated from the investigation process itself. [5] To measure a child's intelligence is to appreciably change the child and his parents, as well as to affect the way in which teachers and others come to view the child.

If, as is asserted here, the process of evaluation has an effect on the learner and the teacher, as well as on others involved in education, it is necessary to understand the possible effects and to deal with them intelligently. If these effects are understood and utilized properly, they can do much to enhance the student's learning as well as his regard for himself. If the effects are not used well, they can do great damage to the student as well as to the educational system. The point to be made is that the effects of evaluation can be maximized or minimized, but they cannot be entirely controlled. Also, the effects can be positive or negative, and only rarely can they be entirely neutralized.

Some of the effects of evaluation take place in advance of the

5. D. A. Goslin, *The Search for Ability* (New York: Russell Sage Foundation, 1963).

actual use of the evaluation instrument. In England, children begin to prepare for the "11+" examination a year or two in advance of the actual time of the examination. In the United States, college entrance examinations have a similar influence. Teachers also anticipate an examination, especially an external examination, and they direct some of their teaching effort (both group and tutorial instruction) to preparing their pupils for the anticipated examination. Parents also do whatever they can to increase their children's chances of successfully completing an anticipated examination, including placing their children in schools which they believe will give them the best preparation, coaching their children, or using whatever other tactics they believe will be efficacious.

The effects on the students at the time of the examination may be relatively small, except for anxiety aroused by the examination and frustration, self-doubt, or a sense of accomplishment engendered by the student's interaction with the examination. There is no doubt that many students are exhausted at the end of an important examination, but most of these effects disappear relatively quickly.

The postexamination effects may be very profound, depending on the uses made of the examination results. The result of some examinations, such as an intelligence test or a major external examination, may be to mark an individual for the rest of his life. An I.Q. index, the results of a school or college entrance examination, or the results of the matriculation examinations in many countries may determine the individual's educational and vocational career, his own view of himself, and the ways in which others regard him. These major examinations create self-fulfilling prophecies in which later success or failure or the educational and vocational openings available are largely determined by the results. It is no secret that teachers may rationalize their difficulties in instruction by pointing to the I.Q. or standardized test scores of their students. Parents also come to judge their children, positively as well as negatively, in terms of their I.Q.'s or other examination results. And the child himself will come to view himself partly in terms of his performance on certain key examinations.

MAXIMAL AND MINIMAL EFFECTS OF EVALUATION

Not all examinations have the same effect on students, teachers, parents, or instruction. Not all examinations have powerful effects on the way in which the student views himself or the way in which others (including employers) view the individual.

Examinations which are regarded as measuring important and relatively stable characteristics of the individual have the greatest effect. Thus, the I.Q. score is regarded as so important because it is widely believed that it is highly stable, that it determines the individual's capacity to learn, and that little can be done to alter it. While each of these assumptions can, in part, be questioned, it is the beliefs of school people and laymen (including the student himself) which make the intelligence test so important and which have such marked influences on the use of the results of such tests. Other tests which may be regarded in the same way are aptitude tests, personality measures, vocational interests tests, and, sometimes, tests of reading ability.

Examinations which are used to make important decisions at major disjunctions in the educational system also have great effects. The examinations which are used for certification of the completion of an educational program, for the selection of students for particular programs or streams of education, and for the determination of which students are to be admitted to advanced programs of education are so critical in the lives and careers of students that they not only have effects on the student and the educational system but they also influence the entire society. Such examinations have a profound effect on the curriculum and instruction: They determine who will have certain opportunities and who will not, and they determine the type of person who will be admitted to (or denied entrance into) particular occupations and professions. In the larger sense these examinations help to shape the society's view of itself and of the variations among the members of the society.

Examinations for which the results become part of the student's permanent record or which are made public also have great effects. If the results of a particular examination are referred to repeatedly in making critical decisions about the student (or adult), the examination will have a marked influence on the student and on the adults who are interested in or concerned with him. Here is the whole issue of invasion of privacy. Insofar as examination results are made a part of the permanent record of the student and such a record may be made available to other teachers, school authorities, and employers, they must be regarded as important by the student, and to do well or poorly on them is a matter of vital concern to the student and others. It is quite possible that administrative convenience has led to an overemphasis on some examinations. Undoubtedly, administrative convenience has led to the creation of a few landmarks in the student's records rather than to the development of a truly cumulative record which highlights the pattern of development of the individual over his entire educational career.

Examinations which are used to judge the effectiveness of teachers, schools, or systems of education have great effect on the institutions involved. While such examinations may have little direct influence on the students tested, they may have marked influence on the curriculum, on the patrons of the institution, and on the staff and administration of the institution. Undoubtedly, the responsiveness of the institution and the staff to the examination results is determined by the extent to which the results are made public and the extent to which the results can be related to specific practices and persons in the institution.

It is possible for examinations to have minimal effects on students, staff, and patrons. *Perhaps the least effect is likely when the examination results are not related to individuals, practices, or institutions.* If the examinations are related to anonymous individuals and institutions with a minimum of comparison among individuals or institutions and with a minimum of publicity, the results are unlikely to have much effect on either individuals or institutions. *Examinations are likely to have little effect if they are considered to be measuring trivial things which are not regarded as important by the students, teachers, patrons, and others.* Thus, a test of handwriting elegance is unlikely to have much influence on students or schools at present, while sixty years ago it might have been regarded as of the utmost importance. *Finally, examinations which are not used for making significant decisions by or about individuals or institutions, and where this is known in advance by the examinees, are likely to have minimal effects on the individuals and institutions.*

Perhaps the main point to be made about the effect of examinations is that it is largely a perceptual phenomenon. That is, if students, teachers, or administrators believe that the results of an examination are important, it matters very little whether this is really true or false—the effect is produced by what individuals perceive to be the case.

POSITIVE VERSUS DESTRUCTIVE EFFECTS OF EVALUATION

Evaluation is a two-edged sword which can enhance student learning and personality development or be destructive of student learning and personality development. It can have positive or negative effects on teachers, curriculums, and school systems. While it is unlikely that examinations and other methods of appraising the learning progress of students can be eliminated, it is possible to use evaluation procedures wisely, so that they may have a beneficial effect on learning and teaching. This is a matter of designing and using evaluation with a clear awareness of its possible effects and with a sensitivity to the ways in which the evaluation will be perceived by students, teachers, school authorities, and school patrons or the public.

If the primary use of evaluation is to render judgments of pass or fail, good or poor, the person being evaluated is likely to respond as one who is being tried by a judge. He is concerned about the fairness of the decision. Where students or teachers believe the evaluations to be unfair, they either overtly express their sense of mistreatment or brood about it and feel resentment against the evaluation process as well as the educational system which has used the process. Where students have no way of determining the fairness or soundness of the evaluation and where it is used repeatedly to indicate failure, poor performance, or other negative judgments about students, they are likely to develop a sense of frustration and their motivation for learning must suffer. Thus, some colleges may use achievement examinations at the end of the Freshman year to arbitrarily eliminate as high as 40 per cent of the entrants. Under such conditions, the students are penalized by their rank order on the examinations rather than by the inadequacy of their performance. When the examination system is "rigged" in this way, the students are placed in a competitive system in which "beating the system" and survival are more important than the learning which is presumably being tested. To "win" under such conditions is to lose in terms of one's view of himself and of his relations with others, and to suffer some deterioration in personal values. This is especially true where passing the examination by cramming, studying the tricks of examiners, memorizing material just for the examination, and other examination-taking strategies are separable from learning the subject.

Quite in contrast is the use of evaluation procedures which are regarded as valid by teachers and students, where the system of grading or marking is regarded as fair and just, and where there is a clear relation between what is taught and what is examined. Under such conditions, the students and teachers can enter into the learning process with a clear sense of purpose, and the appraisal of what has been learned may be regarded with concern and anxiety but, at the same time, as relevant and fair. Motivation for learning can be very high under such conditions, and students can give their efforts to those aspects of the learning which they regard as important. To pass or to do well on such examinations is likely to be regarded by the students as worthwhile, and this success is likely to lead to a strengthening of the student's sense of adequacy and of his commitment to the learning. Even to fail such an examination leaves the student with the sense of having entered into a worthwhile learning process and no great feeling of disgrace if one has done his best.

The basic questions to ask about examinations and other evaluation procedures are whether they have a positive effect on student learning and instruction and whether they leave both teachers and students with a positive view of themselves and of the subject and learning process. A primary task of teachers and examiners is to design the examinations and the evaluation process so that they will have these positive effects. We are able to state a few of the necessary conditions for this to take place. First, the examinations must be valid in the sense that they must examine for those aspects of the learning which are regarded by teachers and students as important and desirable learning outcomes. The examinations must also be valid in that they examine for these learning outcomes by the most direct methods. The evaluation techniques—whether they be observations of processes, products (such as term papers), reports of observations or experiments; recall or recognition questions; open-book or closed-book examinations; viva voce; etc.—must be seen by students and teachers as directly related to the learning or performance desired. Second, the examinations must be regarded as reliable and objective in the sense that chance and error must play a minimal part in determining the adequacy of each examinee's performance. That is, the sampling of the learning outcomes must be adequate enough to minimize the likelihood that chance failures or successes determine the final outcomes, and the scoring procedures must minimize subjectivity on the part of the readers or scorers. Finally, the standards for grades or pass-fail must be defined in terms of adequacy of learning rather than in terms of rank order of students and competition. That is, the student must be left with the sense that he has been judged in terms of what he has been able to do rather than in terms of who else took the examination at the same time as he did.

In addition to these elements, a well-designed examination with adequate previous indications to the student of what is to be expected of him can leave the student with a feeling that his preparation for it was eminently worthwhile. Such an examination can make the preparation for the examination an important learning experience if it requires him to bring the parts of the subject together in new ways—that is, if the examination causes him to interrelate and integrate the elements of the subject so that he finally perceives them in ways different from the ways he experienced them as he learned the parts or elements separately. This of course requires that the examining art be brought to its highest level and that the expectations for the learning be adequately communicated to the students in advance of their special preparation for the examination.

Formative Versus Summative Evaluation

Much of what we have been discussing in the section on the effects of examinations has been concerned with what may be termed "summative evaluation." This is the evaluation which is used at the end of the course, term, or educational program. Although the procedures for such evaluation may have a profound effect on the learning and instruction, much of this effect may be in anticipation of the examination or as a short- or long-term consequence of the examination after it has been given.

Quite in contrast is the use of "formative evaluation" to provide feedback and correctives at each stage in the teaching-learning process. By formative evaluation we mean evaluation by brief tests used by teachers and students as aids in the learning process. While such tests may be graded and used as part of the judging and classificatory function of evaluation, we see much more effective use of formative evaluation if it is separated from the grading process and used primarily as an aid to learning.

Frequent use of formative evaluation during a course may be very effective in pacing student learning. Each student is faced with many competing demands on his time and energies. Unless he is unusually well organized and purposive, he is likely to give his major efforts to those demands which are most compelling and less attention and care to those demands which he believes can be postponed to some later time. In highly sequential learning, especially, it is of the utmost importance that the student learn one task before another if he is to master the entire sequence. The use of formative evaluations after each separable unit or task in the learning process can do much to motivate the student to the necessary effort at the appropriate time.

Another use of formative evaluation is to provide feedback to the instructor after the completion of each unit in the sequence of instruction. Where a significant proportion of the students have made particular errors or have had difficulty with an important element of the learning tasks, this should be taken as a symptom of weakness in the instruction or instructional material. If these errors are regarded as critical, especially for later learning tasks, it is most desirable that the instructor review the ideas, preferably through alternative ways of explaining or describing the element in question. Ideally, the instructor should probe to determine why the idea was not understood or should seek other ways of clarifying what has gone wrong. The use of formative evaluation for this purpose requires that the instructor analyze the accuracy of item responses rather than be content with a description of the distribution of scores on the total test. Formative evaluation used in this way is a healthy corrective to the teaching process, since it finds difficulties early enough to do something about them as the sequence of learning-teaching develops.

Probably the most effective use of formative evaluation is to provide feedback to students on their learning of particular portions of the learning sequence. If a student has mastered all or a high proportion of the test items in the formative test (perhaps 85 per cent or more of the items), this can assure him that his learning is going well and that he should continue his present learning procedures. Such mastery information can serve to reinforce the learning (and the learning process) and can do much to decrease the student's anxiety about his learning. Since it is likely that high performance on a number of formative evaluation tests will be predictive of high performance on the summative evaluation instruments, the student who does well on the formative tests can be confident of his learning even in advance of the summative evaluation.

For students who have not mastered a particular unit of learning, the formative evaluation can provide feedback as to precisely where he is having difficulty. Here the formative test must be analyzed to indicate the particular elements still to be learned as well as the relation of these elements to other elements in the unit of learning. Such feedback to the student is most useful when it not only identifies what the student must still learn but also suggests very specific instructional materials and procedures that he should use to learn these ideas. If the students can be motivated to correct their difficulties and if the appropriate resources are made available to them (including tutors, special materials, etc.), it is quite likely that the majority of them can achieve mastery over each unit in the sequence of instruction.

We have found that such formative evaluation procedures are most effective when they are separated from the grading process and are presented primarily as aids in the teaching-learning process. Thus, when each formative test is graded, it is likely that those students who repeatedly receive C grades or less will match their efforts in the course to the final grade they expect. In contrast, when students are assured that they can learn the material if they will correct their difficulties during the progress of the course, they can be motivated to put forth the necessary extra effort at the appropriate time in the course. Further motivation for this extra effort can be produced if there is any assurance that their efforts will eventually be rewarded by high grades on the summative evaluation instruments as well as by the thorough mastery of the subject being studied.

The use of formative evaluation suggests that evaluation in relation to the process of learning and teaching can have strong positive effects on the actual learning of students as well as on their motivation for the learning and their self-concept in relation to school learning. Much can be written on the process of testing and test construction in formative evaluation, but the main point being made here is that evaluation which is directly related to the teaching-learning process as it unfolds can have highly beneficial effects on the learning of students, the instructional process of teachers, and the use of instructional materials by teachers and learners. This is one method by which individualization in the learning process can be related to the attainment of a common set of objectives by a large proportion of students.

CHAPTER IV

The Uses of Evaluation in Guidance

RALPH F. BERDIE

Educational and psychological evaluation, assessment, and measurement are considered by this author as essential functions of the guidance program. The role of evaluation in guidance is minimized by such writers as Arbuckle,[1] Rogers,[2] and Boy and Pine[3], and emphasized by Traxler,[4] Williamson,[5] and Super and Crites.[6] The emphasis placed on evaluation in a guidance program depends in large part on the stated objectives and on the personal and professional values of the guidance staff. Brim (see footnote 7) refers to John Gardner's distinction between three social organizations, one based on an equalitarian philosophy, one based on an inherited aristocracy, and one based on open competition. Brim notes that ability tests are incompatible with the equalitarian viewpoint that men are equal insofar as ability tests assume the presence of individual differences which, according to the equalitarian point of view, are non-existent. Testing is inappropriate according to the second point of view insofar as tests serve to open avenues of achievement according to biological inheritance rather than to so-

1. Dugald S. Arbuckle, *Counseling: Philosophy, Theory and Practice* (Boston: Allyn & Bacon, 1965).

2. Carl R. Rogers, *Client-centered Theory* (Boston: Houghton Mifflin Co., 1951).

3. Angelo V. Boy and Gerald J. Pine, *Client-centered Counseling in the Secondary School* (Boston: Houghton Mifflin Co., 1963).

4. Arthur E. Traxler, *Techniques of Guidance* (New York: Harper & Bros., 1945).

5. Edmund G. Williamson, *Counseling Adolescents* (New York: McGraw-Hill Book Co., 1950).

6. Donald E. Super and John O. Crites, *Appraising Vocational Fitness* (New York: Harper & Row, 1962).

cial inheritance, and consequently they challenge the established aristocratic social order. The view of society as competitive leads to the conclusion that evaluation is acceptable.

In each generation a talented elite should rise to the top, to be replaced next generation by others bearing no necessary blood relationship to them. Each individual has the right to contribute to society as much as he is able, according to his talents. Since tests identify the talented and make it possible to provide them with opportunities for full development of their capacities, a favorable view of intelligence tests should follow.[7]

Brim and also Berdie have explained attitudes toward evaluation by referring to the personality characteristics of the guidance staff. Again, to quote Brim: "It is likely . . . that strong opposition exists among those people who are distinctly hostile to any self-examination, introspection, or self-understanding. These are the people who are also authoritarian in interpersonal relations, intolerant of diversity in ideology or beliefs, and strongly opposed to most forms of social change."[8] Of course, many other factors, particularly personal experiences, help explain attitudes toward testing.

The more the guidance program's emphasis is on the student's emotional acceptance of himself and on his ability to establish empathic relationships with others and the less its emphasis is on rational understanding of his own behavior and the sensibility of his educational and vocational decisions, the less is the attention that will be given to systematic evaluation. Perhaps only a few guidance programs place major emphasis on objectives related to these empathic, intuitive, and emotional processes. A few more programs tend to place almost exclusive emphasis on the processes related to the guidance staff's and the student's perceptions of measurable and observable student characteristics. The philosophies of most professional guidance personnel lead them to recognize the importance of both the cognitive and non-cognitive processes which constitute student behavior.

Consideration of the function of evaluation in guidance requires

7. Orville G. Brim, Jr., "American Attitudes toward Intelligence Tests," *American Psychologist*, XX (1965), 125-30.

8. *Ibid.*; See also Ralph F. Berdie, "Science, Values, and Psychometry," *Teachers College Record*, LXIV (December, 1962), 199-203.

us to consider the purposes of guidance programs. These purposes can be perceived both as they are related to the student and to society. As far as objectives related to the student are concerned, the guidance personnel can easily adjust to Dewey's perception of education as continuing experience. The function of the guidance staff is to make available to students experiences that have social and personal significance, essentially experiences that will lead to other experiences which, in turn, are part of a continuing experiential process. The guidance program serves to extend the range of educational experiences available in the school beyond those traditional experiences historically located in the classroom. The program aids students and others in the school to select opportunities for experiences and to help make them meaningful to students. The processes of selecting experiences and making them meaningful require that the student and others in the school be provided with information about the student and with normative information which is essential if information about the individual is to have any impact on his education.

No lasting distinction can be made between purposes of guidance related to the student and those related to society, but consideration of both the personal and social implications of guidance leads to a better understanding of the function of evaluation in guidance. The guidance staff, along with everybody else in the school, shares responsibility for providing society with an educated citizenry capable of assuming the roles of parents, voters, and participating members of society. Along with this responsibility is the responsibility for providing productive citizens who are trained and educated to make available the needed materials and services on which we depend.

Society also has assigned to the guidance program a somewhat different responsibility; one might describe this as a responsibility for aiding in the reduction of social conflict. For example, if our social processes are to function effectively, mental health problems must be identified, treated, and prevented. Many such problems have their origins in childhood and are closely related to school experiences. The guidance program is becoming one of society's chief instruments in improving and maintaining the mental health of the nation. Delinquency and crime are other expressions of social conflict closely related to mental health; these problems also are becoming of increasing concern to guidance personnel.

In a sense, many of these responsibilities can be subsumed under the more traditional assignment of helping society maximize the use of individual talent. The welfare of the individual and the efficiency of society depend in large part on the extent to which persons are available to perform necessary jobs, the extent to which energies and effort are not wasted on non-productive and destructive activities, and the extent to which individuals can identify, develop, and express their talents, interests, and needs.

No attempt will be made here to describe the functions included in a guidance program. These include such things as the admission and selection of students, the classification and educational placement of students, educational and vocational planning with and for students, care of the physical and mental health of students, participation in non-classroom educational experiences, placement and employment, and discipline of students. Many persons in the school are involved in all or most of these functions, including teachers, administrators, and counselors. Many other specialized staff members have more restricted responsibilities, such as social workers, school nurses, psychometrists, school psychologists, and, in higher education, specialists, dealing with housing, financing, unions, and admissions.

Guidance personnel maintain working relationships with students and their families, with teachers, with administrators, with the community, and with other persons on the guidance staff. Guidance personnel spend much time talking with individual students and parents, working with groups, and consulting with other persons in the school and the community. Much of the guidance staff's time is devoted to observing students, giving tests, observing and structuring field situations, and writing reports. Perhaps most of their time is devoted to individual interviews with students, parents, and other persons in the school in order to achieve the purposes we have discussed.

Purposes of Evaluation in Guidance

Evaluation is used in guidance to aid in decision-making processes and to facilitate self-understanding on the part of the student. The decisions regarding students can be arbitrarily categorized as educational, vocational, and personal. Of these three types of decisions, educational decisions are perhaps the easiest to evaluate insofar as some criteria of educational success are available, such as school grades, persistence in school, graduation or completion of course study, and accomplishment as shown by tests of educational attainment. When matched against the stated objectives of most educational programs, these criteria provide bases for no more than indirect inferences of educational success. One can infer something regarding the effectiveness of a school or a guidance program from how well students do on achievement tests or how long they remain in school, but most educational objectives have considerably more breadth than do these criteria.

Criteria for evaluating the effectiveness of vocational decisions also are available, although they are even less adequate than the criteria pertaining to education. Income, eminence, persistence, productivity, or success and satisfaction as rated by self or others all have implications for vocational success, but each of these is subject to so many influences and is a result of so many determinants that any inferences made must be highly tentative.

Personal decisions involving such things as marriage, family, military service, community participation, selection of the area of the country in which to live, and other behaviors closely related to the individual's style of life are even more difficult to evaluate. Knowledge about the relationships between the characteristics of the individual and these personal behaviors is available only for carefully selected samples and is amenable to little generalization. The studies of Terman and Oden [9] and of Kelly [10] are examples of the better types of these studies. In the near future, additional information should be available concerning the relationships between many types of individual differences and subsequent behaviors

9. Lewis M. Terman and Melita H. Oden, *The Gifted Child Grows Up* (Genetic Studies of Genius IV [Stanford: Stanford University Press, 1947]).

10. E. Lowell Kelly, "Consistency of the Adult Personality," *American Psychologist*, X (1955), 659-81.

through follow-up studies of persons first studied as children in the 1920's and 1930's.[11]

One use of evaluation in the prediction and decision-making processes is best exemplified by the use of prediction, probability, or expectancy tables used to predict success in college. This approach requires that assessment data be gathered on a large sample of prospective college students. After a specified length of time in college, these students are grouped according to various behaviors demonstrated in college. For example, they may be divided into students who remain in college and those who leave. They may be divided into students who do successful work as opposed to those who are unsuccessful or divided into students who have average grades of A, B, C, D, and F. They may be divided into students who are admitted to professional schools and those who are not, or into students who graduate from one curriculum as opposed to others. The relationships then are observed between the assessment information gathered prior to college and the subsequent collegiate behavior, and statements of probability are made concerning expected college behaviors of groups of students with varying entrance characteristics.

The *College Expectancy Tables* used in Minnesota provide one example.[12] All high-school Juniors in Minnesota are given the *Minnesota Scholastic Aptitude Test*, a fifty-minute scholastic-ability test, and test scores and high-school percentile ranks are available for all of these students. At what is normally the end of the college Freshman year, lists are prepared showing which of these students entered each college in the state, and in each college the students are divided into three groups, those obtaining grades of B or higher, those obtaining grades of C or higher, and those obtaining grades of D or higher. Then, in each college, the students are divided into five groups according to their high-school percentile rank. One group of students consists of those with high-

11. Nancy Bayley, "Behavioral Correlates of Mental Growth: Birth to Thirty-Six Years," *American Psychologist*, XXIII (1968), 1-17.

12. E. O. Swanson, J. C. Merwin, and R. F. Berdie, "Expectancy Tables for Freshmen Entering Minnesota Colleges" (Minnesota Test Norms and Expectancy Tables [St. Paul: Department of Education, State of Minnesota, 1967]).

school percentile ranks of below twenty; the second group consists of those with high-school percentile ranks from twenty to thirty-nine, and so on. Then, in each of these percentile groups, the per cent of students who fall into each of the three groups divided on the basis of college grades is determined. As an example, the table below shows the men and women who completed their Freshman year in the College of Education of the University of Minnesota in the springs of 1960 and 1962. Of the students in the upper 20 per cent of their high-school class, 97 per cent received an average grade point of D or higher, 70 per cent an average grade point of C or higher, and 15 per cent received an average grade point of B or higher. Of the few students with a high-school percentile rank of less than 40, 75 per cent received a grade-point average of C or higher but none received average grades of B or higher.

TABLE 1

EXPECTANCY TABLES FOR FIRST-YEAR GRADE-POINT AVERAGE BASED ON FRESHMEN (MALE AND FEMALE) ENTERING UNIVERSITY OF MINNESOTA COLLEGE OF EDUCATION IN THE FALL OF 1959 AND THE FALL OF 1961 (PREDICTIONS BASED ON HIGH-SCHOOL RANK)

HIGH-SCHOOL RANK QUINTILE GROUP	CHANCES IN 100 OF A FRESHMAN OBTAINING AN AVERAGE GRADE OF:			SIZE OF GROUP
	D or higher	C or higher	B or higher	
80 or more	97	70	15	Over 100
60–79	92	46	—	Over 100
40–59	88	29	1	From 50 to 100
20–39	75	—	—	Less than 10
19 or less	—	—	—	—

Similar tables using test scores and other data are available. Presentations such as these relieve the counselor of much of the necessity for incorporating into his test interpretation explanations of the concepts of the standard error of measurement and the standard error of estimate insofar as the probability statements implicit in the table explain these for him. For example, the tables demonstrate to the student that those students with extremely low test scores have some probability of outstanding success even if it is a small probability, and the tables also demonstrate that students with high test scores have some probability of failure.

Prediction tables have been made available in several places in the country. Expectancy tables based on SCAT and STEP are available for predicting success at the University of New Mexico.[13] Hills[14] has published several expectancy tables for high-school counselors working with students planning to enter any of the colleges in Georgia. The counselor enters Hills' expectancy tables with an index obtained from combining several predictors. Prediction tables based on regression equations are available for counselors to use with students considering attending Utah colleges and technical institutes.[15]

Gelatt and Clarke discuss some of the subjective probabilities of the decision process. On the basis of a review of much literature, they conclude:

The evidence suggests that many students may well be quite capable of basing their subjective probabilities on an objective assessment of their own experiences and on factual data concerning the nature of the situation and the experience of others. It would appear, then, that a primary function of an effective guidance program would be the gathering and organizing of a broad base of relevant factual data to be used by students in formulating probability estimates.[16]

The counselor's responsibility for aiding the student to make a decision encompasses more than providing him with information concerning the probabilities of various outcomes. Once the student obtains some realization of these probabilities, he then faces the task of deciding which risks he wishes to assume. Some students will quickly decide that, if they have at least one chance out of ten of succeeding in a certain choice, they will take the risk. Other students will require assurance that at least eight or nine out of ten persons similar to themselves succeed in a certain course before

13. A. A. Wellck, "State-wide Tests and Academic Success at the University of New Mexico," *Personnel and Guidance Journal*, XLII (December, 1963), 403-5.

14. John R. Hills, "College Expectancy Tables for High School Counselors," *Personnel and Guidance Journal*, XLII (January, 1964), 479-83.

15. F. B. Jex, *Predicting Academic Success beyond High School* (Salt Lake City: University of Utah, 1964).

16. H. B. Gelatt and Robert B. Clarke, "Role of Subjective Probabilities in the Decision Process," *Journal of Counseling Psychology*, XIV (1967), 332-341.

selecting it. Often these decisions are not easily made and, as students vacillate, consider alternatives, and react to tentative choices, counselors can aid them in understanding their own needs and also help them provide for many contingencies.

Although the use of evaluation in guidance for purposes of decision-making assumes a need for self-understanding on the part of the student, some guidance personnel and some counseling theories regard this need as quite apart from the process of decision-making. Knowledge of self has been stated as a life goal by many of the world's wise men: Plutarch, Diogenes, Plato, Chaucer, Shakespeare, Cervantes, Pope, and so on. These and others have assumed self-knowledge to be an essential quality of humanity and a principle purpose of education, and guidance may be viewed as the development of self-knowledge.

Self-knowledge can have validity and meaning only in light of the individual's knowledge of others and his perception of the world surrounding him. A test score means little or nothing without norms; awareness of one's own behaviors and proclivities means little outside of the reference provided by knowledge concerning others.

Several attempts to assess the impact of guidance in counseling on students have observed changes in self-knowledge. Singer and Stefflre[17] have reviewed some of the problems inherent in such research and have revealed incidentally that changes in correlations between precounseling and postcounseling self-descriptions and test scores may not provide an adequate basis for evaluating the impact of counseling. They indicate that the self-description technique should reveal whether the individual deviates more or less from his actual "observed" status after counseling than he did before. Such discrepancies may occur not only in terms of mean values but also in terms of variance, and similar methods of counseling may have quite different impacts on students with varying characteristics.

Most authors agree that knowledge of self is not sufficient to influence behavior. Acceptance of self, as contrasted to knowledge of self, may be a more relevant concept, and persons' attitudes of

17. Stanley L. Singer and Bufford Stefflre, "Analysis of Self-Estimate in the Evaluation of Counseling," *Journal of Counseling Psychology*, I (Winter, 1954), 252-55.

acceptance and rejection may change considerably with no observable change in self-knowledge, as shown by one's realization of his own characteristics as compared to the characteristics of others. Even counselors who are mainly concerned with increasing the level of self-acceptance, however, spend considerable time discussing with counselees the behaviors and attitudes characterizing the individual.

The process of decision-making on the part of both the student and the school should be a continuous one, and only seldom in a student's life is a decision "made." Decisions tend to evolve or develop, and, just as values and attitudes rarely spring forth full-blown, decisions emerge as a student experiences the world about him. Knowledge about self also develops in this way, and the relationships between self-knowledge and educational, vocational, and personal decisions obviously are important but as yet relatively little is known about them.

The roles of the counselor and the counselee in using information obtained from evaluation involving tests and other means can be specified further. The counselee has final responsibility for judging the meaning of the information. He and the counselor consider its implications, its accuracy, and the many ways in which it can be interpreted, but the counselee accepts or rejects as he sees fit from the many meanings of the information.

The counselor has a primary responsibility, which the counselee shares, for using evaluation data to construct and verify hypotheses. In a sense, this resembles the counseling process described by the Pepinskys,[18] and the author proposes it again in spite of some suggestion from Parker's research[19] that many counselors may not proceed in this fashion. Perhaps many do not but should.

As some examples of this approach, consider the counselor who is discussing with a high-school Senior the probability of his success in an arts college having highly selective admissions requirements. The counselor may look at the boy's high-school record and, on the basis of the student's being in the upper 3 per cent of a

18. Harold B. Pepinsky and Pauline N. Pepinsky, *Counseling: Theory and Practice* (New York: Ronald Press, 1954).

19. Clyde A. Parker, "As a Clinician Thinks . . ." *Journal of Counseling Psychology,* V (Winter, 1958), 253-61.

large graduating class, hypothesize that the student has a reasonable chance for success in that college. This is his initial hypothesis. The counselor and the student then search for additional information that may or may not support it. They consider the student's score on the *College Entrance Examination Board Tests*, and find that the SAT score is 498. The average SAT score for Freshmen entering the college being considered is 610. This evidence leads the counselor and the student to question the validity of the original hypothesis. The counselor and the counselee continue their search for evidence and begin to consider the scores the student obtained on other tests extending back into the elementary grades. On the basis of high scores, the counselor realizes that the SAT score is not an adequate reflection of what the boy's true score well might be. On the other hand, he may decide to reject the original hypothesis and conclude that most of the available evidence indicates the boy would have considerable difficulty in the college being considered.

Another example is found when a counselor and a student are discussing educational and vocational alternatives. The student has described the satisfaction obtained from working in a local garage and using his father's basement shop equipment. He expresses an interest in engineering, and the counselor and the student hypothesize that on the basis of available information this might be an appropriate choice. Then they consider information provided by the *Strong Vocational Interest Blank* and a mathematics achievement test. The scores on scales related to engineering are all C; the scores on occupations involving mechanical work are high. The mathematics test score is slightly above average for high-school graduates but considerably below average for engineering students. In this way the information about the student's hobbies, work experience, and academic achievement, as obtained from interviews, school records, tests, and inventories, is all used in the process of making and verifying hypotheses.

EVALUATION OF COUNSELING AND GUIDANCE

Attention should be given not only to the use of evaluation in counseling and guidance but also to the evaluation of counseling and guidance. Assessment instruments are used to provide information about individuals, to further self-understanding, and to aid in decision-making, but somewhat different evaluation concepts are applied when the counselor attempts to learn more about the impact of counseling and guidance on the individual and on the groups to which he belongs. Does guidance have such an impact? How effective are different guidance and counseling systems, programs, and methods in comparison to one another? What are the relationships between such effectiveness and characteristics and needs of students? How does the value of the impact of guidance compare to the cost of providing it?

One of the most complete and systematic discussions of outcome research is contained in the volume by Volsky, Magoon, Norman, and Hoyt.[20] These authors discuss problems of counseling research, methodological considerations in outcome studies, the relevance of the philosophy of science to such evaluation research, and problems involved in the design and analysis of outcome studies. They present a conceptual framework that provides a basis for a nicely designed, controlled study of the outcomes of counseling. In their research, discussions with counselors led to the postulation that three types of behavior changes might be related to counseling: reduction in anxiety, reduction in defensive behaviors, and increase in personal problem-solving ability. Tests and inventories then were devised to evaluate changes in these behaviors as they might be observed in college-student counselees, and then an experiment was designed in which matched students were randomly assigned to counseled and non-counseled groups, given pretests, and—after counseling for the experimental group—given posttests. The results failed to show significant differences between the experimental and control groups on the specially designed instruments, but the evidence did suggest that those in the experimental group were able to solve highly individualized and specific problems; a later follow-up study revealed that 74 per cent of the counseled group had made satisfactory progress in the university, as compared to only 35 per cent in the non-counseled group. The study deserves attention mainly because it so well illustrates the complexity of evaluating the guidance process and because it describes the development of instruments designed to accomplish this purpose.

20. Theodore Volsky *et al.*, *The Outcomes of Counseling and Psychotherapy* (Minneapolis: University of Minnesota Press, 1965).

These examples may help explain the purposes and general approach of the counselor in using evaluation data. Many questions can be raised, however, concerning what guidance personnel actually do with information, and problems of interpreting test and other data need to be reviewed.

Interpretation of Data

The research on and the discussions of interpreting data in counseling have been directed largely to the interpretation of test scores. Several papers discuss possible frameworks and problems involved in test interpretation. Some describe and attempt to evaluate single methods of test interpretation. A few compare the relative impacts of two or more methods.

Horst deals with the general problem of whether or not students should be given information and how much data should be provided to them. He concludes not only that the counselor can but also that he must provide test results to students.

We can take the point of view that it is up to the counselor to state the facts to the student and then it is up to the student to do as he pleases. I think this counseling philosophy is too narrow. It assumes that what a student does is his own business so long as he has been informed of the best available facts and that it is his responsibility and his alone if he decides to act contrary to these facts. This again is in the tradition of so-called democracy and individual freedom. It is a permissive point of view in counseling. I think it fails to take into account the broader social consequences when students go contrary to indications of tests and test results. Have counselors or advisors really discharged their responsibilities toward the student when they have given him all the information available about his possibilities for success or failure in various academic or vocational areas or any other kinds of activities which are of importance to the person being counseled? . . . I would say, further, know on the basis of past experience what the test scores mean; second, tell the student what his test scores mean; and third, do your best to get the student to act accordingly.[21]

In an analysis of counselors' errors in test interpretation, Lister

21. Paul Horst, "How Much Information on Test Results Should Be Given to Students: Views of a Research Psychologist," *Journal of Counseling Psychology*, VI (Fall, 1959), 218-22.

and McKenzie[22] list: too early presentation of test results, interpretation without reference to criteria, erroneous assumptions of validity, and presentation in terms students cannot understand. They state that some of these errors can be reduced by counselors' emphasizing the student's felt need for information, helping him state his questions operationally, using statements of empirical validity, and adequately communicating. The focus of evaluation should be on student recall, understanding, and acceptance of predictions derived from test results. Lifton[23] suggests that counselees can incorporate test information best when it involves a minimum of transfer, does not conflict with their security needs, and is perceived by students as necessary information for achieving a goal.

Berg[24] studied test score misunderstandings identified in a group of thirty adults who received vocational counseling. He reported the following distribution of errors:

Centile confused with I.Q. 4
Confusion over what I.Q. means......................... 5
Norm group confused.................................... 12
Confusion of interest and aptitude....................... 15
Scores guarantee success............................... 17

Berg emphasizes the need to verify and learn what scores mean to counselees at the end of interviews.

Several observations have been made of the impact of undifferentiated test interpretations on students. Froehlich and Moser administered the *Differential Aptitude Tests* to 150 ninth-graders and then interpreted the tests in group and individual sessions. Immediately after the interpretation and again fifteen months later, each pupil drew his profile, and the profiles were compared to the obtained scores. The authors concluded that, "A large proportion of students in this study did not accurately report their percentile

22. James L. Lister and Donald H. McKenzie, "A Framework for the Improvement of Test Interpretation in Counseling," *Personnel and Guidance Journal*, XLV (September, 1966), 61-66.

23. W. M. Lifton, "Counseling Theory and the Use of Educational Media," *Vocational and Guidance Quarterly*, XIII (1964), 77-82.

24. Irwin A. Berg, "Test Score Interpretation and Client Confusion," *Personnel and Guidance Journal*, XXXIV (May, 1956), 576-78.

rank on the several tests of the DAT battery."[25] These students tended to avoid recalling both high and low scores and the variance for the recall scores was smaller than that for the obtained scores. Coefficients of correlations for the eight tests between recall and obtained scores ranged from .41 to .57.

Another study of the extent to which interpreted test scores were recalled was reported by Fernald.[26] Tests were given to fifty-nine college students who were provided with individual test interpretations. The results showed high immediate recall but marked variability and distortion on delayed recall. The distortion consisted of students overestimating their scores, perceiving scores closer to the average range than they actually were.

The effect of test interpretation on self-understanding or self-perception was studied by Lister and Ohlsen.[27] These authors varied the orientation of the students to testing and then observed accuracy of self-estimates as related to motivation. The differences in orientation to testing were not related to any increases in self-understanding, but the interpretation-of-objective tests appeared to increase accuracy of self-estimates of achievement, intelligence, and interest, at both secondary- and primary-school levels.

In a somewhat similar study by Hills and Williams,[28] forty-five counselees rated themselves both before and after counseling. The authors concluded that communication of test results did not lead to a positive change in self-perception but rather that the test results which differed from clients' preconceived notions of themselves had a negative effect. The impact of test interpretation on the attitudes of students and their parents toward counseling was reported by

25. C. P. Froehlich and W. E. Moser, "Do Counselees Remember Test Scores?" *Journal of Counseling Psychology*, (Fall, 1954), 149-52.

26. L. Dodge Fernald, Jr., "Client Recall of Test Scores," *Personnel and Guidance Journal*, XLIII (October, 1964), 167-70.

27. James L. Lister and Merle M. Ohlsen, "The Improvement of Self-Understanding through Test Interpretation," *Personnel and Guidance Journal*, XLIII (April, 1965), 804-10.

28. David A. Hills and John E. Williams, "Effects of Test Information upon Self-Evaluation in Brief Educational-Vocational Counseling," *Journal of Counseling Psychology*, XII (Fall, 1965), 275-81.

Herman and Zeigler.[29] They found that a group counseling program increased favorable attitudes toward counseling and resulted in many parents reducing the personality and academic ratings of their children. The treatment appeared to produce favorable attitude changes toward counseling.

A more sophisticated research approach, and one providing a comparison of different methods of test interpretation, was reported by Dressel and Matteson.[30] They were interested in the relationship between client participation in the test-interpretation process and increases in self-understanding. First, they developed and published a scale for identifying the extent of client participation in test interpretation. Then they used an experimental design in which seven counselors each counseled seven students. The students first were given a test of self-understanding, then were administered the test, then were interviewed with the interviews being recorded, and immediately after the interview were given the test of self-understanding again. The self-understanding test was readministered two months later.

This study revealed that counselors who involved students more in test interpretation also had students who improved more in self-understanding, but for any given counselor there was no relationship between counselee participation and increase of self-understanding. Perhaps the counselor characteristics that result in more counselee participation also are the characteristics that result in more counselee gain. Although counselee participation was not related to satisfaction with counseling, a positive and significant correlation was identified between amount of participation and certainty of vocational choice at the conclusion of counseling.

Other investigators have attempted to vary systematically the methods of test interpretation. Walker[31] reported that greater

29. Louis M. Herman and Martin L. Zeigler, "The Effectiveness of Interpreting Freshman Counseling-Test Scores to Parents in a Group Situation," *Personnel and Guidance Journal*, XL (October, 1961), 143-49.

30. Paul L. Dressel and Ross W. Matteson, "The Effect of Client Participation in Test Interpretation," *Educational and Psychological Measurement*, (Winter, 1950), 693-706.

31. Joseph L. Walker, "Four Methods of Interpreting Test Scores Compared," *Personnel and Guidance Journal*, XLIV (December, 1965), 402-3.

personal acceptance of test scores resulted from individual interpretations using verbal methods and printed materials than from group discussions making greater use of audiovisual aids. Holmes[32] tested 154 college Freshmen with a variety of tests and divided them into four groups. Interpretation methods involved (*a*) test descriptions and referral to the student's profile; (*b*) students rating themselves on a test profile before receiving scores and then discussing scores with counselors; (*c*) counselors selecting tests to be interpreted and exploring, clarifying, and reflecting; and (*d*) mail reports. One week later, counselees completed forms revealing their attitudes toward the counselor and the value of the information. No significant differences in attitude toward the counselor were found, although the counselors themselves expressed preferences. Students who had not seen a counselor but received their results by mail appeared to have less favorable attitudes toward guidance than did the other students.

A study by Folds and Gazda[33] compared three different methods of test interpretation—individual, small group, and written. All experimental groups were more accurate in self-estimates of test scores than were control groups, and students receiving individual interpretations expressed greater satisfaction with that procedure. All groups, including the control groups, made significant changes in concepts of self and others, but no such significant differences were found among groups.

Attempts to compare the differential effectiveness of various methods of interpretation are marred by lack of knowledge concerning how well such interpretations are done. Peckens and Bennett[34] observed interviews between twenty-five certified full-time high-school counselors and twenty college Freshman women who had been tested. Interviews during which counselors interpreted

32. June E. Holmes, "The Presentation of Test Information to College Freshmen," *Journal of Counseling Psychology*, XI (Spring, 1964), 54-58.

33. Jonell H. Folds and George M. Gazda, "A Comparison of the Effectiveness and Efficiency of Three Methods of Test Interpretation," *Journal of Counseling Psychology*, XIII (Fall, 1966), 318-24.

34. Russell G. Peckens and Lloyd M. Bennett, "A Study of the Effectiveness of the Secondary School Counselor in Test Interpretation," *School Counselor*, XV (January, 1968), 203-8.

test scores to students were recorded and each sentence of each interview was categorized according to relevance, generality, and specificity. The results suggested that test interpretations were not well done; they were irrelevant, overgeneralized, and avoided pertinent information. Many subjects retained so little of the interpretation that the interpretations could be considered worthless, and lack of learning resulting from interpretation well might have been due to the inadequacies of interpretations.

The results of studies lead to the conclusion that the effectiveness of test interpretation in counseling is a function of many things, including counselor characteristics, student characteristics, method of presentation, personality characteristics being evaluated, tests used, counselee's perception of self as related to test scores, and expectations and attitudes of both counselee and counselor toward counseling.

Research needs to be done on the vocabulary appropriate for use in interpreting data to different students, the relative effectiveness of methods of score presentation, students' understanding of probability concepts, the relationship between effectiveness of interpretation and counselors' understanding of the information being interpreted, and the adequacy of interpretation as related to relevancy of the information being presented.

Lack of this kind of information suggests why Goslin can conclude:

> Obviously, individuals make use of many different types of information in arriving at an estimate of their abilities; standardized test scores are only one of many ways in which individuals get information about their capabilities. Data from a national sample of high school students indicate further that test scores are of relatively minor importance in shaping self-estimates of ability in comparison with such things as school grades, comments made by one's peers and parents, and contact with teachers.[35]

Some Conceptual Problems

Some conceptual problems are directly related to the interpretation of evaluative information in guidance. These conceptual

35. David A. Goslin, "What's Wrong with Tests and Testing—Part II," *College Board Review*, No. 66 (Winter, 1967-68), 33-37.

problems have implications for the use of evaluation for other than guidance purposes, and the problems are not independent of one another.

A major problem concerns the nature of personality. Common observation reveals that persons operate as entities, and, if we are to understand most interactions among persons, individuals must be considered as "whole" persons. Yet most evaluation is based on analysis of the individual, and we use the concept of traits in making inferences about persons. These traits, as Allport has emphasized,[36] are intervening variables and are never directly observed, only inferred.

Trait theory requires us to assume that small behavior patterns can be grouped rather consistently into larger patterns and that some smaller patterns fit into some larger patterns but not into others. It assumes a certain amount of independence of one larger pattern from other patterns and some dependence among the smaller behaviors within a given pattern. Thus it assumes some generalizability of behavior and some specificity. We group certain behaviors together and call them aptitudes, others we group and call interests, and so on. Within the broad category of aptitude, some behaviors are classified as mechanical aptitude, some as clerical aptitude, and some as academic aptitude. We realize the inferential nature of our categories when we observe empirically that some behaviors we define as aptitudes in one area are predictive of behaviors in other areas. The counselor, as he uses evaluation data, must be concerned with the extent to which generalizations can be made about specific behaviors, and he must realize that the extent to which the "clustering" of specific behaviors occurs varies from individual to individual, from behavior to behavior, and even from time to time.

Another conceptual problem facing the counselor involves the question of clinical versus actuarial prediction. Extensive attention was first given to this problem by Meehl,[37] and the later reports by

36. Gordon W. Allport, "Traits Revisited," *American Psychologist*, XXI (1966), 1-10.

37. Paul E. Meehl, *Clinical versus Statistical Prediction* (Minneapolis: University of Minnesota Press, 1954), p. 14.

Watley[38] demonstrate the significance of the problem for counselors. Meehl posed the question as to whether behavior could best be predicted on the basis of quantified data treated statistically or of data treated clinically, subjectively, or intuitively. He concluded that such behaviors as school performance and response to psychiatric treatment could be predicted best actuarially. Watley's work suggests that, in most situations and for most predictors or persons, Meehl's conclusions are valid, but in certain situations some persons are able to predict at least as well as statistical means, and perhaps slightly better.

What we know about the effectiveness of such predictions has at least two implications for the guidance program. At first, considerable effort must be directed toward transforming what traditionally have been clinical predictions into actuarial predictions. Many systematic observations must be made and recorded regarding relationships between behaviors considered predictive and outcomes. For example, in light of the number of hours a student will work, where he will live, how much time he will spend commuting, his marital status, or his medical condition, high-school and college counselors sometimes alter actuarial predictions of college success that have been based on high-school grades and test scores. These are all variables which can be observed, classified, and recorded, and relationships can be empirically determined between these conditions and academic success. Prediction and expectancy tables and regression equations can include many of the variables which presently are handled clinically.

The second implication is that the guidance program needs to give much greater attention than it has in the past to developing effective and appropriate methods for using actuarial data and predictions. Do students and their parents know enough about probability to interpret prediction data? How can such knowledge be imparted? What methods of presentation provide appropriate com-

---

38. Donivan J. Watley, "Counselor Confidence in Accuracy of Predictions," *Journal of Counseling Psychology*, XIII (Fall, 1966), 62-67; "Counselor Variability in Making Accurate Predictions," *Journal of Counseling Psychology*, XIII (Fall, 1966), 53-61; "Predicting Freshman Grades and Counselors' Prediction Style," *Personnel and Guidance Journal*, XLVI (October, 1967), 134-39.

munication? How are such data accepted, rejected, and, in general, reacted to emotionally?

The counselor also is concerned with the problem of breadth versus depth of evaluation in guidance; Cronbach and Gleser[39] treat this problem in considerable detail. As far as the counselor is concerned, he must decide whether he will observe a broad range of behaviors relatively superficially or more exhaustively observe a less extensive range of behaviors. The counselor's decision must depend on the relative costs of various types of observations, the significance of decisions to be made, and the alternatives being considered. This author proposes that the counselor soon reaches a point beyond which intensive evaluation of a limited range of behaviors is no longer as profitable as evaluation encompassing new and different behaviors. Bartlett and Green's research[40] suggests that this opinion can be questioned. They found that six psychologists who predicted first-year grades for forty university students did better when they used four predictors than when they used twenty-two.

Concepts related to factor analysis have many implications for the guidance program and are closely related to the concepts already mentioned. The extension of trait theory suggests that not only can predictors and characteristics inferred from them be grouped into meaningful and relatively independent "bundles" but also that the behaviors which are to be predicted can be grouped accordingly and that close relationships will be found between predicting factors and corresponding criterion factors. Much more research has been devoted to factor analysis studies of predictors than of criteria, but, in spite of the paucity of the latter research, at present the statement seems justified that the data we use for prediction purposes can be more meaningfully factor analyzed and "bundled" than can be the factors that we are attempting to predict. Most research of this kind has observed relationships between factor-analyzed predicting data and non-factored criterion data. In

39. Lee J. Cronbach and Goldine C. Gleser, *Psychological Tests and Personnel Decisions* (Urbana: University of Illinois Press, 1957).

40. C. J. Bartlett and Calvin C. Green, "Clinical Prediction: Does One Sometimes Know Too Much?" *Journal of Counseling Psychology*, XIII (Fall, 1966), 267-70.

general, the evidence is that factor scores empirically weighted in multiple-regression analyses predict available criteria no better than do total scores.[41] The relative ineffectiveness of combining in a sophisticated fashion multiple and complex data in order to predict academic success is demonstrated by a study of Calia,[42] who used the *Differential Aptitude Tests*, the *Kuder Preference Record*, and other instruments in an attempt to predict the academic success of Boston University junior-college Freshmen. The fact that verbal indices made the major contribution to the prediction may reflect only that academic success is inferred mainly through a student's verbal behavior.

Many methods have been used for combining prediction data. Calia used discriminant analyses. Simple regression analysis have been used most often,[43] and usually assumptions are made, although not explicitly recognized, that the data so analyzed are characterized by rectilinear relationships and that samples are homogeneous enough in terms of relevant characteristics to make a single regression line the most appropriate one for a large number of persons in the sample. Frequently recognition is given to the possibility that different regression lines for boys and girls may be appropriate, and different sex analyses are presented, but seldom is recognition given to the possibility that separate regression lines may better characterize persons in different socioeconomic groups, of different personality characteristics, and with different motivations.

The concept of the moderator variable here has implications for the guidance program. Saunder's paper[44] demonstrates how predictions for a total group may be quite different from predictions for the group divided into meaningful subgroups. Seashore's

---

41. Joseph T. Impellitteri, "Predicting Academic Achievement with the High School Placement Test," *Personnel and Guidance Journal*, XLVI (October, 1967), 140-43.

42. Vincent F. Calia, "The Use of Discriminant Analysis in the Prediction of Scholastic Performance," *Personnel and Guidance Journal*, XXXIX (November, 1960), 184-90.

43. David E. Lavin, *The Prediction of Academic Performance* (New York: Russell Sage Foundation, 1965).

44. David R. Saunders, "Moderator Variables in Prediction," *Educational and Psychological Measurement*, XVI (Summer, 1956), 209-22.

paper[45] reviews sex as a moderator variable. The research of Berdie[46] shows the possibility of using intra-individual variability as a moderator variable, and that of Ghiselli[47] shows how moderator variables can be extracted from the prediction indices themselves. Not only may further research on moderator variables improve prediction for subgroups in our total population, but information so gained may provide suggestions as to how our prediction models can be varied and how new criteria may be more appropriate than some we presently use.

The effective use of evaluation in guidance presupposes the existence of meaningful criteria. The criterion concept and problem present real dilemmas, not only because of the difficulty of determining what criteria are relevant but also because of the difficulty of obtaining criterion measurements. When a counselor uses a test score and other data to help a student make decisions, is he concerned with predicting whether the student will be admitted to a program, what his grades will be, whether he will persist in the program, whether he will eventually graduate, whether he will learn anything from the experience, or whether he will derive satisfaction from it? In vocational counseling, to what extent are the student and the counselor concerned with employability, financial return, advancement, persistence, satisfaction? In predicting personal adjustment, how does one take into account criteria such as happiness, morale, virtue, reliability, ambition, and energy?

Even when one selects what has appeared to be a relatively simple criterion, school grades, a problem is present. Hood and Swanson[48] demonstrated that the distribution of grades in one college did not resemble the distribution of grades in other colleges, and that in a group of colleges little relationship appeared between

45. Harold G. Seashore, "Women are More Predictable than Men," *Journal of Counseling Psychology*, IX (Fall, 1962), 261-70.

46. Ralph F. Berdie, "Intra-Individual Variability and Predictability," *Educational and Psychological Measurement*, XXI (Autumn, 1961), 663-76.

47. Edwin E. Ghiselli, The Prediction of Predictability," *Educational and Psychological Measurement*, XX (Spring, 1960), 3-8.

48. Albert B. Hood and Edward O. Swanson, "A Look at Student Achievement in Different Types of Colleges," *Personnel and Guidance Journal*, XLIV (November, 1965), 282-85.

mean ability levels of Freshman classes and their mean grade-point averages. Not only do mean grades vary from one school to another, but the shapes of the grade distributions vary: in two colleges the mean grade may be C, but in one college high proportions of students may receive A's and F's, and in the second college few students may receive these grades.

College persistence as a criterion was studied by Prediger[49] who tried to predict college dropouts from measures of academic aptitude and achievement and from biographical data. The academic predictors had some usefulness, the biographical data little. Williams[50] using a much smaller sample, tried to differentiate between dropouts and persisters and found that his original validity groups could be differentiated, but the variables that differentiated the original groups did not differentiate similar cross-validity groups. Watley's research[51] suggested that a distinction must be made between students who leave college with poor academic records and those who leave college with satisfactory records. He found that the latter group was characterized by favorable college aptitude scores but by personality inventory scores suggesting that students in good academic status who left the college were more emotionally disturbed than were students who persisted or who dropped out while having academic difficulty.

New Developments Relevant for Guidance

In response to changing social conditions and technical developments, emphasis on assessment in guidance has shifted and expanded. Increasing attention is being devoted to procedures appropriate for groups of persons other than typical students. Adults, women, persons with unusual cultural backgrounds, and students in other than the traditionally academic avenues are some of these groups.

49. Dale J. Prediger, "Prediction of Persistence in College," *Journal of Counseling Psychology*, XII (Spring, 1965), 62-67.

50. Vernon Williams, "Difficulties in Identifying Relatively Permanent Characteristics Related to Persistence in College," *Journal of Counseling Psychology*, XIII (Spring, 1966), 108.

51. Donivan J. Watley, "The Minnesota Counseling Inventory and Persistence in an Institute of Technology," *Journal of Counseling Psychology*, XII (Spring, 1965), 94-97.

The *General Aptitude Test Battery* of the United States Employment Service has been examined carefully in light of its use with first adults and then students entering a variety of training programs. Droege, Crambert, and Henkin[52] have presented data showing the relationships between GATB scores and age. In a broad sample of men and women from four states, they studied differences occuring at ages from seventeen through seventy-four years. They reported differences on all aptitudes except the verbal; on this they found no decline with age. Ingersoll and Peters[53] reported an extensive analysis of the relationships between GATB scores and high-school grades and found that scores combined in a multiple regression equation could be used with considerable effectiveness. Cooley[54] described the relationship between the GATB scores and the scores on the tests used in Project TALENT. In light of the great amount of research information becoming available on Project TALENT, Cooley's reports will provide a considerable basis for making inferences about GATB.

Work on vocational interest measurement has expanded considerably from preoccupation in the past with upper-level occupations and professions to increasing attention to the measurement of interests of persons in lower-level occupations. Clark and Campbell's[55] publication of the *Minnesota Vocational Interest Inventory* and Clark's book, *The Vocational Interests of Non-Professional Men*[56] serve as landmarks in such work. Clark demonstrated that the vocational interests of men in a broad range of occupations can

---

52. Robert C. Droege, Albert C. Crambert and James B. Henkin, "Relationship between G.A.T.B. Aptitude Scores and Age for Adults," *Personnel and Guidance Journal*, XLI (February, 1963), 502-08.

53. Ralph W. Ingersoll and Herman J. Peters, "Predictive Indices of the GATB," *Personnel and Guidance Journal*, XLIV (May, 1966), 931-37.

54. William W. Cooley, "Further Relationships with the TALENT Battery," *Personnel and Guidance Journal*, XLIV (November, 1965), 295-303. This is a continuation of "The Project TALENT Tests as a National Standard" by Cooley and Judy D. Miller, pp. 103-44 in the June, 1965 issue of this Journal.

55. Kenneth E. Clark and D. T. Campbell, *Manual for the Minnesota Vocational Interest Inventory* (New York: Psychological Corp., 1965).

56. Kenneth E. Clark, *The Vocational Interest of Non-Professional Men* (Minneapolis: University of Minnesota Press, 1961).

be differentiated and that counselors working with young persons considering entering skilled-trades occupations have a responsibility to be concerned with the measured interests of these persons as well as with their measured aptitudes. Barnette and McCall[57] reported a relevant validation study of the *Minnesota Vocational Interest Inventory*, using as subjects vocational high-school boys. At present, the available evidence indicates that the concept of vocational interest and procedures for its measurement are appropriate for counselors working with all young persons, regardless of the level of occupations being considered.

The educational and occupational problems of women are receiving increasing attention, and research regarding evaluation techniques for women is increasing. Harmon[58] has demonstrated that the interests of a group of women who worked most of their lives were not different twenty-five years earlier from those of women who retired shortly after marriage. Nolting[59] has demonstrated that the *Strong Vocational Interest Blank* has validity for women comparable to that it has for men. His study was a follow-up of a group of women college graduates tested as high-school seniors or college Freshmen. Harmon[60] has given considerable attention to the techniques of measuring women's interests and has studied particularly the problem of including married women in the criterion groups. Wagman[61] reported that the *Strong Vocational Interest Blank* and *Study of Values Scores* differed for undergraduate women planning on careers from those planning on homemaking. The

57. W. Leslie Barnette, Jr., and John N. McCall, "Validation of the Minnesota Vocational Interest Inventory for Vocational High School Boys," *Journal of Applied Psychology*, XLVIII (1964), 378-82.

58. Lenore W. Harmon, "Women's Interests—Fact or Fiction?" *Personnel and Guidance Journal*, XLV (May, 1967), 895-900.

59. Earl Nolting, Jr., "A Study of Female Vocational Interests: Pre-College to Post-Graduation" (unpublished Ph.D. dissertation, University of Minnesota, 1967).

60. Lenore W. Harmon, "Women's Working Patterns Related to Their SVIB Housewife and 'Own' Occupational Scores," *Journal of Counseling Psychology*, (Winter, 1967), 299-301.

61. Morton Wagman, "Interest and Values of Career and Homemaking Oriented Women," Personnel and Guidance Journal, XLIV (April, 1966), 794-801.

Strong blank for women is now being revised in somewhat the same way the men's blank was revised in 1966.

The development of the aptitudes of women also has been studied. Droege,[62] in a series of reports on the *"General Aptitude Test Battery,"* found that the average increases in GATB scores were the same for boys as for girls and that the test-retest correlations were similar for the two sexes.

The test scores of persons from minority groups, particularly racial groups, have been of concern to guidance persons for several years. A paper by Deutsch *et al.*[63] emphasizes the responsibility of the person who is using tests to take into consideration the previous experiences of the testees, because experience has been found to be related to performance on tests. Greater attention also must be given to determining the validities of tests for special groups. For example, do tests that predict well for non-handicapped persons also predict well for physically handicapped persons? Do tests that predict well for children coming from southern rural areas predict well for those coming from southern urban areas?

The discussion in this chapter has emphasized the use of tests in evaluation. Other evaluation devices also have to be given careful consideration. Perhaps one of the most important evaluation tools is the student's record. Little research has been done on the effectiveness of using records in guidance, but two studies suggest the possible value of records in systematic evaluation. Warnken and Siess[64] have shown that cumulative records of young children have remarkable value in predicting whether these children will become schizophrenic and also in predicting their adult interest patterns. Theirs is one of the few reports indicating the predictive value of observations made in the early grades. Tennyson, Blocher, and

62. Robert C. Droege, "Sex Differences in Aptitude Maturation during High School," *Journal of Counseling Psychology,* XIV (1967), 407-11.

63. Martin Deutsch *et al.,* "Guidelines for Testing Minority Group Children," *Journal of Social Issues,* XX (1964), 127-45.

64. Robert G. Warnken and Thomas F. Siess, "The Use of the Cumulative Record in the Prediction of Behavior," *Personnel and Guidance Journal,* LXIV (November, 1965), 231-37.

Johnson[65] discuss several principles to be considered in organizing a records system and call attention to the problems of establishing reliability and validity for reported information just as for other types of information used in evaluation.

Biographical information has been examined both as a predictor and a criterion. Dailey[66] has discussed the life history as a criterion of assessment, and the relationship between biographical information and academic achievement has been observed by Myers.[67] Siegel[68] has published one example of a biographical inventory for use with students. An interesting but somewhat unsystematic treatment of autobiographical data as psychological predictors is included in a conference report prepared by Henry in 1965.[69]

Some useful examples of the application of the biographical information method are reported in studies from the National Merit Scholarship Corporation and the American College Testing Program. Richards *et al.*[70] have designed a questionnaire to assess non-academic accomplishments of college students and have described methods for obtaining scores from this questionnaire. Records of non-academic achievement, similarly taken, and measures of academic success are not correlated, as demonstrated in a report by Holland and Richards.[71] This report reveals that non-academic

65. W. Wesley Tennyson, Donald H. Blocher, and Ralph H. Johnson, "Student Personnel Records: A Vital Tool But a Concern of the Public," *Personnel and Guidance Journal*, XLII (May, 1964), 888-93.

66. Charles A. Dailey, "The Life History as a Criterion of Assessment," *Journal of Counseling Psychology*, VII (Spring, 1960), 20-23.

67. Robert Cobb Myers, "Biographical Factors and Academic Achievement: An Experimental Investigation," *Educational and Psychological Measurement*, XII (Autumn, 1952), 415-26.

68. Laurence Siegel, "A Biographical Inventory for Students: I, Construction and Standardization of the Instrument," *Journal of Applied Psychology*, XL (1956), 5-10.

69. E. R. Henry, "Research Conference on the Use of Autobiographical Data as Psychological Predictors" (Richardson Foundation, 1966).

70. James M. Richards, Jr., John L. Holland, and Sandra W. Lutz, "The Assessment of Student Accomplishment in College," *Research Reports, American College Testing Program*, II (March, 1966).

71. John L. Holland and James M. Richards, Jr., "Academic and Non-academic Accomplishment: Correlated or Uncorrelated?" *Research Reports, American College Testing Program*, No. 2 (April, 1965).

accomplishment can be predicted to a useful degree but that non-academic accomplishment is quite independent of both academic potential and achievement.

The availability of document readers and computers makes feasible large-scale research using biographical data and experience reports, both as predictors and as criteria. The available evidence suggests that relationships involving these data are quite specific to populations and situations and that one must be even more careful when using biographical data than when using test scores in generalizing from results derived from samples to other samples.

Systematic observation and assessment of the educational environment have received delayed attention, but, since the work of Pace and Stern,[72] several diverse procedures have been developed for describing what might be called "school atmosphere" or "institutional climate." The *College Characteristics Index* by Pace and Stern and the *College and University Environment Scales* by Pace depend on statements made by students which describe their schools.[73] Astin and Holland[74] derive institutional indices from data descriptive of students—their test scores, college majors, and experiences—and from data such as school size, support, and financial resources. Much of this work has as its purpose providing information to students and counselors indicating to them the appropriateness of different colleges for the different students.[75]

Essentially, the problems and concerns of the guidance person using evaluation are no different from those of other persons who measure and assess behavior. Such questions as what behavior we are trying to understand, what information we should gather, how

72. C. Robert Pace and George G. Stern, *A Criteria Study of College Environment* (Syracuse: Psychological Research Center, Syracuse University, 1958).

73. C. Robert Pace and George G. Stern, *College Characteristics Index* (Syracuse: Psychological Research Center, Syracuse University, 1958); C. Robert Pace, *College and University Environment Scales* (Princeton: Educational Testing Service, 1963).

74. Alexander W. Astin and John L. Holland, "The Environmental Assessment Technique: A Way to Measure College Environments," *Journal of Educational Psychology*, LII (December, 1961), 308-16.

75. Alexander W. Astin, *Who Goes Where to College?* (Chicago: Science Research Associates, 1965).

the information should be evaluated and interpreted, how valid and reliable the information is, what difference the use of the information makes in the broader social process—these are all questions of concern to everyone using evaluation. If anything does distinguish the concern of guidance persons, it is the fact that they are more immediately and more often concerned than others with the impact of evaluation on the individual with whom they are working.

CHAPTER V

Research in College Admissions

DEAN K. WHITLA

In many ways this report is dated as it is being written. In a very real sense it is inappropriate to use the library style of research for an article on research in admissions. Much of the good work in this area is done, not by the scholars of the field, but by the effective working pragmatists who see a problem, collect some data, make analyses, interpret the results in the context of the situation they know so well, revise their operating procedures and proceed to apply them. This approach leaves behind it none of the academic fallout. No papers are written; none is cited. There is no record except the hazy recall of the central figure—the person who did the work. He rejects the thought of recording his work, for the rationale was superficial, the experimental design ragged, the findings localistic. Even though his findings may be interesting, he does not have time to enlarge the setting to make the idea worthy of setting out in print.

There is also a second aspect which makes a chapter such as this inappropriate. In the past, there has been a short half-life to much research done in admissions and institutional areas. As the author looks back to pieces of research on which he worked only five years ago, he can see how dated they are in the ongoing process of his own university, which, with its three-hundred-year history, one would expect to be as stable and even as encrusted as any. The pieces of research that have been used in admissions, turned into faculty legislation, or even swept under the table are by and large out of date today. The materials reported in this chapter will seldom be the current work of colleagues in the field, but will be taken primarily from journals and books in which they have been published and will of course reflect the delay involved in publication and in preparation for publication.

This normal delay has been accentuated by the very rapid change which is reflected in admissions and in undergraduate bodies. Where are the studies relating what is known about students at the time of admission to their subsequent academic performance and general college behavior? The admissions office plays a critical role in the makeup of a class. It can, if it chooses and if it is lucky, put together an incoming student body with a variety of characteristics which will markedly influence the college scene. This is a relevant area for research and an area in which research has yet to be done.

The review of past research will be parsimonious. It should provide the reader with a basic understanding of some of the primary activities that have been pursued with diligence in the field of admissions research within the last decade. This review will be presented under four headings: (a) the measurement and prediction of academic performance, (b) personality measures in admissions, (c) demographic factors, and (d) the psycho-social approach to college evaluation.

Measurement and Prediction of Academic Performance

There has been more research directed toward the prediction of students' grades than toward any other aspect of admissions research. Since the *Scholastic Aptitude Test* of the College Board became available in the late twenties, there has been a continuous parade of research studies investigating the relationship of scores on this test and of secondary-school performance to college grades. The College Board organization has advocated that institutions investigate the relationship of these scores to grades in their own local setting. The published studies exploring these relationships have been prodigious and even so they represent only a small fraction of the total number of such studies that have been conducted. The number of such studies increased after the College Board staff established a prediction-validity seminar service following World War II. At that time the Board invited member colleges to send representatives to a week-long session to which they brought data from their own institutions. Through the use of appropriate computer programs, both ACT (American College Testing Program) and the College Board now conduct studies for colleges assessing the effectiveness of scores and secondary-school records as predictors of college grades. Both of these organizations conduct these studies without charge to the colleges. It is therefore unnecessary for any college admissions staff to be without this information.

How effective are the predictors of college grades? There are several ways to examine this question. One answer is to report the correlations between test scores and college grade-point averages. A second is to determine the multiple correlations of test scores and the secondary-school record as predictors of college grade-point average. This would be the correlation of a series of measures combined in an optimal predictive fashion. A third method would be to estimate the effectiveness of the grade predictors if no selection had been made on the basis of scores or secondary-school record. A major limitation of almost all studies reported is that they contain correlations computed on the students enrolled in college, and one can understand this necessary limitation. However, especially for the admissions process, one is interested not in the correlation based on measures of those enrolled but in what the correlation would have been had there been no selection made at the time of admissions. If there is useful information in score data for the prediction of college grades, then it is appropriate that much of that information be used in the process of admissions, i.e., that those who are predicted to fail be rejected. Therefore, those enrolled in college are predicted to be successes, so that the correlations as typically reported based upon data of enrolled students are, as a consequence, much smaller than if total group data had been used. Estimates can be made of the magnitude of the correlation had the total group been admitted.

In reviews of studies by Cronbach,[1] Henry,[2] Dyer,[3] Fishman,[4]

1. Lee J. Cronbach, *Essentials of Psychological Testing* (New York: Harper & Bros., 1949).

2. Ervin R. Henry, "Predicting Success in College and University," *Handbook of Applied Psychology*, eds. Douglas H. Fryer *et al.* (New York: Rinehart & Co., 1950), pp. 449-53.

3. Henry S. Dyer, *College Board Scores* (New York: College Entrance Examination Board, 1955).

4. Joshua A. Fishman, "1957 Supplement to College Board Scores, No. 2" (New York: College Entrance Examination Board, 1957).

Lavin,[5] and Whitla,[6] college test scores were found to correlate .35 to .55 with college grade-point average. If one adds measures of secondary-school performance to scores on ability tests, the multiple correlations for predicting college grade-point averages run in the range of .40 to .80 and tend to average about .60. The square of a correlation coefficient represents the variation in grades that can be predicted by these variables. Here we see that approximately 25 per cent of the variation can be predicted by test scores, approximately 40 per cent by the combination of secondary-school record and test scores. Predictions of college grades are poor for a number of reasons. First, grade-point average is a very complex criterion. As Burnham recently stated, thirty years ago the members of the Freshman class at Yale might have been enrolled in something like twenty courses in a total of 12 to 15 departments. The present Freshman class is represented in 148 different courses in 39 different departments. Clearly, the grade average, which is a simple numerical summary of this complex assessment does not adequately represent student knowledge. Is an A an A an A if reported for Mathematics 1, 20, and 200? Considerable evidence has also been accumulated to show that college grades are not themselves a highly reliable measure. The accidents of a particular professor, the way the blue book was graded, and the motivation of the student operate in such a way as to reduce the reliability of the college grade.

The admissions process itself is a second major reason why we can predict only 40 per cent of the variation in college grades. There are a series of selection mechanisms operating for almost all colleges. One never sees a distribution of applicant scores that corresponds to the total national distribution. There is much self-selection of colleges by students. Further, in many colleges there is much selection by the admissions committee. In the process much of the useful variation in test scores is removed. As students become more homogeneous, scores become less effective as predictors of college grades. Let us, for example, use Sanders' illustra-

5. David E. Lavin, *The Prediction of Academic Performance* (New York: Russell Sage Foundation, 1965).

6. Dean K. Whitla, *Handbook of Measurement and Assessment in Behavioral Sciences* (Reading, Mass.: Addison-Wesley, 1968).

tion: all members of a basketball team are over seven feet tall; therefore, height has little correlation with basketball ability. So it is with test scores and other academic measures. When students become very homogeneous, the little variation that exists among them does not effectively predict college grades. As one example, the correlation between predicted grades and actual grades at Harvard College was .62; the estimate of the correlation between predicted grades and actual expected grades for the total applicant group was .78. If we square these correlations we find that the former would predict 38 per cent of the variation in college grades, the latter 61 per cent, a marked increase.[7]

In summary, the second major reason why test scores and secondary-school record are not better predictors of college-grade achievement is that they are an artifact of the method of computation (but, in fact, they are more powerful than they appear to be upon initial investigation). Later in this chapter, we will discuss the domains of institutional environment and student personality in the college setting. The part these factors play in explaining the unpredictability of college grades is a moot question.

Before proceeding into other areas of research in college admissions, it is appropriate to comment on several studies that have been made about the importance of college grades. Grades have been found to have very little relationship to success in life, or as McClelland has phrased it, "grades in life." [8] He used the Roe study of eminent scientists to support his position. For the eminent scientists studied, the average score on intelligence tests was very high, but it was true that a number of scientists tested had intelligence scores only moderately above average. Some interpret these data to support the position that extremely high scores are necessary for outstanding achievement in science. Others, including Roe, have interpreted these findings to indicate that it is possible, given moderately high intelligence, to be one of the world's great living scientists.

7. *Testing and the Freshman Year* (Cambridge: Office of Tests, Harvard College, 1968).

8. David C. McClelland, "Issues in the Identification of Talent" in *Talent and Society*, ed. David C. McClelland *et al.* (Princeton, N.J.: D. Van Nostrand Co., 1958).

In a National Science Foundation study of research fellows, those who were found to be most effective when back at work were those who had been selected through the use of references (i.e., evaluations made by their superiors at the time of their selection for the NSF fellowship) rather than those selected on the basis of college grades. College grades had no correlation with on-the-job performances. This finding held true even when adjustments were made for the quality of the college from which the research fellows had graduated. McClelland in a study done at Wesleyan University found no relationship between the performance occupationally of students and their grades in college.[9] He also found that as many with poor grades as with high grades went on to graduate work.

A study at the Bell Telephone Company revealed that there was a substantial correlation between college grades and Bell Telephone assessment of performance when there was control for the college attended. This study seems to be rare among those investigating this problem. MacKinnon's studies of creative research scientists and architects indicate that they seldom had outstanding college grades, and in fact were often quite mediocre.[10] Holland has found that for National Merit Scholars those factors predictive of high performance tend to be negatively related to creativity.[11] (Clearly, there seems to be a need for clarification in this area in which criterion problems are extremely complex.) With very rare exceptions, there seems to be little relationship between academic, scholastic ability and vocational success. Should these findings be confirmed (and we anticipate that they will be), grades in college must become their own reward, not keys to preferment after student days are over.

One method of trying to improve the predictive power of tests and secondary-school records has been to use a differential prediction technique; predictions are made for the several discip-

9. *Ibid.*

10. D. W. MacKinnon, "Genus Architectus Creator Varietas Americanus," *Journal of American Institute of Architecture*, XXXIV (September, 1960), 31-35.

11. J. L. Holland, "The Prediction of College Grades from Personality and Aptitude Variables," *Journal of Educational Psychology*, LI (October, 1960), 245-54.

lines in which students take courses. Horst was an early contributor to this work.[12] His results at the University of Washington showed that the median correlations are about .50, ranging from .13 to as high as .89. Cronbach, however, has asserted that multifactor tests add little to the predictive power over that which is provided by general measures of ability.[13] Berdie confirmed this finding, coming to the conclusion that limited improvement can be made in predicting grades by using differential aptitudes.[14] Eells also found that a differential battery of tests added so little over that obtainable from a standard battery in the prediction of grades that inclusion of the longer, more complicated testing was not justified.[15]

Findings that have been supported in a variety of studies have shown that ability is related to school performance in a linear fashion; an increment any place on an ability scale is equally valid and useful in the prediction of college grades. This is quite contrary to the generally stated theory of thresholds from which it has been hypothesized that, above a certain point on the ability continuum, other factors predominate. While this theory seems to have some documentation in the vocational world, contrary findings predominate with reference to college grades.[16]

In an analysis of the decision process, Whitla studied the dimensions upon which decisions were based in the admissions of candidates. This study, continued over a decade, analyzed the changing weights given to admissions variables by the Admissions Committee; and it showed that, as the numbers and strengths of applicants increased, the committee chose to emphasize personal qualities more heavily in its decisions.

12. Paul Horst, "Differential Prediction in College Admissions," *College Board Review*, XXXIII (No. 4, 1957), 19-23; Paul Horst, *Differential Prediction of Academic Success* (Seattle: University of Washington, 1959 [mimeo.]).

13. Cronbach, *op. cit.*

14. Ralph F. Berdie, "Aptitude, Achievement, Interest, and Personality Tests: A Longitudinal Comparison," *Journal of Applied Psychology*, XXXIX (1955), 103-14.

15. Kenneth Eells, "How Effective is Differential Prediction in Three Types of College Curricula?" *Educational and Psychological Measurement*, XXI (Summer, 1961), 459-71.

16. Whitla, *op. cit.*

Personality Factors in Admissions

Since we are able to account for less than half of the variation in grades by academic predictors, it is appropriate to explore other methods and instruments to see if we can understand more precisely the nature of the academic experience. A wide range of such instruments has been made available for the use of admissions officers, and, in addition to these, numerous instruments have been tried over the period of the last decade as predictors of achievement in college. This research in admissions has been of two types. First, and most common, are those studies which correlate the scores on the instrument with college grades. The second and more useful method is that by which these results are used in combination with academic measures for the prediction of college grades. In such studies it is possible to see the unique contribution of the personality measures. Academic measures are commonly available; hence, the real question is, does the new measure contribute significantly and importantly to the information that is already available? Lavin in his book, *The Prediction of Academic Performance*,[17] provides a series of excellent summaries and studies from which this review has drawn heavily. Stein's review, *Personality Measures in Admissions*, is also a very notable work.[18]

Kerns found a tendency for overachievers to attend college for intellectual reasons and for underachievers to attend for negative reasons such as getting away from home.[19] Results from an inventory developed by Brown and Holtzman called "Survey of Study Habits and Attitudes" produced a mean correlation with grades of about .40 for males and females; the multiple correlation was about .70 when ability measures were combined with "Survey of Study Habits and Attitudes" results to predict college grades.[20]

17. Lavin, *op. cit.*

18. M. I. Stein, *Personality Measures in Admissions* (New York: College Entrance Examination Board, 1963).

19. Byron L. Kerns, "A Study of Under-achieving and Over-achieving First Semester College Freshmen as Revealed by the Way in Which They View the College Situation and Themselves as College Students," *Dissertation Abstracts*, Vol. 17, 1957, p. 2500.

20. William F. Brown and Wayne H. Holtzman, "A Study-Attitudes Questionnaire for Predicting Academic Success," *Journal of Educational Psychology*, XLVI (February, 1955), 75-84.

Ahmann later used the inventory and found that it did not add significantly to a battery of intellectual measures in predicting college grades.[21] Another study revealed that it did not differentiate probationary students from non-probationers.[22]

Cronbach has stated that substantive interest measures can improve the prediction of grades even though results on these measures have low correlations with grades.[23] Travers found that interest tests were of some value for predicting grades in courses within areas of interests.[24] Hewer found that, when ability was controlled, there was little relationship between the physicians' key on the *Strong Vocational Interest Blank* and grades of male premedical Freshmen, but there was some evidence that differences between grades in certain courses were related to the predictor.[25] In Melton's study, the physicians' scale score was uncorrelated with academic performance. In a study of engineering students, interest-test scores were unrelated to performance.[26] In one study, underachievers were found to have stronger interests in social activities than in intellectual activities, and the opposite was true for overachievers. Rust and Ryan found that overachievers in college tend to have higher interest-scores in high-prestige occupations.[27] Choice of a major field is directly related to academic performance in the case of males,

21. J. Stanley Ahmann, William L. Smith, and Marvin D. Glock, "Predicting Academic Success in College by Means of a Study Habits and Attitude Inventory," *Educational and Psychological Measurement*, XVIII (Winter, 1958), 853-57.

22. Robert P. Anderson and James E. Kuntz, "The 'Survey of Study Habits and Attitudes' in a College Counseling Center," *Personnel and Guidance Journal*, XXXVII (January, 1959), 365-68.

23. Cronbach, *op. cit.*

24. M. W. Travers, "Significant Research on the Prediction of Academic Success," *The Measurement of Student Adjustment and Achievement*, eds. W. T. Donahue *et al.* (Ann Arbor: University of Michigan Press, 1949).

25. Vivian H. Hewer, "Vocational Interest-Achievement-Ability Interrelationships at the College Level," *Journal of Counseling Psychology*, IV (1957), 234-38.

26. Richard S. Melton, "Differentiation of Successful and Unsuccessful Premedical Students," *Journal of Applied Psychology*, XXXIX (December, 1955), 397-400.

27. Ralph Rust and F. J. Ryan, "Relationship of Some Rorschach Variables to Academic Behavior," *Journal of Personality*, XXI (1953), 441-56.

but no significant relationship pertains with regard to females. In general, in those studies controlling for ability and interest measures, these measures were found useful in predicting academic performance. Expressed interest, however, did not seem to be related to academic performance for females as it was for males.

Achievement motivation.—McClelland[28] found that, for a sample of male students, correlation between grades and achievement motivation as measured by the *TAT* (Thematic Apperception Test) was .39. Weiss, Wertenheimer, and Grossbeck[29] found that the *TAT* measures correlated .34 with grades and, combined with aptitude measures, produced a multiple correlation of .63. Burgess found that overachievers were significantly higher on need achievement than underachievers.[30] Chahbazi[31] found that the achievement motivation measure added to measures from a battery of six tests (*Cooperative Reading, Cooperative Science, Cornell Mathematics Test, Ohio State Psychological Test,* and the *Cornell Orientation Inventory*) raised the correlation from .51 to .63. Lavin found five other studies showing that achievement motivation was unrelated to academic performance.[32] These studies were conducted by Walter,[33] Haber,[34] Krumboltz and Farquhar,[35] Parrish and Reth-

28. McClelland, *op. cit.*

29. Peter Weiss, Michael Wertheimer, and Byron Groesbeck, "Achievement Motivation, Academic Aptitude, and College Grades," *Educational and Psychological Measurement,* XIX (Winter, 1959), 663-66.

30. Elva Burgess, "Personality Factors of Over- and Under-Achievers in Engineering," *Journal of Educational Psychology,* LXVII (February, 1956), 89-99.

31. Parviz Chahbazi, "Use of Projective Tests in Predicting College Achievement," *Educational and Psychological Measurement,* XVI (No. 4, 1956), 538-42.

32. Lavin, *op. cit.*

33. Verne Arthur Walter, "The Effect of Need for Academic Achievement on the Performance of College Students in Learning Certain Study Skills," *Dissertation Abstracts,* Vol. 17, 1957, p. 1384.

34. Ralph N. Haber, "The Prediction of Achievement Behavior by an Interaction of Achievement Motivation and Achievement Stress," *Dissertation Abstracts,* Vol. 17, 1957, pp. 2686-2687.

35. John D. Krumboltz and William W. Farquhar, "Reliability and Validity of the N-achievement Test," *Journal of Consulting Psychology,* XXI (1957), 226-28.

lingshafer[36] and Mitchell.[37] In part, the negative results were attributed to the low reliability of the *TAT* scoring.

In the preceding studies, "achievement motivation" (which refers to the need of an individual to achieve) was investigated using the *Thematic Apperception Test* which presents students with pictures and asks them to write stories in response to the pictures presented. The scoring system is in terms of the presence of themes representing achievement. A series of experiments has also been conducted using a questionnaire method of investigating achievement motivation. In a number of such studies at the college level, the *Edwards Personal Preference Schedule* was used; there was found to be a correlation between achievement motivation and academic performance. Using the projective methods of the *TAT* for assessment of need-achievement, we find the results are inconsistent. In those studies using questionnaire methods to assess achievement motivation, small positive relationships were always found. They were significant but not important in terms of accounting for variation of students' academic performance.

Measures of independence have also been investigated as predictors of academic performance. These measures are based on items such as "plans alone without suggestions or discussion," and "usually faces troubles alone without seeking help." Independence, as this dimension is measured, is positively related to academic performance as found in studies by Weigand.[38] These studies, however, raise another question, for they seem to be correlated with the concept of achievement motivation.

From findings on measures of impulsivity, it seems that the willingness to defer gratification in pursuit of a long-range goal is essential in our educational process. Merrill and Murphy found a correlation between the endurance-scale score of the *Edwards Per-*

36. John Parrish and Dorothy Rethlingshafer, "A Study of the Need to Achieve in College Achievers and Non-Achievers," *Journal of General Psychology*, L (April, 1954), 209-26.

37. James V. Mitchell, Jr., "An Analysis of the Factorial Dimensions of the Achievement Motivation Construct," *Journal of Educational Psychology*, LII (August, 1961), 179-87.

38. George Weigand, "Goal Aspiration and Academic Success," *Personnel and Guidance Journal*, XXXI (1953), 458-61.

sonal Preference Schedule and the academic record.[39] This *EPPS* also seemed useful in Krug's study of over-and-underachieving Freshman engineering students.[40] General measures of anxiety do not seem to be directly useful for the prediction of academic performance. Measures of introversion, however, are positively related to college grades, for introverted students appear to have time and inclination for academic affairs.

Yeomans and Lundin administered the *Minnesota Multiphasic Personality Inventory (MMPI)* to the top and bottom quarters of the Freshman and Senior classes at Hamilton College.[41] Poorer students in both classes were more maladjusted, particularly as shown on the psychopathic, deviate, and hypomania scales. The authors stated, "These students in general probably are more poorly motivated, irresponsible, and too active in other affairs to spend necessary time and effort in their scholastic endeavors." In follow-up work, Lundin and Kuhn found that the Freshmen in the lower quarter did not show significant improvement in their *MMPI* scores over a four-year period.[42] On the other hand, students who were originally in the top quarter of their Freshman class showed definite improvement. "By the time the senior year is reached, the better students have become less worried about their personal health, less anxious, and more self-confident and reliable."

From these studies, we can summarize as follows: Academic performance seems to be higher for students who have better study habits, more favorable attitudes towards school, greater interest in the course area, and a greater degree of achievement motivation; who tend to be more independent, to have more impulse control,

39. Reed M. Merrill and Daniel T. Murphy, "Personality Factors and Academic Achievement in College," *Journal of Counseling Psychology*, VI (Fall, 1959), 207-10.

40. Robert E. Krug, "Over- and Under-Achievement and the Edwards Personal Preference Schedule," *Journal of Applied Psychology*, XLIII (1959), 133-36.

41. W. N. Yeomans and R. W. Lundin, "The Relationship between Personality Adjustment and Scholarship Achievement in Male College Students," *Journal of Genetic Psychology* (1957), 213-18.

42. R. W. Lundin and J. P. Kuhn, "The Relationship between Scholarship Achievement and Changes in Personality Adjustment in Men after Four Years of College Attendance," *Journal of Genetic Psychology*, XI (1960), 35-42.

to have less anxiety in test-taking situations; who are more introverted, have a more positive self-image, have greater cognitive
flexibility, are less hostile and less defensive about revealing personal inadequacies, and are more conforming. These findings are
more representative of males than females in those studies which
noted a difference between them. The problem with this research is
that the differences among the groups are so small and tentative
that they cannot be used confidently for practical purposes such
as college admissions.

Lavin has proposed a summary in factor form for the great
variety of studies that have been made. Under six basic dimensions,
he summarizes twenty-six variables. They do provide a useful
rubric in thinking about this problem. The dimensions are as follows: (*a*) social maturity in the student role; (*b*) emotional stability; (*c*) achievement-motivation syndrome; (*d*) cognitive style;
(*e*) achievement via conformance; (*f*) achievement via independence. Lavin states that in most cases the relationships between personality variables and academic performance are quite weak.[43] And
the findings are often inconsistent. "Essentially we think that the
literature presents a somewhat disappointing picture." Holland,
after having conducted a series of studies on National Merit Scholars, concluded that personality measures did not add significantly to
academic measures in the prediction of college grades.[44] This
writer shares these evaluations. There is little need for further investigation and corroboration through more studies such as these.
New ideas, new measures, and new techniques are necessary before
more research is undertaken.

Demographic Characteristics

Socioeconomic status (SES) is found to be positively associated
with both intelligence and academic performance in a wide variety
of studies. SES even seems to be predictive of college grades when
ability is controlled. These general findings have been contradicted,
however, in a few studies conducted at institutions (e.g. at Princeton) in which a large number of upper-class students were en-

43. Lavin, *op. cit.*

44. Holland, *op. cit.*

rolled.[45] In these studies SES has been inversely related to performance even when intelligence has been controlled. The variable quite apparently has a curvilinear relationship with achievement in general, though that relationship is seldom found in any one college. In earlier studies, those of middle SES performed better than those of low SES. In colleges where there were significant numbers of upper-class students, the middle SES students still performed better.

McArthur's very effective studies of students from public and private schools stress the difference in value orientation of these two groups. When examined in the context of competitive college climates, the public school graduate is oriented towards the future, the individual, and achievement. McArthur has called this the "doing" oriented syndrome. The private school syndrome has reference to inherited status and stylistic qualities, and hence is "being" oriented. A few years ago these differences were closely associated with differences in college performance. However, more recently those differences have begun to disappear. As Riesman has said, "The college is owned by the public school graduate." The press of graduate schools also seems to have prevented the prep-school type from enjoying the gentlemanly attributes of the college career and deferring work until the "chips were down," i.e. until admission to law school or medical school. The differences that McArthur described are still present but much more subtly than before, typically being demonstrated by the difference in quantity of output—public school students being very productive, and private school students tending to emphasize quality.

McArthur says in summarizing his own work:

Not only do members of American sub-cultures have different traits but different psychodynamics underlie these traits. Not only do they have different memories but they obey different laws of memory. Not only do they have different learnings, but these may have been acquired by means of different laws of learning. All of these sub-cultural effects on personality show up within and between college student populations.[46]

45. Junius A. Davis and Norman Frederiksen, "Public and Private School Graduates in College, *Journal of Teacher Education*, VI (March, 1955), 18-22.

46. Charles McArthur, "Sub-Culture and Personality during the College Years," *Journal of Educational Sociology*, XXXIII (February, 1960), 260–68;

McArthur goes on to say that an 18-year follow-up study with *Strong Vocational Interest Blank* indicated that it predicted well the public students' careers but predicted very little about the future of private students. For the latter, the best predictor was simply to ask them while in college what they were going to be doing twenty years later. Public school boys chose items that had to do with success and science while private school students chose clusters of social, esthetic, statusful, and romantic outdoor activity items. McArthur suggests these young men had read Parsons on the ascribed versus the achieved status and then had filled out their *Strongs* accordingly.

Some other miscellaneous findings with regard to ecological and demographic characteristics are that Jewish students out-perform non-Jewish students, Northern students out-perform Southern students, and urban students out-perform rural students.[47] Successful students are likely to come from a family in which parents show warmth and interest, in which the child has had a relatively strong voice in decision-making, and in which the family tends to agree upon issues it defines as important.

Used as they have been in research studies, the masculinity and feminity dimensions are not part of a continuum. They are separate variables and confusing to all of us since they do not imply a psychological, bisexual orientation as the words themselves might indicate. Bruner has made the remark in the past, somewhat humorously, that girls are the non-fidgety type but, in a more serious vein, goes on to say that maybe they are more educable. It would seem that our society has been singularly unsuccessful in engaging the talents of a group as talented and as learned as women students.

Male students, to have high achievement, need to have characteristics which in the research have been categorized by the term "femininity," a term used to indicate a combination of such traits as cultural interests, receptive attitudes, sensitivity, awareness of

---

see also McArthur's "Personalities of Public and Private School Boys," *Harvard Educational Review*, XXIV (Fall, 1954), 256-62.

47. H. G. J. Gerritz, "The Relationship of Certain Personal and Socio-Economic Data to the Success of Resident Freshmen Enrolled in the College of Science, Literature, and the Arts at the University of Minnesota," *Dissertation Abstracts*, Vol. 16, 1956, 2366.

feeling, and artistic interest. It would seem more appropriate if these traits were couched in terms of cultural interest or aesthetic interest rather than being designated by the term, femininity. Correspondingly, girls do better in college if they score high on a masculinity scale, a scale which really describes an individual with regard to capacity for action, assertiveness, and orientation towards external objects.

Psycho-Social Approach

One of the classic studies of the interaction between students and the college environment was conducted by Stern, Stein, and Bloom using Murray's need-press schema—essentially that personality is defined in terms of needs and the environment is viewed as a series of presses.[48] The authors differentiated their students into three major personality types: stereopaths, non-stereopaths, and rationals. A stereopath is one who is characterized by depersonalized and codified social relationships, pervasive acceptance of authority as absolute, inhibition and denial of impulses, and rigid orderliness and conformity in behavior. In their study of these personality types in the general education programs at the University of Chicago, the researchers found that over two-thirds of the stereopaths expressed an interest in instrumental activities (accounting, engineering, business, law, and medicine) while two-thirds of the non-stereopaths expressed interest in pursuits such as psychology, sociology, teaching, music, art, and literature. Stereopaths were more active participants in the classroom process than were non-stereopaths, and in addition, they engaged in covert behavior in the classroom which was predominantly critical and hostile. They made a poor adjustment to college as indicated by the comments of their student advisors. A significantly larger proportion of the stereopaths was found to have withdrawn from the college.

Using an outgrowth of this original study called "The College Characteristics Index," Thistlethwaite attempted to assess the press of colleges and universities attended by National Merit Scholars.[49]

48. George G. Stern, Morris I. Stein, and Benjamin S. Bloom, *Methods in Personality Assessment* (Glencoe, Ill.: Free Press, 1956).

49. Donald L. Thistlethwaite, "College Press and Student Achievement," *Journal of Educational Psychology*, L (August, 1959), 183-91.

Making the assumption that the institutions had remained the same over time, he found a series of differences between those that tended to be high in producing Ph.D.'s in natural science and those that were high in the productivity of Ph.D.'s in the arts, humanities, and social sciences. The latter group of universities exhibited a student climate characterized by humanism, breadth of interest, reflectiveness, low participation in large-group social activities, and low aggression. The faculty was characterized by high energy, controversy in instruction, informal contact with students and flexibility in relation to the curriculum. Science-productive institutions exhibited high press of aggression and scientism on students and were low in press toward social conformity. The faculty was low on such characteristics as directiveness of teaching methods and close faculty supervision.

Disadvantaged youth.—One of the more sorely needed areas for research is that of the disadvantaged. Clark and Plotkin published a study in which they concluded that the *College Board Aptitude Tests* either fail altogether to predict academic performance of Negroes at integrated colleges or underestimate the performance of Negroes as compared with whites.[50] For those who have tried actively to recruit and admit black students, this is heart-warming evidence. However, it fails to be corroborated by other studies. Roberts,[51] Stanley,[52] Cleary,[53] and others [54] have all analyzed the use of *College Boards* with Negro students, sometimes in Negro colleges and sometimes in predominantly white colleges. Their results have shown conclusively that the *SAT* is as powerful a pre-

50. *The Negro Student at Integrated Colleges* (New York: National Scholarship Service and Fund for Negro Students, 1963).

51. *Studies in Identification of College Potential* (Nashville, Tenn.: Fisk University, 1962).

52. "Relative Predictability of Freshman Grade-Point Averages from SAT Scores in Negro and White Southern Colleges" (Madison: Laboratory of Experimental Design, University of Wisconsin, 1966 [mimeographed]).

53. *Test Bias: Validity of the Scholastic Aptitude Test for Negro and White Students in Integrated Colleges* (College Entrance Examination Board Research and Development Reports, No. 18 [Princeton: Educational Testing Service, 1966]).

54. J. R. Hills, J. A. Klock, and M. L. Bush, *Counselors' Guide to Georgia Colleges* (Atlanta: Office of Testing and Guidance, University System of Georgia, 1965).

dictor for black students as for whites. In fact, in Cleary's study, which was then reanalyzed by Linn, the *SAT* overestimated the college grades of Negroes.

Linn speculates about these findings as follows:

"It is of course possible that Negroes tend to obtain higher test scores than their white counterparts with equal 'true' ability. I find this explanation extremely hard to believe. Unfortunately, a more realistic alternative explanation might be that instructors of the school tend to give lower grades to Negroes than to whites for the same performance. Another possibility might be that Negroes are not as well off financially as the whites and are required to hold more part-time jobs, thus leaving them less time to study." [55]

This explanation has no special charm for the writer, though unfortunately he has no ready alternative to offer. What Linn has produced is some documentation of the fact that no correlation exists between the scores and the performance of black students. This fact has given rise to the methods of selection which have little relationship to scores themselves. Such dimensions as high energy (evidenced by participation in a great number of school activities, employment, etc.), some strong teacher recommendations, and an ability to write an essay which is convincing as a literary exercise and which also indicates a reasonable perspective from a personal standpoint seem to be the effective factors (albeit hard to document) in success of black students at Harvard College. Two topical articles addressing this problem and helpful in formulating these remarks were written by Dyer[56] and Kendrick.[57]

Clearly the unfortunate cyclic pattern in the lives of the disadvantaged is one of the nation's biggest internal problems and one that research must help to solve.

Our hope these days seems to be tied to some of the newer pro-

---

55. "Reanalysis of the Data of Miss Cleary's Predictive Bias Study" (Princeton: Educational Testing Service, March, 1967 [mimeographed memorandum]).

56. Henry S. Dyer, *Recruiting the Disadvantaged: An Urgent Need* (College Admissions Policies for the 1970's [New York: College Entrance Examination Board, 1966]).

57. S. A. Kendrick, "The Coming Segregation of Our Selective Colleges," *College Board Review*, LXVII (Winter, 1967-68), 6-13.

grams underway, such as those of Deutsch[58] and Bereiter[59] as well as other programs around the country. It is yet too early to generalize about the effectiveness of such programs in raising the achievement of the disadvantaged.

Constructive approaches.—Recent essays have been written about college environments by Riesman and Jencks[60] and by Trow.[61] Pace's *College Characteristics Index* (CCI) approached this same problem through quantitative methods.[62] It contains items about students' activities in art, music, or the theater. Students are asked to indicate the frequency with which they would subscribe to such items. Colleges are then characterized by the degree of intellectual, aesthetic, social, and other interests that students feel are present.

There are several new instruments that are now available for use in the admissions process and for admissions research. They include a new and improved version of the *CCI* called *CUES* (*College and University Environment Scales*), and *OAIS* (*Opinion, Attitude*, and *Interest Survey*).[63] These are now available for examining both the college press and students' values. Much interesting work has gone into these instruments; we must await the test of time to judge their full usefulness.

One of the constructive ideas with which admissions research must come to grips very shortly is the concept of building a class. We, in Cambridge, have given some thought to the process, as has everyone, and hope we have become a little more sophisticated than to use simple variables such as economic diversity, geographic dis-

---

58. Martin Deutsch, *Disadvantaged Child* (New York: Basic Books, Inc., 1967).

59. Carl Bereiter and S. Engleman, *Teaching Disadvantaged Children in Preschool* (Englewood Cliffs: Prentice-Hall, Inc., 1966); Deutsch, *op. cit.*

60. David Riesman and Christopher Jencks, "The Viability of the American College," *The American College*, ed. Nevitt Sanford (New York: John Wiley & Sons, 1962), pp. 74-192.

61. Martin Trow, *Reflections on the Recruitment for College Teaching* (mimeo; Berkeley, Calif.: University of California Center for the Study of Higher Education, 1964).

62. C. Robert Pace, "Five College Environments," *College Board Review*, XLII (Spring, 1960), 24-28.

63. Benno G. Fricke, *Opinion, Attitude and Interest Survey Handbook* (Ann Arbor: University of Michigan, 1963).

tribution, and anticipated college major. In thinking about this process, we have found it useful to consider the psychological impact of the academic standing of a student in his class. Glimp has called this the search for the happy bottom-quarter type.[64] There are students who, because of their previous performance, come expecting to rank very well in their college class. When they, in fact, find that there are many students above them, they feel second rate. The psychological impact of their averageness becomes even more pronounced near the bottom, especially when students are interested in going to graduate school. There also seems to be an inadequate supply of psychic reward for these students. In an attempt to discover some solution, we struck upon the idea of admitting students whose talents do not lie especially in the area of academic work, but whose great strength in other areas more than compensates, making them attractive individuals personally and effective persons in their own area. We hope that such students will not be disturbed by their rank but will go through their undergraduate years enjoying the experience of college and getting a great deal out of it. Later, they should make a marked contribution to the world despite the fact that they do not graduate with honors. In contrast, men whom we might have taken in their places have gone elsewhere, where they can achieve many distinctions that are rightfully theirs. In our search for those whose ego strength is strong enough to tolerate a relatively poor ranking, we feel that we admit one of the interesting sectors of Harvard classes.

Multiple applications.—In a recent study of overlapping candidates in admissions, Whitla demonstrated that for 43 colleges the number of applications per candidate was 1.65 and that 62 per cent filed only one application and 21 per cent only two applications.[65] More applications were filed by students who had high scores than by those who had low scores, and more were filed by those from private schools than by those from public schools. The number of admissions tickets received was highest for those with high scores but equally frequent for those from public and private schools, if

64. Fred L. Glimp, *Report of the President of Harvard College* (Cambridge: Admission and Scholarship Committee, 1967).

65. Dean K. Whitla, "Candidate Overlap Studies and Other Admissions Research," *College Admissions Policies for the 1970's* (New York: College Entrance Examination Board, 1968), 137-65.

score level was controlled. Factor analysis of the applicant patterns indicates that students tended to file a number of applications to the same style of institution, and that their perceptions about the colleges (as indicated by their patterns of filing applications) grouped institutions in a fashion which is quite typical of perceptions of admissions people in general. This study has been replicated for 107 colleges, and the preliminary analysis seems to confirm the earlier findings.

Summary

There is no evidence from the research cited that would provide colleges with bases for new directions in assessing personal qualities. What this review then concludes is that there is great need for research on student typologies, on class mix (with particular attention to the current scene), and on the disadvantaged.

Of these problems, only that of the disadvantaged has been undertaken in a serious way by researchers. Admissions will continue to operate using many of the standard academic measures. Everyone is aware that much of the variation in grades is unaccounted for by these or any other variables that have yet been ascertained. There are even doubts that academic performance is a reasonable criterion. The upshot is that, after a decade of frenzied research activities, the field is wide open for new criteria and for new predictors. Currently, there are two approaches to the problems of admissions. One set of admissions officers thinks there is veracity in men; and they react by giving credibility to teachers' reports, counselors' reports, and students' own statements. This style incorporates the human dimension by making assessments of personal qualities on the basis of these personal reports. There are older and more disillusioned men who take another view. They distrust the counselor's evaluation, for they know he may exaggerate to get students into college. They distrust the student's own essay, for they know it could have been written by a New York ad man. They distrust the interview, because they recognize the effects of their own grumpy days. And so they choose to enter the personal side of admissions on the basis of randomness. There is just enough truth yielded by each of these styles to keep them alive. This writer, however, opts for the former style. At this moment, the nature of future admissions research is not clear.

CHAPTER VI

Evaluation and the Award of Scholarships

JOHN M. STALNAKER

Scholarships, like virtue and decency, are generally favored, even though few agree on precisely what they are. For the purposes of this discussion, a scholarship is an award made to a student for outstanding attainment of some type in the intellectual or performance fields. Typically, the attainment is believed to predict success in some aspect of desired college behavior. The scholarship usually, but not always, carries with it a grant of money to aid the recipient in financing his college education. The amount of money accompanying the scholarship may be a set amount given as a prize for attainment of some sort; or it may be based on the recipient's family financial situation, on the cost of attending the selected college, or on a combination of the two—the latter being the plan most commonly followed by colleges today.

Some use of financial need as a basis for stipend-setting is characteristic today of scholarship programs—government or private. Financial need itself may be determined in accordance with one of several schools of thought. Financial need is more a personal matter than a universally applicable dollar figure, especially with incomes above the subsistence level. What is one man's need can be another man's luxury.

Scholarships can be entirely honorary—a recognition of attainment without any provision of money. Such an award may be highly prized, publicly recognized, and honored. The program of Presidential Scholars, established by President Lyndon B. Johnson, is an example of a scholarship program which is entirely honorary. Certain scholarships awarded by universities to students of unusual attainment whose families are judged by the institution as not needing financial assistance (the parents not always concurring) are another example of awards bearing no financial commitment.

Purpose

The selection procedures followed in a scholarship program depend upon the purpose of the program. Scholarships are merely a means to aid in achieving a goal. Because scholarships serve many purposes, there are no universally appropriate selection procedures independent of the purpose of the scholarship.

Selection procedures, for example, are obviously different for a scholarship program financed by an alumni group which is avid to attract better athletes from one which is designed to draw promising students to the study of mathematics. A regional scholarship program of an institution may seek to make the institution better known throughout the country, and whether the winner from one region is "better" than the one from another is of no great consequence.

Another type of scholarship program is the one a state institutes to keep more of its top-flight students from going out of the state to college or to divert more of its students from public to private institutions within the state (to reduce expenditures for the public institution). The success of such programs depends upon what criteria are used to define "top-flight students," and upon what happens to such students.

A scholarship program to recruit Negro students to a particular college will aim to attract those Negroes who will complete the work of the college and graduate. Success is measured by the proportion who graduate.

The scholarship offered to the winner of a beauty contest frequently is used to give the contest an air of respectability. In the case of science fairs and many other intellectual contests, scholarships are a feature to attract greater participation and to provide prizes for the winners.

One of the common purposes which scholarship programs have served is that of providing help to able students from impoverished backgrounds. Indeed, the general public usually assumes that scholarships are primarily a device to equalize educational opportunity. The federal government has a program of opportunity grants which are explicitly directed toward this end.

The GI Bill, while not called a scholarship program, provided a grant of money for educational purposes, and it did make a college education possible for those GI's inclined to go that route. The original GI Bill (at a cost of over $15 billion) probably did more to equalize educational opportunity than any other single program and ranks in this regard with the Morrill Act of 1862. The amount of money given was not based on need, as is popular today, but the availability of the GI money made a college education attractive and possible for hundreds of thousands, a substantial proportion of whom would not otherwise have attended college. Eligibility for these grants was based on the length of military service to the country rather than on academic potential or attainment.

Compensatory scholarship programs, like the National Achievement Scholarship Program for outstanding Negro students and many special college programs, are designed to increase social mobility and integration by making a college education available to special classes of individuals who may not meet the level of the highly selective, open competition.

Another purpose scholarships serve is to reward unusual or distinguished performance regardless of the economic background of the participants. The most obvious example is the athletic scholarship given overtly or covertly to a young man because of his demonstrated athletic prowess. Today, as in the past, in spite of codes and pacts of various sorts, a good halfback can anticipate many scholarship offers, including some from distinguished universities. As long as college athletic events draw thousands of paying spectators and serve as a rallying point for alumni and the public, scholarships will likely be used to attract promising athletes to colleges. The basis for selection is past performance in the sport, and while no studies have established the validity of the selection, it is undoubtedly very high. The star scorer on the all-state, high-school basketball team is very probably going to be a superior player in college.

But athletic prowess is not the only skill recognized and rewarded by scholarships. The intellectually apt student who scores well on tests and has a high academic standing among his classmates is now much in demand. The strength of the demand, like that for athletes, is much greater for the very distinguished and trails off sharply as one moves down from the very top. The demand for those at the 95th percentile is slight when compared with the demand for those at the 99.5 percentile, and those at the 75th percentile must possess some very special attributes to have a chance for an open scholarship.

A third type of purpose which scholarships serve is to attract students to a specific field or to a particular college. If a group having adequate funds wishes to use scholarships to attract able students into the field of chemistry, for example, a scholarship program can be established and restricted to very able students who agree to do their major work in chemistry. Even more common is the use of scholarships to attract very able students to a particular college. In fact, most college-controlled scholarships are used to divert college-bound youth from one college to another. Some of the large prestige institutions will give hundreds of thousands of dollars to entering Freshmen in the form of scholarship aid. Most of the recipients were college bound but their choice of a college was determined largely by the award of the most attractive scholarship. While the use of a common need base for determining the amount of money to accompany the scholarship restricts the dimensions of the competition, students are attracted by the larger dollar awards, and the institutions that have the highest student costs tend to benefit because the size of the monetary award is higher in those institutions.

The use of financial need as a basis for determining the scholarship stipend is a type of price-fixing which might be said to reduce or control the price that able students can command from institutions desiring them. Without scholarships or other forms of financial aid, the institutions offering these aids would not attract as many of the students they believe to be highly qualified as they now do.

A fourth common purpose is found in the scholarship program designed to influence both the recipients of the awards and other students who compete for the awards to raise their educational sights and thus motivate them to try harder. The Merit Scholarship Program has this as one of its purposes. Such programs can also motivate parents and teachers. Comments are heard to the effect that the teacher or parent knew that the winner of a highly competitive scholarship was good, but they did not know that he was as good as winning the competition indicated. As a result, the efforts to further the education of this student are greatly increased.

Large scholarship programs which are publicized widely can influence the public in its attitudes about bright students and about higher education.

Selection Criteria

Up until the last decade or two, scholarships were largely controlled by the colleges. More recently, government interest in the field of financial aid for students has greatly increased. State-supported scholarship programs have multiplied, and the federal government (long active in the fellowship field) has now entered the financial-aid field for undergraduates—more with loans than with cash grants. The government programs tend to have a broader base than the institutional ones, but the criteria for the selection of the recipients are largely the same.

In spite of the great diversity of purposes which scholarship programs serve, the vast majority of the scholarships in existence today, as judged by the monetary value and the number of scholarships offered, are for students who will do distinguished work in college classrooms. Distinguished work is indicated by the grades earned in college. The bright, academically oriented student who learns academic material quickly and thoroughly, who enjoys the classroom situation, and who takes pleasure in succeeding in the eyes of the teacher will frequently be chosen. The well-rounded person rather than the one-sided, highly specialized or non-conforming student will be offered a scholarship.

The criteria for these programs are controlled by the requirements for success set by the college. What type of students receives "A" grades in college? What is the college's image of the ideal student? The answers to these questions—as determined by a study of what actually goes on in the college—suggest how scholarship recipients should be selected from a pragmatic point of view.

Where there is competition for a scholarship—and competition exists for virtually every scholarship of a general nature which carries honor or financial award—the typical criteria are:

1. The record of past scholastic behavior as indicated by grades (or rank in class), the pattern of subjects studied, the record of school activities, the leadership roles played at the school, etc. A comprehensive school record gives this information.

2. Scores on a test of scholastic aptitude or on a test of general educational development, such as the *Scholastic Aptitude Test* of the College Entrance Examination Board, the *American College Testing Program,* or the *National Merit Scholarship Qualifying Test.*

3. Estimates of loosely defined but desirable personality characteristics as evaluated from interviews, recommendations, or written responses by the applicant. Some colleges still include such banal questions as, "Why do you want to go to college?" or "What do you expect from this college?" or "How have you spent your summer?" Some colleges ask for a brief autobiography.

4. Evidence of the possession of specific characteristics desired by the donor of the scholarships, such as place of residence (where geographic spread is desired), socioeconomic background (where a cross section of economic classes is desired), special non-academic skills (such as in athletics), or academic potential in specified fields (such as science, modern languages, or mathematics).

In actuality, if one is to generalize, the heavy emphasis in the selection of winners in large scholarship programs—state, federal, independent or college-controlled—has been on grades (relative class standing), test scores, and specific characteristics set by the donor.

Research Criteria

No major or noteworthy research has been undertaken on the selection techniques used in specific scholarship programs. Innumerable elementary studies have been undertaken over the years on the relationship between test scores and secondary-school standing on the one hand and college success as measured by grade-point averages on the other. By and large, secondary-school grade-point averages predict averages in college (usually for the Freshman year) better than any other single indicator, but still the level of prediction is not high enough to suggest that other techniques are not needed. The more similar the secondary school is to the college in the quality of its students and its standards, the more accurate the prediction. Test scores are said to add a common element inasmuch as all candidates take the same test, and, while they predict somewhat less well than grade-point averages, they do add something to the total predictive picture when used in conjunction with grades.

From a broader point of view, predicting grades in college is a sterile business of little social or practical significance. Grades are a relative index based on the quality of the competition in a particular class at one college, not on a fixed standard of achievement. As our society is now structured, the important thing is to get over certain hurdles in formal education. Education is a great sorting process in which the labels count. If one graduates from college, one is a college graduate, and that fact is noted by the public. That one was an anchor man in one's class is usually not known.

Because scholarship students are generally selected for academic promise, the use of college grades as a criterion is logical, even if not very socially significant. The selection measures of grade-point averages and of high-school test scores are available and can be related to college grade-point averages. However, scholarship recipients are a very select group representing a restricted range of the measures used. Consequently, the resulting correlations when limited to the scholarship winners tend to be low. More meaningful measures of validity are more difficult to obtain and thus the lack of research involving such measures.

If the scholarship is designed to select individuals who will be leaders or successful producers in business, science, scholarship, or government, then the time lag is great between the selection of the winners and the date when they will have an opportunity to be effective in other than the student role. For some of the professions, a period of as much as twelve years or more of preparation is required, and longitudinal studies of this span require a measure of funding and planning which is difficult to obtain. Thus, such studies are almost non-existent.

If one wishes to add such characteristics as creativity, independence, leadership, and the like, measures of success are extremely difficult to determine, and the time span for gathering the data is a problem of even greater magnitude.

The Merit Program

THE SELECTION OF SCHOLARS

The National Merit Scholarship Program which has been in operation since 1955, is an example of a large, private, independent scholarship program. The purpose of the Merit Program is to identify and honor high academic talent without regard to its origins or its interests. The Merit Program informs the public of the nationwide distribution of unusual intellectual talent and attempts to create respect for such students. What a nation recognizes and honors tends to prosper and to grow. Because the need for educated intellectual talent has never been greater, the Merit Program serves an important national function.

The success of any selection procedure depends, first, upon attracting an appropriate group of available applicants. Obviously, unless one has more applicants than scholarships, selection is not required. Also, unless some of the applicants possess the desired characteristics, no selection procedure can be satisfactory. Therefore, the recruitment of a suitable group of applicants is essential to any selective scholarship program.

The Merit Program obtains a large applicant population by inviting all secondary schools in the United States to participate. In recent years over 17,500 schools have taken part. These secondary schools enrol over 95 per cent of all Seniors. The number of students in a given class who participate is determined by school officials. The schools generally see that their most able students enter the program; few schools exclude anyone who is interested. In some schools the entire class takes part.

There are about 800,000 applicants each year and, of these, about 55,000 are honored. Between 35,000 and 45,000 are designated as "Commended" and another 15,000 as "Semifinalists," almost all of whom become "Finalists." The scholarship winners are selected from the "Finalist" group. The winners of paying scholarships have numbered around 3,000 in recent years.

Reducing the applicant population of 800,000 to the 55,000 who are recognized in some way requires a method which is relatively inexpensive and yet acceptable as fair and appropriate to the high schools, the colleges, and the public. Thus far, the method which best meets this requirement is one involving a test of educational attainment. The test must be general enough not to dictate school curriculum or to exclude students from a school unable to offer a broad curriculum, yet specific enough to separate the academically apt from those less able. The *National Merit Scholarship Qualifying Test*, given by the schools in February or March of the Junior year, has met these requirements.

The Commended students, numbering 39,000 in 1968, are selected exclusively by test score without regard to geographic location or any other factors. They are sent a "Letter of Commendation." Typically, in test performance the Commended students stand among the top 7 per cent of the students entering the program and among the top 2 per cent of the students who graduate from high school. Some states have a much higher proportion of their school population attaining this honor than do other states.

The 15,000 Semifinalists are selected on the basis of test scores *and* geographic location. These students are selected separately for each state because states control public education, and they vary on such factors as the quality of education offered, per pupil expenditure for education, per capita income, and the educational level attained by the adult population, as well as in other important ways. The number of Semifinalists in a state is slightly over one-half of one per cent of the graduating secondary-school Seniors in that state. This method of selection has been accepted by the public and has resulted in a very high quality of students from every state.

The 15,000 Semifinalists take a second validating test given under supervised conditions and supply certain detailed information about themselves. The school also supplies additional information and recommendations. Almost all Semifinalists meet these requirements and become Finalists.

The winners of the National Merit Scholarships, which carry no restrictions as to choice of college, field of study, employment of parent or financial status, are selected on a state basis by a selection committee composed of college-admissions officers and school counselors. The selection committee is under no instructions regarding how it should operate, except that all selections are to be approved by at least two members. Unpublished research studies have shown that the dominant factors in selection are test scores and rank in class. However, neither high test scores nor high class ranking insure selection. The selection committee governs in all instances.

The Merit Program also includes a large number of sponsored Merit Scholarships. The sponsor has the right to set criteria over and above those of the National Merit Scholarship Corporation. The sponsor may select any Finalist, since all are considered fully qualified for a Merit Scholarship. All have scored very high on the test and have been recommended by their schools. The typical criteria used by sponsors are (*a*) employment of parent, (*b*) field of study, and (*c*) college choice—the latter being a requirement of college-sponsored Merit Scholarships.

In general, Merit Scholars succeed academically in college. They attend colleges ranging from the highly selective to the non-selective, with the former type attracting most of the winners. Their fields of interest cover the entire range, with the science fields attracting the largest numbers. In 1967/68, scholarship aid was provided by the Merit Corporation to over 9,300 students enrolled in 650 different colleges. The annual reports of the National Merit Scholarship Corporation give the basic statistical information about the program.

CHARACTERISTICS OF SCHOLARS

Over 90 per cent of Merit Scholars graduate from college, and of the graduating group, almost 90 per cent of the boys and almost 70 per cent of the girls then enter graduate or professional schools.[1] A high proportion are honor students, even though most of the winners attend highly selective colleges for which not all are adequately prepared.

1. Robert C. Nichols and Alexander W. Astin, "Progress of the Merit Scholar, an Eight-Year Follow-up," *Personnel and Guidance Journal*, XLIV (March, 1966), 673-81.

Probably no changes in selection procedures would result in any major increase in the proportion of Merit Scholars graduating from college or winning honors. Most of the winners are free to select any college of their choice (which will admit them) and to study any subject of interest to them. Under these conditions, a few academic failures do occur and a few of those selected experience mental and physical health problems which interfere with their progress. Marriage takes some of the girls from the academic scene, although most Merit Scholars who marry continue with their education.

Merit Scholars are characterized by diversity in almost every respect except that all have a quickness of mind, an interest in the intellectual side of life, and a sense of great satisfaction in classroom success. They vary in appearance, social sophistication, poise, mannerisms, and interests. They come from a range of economic backgrounds and home environments (i.e., some parents have little formal education while others possess professional degrees). Some are from small schools; some, from large. Some are from large cities; others, from rural areas.

Research studies which show that this group differs on the average from a randomly selected group of high-school students in almost every way must not obscure the enormous range in behavior and personality characteristics which are to be found in students of unusual intellectual capacity and promise. For example, Merit Scholars come more frequently from highly educated parents than from parents whose education stopped at the grade-school level, from the higher socioeconomic level more often than from the lower, from parents in the professions more often than from parents who are unskilled laborers, from suburban areas more often than from the inner city. Yet, in every class of Merit Scholars, there are a substantial number of exceptions to these generalizations.

The detailed research reports concerning the Merit Program are published and available. A recent report of the National Merit Scholarship Corporation includes abstracts of the studies completed to 1966.[2] Research reports are published at irregular intervals by the Corporation.

2. *Tenth Annual Review of Research* (NMSC Research Reports, Vol. II, No. 11 [Evanston, Ill.: National Merit Scholarship Corporation, 1966]).

The traditional methods of selecting scholarship recipients undoubtedly result in rewarding those students who fit the academic and behavioral patterns which our schools and colleges encourage and reward. Such students are not dull and uninteresting. Research shows that Merit Scholars are generally more independent, assertive, idealistic, unconventional, skeptical, rebellious, and argumentative than students of less ability in the traits on which the selections are based. Student uprisings contain their share of Merit Scholars. Not all Merit Scholars restrict their activities to libraries and laboratories. Some Merit Scholars are less respectful of campus routine than college administrators would like. Some are quite capable of cutting classes, of arguing with teachers, and, indeed, of sleeping or day-dreaming when the "going" in class seems dull. By and large, they are liberal politically, unhappy with the status quo, and more likely to attract attention than the average student. Although selection procedures tend to rule out the overtly independent and outwardly non-conforming, among the individuals who get through the screen are a few who become extremists in their college days by assuming roles in leading movements and by supporting ideas not popular with college administrators.

Problems

The greatest shortcoming of the present widely used selection techniques is that they favor the well-rounded, academic-type person at the expense of the individualist, the person of broad interests at the expense of the very specialized but highly talented, lopsided person. The diversity of talent is not recognized or its development fostered by most scholarship programs (or by most colleges) today. The values of diversity are discussed by Wolfle in his Bingham lecture.[3]

The current selection procedures in most common use are aimed to select individuals who will do distinguished work as measured by grades in college courses. The tacit assumption is either that high grades are an end in themselves or that high grades—and the level of ability and learning they represent—augur for success in what-

3. Dael Wolfle, "Diversity of Talent," *American Psychologist*, XV (1960), 535-45.

ever field the student enters after college. These are questionable assumptions. At least the evidence is at best inconclusive. Studies of the relationship between college success and success in later life are few, and most of them are neither convincing nor broad enough to support generalizations of practical value.

From observation, one can note that many of the characteristics which contribute to success outside the classroom do not contribute in the same degree to success inside the classroom. An obvious example is the ability to get along with others, to be interested in and to be empathetic with one's associates—in short, to be a likeable fellow. Individuals differ in major ways in this ability, and the ability is probably somewhat stable at the adult level. Its value is evident in most situations today in which co-operation with associates is an element contributing to the productivity of an individual, an office, a group, an academic department in a university, or even a research staff. The day when the individual could work with complete independence from others has passed.

There are numerous other illustrations one can offer to suggest that classroom work is not a sample of life. Success in the classroom, therefore, should not be expected to predict success in many life situations. Fortunately, positive traits tend to go together, but current selection techniques may be excluding groups of individuals who will be productive, effective, and perhaps creative in important work in later life.

To broaden current selection procedures for scholarships to include assessment of characteristics believed to be predictive of success beyond the narrow confines of the classroom would require establishing targets other than grades. To develop procedures for selecting individuals who will be able to hit these new targets requires numerous extensive, well-designed, longitudinal studies— studies which are expensive in time as well as in talent and money. The snapshot must be supplemented with time-lapse photography.

This long-range type of research can produce practical results. Without it, we are very much limited in what we can do. When the results of such long-range research are available, scholarship selection can be augmented to meet new criteria. That day is not close at hand, but, unless a start is made, it will not arrive.

CHAPTER VII

The Evaluation of Group Instruction

HERBERT A. THELEN

Evaluation plays a part in all strategies of instruction. The strategy discussed in this chapter is to "reach" the individual learner by influencing his participation in the activities of the classroom group. The strategy of instruction discussed in the next chapter is to direct the learner to make the appropriate ("individualized") sequence of choices throughout a programed course of study.

In both strategies, evaluation includes the functions of feedback, diagnosis, and steering. Evaluation concerns itself with "where" the class is within an emerging sequence of activities; or "where" the individual is with respect to the systematic development of a prescribed repertoire of verbal skills. The diagnosis of "location" is followed by "trouble-shooting" and planning decisions about the next step of action.

In teacher-led group instruction (discussed in this chapter), evaluation is conducted by the teacher with the help of the class, and their joint effort, however subjective, is successful to the extent that it results in decisions which turn out to have educative consequences. In "individualized" instruction programed by materials (discussed in the next chapter), evaluation is the utilization of the student's latest response in order to direct him to one of several possible next steps built into the program by its makers.

Both chapters deal with instructional systems. In the one case, the system is the miniature society of the classroom, with its full range of expressed feelings, language, and action; in the other case, the system is confined to the interface of the "man-machine" (or "man-program" combination)—a sort of mechanical tutoring dyad.

Neither chapter is much concerned with what, to many people, is orthodox educational evaluation—a technique for getting students to demonstrate *what* they have learned at some time well after the bulk of the learning has occurred (e.g., the end of the year). Instead, the evaluation considered in these chapters is made while learning is in process, and testing is in small segments at frequent intervals. There is nothing in either chapter—or in the "systems" approach generally—to argue against giving year-end tests of any or all behaviorally defined educational objectives. Such tests are not considered in this chapter because their purpose is not to guide instruction. They are useful for giving grades, and they serve a number of other interests of such non-participants (in instruction) as parents, school boards, taxpayers, and college admissions staffs. For these fateful, non-instructional purposes, a high level of validity and reliability is essential; and therefore evaluation has in practice been restricted for the most part to those fragments of the educational product the measurement of which, in the present state of the art, can be alleged to lend itself to these qualities. Evaluation for guiding instructional processes rather than for appraising products has little to do with statistical formulas, item discrimination, and intricasies of scoring. It has instead to do with interpretations of discrepancies between anticipation and performance, and the test of good evaluation is pragmatic, not technical.

The art of test construction has contributed very materially to the development of programed materials (see next chapter) because of their verbal and cognitive (test-like) flavor. But when it comes to assessment of the existential world with which the creative teacher is concerned, procedures of test construction are less useful, although the *discipline* of evaluation, which should underlie the art of test construction, has much to offer.

Let us now proceed to the major business of this chapter: to expose the nature of evaluation as feedback, diagnosis, and troubleshooting in a complex, ongoing social system. As our starting point, we shall consider the simplest possible instructional system: its structure is a teacher-pupil dyad and its process is tutoring. (We note in passing that this system is often claimed to be the archetype for individualized instruction by programed materials.) We shall see how the simple system changes by a large, conceptually discontinuous leap when it is increased to a group; and, still speaking generally, we shall offer a beginning overview of diagnosis and troubleshooting in the group. Under the "diagnostic tool" we shall define "validity" as referred to feedback, and we shall see why the teacher and class together should evaluate their system. With these definitions and overviews out of the way, we shall analyze three species of group instruction along with their corresponding methods of evaluation. Finally, as a kind of epilogue, certain somewhat unsystematically selected conceptual problems in the evaluation of group instruction will be discussed.

Overview: Instructional Systems

THE DYAD

The purest form of individualized instruction presumably would be one highly responsive teacher dealing with one pupil. The teacher, in this relationship, would continually try to adapt his own performance to that of the pupil, and he would not only correct and judge but would also support, empathize, and personalize. While the teacher and pupil together might be viewed as a social system (a dyad) for most purposes, the system properties would be much less salient than the processes of interaction between teacher and student and between student and materials and problems. There would be little point in distinguishing between the roles of the student as learner and as dyad member. Indeed, the child ideally would be seen as a complete person, and the concept of "role" would be superfluous. The teacher would deal with the learner, citizen, and group member all at once, without any need to sort out these aspects of the person. The teacher would theorize about the state of rapport he had with the student, about the student's apparent motivations and competencies, and about productive strategies to follow in order to keep the student's attention concentrated on the matter to be learned. He would over time gradually find out these things about each individual and govern himself accordingly. And, by dealing with each student separately from the others, he could give his own full attention to that one child and do exactly what he thought best for that child without worrying about the possible effects of his behavior on other children.

This sort of individualized dyadic instruction is tutoring. The fact that children often tutor each other quite effectively suggests that intuitive or spontaneous responsiveness (the sort of thing that children are capable of) is an important component of teaching and that sophisticated insight, rational alternatives, and explicit verbalized principles are correspondingly less important. This is another way of saying that the "theory" of dyadic teaching can (whether desirably or not) be rather minimal. Diagnosis and trouble-shooting can be made conceptually complex, but the one-to-one situation is in fact so easy to modify that our twelve-year-old student tutors, for example, typically substitute experimentation (trial and error) for diagnosis and trouble-shooting. If a technique, question, flash-card, or exercise does not "work" (in the sense of keeping the learner productively absorbed), they simply try something else. If teaching still gets nowhere, they give up teaching temporarily and take the role of friend, co-conspirator, hobbyist, or any other role through which they can reach the tutee. The explicit rationale of teaching is one which centers around activities and games through which the learner is exposed to and invited to practice desirable performances, but the social system, personalities, culture, group standards, etc., can all be ignored as objects of conscious attention even though they are responded to by the teacher.[1]

We have portrayed the dyad as a rather free-wheeling, mutually accommodative situation in which the teacher gradually finds out about the child and does what he thinks best for the child. This, of course, is the responsibility of any *professional* person working with children in any situation. But it is further required of the professional that he discharge his responsibilities in a sophisticated, informed way and, on this score, "gung-ho" evaluators frequently question the reliability and validity of the teacher's "subjective" judgment. Since the teacher's subjective judgment more often than not is the "outside criterion" against which these same evaluators judge the validity of *their* instruments, it might seem that their question could be narrowed to focus on reliability, and that the systematic use of repeated observations would take care of that. But the matter is much more complicated than that; what is involved here is not simply the difference between objective, reliable,

1. For an exposition of the dyad as a social system, see John W. Thibaut and Harold H. Kelley, *The Social Psychology of Groups* (New York: John Wiley & Sons, 1959).

and valid evaluation (which nobody is against) and idiosyncratic, unstable, and biased opinion (which everyone is against).

What is involved here is feedback from a total experiential flux, the salient dimensions of which vary continually versus appraisal of some pattern of traits of the child to which most of the variance in the situation can be attributed. The purpose of the feedback is to enable the teacher to make wise judgments about what to do next in the classroom; the purpose of the appraisal is to describe some state of need, readiness, or ability on the part of the child. These purposes are entirely different and therefore the fact that they are achieved through different procedures seems reasonable. These differences may be noted: (*a*) In feedback, the decision about what data to collect can be finally made only at the moment of collection, whereas, in appraisal, the decision can be made independently of the situation. (*b*) In feedback, the object under scrutiny is the activity of a complex system, whereas, in appraisal, it is an aspect of the personality structure of an individual. (*c*) In feedback, the categories must be useful to the teacher and usually will be expressed in her vocabulary, whereas, in appraisal, the categories should fit coherent theory and are often intelligible only to the researcher or some other non-participant. Still other differences will become apparent as we extend our examination to the group.

THE GROUP

Group instruction introduces new complications for instruction and evaluation. The free and easy experimentation with materials and the almost automatic accommodations that two persons of good will can make to each other are much harder to come by and usually do not exist until after a great deal of group "growth" has occurred. Persons are no longer free to change the subject at will, to indulge in free associations, to play back ideas to check understanding. Instead, they must worry about wasting time, being lucid to everybody, avoiding semiprivate jokes and personal remarks, not asking stupid questions, and so forth. And, to govern a society, the teacher needs clear policies and principles, not just a few interpersonal attitudes to act out toward one other person.

The target of the teacher's actions is the group. To some extent, any one child is always a representative of or delegate from the class. And to that extent the teacher tends to respond to him, not as a complex individual, but as a member of the class—more or less interchangeable with any other member. The child in the group is anonymous, not in the sense of being unknown or invisible so much as being a non-individual, a duplicate of other children with respect to the aspects of classroom life regarded by the teacher as being most salient. The salient aspects, usually prominently related to group management, have been encoded, formalized, and ritualized in the role of the student. The child's "education" is an accumulated by-product of his continual enactment of the role of the student over a period of years.

The teacher, then, addresses himself to diagnosing and trouble-shooting the role of the student, or, more precisely, to defining, delimiting, correcting, activating, and reinforcing that role. The major behavior of the teacher is that of stating and reiterating general and specific expectations. Instructions for each activity limn short-range or procedural expectations; moral criteria, citizenship standards, and social policies tend to be longer range, and through their consistency they give stability to the group; values, philosophical orientations, and commitments to general purposes are basic assumptions or themes with which the child is indoctrinated and through which his culture is transmitted to him.

The child has to produce the role of student. When problems of obeisance to expectations held by the teacher and supported by other children and parents occupy much of the child's attention, he may feel that the group is a demander of conformity, a stultifying trap. When the expectations to be met are discussed and when decisions are felt to be in response to the suggestions of individuals, the legislated boundaries, deadlines, product specifications, etc., may serve to define the situation in such a way that the child can cope with it meaningfully. When the role expectations include not only task structures, but also agreements on a great many further procedural choices that each child, invested with the authority of common purposes, can settle for himself, then the student is made "free." In this case, expectations are seen as being inherent in the *situation*, rather than merely in the demanding personality of the teacher. And such impersonal expectations provide a secure platform from which each child can take off on his own.

It might be said, then, that the role of "group member" stimulates and co-ordinates a large number of internalized roles: manager, artist, rebel, warrior, teacher, friend, baby, team player, and so on.

For the most part, the children and teacher lead public lives in the classroom. Their public is their image of the classroom group; and their behavior is directed to this image at times, as well as to certain individuals. Thus, when a single child "acts up," the teacher reacts to the fact that one of the rules is being violated, and making the child desist is also seized upon as an occasion to reinstate or reinforce the rule for all. The time for noticing a child, then, is when his conduct deviates from group standards, common expectations, and public policies. That part of his behavior we call "citizenship" is defined by legislated laws, and these in turn are operationally or behaviorally defined; and for that reason practically all antisocial behavior can be spotted and thus the classroom can be an effective setting for socializing the child. Processes of learning (as distinguished, perhaps, from demonstrable symptoms that learning has occurred) go on inside people and are, for the most part, not observable nor operationally definable. Therefore "laws" or behavioral expectations cannot be formulated and deviancy during learning cannot be spotted. In the group it is not possible to have the dyad's continual interaction which serves to check what has been learned each moment—tantamount to assessing the effectiveness of the ongoing processes of learning. The teacher has to substitute criteria of overt participation for criteria of learning; this means that the most informative activity is one in which the children act out their new information and skills as they are acquired.[2]

Overview: Diagnosis and Trouble-shooting in Group Instruction

If Johnny is adding $2 + 2$, his teacher can ask for his answer, correct it or commend it, say something humane, and let it go at that. The answer, 4, tells the teacher both that Johnny is learning the required matter and that he is participating effectively with his

---

2. Jacob W. Getzels and Herbert A. Thelen, "The Classroom Group as a Unique Social System," in *The Dynamics of Instructional Groups* (Fifty-ninth Yearbook of the National Society for the Study of Education, Part II [Chicago: Distributed by the University of Chicago Press, 1960]), pp. 53-82.

workbook (on the possibly leaky assumption that successful participation in carefully set-up learning activities practically guarantees that the anticipated learnings will occur). But, with twenty-five Johnnies, the teacher can at best only sample each child's answers; and, even if he spent all his time at it, each child would be unsupervised 96 per cent of the time. To know when to intervene with a child, the teacher must rely heavily on data that can be rounded up simultaneously and easily from everyone.

THE STRUCTURED CLASS

In a group, the time-honored way for a child to bring—nay, force—data to the teacher's notice is to stop paying attention or to bother some other child. Both these behaviors are easily spotted from the teacher's desk, and the amount and distribution of such behaviors is the basis for diagnosing how well the activity is going. It is presumed that one is not learning if he is inattentive, and that unauthorized conversation likewise is not conducive to learning. The presumptions approximate the truth when the task, materials, and procedures are specified in detail and when individuals compete with each other so strongly that all forms of co-operation are regarded as cheating. Thus, when the group is engaged in highly *structured* activity, diagnosis means what it meant in ancient Greek times: "the process of determining by examination (of symptomatic behavior of individuals) the nature and circumstances of a diseased condition" (i.e., ineffective activities in the group). The prototype of diagnosis in highly structured (totalitarian) classrooms is the attention chart, whereby each person's lapses of attention are tallied.

If all classes were structured, evaluation would be easy. One would make check sheets on which to tally the behaviors of the student which deviate from the role of the (good) member. Instances or intensities of "goofing off," non-attention, presumably deliberate provocation, irrelevant "contributions" (and so on) would be counted or judged. Categories of teacher behavior (usually verbal, oral) would be defined along certain continua from desirable to undesirable (e.g., student- to teacher-centered, democratic to authoritarian, indirect to direct influence, etc.); samples of classroom discussion would be observed and the behaviors of the teacher tallied. (Behavior of the students could also be tallied, but it is generally so consistent with that of the teacher that it would be useful mostly to differentiate among individuals rather than to get feedback for activity.) The point, of course, is that the *student* or member role and the *teacher* style are in fact defined by traditional expectations which fit the traditional, basically authoritarian classroom. Extensive chapters of a recent volume indicate the sorts of devices one uses in the structured classroom.[3] For the most part, the instruments discussed in these chapters purport to help record what happens rather than the deviance between what happens and what is wanted. If they describe what happens, they can be useful in any classroom no matter how structured; if they describe only deviance, then they can be most useful in any classroom, however structured, in which the teacher's purposes are congruent with the evaluator's biases.

THE UNSTRUCTURED CLASS

In an *unstructured* group, diagnosis obviously cannot be defined as the description and interpretation of deviancy. Purposes, procedures, materials, and required behaviors are not so well defined that deviations from them can be ascertained (except with regard to group standards about the expression of emotion, loyalty, respect for the leader, and management or housekeeping aspects). It is not possible to describe "health"; therefore, it is not possible to specify "disease," and hence it is not possible to know what symptoms (individual behaviors) to look for. Under these wide-open conditions, one cannot assert what ought to be true and then check to see how true it is (e.g., everyone ought to be paying attention to the teacher's blackboard work, but, in fact, half the pupils are not). The assertive "dialectical" or Platonic approach gives way to the problematic approach[4] which addresses itself to the question:

3. Donald M. Medley and Harold E. Mitzel, "Measuring Classroom Behavior by Systematic Observation," *Handbook of Research in Teaching*, ed. N. L. Gage (Chicago: Rand McNally Co., 1963), pp. 247-328; John Whitehall and W. W. Lewis, "Social Interaction in the Classroom," *ibid*, pp. 683-714.

4. These terms, plus "logistical" and "operational," are used by Richard P. McKeon to characterize major methods of inquiry, the subject of a forthcoming book.

"What is going on in the group that would account for my feeling (as a professional teacher) the way I do at this point?" It is assumed that *all* behavior is relevant or symptomatic, and that the diagnostic task is to propose an underlying trend or condition which would account both for the behaviors in the group and for the teacher's sensitive awareness of "problems." The process of diagnosis will clearly involve a movement from an undiagnosed sense of impatience, apprehension, joy, or other feeling to a diagnosis in words of "the cause or nature of a problem or situation"; and from the *private* sensitivity of one person to a *publicly* designated and consensually objective circumstance or purpose, value, or cause, that makes sense out of the behavior of all the members.

THE DIAGNOSTIC TOOL

As the teacher observes tell-tale behavior, he attempts to make sense of it. He is helped by knowing how to think about situations. Thus it is useful, first of all, to realize that, in a group, energy may be put into a job to be done or a purpose to be realized (productive system), into developing and maintaining the group as an organization through which required task behaviors can be elicited and used (managerial system), and into protecting the privacy, diversity, and autonomy of individuals (interpersonal system). It is also useful, in the second place, to know what to expect in a variety of circumstances: to anticipate the appearance of boredom and to know its behavioral manifestations, to understand why decisions tend to come unstuck at the point of having to act on them, to recognize the sorts of stress under which most people just naturally turn to a friend. And, third, it is useful for the teacher to have calibrated himself: to know under what circumstances he can count on himself to become passive, to get angry, to feel warmth, and so forth. He may have discovered, for example, that he becomes annoyed when asked to hand down a decision about which he is unsure, or that he becomes impatient and punitive when the group seems to have lost its thrust, or that he tends to withdraw from discussions when children start picking on each other. He, having found these probabilities about his own behavior, is predisposed to suspect, whenever he becomes aware of his annoyance, that he is saying things in which he has no confidence. Recognition of his impulse to punish may suggest that purposes are unclear; the tendency to withdraw (once he is aware of it) may suggest interpersonal disharmony.

The calibrated and highly-educated human nervous system is the diagnostic "tool," and, considering the dangers of mere projection, psychologizing, ex-cathedra evaluation, and (if I may say so) downright arrogance of some "observers," one needs some further methodological idea that will indicate when a diagnosis is dependable. That idea is an ideal of truth. What is truth in a diagnosis? How can it be recognized? The answer is simple in concept: *the closest possible approximation to the truth of "what is going on in the group" is a theoretical reconstruction that explains why everyone in the group feels and acts the way he does.* This definition implies: (*a*) that there is some underlying condition (e.g., source of frustration, threat, eagerness) in the group and that all the members are affected by this condition; (*b*) that they are all affected differently or individually (it makes one angry, another nostalgic, another pleased, etc.); (*c*) that each person in the group has been calibrated in the sense described above, so that the sort of thing to which each would react with fear, flight, intimacy-seeking, dependency, etc. is known. Under these conditions, a diagnosis is produced by finding out how each person reacted to or felt about the period to be diagnosed, and then by imagining a condition X as the most likely single condition that would explain why each person reacted the way he did. Condition X, then, is the "true" condition.

Diagnosis can arrive most closely at the truth when the group is sufficiently cohesive that individuals feel secure in expressing their own reactions; when each person has participated enough to emerge as a known individual in the minds of others; when diagnosis follows closely on the heels of the situation to be diagnosed; when diagnosis is made a normal part of operation; and finally, when the classroom group considers itself a laboratory in which to investigate its own problems of work, resistance, communication, and so forth.[5]

5. Supportive concepts are found in: Henry A. Murray, *Explorations in Personality* (New York and London: Oxford University Press, 1938); *Assessment of Men: Selection of Personnel for Office of Strategic Services* (U.S. Office of Strategic Services Assessment Staff [New York: Rinehart & Co., 1948]); Norman Polansky *et al.*, "Problems of Interpersonal Relationships in Research on Groups," *Human Relations*, II, no. 3 (1949), 281-91.

Diagnosis, when performed co-operatively by teacher and class, is realized through suitable activities. During class discussion, one may invite the group to consider whether the speakers are all saying substantially the same thing—but in different vocabularies and in relation to different referents—or whether there are several points of view and genuine issues. One can set up role-playing scenes (such as a group of students waiting for the teacher to arrive and open the door) into which their feelings about school authority will be projected. Horowitz and Henry developed a picture projective test, in which the group makes up stories together and projects its attitudes toward loneliness, authority, ambitions, and the like. The teacher may set up a panel of red and green lights which can be turned on and off by students and thus get simultaneous non-verbal feedback from everybody as the discussion proceeds. He may invite the class to divide into subgroups to come up with suggestions about what activity to undertake next—and underlying these suggestions will, of course, be some implied purposes. He may wait until the last few minutes of the period and then have the class fill in a "post-meeting reaction sheet," eliciting feelings about how well the meeting went, how freely one could express opinions, what was the most interesting or valuable activity, and so forth. Then, at the beginning of the next period, he can feed back to the class a tabulation of its answers and invite the class to interpret the data— as useful hypotheses about the state of need and readiness. Although the procedures of co-operative feed-back evaluation by a group bear little resemblance to rigorous test construction and scoring, the same basic *discipline* of evaluation underlies both, having to do with: the nature of discrimination, the identification of prototypical situations, the tracing of connections between phenotype and genotype, the distinctions between familiar and "new" situations, the correspondences and differences between verbal and non-verbal behaviors, and the relationships between habitual behaviors and "significant" incidents.

Trouble-shooting is concerned with means or procedures in contrast to diagnosis which traffics in ends or purposes. Diagnosis asks how far we have progressed toward our stated goals (closed situation), or what our apparent goals are as judged by what we are doing (open situation). Through diagnosis in the closed situation, a discrepancy may be found between "where we are and where we ought to be," and trouble-shooting would attempt to see what caused the discrepancy and what action would remove it. Some form of correction, stimulation, restructuring, reward enhancement, or seating change may be called for. Diagnosis in the open situation yields a theory about "what the group is trying to do," and evaluation of this direction in the light of larger purposes or more appropriate responses would result in a definition of the "trouble" (if any) with which trouble-shooting would be concerned. The interpretation of the diagnosis, the evaluation of the presumed direction, and the suggestion of what ought to be done about it would best come about through group discussion. Trouble-shooting in the open situation, like diagnosis, is most effective when it is a normal part of group operation and when the method of teaching in the microsociety builds in diagnosis and trouble-shooting as parts of its own steering mechanism.

We shall consider diagnosis and trouble-shooting more fully in connection with the three views of the group as: (a) a collectivity, (b) an interpersonal network, and (c) a microsociety.[6]

Collective Individual Instruction

The typical classroom, if there were such a thing, would be a collection of children all being taught and tested on the same things at the same time and at the same rate. Each child would be involved in a quasi-contractual relationship with his teacher—so much work at such and such a level in return for such and such a grade. The children would have some discussion with each other during waiting periods between activities, but for the most part conversation would be discouraged during "learning" activities; and talking during some activities would be called cheating and would be liable to punishment. It would be recognized that some children are faster than others, and that some are more responsive, more motivated, or more skillful, but what, if anything, would be done about these individual differences would be up to the teacher. He could punish and slow down the fast or bright children by giving them extra work; he could speed up the slow or dull children by eliminating

6. Dorothy Stock and Herbert A. Thelen, *Emotional Dynamics and Group Culture* (Washington: National Training Laboratories, 1958), pp. 225-38.

part of the work (usually the more interesting parts). He could make much use of seat work in which the children would be occupied and directed by programed syllabuses or workbooks, and he could wander about trying to help those children who seemed to need it. He could respond differently to each child, being in turn kind, cruel, equable, noisy, etc., hoping thus to adapt his own expression of affect to support or curb the child. He could find indirect ways to "jack up" the self-esteem of unmotivated pupils by letting them run the projector, take the roll, etc., and he could even give "credit" for such services as if they were tantamount to the more subject-centered learning activities. By and large, his thinking would tend to center around THE STUDENT, a sort of averaged-out imaginary character whose needs exactly fit the curricular opportunities, whose attitudes support the teacher, and whose performance is rational and predictable. It is assumed that all students are like THE STUDENT until they reveal themselves to be otherwise, and that deviations and discrepancies will call for techniques of "adjustment" through which the child will be persuaded to go along with the work and, hopefully, even to enjoy it and to learn something from it.[7]

TEACHING STRATEGIES

In collective instruction, the two major questions are: "What shall we teach THE STUDENT?" and "how shall we deal with diversity or individual differences?" The three alternative strategies open to the teacher in responding to these questions are:

1. Specify the purposes and procedures and use whatever force (of persuasion or policing) that is required to make everyone meet specifications.

2. Specify the purposes, but leave open some or all of the procedures; use some information from the children in order to decide

7. See any chapter on "classroom management" in any educational psychology textbook; for "*the* learner," see also Jerome S. Bruner (ed.) *Learning about Learning: A Conference Report* (Cooperative Research Monograph No. 15, Office of Education, U.S. Department of Health, Education and Welfare, 1966); also "autocratic methods," in Ralph K. White and Ronald Lippitt, *Autocracy and Democracy* (New York: Harper & Bros., 1960).

which of the available alternatives makes sense for each boy or girl, each subgroup, or the total class.

3. Specify neither purposes nor procedures but have in mind the major principles the course is supposed to teach; use classroom procedures which enable the necessary decisions about curriculums to be made on the basis of evidence, much of which is obtained especially for that purpose.

These strategies of *assignment, adaptation,* and *emergence* respectively correspond to three drastically different teaching styles and pedagogical theories, and, within these, to correspondingly different views of diagnosis and trouble-shooting.

ASSIGNMENT

The method of teaching in the *assignment* strategy is dialectical. The teacher has to act as if he truly knows what ought to be taught to everyone. He then asserts this knowledge by acting on it and discovers that the performances of individuals differ in the extent to which they meet the teacher's expectations. Making such discoveries is *diagnosis*. The teacher then has to evaluate his diagnosis and decide whether to accept the differences and record them in different grades for each student (achievement assessment) or whether to take further persuasive or police action of some sort; this latter process is *trouble-shooting*. Trouble-shooting ranges from imaginative innovation to cut-and-dried schemes of reward and punishment.

For a totalitarian teacher, who believes that his assignment specifies all aspects of permissible behavior, trouble-shooting is confined to finding the culprit and deciding on the stick or carrot to be applied. The application may be made in class or in private. (One can get rather exquisite nuances of gratification or punishment by dealing with the whole class even when the main target is individuals. Then there is the intriguing question of who the teacher is *really* talking about when she addresses the class and the multiplication effect [or tossing-to-the-wolves effect] that ensues from punishing the whole class for the sins of the few. Likewise, the whole class may be rewarded for the accomplishments of the few, but this is unlikely to be done by the totalitarian teacher because he keeps reward in scarce supply in order to encourage competition.)

One pseudo trouble-shooting device employed for totalitarian or collective teaching is put into effect before the teaching actually begins. This is ability-grouping, and in the author's view a consequence of pseudo trouble-shooting, first, because it is based on experience with other earlier groups rather than with the present group and, second, because it is not based on data—only on "common sense." The research evidence, which is sufficiently conclusive demonstrates that segregating children on the basis of ability is no more likely than non-separation to result in better achievement. Nevertheless, because ability-grouping is also socioeconomic grouping, it facilitates indoctrination for college or welfare, for affluent or poverty societies; and thus the "top" parents (who come to school) like it and the "bottom" parents (who do not come to school) are ignored.[8]

SEMIADAPTATION

For a less totalitarian teacher, who does not intend for his assignments to go beyond thought-control or cognitive aspects of performance, diagnosis is about the same, but trouble-shooting can lead to formulation of alternatives in realms not covered by the assignment (social interaction, organization, leadership, and others). Although the strategy of *assignment* is maintained for task-related aspects of school life, the strategy of *adaptation* is adopted to some extent for its social, organizational, and managerial aspects. Thus the teacher may divide the class into small groups, all of which must ultimately cover the assigned work, but which are not required to do so at the same rate. If the assigned work forms an invariant sequence, then it is possible to divide the sequence by the number of school years it covers and allow each section to take the time it needs to cover each "year" of the sequence. Thus some children would take eight calendar years to do six grades; others would take

8. Harry A. Passow, "The Maze of Research on Ability Grouping" and other chapters in *Grouping in Education* (Report sponsored by the UNESCO Institute for Education, Hamburg [New York: John Wiley & Sons, 1966]); and Ruth B. Ekstrom, *Experimental Studies of Homogeneous Grouping: A Review of the Literature* (Princeton, N.J.: Educational Testing Service, 1959).

four years. This design, called "non-gradedness," represents a rather minor adaptation of the inflexible-assignment strategy.[9]

For the most part, trouble-shooting in the semiadaptive-assignment strategy addresses itself to the question of how to get the children to influence each other to accept the teacher's assignments. The development of the proper "set" through identification and involvement techniques, the overview of "advance organizers," the imbedding of learning in "games," the use of gold stars and achievement thermometers, the display of exemplary written work on the bulletin board—these devices use public means to effect private results. A fascinating recent development is the use of older children to tutor younger ones. As a semiadaptive strategy, the material to be learned may be the same as that which the regular teacher would use, but the culture, generation, and authority barriers that separate the adult teacher from the small child may be virtually overcome.

In the collectivity, then, the teacher checks on the achievement of each pupil, and he relates this information to his observations of how the child participates. The teacher believes that if an underachieving student would only participate more normally he would achieve adequately; hence, the first aim of diagnosis and troubleshooting is to bring the behavior of the deviate into conformity with the others. If this does not clear up the problem, the teacher has to diagnose the particular "individual difference" that is being so stubborn and possibly transfer the child to a more suitable class, find him a buddy, institute remedial instruction, or take some other action.

CERTIFICATION

In the broadest terms, the function of evaluation as applied to the collectivity is certification. What is certified is that the child has had a prescribed set of experiences covering the right number of years—that he has completed school and has survived a standard regimen that was imposed on all his age-mates as well. Because of the relative inflexibility of the assignment strategy, the child has had to do most of the accommodating; and the child who cannot

9. John I. Goodlad and Robert H. Anderson, *The Nongraded Elementary School* (New York: Harcourt, Brace & World, 1959).

submit to or take advantage of this "socialization" drops out of school—as well as out of possible participation in the affluent society. While the demands of the learning activities create difficulty for children, even greater and more traumatic problems are likely to center around the member role in the classroom society. The degree of incongruence between the culture of the classroom and that of the home is probably the best predictor of the difficulty the child will experience in both learning and accommodating. For the child of poverty, the high-school diploma is the passport into the affluent society, for it testifies that he has survived his probation in the junior establishment.[10]

Interdependent Interactive Learning

In discussing the collectivity, it has been indicated that spontaneous conversation among children tends to be seen as irrelevant to classroom purposes and that voluntary serious discussion is likely to be regarded as cheating. Since these and other informal interactions are simply to be prevented, the conception of the collectivity has no scope for considering the constructive or even essential character of informal person-to-person conversation among children.

In this section we are interested in the informal interpersonal network both because it influences the behavior of children and because it can serve useful purposes. These are: reduction of individual stress so that children can overcome temporary upsets, anxieties, and excitements that otherwise would block the operation of intelligence; support for each individual through complementation of his own resources by those of other children; and reinforcement of assigned task-work by interpersonal striving. Each of these uses is formed by diagnosis and directed by trouble-shooting or feedback.

STRESS REDUCTION

One of the salient dimensions of group life is morale. A high-morale group is responsive, non-distractable, good-humored, and productive. All groups have slumps in their morale, and the leader

10. See, for example, chapter vi in Kenneth B. Clark, *Dark Ghetto* (New York: Harper & Row, 1965).

at such times notes apathy, sullenness, inability to understand instructions, doggedness, interpersonal aggression, expressions of inadequacy, and the like. When he "trouble-shoots" the situation, he
is likely to find that the class is under stress; it has become discouraged by the boredom of the work, it feels that nothing the
members do will be really appreciated or rewarded, or it concludes
that the members really have no role or "place" since the teacher
does all the thinking, acting, and talking. Under such conditions,
the teacher's strategy will range somewhere from thinking everything out by himself and privately resolving to behave differently
(manipulative approach) to inviting the class to form into small
groups to diagnose the situation and think about the qualities they
would like to see more prominent in the classroom life (inquiry
approach).

Sometimes the problem for the teacher is that the group seems
to have too much morale; that is, they are in the grip of excitement
and all want to talk at once. Anything from a bathroom word to
an exciting movie can produce this effect. It is as if each person is
reacting to the same stimulus at the same time, and the quality that
frightens the teacher is probably the non-communicativeness of the
interaction. Each child thinks aloud and does not really expect to
be listened to or responded to. Under these conditions it seems
sensible to suggest that the children form into small groups and
interact with each other. Then, after the catharsis is over, they can
see what ideas they wish to report to the whole group. In both
cases, group depression or group mania, the individual is under
stress and he will do something about it if the opportunity is there;
what he will do is to turn to one or more special people (friends)
with whose help he will "get hold of" his thoughts and feelings.

COMPLEMENTATION

Children also turn to each other for help on tasks. In one experiment, for example, it was found that about a quarter of the students
in an algebra class preferred to work their homework assignments
together and that they not only worked the problems, but also
compared notes on the teacher, the class, mutual friends, the "Man
from U.N.C.L.E.," and so forth. But, whatever other purposes may
have been served, the reason for the small groups was that members

felt insecure, inadequate, or unmotivated to do the work individually. By acknowledging anxiety and finding that others felt the same way, the anxiety was reduced. In addition, they had among them the necessary ideas for getting the work done; there was a multiplication of resources.

One frequently observes pairs of children who seem inseparable and who obviously support and "complete" each other: the domineering boy or bully accompanied by an obsequious "egger-onner," the two unpopular, minority-group girls who present a defensive coalition, the lively boys whose energy wears everyone out and who need each other to absorb their initiations, the children with strong common interests in sex or in hobbies who are always ready to channel dull classwork into lively discussion, and just plain people who need, as does everyone, to be responded to as individual persons at least once in a while.[11] The easiest way to deal with these attractions and sought-for associations is to allow children to work together and to choose their work partners. Then, if the relationship is not productive, the teacher might discuss it with the children involved and suggest that a different team be formed next time. Generally speaking, giving the students the responsibility of deciding to work alone or to work with others (and with whom they will work) is a useful way to increase their autonomy and to mobilize resources over which the teacher otherwise has little control.

REINFORCEMENT

The third function of interpersonal associations is suggested by the fact that persons not only use each other to help see them through difficult situations, but they also appear to have longer-range goals with respect to each other. That is, there are certain persons one wants to know more about, and gaining information and having experiences with such persons become strong purposes. When, for example, an older but inadequate student tutors a younger one, the older student has domination of the younger one very much on his mind, and the transmission of material and skill may only be the vehicle through which dominance may be

11. Thomas Howell Hawkes, "The Emotional Dynamics of Reciprocal Sociometric Choices" (unpublished Ph.D. dissertation, University of Chicago, 1967).

achieved. One validates, confirms, and strengthens his self-image and sense of identity by living in accordance with it; if his image is that of kindness, power, knowledge, or skill, he needs a suitable person to whom he can be kind, whom he can dominate, whom he can tell, or to whom he can demonstrate. Thus selected people are not only part of one's supportive milieu; they are also targets of purposive strategies.[12]

The interpersonal network is a spontaneous, voluntary, mostly private informal organization. It is activated by students when their personal needs are strong. It serves the purpose of helping them get through situations more adequately and less anxiously. The more impersonal, "hardnosed," unreasonable, unjust, or undependable, and so forth the environment, the more people need and turn to each other voluntarily.[13] The interpersonal dynamic is the major means of *self-help* and adaptation, and a teacher who can determine when self-help is needed and can make it accessible to those who need it has the first requisite for success. The strategy here involved is the *adaptive* as described in the discussion of the collectivity (see type b). The purpose is made clear, primarily by describing the state of disorganization, apathy, etc., that exists, and the children are invited to act out and rehearse their own solutions. But the teacher can facilitate this interaction (*a*) by explicitly commenting on how the small groups or pairs are to be formed, (*b*) by saying what will happen after the small groups have finished their meetings, and (*c*) by indicating what report, if any, will be made and how future action of the class may be affected.

TEACHABLE CLASSES

In all departments of classroom life, the teacher is profoundly influential. His influence is both private and public, unconscious

---

12. See chapters in *Person Perception and Interpersonal Behavior*, ed. Renato Taguiri and Luigi Petrullo (Stanford: Stanford University Press, 1958)—especially: Urie Bronfenbrenner, "The Study of Identification through Interpersonal Perception," pp. 110-30; O. K. Moore, "Problem Solving and the Perception of Persons," pp. 131-50; Edward E. Jones and John W. Thibaut, "Interaction Goals as Bases of Inference in Interpersonal Perception," pp. 151-78.

13. See chapters x, xi, and xiii in Helen Hall Jennings, *Leadership and Isolation* (New York: Longmans, Green & Co., 1950).

and planned. His private influence is informal and voluntary, and falls into all the categories we have been discussing. In short, he has his own personality and his own need for other persons and for maintenance of his self-image, identity, or basis of personal security and self-esteem. With some students, the teacher is effective, strong, and happy; with others he is dull, weak, worn out. The most important single thing the principal can do to help most teachers is to give them "a class they can teach," a compatible class. In the one major experiment with compatibility grouping, it was discovered that the "teachable" or "composed" classes had high *solidarity* as compared to the control (more or less typical) classes. And this higher solidarity contributed very markedly to the effectiveness of adjustment through the interpersonal network.[14]

The development of procedures for composing "teachable" or teacher-compatible groups is a fine challenge to diagnostic and trouble-shooting ingenuity. In our experiment, we asked each teacher to give us the names of students who got a lot out of class and those who got little. We then tested the students of both lists on a very comprehensive battery covering everything we could think of that might be relevant to personal effectiveness, ranging from projectives to preferences for kinds of activities. The responses that differed significantly for the two lists were made into a scoring key, different for each teacher, and all the students available for the next year's classes were tested and scored using the compatibility-discriminating key. The teacher's "teachable" class was composed of the high scorers.

This procedure attempts to do the whole job of matching before the classes meet. The opposite kind of procedure would be to assign students and teachers to each other at random and shift students around from class to class as the need arose. A combined technique, beginning with a good guess and then making modifications as more information is obtained or as growth occurs to change the situation, should be employed, and it should be based on adequate data about the effectiveness of each pupil in the social environment of his particular class.

14. Herbert A. Thelen, *Classroom Grouping for Teachability* (New York: John Wiley & Sons, 1967).

PEDAGOGICAL POLICY

The public, planned influence of the teacher comes about through the realization of his pedagogical and management policies. Of special interest is his own accommodation and attitude toward the interpersonal aspects of interaction. He may pointedly ignore, suppress, or encourage these; and he may do it selectively, differently, or even oppositely from one kind of occasion to another. He encourages the informal structure: (*a*) by having a wide range of activities through which students can discover each other's strengths and weaknesses as persons (*b*) by participating in the informal interchanges "as a person"—which means expressing genuine personal feeling once in a while, (*c*) by explicitly recognizing the need for subjective opinions as data to be interpreted by the class, (*d*) by noting cues the children give as to when they most seem to need each other, and (*e*) by accepting expressions of personal likes and dislikes as reasonable, proper, and potentially constructive.

Basically, the possibility of revising decisions about who should work with whom, on what, for how long, to what end, and with what product resulting is always open. All classroom behavior is "processed" or screened for elements of feedback or trouble-shooting that will confirm or challenge existing arrangements and suggest better ones.

PROCESS

Awareness of the interpersonal, ameliorative, adaptive aspects of classroom life is what is usually meant by sensitivity to "process." It implies that the teacher is putting himself in the place of the student, has some feeling for what it is like to be a student, and has some feeling for the qualities of life he wants to obtain and maintain in the classroom. The view is basically religious; one continually *lives* by the values he professes, and, in the effort, he comes to understand more fully what these qualities are. Thus the teacher is sensitive to that bored, loose-end feeling, to self-pity and sadness, to vigor and excitement. And he respects absorption in work, perseverance, and creative impulses. He is glad when children say what is on their minds, when they listen to each other, and when they try to plan wiser policies of self- and other-autonomy.

It is highly instructive to compare the collectivity and the interpersonal network with respect to product and process. Private and interpersonal needs or frictions activate the network, and it operates to do whatever is required to maintain individual adequacy—which means effective participation. The interpersonal network maintains desired qualities of process, and it is assumed that, if the process is informed and appropriate, the product, whatever it is, is bound to be good. In the extreme view, it is even assumed that it is arrogant of the teacher to judge the product or pass on it. The fact that the individual was absorbed productively is sufficient validation of the worth of the product; and to judge the product by preconceived expectations must, in the long run, destroy the adaptive process, the responsive way of life, that is so important.

In the collectivity, the view is simpler. Once the desired product has been specified, the teacher can deduce the procedures the student must follow to obtain it. The teacher tends to believe that learning is a direct reflection of procedures or techniques (e.g. "study skills"). Actually, achievement tests typically used in schools are notoriously insensitive to instructional methods; as a result, there is not a close relationship between the qualities of learning processes and measured "achievement." It is possible that what is measured and called achievement represents only a trivial and inconsequential part of the educational outcome. It is even possible that important things were learned but were not measured at all.

What is needed, then, is the kind of task clarity and objectivity of the collectivity along with the pupil self-help and process sensitivity of the interpersonal network—in short, a conception that makes room for both the formal and the informal structure and processes of the classroom group. Such a conception has to be larger than either, and the concept that fills the bill is that of the microsociety.

Purposive Inquiry in the Classroom Microsociety

The third major concept of the classroom group is that it is a miniature but complete society.[15] All the political, sociological, eco-

---

15. For more on the group as a microsociety, see Daniel Katz and R. L. Kahn, *The Social Psychology of Organizations* (New York: John Wiley & Sons, 1966).

nomic, religious, and other concepts of the sciences of society can be applied to the phenomena and structures of the classroom. In this view, the classroom is to be regarded as having all the characteristics of a society, not just the ones the teacher finds convenient to recognize; the teacher must understand that he did not create the society nor can he rub it out. It is a part of the larger society; it is swept by the same controversies, issues, anxieties, and frustrations, even though the forms in which they are made manifest are only those available to children. The reason for the overlap is, of course, that the students and the teacher do in fact live in the larger community, and they bring its cultures, which they have internalized, into the classroom with them. And because of this overlap, incongruent or high-impact classroom experience can invest outside experiences with new meanings.

CULTURE

An interesting question for the classroom and for the larger society is that of which culture will dominate. One usually imagines that it will be a WASP middle-class culture—a tribute both to the teacher's power and to his provincialism. In a school which is both poor and Negro, the WASP teacher is usually only partially successful in establishing her culture. Through force it is possible to get outward conformance to middle-class behavior, but the achievement motive is likely to remain unaffected. What is needed, of course, is an emergent culture developed through dialogue initiated in response to the alternatives brought in by all those concerned; and a major component of an emergent culture is the understanding that it is emergent—and properly so.

Changes of cultural aspects such as language, attitudes toward social roles, nature of accepted authority, use of myths, and degree of rigor in thinking are changes in the way of life of the group. Cultural conflict, whether manifest or hidden, is an important object for diagnosis, both as feedback to guide decisions and as evidence of group growth. Clearly, decisions about activities should bias the group toward the way of life of educated men. If such shifts do not occur, one may assume that the microsociety was treated as a collectivity, and that educational aspirations were compressed into mere cognitive and verbal outcomes.

All classrooms shake down a set of expectations which become sufficiently well established that people can see how to relate to and communicate with each other. But it is a mistake to assume that all possible underlying themes are necessarily educative. Classroom cultures can indeed be organized around the themes of achievement and inquiry; but they can also be dominated by the quest for comfort, for reassurance of the teacher, and for toilet training (behavioral conformity to absolute standards of order, respect, quiet, and punctuality).[16]

COMPONENT SYSTEMS OF THE CULTURE

The (cultural) way of life of classroom and larger societies may be seen as produced and maintained by three component systems: (a) the productive-distributive, (b) the managerial-legislative, and (c) the interpersonal-informal.[17]

Productive-distributive system.—The productive-distributive system is oriented toward making something and then distributing the earned rewards. In the larger society, what is produced can be exchanged for money, and the money can be divided and spent for whatever things money will buy. In the classroom, what is made can be exchanged for approval by the teacher, and this in turn can be translated into grades, privileges, and a variety of psychic rewards. One important difference between the classroom and the larger society is that in the latter the production goals are reached through co-ordinated and concerted effort, whereas in the classroom the goal of "behavioral change" of each student is not one toward which co-operation of the whole class can be effectively directed. Any collective goal simply does not function to give the group cohesion or authority; it is an inadequate *raison d'etre* for a group—a point to which we shall return.

Managerial-legislative system.—The managerial-legislative system is concerned with the maintenance of the classroom society as

16. See also Dorothy S. Whitaker and M. A. Lieberman, *Psychotherapy through the Group Process* (New York: Atherton Press, 1964).

17. Talcott Parsons, "Some Ingredients of a General Theory of Formal Organization," in *Administrative Theory in Education*, ed. Andrew Halpin (Chicago: Midwest Administration Center, University of Chicago, 1958), pp. 40-72.

an organization as distinguished from maintenance of an internalized "way of life" (culture) or a purposive goal-directed strategy (production). The distinction among these three concerns can be illustrated: the value of personal safety in the sense of prevention of accidental death is fairly well ingrained in our *culture*. The *productive* system turns out automobile seat belts. The *legislative-managerial* system attempts through laws, propaganda, and persuasion to get people to use the belts. Or again: the cultural theme in the classroom group, let us say, is verbal learning; the productive system defines a great many performances to be produced; and the managerial-legislative system contains the machinery of roles and power through which decisions are made, conflicts adjudicated, communicability protected, rights upheld, recourse provided for individuals, and agreements (both implicit and explicit) reached.

Interpersonal-informal system.—Finally, there is the interpersonal-informal system whose properties were discussed extensively in the preceding section.

SYSTEM RELATIONSHIPS

The way these systems relate to each other determines the results, educational and otherwise, of group instruction; therefore, the relationships among the systems must be continuously diagnosed and corrected, as necessary, through trouble-shooting.[18] One way in which the relationships can differ is with respect to which system dominates the microsociety. Suppose, for example, the interpersonal-informal system is the "leading" one, and that therefore the productive-distributive and legislative-managerial systems must adapt to it. The dominant demands are for active celebration of friendships or other personally important relationships. The required learning (productive) activities are those through which interpersonal preferences can be explored and revealed as, for example, when a self-selected small group of three friends decides what they would like most to do and how they wish to do it. Managerial-legislative arrangements would be required to facilitate the break-up of the class into small groups, the provision and pro-

18. Much of the work that underlies this chapter may be found in Herbert A. Thelen, *Dynamics of Groups at Work* (Chicago: University of Chicago Press, 1954).

tection of the "territory" of each, and the control of noise, competition, and reward among them. The "purest" example of the whole organization's being dominated by the informal structure is probably the collection of "bull sessions" going on in a college dormitory almost any evening. The dormitory residents produce and maintain the rules of conduct (parietal, managerial-legislative); the small groups select such topics as will enable them to get to know each other in ways that are personally important; and the conversation may or may not result in planning and executing activities (i.e., projects such as parties, expeditions, and protests, etc.).

Domination by the managerial-legislative system is perhaps best revealed in the common wail that "you have to be able to manage the class before you can teach it" and in the insistence that children must "respect" the teacher, sit quietly during transitions between activities, take turns (regardless of intensity of need or interest), be treated without favoritism, and so on. Many classrooms apparently exist primarily to be, or to celebrate the virtues of quiet, order, punctuality, and respect. In such classrooms, the learning activities (productive system) selected are unexciting, unfrustrating, easily supervised, fair, and readily justified. In a sense, participation comes under the aegis of citizenship rather than learnership or inquiry. The emotionality that might, if encouraged, threaten classroom quiet and teacher tranquillity is further kept in low key by suppressing interpersonal spontaneous interaction. In short, the interpersonal network is spiked. This sort of classroom is most likely to be found wherever the teacher has given up the effort to teach—in many inner-city schools, for example. But one does not have to go to the slums to see the managerial system dominant in the classroom, for this feature is incorporated in the traditional view of teaching. Many adults take it for granted that the worst crime in the book is to cross the teacher, and the brutality with which the rules are maintained in the English public schools seems to be worn as a proud badge of courage.

DOMINANCE OF PRODUCTIVE SYSTEM

A great variety of considerations converge in the third notion that the productive system should be dominant in the classroom. In the first place, this is what teachers almost always claim is in fact the case—even when they are martinets or non-directives, so that all that remains for them is to fit their actions to their words. Second, as Jennings pointed out, groups form spontaneously (naturally) to produce such things as everyone wants, but which none can get as well by himself.[19] Third, for people to know what is appropriate, relevant, or helpful to do in a group, they must have an idea of its purposes and tasks. Fourth, a purpose has as a target some condition in the environment; and such a target is externalized, objective, and impersonal. This means that it can be thought about explicitly, consciously, and non-defensively; alternatives can be suggested and tested; and progress can be seen and demonstrated. (Consider the ineffectiveness of wiping out prejudice as compared with attacking discrimination.) Fifth, the greatest individual reward is in having one's own contributions picked up and used by the group, and this of course is not possible if the group has no goal or aim it is trying to reach. Many individual products or actions such as looking up information, writing essays or stories, outlining, planning, taping, drawing, etc., acquire meaning and consequence when they are part of the goal-seeking sequence of actions in the group. Sixth, until the group can articulate clear goals or purposes, it must engage in exploring its own attitudes and feelings, and its discourse remains semiprivate and parochial. But, once its purposes are conceived in public language, warranted knowledge can, for the first time, be applied and learned. Learning or knowledge-using behaviors, like other behaviors in the group, are legitimized and made examinable only when the group has and acts on related purposes. (Looking at the children's arithmetic skills, for example, would appear to be of doubtful legitimacy if the group's major purpose is to get out of the arithmetic class.)

Seventh, and quite apart from the above more or less "educational" reasons for making the productive system dominant, is the demand in modern society for avoiding all forms of socioeconomic grouping, such as homogeneous ability-grouping tends to be. We must figure out some way to deal with a heterogeneous class, in fact, to *capitalize* on heterogeneity. The principle is clear: if everything is specified at the level of exact procedures, diversity is a

19. Jennings, *op. cit.*

nuisance; but if all that is specified is a broad purpose, then a broad range of different behaviors may contribute. A shared commitment to common purposes makes diversity tolerable, and the clearer and stronger the commitment, the more diversity can be tolerated and made a source of strength.

EMERGENT PURPOSES AND INQUIRY

Purposes emerge when persons who are together in a situation share their concerns with each other, try to diagnose what there is in the situation that gives rise to their concern, and begin to reinforce each other's belief that they can do something about it. The emergence of shared concern is a complex process and bears very little resemblance to the teacher's telling the class that the homework for tomorrow will be the first twelve problems on page 156. The development of common concern proceeds through the development of common perceptions, the sharing of feelings, the raising of questions and alternatives, and the interpretation of diverse remarks in a quest for the "sense of meeting." The process can be initiated by the teacher through setting up situations that invite speculation, that overwhelm and require abstraction of organizing principles, or that violate the children's expectations. Examples are, respectively: reconstructing a community from a single letter, picking out the most important point made by a dramatic movie, figuring out what to do when a chemical experiment planned by the class fails. In such situations, everyone's attention is arrested, feelings are aroused, and thoughts are engendered.

The obvious next step is to invite the children to go into small groups to share their ideas and feelings, to think out loud, and to decide how to put into words what the confrontation meant to them. Back in the class, these rehearsed notions are listed on the board. The class is directed and helped to look for underlying commonalities. The basic question is: "In this list, are the different items all saying different things or are they all saying the same thing in different ways?" If they are saying the same thing, then that thing is easily converted into a series of individual investigations to be undertaken as learning experiences. The results are then put together and compared with the initiating purpose, and further steps can then be planned.

An example may clarify the way the systems enter into the development of purposive inquiry when the classroom is viewed as a microsociety. Each pupil is given a facsimile of a letter written in an unfamiliar hand. The students are told to reconstruct in mind's eye the community out of which the letter came. They work alone until tension gets high (usually about five minutes) and then in self-selected small groups (usually rapid-paced and fun). Their ideas are then listed on the board by the teacher, and the class is asked to characterize the community that seems to be emerging in the speculations. This development represents the first level of commonality, namely agreed-upon *perceptions* (e.g., that the community was small, that the people were friendly, that they trusted each other financially, and that handcrafts had not yet been displaced by mass production). The children are then confronted with their own word-picture and the question: "How would you like to live in a village like that?" They talk with each other and formulate the questions they would want to ask in order to make up their minds. These questions are listed on the board, and a common concern is sought. The common concern that emerges is whether one would be able to live the way he would like to live; and the point at issue is the kind and amount of freedom the individual would have. The investigation of freedom, its initiating and maintaining circumstances, is then announced as the *purpose* of this class.

The concept of freedom is then broken down into its components: freedom of whom with respect to what (e.g., boys, merchants, slaves, females, etc., with respect to participation in activities—political, economic, religious, commercial, and so forth). This generates a great number of small investigatable questions, and each child is helped (by discussion in small groups and in class) to find the question that most interests him. The individuals make their investigations and finally put them together, not as a series of reports in which no one is interested, but as a series of applications to a new, more comprehensive product. Thus, for example, the class could get out a "newspaper" to which each of the researchers could contribute an article. The whole class, as a board of editors, would be concerned with the authenticity of each article, and in the ensuing discussion, there would be considerable learning from each other. Even more intriguing would be a re-enactment of a civil suit in the legislative chamber, with each person contributing his special knowledge through taking the role of plaintiff, counselor, witness, technical expert, *amicus curiae*, and the like. Again, the whole class would be concerned with the authenticity of the performance, for they would understand that the discipline of history is in the present re-enactment of events from another time and place.[20]

"BUILT-IN" EVALUATION

The major diagnostic question in the microsociety is: "What are the explicit and hidden purposes of the society, and how effectively is each being achieved?" This question is answered by attempting to describe the state of the productive-distributive, managerial-legislative, and interpersonal or informal systems in relation to each other and to the criteria that must be met by acceptable learning processes. Trouble-shooting involves decisions as to which of the manipulatable elements in the situation should be changed—in other words, decisions as to what restructuring is needed to keep the classroom society functioning effectively to meet the process criteria. The range of choices is by no means infinite, and the major ones, it appears, have to do with social organization and with kind of knowledge. Thus the teacher may decide at any time to have the students work alone, in self-selected small groups, in official committees, or as a total class. The teacher may also direct the discussion to the "official" subject matter in the book or to the personal opinions of each student, without regard for their warrant or validity. Generally speaking, when the class has lost thrust and its purpose is no longer compelling, one tends to allow the informal structure (meaning friendship groups) to take over, and exchanges of opinion are invited to provide a psychological "bootstrap" operation through which group purposes can be recovered. When pur-

20. For elaboration of the views on inquiry sketched here, see Herbert A. Thelen, *Education and the Human Quest* (New York: Harper & Bros., 1960), especially chapter vii; see also his "Insights for Teaching from Interactive Theory," in *The Nature of Teaching: Implications for the Education of Teachers* (Proceedings of an invitational conference sponsored by the School of Education, under a grant from the Uhrig Foundation, October 21, 22, 23, 1962 [Milwaukee: University of Wisconsin, 1963]), pp. 19-32; and his "Group Interactional Factors in Learning," in *Behavioral Science Frontiers in Education*, ed. Eli M. Bower and William G. Hollister (New York: John Wiley & Sons, 1967), pp. 257-88.

poses are clear and compelling, bureaucratic organization, rational action, and systematic data-collection are germane.

It is clear that diagnosis and trouble-shooting in the microsociety are built into the pedagogical method and that a "complete" rationale for teaching would be a member of the family of systems theories, in company with Lewin's Reconnaisance Cycle, Werner's Cybernetics, Pribram's TOTE, Thelen's Inquiry, and others. In all these cases, examination of one's own behavior and its perceived consequences provides some of the data needed for deciding on next behaviors. In the classroom as a microsociety, each person is expected to make his own contribution to group purposes and understandings; therefore, the students should be involved in the processes of diagnosis and trouble-shooting. All members need to participate in these functions at such times as their own thoughts, feelings, or actions are to be examined as the basis for decisions. The basic sequence is planning, action, feedback, planning, action, and so on. Each of the three is incomplete and meaningless without the other two, and the overarching wholistic concept to which the three parts are referred is purposive inquiry by the class as a microsociety.

Evaluation: Conceptual Problems

The decision of what to evaluate, how to evaluate it, and what role to assign to diagnosis and trouble-shooting depends on concepts of the classroom group and of the pedagogical undertaking. We have seen that when the group is viewed as a collectivity, then diagnosis ascertains "where the different students are" with respect to stated learning goals; and trouble-shooting tries to accommodate individual differences within a single image of THE STUDENT. The tools for diagnosis depend on the academic attainments to be assessed, and the trouble-shooting kit depends on what sorts of individually adjustive actions may be visualized as potentially feasible. Such actions may cover quite a range. Thus when a student is too far behind in reading, any of the following actions could be considered by the trouble-shooter: (a) having an adult shoot baskets with him after school; (b) inviting him to substitute his own reading materials for the prescribed ones; (c) having an older student, instead of the teacher, tutor him; (d) giving him a do-it-yourself model airplane kit whose instructions he will have to decode in order to assemble the plane; (e) making him part of a team competing with other teams to bring up the reading scores of their members; (f) giving him a large number of physiological and functional tests, and then telling him he will start "blooming" this year; (g) letting him drill with pins, prisms, and eyepushers under laboratory conditions; (h) teaching him the theory that if he could tap his finger faster he could read better, then drilling him on finger tapping; (i) offering money or beatings, and so forth.

The view of the classroom group as an *interpersonal network* is, admittedly, an incomplete view, and many teachers round it out with the further view of the classroom as a collective. This makes considerable sense because the interpersonal network is the most natural and potentially potent mechanism for individuals to use to adapt to bureaucratic, totalitarian, or unresponsive societies. Diagnosis, then, considers the state of stress in the group and the sort of private needs that may be diverting the individual's energy away from tasks. Trouble-shooting ascertains what social organization (individuals, small group, total class) is appropriate to the state of stress or emotion and also which individuals might be most useful to each other—that is, in helping each other adapt to the situation.

The group as a microsociety is complete, and the diagnosis is concerned with the effectiveness of ongoing processes and the way the three component subsystems reinforce or dominate each other. Trouble-shooting is built-in feedback that enables the teacher and the group to see how they need to modify their activity to bolster or soft-pedal events in each subsystem. As compared to the other two views, the microsociety theory helps one see a vast array of resources and activities that can be mobilized within the group, and the variety is so great that taxonomic or logistic concepts are needed just to sort them all out. But, basically, the teacher is invited, when processes do not seem effective, to consider whether the problem lies in the area of *work*, of *group management*, or of *personal feelings*. The kinds of actions to consider are respectively: clarification, examination, demonstration of task procedures and products; discussion of what the class members expect from the teacher and from each other, and vice versa; and development of semi-private dyadic conversation between selected individuals, including, possibly, the teacher.

SUCCESS

In each of the three views there is some concept of success, and diagnosis and trouble-shooting are the functions by which sensed or suspected shortcomings can be identified and corrected. In the view of the collectivity, success means the smooth operation of the programed lesson, with everyone seeming to be busily occupied with it and with the stipulated products being turned out. In the interpersonal network, success means "personal meaningfulness," a continuing sense of self-discovery and of relationship between self and the matters under scrutiny in class. In the microsociety view, success means "full" functioning of everybody, or maximum utilization of human and other resources in the service of complex strategies of inquiry or of "growing up."

As applied to a single *activity*, such as a class discussion, small group project, or individual composition, success in all three views would mean that (*a*) the activity achieved its specific purposes within the sequence of preceding and following activities, (*b*) it developed anticipation and readiness for the next activity, and (*c*) it facilitated constructive and purposive behavior on the part of each child.

As applied to lists of educational *objectives*, success, regardless of pedagogical method, would mean that the child had gained a sufficient increment of specified skill, attitude, interest, or information. The child's status with respect to an objective is his level of proficiency or intensity as compared with that of his classmates; the child's learning is the amount of gain during the course of whatever learning activity is to be evaluated. Most teachers have inadequate preactivity measures, so most statements, supposedly about learning, are actually about status. And when teachers do have preactivity measures, the period over which the gain takes place is often so long that it is extraordinarily difficult to decide what contribution classroom activities made to the change.

As applied to pupil growth, incremental gains toward educational objectives tell part of the story but usually miss the most vital part having to do with increased ability to cope adaptively with molar situations. Thus, for example, one can memorize one thousand French words—certainly a desirable outcome in foreign language. Yet this might not represent growth; it would depend upon the meaning of this learning to the child and its place in an over-all strategy of dealing with the classroom or learning situation. Thus, learning the one thousand words could be the easiest way to get a demanding teacher "off one's back"; the meaning is submissiveness, and the new words will be forgotten as soon as the course examination is passed. On the other hand, the new vocabulary could be learned voluntarily in conjunction with deciphering a French story, game instructions, recipes, etc.; the meaning would be an access of new-felt power, and the words would fit into a conceptual language "tree" and serve to make further word acquisition even more enjoyable and efficient. Learning of either sort would be measured as an educational gain; but only in the latter circumstances would one regard the learning as a part of "growth."

In addition to new powers to cope with increasing challenges, one could also study development of the child's *repertoire of roles:* citizen, consumer, conservationist, idea-giver, group member, and so forth.

As applied to the *teacher,* success would mean increase of professional understanding and skill. The most generalized or universal aspects of teaching have to do with maintaining a supportive yet challenging climate in the classroom. More specific aspects revolve around correspondingly specific purposes: to draw out shy children, to respond adequately to fragmentary contributions, to reflect on discussion in such a way that broader implications can be seen. Such success is possible only when the teacher has a consciously acknowledged goal of self-improvement.

Thus "success" is the extent to which specific anticipations or hopes are realized by an activity, a child, the class, or the teacher. "Failure" may show that any of these agents is at fault or that the anticipations were ridiculous and unrealistic. Appropriate expectation-setting is an important outcome of diagnostic evaluation, and the expectations ought to be considered separately for all of the parties involved in the system.

WHEN TO DIAGNOSE AND TROUBLE-SHOOT

Diagnosis and trouble-shooting are part of any complete rationale of teaching. They are especially useful:

1. When the group does not know what to do; when pace, thrust, and confidence have bogged down in inconclusiveness.
2. When choices must be made among alternatives.
3. When the group is consciously concerned with self-training, and wishes to experiment with agreements, roles, procedures, and expectations that might improve its own operation.
4. When the group has finished some phase or task and now needs to get a "fix" on appropriate next purposes.
5. When the teacher adds to professional insight by trying to decide under what circumstances the present activity seems actually or potentially most appropriate and the children for whom it seems most helpful or contraindicated.

MANIFEST VERSUS HIDDEN PURPOSES

It appears that the most severe and widespread difficulty teachers and researchers encounter with diagnosing group instruction is their failure to see a *group*. The group can only be seen in the mind's eye: a group is a theoretical construct. Nevertheless it must be talked about as if it were real, and if one defines what is real by what makes a difference, then the group is "real." But to think about a group rather than just a collection, one has to assume that a group can and does have *purposes* and that the purposes may not necessarily be known to the members. This is another way of saying that the "actual" purposes of the group are arrived at by interpretation of behavior: What purpose, if held by all the members, would account for the pattern of their behaviors? The notion that there may be hidden or unacknowledged or even denied purposes has its parallel in theories of individual behavior.

What one may mean by a "group purpose" presents severe conceptual problems. The notion that a group purpose is any goal or even demand stated by the teacher is, of course, ridiculous—unless the statement sums up the "sense of meeting" which has developed over some time. The usual statement of purpose by the teacher is an *expectation* which she says she holds for the performance of the class, and it is also a warning to the class that she is about to make her expectation come true. But a "real" group purpose is something that is being sought voluntarily by the children together; they are all contributing to the seeking. In the writer's opinion, group purposes are *qualities* (or models) *of experience that the group has tasted and of which it wants more.* Thus, a group which enjoyed a movie may put forth considerable effort to get another movie, or more generally, it wants to repeat kinds of activities that it enjoyed. But it can also be much more selective, as when a class finds that it was gratifying for each student to select the topic of his own report—and now the class members are eager to have more opportunities to make choices or take on responsibilities for themselves. Presumably, purposes in this sense refer to the future and can be diagnosed and sought through planned strategies.

Hidden purposes frequently refer to the present rather than to the future; they are directed toward maintaining some condition of balance, morale, power, etc., in the group. Prominent examples of hidden purposes are Bion's "basic assumption cultures." [21] Thus it may be that the group is using its energy to evade coming to grips with real problems. This may be seen as "flighting" (running away through joking, sleeping, withdrawing, academic lecturing, etc.,) as "fighting" (attacking the leader, the definition of the problems, scapegoats, themselves, etc.), as "dependency" (hunting for a stronger person or leader, past legislation, or report of somebody else's practice to "pull them through" without having really to study the situation themselves), or "pairing" (pulling closer together in the interpersonal network for the sake of reducing stresses and anxieties felt by individuals). Opposed to these hidden agendas is the purpose of "working," which means not merely doing tasks, but trying to cope realistically with the complete situation, of which the task is but a part.

21. Wilfred R. Bion, *Experiences in Groups* (New York: Basic Books, 1961): *Assessment of Men, op. cit.;* Elliot Jacques, "Interpretative Group Discussion as a Method of Facilitating Social Change," *Human Relations,* I, no. 4 (1948), 533-49.

BAROMETRIC INDIVIDUALS

Just as different individuals have special skills that can be put at the disposal of the group, so different individuals have different levels of responsiveness which, when understood, are powerful diagnostic tools. The most general observation is that participation in a group is seldom evenly distributed, and that usually, at any one time, only a few members account for most of the participation. Further, although certain members may be heavily participant all the time, the participation of others depends on the situation in which the group finds itself. Thus certain of these latter individuals are more likely to be participating when the mood of the group is "flight"; others are more likely to express dependency, and so on. Teachers note the child whose approval of a plan means it will be adopted by the group and the slow child whose grasp of a point tells the teacher the class is ready to move on. Teachers learn to spot the children whose behavior provides a barometer of some group condition which they consider to be especially salient. Persons who respond consistently but selectively—rather than compulsively—can be "calibrated" by observation; and after that, as Ben-Zeev [22] has shown, change in the pattern of participants is likely to index change in the dynamics of the group's interaction.

GROUP LEARNING

Another badly misunderstood concept is that of "group learning." What does it mean to say "the group learned the multiplication table through the sevens" or "the group learned to operate democratically?" And, of course, if one decides that the group learned something, can one assume that all—or even any—of the members did too?

There are two ways by which the group could gain greater effectiveness. One way requires learning; the other way does not. Suppose, for example, that the class is now reaching better decisions on the basis of more alternatives weighed more realistically. In terms of learning, one would explain that each person (or most of

22. Saul Ben-Zeev, "Construction and Validation of a Method for Unitizing Sequences of Group Interaction" (unpublished Ph.D. dissertation, University of Chicago, 1955).

the persons) in the group must have become more creative and rigorous in his thinking, that each person must have acquired new, similar skills. The "non-learning" explanation fits the writer's experience with group growth—that no individual has changed, but that somehow the group more efficiently activates the member who can help it most at any moment. The only "learning" has been to co-ordinate more effectively the different resources of individuals: The group somehow activates the original thinkers when new ideas are required, the cynics and pessimists when reality-testing is required, and the most judicious person when probabilities are to be estimated. It is not, of course, impossible to tell which process of "growth" has occurred: If the individual learned anything he should behave differently in a further and different situation; if he only improved his timing, the nature of his contributions in further situations should be substantially unchanged.

COPING

One is reluctant to accept the notion that the group can grow without individuals becoming more productive. It is here that the conception of the three systems comes into its own. Assuming no significant "learning" in the productive-distributive system, what about the managerial-legislative and the interpersonal-informal? Clearly, the growth of the group through better knowledge and co-ordination of individual resources is a change in the managerial-legislative system, possibly supported by changes in the interpersonal system as well. In short, group growth may come from increased skills of membership and from personal self-confidence rather than from "achievement" as usually tested in school subjects.

What we have been illustrating is that the roles of producer, member, and "individual" can be distinguished, and that all of them play a part in coping with a situation. Achievement testing has been primarily concerned with the skills believed to be necessary for "production"; and secondarily with such attributes of "the member role" as can be rationalized: proper attitudes, interests, responsibility, and the like. Aficionados of "mental health" are usually made acutely uncomfortable by such tests. As for "personality," that has not been considered among educational objectives; it is something to fall back on, with the help of a clinician, in order to prove that school failure is at least as much the fault of the child as of the school; and, anyway, to assess personality would be an invasion of privacy.

In customary achievement terms, we see that the part of the "educational product" which is evaluated is confined to the "low-level" (verbal, rational) abilities within the producer role; and that the rest of the whole child—which, it may be said, has at least as much to do with coping successfully with the world—is either ignored or left to the teacher's subjective judgment. The position of this chapter is that the member role and the individual are at least as educationally relevant as the producer or typical "learner" role and that only the concept of the microsociety is broad enough to comprehend all three in their relationships to each other and the environment. As pedagogical principles are extended to the notion of the classroom as an educative community, diagnosis and feedback will be seen as the navigational or steering system, and the "process" point of view—that teaching is judicious intervention in a complex social system—will begin to pay off. The evidence that a person is becoming educated will be that he is developing his own somewhat unique style of coping with increasing success with more and more complex, challenging, and socially significant situations. And a proper "evaluation" will consist of describing the situations with which he can cope rather than measuring fragmentary producer skills that "everybody should have," even though they represent only a small and uncertain part of the complete armamentarium with which individuals cope with the world.

CHAPTER VIII

The Role of Evaluation in Programs for Individualized Instruction

C. M. LINDVALL
and
RICHARD C. COX

Preceding chapters have discussed the role of evaluation with respect to a variety of aspects of the educational program. From this discussion it is quite obvious that educational evaluation takes many forms and serves a great number of functions. Evaluation can mean the assessment of pupil achievement and the use of such information for making decisions about students or for making decisions about the quality of instruction. It may also refer to the gathering of many types of pupil data, of which achievement measures would be only one part, for the purpose of planning learning activities suited to the individual. The term "evaluation" has also been used to describe the study of teacher performance for the purpose of improving it and to indicate the assessment of an entire curriculum for the purpose of making decisions concerning its worth. Because of the many uses of the term it may be clarifying to specify how it will be used in the present chapter. For the most part it will be used in two ways.

Evaluation as a procedure for gathering pupil data to use in planning and monitoring individual programs.—Planned programs for individualizing instruction require extensive diagnostic data concerning pupil aptitude, achievement, interest, learning styles, and other qualities having implications for the planning of educational programs. An evaluation program of this type must include not only the plans and procedures for gathering data but also rather detailed suggestions for the use of each type of data collected.

Evaluation as a procedure for gathering and analyzing data in such a way that it leads to improvements in materials and in the instructional system.—Individualized instruction, with its need for extensive information concerning pupil progress, provides an excellent opportunity for studying and improving instructional resources on the basis of such data. Furthermore, the effective functioning of an individualized system probably requires this type of continuing improvement even to a greater degree than does conventional group instruction.

Early Models for Evaluation in Individualized Instruction

This chapter will deal largely with evaluation procedures used in relatively current plans for individualizing instruction. However, it is to be recognized that most current plans owe much to procedures for individualization and evaluation that were developed at much earlier times. Although several such early programs could be cited as providing important background for present programs, only two of the most significant ones will be described. The first, the Winnetka Plan for individualizing instruction, represents a landmark in the history of the development of individualized programs which has served as a point of departure, or at least of comparison and contrast, for many subsequent activities in this area. The second, the Eight-Year Study, provides in its presentation of evaluation plans and procedures a detailed description of basic rationale and of specific techniques which are or should be carefully studied by all persons concerned with the problem of making a comprehensive evaluation of the characteristics of individual learners.

THE WINNETKA PLAN

Historically, probably the classic program for individualizing instruction was the Winnetka Plan.[1] Most modern programs acknowledge their debt to Burk and Washburne and their associates. In brief, the Winnetka Plan was a procedure for the individualization of instruction involving carefully specified sequences of in-

1. Carleton W. Washburne, "A Program of Individualization," *Adapting the Schools to Individual Differences* (Twenty-fourth Yearbook of the National Society for the Study of Education, Part II [Bloomington, Ill.: Public School Publishing Co., 1925]), pp. 257-72; Carleton W. Washburne and Sidney P. Marland, Jr., *Winnetka: The History and Significance of an Educational Experiment* (Englewood Cliffs, N.J.: Prentice-Hall, 1963).

structional objectives, tests to determine pupil mastery of these objectives, instructional materials for use in achieving each objective, a procedure for developing individual lesson plans, and a procedure for monitoring pupil progression through the curriculum. The program called for each pupil to work through the sequences of objectives at his own rate and largely on an independent basis. In studying arithmetic, for example, the pupil worked with textbooks or mimeographed lesson materials which were largely self-instructional. In working through these materials the pupil corrected his own work, using an answer sheet provided with the lesson. In this way the pupil could quickly evaluate every exercise and receive feedback concerning his progress. If he made mistakes, he was expected to work another set of exercises on the same topic. At frequent intervals a pupil took a diagnostic test covering a number of steps in the curriculum. Before taking the form of this diagnostic test that the teacher scored and used for determining his advancement, the pupil took one or more practice diagnostic tests that were in his book. In that way he was able to conduct a self-diagnosis which provided him with information as to where he might need additional study. When he had answered one of these tests correctly, he was given the teacher-scored test, and the results were used as the basis for teacher diagnosis and subsequent prescription. Also, at periodic intervals, the pupil took review tests designed to measure the extent to which he had retained abilities acquired over some extended period of time.

In the Winnetka Plan each child had a goal book in which was recorded the date on which he passed each test of a sequence. This provided both the teacher and the pupil with readily available data concerning the pupil's progress.

The Winnetka Plan involved a careful procedure for evaluating pupil achievement and for guiding progress. This procedure and the associated record-keeping system were essential ingredients in making it a successful program for the individualization of instruction.

THE EIGHT-YEAR STUDY

Although the justly acclaimed Eight-Year Study was not basically concerned with the individualization of instruction, guidelines developed during the study offer many specific suggestons concern-

ing the role of evaluation in achieving individualization. Because of
the impact of this study, particularly on persons concerned with
testing and evaluation, it is safe to state that its suggestions have
been, either directly or indirectly, a major source of guidance
for persons currently working on procedures for evaluation in
programs of individualized instruction. In describing the roles of
evaluation in schools, one of the volumes reporting the Eight-Year
Study states:

A third important purpose of evaluation is to provide information
basic to effective guidance of individual students. Only as we appraise
the student's achievement and as we get a comprehensive description of
his growth and development are we in a position to give him sound
guidance. This implies evaluation sufficiently comprehensive to appraise all significant aspects of the student's accomplishments. Merely
the judgment that he is doing average work in a particular course is
not enough. We need to find out more accurately where he is progress-
ing and where he is having difficulties.[2]

In a later chapter in the book describing the evaluation activities
of the study, Taba illustrates the use of the case-study technique
for using data to make a careful diagnosis of individual student
needs.[3] Her work pointed the way toward using comprehensive
student data for the individualization of a student's program. The
evaluation work on the Eight-Year Study has also come to represent
a landmark in describing specific ways for measuring pupil variables
other than simple achievement measures. One indication of the
acknowledged excellence of this latter contribution is found in the
number of current texts on testing and evaluation which go back
to this thirty-year-old study to cite examples of how to measure a
variety of types of pupil variables. It might be suggested that many
current programs for individualized instruction could strengthen
their evaluation procedures in terms of the breadth of student
characteristics measured by adopting many of the techniques developed or described in this study.

2. Eugene R. Smith, Ralph W. Tyler, and the Evaluation Staff, *Appraising
and Recording Student Progress* (New York: Harper & Bros., 1942), pp. 8-9.

3. *Ibid.,* pp. 403-43.

A Structured-Curriculum Model for Individualized Instruction

Most teachers are aware of the range of individual differences represented by the students in their classes and probably make some type of effort to individualize instruction. This individualization may take such forms as are represented by the elementary teacher who tries to go from pupil to pupil to provide individual help during a period in which the class is working on a common assignment or by the college professor who uses the lecture method in his class sessions but gives each student some choice in selecting the topic for a term paper. Although such relatively unstructured procedures as these can, when used by a skilled teacher, achieve a considerable degree of individualization, the term "individualized instruction" is usually reserved to denote procedures which provide for having each pupil working on an individualized assignment in the classroom and proceeding through his work at a pace suited to his own needs and abilities. It is procedures of this latter type that are considered in this chapter.

Individualized instruction can be achieved, at least theoretically, through a number of different patterns.[4] Some patterns call for different educational goals for different students, with the goals selected on the basis of pupil needs, interests, abilities, and certain other relevant factors. Much of the instruction that a child receives in the home is of this type. It is also characteristic of certain advanced graduate programs in which the candidate carries out much of his work through independent study. However, this pattern is not too feasible for typical school situations. Programs for individualized instruction which have actually been carried out in the schools usually involve a structure of learning goals or objectives, and the individualization takes the form of variations in the way in which each pupil progresses through these established objectives. This type of individualization may be termed the "structured-curriculum" model. There are several variations in the employment of

4. Lee J. Cronbach, "How Can Instruction Be Adapted to Individual Differences?" in *Learning and Individual Differences,* ed. Robert M. Gagné (Columbus, Ohio: Charles E. Merrill Books, 1967), pp. 23-39; Glen Heathers, "Teacher Education for Individualized Instruction" (Working Paper No. 42, Learning Research and Development Center, University of Pittsburgh, 1968).

this model. Some applications of it involve having all students going through all objectives and studying from the same materials, with the only provision for differentiation being that each pupil is permitted to proceed at his own rate. The simplest example of this is instances in which all pupils work through the same programed text (using a strict linear programing format) but each is permitted to work at his own pace. In another variation all pupils master the same objectives but each may work with different instructional materials. Still another variation permits pupils to work through the objectives in different orders or to skip some objectives when this is deemed feasible and desirable. But in all of these variations the basis for planning and instruction is some type of curriculum structure, and it is this structure that provides the framework for pupil evaluation and diagnosis. Basically, the structured-curriculum model for individualized instruction involves the following elements:

1. Sequences of instructional objectives to define the curriculum
2. Instructional materials to teach each objective
3. An evaluation procedure for placing each pupil at the appropriate point in the curriculum
4. A plan for developing individualized programs of study
5. A procedure for evaluating and monitoring individual progress

DEFINING INSTRUCTIONAL OBJECTIVES

Formal instruction of any type and any degree of complexity is designed to help the learner progress through a sequence of steps in acquiring given skills and abilities. These steps and these skills and abilities constitute the objectives of instruction. In certain types of group instruction, a teacher may have a final goal for a day's, week's, or term's lesson spelled out with some concreteness and then take his students through the steps necessary to reach this goal merely by having all of these steps in his mind. However, if a curriculum is to be structured in such a way that pupils are able to progress toward learning goals on an individual and independent basis, all of the steps or objectives must be spelled out in detail and must be available in a form which permits their use in the development of lesson materials, diagnostic procedures, individualized lesson plans, and evaluation instruments. Individualized instruction requires a framework of skills and content through which the pupil is to proceed on an individual basis, and this framework is provided by the sequences of instructional objectives.

Objectives that have been found to be of most use in the development of programs for individualized instruction are those that are stated in specific behavioral terms—that is, in terms of what the pupil will be able to do to indicate his mastery of a given ability. This type of specificity is essential if the objectives are to provide a clear and common description of what is to be learned—to the curriculum developer, the tester and diagnostician, the teacher, and the pupil. The exact form and the importance of objectives of this type have been discussed by a number of writers.[5]

Not infrequently, this emphasis on defining objectives in terms of pupil behaviors is criticized as placing a serious limitation on the kinds of learning that can be involved. Critics of such a definition contend that it limits one to objectives that deal with knowledge only or to objectives that can be assessed only by paper-and-pencil performance. This claim is far from justified. Behavioral objectives may deal with learnings of any degree of complexity or sophistication—applications, appreciations, understandings, attitudes, values, and a variety of skills. What is required is that the person developing the objective phrase it in terms of how the pupil will display the desired quality or ability. The purpose of such statements is preciseness and clarity in communication. Everyone involved must know what is meant by a general goal such as "the pupil will understand . . . (a given principle)." This type of clarity is of crucial importance in an individualized system. Here any objective must mean essentially the same thing to the student, the teacher, the curriculum writer, the test developer, and the evaluator.

It should also be emphasized that careful specification of objectives does not mean that these are the only things that a student can learn or that an instructor can teach. They serve merely to define the core structure of the program. In a conventional classroom this structure is provided by a textbook, a course outline, or by a teacher's lecture notes. The careful definition of sequences of in-

5. C. M. Lindvall, *Defining Educational Objectives* (Pittsburgh: University of Pittsburgh Press, 1964); Robert Mager, *Preparing Instructional Objectives* (San Francisco: Fearon Publishers, 1962); Ralph W. Tyler, *Constructing Achievement Tests* (Columbus: Ohio State University Press, 1934).

structional objectives is merely an effort to develop this structure in a more systematic manner. Teachers still have the opportunity to supplement these learnings on an individual basis and students will still learn many things (both good and bad) in addition to those abilities that are specified.

ORGANIZING OBJECTIVES

Sequencing and organizing objectives are key steps in the design of a program for individualized instruction. Some type of order is essential for determining how far advanced each pupil is within the curriculum, for planning his next learning experiences, and for monitoring his progress. Much of the organization will be determined by the hierarchical or prerequisite nature of the objectives. For example, a pupil must learn to read words before he can read sentences and must be able to comprehend sentences before he can be expected to interpret the meaning of paragraphs or longer passages. On the other hand, many decisions on the ordering of objectives may be relatively arbitrary—for example, the decision as to when a pupil should interrupt his progress in learning increasingly difficult steps in addition in order to begin the study of subtraction.

Of course, the ordering or organizing of objectives does not dictate the order in which every pupil will master the abilities involved. They may merely provide the basic organization from which various paths may lead.

The considerations involved in sequencing may be illustrated by reference to Figure 1. It presents a small portion of the objectives for the reading curriculum for Grades K-VI of the Individually Prescribed Instruction Project being developed at the University of Pittsburgh.[6] In this curriculum a type of "spiral" progression is employed so that the student will move through many of the same topics (vocabulary development, literal comprehension, etc.) at successively higher levels (A, B, C, D, E, and so on). The or-

6. C. M. Lindvall and John O. Bolvin, "Programed Instruction in the Schools: An Application of Programing Principles in Individually Prescribed Instruction," in *Programed Instruction,* ed. Phil C. Lange (Sixty-sixth Yearbook of the National Society for the Study of Education, Part II [Chicago: Distributed by the University of Chicago Press, 1967]), pp. 217-54.

Level C

Vocabulary Development

1. Identify words that have similar meanings.
2. Identify words that have opposite meanings.
3. Select words that rhyme with a written or pictured word.
4. Identify the correct meaning of a word from the context of a sentence.

Literal Comprehension

1. Match words that form an associative pair.
2. Copy statements answering recall questions.
3. Answer questions requiring recall of facts from written passages.
4. List main characters from a story after reading it silently.

Interpretative Comprehension

1. Order sequentially two to four sentences.
2. Select the event that happened first in a short story just read.
3. Read a sentence silently and write what might happen next.
4. Read a poem or story and indicate, in writing, the mood expressed.
5. Read a story and write a description of the idea expressed.

Level D

Vocabulary Development

1. Mark consonants and consonant blends for dictated or pictured words.
2. Draw picture to illustrate meaning of new words.
3. Match pictures with sentences or paragraphs which they illustrate.
4. Select the word which correctly completes a sentence.

Literal Comprehension

1. Complete a statement based on content read.
2. Select words to complete statements based on recall of material read.
3. List, in order of occurrence, the main events of a story read.

Interpretative Comprehension

1. Underline part of a sentence that answers a given question.
2. Describe a story he has read as happy, sad, funny, or exciting.
3. Select the sentence describing the main thought of a story.
4. Give oral account of a story read.
5. Explain cause-effect relationships in stories read silently.

FIG. 1.—Objectives for selected units at levels C and D in the Individually Prescribed Instruction (IPI) reading curriculum

ganization is such that a level C topic should be studied prior to the same topic at level D. There is an attempted hierarchical ordering across levels. Also there is some attempted ordering within levels so that, for example, the vocabulary development unit is prerequisite to the literal comprehension unit which, in turn, is prerequisite to the interpretative comprehension unit.

In this curriculum the hierarchical structure is only approximate, and, in many cases, the ordering of units and objectives is largely arbitrary. However, the basic goal is that of any plan for organizing a curriculum for individualized instruction. This is to provide a structure, involving as much sequence as possible, which can serve as a framework for determining the student's present status and for planning his future path.

Of course, the same considerations regarding sequencing also enter into the ordering of objectives within a unit. In some cases the objectives within a unit can be sequenced in such a way that objective 1 is prerequisite to 2, which is prerequisite to 3, and so on. This may be due to the nature of the content within the unit. In other cases the objectives within a unit may be such that all are prerequisite to work in subsequent units but that no one objective is prerequisite to another objective. In this case it would not make any difference in which order the objectives were mastered, and their ordering within the unit is entirely arbitrary.

A rather carefully defined procedure for developing sequences of objectives for a program for individualized instruction has been described by Resnick. Her procedure calls for analysis, termed "component analysis," to start with an objective and work backward through the necessary prerequisite chain.

Component analysis begins with any desired instructional objective, behaviorally stated, and asks, in effect, "To perform this behavior, what prerequisite or component behaviors must the child be able to perform?" Several new behaviors are identified in this way. For each behavior so identified, the same question is asked, thus generating a hierarchy of objectives based on behavioral prerequisites.[7]

7. Lauren B. Resnick, "Design of an Early Learning Curriculum" (Working Paper No. 16, Learning Research and Development Center, University of Pittsburgh, 1967).

The procedure described by Resnick could be applied in the development of a structure such as that of the IPI curriculum as exemplified in Figure 1. Here the sequencing technique could be used both in sequencing the units and in sequencing the objectives within each unit. This would involve first defining some type of terminal goal that the student is to achieve by the time he completes his work in any given topic (vocabulary, literal comprehension, and so on). Working backward from this, a broad objective would be defined for each unit. These latter objectives, in addition to providing the basis for sequencing units in the proper order, would also represent the terminal objective for each unit. The sequencing within a unit would then involve working backward from this terminal objective to list all prerequisite subobjectives, going back as far as the abilities that the student would acquire in preceding units.

The foregoing rather extended analysis of what is involved in the development of a curriculum sequence for individualized instruction may, at first glance, appear to be only peripherally related to the problem of evaluation and diagnosis. However, such is not the case. The basic diagnostic instruments in programs of individualization must be the tests and other techniques that provide information concerning where the pupil is in the curriculum and what progress he is making. These instruments will be useful only to the extent that they are referenced to specific objectives and specific units and consequently to the instructional materials that teach these abilities. Tests that are useful for individualization must tell the student (and his teacher), "If I have test scores of this type, then I should start my study here," and "If I do poorly on this test, then I should endeavor to acquire this ability by studying these materials." All teachers have been told many times that results from standardized tests and from a variety of other sources provide them with information about individual pupils which they should use to help them fit instruction to the needs of each pupil. Unfortunately, the teacher is then left to his own devices in determining how he is to accomplish this highly complex and difficult task. The result is that the use of such a recipe for individualization is almost uniformly unsuccessful. Evaluation and diagnosis that is to be useful for individualizing instruction should begin with a careful specification, sequencing, and structuring of detailed instructional objectives.

INSTRUCTIONAL MATERIALS AND THE DIAGNOSTIC PROGRAM

A second major step in the development of a program for individualized instruction is the development or selection of instructional materials and activities for teaching each objective. Although such materials, strictly speaking, are not a part of the diagnostic program, their proper selection and use are essential to meaningful diagnosis. As suggested in the preceding section, each piece of lesson material and each specified learning activity must be keyed or referenced to some one objective. This type of identification must take such a form that when it is known that a student is to work on the mastery of objective 6, he can do this by studying materials R, S, T, U, V, or W. Only when this is the case can diagnosis lead to meaningful prescription of an individualized lesson plan.

However, the development of lesson materials probably must involve more than this. Effective individualization should be based on something more than having each pupil work at his proper point in the curriculum continuum. He should be engaged in activities suited to his interests, aptitudes, learning style, and other relevant personal qualities. Diagnosis that leads to individualization on such bases is dependent on the availability of materials and learning experiences adapted to differences in such qualities. Unfortunately, not enough is known about how to adapt to such differences. However, some things are known and many others can be explored within the context of the development and improvement of an individualized system. A key place to start this type of exploration is in the provision of a variety of types of materials for teaching each objective. Some students may learn certain concepts and principles quite readily from verbal materials alone. Other pupils may be able to achieve mastery only through the help of diagrams and pictures. Still others may require learning experiences involving the physical manipulation of objects and devices. Some students may learn most things readily by working quite independently; others may require considerable interaction with a teacher or with other students. These and many other pupil differences should be taken into account in building the lesson materials and the specified learning activities for each objective and unit. Without the availability of this variety in the learning experiences that can be employed, diagnostic procedures will be of little use. Every teacher has an almost infinite store of information concerning ways in which his students differ. A successful program for individualized instruction must provide ways for adapting learning experiences to the most meaningful of these differences.

EVALUATING PUPIL PERFORMANCE
IN A STRUCTURED CURRICULUM

Given that the learning objectives are carefully defined in behavioral terms and are sequenced in learning continua and organized in other meaningful ways, it is then a requirement of the proposed general model for individualizing instruction that pupil performance be assessed in reference to these objectives. The major purpose of this assessment is to provide the teacher with sufficient information to adapt instructional activities to each pupil's individual learning requirements. It is important that the evaluation of pupil performance be related to the learning continua in such a way that diagnosis of pupil performance can lead to the careful prescription of learning tasks based on the available instructional resources for each continuum.

The identification and clear specification of the level of individual pupil performance is a crucial aspect in an individualized instruction model. Diagnosis of performance is important not only for assessing what each pupil is able to achieve at any given time but for identifying the next instructional assignment for that pupil. This requirement indicates the need for content- or criterion-referenced measures as opposed to norm-referenced measures.[8] Norm-referenced measures indicate a pupil's relative position with respect to other pupils in some norm group. For example, standardized achievement tests yield norm-referenced scores in the sense that they tell how pupils in a given class or school rank in comparison with the pupils in the test-standardization group. They do not pro-

8. Robert Glaser and Richard C. Cox, "Criterion-Referenced Testing for the Measurement of Educational Outcomes," in *Instructional Process and Media Innovation*, ed. R. A. Weisgerber (Chicago: Rand McNally & Co., 1968), pp. 545–50.

vide information as to what the pupil can perform in reference to a specified area of content.

On the other hand, a criterion- or content-referenced measure indicates how pupil proficiency corresponds to some desired criterion. In the individualized instruction model being proposed, the detailed behavioral objectives define the criterion behavior which is expected of pupils. Measurement of pupil performance must, therefore, be accomplished by using tests clearly referenced to the content objectives within each learning continuum.

Tests of pupil performance which are currently in general use are typically not appropriate for use in the individualized instruction model being proposed. What is required, then, is the development of tests which provide measures referenced to the sequences of instructional objectives. Performance measures which are to be useful as a basis for the continuous planning of instructional experiences for individual pupils in a program for individualized instruction should include (*a*) placements tests, (*b*) diagnostic tests for given units, and (*c*) curriculum-embedded tests for monitoring pupil progress.[9]

EVALUATING PUPIL PERFORMANCE FOR PLACEMENT IN THE LEARNING CONTINUUM

One of the first diagnostic requirements for an individualized system is the placement of each pupil in a learning continuum at a level which is commensurate with his performance level. It would be wasteful to have the pupil assigned to a unit of instruction which he had already learned, while, on the other hand, it would be frustrating for the pupil to be given an assignment for which he did not have the necessary prerequisites and which, therefore, he could not accomplish. What is required is a type of placement measure that is criterion-referenced and that will provide the information about the performance level of each pupil that enables the teacher to determine the appropriate place for assignment in the curriculum.

9. To make the description of the evaluation procedures for an individualized instruction program as specific as possible, the writers have based these sections largely on the Individually Prescribed Instruction (IPI) program with which they are associated. The use of comparable procedures in other individualized programs is described in a later section of the chapter.

Placement tests should be administered at the beginning of the school year or when the pupil enters the individualized program. While the results of these measurements must be interpreted for individuals and used for decisions concerning individuals, it is not necessary that the tests be designed for use with individuals only. It may be that placement measures can, for the most part, be group tests. Of course, the test must be logically consistent with the objectives; if, for example, the objective calls for an oral response to be monitored by the teacher, the items to test this objective must be administered on an individual basis.

The major function of the placement measures is to provide a general profile of individual pupil performance over many units of work. What is being suggested is that placement tests should be broad in scope. If the individualized instruction program covers several subjects, the placement test battery must cover all of these subjects. If only the mathematics continuum is being individualized, the only placement tests needed are those for mathematics. It is certainly true that within any grade level there is a great deal of interindividual differences in achievement. The placement measures must therefore span some considerable sequence in the learning continuum.

Placement testing should be efficient, that is, it should yield a maximum of information in a minimum of time. The test constructor must make some decisions about the number, the length, and the type of tests to be used for placement purposes. As already noted, the number of measures demanded will first of all depend upon the number of curriculum areas to be individualized. In addition, the extent to which each curriculum objective is tested will have a bearing on the number of tests required. If each curriculum is really sequenced in the sense that one objective builds upon another, it may be possible to obtain a fairly accurate picture of where a pupil belongs in the continuum without testing him on every objective. That is, a placement test could be constructed by selecting items which test representative objectives along the continuum.

The length of placement measures is subject to the same conditions as cited for the number of tests required. Actually, the test constructor has to play the number of tests against the length of any one test. Once the universe of content to be tested for place-ment purposes has been defined, decisions can be made concerning how this universe is to be subdivided into tests of appropriate num-ber and length. In most cases the length of any one test should be restricted to a time limit that is reasonably consistent with the length of the attention span of the group to which the test is to be given. The validity of the measures for placement should not be dimin-ished by fatigue on the part of the test-taker.

The type of test required also has many conditions to be con-sidered. As previously stated, the test should be content-referenced in the sense that each test item is evaluating a certain curriculum objective and that success or failure on the item indicates profi-ciency or lack thereof in achieving the curriculum objective. Also, the test should, in general, be constructed so that it may be given as a group test with some allowance for some items that must be administered on an individual basis. The major reason for the group aspect of placement measure is a purely practical one. Since this is the first diagnostic procedure for all pupils, the time factor is crucial. If the placement testing is not completed in a minimum time, some pupils may be penalized by not being able to proceed in instructional units only because of time spent in testing. There is another good reason for the efficiency requirement. Having to give many individual tests at the beginning of a school year would place a heavy burden on the teacher who must make individual diagnoses for an entire class. There is nothing to prevent individual diagnoses being made from group tests.

Consideration should be given to certain item types which may accomplish this diagnosis in a most efficient manner. Objectivity is highly desirable. Of course, teachers will make subjective judgments based on the results of tests and on other information available on each child such as general achievement, type of learner, and so on; however, the results of the tests in terms of proficiency in a cur-riculum area should be unequivocal. Certainly, multiple-choice and short-answer items should be considered. This is not to say, by any means, that the format of test items should dictate what is to be tested. Just the opposite is true. If the curriculum objective states that the child should respond by solving a problem or by construct-ing a certain response, the test item should demand this behavior.

What is being suggested is only that, when alternative item types are possible, the test constructor should choose those items which allow for greatest objectivity and ease in scoring.

An example of a placement test battery for use in individualized instruction which illustrates some of the principles that have been cited is the Individually Prescribed Instruction (IPI) placement tests.[10] The IPI system is designed to achieve a certain type of individualized instruction in Grades K-VI in the subject areas of mathematics, reading, and science.[11] Each of the IPI curriculums is defined by a series of behavioral objectives or skills which are organized into content areas and levels. The mathematics curriculum, for example, is divided into the content areas of numeration, place value, addition, subtraction, multiplication, division, combination of processes, fractions, money, time, systems of measurement, geometry, and special topics. It is also structured into nine levels starting with very elementary mathematics at level A and systematically building in difficulty to level I, which is quite advanced junior-high-school mathematics. The objectives for a content area at a given level are defined as a *unit*. This means that each unit is designated with a descriptive title such as "Level A Addition," "Level D Multiplication," and so on. The basic task in placement testing, then, is to determine the level at which a pupil is prepared to work in each of the several areas.

Placement tests have been constructed for each level of the curriculum so that, in a sense, each placement test represents a certain well-specified achievement level which is similar to the achievement defined by a grade level in a graded school. The level-E placement test in mathematics, for example, includes items which test each content area in the curriculum at that level. At the outset of individualization, the teacher must decide which is the most appropriate placement test for each pupil. This decision, in most cases, is made after obtaining information about past achievement of each pupil, examining the content of the placement test, and then matching

10. Richard C. Cox and M. Elizabeth Boston, "Diagnosis of Pupil Achievement in the Individually Prescribed Instruction Project" (Working Paper No. 15, Learning Research and Development Center, University of Pittsburgh, 1967).

11. Lindvall and Bolvin, *op. cit.*

these. This means that, in a given class, pupils will start taking placement tests at a variety of levels depending on achievement variability in that class. (After the individualized system has been in effect for a year, the placement testing provides an indication of retention or lack of retention over the summer months.) In order to cover a wide range of achievement, each pupil typically will be assigned placement tests for more than one level.

Intraindividual differences will readily appear as a result of placement testing. A pupil may demonstrate proficiency in certain content areas and lack of proficiency in other content areas. In order to obtain an achievement profile for each child, certain sections of the next higher- or lower-level test will be administered.

One of the basic assumptions in the IPI system is that instruction should be basically sequential. As explained earlier in the chapter, each curriculum is constructed so that the objectives within a unit, and from level to level in a given area, are sequenced (when appropriate) in the sense that each objective builds on the preceding objective and is prerequisite to those immediately following. This condition allows the test constructor considerable flexibility in the assembling of items for placement tests. A subset of objectives which describe the entire curriculum can be identified by selecting the most representative objectives in a content area at each level. For a given unit, the testing of a single objective may be sufficient for assessing performance in that unit. Successful performance on the test of that one criterion objective will indicate successful performance on all the objectives in the unit if the other objectives are prerequisite to the criterion objective. Selecting and testing these criterion objectives allows the test constructor to achieve accurate placement testing in a highly efficient manner. It is possible to test an entire level of a continuum with a measure that requires only one test administration of reasonable length.

The result of placement testing is a profile of pupil performance over all content areas of the curriculum. Figure 2 shows a mathematics profile for a hypothetical third-grade pupil. Each check mark indicates successful performance in that unit.

The pupil's placement tests are scored in such a way that he is reported as having mastered each area at the highest level at which he exhibited mastery of the items on the test. The hypothetical third-grade pupil mentioned would have "scores" of C—Numeration, C—Place Value, C—Fractions, D—Addition, D—Subtraction, D—Multiplication, D—Division, D—Combination of Processes, E—Systems of Measurement, E—Time, E—Money, and E—Geometry. Such scores are criterion-referenced measures in that they tell where the pupil is in the sequence of levels in each area. As criterion-referenced measures, they provide specific information concerning what abilities the pupil has mastered and at what levels or in what units he is ready to begin work.

Student A

	A	B	C	D	E	F	G	H
Numeration	√	√	√					
Place Value	√	√	√					
Addition	√	√	√	√				
Subtraction	√	√	√	√				
Multiplication	√	√	√	√				
Division	√	√	√	√				
Combination of Processes	√	√	√	√				
Fractions	√	√	√					
Money	√	√	√	√	√			
Time	√	√	√	√	√			
Systems of Measurement	√	√	√	√	√			
Geometry	√	√	√	√	√			

Fig. 2.—Example of a performance profile indicated by mathematics placement tests

DIAGNOSTIC TESTING FOR PLANNING INDIVIDUAL PROGRAMS

Placement measurement in the theoretical model for individualizing instruction provides a broad diagnosis of pupil performance that can be utilized in the identification of instructional units appropriate for each pupil. Placement-test information can indicate the possible curriculum units to which a pupil may be assigned with a high probability of his being successful. This initial diagnosis, however, will not provide detailed information needed for the assignment of exact instructional materials for the unit. What is demanded is a further diagnosis of a pupil's competencies specific to the particular instructional unit which he is about to study.

For each unit of the curriculum there needs to be a pretest of the objectives included in the unit. This measurement is an extension of placement testing for each specific unit in the curriculum. Pretesting must be, as placement testing, content-referenced so that the results of the pretest can be used to indicate the objectives in the instructional unit in which the pupil has or has not indicated proficiency. This is necessary for several reasons. Take, for example, a given instructional unit which contains ten objectives. The placement test has indicated that the pupil should be assigned this unit since he has not demonstrated proficiency on the test item or items representing the entire unit. This is not to say, however, that the pupil needs to be assigned work on each objective in the unit. He may be deficient on only one or two of the objectives. The pretest measures performance on each objective in the instructional unit so that the teacher has information for specific assignments in the unit. It must be possible for a child to pretest out of certain parts of a unit. In fact, as the child proceeds through the curriculum he may pretest out of an entire unit of work. This may result as a function of content learned in a lower-level unit or in a related unit.

The pretests point out, once again, the individual aspect of the theoretical model. Not every pupil who is about to start on a given instructional unit will necessarily be required to go through the sequence in the same way. Pretesting aids the teacher in providing an instructional task which is appropriate for each individual entering the unit.

The number of pretests in a given continuum is dictated by the number of instructional units in the continuum. It is proposed that instructional units be limited to a set of highly related objectives and therefore not be, typically, so lengthy as to negatively affect pupil performance. The length of a pretest will be determined by the number of objectives in the instructional unit and by the number of items used to test each objective. In general, the number of items testing the same objective must be examined in light of each objective. For example, an objective like "the pupil can solve simple addition problems involving all number combinations" will require more items than would an objective like "the pupil must select which of three triangles is equilateral." Certain objectives may be stated in such a manner as to limit the ways in which successful performance can be tested. If only one item per objective is used, the test will generally be less reliable than if more items are used. On the other hand, it may be assumed that, if a pupil can perform well on five or ten items of similar content, he can perform well on twenty or fifty such items.

Item types for unit pretests can be more varied than those suggested for placement measures. Again, the items must be content-referenced for ease in interpretation and should be as objective as possible for ease in scoring. Also, they must accurately test the objective; if oral responses are called for in the objective, oral items must be used. Since unit pretests provide the basic diagnostic information for the planning of individual instructional assignments, the tests should evaluate in detail the performance dictated by each objective in the unit.

Again, in a form similar to that used in the case of placement tests, unit pretest results are reported in terms of the student's mastery or lack of mastery of each objective. For example, the results for a given pupil taking the unit pretest in D-Multiplication may show that he has mastered objectives 1, 2, 4, and 8 but has not mastered objectives 3, 5, 6, and 7. This type of report represents a criterion-referenced measure since it provides specific information concerning pupil mastery of the curriculum.

The results of the unit pretest are not the only information on which the teacher prescribes work in the curriculum. In the individualized model being proposed, a case-study approach needs to be taken for each child. In order to prescribe instructional materials suited to each learner, the teacher should know not only the pretest results but also the general performance level of each child as defined by such measures as the placement tests, standardized achievement tests (when relevant), and by general intelligence measures. Reading level would certainly be a consideration in assigning instructional materials in any content area. Pupil interests and learning styles should also be considered. Pretests indicate to the teacher only the objectives in which the pupil is deficient, not which instructional materials are appropriate for this given pupil. The continuous planning of individual programs must be based on a combination of variables and must be updated as a pupil proceeds through the curriculum.

EVALUATION IN THE MONITORING
OF INDIVIDUAL PROGRESS

As a pupil proceeds by working on specific objectives in the units of the curriculum, there is a need for evaluation of the required criterion performance. Two types of measures are demanded for this evaluation. The first of these is what may be called "curriculum-embedded tests," which are an integral part of the instructional sequence. A curriculum-embedded test (CET) is a measure of performance on one particular objective in the sequence. It is used to assess performance on the skill stated in the objective so that the teacher has information with which to make a decision to advance the pupil to the next objective or to assign additional instructional exercises for the same objective. A CET will be prescribed for each pupil at specified intervals in the sequence of instructional materials for the objective.

The CET, like placement and preunit tests, must be content-referenced to the particular objective it is intended to test. Since only one objective is being tested, these tests will, in general, be quite short and should be considered as just another task in the instructional sequence, i.e., a part of the curriculum. The item types need not be limited in any way, except that they follow logically from the objective being tested. Behaviors required by the test items should be quite similar to the learning tasks defined for that objective. Since this is the measurement for the most basic curriculum element, the objective, the tests should specifically evaluate the criterion behavior specified in the objective.

A second type of evaluation used to monitor individual progress in an individualized model is the postunit test. The pupil proceeds by attaining proficiency on the CET's for the objectives in his instructional sequence. When satisfactory performance has been attained on all the objectives in an instructional unit, there is a need for reassessment of performance on the unit as a whole. This is another decision point for the teacher. Diagnosis of performance is required so that information is available to help the teacher decide whether or not the pupil should proceed to the next unit of work in his program. Success on the posttest indicates that the pupil has the prerequisites for subsequent units; failure indicates that remedial work is necessary on one or more objectives.

In most cases the postunit test will be an alternative form of the preunit test. If there is an interest in whether or not a pupil can apply the knowledge learned in the instructional unit to another situation, an item testing this ability may be included in the posttest. Remediation of failure on this type of items would be difficult, however, unless these objectives and instructional materials are part of the curriculum.

Evaluation of pupil performance as required by the general theoretical model for individualized instruction has as a basis two types of measures. First, there are those measures for diagnosis of individual pupil performance designed to identify the units and the objectives within units for which instructional activities should be prescribed. The placement and preunit tests serve this function at different levels, the placement measures identifying general pupil performance over many instructional units and the preunit measure identifying more specific pupil performance over objectives within an instructional unit. Second, there are measures for monitoring pupil performance so that each pupil can progress through the curriculum at a rate appropriate for him. The curriculum-embedded test provides an end-of-objective measure while the postunit test provides an end-of-unit measure. Both are used to assist the teacher in making a decision on instructional materials to be prescribed for each pupil.

The function of each test may be seen by examining the flowchart for the IPI system as presented in Figure 3.

The Role of Evaluation in the Improvement of Individualized Programs

As has been emphasized thus far in this chapter, the major function of evaluation in programs for individualized instruction is to diagnose pupil performance and other pupil qualities in such a way as to adapt the pupil's educational program to his individual requirements. Attention has been given to the need for an organized curriculum sequence, instructional activities and materials to teach each objective, and a testing and evaluation program to place pupils and to monitor pupil progress. Evaluation and diagnosis

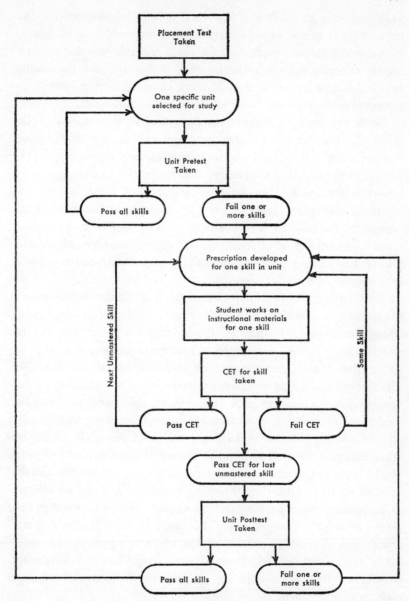

Fig. 3.—Flow-chart of steps in the cycle for evaluating and monitoring of pupil progress in the IPI procedure

permits the development of individualized study programs which make optimum use of the curriculum and materials. However, evaluation has an additional key role to play in programs of this type. This is in the improvement of the program itself. Adapting to individual requirements should involve not only the best possible use of available materials and procedures but also the continuing development and modification of these elements so that individualization is made more and more effective.[12]

Such continuing improvement is crucial to the success of individualized programs. In such programs the quality of diagnosis and prescription is judged on the basis of how well the pupil performs. If the pupil does poorly, not because diagnosis and prescription are invalid but because instructional materials are inadequate, his performance may be incorrectly interpreted as suggesting the need for changes in diagnosis. That is, in a complex system of instruction, all elements are highly interdependent, and proper functioning requires that all parts be characterized by a high degree of effectiveness.

Fortunately, a structured system of individualized instruction is typically one which continually provides data concerning the effectiveness of each part of the system. With tests that are clearly and definitely referenced to specific objectives, it is easy to gather data concerning the general effectiveness of the materials and activities designed to teach a given objective. Likewise, if the system calls for scoring each lesson sheet, this assessment can be used to judge the quality of each such item. Data such as this may suggest modification or replacement of given materials. Similarly other data may be used to indicate needed changes in other aspects of the program. Since individual prescriptions are usually developed in written form, they provide a record which can be related to subsequent pupil performance in such a way as to suggest the points at which changes might be made in prescription-writing procedures. An earlier section of the chapter suggested the need for a continuing investigation of new bases for individualizing instruction. Evaluation data are essential to the appraisal of any such new procedures.

12. These two roles for evaluation in an individualized system have recently been discussed by Robert Glaser, "Evaluation of Instruction and Changing Educational Models," in M. C. Wittrock and D. Wiley, (eds.), *Evaluation of Instruction* (New York: Holt, Rinehart, and Winston, 1969 [in press]).

In summary, then, an individualized system can achieve its true potential only if all of its elements are evaluated on a continuing basis and if information acquired is used as feedback for improvement. Hence, such a system should involve a planned program for gathering and analyzing data to accomplish this purpose.

Examples of the Role of Evaluation in Current Programs for Individualized Instruction

The foregoing sections have described one basic model for using an evaluation program in implementing individualized instruction. The use of this general model, with a variety of modifications, is relatively widespread at the present time. The basic elements of the model have been described as consisting of sequences of educational objectives, materials to teach each objective, and a program of testing and evaluation for diagnosing the needs and guiding the progress of pupils. As has been indicated, the specific materials and procedures that have been presented in foregoing sections as examples of how the model may look in actual operation are those used in the Individually Prescribed Instruction procedure. The use of this program as an example is largely a result of the fact that the writers have been involved in the development of IPI and hence are intimately acquainted with it. Its use may also be justified on the basis of the fact that it is a relatively highly structured program and hence provides a rather detailed example of how an evaluation program for individualized instruction may be carried out. The reader should recognize, however, that the use of placement tests, unit pretests, curriculum-embedded tests, unit posttests, and prescriptions as described in this chapter are somewhat unique to IPI. The basic functions that they are designed to serve, however, are characteristics of the general model and are found in a number of programs. To show how these functions enter into other individualized programs, the following paragraphs present brief descriptions of other procedures designed to achieve similar goals.

COMPUTER-BASED INSTRUCTION

Computer-based or computer-assisted instruction, which is being developed and tried out in a number of laboratories throughout the country, may eventually represent one key to the effective and efficient individualization of instruction. Efforts to develop programs of this type represent attempts to capitalize on the storage capacity and the speed of data analysis and retrieval of the computer in order to carry out the data-processing and decision-making activities necessary for the achievement of individualized programs. In these systems, the computer carries out the processes of evaluation, diagnosis, and prescription. Wilson and Atkinson have described a computer-based program for word-list learning.[13] This program takes the pupil through a series of paired-associate tasks which are to enable him to acquire the criterion behavior of being able to identify a word in a word list when he hears it pronounced. He is brought to this ability by working through a sequence of four types of tasks or "problem types": the first provides picture, orthography, and audio cues; the second, picture and audio cues; the third, audio only; and the fourth, picture only. The fifth problem type is the criterion test and provides audio cues only. In each task the computer console presents the pupil with the cue, and he is to touch the proper word on a cathode ray tube. As with most computer-based instructional systems, evaluation and feedback are parts of every step in the program. With each response, if it is correct, the student receives that information; if it is incorrect, he is shown what the correct response is. When the pupil makes an error, he is required to make a correct response before going on, or he is branched into a remedial sequence. This latter step represents a simple type of diagnosis and subsequent prescription. When the student has worked through the four problem types that represent the learning exercises, he is presented with the criterion test. If the student passes this, he moves on to another learning task. If he does not meet criterion, he is recycled through parts of the learning sequence to learn the words that he has not mastered.

It can be seen that a computer-based instructional system can give the pupil some of the same type of individual attention and

13. H. A. Wilson and R. C. Atkinson, *Computer-based Instruction in Initial Reading: A Progress Report on the Stanford Project* (Technical Report No. 119 [Stanford, Calif.: Institute for Mathematical Studies in the Social Sciences, 1967]), pp. 22-26.

diagnosis that he would have if a teacher were constantly looking over his shoulder. Evaluation, diagnosis, and prescription can be continuing features that characterize every step in the learning process.

THE BUCKNELL CONTINUOUS PROGRESS PLAN

An interesting program for individualizing instruction at the college level has been developed at Bucknell University.[14] Work is being done in five departments—biology, psychology, philosophy, religion, and physics—and the individualized programs are designed to cut across conventional course boundaries so that individual progress is not stopped with the mastery of the content of a given course. Unlike other procedures described in this chapter, the Bucknell plan provides for having students study independently rather than having them meet for formal instructional sessions. At the start of the school term, the students are assembled for one class period to have procedures explained to them, to receive a copy of the objectives for the course, and to obtain instructional materials for the first unit. Units and accompanying unit tests constitute the elements used in monitoring student progress through the curriculum. When a student decides that he is ready to take the test for a unit, he requests this from the instructor. After the unit test has been taken and scored, the student arranges a conference with his instructor to discuss the results, to diagnose strengths and weaknesses, and to plan his next learning experiences. If the student has not shown mastery on the unit test, plans will be made for additional study and counseling on those things he has not mastered. If he passes the unit test, he is given his objectives and materials for the next unit. In this way a student works through a sequence of units, each of which must be mastered before he goes on to the next.

It is obvious that, in this program, much of the day-by-day and week-by-week monitoring of pupil progress is done by the student himself. While he is working within a unit, he determines how well he has mastered each element of instructional material and when he is able to move on to something else. At this level the

14. J. William Moore, "The Application of the Continuous Progress Concept to the Natural Sciences in Higher Education" (paper presented at the Research for Better Schools Forum, December 8, 1967).

student is carrying out self-evaluation and prescribing his own study schedule. At the time of the unit test, he receives additional assistance from the test results and the conference with the teacher. It might be suggested that some of the more structured plans used with elementary pupils are a natural preparation for this more independent type of evaluation and diagnosis that can and should characterize programs for higher level students.

PROJECT PLAN

Another procedure for individualizing instruction, Project PLAN, has been developed by the American Institutes for Research in collaboration with the Westinghouse Learning Corporation and a number of school districts.[15] This model involves the use of a structured curriculum including sequences of objectives, evaluation instruments, procedures for planning individualized programs, appropriate learning materials, and management procedures. A basic element in the PLAN operation is a computer terminal in each school, connected to a central project computer and serving as the main source for student data. Extensive information on each pupil is stored in the computer, and this is added to on a regular basis as a pupil proceeds with his study. A student's school year is started by his obtaining (along with the teacher) a printout of his past performance and other pertinent characteristics. These data are used as a basis for making decisions concerning the pupil's work for the school year and for joint selection of the student's first units of work. These decisions include selecting, with the aid of suggestions from computer printouts, the immediate objectives toward which he will work and the learning exercises in which he will engage in order to master these objectives. When it is felt that the student has mastered his first set of objectives, his achievement is assessed through the use of an appropriate evaluation procedure. These results are then used in making decisions concerning what the pupil will do next. It is evident that PLAN involves a curriculum which has considerable structure but within which a student has some choice in determining his goals. It includes an evaluation procedure which uses extensive pupil data as an aid in determining

15. John C. Flanagan, "Functional Education for the Seventies," *Phi Delta Kappan*, XLIX (September, 1967), 27-32.

what the pupil should study and which monitors each individual's progress through the curriculum. With the aid of the computer with its capacity for high-speed data analysis and retrieval, this evaluation procedure should enable the PLAN system to become increasingly adaptive to individual pupil needs as more is learned about relevant individual differences.

Some Suggested Future Directions for Evaluation in Programs for Individualized Instruction

The principle type of evaluative information described in this chapter which is used to adapt instruction to the individual is information concerning pupil achievement. Undoubtedly, the basic reason for this emphasis is the fact that measures of a pupil's level of achievement have rather clear implications for the planning of his educational program. The fact that a pupil has mastered skills and content up to a particular point in the curriculum suggests that he is probably ready to start his study at that point. The application of this procedure to the problem of adapting instruction to individual needs appears to be relatively straightforward and simple, although achieving even this modest degree of individualization has been found to be a major undertakng by persons who have developed these programs. However, these persons recognize that the present form of their programs represents only a first stage in fitting instruction to the personal characteristics of each pupil.

A major handicap in trying to use other pupil variables in individualizing instruction is a lack in fundamental knowledge concerning the implications of differences in such pupil variables for differences in educational needs or instructional treatments. That is, there is an almost countless number of tests that can be used for measuring various dimensions of aptitude, interest, attitude, personality, and many other personal variables and a great number of procedures for obtaining information on a variety of background factors, such as socioeconomic status, family background, educational experience, and so on. However, little work has been done on determining exactly what these variables mean for differences in the instructional experiences that should be prescribed. It is to be hoped that future work on individualizing instruction will involve both basic research on the instructional implications of many of these pupil variables and development efforts based on such implications.

It should also be emphasized that the general model for individualization that underlies the programs described here facilitates the introduction of new evaluative data as a basis for fitting instruction to each pupil. Each program has a structure which provides for obtaining specific data on each pupil and using such data for prescribing an individualized study plan. Although presently such data consist largely of measures of achievement, the structure is such that any new meaningful measures could easily be incorporated into the system. In fact, some non-achievement measures are already being employed, albeit on a relatively unstructured basis. For example, IPI teachers are encouraged, when they develop prescriptions, to take into account a variety of types of non-test information which they have available concerning their students. Experienced IPI teachers have found that some pupils are slow but careful workers, while others work quickly but with rather casual attention to what they are doing. The former type of student seems to require a relatively short prescription to master an objective, while the latter requires a greater amount of work. An immediate goal of research related to the IPI Project is to learn much more about such learning-style phenomena and to use such information quite extensively in developing pupil prescriptions.

Most of the models for individualizing instruction also place an emphasis on the need for greater attention to differences in pupil aptitudes and interests. First steps have been taken in making available a variety of types of materials for mastering each instructional objective. When this effort is fully developed, it will mean that some students may study with materials that are largely verbal, others with visual presentations, still others with manipulative materials, and so on. Progress in this area is impeded by both the paucity of basic knowledge concerning the relevance of differences in modes of presentation and the great investment required to produce instructional materials for individualized instruction which employ various modes. However, it is likely that, in the future, evaluation procedures for programs of individualized instruction will use measures of differential aptitudes as basic diagnostic devices.

The availability of a greater variety in instructional materials and procedures, as mentioned above, should also enhance the possibility of giving greater attention to information on pupil interests. If pupils have a variety of approaches from which to choose, they can make selections on the basis of their own interests. Likewise, the teacher can accumulate information on pupil interests and employ this in suggesting or prescribing instructional procedures.

Evaluative information concerning interests may be derived partially from tests or interest inventories, but it is likely that even more valid data will be obtained from accumulated data based on teacher observation and on performance records. Information that has been employed thus far has been quite informal in nature, but it can be hypothesized that, in the future, diagnostic evaluation programs will incorporate data on pupil interests as an essential part of the program.

Summary

This chapter has been concerned with the role of evaluation in programs for individualizing instruction. The adaptation of instruction to the needs and interests of the individual student requires that one have available considerable information concerning the student. The role of evaluaton is to gather this information and to make the proper use of it. A variety of procedures have been explored by educators in the effort to achieve individualization. Of these procedures, perhaps the general model that has been most widely used is what has been described in this chapter as the "structured-curriculum" model. The essential feature of this model is that it is based on an organized structure of carefully defined instructional objectives. Efforts to implement this model span the period of time from its early use in the Winnetka Plan up to the most current programs of computer-based instruction. The evaluation program that must be a basic part of this model makes extensive use of criterion-based measures of pupil achievement—that is, of measures that provide a maximum of information as to exactly where a student is in the curriculum sequence rather than how he ranks in comparison with other students. How this type of evaluation program is carried out has been described by using the program for Individually Prescribed Instruction (IPI) as an example. This program uses (a)placement tests to start the pupil at his proper point in each curriculum sequence, (b) diagnostic unit tests to determine the student's specific strengths and weaknesses before planning his individualized lesson plan for the unit, and (c) curriculum-embedded tests for frequent monitoring of his progress through a unit. Other programs for individualizing instruction, together with their provisions for evaluation, that have been discussed in the chapter include computer-based instruction, the Bucknell Continuous Progress Plan, and Project PLAN. All of these were seen as programs that involve considerable structure in their curriculum sequences and that require well-planned procedures for pupil evaluation. It must be assumed that all current efforts in designing individual learning experiences for each student on the basis of a continuing comprehensive evaluation of all relevant characteristics represent only a first stage in the development of such programs. However, the emphasis of all of these programs on the careful study of the individual and of his performance in the learning situation offers great promise for an increased understanding of the learning process and the development of increasingly effective instructional programs.

CHAPTER IX

The Relationships between Research and Evaluation Studies

JOHN K. HEMPHILL

Introduction

The relationships between research and evaluation studies need to be made explicit. It is evident that many of the activities associated with evaluation in education are also associated with educational research. In many instances, no distinctions are made between evaluation and research. Are evaluation studies to be considered simply a subset of the more general set of activities denoted by the term "research," or are there characteristics of the activities involved in evaluation that can or should be used to distinguish it from research?

Let us first look at the broad objectives of research and of evaluation as they can now be observed in the field of education. It appears to be well agreed that the objective of educational research is to add to our knowledge of the practices and methods of education. Less agreement is evident, however, as to whether new knowledge created by educational research should have some immediate usefulness or whether such research is sufficiently justified by the potential value of any new knowledge or by the satisfaction of any "idle curiosity." [1] Distinctions between "applied research" and "basic research" are often based on considerations of immediate utility as opposed to a concern for the possible usefulness of specific new knowledge. Evaluation studies are made to provide a basis for making decisions about alternatives and, therefore, in undertaking an evaluation study, one at once addresses himself to questions of utility. It may be objected, however, that this is too

1. Thorstein Veblen, *The Place of Science in Modern Civilization and Other Essays* (New York: Viking Press, Inc., 1919).

idealistic a view of the purpose of evaluation studies. In fact, it may be that the great majority of evaluation studies in education are not concerned with the alternatives per se, but instead deal with the simple question, "Does treatment X work?" At best, there may be an implicit assumption that if X does not work, something else must be tried; but this is as far as thinking about alternatives may go. Regardless of the lack of precision in thinking, providing information for choice among alternatives remains the basic and utilitarian purpose of evaluation studies. It appears that in this respect, at least, it is necessary to regard research, particularly basic research, as having a distinctly different objective than evaluation. Often the information to be provided by an evaluation study is needed because a decision *must* be made. This decision-making is not usually an integral part of the evaluation study itself, but a subsequent activity and one to be engaged in by parties not involved in the study. This fact might lead to the conclusion that an evaluation study could avoid questions of value and utility, leaving them to the decision-maker, and thus not need to be distinguished from research, either basic or applied. The crux of the issue, however, is not *who* makes a decision about what alternatives or *what information* serves as the basis for a decision; rather, it is *the degree to which concern with value questions is part and parcel of the study*. Decision-makers can and frequently do make use of information developed through research, but this act does not thereby transform a research study into an evaluation study.

Evaluation studies differ from research in the manner in which value questions are involved—especially value questions that undergird choices about what information or knowledge is sought. The implications of primacy of utility in evaluation studies and the relative unimportance of such considerations in research are profound. Although there are differences in points of view among behaviorial scientists, an "ideal" research study is one in which:

1. Problem selection and definition is the responsibility of the individual doing the research.
2. Tentative answers (hypotheses) to the problem may be derived by deduction from theories or by induction from an organized body of knowledge.
3. Value judgments by the researcher are limited to those implicit in the selection of the problem.

4. Given the statement of the problem and the hypothesis, the research can be replicated.
5. The data to be collected are determined largely by the problem and the hypothesis.
6. Relevant variables can be controlled or manipulated, and systematic effects of other variables can be eliminated by randomization.

The evaluation study may be described in terms of characteristics almost the reverse of those outlined above:

1. The problem is almost completely determined by the situation in which the study is conducted. Many people may be involved in its definition and, because of its complexity, the problem initially is difficult to define.
2. Precise hypotheses usually cannot be generated; rather the task becomes one of testing generalizations from a variety of research studies, some of which are basically contradictory. There are many gaps which in the absence of verified knowledge must be filled by reliance on judgment and experience.
3. Value judgments are made explicit in the selection and the definition of the problem as well as in the development and implementation of the procedures of the study.
4. The study is unique to a situation and seldom can be replicated, even approximately.
5. The data to be collected are heavily influenced if not determined by feasibility. Choices, when possible, reflect value judgments of decision-makers or of those who set policy. There are often large differences between data for which the collection is feasible and data which are of most value to the decision-makers.
6. Only superficial control of a multitude of variables important to interpretation of results is possible. Randomization to eliminate the systematic effects of these variables is extremely difficult or impractical to accomplish.[2]

Evaluation studies are often undertaken in response to a need to know the usefulness of an invented alternative to an existing mode of action which has resulted from some combination of old and new knowledge, or they may be undertaken to determine how well an existing mode of action is working. Is a new method of training teachers an improvement over a presently used method? Is a specific head-start program effective in preparing disadvantaged youngsters to enter school? New alternatives are likely to have

2. I am indebted to Dr. Richard Watkins for the major portion of this analysis.

been based, at least in part, upon generalizations from research findings and results. To the degree that this is true, an evaluation study can provide a test of the generalization and thus go beyond the point at which most research stops—the verification of hypotheses within only a very controlled and restricted situation. In this respect, evaluation can contribute side by side, but in a distinctly important way, to the development of a science of education.

Research and evaluation studies share many characteristics of method and approach. Both add to new knowledge. Both profit from and stimulate the development of theory. Both can contribute to a science of education and perhaps both are required for its orderly development.

The remainder of this chapter includes two major sections (that may not appear as being obviously related to each other) and a summary. The first of these sections looks at evaluation studies and research studies from the point of view of the major territory they share in common. The emphasis will be upon a relationship between the two that may be viewed as symbiotic. A specific evaluation study will be used as an example and as a means of making these relationships concrete and explicit. Following the presentation, this specific evaluation study itself will be subjected to a brief evaluation. The next section introduces statistical decision theory as a more appropiate framework for appraising evaluation studies than is the "research" framework most often employed. In this section, a scenario will be developed to explain the framework's major features. For the reader's convenience, the scenario utilizes as an example the same specific evaluation study described in the preceding section. In the summary section, the relationships among the various sections of the chapter, hopefully, will be made apparent as the similarities and differences between research and evaluation studies are viewed from perspectives that are appropriate to each.

The New Nursery School[3]

In exploring the relationship between evaluation studies and

3. I particularly wish to express my appreciation and indebtedness to Dr. Glen Nimnicht for his willingness to permit me to select from, paraphrase, and perhaps unintentionally distort the description of his work and evaluation study.

research, it is perhaps more useful to stress the many ways in which one may enrich the other, than it is to dwell at length upon their basic difference. To facilitate this exploration, we shall draw upon a specific evaluation study of an educational program, a study in which is found many, if not most, of the problems that confront educational evaluation.

DESCRIPTION OF THE SCHOOL

The selected study (from which pertinent examples have been drawn) was designed to evaluate the effectiveness of the New Nursery School, located in Greeley, Colorado. The program of the School has been developed under the direction of Dr. Glen Nimnicht at Colorado State College and has been supported by grants from the Office of Education, the Boettcher Foundation, and the Office of Economic Opportunity. It represents one of the few model head-start programs that has been selected for extensive study in the current Follow Through Program. Thus, it is a significant educational innovation brought into being to meet demands for more meaningful education for a neglected portion of the nation's children.

It is impossible in the space available to describe this study in detail or to report its findings completely. Parts of the study will be used as examples representative of the many educational evaluation problems that are becoming increasingly apparent as more and more studies, stimulated by the impetus today toward the massive improvement of the educational enterprise, are undertaken.

The particular focus of the New Nursery School is upon three- and four-year-old Spanish-surnamed children from low-income homes. These children are at a disadvantage at the time they enter traditional school programs, not only because of environmental deprivation, but also because they have a different culture and language than that which they will encounter in school. In developing the New Nursery School, Nimnicht reasoned that, if it could be demonstrated that a carefully designed program was effective for these children, it would be possible to assume that similar programs would benefit other educationally disadvantaged children.

The general objectives of the New Nursery School are as follows: (*a*) to develop a positive self-image within each child;

(*b*) to increase the child's sensory and perceptual acuity; (*c*) to improve his language ability; (*d*) to improve his problem-solving and concept-formulation abilities. These specific objectives were selected for the New Nursery School because previous research studies [4] seemed to indicate that they represent areas within which disadvantaged children show a large deficit at the time they enter the formal education system.

The programs of the New Nursery School are organized to provide an autotelic responsive environment. An autotelic environment is one that is self-rewarding. The School's programs avoid as much as possible rewards and punishments that have no inherent connection with activities that go on within the environment. A child in such an environment takes part only in those activities in which *he* wants to participate and not in activities that an adult decides he is ready for or should do. Nimnicht, following the work of Anderson and Moore,[5] specifies the following conditions which must be satisfied if an environment is to be considered responsive:

1. The learner can explore the environment freely.
2. The environment is so structured that it immediately informs the learner of the consequences of his actions.
3. Events happen within the environment at a rate determined by the learner.
4. The environment is structured to permit the learner to make full use of his abilities to discover relationships.
5. The structure of the environment provides opportunities for interconnected discoveries about basic relationships in the physical, cultural, and social worlds.

The requirement that a responsive environment informs the learner immediately of the consequence of his action does much to determine the selection of material and equipment placed within the environment, the way the equipment, material, and facility are used, and what the teacher and her assistant do.

---

4. See for example, Benjamin S. Bloom, Allison Davis, and Robert Hess (eds.), *Compensatory Education for Cultural Deprivation* (New York: Holt, Rinehart & Winston, Inc., 1965); Martin Deutsch, "The Disadvantaged Child and the Learning Process," *Education in Deprived Areas,* ed. A. Harry Passow (New York: Bureau of Publications, Teachers College, Columbia University, 1963), pp. 168-71.

5. Allen R. Anderson and O. K. Moore, "Autotelic Folk Models," *Sociological Quarterly,* I (1960), 203-16.

When a child is in an autotelic responsive environment, he is free to explore and is never encouraged to stop one activity in order to start another. Control of the child's learning experience at the New Nursery School is effected in a large measure by choices that are made concerning what is included in his environment.

The teacher assumes a new and different role that further develops the responsiveness of the environment. She does not direct; rather, she facilitates the child's learning as he spontaneously encounters and manipulates his surroundings.

The details of the curriculum of the New Nursery School and the manner in which its contents are introduced to provide an autotelic responsive environment cannot be described fully in this paper. In general, the curriculum of the School has been developed to form sixteen major units, each involving a number of related learning episodes. Each episode has a set of specific objectives.

A more detailed description of the New Nursery School program has been published, but this brief description is perhaps sufficient for our purpose of examining how the total program is being evaluated.[6]

THE EVALUATION STUDY

The evaluation study [7] is an integral part of the entire development procedures that were used to create the New Nursery School, and began with the admission of its first group of children in the fall of 1964. The first year's activities at the School were focused upon the development of curriculum and procedures. Specific learning episodes were designed or invented, tried out with a small number of children, revised, retested, and revised again. This type of development work has been continuous throughout the program but has become a less dominant theme as the program has matured.

6. Glen P. Nimnicht and J. Meier, "A First Year Partial Progress Report of a Project in an Autotelic Responsive Environment Nursery School for Environmentally Deprived Spanish-American Children," *Journal of Research Services*, II (1966), 3-34.

7. The evaluation study is described in detail in an unpublished report by G. P. Nimnicht, J. Meier and O. McAfee, "A Summary of the Evaluation of the Experimental Program for Deprived Children at the New Nursery School," (Far West Laboratory for Educational Research and Development, 1967) and is extensively summarized and used selectively in this section.

Evaluation in a general sense is implicit in this early part of the development of a new program, but usually the specific data upon which judgments are based and the reasoning associated with their interpretation are not formally recorded for review. Although such informal evaluation serves the important function of providing immediate feedback to aid the process of educational development, our concern here will focus upon the more formal evaluation studies that were carried out to estimate the value of the program as a whole.

Formal evaluation of the New Nursery School program is not yet complete, since its basic design is longitudinal and the School staff is continuing to collect information about the children involved as they progress through their subsequent schooling. Data referred to in this discussion are those collected as of the spring of 1967.

Several distinguishable groups of children have been involved in one way or another in the evaluation study. Each group is small in number. These groups are as follows:

1. A group of 14 three-year-old children with disadvantaged backgrounds who entered the School in the fall of 1964
2. A group of 13 four-year-old children with disadvantaged backgrounds who entered the School in the fall of 1964
3. A group of 8 three-year-old children from disadvantaged backgrounds who entered the School in the fall of 1965
4. A group of 9 four-year-old children from disadvantaged backgrounds who entered the School in the fall of 1965
5. A group consisting of 12 of the 14 children from Group 1 who returned to the New Nursery School in the fall of 1965 for a second year
6. A group of 27 three-year-old children from disadvantaged backgrounds who entered the School in the fall of 1966
7. A group of 18 four-year-old children from disadvantaged backgrounds who entered the School in the fall of 1966
8. A group consisting of 7 of the 8 children composing Group 3 who returned to the School in the fall of 1966
9. A group of 11 three-year-old children from non-disadvantaged backgrounds who entered the School in the fall of 1965
10. A group of 11 four-year-old children from non-disadvantaged backgrounds who entered the School in the fall of 1965
11. A group of 8 three-year-old children from non-disadvantaged backgrounds who entered the School in the fall of 1966

12. A group of 17 four-year-old children from non-disadvantaged homes who entered the School in the fall of 1966

13. A group consisting of 5 of the 8 children composing Group 11 who returned to the School in the fall of 1966

14. A group of 22 five-year-old children with backgrounds comparable to the 1964 four-year-old disadvantaged children who attended kindergarten in 1965 as cohorts but who did *not* attend the School

15. A group of 28 five-year-old disadvantaged children (with backgrounds comparable to the 1965 four-year-old disadvantaged children) who attended kindergarten in 1966 as cohorts but who had not attended the School. These children composing the last two groups (14 and 15) were comparable to the New Nursery School children in the sense that (*a*) they were Spanish-surnamed children, and (*b*) they came from low-income homes.

These fifteen groups of children afford the possibility of making contrasts that yield information relevant to judging the School's effectiveness. Comparisons between disadvantaged and non-disadvantaged children can point to particular deficits that the School may meet (e.g., comparison of Group 4 with Group 10). Comparisons with the "comparable group" provide an estimate of how effective the School may be (e.g., comparison of Group 2 with Group 14).

The development of the study design (research design) of an evaluation study demands the best of research methodology and analysis. How can inferences about the New Nursery School's effectiveness, for example, be made in the face of the practical situations which yield such a small number of cases and permit only partial controls, and in which relevant data must be gathered over a period of years? Insistence on "better" designs does not help persons faced with the very practical problems inherent in such studies. However, suggestions made by Campbell and Stanley [8] regarding quasi-experimental designs can be helpful to the designer of evaluation studies in education.

It will be recalled that the stated objectives of the New Nursery School were (*a*) improvement of the child's self-image; (*b*) development of his sensory and perceptual acuity; (*c*) improvement of

8. Donald T. Campbell and Julian C. Stanley, "Experimental and Quasi-Experimental Designs for Research on Teaching," *Handbook of Research in Teaching*, ed. N. L. Gage (Chicago: Rand McNally & Co., 1963), 171-246.

his language abilities; and (d) the development of his concept-formation and problem-solving abilities. Major problems face an evaluator who undertakes the task of securing evidence which reveals the degree to which such objectives have been achieved. First is the problem of explicating and defining those specific behaviors of children which can provide evidence that each of the general objectives has been achieved. Objectives stated in the manner of these four goals for the New Nursery School must be made much more explicit and then expressed in behavioral terms before the degree of their achievement can be assessed. Definition of objectives in "behavioral" terms, following the leads provided by Mager,[9] finds ready application at this point. Second, some form of measurement procedures must be found or devised which yields information that can be considered relevant. Problems of measuring abilities of children at ages three and four, although not neglected by research, have not been sufficiently resolved to permit one to readily select appropriate and ready-made measurement tools for the task. How, for example, is one to measure the degree to which a language-handicapped child has developed a positive self-image at age three? These problems of inventing, developing, and validating measurement procedures and instruments represent one large area of concern shared by the researchers interested in child development and the evaluators of educational programs designed for young children.

DEVELOPMENT OF A POSITIVE SELF-IMAGE

A new technique developed by Brown at the Institute of Development Studies at New York University was tried in an attempt to evaluate the achievement of a positive self-image.[10] It was hoped that this technique would serve the needs of the evaluation study and also that the technique itself might be better understood, refined, and developed.[11]

9. Robert F. Mager, *Preparing Objectives for Programmed Instruction* (San Francisco: Fearon Publishers, 1962).

10. B. R. Brown, "The Assessment of Self-Concept Among Four-year-old Negro and White Children," a Comparative Study Using Brown's *IDS Self-Concept Referent Test* (unpublished paper, a shorter form of which was presented at the Eastern Psychological Association meeting, New York, 1966).

11. As is often the case, the investigators conducting the evaluation study were also motivated by a desire to contribute to research and thus the study actually embraced both research and evaluation as objectives.

The procedure involves showing the child a snapshot of himself and then asking him a standard set of questions, examples of which are:

Is Jose happy or sad?
Is Jose clean or dirty?
Does Jose's mother think he is happy or sad?
Do other kids like Jose to play with them?
Does Jose's teacher think Jose is clean or dirty?

This test was administered to twelve kindergarten children who had been enrolled in the New Nursery School and sixteen children from the comparable group (Group 15). The children in the New Nursery School group gave slightly fewer negative responses on the average, but the differences were small. Later this test was judged to be inadequate in its present form for use in the evaluation study. Its major weakness was that it focused upon a small part of what is generally included in the concept of self-image,[12] and perhaps upon a relatively insignificant part of the total. As of the present time, no satisfactory procedure for assessing the total concept of a *positive self-image* has been found for use within the New Nursery School setting. An adequate assessment of the concept of self-image will require further clarification of the basic concept, additional research, and solution of the many problems involved in its measurement. Although the concept of self-image has interested many of those designing new educational programs for disadvantaged children, it is doubtful that a satisfactory assessment in this area is presently possible.

DEVELOPMENT OF SENSORY AND PERCEPTUAL ACUITY

Progress toward measuring the objective of developing sensory and perceptual acuity was made. One successful technique was designed to measure the child's ability to identify and name nine colors: black, white, red, orange, yellow, brown, green, blue, and purple. The procedure required the child to point to a color painted on a card after the name of the color was given by the examiner.

12. See for example, Ruth C. Wylie, *The Self-Concept* (Lincoln: University of Nebraska Press, 1961); J. Parker, "The Relationship of Self-Report to Inferred Self-Concept," *Educational Psychological Measurement*, XXVI (1966), 691-700.

The child was also asked to give the name of a color presented to him with the question, "What color is the paint on this card?" This test has the obvious weakness of confounding perceptual ability with language ability and therefore cannot be regarded strictly as a test of achieved ability to perceive color. Since the New Nursery School also has the objective of increasing the child's language skills, performance on the test is relevant to the general objectives of the School, if not to this specific objective of developing perceptual acuity. Table I shows the number of colors identified before and after one year of the New Nursery School experience by six groups of children tested in the year 1966-67.

This attempt to evaluate the achievement of an objective of the New Nursery School illustrates a general difficulty associated with finding or creating a measurement procedure that can be used to assess change along a single dimension within a multidimensional set of educational objectives. If one speculates about what might result should he conduct a factor-analysis study of a battery of measures related to the complex performance implied by the four general objectives of the New Nursery School, it is likely that a test requiring the naming of colors, if included as one of the measures in the battery, would produce substantial loadings on more than a single factor. Even if one had achieved a reasonable understanding of the dimensions of performance in the complex domain of sensory and perceptual abilities, it is not clear that these dimensions would be those along which children develop with school experience. Much research will be needed before the dimensions of change in performance, which describe the process of early learning, can be identified. This, too, is an area in which interest associated with evaluation may stimulate research; in fact, research work in identifying these dimensions of change in performance is now being pursued at the Center for the Study of Evaluation of Instructional Programs at the University of California, Los Angeles.[13]

The data shown in Table 1 are perhaps more significant as evaluation data for the New Nursery School than their limitations, their complexity, and the small number of cases involved would

13. Merlin C. Wittrock, *The Experiment in Research on Evaluation of Instruction* (Working Paper No. 2, Center for the Study of Evaluation of Instructional Programs [Los Angeles: University of California, 1966]).

TABLE 1
Colors Named by New Nursery School Children

Group	N	Number of Colors Named	
		Before	After
Disadvantaged three-year-old children............	15	2.00	5.20
Disadvantaged 1st year four-year-old children.....	11	1.45	6.66
Disadvantaged 2nd year four-year-old children.....	5	7.80	9.00
Non-disadvantaged three-year-old children........	6	4.50	7.84
Non-disadvantaged 1st year four-year-old children..	10	6.40	8.00
Non-disadvantaged 2nd year four-year-old children.	4	7.25	8.25

suggest. First, we note that the disadvantaged children who had not had previous school experience, regardless of whether they were three or four years of age, were able, on the average, to name only two of the nine colors. But they were able to name five or six after one year of nursery school and continued to master this task through the second year at the School. Non-disadvantaged children entered the New Nursery School with the ability to identify and name five or six of the colors and their performance also appears to improve with experience in the School. The general implication of the pattern of data in this table is of a deficit on the part of the disadvantaged children, but one that is readily remedied by experience in the School. Children who have spent two years at the New Nursery School no longer show this specific deficit in comparison with the more advantaged group.

DEVELOPMENT OF LANGUAGE ABILITY

Scores yielded by the *Metropolitan Reading Readiness Test*, which was administered to all kindergarten students in the Greeley Public Schools at the end of the 1966-67 school year, provided a relevant source of data for evaluating the School's achievement of objectives in the language-ability area. Table 2 shows the scores of

TABLE 2
Average Raw Score on the Metropolitan Reading Readiness Test of Two Groups of Disadvantaged Children

Score	New Nursery School Group		Comparison Group	
	N	Raw Score	N	Raw Score
Reading.............	16	55.3	28	46.6
Arithmetic..........	16	17.0	28	12.9
Total...............	16	78.9	28	64.4

16 New Nursery School children and 28 children from a comparative group (Group 15). Both groups, it will be recalled, were from low-income homes and had Spanish surnames. Because the New Nursery School children were selected from the extreme of the population from which both groups were drawn, they, in all probability, were somewhat more disadvantaged than the comparison group. The mean total score of 78.9 for the New Nursery School group is at the 70th percentile on the norms of the test, while the mean total score of 64.4 earned by the comparison group is at the 35th percentile. These data provide further evidence of the effectiveness of the program, together with the facts that (*a*) two of the 16 children in the New Nursery School group could not be tested on either the *Peabody Picture Vocabulary Test* or the *Stanford-Binet* at the time they entered the School; (b) three others tested 79, 75, and 50 on the *Peabody* but could not score on the latter; and (*c*) one child tested 57 and 61 respectively on these two tests.

These data presented as evidence of the School's effectiveness in the language area illustrate some additional problems in evaluation. First, evidence was obtained from normal settings or operations, e.g., from tests, administered routinely in school operations, that are meaningful as evaluation information but which may not be exactly of the type or of the quality that would be most desirable if their use as evaluation information were primary. Second, control groups are seldom available that can be considered entirely comparable. The "control" group represented in Table 2 was defective in a very significant way; it consisted of a number of children who remained after the more extreme individuals, as judged on the basis of the defining criteria, had been removed and included in the "treatment" group. To the extent that selection based on the criteria was done in a valid manner and the measures of performance were related to these criteria, the comparison provided by the control group is biased in a way that attenuates the apparent effectiveness of the New Nursery School. Third, difficulties arose from the use of data of a "case" or of a "clinical" character which nonetheless were utilized because they added significant information for the evaluation. Much rigor was sacrificed, and clear and unambiguous procedures for drawing inferences from these types of data were not available. Research on methods of analysis and on interpretation of information gathered in relatively "messy" situations could add to the usefulness of an evaluation study.

DEVELOPMENT OF CONCEPT-FORMATION
AND PROBLEM-SOLVING ABILITY

The evaluators of the New Nursery School program searched widely for measurement procedures appropriate for use with these groups of children in the areas of concept formation and problem-solving. They became interested in possibilities suggested by instruments being used in research conducted by Banta,[14] of the University of Cincinnati. Banta had made substantial progress toward the development of a battery of measures, called the *Cincinnati Autonomy Test Battery*, suitable for use with young disadvantaged children. These tests grew out of a study of the development of children, ages three to five.

Of Banta's tests, the five that seemed to hold most promise were as follows:

1. "Curiosity." An interesting looking box, covered with attractive objects and provided with a peephole and holes big enough for a child's hand to explore the interior, is placed before a child. The child's score reflects the amount of manipulation, of tactile and visual exploration, and of verbalization in the child's response over a period of five months.
2. "Impulse Control." The child is instructed to draw a line "fast" and then "very fast." Next he is shown how to draw a line slowly. Finally, as a test of his control of motor activity, he is asked to draw three lines, each very slowly. His score is based on how long he takes to draw three eight-inch lines "very slowly."
3. "Intentional Learning." A series of ten familiar drawings is presented and the child is requested to name each as it is presented. The test then requires the child to recall the drawings he has just named.
4. "Innovative Behavior." A cardboard the size of a checkerboard is presented upon which are four small "houses" near each of its four corners. There is space between each "house" and the edge of the board. A toy dog and a bone are also provided. The dog is placed in front of the child and the bone at the other edge of the board. The

14. Thomas J. Banta, "Tests for the Evaluation of Early Childhood Education: The Cincinnati Autonomy Test Battery (CATB)," *Cognitive Studies,* I (in press), 1968.

examiner demonstrates two ways the dog can reach the bone: (*a*) by going in a straight line; and (*b*) by going around one of the houses. The child is asked to show another way the dog can reach the bone. He has ten trials and earns one or two points depending upon the complexity of the route for each unique way he finds.

5. "Field Independence." An embedded figure test is used. The child is asked to place a cone-shaped piece of paper over the same shape in a series of pictures within each of which the figure is embedded. There are fourteen pictures and one point is scored for each correct response.

Table 3 presents the results of the administration of these five tests to groups of New Nursery School children (1966-67 groups).

TABLE 3

MEAN SCORES ON FIVE TESTS FROM THE CINCINNATI AUTONOMY TEST BATTERY FOR SIX GROUPS OF NEW NURSERY SCHOOL CHILDREN

Group	N	Test				
		1	2	3	4	5
Disadvantaged three-year-olds............	20	17.32[a]	.83[b]	2.30	3.58[b]	5.05
Disadvantaged 1st year four-year-olds.....	13	11.36[c]	.64[c]	2.62	4.85	7.00
Disadvantaged 2nd year four-year-olds.....	6	18.17	.57	4.50	8.00	6.00
Non-disadvantaged three-year-olds........	5	27.80	.69	2.80	9.00	5.80
Non-disadvantaged 1st year four-year-olds.	12	21.50	.48	2.33	8.92	8.58
Non-disadvantaged 2nd year four-year-olds	4	29.75	.30	2.75	9.50	10.00

[a] N = 22   [b] N = 19   [c] N = 14

Test 1, "Curiosity," yields higher scores for the non-disadvantaged children, but provides no evidence that the School (New Nursery School) experience increased curiosity as measured.

The scoring of Test 2, "Impulse Control," is reversed so that a low score indicates greater control. Disadvantaged children show less control than the non-disadvantaged. Older children show greater control, and School experience appears to favor development of control.

The results in the case of Test 3, "Intentional Learning," are mixed; however, the highest average score was earned by the six children from disadvantaged backgrounds who had two years of the New Nursery School experience.

Scores in Test 4, "Innovative Behavior," show a pattern consistent both with the notion of a major deficit in this area on the part of disadvantaged children and with the effectiveness of the School in overcoming it.

Test 5, "Field Independence," yields a pattern of scores suggesting some deficit on the part of disadvantaged children but little or no evidence of the School's effect on such a deficit.

The data yielded by the *Cincinnati Autonomy Test Battery* provides some evidence favorable to the effectiveness of the New Nursery School, but there is reason to question whether any one of the five tests that were used were particularly relevant as measures of the stated objectives of the School. It is not clear that curiosity, impulse control, innovative behavior, field independence, or even intentional learning (each as measured) require abilities that are other than tangentially related to either the ability to form concepts or the ability to solve problems. Were they available, measures more directly related to the objectives of the School may or may not have shown different results. The question of the relevance of a measure to the objective of a school experience underlies a real problem faced by evaluation studies—the problem of securing measurement tools based upon their relevance to the task at hand rather than upon their mere availability which sometimes dictates choice of tools because of lack of time, resources, or even skill.

Evidence regarding the effectiveness of the School that is less tangential than are the Banta test data is provided by a test developed on the spot by the staff of the School and given the title, "Classification Test." In administering this instrument, the examiner presents the child with the following objects that have been placed upon a table before him by pointing to each object one at a time, and naming it: an apple, toy car, bowl, shoe, toothbrush, crayon, cigar, dollar bill, screwdriver, and light bulb. These are the "response" items. The examiner next holds up one of a set of stimulus objects and asks, "Show me the thing that goes with this orange." The stimulus objects are respectively: an orange, doll, cup, glove, comb, pencil, cigarette, penny, hammer, and flashlight. The child's score is the number of stimulus objects that he is able to match with the "correct" response objects. The selection of specific objects to be used in the test required much pretesting to eliminate unfamiliar items and items that could be matched (correctly or incorrectly) on superficial elements (e.g., a red glove and a red crayon). It can readily be seen that this test is directly related to the School's objective, of concept formation, since ability to match an orange with an apple implies that the child has formed and can demonstrate the ability to use a class or categorical concept such as "fruit" or "food," and the like.

Table 4 presents the data from an administration of this test to New Nursery School children in 1966-67.

TABLE 4

MEAN SCORES ON THE "CLASSIFICATION TEST"
FOR NEW NURSERY SCHOOL CHILDREN IN 1966-67

GROUP	N	MEAN SCORE
Disadvantaged three-year-olds	23	1.67
Disadvantaged 1st year four-year-olds	13	3.77
Disadvantaged 2nd year four-year-olds	7	5.86
Non-disadvantaged three-year-olds	7	3.71
Non-disadvantaged 1st year four-year-olds	7	4.71
Non-disadvantaged 2nd year four-year-olds	3	5.00

The pattern of these data is clearly consistent with the notion that concept-formation ability is an area within which disadvantaged children show a deficit and that it generally develops between ages three and four. The scores presented in the table also clearly show that the ability to form concepts improved during the New Nursery School experience. Comparison of the results of this homemade test, which was designed to be directly relevant to the objective of the School program, with those of the "borrowed" test of questionable relevance suggests the importance of careful attention to the problem of *what* is measured in carrying out an evaluation study.

FOLLOW-UP INFORMATION

The final example of types of information that were collected in the evaluation study of the New Nursery School to be discussed is provided by a small set of longitudinal data. These data illustrate another possibility that is too often neglected but which can be useful in forming a judgment about the value of an educational program.

Progress of some children who had attended the New Nursery School was followed in kindergarten and first grade. Twelve of the thirteen disadvantaged four-year-old children (Group 2) who had attended the New Nursery School in 1964-65, entered kindergarten the next year. The teachers were asked at the end of the first five weeks to judge whether each child (*a*) would be very successful in school, (*b*) would have average success in school, or (*c*) would have difficulty in school. The teachers judged that (*a*) two would be very successful; (*b*) eight would experience average success, and (*c*) two would have difficulty. Since most of the other children in each teacher's class were from non-disadvantaged backgrounds and since there is much evidence that disadvantaged children generally enter school with major deficits, these judgments, which suggest that the New Nursery School children (having disadvantaged backgrounds) were not regarded as likely to be less successful than others, are consistent with the notion of the positive effect of the School.

In February of the following year (1967), at which time the same twelve children were in the first grade, their teachers were asked again to judge their progress. For purposes of comparison, those children among the 22 in the "control" group (Group 14) who were in the same classroom with the twelve former New Nursery School children were also judged. The teachers rated each child as (*a*) in the upper 10 per cent of the class; (*b*) in the next 20 per cent of the class; (*c*) in the middle 40 per cent of the class; (*d*) in the next lower 20 per cent of the class; or (*e*) in the lowest 10 per cent of the class.

The children were judged on reading, arithmetic, independence, attention span, good behavior, and total success in school. The ratings for reading, arithmetic, and "total success" were as follows:

TABLE 5

Teachers Ratings of the Progress of
Pupils in Terms of Position in Class

RATING	NEW NURSERY SCHOOL N = 12			CONTROL N = 10		
	Reading	Arithmetic	Total Success	Reading	Arithmetic	Total Success
Upper 10%....	1	2	1	1	0	0
Next 20%.....	0	1	0	1	2	4
Middle 40%...	5	4	6	3	3	3
Next 20%.....	4	2	3	1	4	0
Lowest 10%...	2	3	2	4	1	3

There is little or no difference between the ratings of the two groups on reading, arithmetic, and total success; nor was there a difference between the groups on independence, attention span, or good behavior. In general, both groups were judged to be slightly below their classmates. From one point of view, these results can be interpreted as supportive of the effectiveness of the School; but from another, there is room for doubt. The fact that twelve children (many of whom could not be tested on standard intelligence tests when they entered the New Nursery School, or, if testable, were judged to have I.Q.'s in the 40's to 60's) were performing only slightly below the average of their classmates supports the judgment that the School was effective. Yet the children in the control group, also disadvantaged (perhaps not as much as the New Nursery School children) but who had not attended the School, were judged as doing equally as well. Perhaps the effect of the "head start" given the children by the New Nursery School experience and which seemed to be evident at the kindergarten level had been lost by first grade. Perhaps, also, teachers were not capable of perceiving and judging differences among students at these early ages. In any event, it is difficult to draw conclusions from the follow-up information available regarding the value of the New Nursery School experience at this point in the study.

EVALUATION OF THE EVALUATION STUDY

If one were to apply conventional research standards to the evaluation study of the New Nursery School, he probably would conclude that:

1. The study was poorly done—specifically, the design of the study was deficient in many respects (or perhaps absent); controls were inadequate, confounding, rampant; and measurement, inexact or inappropriate, and so on.
2. Drawing conclusions from the study is next to impossible because its design and execution are deficient, and because the hypotheses are not stated or the objectives clearly defined, and because the evidence presented in the study is not convincing.

However, as an evaluation of a new educational program, this effort certainly compares favorably with the best. This paradox may be viewed to suggest, therefore, that conventional standards for research work are not appropriate if applied to evaluation studies in education. A new framework of conventions and a new way of viewing evaluation studies may be needed. In the next section, some notes concerning a different framework and a different basis for standards will be offered.

Evaluation Studies within a Framework of Decision-Making

Evaluation studies in education can be viewed more appropriately within a context of decision-making than within a framework provided by purposes and conventions of research. Recent developments in statistical decision theory, especially the development related to business administration, appear to be applicable in education but as yet have not been so employed to any significant degree. Perhaps the newness of these developments rather than lack of relevance accounts for their infrequent application. In this section, we will examine in a very general manner how evaluation studies in education may fit into the structure of statistical decision theory.[15]

Those who make decisions about the alternatives in allocating resources to carry out an educational program share a large responsibility. How school administrators act in making such decisions has been the subject of research study in the past,[16] and it is likely that in the future we will see, as a result of current interest in better educational planning, even greater attention being given to this process. But how educational decisions *are made* is less important than how such decisions *should be made*, if they are to be rational rather than intuitive and capricious. How decisions should be made is the prime focus of statistical decision theory.

As an aid to introducing the basic concepts of statistical deci-

---

15. A few useful references include: Leonard J. Savage, *The Foundations of Statistics* (New York: Wiley, 1954); Howard Raiffa and R. O. Schlaifer, *Applied Statistical Decision Theory* (Boston: Division of Research, Harvard Business School, 1961); Charles Jackson Grayson, Jr., *Decisions under Uncertainty: Drilling Decisions by Oil and Gas Operators* (Boston: Division of Research, Harvard Business School, 1960).

16. See for example: Keith Goldhammer, *et al., Issues and Problems in Contemporary Educational Administration* (Center for Advanced Study of Educational Administration, University of Oregon, 1967); *Behaviorial Science and Educational Administration*, ed. Daniel E. Griffiths (Sixty-third yearbook of the National Society for the Study of Education, Part II [Chicago: Distributed by University of Chicago Press, 1964]).

sion theory, we shall continue to use the evaluation study of the New Nursery School as a general example and attempt to place it within this framework. For clarity, we will need to simplify and be concrete; hence, we shall develop a scenario around an assumed decision situation in which whether or not to install a head-start program, specifically a program on the New Nursery School model, is the central issue.

Let us assume that Superintendent Brown of Big City Unified School District has data that show his district contains approximately 5000 youngsters of age four from disadvantaged homes. His Board is sensitive to the many pressing social problems that give popular support to the desirability of a "head start" for these youngsters. However, they are also sensitive to a strong feeling in the community that taxes have already risen as high as they can go. Superintendent Brown's estimate of the cost of providing a head-start program in his district along the lines of the New Nursery School is about $800 per pupil. This estimate includes both operating costs and amortization-of-facilities costs. Thus, he is faced with the decision of whether or not to suggest to his board the inclusion in the budget of a $4 million item ($800 x 5000 students) to support a new head-start program. How can he justify such an item, particularly in view of his awareness of the "values" of the board? He knows that there is no chance of convincing enough members of the board by arguing, as he has in the past, the general values of education. Many board members would concede that the value of education cannot be measured in dollars, but Mr. Brown knows that a decision of the board to initiate a new program will depend largely upon costs to the taxpayers. He believes that his board can be influenced to embark on a new program only by evidence that the new venture can improve the total school program in his district, without adding to the tax burden. In other words, Brown faces the problem of making up his own mind and then of convincing the board that $4 million spent on a head-start program would be saved by its direct effects upon other costs of the total school program. He is enthusiastic about the potential of the New Nursery School program, believes intuitively (but doesn't really know) that this type of program might be just what Big City needs, and (fortunately for our example) Mr. Brown has a grasp of the principles and procedures of statistical decision theory. Let us see how he proceeds to apply this approach to decision-making and note how an evaluation study of the New Nursery School program could fit into the systematic attack he makes upon his problem.

As his first step, Brown begins to build a "payoff" matrix. This matrix is a simple chart showing the relationships between the alternatives of (*a*) *not deciding* to install a head start program, or (*b*)*deciding* to install such a program, and the best estimate he can make of the "dollar" payoff of his chosen alternative as compared with the payoff of the other alternative. His matrix is laid out to look like this:

TABLE 6

IF: ↓ ACTION	THEN: → CONSEQUENCES			
	The Program Has a Small Negative Effect	The Program Has a Small Positive Effect	The Program Has a Moderate Positive Effect	The Program Has a Strong Positive Effect
The program is installed...	$?	$?	$?	$?
The program is *not* installed	$?	$?	$?	$?

Note that Mr. Brown's matrix at this point has no entries in its cells; he has merely identified his two choices and provided categories for considering the consequences of his choice. In order to proceed, Brown must decide how he can best consider and express the outcomes of his actions—the consequences. He decides to look at the outcomes in terms of how his choice affects the large costs of special educational programs which the district provides for children who have difficulty with the regular school program. He might have selected some other outcome, e.g., possible reduction of school-dropout rate, but he believes that the board's values can be most effectively addressed by emphasis on costs.

Operating records show that the cost of instructing a child in a typical special program is about double that for a regular program: $1000 per special student in contrast to $500 per regular student. He then estimates (upon the basis of the records for the past five years) that 4000 of the 5000 children with disadvantaged backgrounds in his district who will be entering school each year will present educational problems that will require their entering some special program. He sees in the possibility of reducing the costs to the district of these special programs the type of "payoff" he could use effectively in considering what his recommendation to the board should be. If he could save $500 per year on the cost of providing special education for each of 4000 students, this would represent a saving of $2 million the first year, and, since each child who needs such a program can be expected to remain in school for about ten years, the saving to the district eventually could be as large as $20 million per year.

The $20 million potentially to be gained each year through the introduction of a head-start program must be discounted because it cannot be realized immediately but would accrue year by year over the ten years the 4000 children remained in school. Thus, for the first year only $2 million could be saved; at the end of two years, $4 million, and so on. Brown then estimates the "present value" of $20 million to be gained at the rate of $2 million per year over ten years. The "present value" of $20 million is dependent upon the rate of return expected on an investment which is to be made now and realized up to ten years later. Mr. Brown is confident that his board would consider a 10 per cent return per year on an investment as satisfactory and calculates the "present value" of $20 million returned at the rate of $2 million per year over a ten-year period to be approximately $13 million.

Mr. Brown is not yet in a position to complete his "payoff" matrix. First, he defines "a small negative effect" as one creating 10 per cent more requirements for special education programs (i.e., he would have to provide for special programs for 4400 rather than 4000 students). It is just possible to reason that a head-start program would make the situation worse instead of better. Mr. Brown does not really believe that this negative outcome is a likely one, but he reasons that it is not impossible, and so includes it in his analysis. He defines "a small positive effect" as a 10 per cent improvement (he would need to spend 10 per cent less for special programs, i.e., provide special programs for 3600 students rather than for 4000), a "moderate positive effect" as 20-per-cent improvement, and a "strong positive effect" as 50-per-cent improvement. Now he finds he is ready to calculate "payoff" values for each cell, bearing in mind that (*a*) it would cost the district $4 million ($800 x 5000 children) per year to mount and operate the head-start program if it were to be initiated, but nothing, of course, if it were not begun; and (*b*) that, if the program is *not* undertaken, its "payoff" (in terms of the board's values as he sees them) would likewise clearly be nothing. The results of his calculations are as follows:

TABLE 7

IF: ↓ ACTION	THEN: → CONSEQUENCES			
	The Program Has a Small Negative Effect (−10%)	The Program Has a Small Positive Effect (+10%)	The Program Has a Moderate Positive Effect (+20%)	The Program Has a Strong Positive Effect (+50%)
The program is installed...	−$5.30M*	−$2.70M	−$1.40M	+$2.50M
The program is *not* installed	0	0	0	0

* Calculation:

−$4M (cost of head-start program) + (−.10 × $1.3M, annual gain from program) = −$5.30M

It is clear to Mr. Brown from this "payoff" analysis that a program having a *strong positive effect* might be defended before his board as being of great benefit to the district. It is equally clear that, if it does not have a strong positive effect, the district would need to underwrite the program with additional school taxes. But will the program really prove to be one that produces the "strong positive effect" required or will it lead to one of the less desirable consequences? After much thought, reflection, and consultation with his staff, and upon the basis of his knowledge of the New Nursery School program, Mr. Brown forms a professional judgment about the probability of occurrence of each of the four outcomes. He feels very uncertain about these subjective and personal estimates, but clearly he must deal with such probabilities. These estimates represent the best that he can do to rationally assess the possible outcomes under the uncertainty in the situation he faces. His personal probability estimates are:

The program would have "a small negative effect"...........1
The program would have "a small positive effect"............1
The program would have "a moderate positive effect"........4
The program would have "a strong positive effect"..........4

Mr. Brown then takes the next logical step to reach a conclusion about what action to take. He weighs the consequences of each possible outcome by his estimate of the probability of the outcome occurring. The results are an expected "payoff" of —*$360,000 per year*[17] *if he installs the head-start program and $0 if he does not install it.* Clearly at this point, Mr. Brown cannot visualize himself trying to defend before his board the proposition of installing the head-start program in his district. Yet he dislikes the possibility that, by taking no action, he could lose the opportunity to have a program that would be of great benefit to the children in his district and one that has a good chance (four to ten) to "pay off." Here is where the value of further information about the potential of the New Nursery School becomes very clear. Mr. Brown knows that a good evaluation study of the effects of a program such as that represented by the New Nursery School would be of assistance to him in reaching his decision by reducing some of the uncertainty he has about the effects of the new program, but such a study would necessarily have its costs. Would investment in such a study be worth the costs?

Inquiry reveals that he can contract with a respected firm for an evaluation study of the effectiveness of the New Nursery School (as it might be adapted and installed in *his* district) for the sum of $100,000. The question at this point is whether he can justify recommending to the board that it enter into such a contract. Could the investment of $100,000 before deciding *not* to install the program be defended? Before actually having the results of the evaluation study, the best anyone can do is again to make use of the best professional judgment about its probable outcomes and their implications. Relying upon his past experience and the assistance of his staff, Mr. Brown makes the following estimates of the probable outcomes of the evaluation study:

Positive 6
Mixed 3
Negative 1

Thus, Mr. Brown and his staff expect that an evaluation study of the

17. $(.1 \times -\$5.3M) + (.1 \times -\$2.7M) + (.4 \times -\$1.4M) + (.4 \times \$2.5M)$
$= -\$.36M$.

adaptation of the New Nursery School program will indicate that the study will have positive effects rather than negative ones, but again he is not certain. Positive outcomes of the study were defined by Mr. Brown to mean that at least 90 per cent of the findings of the evaluation study would be interpretable as favorable. He would regard as negative an outcome for which 50 per cent or more of the indications from the study pointed in negative directions. Mixed outcomes then include all the outcomes between these two extremes. The question remains, however, as to how the three types of outcomes of the evaluation study are related to the four consequences of installing the program. Again, Mr. Brown relies upon his prior experience and professional judgment as he systematically re-assigns probabilities to each of the four consequences—but this time probabilities that are *conditional* upon each of the three outcomes of the contemplated study. His conditional probabilities are as follows:

TABLE 8

IF: ↓ STUDY OUTCOMES	THEN: → A Small Negative Effect	CONSEQUENCES A Small Positive Effect	A Moderate Positive Effect	A Strong Positive Effect
Positive......	.0	.1	.3	.6
Mixed........	.1	.1	.7	.1
Negative.....	.6	.2	.1	.1

At this point, Mr. Brown decides to use a device called a "decision tree," not only to make it easier for himself to follow the process of his decision-making, but also in order better to present his case to the board. (See Figure 1.)

Let us follow some of the branching along Mr. Brown's tree to trace the implications of the various choices he might make. On the one hand, if he were to decide to forego the evaluation study and install the head-start program and then it should turn out that the program actually had a small negative effect, his "payoff" would be the loss of $5.3 million per year. As has been noted, should he use his best guess of the probability of the four consequences without benefit of the evaluation, he would *expect* to lose $.36 million per year. Clearly, the choice of not installing the program and thus risking neither a gain nor a loss ($0 payoff) is the more rational one. On the other hand, if he were to invest $100,000 for an evaluation and install the program *only if* the study produced "positive"

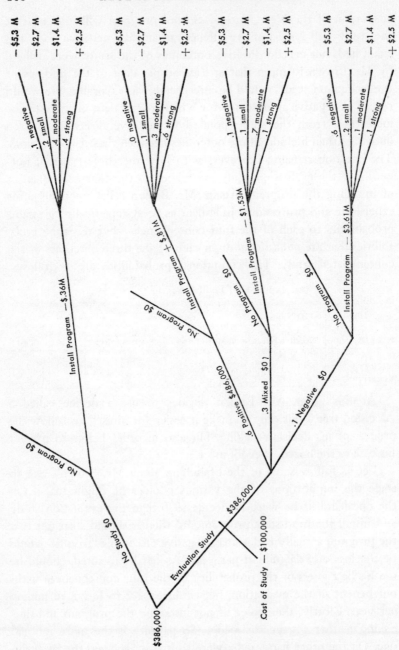

FIG. 1.—The decision tree drawn from the data presented.

results, he would expect to gain $.81 million as the "payoff." Note, however, that should the program, despite the indications of the evaluation study, actually have a negative effect, the consequences are still the same, i.e., a loss of $5.3 million. But this is not what he can reasonably expect to be the outcome, should the study be positive, and, furthermore, he expects the evaluation study to be positive (0.6). His expectation, with the benefit of knowing the results of the evaluation study before he makes a final decision, is to gain $.48 million rather than to lose $.36 million. How can this be so? The answer is that he has a means of taking a second look at the decision before he chooses, a look provided by the outcome of the evaluation study.

The results of the analysis depicted by Mr. Brown's decision tree lead him to recommend to his board that $100,000 be invested in an evaluation study of an adaptation of the New Nursery School program for his district and further, that, if the study yields positive results, the board install the program throughout the district. He notes that, if the study is undertaken and if the results are positive, the district can expect to save approximately $486,000 per year by installing the program district-wide. If the evaluation study yields negative results, then, as a result of having invested $100,000, the district can avoid the mistake of undertaking a program which would prove to be much more costly.

It is important at this point to stress the fact that Mr. Brown's conclusions concern what *probably* would happen and not what actually *will* happen. This is a characteristic of all decisions that require action to be taken in *uncertain* situations. It is also important to note that this particular scenario of Mr. Brown's procedure in making this decision is much simplified and does not reflect fully the complexity or the power of statistical decision theory. It does, however, illustrate the framework within which educational evaluation studies can be viewed. This framework quite clearly is not the framework of research in which conventions designated by such concepts as "level of significance" (i.e., the .01 level or .05 level) are employed as guidelines in interpreting the results, the prime purpose of which is to add to the store of verified knowledge of the general orderliness in nature.

Evaluation of evaluation studies based on the statistical decision theory framework is made in terms of the "payoff" value of the information the study yields in a specific decision situation. Nothing about this framework detracts from the need to design and carry out evaluation studies with care and precision. The better (i.e., the more relevant, precise, unbiased, accurate, complete, etc.) the information yielded by the evaluation study, the more value it is likely to have for the decision-maker who incorporates the information into his personal estimates of the probability of the occurrence of uncertain outcomes or events. Thus, in this respect, good research studies and good evaluation studies share common territory.

Summary and Outcomes

Studies with the objective of evaluating educational programs share much common territory with research studies in education but cannot be viewed simply as a subset or special type of research studies. To do so would imply that evaluation studies be subjected to the same criteria of excellence that are applied to research studies. The purposes served by the two types of studies are not identical and diverge most sharply at those points at which *value* and *choice* become central issues. Concerns with value and utility are generic to evaluation but do not play as important a role in research, even to the point of deliberately being excluded or denied as relevant. In using, as an example, parts of an evaluation study of the New Nursery School, we have seen that there are many common points of interest and method between evaluation studies and research studies. Progress on the part of one can facilitate progress on the part of the other, but they have distinctly different roles to play. It is to be regretted that evaluation studies have earned the reputation of being poorly conceived and executed research. Despite the fact that precision, care, discipline, and logical thought are marks of "good" evaluation as well as of "good" research, there is no requirement that evaluation studies must be judged on the same basis as that on which research studies are now conventionally judged. It is suggested that the criterion of the worth of an evaluation study is to be found in its contribution to a rational decision process in situations in which it is necessary to estimate the probability of a desirable but uncertain outcome of an action chosen from a number of alternative actions.

If we accept the proposition that the basic reason for undertaking an evaluation study is to develop information that will assist a decision-maker in choosing rationally among alternative courses of action, then the value of an evaluation study is to be viewed from a perspective quite different from that of a research study. The need to act (inaction is also an act in the world of the decision-maker) and then to live with the consequences of the action taken is not an overriding concern of the researcher (particularly in his conduct of research) but it is a concern of the decision-maker. From the point of view of the decision-maker, "refuting a null hypothesis" carries little or no useful meaning, since for him to know that he *cannot* reasonably consider some situation or condition (which is not stated in the hypothesis) provides little guidance in the choice he must make. Confidence in a conclusion, as represented by the research convention implied by the general acceptance of the ".05 or .01 probability level" as the criteria for "belief" of a research finding, is a luxury a decision-maker seldom can afford. Rather more frequently he faces situations where any information more dependable than that provided by a "flip of the coin" is desperately needed. The concept of "sampling" a domain of problems, of which the unique problem he faces in making a particular choice is only one case, is simply not applicable to the decision situation but is the foundation of research design.

We have suggested that statistical decision theory provides a framework for evaluation studies. Within this framework, an evaluation study becomes a process of acquiring further information (or new information, at least from the point of view of the person making the decision) that can be used by the decision-maker as a conditional modifier of his present information. The decision-maker's probability estimates of the consequences of his contemplated acts can be changed or modified as a direct result of expectations regarding the outcomes of an evaluation study. The outcomes in turn are uncertain but also have an estimable probability. This fact makes it possible for decision-makers to step back a step and make a reasonable decision about whether an evaluation study would likely be worth what it costs. Thus, we see that the value of performing an evaluation study is determined by the same criteria that are used to judge the consequences of major choices of action confronting the decision-maker. This criterion is *not* the criterion of the research worker who finds his "payoff" in the creation of "new knowledge" but is the "payoff" in the world of the decision-maker.

The consequence of the differences between the proper function of evaluation studies and research studies is not to be found in differences in the subject interest or in the methods of inquiry of the researcher and of the evaluator. It is to be found in the manner in which the outcomes of the two types of studies are used and regarded.

CHAPTER X

The Uses of Educational Evaluation in the Development of Programs, Courses, Instructional Materials and Equipment, Instructional and Learning Procedures, and Administrative Arrangements

JOHN C. FLANAGAN

For many years now, change and innovation have been key words in American education. The most notable trend in this area in recent years has been the growing insistence of administrators and other leaders on quality and improvement in education rather than on mere change. The systematic evaluation of new developments has supplied the basis for insuring that new developments represent genuine improvements. The over-all comparison of a new approach with a more conventional one is currently being referred to as a "summative evaluation." The application of systematic procedures to provide the basis for important decisions regarding the components of a new program during the process of development is termed "formative evaluation." Thus, evaluation during the developmental program is formative evaluation, and the final evaluation of the program resulting from the developmental work is summative evaluation. In the present state of knowledge regarding the principles and practices of education, it is clear that formative evaluation represents a much more powerful tool than summative evaluation to anyone wishing to improve education.

Although the logical requirements for sound evaluation are the same as they always have been, developments in mathematical statistics and operations research have placed greater emphasis on certain aspects of evaluation. The development of a sophisticated decision-theory has broadened the aim of the evaluator from a simple determination of the existence of a relationship to a comprehensive consideration of all of the factors in the situation and their effect on the consequences of making various decisions in terms of the outcomes. The concepts of decision-theory have required a more rigorous comparison of several possible developments on the basis of a systematic tabulation of benefits and costs associated with each of the possibilities. This has tended to broaden the view of program-developers to emphasize the effectiveness of the total system with respect to the achievement of all desired outcomes rather than the development of solutions for specific aspects of a total program considered out of the context of the complete system.

A variety of procedures developed in accordance with these basic concepts have been applied in many fields, and these applications have been given various names such as "cost effectiveness," "systems analysis," and, in the federal government, "planning-programing-budgeting." In all cases the essential elements of a modern approach to evaluation include: (*a*) the definition of all of the outcomes of the system, including the objectives or aims and also possible unplanned effects; (*b*) the systematic analysis and study of various possible procedures for achieving the objectives as defined (The analysis should include the appraisal of all conditions which might affect costs and benefits resulting from the various decisions which might be made. A very important part of this analysis is the detailed description of the inputs of the system. These inputs in the field of education consist primarily of characteristics of the students. However, teaching staff, facilities, instructional materials and methods, observation and measurement procedures, and available technological assistance must also be included); and (*c*) a plan and decision based on this analysis and an over-all evaluation of the final program.

An important current development in evaluation is to identify objectives very precisely and to assess accurately the extent to which they have been achieved. It is not adequate to indicate that we want a student to become a good citizen. It is essential that we make explicit the specific behaviors which result in a person's being designated a good citizen. On the basis of this type of detailed definition of a good citizen, we must then establish procedures for observing and recording the behavior of the individual in the types of situations so defined.

Another identifiable trend in modern evaluation is the separate evaluation of objectives. Composites require the arbitrary assignment of weights for each of the specific objectives. Since there is not universal agreement on appropriate weights, an evaluation program which provides separate measures has much more universal applicability. A parallel development is the trend towards the separate evaluation of each student. Modern educational programs are developed in terms of separate objectives for individuals of various types. Thus, skill and appreciation in music and art might be of very slight importance for one individual, but of great importance for another. Similarly, knowledge of internal combustion engines might be very important for some individuals but of little value to others. The emphasis in evaluation programs in the future will not be on how well a new educational program has done for the average student but rather on how well the educational program has developed the unique talents and met the specific needs of each individual in preparing him for his most satisfying and appropriate role in society.

To illustrate the application of modern evaluation procedures in developmental programs, several examples are discussed below in some detail. Several of these examples are taken from studies of the American Institutes for Research in the Behavioral Sciences because of the author's familiarity with these studies and because they are not well known to readers of the educational literature.

Evaluation in a National Assessment Program

Following a series of planning meetings in 1964, work was begun in 1965 on defining educational objectives and developing assessment procedures to evaluate American education. This work was done under the general supervision of the Exploratory Committee on Assessing the Progress of Education, of which Ralph W. Tyler was chairman. Grants from the Carnegie Corporation and the Ford Foundation supported the developmental phases of this program. The Palo Alto Office of the American Institutes for Research developed the educational objectives in the field of citizenship. The report prepared by Campbell and Nichols describes the procedures used in developing these objectives.[1] An initial set of citizenship

1. Vincent N. Campbell and Daryl G. Nichols, "Citizenship Objectives" (Report No. AIR-E62-10/65-RP2 [Palo Alto, Calif.: American Institutes for Research, 1965]).

objectives was constructed for various age levels by reviewing previous discussions of the topic and discussing these with teachers. To evaluate and revise this list, more than a thousand critical incidents on citizenship were collected from fourth-, eighth-, and twelfth-grade students in the public schools, from advanced college students, and from members of adult-education classes. The revised list of citizenship objectives based on these materials was submitted to review by an advisory committee consisting of scholars and leaders in civic education, educational measurement, and related social sciences. Resulting objectives received a final review by panels of concerned laymen throughout the country to insure that the objectives represented important common goals.

To develop methods for assessing the achievement of these educational objectives, the investigators used the method of explicit rationales. For example, the first objective for nine-year-olds was "to show concern for the welfare and dignity of others," and the first behavior listed under this objective was "to treat all individuals with respect." Each rationale consisted of a description reporting specific behaviors observed as evidences of behavior in accordance with this objective and as examples indicating failure to have achieved this objective. The other section of the rationale included an analysis of the behavior and recommendations for procedures for assessing the behavior.

The rationales and the assessment procedures developed from them were reviewed by various groups before they were tried out on an experimental basis. The development of the procedures for administration of the assessment program included the experimental evaluation of several critical features of the program. A factor which was carefully evaluated was the method of administering the items. The procedure of having the subject read a question and then answer it was specifically compared with that of giving the question by an interviewer and having the subject answer it orally, and these were also compared with the procedure of using a tape to give the question and also to record the response. Important differences were found in the results obtained from the various methods with certain types of students. These appeared to result mainly from differences in reading skills and vocabulary.

In general, the approach to assessment which was developed in this program was based on the assumption that the most meaningful measures of children's achievement of citizenship objectives are their typical behaviors in the home, at school, and in the larger community. Therefore, the larger portion of these assessments are of behaviors which can be observed, reported, or recorded. The measures include overt behaviors and also knowledges, values, and ways of thinking. Although the assessment of behavior is strongly favored, it is believed that some of the knowledges, values, and ways of thinking which are fundamental to good citizenship have little chance of being exhibited by a nine-year-old child in his typical environment. They are, nonetheless, important as preparation for adult activities, and it is therefore proposed that they be measured as bases for good citizenship rather than as good citizenship itself.

Evaluation in the Development of Instructional Materials and Methods

An example of a modern approach to the use of evaluation in developing instructional materials is provided by a project recently completed by Markle in the Palo Alto Office of the American Institutes for Research.[2] The objective of the program was to develop a $7\frac{1}{2}$-hour first-aid course which would prepare people for Red Cross certification in basic first aid. With the assistance of the American Red Cross, the objectives of the course were developed, including approximately 500 items of specific information, skills, and concepts. These were based on the analysis of thousands of accidents by the Red Cross and were grouped under twenty-two main headings. After preparing the test, a sample of persons typical of those who would be taking the course was assembled and given the test without any training. It was found that this group, without specific training in first aid, was able to answer about 29 per cent of the items correctly. The application of the test to persons who had just received training from one of the previously developed first-aid courses indicated that they were able on the average to answer correctly between 40 per cent and 50 per cent of the items.

After removing the items known to nearly all of the typical

2. David G. Markle, "The Development of the Bell System First Aid and Personal Safety Course" (Report No. AIR-E81-4/67-FR [Palo Alto, Calif.: American Institutes for Research, 1967]).

trainees, the information and skills were grouped into a series of topical units. For each unit the developmental program consisted of preparing a preliminary version of the program, trying it out on typical trainees one at a time, and testing their achievement of the objectives using the relevant questions. Several weeks of work of this type led to a fairly standard format for each of the units, consisting of one or more short instructional films, a short session of practicing newly taught skills, and a study session with a workbook.

In the case of each of these materials, trials were made using preliminary versions with small groups who were immediately tested to see whether or not the materials were effective. Ineffective materials were revised and the new units tried out again. Motion picture films were shot, edited, tried out and re-edited and frequently the cycle was repeated with another filming, editing, and tryout. The process grew more efficient as experience in predicting effectiveness provided better initial decisions. The final 7½-hour training program resulted in the trainees answering, on the average, 81 per cent of the items correctly. Nearly all trainees under the new training program obtained higher scores than did any of the trainees under the previous programs.

An interesting aspect of this program was its efficiency. Since only 7½ hours were available, it was regarded as very important not only that each unit of the training program be effective, but also that the training program be the shortest that would be effective. A deficiency of the typical summative evaluation is that it indicates whether or not the individual has achieved the objective, but not whether he has wasted a large fraction of his time in the training program. To achieve a program which was as efficient as possible, a systematic effort was made to develop units which seemed likely to err on the side of insufficient learning. By starting with a program from which the students did not quite learn and adding small increments, it was believed that an effective program was provided which was very close to the minimum requirement with respect to time.

A second example of development of a training course is provided by a study recently completed for the same company by the

Pittsburgh Office of the American Institutes for Research.[3] The aim of the study was to develop a more efficient self-instructional fundamentals training course for a large subgroup of employees. The first phase of the study was to develop the training objectives for the new course. This was done by observing the men at work on their jobs and analyzing the requirements of the job. The course in use at the start of this developmental program required forty-five working days to complete. On the basis of the study of the important job requirements, a first trial course was developed requiring twenty days. This trial course was a relatively conventional lecture-demonstration course presented to a group of students at a fixed pace, and it differed from conventional courses in two important ways: (a) students made many written responses during lectures and demonstrations, and (b) tests were administered after each lesson to determine the lesson's effectiveness. These procedures made possible the evaluation of each lesson and, because of the written responses during lectures and demonstrations, of each part of each lesson.

On the basis of these results, a new course was developed which was completely self-instructional. Individual students could work through the course at their own pace and finish the course whenever they had successfully completed all of the assignments. The trainees were able to complete this new self-instructional course in ten to thirteen days while still maintaining the very high standard of performance on the tests achieved by the group which required twenty days.

On the basis of a careful analysis of the results of each of the experimental students on the second revision of the course, a third revision was prepared. In this final revision an effort was made to increase training efficiency by reducing the training time whereever it seemed possible. The new training course was tried out with twenty-four individuals proceeding at their own pace. Two finished it in six days and one required fifteen days. The median number of days required was nine. In the revised course, 91 per cent of all of the scores on unit tests by the twenty-four students were

3. The study was directed by Short. See Jerry G. Short et al., "Strategies of Training Development" (Report No. AIR-E97-2/68-FR [Palo Alto, Calif.: American Institutes for Research, 1968]).

above 90 per cent. As in the case of the first-aid course, an effort was made to maintain the students' interest and motivation. In the fundamentals training course, this was done by using tapes, handbooks, printed materials, and special equipment. At the end of the course, in response to a questionnaire, 86 per cent of the students stated that it was the best course they had taken, and 14 per cent said that it was better than most courses. None of the students said that it was average or below. This was regarded as important, since the students worked for approximately two weeks on a relatively independent basis.

The very great improvement in the efficiency of these training courses through the use of intensive evaluation of the effectiveness of each unit of instruction presents an excellent model and challenge to typical educational instructional programs.

Evaluation in the Development of an Educational Program

As the last example, the use of evaluation in the planning and development of an educational program will be described. The first step in the developmental program was the formulation and administration of a comprehensive two-day battery of tests of aptitude, ability, and achievement along with a detailed inventory of background characteristics and plans which was administered to 440,000 students in secondary schools throughout the United States in March of 1960. This study was supported by the United States Office of Education and other government agencies and was greatly aided by the effective co-operation of the 1353 secondary schools included in the sample. The study is called Project TALENT and its design includes the follow-up of this large group of students one, five, ten, and twenty years after their graduation from high school.

This study provides very important evaluative information with respect to both student characteristics and the deficiencies of current educational programs. One of the most important student characteristics which relates to the development of any educational program is ability to read and understand verbal materials. The results from the Project TALENT reading comprehension tests are reported in terms of the student's ability to read and understand the writings of ten standard literary authors and also the contents of ten popular American magazines.[4]

It is difficult to evaluate and communicate in meaningful and precise terms a description of the student's understanding of these materials. Each of the selections for a particular author was judged to be typical of his writing. For each such selection, the items testing comprehension included: a very simple point, a point of average difficulty for the passage, an item measuring general understanding of the passage, an item on the most difficult point in the passage, and an item measuring a student's appreciation, application, or ability to make an inference based on comprehension of some aspect of the passage. For these items, it appears that a criterion of 50 per cent of the items correct for a particular author would represent a minimally satisfactory understanding of the author.

Using this criterion, it was found that about 60 per cent of the ninth-grade students and 85 per cent of the twelfth-grade students can read and understand the writings of Louisa May Alcott fairly well. The corresponding figures for Robert Louis Stevenson's writings were 42 per cent for Grade IX students and 72 per cent for Grade XII students. They were 17 per cent and 44 per cent respectively for Rudyard Kipling's writings, and 12 per cent and 35 per cent for those of Joseph Conrad. For the writings of Thomas Mann, the most difficult author of the set of ten, less than 1 per cent of the students in Grade IX achieved a minimally satisfactory understanding of the author, and only 4 per cent of the students in Grade XII achieved this level of understanding.

Applying the same criterion of understanding to the passages from the magazines, it was found that 75 per cent of the Grade IX students and 92 per cent of the Grade XII students have a satisfactory comprehension of what is in the movie magazines. However, the very popular *Reader's Digest* passages were understood in terms of this criterion by only 18 per cent of the Grade IX students and 45 per cent of the Grade XII students. The understanding of *Time* magazine was even less, with only 7 per cent of the ninth-grade students and 25 per cent of the twelfth-grade students

4. John C. Flanagan *et al.*, *The American High-School Student* (Final Report, Cooperative Research Project No. 635, U.S. Office of Education [Pittsburgh: Project TALENT Office, University of Pittsburgh, 1964]).

attaining the criterion degree of comprehension. On the passages from the *Saturday Review*, less than 1 per cent of the ninth-grade students and only 4 per cent of the twelfth-grade students achieved what might be considered an acceptable degree of comprehension of typical paragraphs.

The foregoing results refer to important practical goals. To check on the current reading performance of these students, they were asked specific questions. That the current textbooks are unsuited to a large proportion of the students was attested to by the students' answers to the question, "How often do you read material over and over again without really understanding what you have read?" Sixteen per cent of the boys and 17 per cent of the girls in Grade XII reported that this happened to them most of the time. In this twelfth-grade group, an additional 18 per cent of both boys and girls reported that this happened about half the time.

The ability to learn the meaning of new words or words in a different language is one of the most fundamental in our educational program. Project TALENT gave a list of twenty-four words in a new language and asked students to associate them with the English equivalent, which was also shown. It was found that ninth-grade students were able to learn the meanings of 10.4 words on the average, or about 2.5 words a minute. The twelfth-grade students were able to associate the new words with English words more effectively in this four-minute period. They obtained 12.3 correct answers, or about three words a minute.

Although teachers and others associated with education have always been aware of the very wide individual differences in students within a particular grade, the Project TALENT findings include some very dramatic data regarding such differences. A sample of ninth-grade Project TALENT students was retested in 1963 when they reached the twelfth grade. For English and social studies it was found that about 30 per cent of the students in Grade IX exceeded the performance of the average of this group of students in Grade XII. For most of the tests, the gains between the ninth- and twelfth-grade tests were between 0.4 and 0.8 of a standard deviation. Only the test on information regarding literature showed a gain by the students of more than a standard deviation for this three-year period.

These data demonstrate very clearly that a substantial fraction of the Grade IX students have the ability and information of the typical Grade XII student and, conversely, that a large proportion of the Grade XII students are at a level more typical of ninth-grade students. These evaluative data provide further evidence of the need for individualizing instruction in schools.

Another important student characteristic evaluated by the Project TALENT study was the relative stability of some of the basic abilities over this three-year period. The vocabulary test showed the greatest stability between the scores of persons tested at the end of Grade IX and again at the end of Grade XII. The rank order of the scores of the students on the second test was essentially the same as that of the scores for the first test when allowance was made for sampling errors in the scores. The next most stable measure over this three-year period was the arithmetic reasoning test. The correlation coefficient between the two sets of scores was about .90 when corrected for attenuation. For a large number of the other measures of ability, the correlation coefficient, corrected for attenuation, was on the order of .80. These measures included such variables as reading comprehension, abstract reasoning, visualization in three dimensions, mechanical reasoning, and creativity. The correlation coefficients indicating the stabilities of the tests measuring speed and accuracy of arithmetic computation and clerical checking were surprisingly low.

Several studies, such as that of Super and Overstreet [5] and the survey by Coleman et al.,[6] have corroborated the Project TALENT findings regarding the unrealistic plans of students in today's secondary schools. In the Super and Overstreet study, it was found that more than half of a group of high-school students wished to enter occupations that appeared inappropriate in terms of the intellectual level required. Similarly, Coleman reported that, of a group of Grade XII students, about 48 per cent planned jobs which were labeled as professional, managerial, official, or technical and

5. Donald E. Super and Phoebe L. Overstreet, *The Vocational Maturity of Ninth-Grade Boys* (New York: Bureau of Publications, Teachers College, Columbia University, 1960).

6. James Coleman et al., *Equality of Educational Opportunity* (Washington: U.S. National Center for Educational Statistics, 1966).

only 18 per cent planned jobs in the semi-skilled and unskilled categories.

In the Project TALENT study, it was found that only 19 per cent of the boys who indicated in the tenth grade that they were planning one of thirty occupations as a career following graduation reported the same plans three years later. For the boys indicating their career plans in Grade XII, only 31 per cent reported the same plans one year later. For the girls, the per cent reporting the same plans was about 10 points higher in each case. This seemed to be due to a considerable extent to the restricted set of choices at both times. Three careers—housewife, office worker, and teacher—accounted for about two-thirds of the plans one year after graduation.

The lack of information and understanding about careers appears to be reflected in the students' reports as to the occupations they would most like or dislike. When asked to disregard educational requirements, salary, social standing, or other factors, the twelfth-grade boys indicated they would like most to be an aviator, a professional athlete, a president of a large company, an Air Force officer, or a rancher.

Additional evaluative data regarding a typical current educational program was provided by a study carried out in 1965-66 by the American Institutes for Research. The purpose of the study was to discover ways in which the educational program could be improved in a particular school system. The main points included in the evaluative study were: (a) the learning abilities of the students and their achievement in comparison to comparable school districts in the state and nation; (b) the appropriateness of the subject matter and the instructional methods for individual students; (c) the effectiveness of the staff and teachers in helping the students to select and work toward appropriate goals; (d) the extent to which the students are given an opportunity to develop a sense of responsibility for their own behavior and are stimulated to learn beyond minimum requirements; (e) the provisions for the education of children with exceptional needs.

The first evaluation compared the school system with other school systems serving parents with similar occupational roles in terms of the average achievement of the students on standardized tests. The occupational scale used was a relatively standard one running from professionals, farm owners, proprietors, managers, and clerks through skilled workers, semiskilled workers, laborers, and servants. It was found that the performance of students in various grades in the system evaluated was slightly better than students in comparable systems in both the state and the nation. The students in this school system were also compared for achievement with other groups in which the intelligence or academic aptitude scores were comparable. However, this procedure was discounted as being circular, at least in part, since many of the types of items in the intelligence or aptitude tests are quite similar to some of the kinds of items in the educational achievement tests.

An innovative procedure was used in this study with respect to the evaluation of the educational development of individual students. In each of Grades IV, VI, IX, and XII, a 10-per-cent sample of the students was selected in such a way as to be representative of the total group of students for each of these classes in terms of learning ability. For the students in this sample, various types of data were collected. These included the pertinent information in the cumulative record for each of the students, information regarding their school program which was collected by questionnaire for the Grade VI, IX, and XII students and by interview from the Grade IV students, consultation with teachers and specialists regarding some of the students' problems, and an interview with each student by the evaluator.

On the basis of all the data obtained, the evaluators answered several questions regarding the educational program. In response to the question, "Is instruction suited to the student's ability?", 82 per cent of the interviewers answered with an unqualified "yes." In 14 per cent of the cases they responded, "yes, with some exception," and in 4 per cent of the cases the answer was "no." Another evaluative judgment the interviewers were asked to make with respect to each of the students was in answer to the question, "What is the quality of student motivation for learning?" For the four classes combined, the evaluators rated the motivation for learning as outstanding or excellent for 30 per cent of the students, as fair or good for 60 per cent, and as poor or very poor for 10 per cent. It is interesting to note that there was a very definite downward trend in motivation on the part of the students in the judgment of these evaluators. For example, of the fourth-grade students, 41 per cent were rated as having excellent or outstanding motivation, and of the twelfth-grade students, only 12 per cent were rated as having excellent or outstanding motivation for learning. Other evidence suggests that this finding would be duplicated in most schools throughout the country.

As a final item for each student, the evaluator indicated the over-all effectiveness of the schools in meeting the needs of children in education and guidance. The evaluators reported that the schools were meeting the students' needs "nearly perfectly" for 25 per cent of the students, "in most respects" for 49 per cent of the students, "well in some respects and poorly in others" for 22 per cent, and either "fairly unsatisfactory" or "very poorly" for 4 per cent. The unsatisfactory evaluations were given for such reasons as the school's failure to detect a severe visual handicap, misplacement of the student, failure to provide psychological assistance, lack of remedial instruction in the early grades, and lack of personal counseling.

Although student evaluations are questionable in some respects, it seemed worthwhile to ask these students whether the instruction in a particular class made them want to learn more or not want to learn more about the subject than was required in the course. In replying to this question at the ninth-grade level, the only subject in which nearly half the students felt the instruction made them want to learn more was science. The subject making the poorest showing in this respect was English in which less than one in five students indicated they were motivated to learn more than was required.

In addition to studying a sample of the students in schools, it was believed that useful evaluative information could be obtained from recent graduates. All of the students who had graduated in the classes of 1960 and 1964 in the high school in this system were sent questionnaires in the summer of 1965. With the aid of reminders and further follow-ups over the next six weeks, 84 per cent of the 753 members of the class of 1964, and 72 per cent of the 429 graduates in the class of 1960 returned completed questionnaires. These high rates of return, plus the consistency of the findings from the two classes, indicate considerable reliance can be placed on the findings reported. One of the items on the questionnaire asked students to complete the sentence, "The best thing provided for me by this high school was ————." In both classes the most frequent responses were "a good basic education," and "good preparation for college." In both classes, another frequent response was "good, competent, interested teachers."

Another item in the questionnaire asked that they complete the sentence, "The main thing I believe I needed which was not provided by this high school was ————." Approximately 25 per cent of the students in each class indicated that "guidance and counseling" was the most important unfilled need in their high-school education. The only other comment from the two classes which was made by an appreciable proportion of the students was "assistance in learning how to study." The other replies were scattered over a wide variety of needs.

These graduates were also asked to provide an over-all evaluation of the preparation they received in the schools by answering the following question: "Immediately following graduation from high school, how well do you believe you were prepared to enter into your new role as a paid worker or as a student?" About 30 per cent of each of the classes indicated that they were very well prepared; 45 per cent in each class indicated that they were fairly well prepared; the remaining 25 per cent in the two classes indicated that they were generally prepared but lacked some specific preparation, or that they were not well prepared.

On the basis of a systematic study of all available data from the students and of observations and studies of the curriculum and staff, it was indicated that the greatest improvement in the school program could be expected from focusing on the two concepts of individualization of instruction and increased student orientation, responsibility, motivation, and maturity in planning and preparing for important life roles.

The evaluative data reported in the foregoing paragraphs provided the basis for entering into the planning phase of a developmental educational program. This program, which has been called "A Program for Learning in Accordance with Needs" (Project PLAN), is aimed at correcting some of the present major deficiencies of the American educational system.[7] In accordance with the procedures for developing a system described at the outset of this discussion, the first step in the program was the definition of the objectives of the system. In simple terms, the objective of the proposed system is to make it possible for each individual to obtain those educational experiences which will develop his talents and potentials in such a way as to enable him to achieve maximum satisfactions in his life's chosen activities and roles.

Two points should be stressed here: first, that this educational system clearly focuses on the needs and development of the individual as a unique person and, second, that it is assumed that there is general agreement that the focus of the schools should be broadened to include three major types of goals for each individual. These goals are: (a) to assist him to plan and prepare for an appropriate occupational role, (b) to prepare him for the responsibilities of citizenship, including his personal and social development, and (c) to emphasize those aspects of general education which will help him find deeply satisfying activities for the anticipated increased time available for leisure and recreation.

In developing the specific implications of these three broad objectives, the project staff has based its first detailed program of objectives on the published literature of committees and leaders in education. The ideas derived from this source have been submitted to review by scholars, behavioral scientists, and teachers and administrators in several co-operating school districts.

There are several subsystems in this over-all program for education. Perhaps the most important of these subsystems is the one aimed at developing each individual's ability to take responsibility for, to plan for, and to manage his own learning program in accordance with his needs. This subsystem can be described in terms of six objectives, each of which should be independently evaluated.

(1) Each individual should know and understand the status of his development with respect to abilities, interests, and values. The understanding and appreciation of these facts should include an understanding of individual differences and the basic principles of

7. John C. Flanagan, "Functional Education for the Seventies," *Phi Delta Kappan*, XLIX (September, 1967), 27-33.

learning. This would relate both to the stability of such differences and to the extent to which abilities can be modified. It is proposed that this knowledge and understanding be evaluated by using tests of information and interpretation of these types of data.

(2) Each individual should be familiar with the variety of opportunities in the world of work. This knowledge should include an understanding of the educational requirements for various occupational roles, of special competencies necessary for certain occupations, and of the importance of each available role in relation to the needs of society. This knowledge and the ability to apply it would be tested directly in terms of information and application types of test questions.

(3) Each individual should have a full understanding of his role as a social being, including interpersonal relations with others, the basic concepts of and requirements for effective human relationships, and his responsibilities and rights as a citizen. The sense of responsibility as a citizen and the social behavior of each student would be measured in terms of observations of behavior in relevant real-life situations, by means of situational performance tests involving role-playing, and in terms of the understanding of civic and social regulations.

(4) Each individual should be aware of the great variety of opportunities for leisure and recreational activities and should understand and appreciate the role of such activities in a satisfying life experience. This would be evaluated in terms of both the essential information and observations with respect to the student's ability to select activities which provide a high degree of satisfaction to him.

(5) Each individual should develop appropriate skills and procedures for solving specific problems and for making plans and decisions. These skills would be measured in terms of the individual's ability to solve realistic practical problems and to make appropriate plans and decisions when given the relevant information.

(6) Each individual should accept the responsibility for, plan, and manage his own development with respect to learning and personal and social behaviors. The focus in this objective is on applying the skills and procedures listed in the fifth objective to his own personal situation. The principal procedure for measuring the

attainment of this objective would involve presenting the individual with the facts regarding the personal characteristics and background of several hypothetical individuals, each of whom represented a composite of a large number of persons included in the Project TALENT sample. The consequences of various specific decisions and plans for this person could thus be evaluated in terms of the actual experiences of these students who had been followed up.

A second important subsystem has the function of providing learning methods and materials to enable each student to have the opportunity to develop those skills and abilities and acquire the information and wisdom which will enable him to make full use of his talents. The program is focused on the twelve years of elementary and secondary school. The effectiveness of this aspect of the program will be evaluated in terms of the following three objectives.

(1) Each individual should learn new skills and knowledge at his own difficulty level and at his own rate. In current practice, much time is wasted because students are asked to learn materials which they already know or materials which are much too difficult for them. The achievement of this objective will be evaluated in terms of the number of new objectives mastered in a given period of time, such as a semester or a year.

(2) Each individual should develop those skills and abilities and acquire that information which is most appropriate for him during a given period of time. Under present circumstances, many students spend a large amount of time acquiring information and skills which are of little value to them. It is very important that they be given an opportunity to learn those things most relevant to their plans. The evaluation of the effectiveness of the program in assisting students to attain this objective will be in terms of the number of the planned objectives in a student's program which are achieved in a given period of time.

(3) Each individual should be given the opportunity to learn from materials and from the use of methods which are most efficient for him. It is believed that current educational programs lose much by not taking full advantage of the interests and specific learning styles of the students. The evaluation of the attainment of this

objective will be in terms of the amount of time required to reach the specific objectives.

The third subsystem in this program of education provides measures of the student's progress in terms of placement tests, tests for particular units, and survey tests on objectives related to several units. Each individual needs to be given knowledge as he proceeds through his educational development concerning the extent to which he has achieved specific educational objectives in his program. The various types of assessment procedures used in this subsystem of the educational program will be evaluated in terms of the extent to which they provide valid measures of the objectives indicated.

The fourth subsystem of this educational program relates to classroom learning conditions, including the effectiveness of the teacher. This subsystem has as its objective the provision of effective learning conditions for each individual. This objective is to be evaluated by observing the learning progress of each individual and recording evidences of interference and facilitation of the learning process. It will also be assessed in terms of the comparative achievement of students with similar abilities in the various classrooms.

The fifth and final subsystem of the educational program relates to the storage of information about both the individuals and the materials in the program in such a way that they can be readily matched to facilitate the immediate and long-range planning of the educational development of each individual. Stated as an objective, this proposes that each individual should be able to determine the consequences of each of the various choices open to him for both his immediate and his long-range development in terms of the experience of persons having similar attributes who have made such choices in the past. Evaluation of this subsystem will be in terms of the validity of the predictions given the individuals regarding the various alternatives open to them.

Some Principles Regarding the Use of Evaluation in the Development of Educational Programs

The major trends in using evaluation in developing educational programs are related to the current focusing of educational efforts on the individual and the transfer of responsibility to the student for planning and carrying out an educational development program. Evaluation programs that center on the school district, the teacher, or some other unit have occupied the attention of educators in the past. The new focus on the individual requires an intensive planning program in order to develop suitable educational objectives for a specific student. The student's possible roles and activities in society must be studied carefully in terms of his abilities, interests, values, and potentials. Only on the basis of this type of thorough and systematic study can a set of educational objectives suitable to his development be established and organized. The data for establishing such objectives must come from a careful study of the behaviors of many persons in situations such as those contemplated by the individual student. On the basis of the experience of persons with known characteristics, predictions can be made regarding the suitability of the role or activity for the planning individual.

Educational programs for developing the necessary skills and abilities can then be developed by applying a simple procedure of assessing the student with respect to such skills and abilities, using an instructional program to develop the desired changes in skills and abilities, and reassessing the skills and abilities. Clearly, those procedures which produce the desired results with the least effort in terms of time and costs will be preferred.

Another major generalization is that, although much of the development of educational programs at the present time depends very heavily on trial and error, there is increasing attention to classifying and testing hypotheses and to generalizing, in an effort to develop a science of learning to replace present empirical methods.

Summary

This is a period of great potential for progress in American education. Such progress can only be achieved if evaluation methods are rigorously used in the development of educational programs. Too often in the past, innovation in education has involved change without real, lasting improvement. The principal steps in insuring that new developments represent improvements in the effectiveness of educational programs are outlined briefly in the following paragraphs:

(1) It is essential that the objectives of the program be clearly defined. This definition must be in terms of observable changes in the students. For efficient use of evaluation procedures in developing educational programs, it is important that the objectives of the program be stated in terms of the achievements of specific individuals. It is highly desirable that the goals be directly meaningful in terms of useful abilities and proficiencies. For clear interpretation of the significance of these changes, they must be stated in terms of their relation to the achievement of the goals of the individual with respect to systematically developed plans for his educational development.

(2) In developing an educational program, it is important that each component be separately evaluated before extensive use of this procedure is made in the total educational program. This type of evaluation is sometimes referred to as "formative" evaluation; it provides a series of decisions with respect to components of the system, as compared to a single over-all evaluation of the total system, called a "summative" evaluation. One of the important trends is the recognition that all educational programs are tentative. Therefore, a system of evaluation which provides for continuous improvement of all of the aspects of the educational program is especially important at this time.

(3) In evaluating either a component or a total educational program, it is important that evaluation be in terms of a specific educational objective with reference to a particular individual and with careful study of any possible unplanned effects of the program in addition to the objective sought. Although means or other average measures of achievement often represent useful summary measures, it is of great importance that the ultimate evaluation of the educational program be in terms of how well it is fulfilling the needs of specific individuals.

CHAPTER XI

Evaluation of Ongoing Programs in the Public School System

MALCOLM PROVUS

Introduction

To the school administrator who needs information about the effectiveness of school programs, the word "evaluation" conjures up some unpleasant memories: a report that took "too long" to prepare and overlooked the obvious while concentrating on the trite, a university consultant who proved unintelligible and eventually hostile, an investigator who got in everyone's way and never seemed able to draw definitive conclusions.

It is entirely possible that most public school evaluations are meaningless because they reflect the confusion of administrators regarding educational programs which are equally meaningless. It is also possible that most evaluators do not know their business. No doubt, the weakness of educational programs, evaluation methodology, and the training provided in institutions that prepare both administrators and evaluators are related.

Recent public school programs are marked by a lack of program control and by measured outcomes that suggest there is greater program variation within programs than between programs.[1] A recent unpublished evaluation of team teaching in a large city school system revealed forty different programs in forty different schools, none of which adhered to the essential principles of team teaching as originally conceived by the school system.[2] It is not surprising that students who had been exposed to this kind

1. Matthew B. Miles, *Innovation in Education* (New York: Bureau of Publications, Teachers College, Columbia University, 1964).

2. Esther Kresh, "Team Teaching Program, 1967 Report" (unpublished paper), 1968.

of "team teaching" for six years showed no greater growth in academic performance than did a control group.

A clause of the 1965 Elementary-Secondary Education Act established evaluation as a necessary building block in the design of American educational reform. The evaluation requirements of that act eventually may prove to have greater impact on education than the program itself. The Congress mandated that billions of dollars be spent in new ways to serve new purposes, yet there is reason to doubt that the administrative capacity exists at each level of government to insure that the money is well spent. Perhaps before we can build effective new programs, we must establish creative new ways to monitor and eventually judge the effectiveness of such programs. This capacity to evaluate programs must ultimately depend upon a management theory that utilizes pertinent, reliable information as the basis for administrative decisions.

Those of us from university research backgrounds who started out in September of 1965 to implement the congressional mandate to evaluate ESEA programs did so with good cheer: "At last," we said, "curriculum evaluation has come in to its own." We began our work by oversimplifying the problem—by attempting to determine whether new programs were better than the ones they replaced. We did not then realize that our first problem was to find out what in fact, constituted a new program. We continued our work by applying the quasi-experimental designs that had served us well in research settings. We soon found that these designs were inapplicable. And finally we settled down to grapple with the formulation of better statements of program objectives and the design of new instruments to measure these objectives— largely ignoring the constrictive influence our activity was having on people responsible for making new programs work.

There is surprisingly little theory on which to base good evaluation practice. The theoretical constructs which appear most relevant to the practitioner are derived from studies by Lippitt[3]

3. Ronald Lippitt, Jeanne Watson, and Bruce Westley, *The Dynamics of Planned Change* (New York: Harcourt, Brace, 1958).

and Miles [4] on organizational health and change; Rogers,[5] Lewin,[6] and Corey [7] on self-realization through group work; the work of Silvern [8] on functional analysis of curriculum; Wiener [9] on control and communication systems; and from Tyler's original work on curriculum-development theory.[10]

This is not to say that there is no new work in evaluation theory going on in the country today. Stufflebeam [11] and Guba [12] have published a number of papers which make substantial contributions to the understanding of institutional change and growth and provide a theoretical frame of reference for the assessment of change. However, despite the title of a new educational periodical, *Theory into Practice*, there appears to be very little linkage between program evaluation going on in public schools today and the kind of theory discussed by university theorists.

The Pittsburgh Evaluation Model

The conclusions and techniques described in this chapter are the result of an attempt to apply evaluation and management theory to the evaluation of programs in a large city school system. As a

4. Matthew B. Miles, *Change Processes in the Public Schools* (Eugene: University of Oregon, 1965).

5. Carl Rogers, "Persons or Science? A Philosophical Question," *The American Psychologist*, X (July, 1955), 267-78.

6. Kurt Lewin, "Principles of Re-education," *Human Relations in Curriculum Change*, ed. Kenneth D. Benne (New York: Dryden Press, 1951).

7. Stephen M. Corey, *Action Research to Improve School Practices* (New York: Bureau of Publications, Teachers College, Columbia University, 1953).

8. Leonard C. Silvern, *Administrative Factors Guide to Basic Analysis* (Los Angeles: Education and Training Consultants, 1965).

9. Norbert Wiener, *Cybernetics* (New York: John Wiley & Sons, 1948).

10. Ralph W. Tyler, *Basic Principles of Curriculum and Instruction* (Chicago: University of Chicago Press, 1950).

11. Daniel L. Stufflebeam, "A Depth Study of the Evaluation Requirement," *Theory into Practice*, V (June, 1966), 121-33.

12. Egon G. Guba, "Methodological Strategies for Educational Change" (paper presented to Conference on Strategies for Educational Change, Washington, D.C., November 8-10, 1965); "Evaluation and the New Media" (unpublished paper presented to the Ohio State University Annual Conference on Modern Media, Columbus, Ohio, July 6, 1962).

result of this effort, a model of program evaluation was eventually developed. It serves as the basis for most of the material presented in this chapter.[13]

The purpose of program evaluation is to determine whether to improve, maintain, or terminate a program. Evaluation is the process of (a) agreeing upon program standards, (b) determining whether a discrepancy exists between some aspect of the program and the standards governing that aspect of the program, and (c) using discrepancy information to identify the weaknesses of the program. As a practical matter, it is generally necessary for those concerned with the conduct of education to employ problem-solving techniques once the weaknesses of a program have been identified. These techniques have been widely discussed elsewhere and will be referred to by the author only to indicate their place in the usual sequence of evaluation activity.

Program standards are of two kinds: content and development. These standards are based on the generalizable content and development of educational programs. The content of programs has been classified in a useful way by systems analysts employing the notion that human activity processes inputs to produce outputs.[14] The development of educational programs has received attention from management engineers, but little has been said in their literature about the relevance of stages of program development to the generalization of program standards for evaluation purposes. It is assumed in this chapter that every educational program undergoes an evolutionary sequence of development and that evaluation must take these stages into account by applying standards governing the sequence and rate of program development.

It follows that if types of programs having different developmental characteristics exist, the development standards for these program types also will vary. Therefore, it is important that a typology of programs of varying developmental characteristics be

13. The research described was supported by grants to the author from the Bureau of Research and the Bureau of Elementary and Secondary Education, Office of Education, and the Pennsylvania State Department of Public Instruction.

14. Joseph A. Kershaw and Ronald N. McKean, *Systems Analysis and Education* (Santa Monica: The Rand Corporation, 1959).

attempted. On the basis of the writer's experience, it can be asserted that there are three types of programs exhibiting three different patterns of program development.

The first and most common type of program in public school work is the "instant installation" variety. Most federal programs, especially those funded under Title I of ESEA and often those under Title III as well, are of this variety. They have been quickly formulated without careful planning or design to utilize available resources. Also in the quick-cast category are most of the "new" programs mounted by public school staffs determined to do "something better" on their own initiative. These efforts are rarely planned and defined with sufficient precision to permit adequate evaluations of the new programs.

The second, less common but still widely used, type of program is the "canned" variety. For this kind of program, either a commercial, a public, or a non-profit developer has carefully determined its standards in advance of installation, and guidelines for installation, including staff training, are generally explicit.

The third and least common type of program is that which has been carefully designed by the school system itself. A few school systems have managed to organize the technical skills necessary to do this job successfully. However, in the two instances of such success best known to the author, sizable funds from outside the school system were needed. Of course, the availability of such funds for planning or development purposes, in no way insures that a program's design will be adequate. Vast sums have been wasted as a result of poor design work or of the failure of educators to recognize the necessity for incorporating design activity within the developmental life of a school program in instances in which program specifications were lacking.

For most public school systems, evaluation of school programs consists of efforts to improve programs which were poorly designed and installed and which continue to be poorly administered. The remainder of this chapter deals with explicit methods for evaluating the first of the three forementioned types. The amount of effort, time, and resources needed for a school system to do the kind of "in-process" program-design work that is described in this chapter fully explains the dependence of school systems on independent "canned" program-developers such as the national re-search and development (R & D) centers. Unfortunately, only a few people in the government and the centers themselves seem to be aware of the kind of program-development work and supporting program specifications and standards that are necessary before either regional laboratories, Title III centers, or public schools can move to install and maintain these programs.

The evaluation of a program already staffed and under way contains four major developmental stages and involves three major content categories which in turn can be broken into nineteen sub-categories. The four development stages can for the time being be best described as dealing with (*a*) definition, (*b*) installation, (*c*) process, and (*d*) product. The process of evaluation consists of moving through stages and content categories in such a way as to facilitate a comparison of program performance with standards while at the same time identifying standards to be used for future comparisons.

This process of comparisons over stages may be clarified by a flow chart (Figure 1).

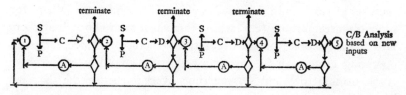

Fig. 1.—A flow chart designed to facilitate comparisons of program perform-ances with standards.

In Figure 1, S = standard, P = program performance, C = compare, D = discrepancy information, and A = change in pro-gram performance or standards. Stage 5 represents a cost-benefit option available to the evaluator only after the first four stages have been negotiated. Notice that the use of discrepancy informa-tion always leads to a decision to (*a*) go on to the next stage, (*b*) recycle the stage after there has been a change in the program's standards or operations, (*c*) recycle to the first stage, or (*d*) termin-ate the project. Discrepancy information permits the program manager to pinpoint a shortcoming in the program the identification of which necessarily leads to a change in the operation of the program or to a change in the specifications under which the program operates. A superintendent of schools or board of education will be as much concerned with the movement of a project through its evaluation stages as with discrepancy information at any given stage. The longer it takes to get to stages 2, 3 and 4, the greater the cost if the project fails. The more rapidly a project moves into advanced stages, the less the risk of its failure.

The generalizable content of a program is shown in Figure 2. To follow Stake, the transactions that transform input into output are emphasized.[15] Equally important are precise estimates of the amount of time and money needed to locate and use resources.

The time and cost columns may be easily understood if one views an educational program as an industrial process. For example, the manufacture of plastic glasses would require raw materials, labor, equipment, and a facility. Time and money would be needed to acquire each of these, and the investments made would be of a fixed amount. Once the actual manufacture of plastic glasses began, both time and money would be required to sustain the operation. As the operation continued, the same time period used to manufacture glasses could be used to assemble and store them for some ultimate purpose (e.g., selling them as they are or making them into some elaborate plastic decorative structure). Hence, although operating costs may be distinguished from cumulate and storage costs, manufacture and storage time overlap (hence the diagonal line in Figure 2).

In all stages of the development and evaluation of an educational program, the content specifications remain the same: input, process, and output relative to time and money. Taken in their form in Figure 2, they represent a taxonomy. At Stage I the evaluation task is to obtain a definition of the program based on the program-content taxonomy. The definition obtained becomes the program-performance information to be compared with the taxonomy. A discrepancy between any component in the program definition and the same component in the taxonomy represents evaluative infor-

15. Robert E. Stake, "The Countenance of Educational Evaluation," *Teacher's College Record*, LXVIII (April, 1967), 523-40.

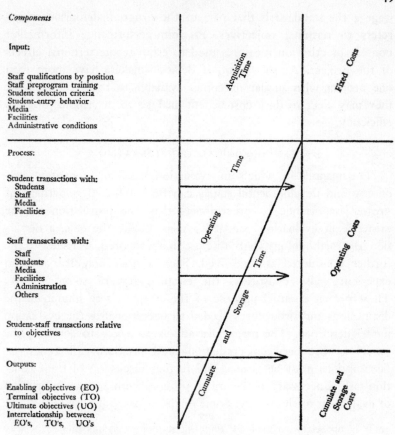

Fig. 2.—Taxonomy of program content

mation to be used by those responsible for the nature and effectiveness of the program. At stage 2 (Figure 1) the standard for comparison is the program definition arrived at in Stage I. Program-performance information consists of observations from the field regarding the installation of the program's components. Discrepancy information is used to redefine the program or to change installation procedures. At stage 3 the standard is that part of the program definition which describes the relationship between program processes and enabling objectives. Discrepancy information is used either to redefine process and relationship of process to interim product or to better control the process being used in the field. At stage 4 the standard is that part of the program definition which refers to terminal objectives. Program-performance information consists of criterion measures used to estimate the terminal effects of the project. At this point, if decision-makers have more than one project with similar outcomes available to them for analysis, they may elect to do a cost-benefit analysis to determine program efficiency.

METHODOLOGICAL CONSIDERATIONS

The manner in which an evaluation based on a content taxonomy and developmental stages can be conducted is perhaps of greater importance to practitioners than the postulation of the existence of evaluation standards. As is usually the case, a discussion of methodology will disclose new theoretical issues to be further considered and resolved. Such a discussion, if based on experience, also constitutes the essential test of sound theory. Therefore an essential purpose of this chapter is to illuminate the distinctions and procedures needed to operationalize the evaluation model described. The major distinction necessary to actualize the model is that between evaluation- and program-staff functions. Assumptions must be posited and further discussion of the evaluation task is necessary if we are to proceed with a clear description of evaluation methodology. Some of the assumptions are as follows:

1. It is necessary to evaluate ongoing school programs in such a way as to make sound decisions as to whether to improve, terminate, or maintain them.
2. There is administrative support for program change initiated by the program staff as opposed to change engineered by authority superordinate to the staff.
3. There is administrative support for making a distinction between program-and evaluation-staff personnel and functions. Program staff is defined as those persons responsible for planning, organizing, and conducting the work of a project.
4. A non-directive, objective evaluation staff can identify and collect information essential to program improvement.
5. Problem-solving activity is required to improve school programs.
6. Problem-solving will be successful only if the program staff is involved in and committed to the change process.
7. A state of tension can be fostered in the program staff which will result in problem-solving activity.

8. Problem-solving success requires pertinent information from the evaluation staff and sound decisions from the program staff.

To distinguish between the functions of the evaluation staff and the program staff, it is necessary to look at the entire web of questions and answers that constitute the problem-solving situation that we call program evaluation. Figure 3 depicts the flow of questions raised in the course of an evaluation and also makes clear how these questions are often nested one within another.

The answer to these questions is as much contained in the criterion used to answer them as in the new information used to obtain an answer.[16] For our purposes it is only necessary that every question implies a criterion (C), new information (I), and a decision (D), and that different functions are involved in answering a question. It is a tenet of our model that these functions should be carried out by different people with different responsibilities. The formulation of the question is the job of the evaluator; the criterion is the responsibility of the program manager; and the information to be used is a function of both evaluation and program-staff activity. The decision alternatives are outlined by the evaluator while the choice between alternatives belongs to the project director. More about this later.

Figure 3 shows that there are five major steps in Stage I. Each step is defined by a question. These are: Step 1—Is the program defined? Step 2—If not, is a corrective action adequately defined? Step 3—Is the corrective action installed? Step 4—If not, is a corrective action defined for securing installation in Step 3? Step 5—Is the corrective action defined in Step 4 installed?

These five steps represent a sequence of problem-solving efforts that may be needed to define an ongoing program. The same steps are used in Stage II to determine whether the program has been installed as defined. Whenever neither a definition nor an installation is obtained, further definition of some new process for definition or installation becomes necessary. If after considerable problem-solving effort the program still is not defined and installed, the principle of diminishing returns dictates program termination.

16. See Chapter IV in preparation by Evaluation Committee, *Phi Delta Kappa Monograph.*

STAGE I.

Step 1. **Is The Program Defined?**

Standard (Taxonomy) (S)
vs.
Performance (Program Description) (P)

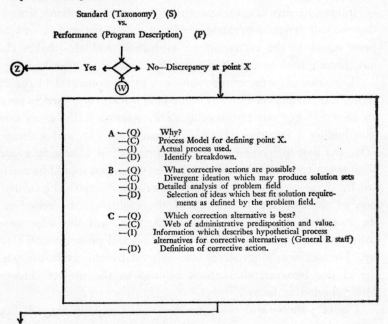

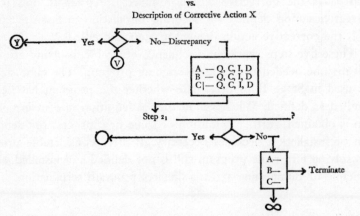

Step 2.   Is The Corrective Action X Adequately Defined?

Standard (Process model for defining corrective action
at point X)

vs.

Description of Corrective Action X

Step 3. Is Corrective Action X_1 Installed?

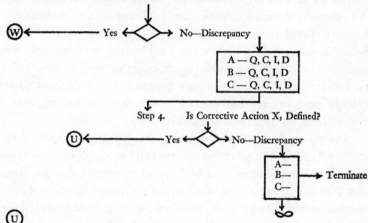

Step 5. Is Corrective Action X_1 Installed?
(Use same installation test as in Step 3)

STAGE II.

Step 1. Is The Program Installed?

Standard (Program description)
vs.
Performance
(Continue by repeating the steps used in Stage I)

STAGE III.

Step 1. Are The Enabling Objectives Being Met?

STAGE IV.

Step 1. Are The Terminal Products Achieved?

STAGE V.

Cost/Benefit Analysis

Fɪɢ. 3.—Flow of questions raised in course of an evaluation

Block Ⓦ in Figure 3 shows the essential problem-solving sequence used to identify a corrective alternative whenever discrepancy information exists as to definition (Stage I), installation (Stage II), process (Stage III), or product (Stage IV). A three-step series of questions is raised: A. Why is there a discrepancy? B. What corrective actions are possible? C. Which corrective action is best? To answer these questions, three elements are necessary: (*a*) Criteria, based on some ideal type or standard for that which is being investigated, which serve to identify relevant information and to provide a framework for interpreting it; (*b*) new information about actual performance or practice; (*c*) a decision to act to change performance based on a comparison of information with criteria and on any resultant discrepancy.

Let us see how Block Ⓦ in Figure 3 might be applied to the study of one of the program components in the content taxonomy; for example, the "input variable"—student-entry behavior. Remember, Block Ⓦ is applied only when a discrepancy exists between performance and standard—in this case, the taxonomy and program description. For example, the program description may fail to provide any information about student-entry behavior. Question A in Block Ⓦ asks, Why does this discrepancy exist? The criteria for this question describe the ideal way in which a description should have been formulated. For example, the staff might study prior to their enrollment in the program the behavior of students for whom the program is intended. The staff could then isolate performance variables which on their face appear relevant to criterion performance. The staff should find ways to measure at least some of these variables in pretreatment subjects and then describe how such information will be routinely obtained as part of the program. Such a process model for defining any component so that it is congruent with the program taxonomy constitutes the essential criterion for answering question A. The information (I) required to answer question A is a description of the process which was actually used in order to arrive at a definition of student-entry level. Perhaps, upon investigation, it is determined that someone was merely told by someone else to "describe students to be enrolled in the program" and in fact this description took the form of age and grade-level measures. A comparison of the process model with actual practice, (C) with (I), makes likely a clear-cut decision (D) as to the cause of the discrepancy. The "Why" question, A, has been answered. Question B, "What corrective actions are possible?" is now pertinent. Again the answer to this question depends on criteria (C), information (I), and a decision (D) based on a comparison of (C) with (I). Continuing with our example, question B asks, "How many ways are there of obtaining a definition of student-entry behavior?" The criteria for this question consist of a variety of ways of generating this type of information under various situational constraints. For example, given no one with a knowledge of tests and measurements in the school system, consultants may be employed. Given no students in the system who have not already been enrolled in the program, students in other systems may be identified and studied, or the behavior of students now in the program may be extrapolated to their level prior to the program. The need under (I) is for the collection of all information from the system which is capable of satisfying the possible ideal courses of action which have been devised under (C). The identification of those courses of action compatible with the existing conditions and constraints of the school system is permitted by (D).

Step C of Block Ⓦ raises the final question in the problem-solving sequence: Given a number of alternative courses of action, which is best? The criteria for this question are located in the judgmental web of the decision-maker. These criteria are rarely explicit, though through introspection they can be made so. Such values as system homeostasis, societal norms, professional standards, the importance of interest groups, and personal expectations are all involved. The decision-maker obtains estimates of the value consequences of each possible alternative under (I) and compares these consequences with his criterion of value. He is thereby enabled to make a decision as to which alternative is best (i.e., optimally satisfies the value web).

It should be noted that the use of the problem-solving Block Ⓦ inevitably raises questions demanding further refinement of criteria. The criterion problem consists of unraveling the values implicit in descriptions of standards, processes, or models needed to identify relevant information for problem-solving. Ultimately, some assumption or absolute is discovered as the basis for an operational criterion and, beyond the identification of this microcosmic value, it is generally not safe for the evaluator to transgress.

Further inspection of Figure 3 will now show that the problem-solving block can be used to resolve discrepancies which arise under each of the five steps for each stage of evaluation. Discrepancies may occur at any of the points at which a comparison is made between the program taxonomy and the program definition. Since there are 21 such points and two interactive factors—time and cost —a total of 57 possible discrepancies may arise for each step. Further, since at least five distinct steps may have to be negotiated, some 285 questions could conceivably be generated for Stage I. As has already been pointed out, the (Q), (C), (I), (D) sequence needed to answer each question raised, necessitates additional questions as to criteria and relevant information. If only one criterion question and one information question are raised (and there generally are several such questions), a total of 855 possible questions exist for Stage I.

Figure 3 suggests that the same five steps exist for Stages II, III, and IV. That is, to answer such a question as, "Is the program as defined in Stage I installed?", it is necessary to compare actual installation, that is, field performance (P) with the program definition, which becomes the new standard (S). If a discrepancy at any point in the program definition is discovered in any of the stages, problem-solving Block Ⓦ must be used, and in turn, Steps 2, 3, 4, and 5 may have to be employed. Hence, another 720 potential questions exist for each stage, cumulating to a total of 3,420 questions.

It may be helpful to look at examples of questions from Stages II, III and IV.

Stage II Examples

(Q) Step II: Has the program been installed?
(C)   Compare program definition with installation information for congruence
(I)   Information about installation obtained from field observations
(D)   Decide if program is congruent with standards for Stage II

Block Ⓦ

(Q)	If program is not congruent, why has the program not been installed?
(C)	Model of program installation procedure
(I)	Description of actual installation procedure used
(D)	Decide where procedural breakdown exists
(Q)	What should be done to install the program?
(C)	Alternative installation strategies of a general nature
(I)	Information about operational constraints on alternative strategies
(D)	Select possible specific strategies
(Q)	Which strategy is best?
(C)	Value priorities of the decision-maker
(I)	Estimates of the actual value consequences of each workable strategy
(D)	Selection of that strategy which optimizes values

Stage III Examples

(Q)	Is the program achieving its enabling objectives?
(C)	Model of relationship of student-teacher interactions to enabling objectives
(I)	Discrepancy information based on actual program performance of students
(D)	Yes, No
(Q)	If not, why not?
(C)	Model of curriculum-analysis procedure
(I)	Actual analysis of learning events and their sequence
(D)	Description of breakdown points
(Q)	What corrective alternatives appear possible under the model?
(C)	Create solution-set alternatives possible within the problem field
(I)	Detailed analysis of actual constraints in the problem field
(D)	Choose from among them the set which meets field requirements
(Q)	What corrective alternative appears best?
(C)	Model of value web
(I)	Information describing value consequences of alternatives
(D)	Choose alternative with best value-configuration fit

(Q)   Is the "corrective action" adequately defined?
(C)   Model of "corrective action," definition-adequacy criteria
(I)   Information descriptive of existing "corrective action" definition
(D)   Determine if corrective action is adequate in terms of the model

(Q)   If not, why not?
(C)   Detailed description or analysis of corrective-action definition-model (also reanalyze previous models)
(I)   Identify definition process actually used
(D)   Describe points at which the definition process has broken down

(Q)   What corrective alternatives appear possible under the model?
(C)   Create solution-set alternatives
(I)   Detailed description-analysis of problem field based on problem-solving model
(D)   Choose from among them that set which satisfies field demands

(Q)   What corrective alternative appears best?
(C)   Model of value web
(I)   Information describing value consequences of corrective alternatives
(D)   Choose alternative with best value-configuration fit

(Q)   Is the corrective action installed?
(C)   Model of corrective action derived from definition of corrective action
(I)   Information descriptive of actual field conditions
(D)   Determine if congruence exists

(Q)   If discrepancy, why? (If not, why not?)
(C)   Restate and reanalyze all previous models from III 1. C to III 9.c
(I)   Describe actual processes used in the field
(D)   Identify breakdown points (actual vs. model discrepancies)

The similarity of the questions raised in an evaluation at different stages should now be apparent. It is the content of the questions which varies across the components in the program taxonomy and across stages of development. A question which asks why in-service training of teachers has not been installed obviously differs from one which asks why administrative support has not been provided. And although the criterion problem is the same, the criteria will also differ. Similarly a question about in-service training installation at Stage II differs from one about the meaningfulness of the processes of an in-training program at Stage III. However, both questions lead to similar questions about the adequacy of definitions and the actualization of these definitions in the program. Again all these questions pose similar criterion problems but most will be distinct in terms of the specific information needed and the basis on which relevant information is identified.

The use of a computer comes to mind as an aid in charting one's decision-making course through an evaluation composed of such a maze of steps. A computer could be used to control the sequence of questions, to store criteria generated by previous decision-makers who faced similar evaluation questions, to store information descriptive of a particular school system or educational program that might be "called up" by criteria, and finally to identify for the decision-maker the alternatives available to him. In fact, except for the need of a human solution to the criterion problem, machines would appear capable of carrying out all necessary decision-making activity. It should be remembered, however, that criteria are dependent on value assumptions and, until a single value system is universal, man will not be dispensable.

IMPLEMENTING THE MODEL

Having described in some detail the steps involved in the evaluation of an ongoing program, let us now turn to a consideration of who takes these steps and how they are implemented.

A few years ago when school systems first tried to decide how they should organize to satisfy the evaluation requirements of ESEA, there was a rather spirited discussion in the literature as to whether evaluation should be the responsibility of an internal unit of the school system or performed by an external organization. The importance of objectivity and credibility was given emphasis at that time. It was said that if a school system subcontracted with a university or a non-profit agency, an evaluation would be free from charges of self-interest and partiality. Now with hindsight it seems safe to say that this strategy has not in fact worked. On the other hand, from somewhat random information coming from throughout the country, it appears that, although the internal evaluation units of school systems are producing highly reliable reports, they are of little real meaning or value to administrators.

Obviously what is needed is a better understanding of how evaluation can serve management as well as the dictates of the canons of research. Whether an evaluation unit be internal or external is perhaps less important than that its functions be clearly defined, its purposes agreed upon by all parties concerned, and its staff adequately selected and trained to do the necessary job. The characteristics that an evaluation takes on when an established institution commits itself to change in the flux of "urban ecology" are critically important. Problems common to big-city-school-system evaluations have been identified, and at least one programatic strategy for their solution has been advanced.

Figure 4 makes clear how evaluation serves as the handmaiden of administration in the management of program development through sound decision-making. (See pages 262-63.)

The evaluator tells the program-manager what decisions must be made and the manager makes these decisions on the basis of information provided by the evaluator. The choice between available decision alternatives as well as the selection of criteria underlying the generation of alternatives is the responsibility of the administrator.

Evaluation is the watchdog of program management. It insures that standards can be used for assessing program performance. It applies to standards the criteria of clarity, internal consistency, comprehensiveness, and compatibility in order that they can be operationalized at each stage of program performance. When standards are not stated clearly, the evaluation unit restates them on its own initiative and then obtains confirmation of the validity of this restatement from the program staff. Only the program staff, however, may reformulate program standards so as to improve their internal consistency, comprehensiveness, or compatibility. Generally, they will not do so unless specific contradictions or omissions in the standard are pointed out to them by the evaluation staff.

Evaluation is also responsible for insuring that the "standard- vs.

performance" comparison is actually made and that any resultant discrepancy information is reported to the program staff. To facilitate this comparison, the evaluation staff stands ready to identify necessary information, collect it, and analyze it for report purposes. Such activity results in "reports of discrepancy" to the program staff.

The problem-solving loop Block ⓦ (Figure 3) is in the province of the program staff. The evaluator's job is to track "the administrator through the problem-solving process, remind him of his methodological alternatives and choice points, and collect and analyze information as needed—though such activity could be carried out equally well by the R and D unit of the school system if one is available to the program-manager.

Skills unique to the evaluator-member of the team permit him to achieve a close working relationship with the program-director and to accomplish productive small-group work with the program staff. Measurement, sampling-report writing, statistical analysis, and other technical functions are generally provided by specialists on the evaluation team.

Evaluation is a team effort, preferably a task-oriented team of the type suggested by Miles.[17] Generally, it will consist of the following team members:

1. Several non-directive evaluation specialists skilled in small-group process work and ethnological techniques each of whom has responsibility for project-evaluation management but all of whom may team up to facilitate group work
2. One or more psychometrists familiar with a wide range of group cognitive and affective instruments and capable of rapidly designing *ad hoc* instruments
3. A research-design specialist capable of drawing carefully-defined samples, designing experiments, and directing the statistical analysis of data
4. One or more technical writers familiar with educational "language" and evaluation concepts
5. A data-processing unit with the capacity for data storage, retrieval, and statistical analysis as directed
6. Subject-specialist consultants
7. A status figure capable of communicating directly with the superintendent of schools and all program directors

17. Miles, "On Temporary Systems," *op. cit.,* pp. 437-92.

Figure 4 shows the interrelationship of the evaluation and the program staff's activity.

Evaluation-Staff Activity	*Program-Staff Activity*
Identify decision points in the entire evaluation process	
Establish and maintain an apparatus whereby staff may formulate standards	
	Identify standards.
	Find ways in which to work with staff to reformulate standards if necessary
Insure the adequacy of standards through the application of explicit criteria	
	Find ways to resolve differences in standards used by the program staff
Communicate statement of standards to staff	
Identify information needed to compare performance with standards	Identify information available or attainable in order to compare performance with standards
Design a method of obtaining program-performance information	
	Provide information descriptive of program performance
Report standard *vs.* performance discrepancy	
	Choose between action alternatives in regard to discrepancy
Identify decision points in the problem-solving process	

Identify kind of information needed to identify cause of program-performance deficiency

Locate information as to cause of program-performance deficiency

Identify decision points in choosing criteria to be used for selecting "possible" and "best" corrective alternatives

Explicate the criteria used to identify cause of discrepancy

Identify available corrective alternatives

Identify information needed to generate alternatives

Locate and synthesize information as requested

Identify criteria u n d e r l y i n g choice of best alternative

Choose "best" alternative for corrective action

FIG. 4.—Relation of activities of the evaluation and program staffs

Public school systems are traditionally monolithic, hierarchical, and monopolistic. Any such organization, be it educational, industrial, or religious, is obviously relatively insensitive to change. Further, if change is to come about, it must be due either to explosive external force or to internally directed, gradual force: a delicately balanced movement that produces within the members of the organization, first uncertainty, then an awareness of discrepancy, self-appraisal, a readiness for change, a commitment to change, and ultimately the satisfaction of actualization and self-realization.

If an evaluation is to provide information effecting change, it follows that the relationship between a program unit and an evaluation unit must be clearly defined and agreed upon by all members of an organization who may be affected by the evaluation.

Further, since an evaluation unit like a program unit derives its reason for existence from the parent school district organization, it is obviously subject to the same organizational constraints as the program unit. Even when the evaluation unit is an outside contractor, it exists within the web of expectations and relationships laid down by the school system. Therefore, interdependence between program and evaluation staff and mutual dependence on the parent structure is generally an evaluation fact of life.

If an evaluation staff is to have the support of the program staff that it seeks to evaluate, it must provide visible assistance to that staff in effecting change. Such assistance must be in a form acceptable to the program staff. The only assurance of such acceptability is that program purposes be defined by the program staff and the methods of change be determined by them as well. There must be maximum involvement of the program staff in every step of the evaluation process. Further, it follows that there must be continual rapport between the program staff and the evaluation staff (fostered particularly by the evaluation staff) resulting in a continuous communication of concern as well as acceptable verbalizations. The relationships to which an evaluation unit submits itself are binding and pervasive; however, it does not follow that evaluation therefore operates at the administrative discretion of the program unit. Evaluation is the handmaiden of program development and the quiet counselor to administrators—but in accordance with its own rules of operation and on an authority independent of the program unit.

An organizational paradigm which makes these intricate and demanding relationships understandable is that of an action system which contains a feedback loop. The processing of input is at the discretion of the program unit. The definition of output and the shaping of input is at the discretion of the parent organization. The management of the feedback loop is in the hands of the evaluation staff. The feedback consists of information concerning the discrepancy between performance and the standard. There can be no evaluation without discrepancy information. There can be no discrepancy without a standard; therefore, the first task of any evaluation is to obtain program standards.

A feedback loop of discrepancy information based on standards derived from the program staff will necessarily be of interest to a

program staff which has been given responsibility for the success
of its program.

What are the specific questions to be raised by an evaluation
unit concerned with adequately executing its own functions as
they have been defined in the preceding pages? How does it know
how to apply criteria governing the adequacy of standards and the
conditions that must be established if evaluation units are to be
successful?

Only after the program's antecedent conditions, transactions,
and purposes have been clearly described in the program definition
can the evaluator be reasonably confident of what he is evaluating.
His second concern is for the clarity, comprehensiveness, internal
consistency, and compatibility of the program definition.

Clarity is judged by an experienced writer or editor. The "comprehensiveness" of a definition is determined by the evaluator and
his supervisor after careful reference to the program-content taxonomy. There is a face validity for the exercise of this criterion
based on the observation of omissions in the program definition.
Internal consistency is often determined by the entire evaluation
team including one or more consultants as well as the program-
manager. Their task is to study the interrelationships of program
components with regard to time and money in order to discover if
inconsistencies exist in the definition of these relationships. Compatibility is judged by the program-manager working in concert
with the evaluator to determine whether the program as defined
conflicts with programs or the support of programs already installed
in a school or system.

Inevitably in the course of an evaluation, an evaluator will ask:
"Is the organization which has been created to conduct the new
program healthy and does it appear capable of executing the purposes of the project?" Pertinent concerns will be (a) staff competence, (b) communication apparatus, (c) flexibility of the program
unit, and (d) commitment to a shared vision. The evaluator will
ask: "Is there compatibility between the purposes and anticipated
procedures of the program unit and the parent school system?" "Is
there an adequate political-economic base available to the school

system to support the program unit and the attainment of its purposes?"

Such questions will be best answered from an attitude of patient optimism—no matter how harried the evaluator.

Most important to the evaluator are his answers to the questions, "Do both the program unit and the parent organization understand the developmental stages any new program must go through before it can be effective?" and "Does the administration of the school system recognize the responsibility of the evaluation unit to independently monitor program-unit activity in order to provide information relevant to management decisions that must be made at each stage of program development?"

A negative answer to the first question indicates the necessity for general in-service training for the program staff on the initiative of the evaluation staff. The dramatic presentation of causes of past system-program failures and of the value of feedback information may be a useful part of a program-staff workshop. A negative answer to the second question will generally mean that the evaluation unit will fail. If the evaluation unit has not been specifically charged with authority to make its own management decisions independent of program-staff and line-authority, its reports will ultimately fail to be objective and hence, whether positive or negative, they will be suspect.

Given the pressure of school board members and community groups for product evaluations, the time constraints placed on evaluations are generally unrealistic, regardless of the acceptance of these limitations by an evaluator. Evaluations must go through the same progressive stages that characterize the development of a project. Too often, evaluators agree to do product evaluation within a one- or two-year period of time. They employ an experimental design borrowed from research methodology and thereby short-circuit the natural stages of program development which provide the only sound basis on which evaluation work can be done. The result is an evaluation beset by classic design problems: (*a*) inadequate sampling, (*b*) faulty instrumentation, (*c*) faulty design, (*d*) lack of knowledge of critical independent variables, (*e*) lack of treatment stability.

The purpose of experimental design is to establish a relationship between treatment and effect. Design represents a method of receiving the experimental and statistical controls necessary to obtain evidence of such a relationship. These controls can be exercised only when a treatment is stable, the conditions of the treatment are under the control of the experimenter, and most of the important factors bearing on the outcomes are known to the experimenter. To apply an experimental design to a situation over which the evaluator has little control and about which he has little knowledge is like trying to practice the art of sailing without wind.

There are conditions prerequisite to the use of experimental design in a school setting, and one of the purposes of the early stages of an evaluation is to secure these conditions—just as in program development the early stages form the base on which later program growth may be realized.

In actual practice, it turns out that movement through the stages of an evaluation requires frequent recycling through those stages which are prior to the stage under negotiation at any point in time. Successive reappraisals of program operations and of the program standards from which program operations are derived are generally consequences of the decisions made by program staff on the basis of discrepancy information reported at Stages II, III, and IV (Figure 3). If a decision is made to reformulate standards rather than to revise program performance, there are immediate implications for the renegotiation of all subsequent evaluation stages. Hence, the soundness of judgment of program decision-makers and the support they derive from their organizational milieu are of prime importance to evaluators.

Stage I work.—In the first stage of evaluation, a documentation of the program staff's description of their program provides the best estimate of the conditions of the experiment.

The evaluation unit facilitates this description by working with the program staff in accordance with small-group techniques. The evaluator uses the content taxonomy to coax from the program staff a comprehensive program description:

1. A description of the client population and the criteria employed in their selection as they are reflected in the program staff's understanding of the program
2. A description of the staff, the criteria for their selection, the level of

their preprogram competency, and the expected level of their competence following any in-service training

3. The major terminal objectives of the program—that is, the behaviors clients will be expected to demonstrate upon completion of the program

4. The enabling or intervening objectives that must be negotiated before terminal objectives can be realized—that is, the intervening behaviors or tasks students must complete as a necessary basis for terminal behavior

5. The sequence of enabling objectives and the nature and sequence of learning experiences that will lead to the attainment of enabling objectives (This sequence generally takes the form of an ordinal list at this first stage of evaluation)

6. Characteristics and entry behaviors of clients—that is, those characteristics or behaviors students should exhibit upon entry into the program

7. A descriptive list of administrative support requirements, facilities, materials, and equipment

8. A description of staff functions and the number and type of positions

9. Finally, the casting of all program activity in a time frame so as to position events relative to each other over time

The program staff must provide these definitions. It is the responsibility of the evaluation staff to insure that such definitions are, in fact, obtained.

Perhaps the most difficult part of defining a program is deciding how much detail is needed in the formulation of educational objectives. The adequacy of criteria for statements of educational objectives has for many years been a controversial question in the literature of evaluation. For most purposes, it is still considered essential that program objectives be stated in behavioral terms. Such definitions constitute the beginning point of most evaluations. However, the complexity and scope of any new program determine the level of specificity at which its objectives can be initially stated. Most ongoing school projects are so very complex that, in the early stages of evaluation, definitions should be oversimplified. There is a relationship between the specificity with which objectives can be stated and the level of understanding of the program staff at various time points in the ongoing program. To define all of the objectives of an educational program with complete specificity at the beginning of a program is recognized as patently impossible by anyone who is engaged in a program of a size and complexity worthy of serious support.

Objectives must be arrived at by a method of successive approximation. In the early life of a new program, only the terminal objectives of a project and the major enabling objectives needed to reach the terminal objectives are usually understood by the staff. As the staff works in the program, it comes to recognize new terminal purposes as well as to discover many intermediate or linking objectives which must be negotiated if ultimate goals are to be realized. Therefore, the definition of program objectives is a continuous and increasingly more detailed effort resulting from program-staff-operations experience.

As goals and program antecedents and processes are gradually better defined, the project moves from a stage of limited and tentative definition to one of comprehensive and reliable definition. This natural evolution of a developing program from adolescent self-discovery to mature self-determination eventually permits Stage III evaluation activity to occur in which the relationship between project outcomes and processes can be systematically studied.

After a comprehensive blueprint of the new program has been obtained by the evaluation staff from the program staff, it becomes possible to submit the design of the program to rigorous analysis. This analysis provides those responsible for the program with new information as to resources required, internal consistency, compatibility with other programs already in existence, and comprehensiveness. Information is presented in the form of a series of judgments which the evaluation staff makes certain have been based on well-defined criteria used by appropriate persons. Judgments may be made by program staff, parents, students, authoritative consultants, or others. All may contribute to a synthesis of judgment, or only those closest to a particular question may provide a judgmental answer.

In any event, the administration is eventually afforded some degree of certainty as to whether or not there is justification for sustaining a program through its next developmental stage. When the human and monetary resources available to a program are obviously below the level required to sustain it, when the program's operating components are inconsistent with one another or with other activity already under way in the school, or when a program after repeated efforts defies comprehensive definition, administrators may terminate a program with some confidence as to the soundness of their decision.

It is important to note that the feedback given to the program staff as to the discrepancy between program definition and standard is necessarily information with negative affect. The program staff is informed of what it has failed to do. Because such reports are always given to all members of the program staff and to all of the superordinates to whom they may report, it is vital that the purpose as well as the tone and intent of the report be understood and accepted. The content of a cover page written to achieve these ends may be of interest to the reader:

EXPLANATION OF THE PROGRAM DEFINITION [18]

What is the Program Definition?

The program definition is a detailed description of an educational program as it is perceived by the staff of that program. The definition is divided into three essential components: (1) the objectives of the program; (2) the students, staff, media, and facilities that must be present before the objectives of the program can be realized; and (3) the student and staff activities that form the process whereby the objectives are achieved. These components are referred to in the definition as OUTCOMES, ANTECEDENTS, and PROCESS.

How is the Definition Obtained?

The definition is obtained at a meeting which is attended by all levels of program staff. The participants are divided into discussion groups where they contribute information about the three essential components of the program. The Office of Research compiles the comments into the program definition, which is then mailed to all members of program staff, with a request for further comments. These comments are incorporated into the definition which is continually subject to updating and modification as the program develops.

What is the Purpose of the Definition?

This definition is used as a standard against which to evaluate the program. After the definition has been obtained, the Office of Research attempts to determine whether the program is operating as the defini-

18. Unpublished paper, Mary Jane Duda and Judith McBroom (Pittsburgh, 1968).

tion specifies. If not, there are two alternatives: (1) either the definition can be modified, or (2) the program can be brought into line with the definition. Only after a definition has been obtained and the adjustment between the definition and the program has been made, can the Office of Research attempt to assess the impact of the program on students.

Have Any Changes Been Made Since the Last Program Definition?

This definition contains a more comprehensive description of the program's objectives for students, teachers, and administrators. The last program definition did not describe any ENABLING OBJECTIVES—i.e., the skills, attitudes, and information which students must acquire during the program to ensure the accomplishment of the major program objectives. These objectives have been specified in this current definition.

Staff functions and duties have been modified and are now stated more precisely. Other minor alterations have been made in the following areas: general description of staff, administrative support, time constraints and communications.

Stage II work.—When an evaluation goes through its *program-installation* stage, it is necessary for the evaluation unit to observe student and teacher activity in order that they may be compared with the appropriate activity program standards.

Evaluation designs in widespread use today call for the comparison of teacher-student activity in a new program situation with such activity in non-program or control schools. The conclusion often drawn is that, if the level or quality of activity is no different in both types of schools, the new program is not effective. Such reasoning assumes that the non-program-school activity is less effective (which may or may not be true) but, more important, it ignores the importance of the only reliable standard against which the program-school activity may be compared—the program specifications themselves. Of course, in instances in which these specifications have never existed and the evaluator has not forced them into existence as prerequisite to his evaluation, other less reliable standards of program activity must be found.

Once the standard for comparison has been determined, the enormous problem of collecting and analyzing reliable and valid information remains. Some standards call for comparisons of non-quantified information such as visual verification of described conditions or behavior. In such cases, the criterion problem is solved simply by referring to the program definition. Other standards require the quantification of comparative data on at least an ordinal scale. In this event, it is possible to encounter psychometric problems which require more time and energy than are available for the entire evaluation. Particularly if one is interested in documenting the nature of student-teacher transactions, instruments relevant to the information needs of the program are less than adequate. Yet this does not mean that estimates cannot be obtained. Reliable judges making repeated observations in carefully defined classroom situations represent perhaps the most effective, expeditious means available to the evaluator to obtain a record of complex human interactions. Such techniques are best used to verify the existence of unexpected variation in teacher activity rather than that differences do not exist, since the latter conclusion assumes an exhaustive classification system.

It is noteworthy that, when the fidelity of teaching associated with a new program has been the topic of careful investigation, the results have almost always shown as much variation within the program as across different programs. It is possible to argue that this finding is due to inadequate and arbitrary schema for classifying teacher behavior. However, the more precise an investigator is in classifying his data and the more discrete his observations of specific types of behavior, the less likely it is that this extreme variation will be due to the artificialities of measurement. That is, the more rigorous the classification constraints imposed on data in order to meet instrumentation standards, the less likely it is that variance within treatment groups will be exaggerated by instrumentation inadequacies.

Instead, we are left with good reason to believe that great variation in teacher behavior exists within many experimental programs and that these behaviors reflect pretreatment sets that are characteristic of teachers not in an experimental program.

When such variation exists, it is a major responsibility of the evaluation unit to document the discrepancy between staff behavior and program specifications. Decisions to be made by the program staff on the basis of this information may direct the retraining of teachers, the redesigning of program specifications, or the termination of the project.

At this point in the life of a project, it is often necessary to build an *ad hoc* staff-training design to compensate for lack of specificity in teacher behavior. When such project activity is initiated, it immediately becomes the responsibility of the evaluation unit to design a training-program evaluation which is predicated on the same stages of program development as those underlying the original program-evaluation strategy.

A study within a study and a program within a program are thus undertaken respectively by the evaluation and program units. Sometimes it is evident that the staff must be expanded to support unexpected training activities. If, as a result of this expansion, available resources should be exhausted, the project's infeasibility is demonstrated.[19]

In Stage II of the evaluation, then, information as to the discrepancy between expected and actual installation is obtained and the program staff is aided in eventually securing effective control over the treatment to which students are exposed.

Stage III work.—In Stage III, the initial effects of the treatment are assessed, further adjustments in treatment based on an analysis of interim product data are made, and greater understanding is achieved as to the relationship between treatment outcomes and the conditions of the experiment. At Stage III, the evaluation staff should collect data describing the extent to which student behavior is changing as predicted. The emphasis should be on validating the enabling objectives rather than the terminal or ultimate objectives. The program staff must be helped to analyze more carefully the behavior it expects students to exhibit as a function of learning activity. Learning activities are appraised for their effectiveness relative to assumptions about student readiness and rate of learning. Such evaluation depends heavily on the production and use of highly specific instruments that provide empirically determined

19. The importance of teacher training in support of almost any conceivable new program and the readiness of the evaluation staff to determine the effect of that training cannot be overemphasized. In-service-training evaluation is, if anything, more complex than preservice-training evaluation which has been the source of considerable uncertainty among professors in teacher-training institutions. See, for example, Malcolm M. Provus, *Teaching for Relevance, On In Service Training Program* (Chicago: Whitehall Publishing Co., 1969).

answers to cause-and-effect questions. As a consequence of this stage of evaluation, the program staff learns whether or not its intermediate-program payloads are being realized on target dates, and if not, why not.

The existence of a data base from which to draw quantifiable, comparable descriptions of students' behavior at various points in time is generally essential at this stage of evaluation. However, rarely is it possible to establish this data base at the initiation of a new program. Instead, the first, second, and third stages of an evaluation must be negotiated before the staff can be reasonably sure of the variables on which data are to be collected.

Hence a data base can be seen as an expanding file which is a function of program description and modification, and of increased staff awareness of related factors. Unfortunately, the data base is often defined prior to treatment, representing data available from student or school records such as standardized achievement results, along with the results obtained from the use of a potpourri of *ad hoc* instruments for measuring such intangibles as attitude, self concept, and creativity. The validity of these instruments (they often have compelling face validity) is less to be questioned than is their acceptability by the program unit or their interpretation by the evaluation unit in the context of the complex maze of program variants and conditions. It would be difficult, for example, to interpret the meaning of "a positive shift in self-esteem accompanied by a lack of significant change in rate of reading" if one did not have knowledge of what had been done to students, of the characteristics of the group that relate to the change data, or of the relationship of such change data to other program outcomes. The argument here is not for more exhaustive and precise statistical analysis but for more understanding of the relevance of data before it is collected. Unless considerable program-definition work has been done, such understanding is unlikely.

Stage III evaluation work generally requires much greater specificity in that part of the program definition dealing with instructional process than has been possible or necessary in previous stages.

In seeking an answer to the question, "Is the program achieving its enabling objectives?", the evaluator must enlist the aid of the program staff in flow-charting the relationship between learning experiences, enabling objectives, and terminal objectives.

Figure 5 shows one format that can be used for this purpose.

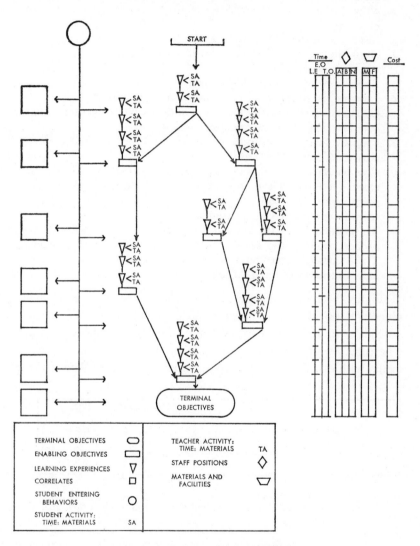

Fig. 5.—Program design analysis

The steps in constructing such a flow chart are as follows:[20]

1. List student and teacher activities associated with each learning experience.
2. Show the sequence of learning experiences leading to each enabling objective.
3. List the sequence of all enabling objectives.
4. Show the structural relationships of all enabling objectives to each terminal objective.
5. Repeat 1 to 4 for all terminal objectives.
6. Estimate the time between each node on the flow chart.
7. Group teacher activities over time into teaching functions. Aggregate functions to define teaching positions.
8. Estimate facilities (includes equipment and media) needed to support teaching activity. List.
9. Cost out facilities and staff requirements relative to nodes on flow chart. (It is possible to prorate fixed staff and facilities cost on a proportional time basis.)
10. Identify entry behaviors of students.
11. Throughout Stage III, correlates of student-entry behavior and in-process, student and teacher behavior will be gradually obtained. These correlates are listed as they are identified and may serve as independent variables in Stage IV.

Figure 6 shows a simplified example of the flow of enabling objectives (solid lines) compared with the actual flow of enabling objectives as determined by evaluation field work (dotted lines).[21] The time line at the bottom permits a comparison of actual attainments with expected attainments at some of the target dates for the

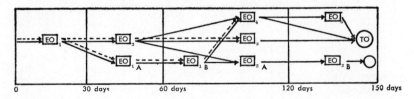

FIG. 6.—Enabling objective attainment and the interim product-flow analysis [21]

20. A number of flow charts are available. See Desmond L. Cook, *Program Evaluation and Review Techniques, Applications in Education* (Cooperative Research Monograph, 1966, No. 17, OE-12024).

21. The flow chart applies to each group of students identified for similar instruction in a given program.

attainment of enabling objectives defined in the program specifications. Such a chart is an essential aid to Stage-III-evaluation procedure. The activities which make up this procedure are described in Figure 7, "Interim product-evaluation-activity sequence." Col-

		A	B	C	D	E	F	Proceed to next E.O.	G	H	I	J
Sequence of E.O.'s	Sequence of Evaluation	Verify administrative feasibility of pre and post instruction	Administer pretest and describe performance	Determine performance levels criteria	Administer learning sequence for E.O._1	Administer posttest and describe performance	Evaluate data relative to performance-level criteria		Identify E.O._1a	Identify learning sequence for E.O._1a	Administer learning sequence for E.O._1a	Subjective approval of E.O._1a learning sequence
Steps	1	2	3	4	5	6			7	8	9	10
EO_1	1											10
EO_2	11							Complete Steps 7 - 10				20
EO_3	21											30
EO_4	31											40

Fig. 7.—Interim product-evaluation-activity sequence

umn A includes a description of who administers what, when, and to whom, and details the activity needed to support administration of both pretest and posttest instruments for an evaluation of the program sequence relative to enabling objective, EO. Column B includes the administration of the pretest and description of the results in terms of levels for each valid subscore. Column C represents performance level on the instrument to be used as program-success criteria. This level is determined as a function of pretest performance estimates of the effectiveness of treatment and estimates of the importance of the enabling objective in the over-all structure of objectives contributing to terminal objectives. Column D represents the administration of program treatment in the form of a learning-activity sequence. Column E calls for the administration of the posttest and data descriptions comparable to those of Column B. Column F compares posttest with pretest and performance-level criteria defined under Column C. As a result of this comparison, a determination is made either to move to EO_2 or to re-examine EO_1. On the assumption that student and teacher activity has been monitored through the continuous operations-research design so as to remain consonant with program specifications, it follows that the predicted relationship between treatment and enabling objective has been faulty. An analysis of EO_1 takes the form of the identification of subobjectives (EO_{1a} and EO_{1b}) subsumed in EO_1 for which learning experiences must be devised. This faulty relationship is generally due to inadequate analysis of student behavior relative to task completion. Having just completed an attempt to produce learning experiences conducive to EO_1 and having information as to the pre- and post-performance of students on criterion tasks, the teacher is in the best possible position to intuitively postulate new behaviors which must be learned as requisite to the achievement of EO_1. These new behaviors become a new set of objectives (EO_{1a} and EO_{1b}), shown in Column G, for which new learning experiences must be devised (Column H) and administered (Column I).

Since no instrumentation is available to measure the attainment of objectives of the class EO_{1a}, evaluation of this second alternative learning sequence must be conducted subjectively by the classroom teacher (Column J). Limited resources and time generally militate against the employment of criterion measures at this level of program development work in a public school setting.

The involvement of the program staff in curriculum-development research is crucial to its success. In many school systems, resources will be insufficient to support such work. However, some systems will value such work highly enough to provide the considerable support necessary.

The discovery by the program staff of new objectives subsumed under previously stated enabling objectives will be a consequence of teaching problems that result from unexpected reactions from students, insights gained from introspection and/or task analysis, and insights gained from successful teaching. Such discovery will no doubt have a bearing on the teacher's incentive to engage in curriculum analysis, and a desire to increase staff initiative may be an important consideration in any administrator's determination to support such work.

The staff may be aware of many layers of underlying enabling objectives but, owing to limited time and energy, fail to state them.

The failure of teachers to utilize their existing knowledge of curriculum and student interaction prior to teaching, of course, results in enormously inefficient programs.

A delicate balance seems necessary between spending time and effort on curriculum analysis *prior* to the teaching of the sequence and *after* obtaining feedback regarding the success of that learning experience. Cost and staff-satisfaction requirements would seem to dictate that minimum resources be used to achieve standard levels of student performance. Since in most cases this minimum cannot be identified prior to feedback about the success of learning experience, it would appear wise to use the collective judgment of the staff in defining objectives at whatever levels of complexity are possible and in determining appropriate learning sequences. Unfortunately such collective judgment is often not considered a necessary part of in-process program-development work.

The time required to complete a learning sequence, the time expected to complete a learning sequence, and the objectives of a program at various levels of complexity are obviously related.

When enabling and terminal objectives are first defined in Stage I, time estimates for their completion are given. However, as teaching difficulties are encountered in Stage III and new subobjectives are discovered or employed, the time dimension of the project must be adjusted to accommodate these changes.

An important in-process set of administrative decisions therefore deals with setting time limits for the attainment of new subobjectives. Herein lies a dilemma. A program can be lost for failure to reach terminal objectives because it bogs down in relation to subobjectives or it can fail to achieve its terminal objectives (even though it completes its entire planned sequence of activity) because of inattention to the achievement of enabling objectives. The captain who reaches port "come hell or high water" may have lost his cargo while the captain who nurses his cargo along may never reach port.

Again, an administrative decision relative to the use of resources over time is critical to program success. Obviously what is needed is periodic information concerning movement toward terminal objectives as well as feedback on new enabling objectives.

The question as to whether to move forward to the next enabling objective (EO_2)in a flow chart (Figure 6) (or to a subobjective (EO_{1a}) is a question of importance. Considerations which bear on this general decision are as follows:

1. The validity of performance data concerning EO_1
2. The time estimated to complete EO_{1a}
3. The time available to reach terminal objectives
4. The ability of staff to identify more efficient learning experiences to reach EO_1
5. The ability of staff to identify alternatives to EO_{1a} (such as EO_{1b} or EO_{1c}) and to estimate their relative time requirements
6. The ability of staff to identify and locate necessary support requirements such as materials and trained personnel, as well as evaluation requirements such as instruments, and so forth

From the foregoing, it appears that the efficiency of the staff in researching the cause of failure and in devising a solution is the overriding consideration.

The problem-solving effort at this point requires careful teamwork between the evaluation and program staffs (see Figure 4 and discussion). The criteria required to answer the research and development (R and D) questions posed by the problem consist of models of learning and curriculum structure appropriate to the particular program under study. These models are suggested by such theoreticians as Gagné [22] and Bloom.[23]

The value of structural analysis of the type proposed by Gagné and Bloom is now obvious. A serious question remains as to the feasibility of such analytic work by a public school staff. Clearly, a research center or university (in conjunction with a public school system) will be best equipped to do this work. Ultimately, public schools may be the recipients of packaged curriculum programs containing precisely defined relationships between instructional process and pupil performance. Then, school systems will more properly devote their evaluation resources to such installation

22. Robert M. Gagné, *Factors in Acquiring Knowledge of a Mathematical Task* (Washington: American Psychological Association, 1962).

23. Benjamin S. Bloom, "Learning for Mastery," *Evaluation Comment*, I (May, 1968); "Peak Learning Experiences," *Innovation for Time to Teach* (Washington, D.C.: Department of Classroom Teachers, National Education Association, 1966.)

activity as pupil selection, in-service teacher training, and the conditions of administrative program support.

Stage IV.—Finally, at Stage IV the evaluator may cast an experimental design for arriving at an answer to the question: "Has the program achieved its terminal objectives?"

Stage IV calls for the kinds of designs we have long employed in educational research and have more recently employed in evaluation. These designs have been "employed in error," not because the quasi-experimental designs of the type described by Stanley and Campbell [24] do not belong in an evaluation strategy, but because they have consistently been used in the wrong stage of a program's development.

In Stage IV, many of the relationships between treatment conditions and effects discovered in Stage III, can be properly expressed as independent variables in the experimental design. The administrative control secured over the new program in Stages II and III ensures treatment stability. Problems of sampling and instrumentation are more likely to be solved as a result of increased staff knowledge of factors interacting with treatment.

Stage V option.—A word about cost-benefit analysis may be in order at this point. There is a lot of "econometrics" discussion today about applying cost-benefit analysis to school system outputs as a method of identifying efficient programs. This discussion is meaningful if the following conditions exist or can be established:

1. The programs that produce measurable benefits are sufficiently well defined to be replicable.
2. There is agreement on both the value and measure of benefit.
3. Antecedent conditions can be sufficiently well defined and measured to determine their effect on output.
4. At least two programs are in existence for which inputs have been "costed out," that share common benefits, and for which comparable data exist describing antecedent conditions.

It may be possible to find programs which meet these conditions, but given the present state of the evaluation art, it is extremely unlikely. Moreover, it must be remembered that cost-benefit analysis

24. Donald T. Campbell and Julian C. Stanley, "Experimental and Quasi-Experimental Designs for Research of Teaching," *Handbook of Research on Teaching*, ed. N. L. Gage (Chicago: Rand McNally & Co., 1963.)

answers the question: "Which program from among two or more that are available achieves its purpose at the lowest cost?" It does not answer questions pertinent to the operation or success of any single program.

Some Old Wives' Tales

At this point, it would seem desirable to dismiss a few old wives' tales about the evaluation process.

1. *The evaluation unit must participate in the planning of a program if it is to be effective.*

   Since most programs have not been planned, it follows that, if they are to be evaluated, they must employ an evaluation strategy which is not dependent on planning. Such a strategy has been described in this article and can be used to capitalize on planning omissions.

2. *It is necessary to wait three to five years before any evaluative judgment can be passed on a new program.*

   On the contrary, the position of this paper is that a whole series of judgments can be passed on a project at various points of its life relative to the various developmental stages through which it goes.

3. *There is inevitable conflict between the interests of program and evaluation staffs.*

   Surely this need not be so. Both staffs have the same mission: either to continue and improve a program or to reject it as soon as there is reliable evidence that its probability of success is very low. In pursuit of this mission, both staffs share the desire to secure and appraise information pertinent to discrepancies between program operation and program specifications.

4. *Evaluation activity gets in the way of program activity.*

   When evaluation is seen as a necessary part of program development, the activity of the evaluator is seen by the program staff as complementary, and that activity of the program staff which is essential to the installation and maintenance of program treatment is always given precedence over evaluation activity by the evaluation staff.

5. *Good evaluation from its inception depends on a sound experimental design.*

   According to the evaluation strategy advanced in this paper, experimental design is irrelevant to evaluation until a program is in its final stages of development. When an evaluation is properly conceived and conducted, it has the power to sound the death knell of a project long before it reaches stability and maturity. Evidence as to excessive cost, inconsistency, unreliability, or the incompatibility of a project at various stages in its development will provide a sound base from which to estimate its probable success at various points in time.

An evaluation which begins with an experimental design denies the program staff that which it needs most: information that can be used to make judgments about the program while it is in its dynamic stages of growth. Furthermore, the imposition of an experimental design in the formulative stages of a program deprives the staff of their desired opportunity to improve a program on the basis of experience. Sound evaluation practice provides administrators and the program staff with information they need and freedom to act on that information.

Conclusion

There is a need for administrators to better understand that the installation of school programs, whether innovative or not, involves high risk of failure. There is a need for evaluators to better understand the kind of information administrators need if the cost of these risks is to be reduced. Both administrators and researchers must see evaluation as a continuous information-management process which serves program-improvement as well as program-assessment purposes. The complexity and concomitant high cost of effective evaluation must be recognized as a necessary management expense somewhat similar to high insurance premiums. Everyone concerned with public education must be willing to spend much larger sums for evaluation if we are to have an adequate management system for protecting federal investments under the present reform strategy of the Office of Education.

Those involved in public school reform through new program development must recognize:

1. The natural developmental stages of any new program
2. The evaluation activity that is appropriate to each stage
3. The dependence of administrators on information obtained through evaluation if they are to make sound, defensible decisions

If a new brand of evaluation can be developed and supported in the years ahead, school programs and evaluation reports are going to look very different than they do today. Our national interest will eventually demand nothing less.

CHAPTER XII

Appraising the Effects of Innovations in Local Schools

HENRY M. BRICKELL

The School As a Complex System

A school may be thought of as a complex system—a series of interlocking components arranged to carry out processes which will ultimately produce learning as an outcome. While a school is not a carefully engineered system and bears little resemblance to a smoothly operating machine, it is a system nonetheless. As a system it has three specific characteristics which have been selected as the concerns of this chapter: (*a*) It has components which could be replaced by others that might be even better than those now being used; (*b*) the present components are so interconnected that changing one will result in changing the others; and (*c*) the processing route is so lengthy that a change in the system will have a delayed effect on the final outcome.

Alternative components.—During a period of energetic modification such as the one that schools are now moving through, a multitude of components compete for a place in the local program. Their availability complicates the evaluation problem considerably. The schools must somehow assess those alternatives and consider them as substitutes for whatever is in current use. Even though local students may be learning quite satisfactorily (not that this is likely), it is always possible that those schools using other approaches may be teaching something of greater value or teaching more or teaching faster or teaching at lower cost. Those possibilities have to be investigated.

Interlocking components.—The parts which make up the school as a system cannot be dealt with singly, each on its own terms. Because the working of each one affects the working of the others, thought must be given beforehand to the way in which any substitute might fit into the system and to what dislocations it might cause if adopted. A change in textbooks, for example, may cause hardly a ripple, while a change to computer-assisted instruction may send a shock wave throughout the system. Unlike the textbook, the computer may take the teacher out of his accustomed role as presenter of information. If the teacher thinks that presenting information is the supreme teaching act, the introduction of the computer can disturb him seriously, cut his productivity, and perhaps drive him to strong resistance. Or, to use another illustration, a modernized test of arithmetic reasoning may be introduced into a school simply because a testing company has withdrawn the old test from the market and replaced it with a new one. If students do poorly on the new test, those results can lead teachers to call for new textbooks, principals to call for new in-service training, and parents to call for an explanation of modern mathematics.

Delayed effects of change.—A change in the school ordinarily takes some time to make its imprint on the students moving through. A new way of teaching observation, classification, and measurement in the primary grades may not have a visible effect on student behavior until the students begin laboratory science courses early in high school. Or the behavior may become visible in the primary grades, but its persistence may not be fully assured until five or six years have passed. A deliberate change in the racial balance of the classrooms may not be accompanied by instant shifts in social groupings, but the school may be perfectly willing to wait a very long time for the desired learning to take place. A new program which trains teachers to diagnose acute pupil learning problems may have to proceed for months before the teachers gain any sure skills in diagnosis. More months may pass before they begin to try new ways of handling pupils who are not learning, and even more months may elapse before measurable pupil learning occurs.

Pressures to Innovate

The pressures upon a school to alter its instructional program vary from time to time, both as to degree and as to source. The evaluation system of the school can itself be a source of pressure by revealing failures in the program. Events outside the school can also lead to changes, even though those events seem disconnected from what the school is doing.

Internal evaluation as a source of innovation.—At a time of relative stability in school programs, the making of instructional decisions by the school can be conceived as an orderly series of steps. In the following admittedly oversimplified model of the decision-making process, the five major phases set forth are common to the design—and modification—of any system:

1. The selection of objectives (*a*) to guide choices about processes, and (*b*) to use as standards in judging final outcomes. In an instructional program, this means the choice of desired pupil behaviors to guide instruction and to judge learning.
2. The selection of processes to produce the outcomes. In the case of instruction, processes of teaching are chosen to cause learning.
3. The description or measurement of the resulting outcomes. In a school this means the reporting or measuring of what pupils have learned.
4. The comparison of the outcomes to the objectives. In instruction, this is the comparison of learned behavior to desired behavior.
5. If the outcomes fail to match the objectives, the selection of an alternative process. In school, if the learned behavior falls short of the desired behavior, a better set of instructional experiences should be selected.

In this model the evaluation procedure itself is envisioned as originating the motive to innovate. Very few schools are actually as systematic in setting objectives or in measuring their attainment as is suggested here. Pressures for change are more likely to come from general faculty or administrative disenchantment with present procedures. But even when the instructional objectives are poorly identified and the evidence of student learning is fragmentary and impressionistic, an evaluation process is at work as the staff senses a discrepancy between objectives and outcomes. At a time when schools use rather similar programs and seem to be doing a satisfactory job, the evaluation process is a major source of pressure to innovate.

External influences as a source of innovation.—At a time of instability and ferment in school programs, while the above model is still fundamentally sound, there are two major inputs from the outside environment thrusting into what at quieter times is a relatively closed system. The first intervening factor is the competition of alternative instructional objectives; the second is the competition of alternative instructional processes. The term "competition" is used because at a time of aggressive experimentation and invention, new goals as well as new content and procedures are generated and brought forcefully to the attention of schools. (At such a time, a school cannot cleave to the status quo simply through ignorance of any alternative; it can only do so through a deliberate decision not to change. In effect, it has to reselect its present program as being better than an array of highly visible alternatives.)

New instructional objectives arise because the surrounding society is changing. A type of job once plentiful may disappear: elevator-operators yield to rows of buttons and parking lot attendants yield to spiral ramps. A technological invention may make entirely new behavior possible: the freezer, the computer, and the pill change life patterns at home, at work, and elsewhere. Political styles shift: the patient Negro entreaties of yesterday are replaced by the black militant demands of today. Values shift: the gifted child is eased aside as the disadvantaged child moves to center stage. World power shifts: the arguments for studying Russian yesterday are repeated for studying Chinese today. Population grows. Knowledge expands. Opportunities multiply. Each change implies new objectives for the schools.

New instructional content and processes arise for just as many different reasons. Television is a medium invented for general communication but converted to instructional use, as was the motion picture forty years earlier. Programed instruction arose directly from experimental procedures originated in psychological laboratories. Team teaching was devised to accommodate uneven talents among teachers. The notable new high-school science and mathematics courses of recent years came about because a number of scholars decided to infuse new content into obsolete high-school courses. Head Start was invented to help disadvantaged children get off to an even start in school. A new "initial teaching alphabet" arrived from overseas because a British publisher wanted to expand his schoolbook market.

Whatever their sources, the new ends and the new means press upon the old system of ends and means. In so doing, they widen the context for local evaluation. Evaluation can no longer be limited to the present system: it must contemplate the possible outcomes of alternative components. Shortcomings in the present system cease to be the only reason for an instructional change; such a change may now come from an apparent superiority in a competing system.

Seeking Alternatives

Once it becomes clear that the configuration of ends and means that comprises the local instructional program is not necessarily ideal, the school is faced with a major decision: If it should decide to change, will it formulate new ends, choose new content, and invent new materials and instructional procedures—or will it adopt those developed elsewhere?

Because very few schools are rich enough in talent and resources (or in motivation) to establish the truly extraordinary conditions needed for the origination of a new program, the discussion in this chapter will be limited largely to the selection and evaluation of novel approaches originated elsewhere. However, before turning away from those schools which do want to devise their own new programs, it would be well to make a few observations about evaluation during the actual development of a new approach. Brief attention will be given to the purposes of evaluation during program development, the probable effects on the participants, and the fitting of the resulting innovation into the existing system.

Developing a program.—Evaluation during development is intended not to assess a final outcome but to shape the process being developed. This leads to the testing of tiny components as soon as they are created, using those components with less-than-full-size classroom groups, conducting short periods of instruction, collecting data through direct observation of the instruction and through interviews, relying heavily on the testimony of students and teachers in judging the success of what has been developed, and returning frequently to the drawing board. In all these respects, the evaluation process during development differs markedly from the assessment of a fully developed program.

Those who take part in developing a new program under conditions of thorough evaluation are likely to experience the following:

1. The objectives they hold for the innovation become noticeably

refined and sharpened; designing the instructional process affects the definition of the objectives as much as the reverse.

2. Because the evaluation concentrates upon the process rather than upon the learner, for the first time it is the instruction which fails rather than the child who fails.

3. The number of acceptable methods of instruction is multiplied, if only because it is so difficult to invent one which is any better than the others.

4. So much doubt arises about any automatic connection between teaching methods and learning outcomes that the participants become thoughtfully critical of the claims made for various innovations.

5. The participants begin to develop the mind-set of inquirers and begin to advance ideas as hypotheses rather than as convictions.

None of these outcomes is of course guaranteed, but they are more likely to arise during the development of a new program than during the evaluation of one developed elsewhere. To repeat, however, few schools will be able to develop their own innovations.

Those few schools which do will probably find that many of the concerns about adopting an outside program which are recounted later in this chapter simply never arise. These concerns include making sure beforehand that the innovation fits the local system, arranging for a hospitable reception, getting an authentic copy installed, making certain that any adaptations are sensible, and seeing that the local system is rebuilt around the innovation where necessary.

Importing a program.—The process of adopting an outside program begins with a search for alternatives to what is presently being done in local classrooms. Information about innovations can be gathered by attending professional meetings and by reading professional literature. Some general-circulation magazines have begun to publish descriptions of new instructional departures as well. Information can also be gathered by visiting the schools which are using a particular innovation. (Program descriptions are customarily available through a visit before they are available from the platform and are available from the platform before they appear in the literature.) Most school people find that an innovation cannot be fully comprehended without visiting and interviewing those who are engaged in it. During the visit, the collection of testimony and sample materials should be supplemented by direct observation in the classroom.

The search for new programs may be carried on in many locations. It may be that in some local classrooms the instructional process is decidedly superior to what it is in others in the same grade and subject: thus the search can begin at home. The search can of course be conducted in other schools—public, private, and proprietary. Moreover, it can be conducted in the fast-growing number of instructional locations outside the schools: those in business and industry (whose instructional costs now approximate half the cost of public education), in the military services, in government, in professional societies, and in temporary projects and programs such as those subsidized by the federal Office of Economic Opportunity and sponsored by assorted non-school organizations. It need not be limited to the subject or grade level for which an innovation is being sought. The reason is that the instructional methods and materials found in other subjects and grades may, with modification, be usable at points in the school program for which they were not originally designed.

Three kinds of information about the innovation should be collected: (a) information about objectives, (b) information about processes, and (c) information about outcomes. It should be remembered that the school will not always be clear and articulate about its instructional objectives—even about those of innovations in which it takes particular pride. Often the most elaborate description of objectives appears in the test instruments the school chooses for assessing learning. Because the objectives which are tested tend to be those toward which teaching is directed, the tests are well worth examining and discussing. The types of evidence which ought to be gathered about the instructional processes used and about their effects on pupil learning are the topics of later sections of this chapter.

Characterizing the Alternatives

A judgment and a decision must eventually be made about each alternative: Will it be adopted, or will it not? The decision will be based on an advance "evaluation," which estimates how the new program would fit into and affect the school itself and estimates how it would affect pupil learning. The following characteristics of each alternative should be noted because they are needed to make such estimates:

GENERAL CHARACTERISTICS OF THE INNOVATION

Magnitude.—What proportion of the total school program does the innovation encompass? How many teachers, how many subjects, how many grades does it involve? A non-graded elementary structure differs markedly in scope from a fourth year of high-school German.

Completeness.—What still has to be added to the innovation—or is it already complete in conception, in classroom procedures, and in supporting materials? Is it a new reading program which requires a huge supply of supplementary library books, or is it a prepackaged kit of science demonstrations?

Complexity.—Is there an intricate series of interlocked procedures, all of which must be used skillfully on a set time schedule, or is the operation straightforward and unembellished?

Convenience.—Simplicity is one thing; convenience is another. Is there, for example, a single piece of equipment which six or eight teachers are expected to share, or a single artifact which all students are supposed to examine intensively, or machine-scored answer sheets which must be shipped out of town for processing?

Flexibility.—Does the innovation depend for its success on the teacher's following a prescription quite closely, or can the teacher deviate and still succeed? Is the instructional television series so cumulative, for example, that not a lesson can be missed?

Distinctiveness.—Is the innovation recognizably different from standard programs? Is it easy to find clear evidence of its presence, or does it differ so little that it can scarcely be distinguished from the ordinary?

Replicability.—Does the innovation owe its existence to something which cannot be duplicated elsewhere—a unique school building, an extraordinary local resource such as an oceanographic laboratory, the charisma of a leader?

Interaction with other programs.—Does the innovation work better in the company of certain kinds of instructional programs?

Is it harmed by the presence of others? What is its effect on each type?

Readiness.—Can it be taken elsewhere immediately and applied, or are further development and testing in the original setting essential?

Trial possibility.—Would the dislocations caused by trying the innovation in a school be so great that it would be difficult or expensive for the school to abandon the innovation and return to the previous program?

Cost.—Many innovations incur initial costs, installation costs, and continuing costs. It is wise to consider each. What is the initial cost of the components—books, equipment, supplies? What will be the cost of actual installation of the new plan in the local school— the highest cost probably being that of training the faculty? After initial purchase and installation, what additional costs will there be? What about training for incoming teachers or refresher sessions for those who stay? What about the cost of evaluation itself: will special observations or new tests be necessary?

SPECIAL CHARACTERISTICS OF THE INNOVATION

Content.—Is wholly new subject matter being taught or is there a sharp shift in emphasis within the usual content? Is the change toward more significant information and skills or is one set of illustrations merely exchanged for another? Do the values being taught deviate from those generally transmitted?

Staff performance.—Are abnormal amounts of teacher energy, enthusiasm, or creativity needed to make the innovation work? What range of teaching competence can the innovation tolerate and still be effective?

Staff background.—Do the teachers using the plan have something in their background so special that it alone could explain their success? Are they, for example, on temporary leave from a nearby university to man a special project?

Staff roles.—Does the innovation cast the teachers chiefly as planners of instruction, as presenters of information, managers of recitations, monitors of a self-instructional process, or evaluators of learning? Can what they do be regarded primarily as professional work, as technical, as custodial, or as clerical?

Social setting.—Do the people in the program exercise considerable independence of action or are they working under the control of others? Do they usually work in a group or in isolation from each other? What sort of recognition do they get for high achievement?

Equipment and materials.—Are the necessary teaching aids included in a single package available from the same source as the instructional procedures or must they be acquired separately from assorted sources? Are they adequate or must they be replaced or supplemented with something better? Are they ready to use or must teachers spend time preparing them further? Is the equipment usable with materials other than those designed for this program? Are the materials usable with equipment other than that designed for this program?

Time.—What are the minimum time requirements—during the year, the week, the day? If these minimums are violated, does the instruction succeed in part or fail completely?

Space.—How much space, and what kind of space, does the new approach call for? How much can this demand be compromised without serious damage to the program?

Assessing the Fit of the Innovation to the Current System

Once the innovation has been characterized in its outside setting, it is possible to contemplate how well it could be fitted into the system as it now exists and to determine what effects it would have on the processes used in the system as well as on the final outcomes in the form of pupil learning. This determination, as indicated earlier, is a form of advance evaluation.

Perhaps the most salient point to be made here is that the probable effects of the innovation *cannot be judged without a deep knowledge of the present system.* The most detailed description of the innovation will be of little use unless one has an equally detailed understanding of the system into which the innovation will have to be fitted. Many decisions about innovations—both adoption decisions and rejection decisions—are less than rational because process and output information is available neither about the innovation nor about the school itself.

It can be said in general about an innovation that it can be more readily added to an existing system if it is small in magnitude, complete in conception and materials, relatively simple, convenient for teachers, flexible, distinctive, replicable, and ready for use. A low degree of interaction with other programs eases the way for adoption. The possibility of trying the innovation without making a permanent adoption decision is desirable. It is favorable for the adoption process if both the initial and continuing costs are low. Few innovations, of course, have all these characteristics. And there are some schools for which certain characteristics are not essential or for which other characteristics would actually be better. Cost will be less important to some schools than to others, for example. Or a school may actually be seeking an innovation of large magnitude which will affect the entire curriculum and all teachers as a way of engaging the total faculty in improving their own work.

If the content offered in the new program is different from that which is now taught, the content in courses which precede or follow it may have to be modified to converge with the new content. If the content falls far out of place in the local curricular sequence, a major reshuffling of the whole program may be necessary. If any new values being taught are in violation of those currently transmitted by the system—views about race, religion, sex, political behavior, and so on—it will probably be difficult to incorporate the innovation.

It may be that the local staff simply does not have the background to match that of teachers in schools where the innovation has been successful, and it may be that no amount of training will equip them sufficiently. It may be that the roles they are called upon to perform are so different from those that are customary, (and from those that they will continue to perform in other parts of the school program) that they cannot or will not undertake the drastic role shifts necessary. For example, if the innovation absolutely requires that the progress of each child be noted every day and that a new instructional decision be made specifically for him, teachers may find this too much of a break from the mass instruction to which they are accustomed. Moreover, if local role norms are supported by similar norms held throughout the profession, the role-changing innovation will have extremely difficult going. In general, as the teacher's role becomes less clerical and custodial and more professional, the change will be welcomed. (This is not to say that all teachers can actually perform at the professional level required.) If the program will not succeed unless the faculty exhibits enormous amounts of energy or enthusiasm or creativity, it will not work in a system where these qualities are rare and cannot be generated initially or sustained over the long haul. Again, if local teachers are accustomed to working with considerable autonomy and independence and in substantial isolation from each other, an innovation that depends for its success upon intensive faculty interaction may never come fully to life in the local classrooms. If by chance the local teachers are accustomed to getting recognition for superb performance but the innovation obscures the teacher's contribution because it is largely self-instructional (or laden with equipment which appears to replace the teacher) or if the teacher's individual contribution is buried in that of a group, the innovation is not a good fit for the present system.

Because teachers are so dependent upon the availability of instructional equipment and materials to carry on the process of instruction, it is desirable that the innovation match or improve upon the quality of what teachers presently have to work with. For most schools it would seem that the more complete and ready-to-use the materials are, the easier it is to undertake the innovation. But the reverse would of course be true in a school where teachers are accustomed to making their own materials; they might object strongly to a "package" which could not be broken open and replaced in part with their own inventions. Innovative materials that can be used with other equipment available in the school and innovative equipment which can be used with other materials (filmstrips to fit the present projectors and vice versa) will be easier to integrate into the system than those that can be used solely with the specific innovation.

If the school is unable to schedule sufficient time for the new approach or to allocate sufficient space to it without serious disruption or damage to the remainder of the instructional program, the innovation will not fit comfortably within the present system and probably should not be adopted.

In the preceding discussion, only the local professional staff has been focused upon. But there is also the board of education and the community itself to consider. Their picture of what a proper school program looks like and their willingness to support change of the kind brought about by specific innovation must be considered. Inasmuch as there is a reasonably good match in most communities between professional expectations of the school program and those held throughout the local community, there will not be a serious problem in the case of most innovations. But certain features of an innovation will arouse more community interest than others. A divergence between professional and community views on those critical features may lead to professional acceptance but to community rejection, a condition which will ultimately be fatal to the innovation. For example, if the new instructional program teaches attitudes toward race or sex which diverge from those generally held in the community, it will not be sufficient that the faculty finds itself comfortable with the new attitudes. While new values may arouse public reaction, many other features of the innovation, such as its convenience for daily classroom use and the easy availability of instructional materials, may well be matters of indifference to the community.

Most local schools do not have a strong tradition of in-service training. Teachers ordinarily get re-educated at their own initiative by taking courses at colleges in no way connected with the local school system. Many innovations depend for their success on a retrained faculty. The school may find upon inspection that the amount of retraining which will be necessary—training for the present faculty and for newcomers who will arrive in later years, training in the substantive content of the innovation as well as in its instructional processes, training in its technical equipment and materials components—is so out of keeping with local traditions that the innovation cannot be successfully installed. Even if teachers would willingly undertake the amount of training necessary, it may be that the school is unable to pay for qualified trainers or to attract them to its location. Unless all the conditions for training can be met, it is quite unlikely that the innovation can ever become a functioning part of the local system.

Assessing the Accommodation of the School to the Innovation

Once the innovation has been adopted and installed, but before it has had time to produce student learning as a final outcome, an interim evaluation can be made. It can be determined whether all the components of the innovation have actually been added to the system and whether the desired processes have in fact emerged in local classrooms. It is useful to distinguish between a component of the system and a process of the system. A component is a structural element which can be built directly into the system; a process is a transaction among components or between those components and something outside the system. Unlike a component, a process cannot be installed into the system directly: it is instead an expected or hoped-for result of putting in certain components. When the chief components are people, as is the case in the instructional system called a school, the hoped-for process may or may not occur. This is the reason that new processes do not always follow from new components: the team teachers may not team teach; the television sets may be turned off; the programed text may be assigned to the whole class a page at a time. It is one thing to ascertain that the components of an innovation have been installed; it is another to determine that the desired instruction is being given.

The first concern in an interim evaluation is with the authenticity of the innovation; the second is with the reasons for any adaptations which have been made in it; the third is with its durability over the long haul as a component of the local school. If the innovation is authentic, sensibly adapted, and hospitably supported, one can conclude that the system has made the accommodations necessary for the innovation to succeed.

THE AUTHENTICITY OF THE INNOVATION

Upon inspection, does the new program in the local school constitute a faithful likeness of the innovation which was selected for adoption? Is the subject content which is transmitted in classroom interactions, contained in the instructional materials, and called for in the pupil tests similar to that in the original? Are the actual classroom operations which teachers employ from day to day strongly reminiscent of those in other schools where the innovation is being used successfully? Does the classroom behavior of the pupils approximate that of pupils receiving the same instruction elsewhere? Are the equipment and materials identical with or similar to those originally designed for the innovation? Are they being employed in the same way?

THE REASONS FOR THE ADAPTATIONS

Undoubtedly the innovation will look somewhat different from what it does in other schools. It is widely believed in the profession that these differences are not only understandable variations to fit local circumstances but are in fact essential to the success of the innovation in each specific setting. Do the local variations actually represent an intelligent tailoring of the innovation to fit local needs, as by adjusting the pace to match the abilities of local children? Or do they represent little more than slack in the system: careless, ignorant, or unintended modifications; misunderstanding of the original; or incomplete adoption? Through interviews with teachers, these questions can be fairly readily answered. Once again, unless the innovation has been accurately characterized before adoption, the local version cannot be compared to the original.

THE MODIFICATION OF THE SURROUNDING LOCAL SYSTEM

It is one thing to look directly at the innovation to see whether it is an accurate copy of the original and to see whether the variations are accidental or intentional; it is another to determine whether the surrounding environment in the school and community has become hospitable to and supportive of the innovation.

Time.—Has the schedule of the school or the allocation of time within individual courses or classrooms been altered in such a way that the remainder of the school program has an adequate time frame? The question is directed not to the time allowed for the innovation itself, but to possible disruption elsewhere in the system. If time has been taken from other valued segments of the program, the teachers directly involved in the innovation or those outside it may resent the time lost from other activities and may be awaiting a chance to recover it. In short, is the innovation living on borrowed time?

Space.—A similar set of questions can be asked about the space allocated to the new program. Have the dislocated programs been crowded into spaces which are really unsuitable? Is a solution for them imminent or is resentment smoldering with no chance for relief? Space competition is every bit as intensive as time competi-tion, especially in the higher grades. To keep any space it has taken, an innovation will have to prove more valuable than what it has replaced or dislocated.

Equipment and materials.—What has happened to the equipment and materials supply system of the school? Has it been possible to equip and supply the innovation without noticeable disruption else-where in the program, or has the innovation monopolized tape re-corders once available to others, soaked up a large fraction of the film rental budget, denied storage space to the equipment and materials needed in other programs?

Formal rules.—Is the innovation illegitimate, living in violation of old rules which have not yet been changed in recognition of its arrival? Is the building locked so that teachers cannot get into preparation rooms to set up new types of laboratory experiments before the day begins? Does the customary one day a year (if that) allowed for faculty travel keep teachers from visiting other places where the innovation is being used? Does the purchasing depart-ment's standard two months to process and fill an order deprive the classrooms of the new items they need? Does the rule pro-hibiting teachers from using the school mimeograph machine keep them from getting the classroom copies they must have? In short, has the innovation had an effect on the rules, rather than the reverse?

Faculty attitudes.—The views of those involved directly in the innovation are salient; so are the views of those not directly involved.

Do the teachers responsible for the new instruction have a clear understanding of the objectives and the nature of the innovation? Does the new behavior expected of them fit their concepts of a professional role for teachers and fit in with national norms as to professional behavior? Do teachers feel a sense of personal responsi-bility for the innovation, associating its success with their success? Has enthusiasm replaced anxiety as the typical emotional response to the new program? Do the teachers feel adequately protected from the risk of failure? That is, do they believe that in case the program should not succeed, the responsibility would be shared by administrators? Do they believe that failure will be attributed to the innovative content and procedures rather than to incompetent teaching? At the other extreme, do they expect personal recognition in case the program should succeed brilliantly?

Do those teachers who are not now involved but who will be when the innovation is extended throughout the school, look upon the first wave of teachers as agents of the entire faculty, experimenting with the program on its behalf? Or does the remainder of the faculty see the pioneers in ways unfavorable to the future of the innovation? For example, the faculty might look upon the first wave as abandoning tried and true local methods, as currying administrative favor, as seeking personal recognition, or as trying to gain unfair access to money, space, and materials.

Those who are not involved (and who do not expect to be) should, ideally, have positive attitudes toward the program. However, neutrality is probably sufficient. Outright hostility could indicate a stormy future for the innovation. In any case, the views of the other teachers are worth collecting.

Administrative attitudes.—To succeed and to endure, the innovation must have administrative endorsement and active support. No evaluation of the accommodation of the system to the innovation is complete if it does not ascertain the administrative posture toward the new content and procedures.

Administrators must value the innovation, favor the fitting of the system to it, believe that it is feasible to accommodate the innovation, and be ready to meet the demands of the innovation as they arise. They must believe that these demands can be met without disrupting the remainder of the school and without disturbing the community. They must feel that the extra costs of the innovation in money, in effort, and in time are well worth the expected benefits of the change. They must stand ready to share the risks of failure and to protect the staff from any hazards that might accompany failure.

Community attitudes.—To the extent that they are familiar with the innovation, members of the general community and the board of education itself should be at least neutral toward the change. While positive attitudes in the general community do not appear to be necessary, negative attitudes would be a definite negative predictor for the future of the innovation.

Student attitudes.—Student reaction to the innovation appears to have an immediate, direct, and powerful influence on teachers' attitudes. It seems likely that student attitudes have a less immediate, less direct, and less powerful but nonetheless influential effect on the attitudes of their parents, if not the community as a whole. Thus, positive student attitudes are a positive predictor for the future of the innovation.

Evaluation system of the school.—Unless the evaluation system of the school has been modified so that it will measure and reward the effects of the innovation, the prognosis for the innovation is in doubt. If the evaluation system ignores the effects of the innovation, the innovation probably will not be influenced; if the evaluation system reflects and rewards the effects of the innovation, the innovation should be enhanced; but if the evaluation system reveals that the innovation has damaged the kind of learning long prized in the school and fails to show the new learning that the innovation is contributing, that innovation is in very deep trouble.

The central component of the typical school's formal evaluation system is the set of achievement tests used to measure pupil learning, particularly those achievement tests which are nationally standardized and which allow a school to compare its results with those of other schools. An innovation which is likely to reduce pupil scores on highly regarded tests will eventually arouse strong opposition. It follows that, if a valued innovation does not match existing school achievement tests, those tests must be made to match the innovation. It may be necessary to eliminate the old tests if none can be found to fit the innovation, but it would be better to locate or develop tests to measure what the innovation seeks to teach. This not only removes a barrier, but also introduces a compelling additional reason to make the innovation work.

The report cards or other devices used to inform parents about pupil achievement should be examined to see whether they have been accommodated to the innovation. To take an example, if the innovation individualizes instruction in such a way that students begin to move through the same material at variable rates of speed controlled by their mastery of the material, report cards which tell parents about the student's *degree of success* in learning the content (usually expressed as letter grades indicating class standing) should have been replaced by new report cards which tell parents about the student's *rate of progress*. Or to take another, if a distinctive new approach for dealing with disadvantaged children means that the immediate objectives for them become different from those established for other children, a report card designed to show comparable achievement in reaching identical objectives should be supplemented by one that lets teachers report the success of this different population in reaching different objectives.

In keeping with what was said earlier, community acceptance of any modified reporting scheme is essential. This is yet another reminder that the school is a complex system indeed and that to introduce an innovation is probably to cause changes throughout the system and even in its surrounding support environment.

If there are other components of the evaluation system of the school, they also need to be accommodated to the innovation. For example, if the school uses some form of teacher evaluation to determine retention, salary increments, or promotion to leadership positions, the new teaching behavior called for by the innovation should be reflected in the scheme for assessing teachers. If the innovation moves the teacher from the lecture platform and converts him into a diagnostician of learning problems, the part of the evaluation scheme which rewards teachers for an outstanding platform performance should be replaced with a section which rewards them for diagnostic skills.

Assessing the Adaptability of the School for Future Innovations

The adoption of an innovation by a school affects its readiness to take on additional innovations in the future. Since it is likely that change will be continuously necessary in the years ahead, it is desirable that the adoption of an innovation leave the school more adaptable than it was beforehand. Evaluation of an innovation, therefore, ought to include an assessment of the school's readiness to change again.

Here are some evidences of favorable effects upon adaptability:

1. The school staff has become more capable of sensing what is happening outside the school, both within the profession and within the larger society. The faculty has taken out new memberships, extended its contact with professional leaders, and increased its

readership of professional journals. Faculty lunchroom conversations deal more often with new approaches to instruction being used elsewhere.

2. The planning capability of the school has increased. The principal has become better at building future faculty meetings around emerging instructional problems; the school office has arranged for spring delivery of next year's materials; the faculty is projecting the coming space needs of an innovation which is moving up through the grades.

3. Communication throughout the school is fuller, freer, quicker.

4. A spirit of "We can do it if it's worth doing" is gradually replacing the spirit of "It's against the rules."

5. Applicants for faculty positions are beginning to say that they have heard that this is a school where teachers can try out new ideas.

6. PTA leaders are showing special interest in having new programs described at their meetings—both those now being used locally and others yet under consideration.

7. Faculty talk about instructional problems is becoming more precise, more discriminating, less directed to whole classes and more attentive to subgroups or even individuals.

8. The school is increasing its repertoire of alternative solutions. If one approach does not work, there are two or three others available. When students do not learn, teachers invent other approaches rather than giving up.

9. Teachers are beginning to *test* things out rather than simply to *try* them out. That is, they are beginning to seek more convincing evidence of the effect of what they do. There is more talk at the beginning about what a new approach is supposed to accomplish and more insistence at the end on measurement.

10. The adoption of the most recent innovation was somewhat easier than the adoption of a similar one sometime before.

11. In bringing in a new program which has been developed elsewhere, teachers are beginning to change it for good reason rather than because they do not know the new content or cannot master the new procedures.

12. Much more than pupil test scores are examined in looking for the effects of a program change. The instructional process itself is assessed even as it is being used, well before the results of pupil learning become available.

Evaluating Learning

This chapter has concentrated upon the impact of a new program upon the school itself rather than upon student learning. It has treated the kind of evaluation that can take place even before an innovation is introduced into the school and the kind of evaluation that can take place before student learning has been influenced by an adopted innovation.

Learning is of course the end product of instruction and has properly been the focus of other chapters in this volume. A change in learning is unquestionably the most important effect of any innovation. An evaluation system which is adequate for assessing learning under the regular program, if modified to take into account any genuinely new learning objectives of an innovation, should be fully adequate for evaluating the learning arising from that innovation.

CHAPTER XIII

Evaluation in Assessing the Progress of Education to Provide Bases of Public Understanding and Public Policy

JACK C. MERWIN and FRANK B. WOMER

Introduction

The project described in this chapter, although it represents a milestone in education, is not the first, nor will it be the last, attempt to develop social indices that are useful in looking at our strengths, progress, and needs. Such indices serve as a basis for future planning and for coping with new situations as they arise. Education is only one area in which such indices have been sought.

In the early 1930's we were without economic guides to provide a basis for dealing with the serious problems confronting our nation at that time. It was in the face of such needs that economic indices such as the gross national product and the consumer price index were first conceived. Similarly, it was some three to four decades ago that the value of systematic development of health indices as a basis for understanding problems and planning courses of action was given serious consideration.

It was nearly a decade ago that consideration was given to the gathering of information based on the outcomes of education. At that time Project TALENT was launched. Four years ago, the project herein described was initiated. This later project serves to illustrate the complexities involved in the development of indices to aid in dealing with social problems on a national scale. Its characteristics point to problems faced by primarily homogeneous societal groups at the state and local levels and by largely heterogeneous groups which cut across international lines as both attempt to get meaningful information about the educational achievements of groups. An international study described in chapter xiv is continuing. A number of state and local groups simultaneously have started seeking educational-outcome information which might be used as an index of progress. The description of the national project, and the complexities and complications that have been unearthed in its development thus far, can serve to indicate the problems and difficulties also faced at local, state, and international levels.

Neither the need for an assessment nor the decision to attempt to meet that need developed overnight. Like most significant educational activities undertaken on a nationwide scale, national assessment is not attributable to any single factor. The work of the Exploratory Committee on Assessing the Progress of Education and the following work by the Committee on Assessing the Progress of Education grew out of a multitude of concerns.

Search as they would, educationally minded individuals could not find comprehensive and dependable data to use in answering questions about the status of or progress being made in education in this country. During 1963 this paucity of information was on the minds of many people who were considering the important educational decisions that lay ahead. They concluded that it was essential to develop a systematic program that would provide comprehensive, dependable data on levels of educational accomplishment over the years. These data then could serve as a basis for public understanding of educational problems to be faced, of progress being made, and of aspirations not yet fulfilled.

It was during this time that the then United States Commissioner of Education, Francis Keppel, noted that one of the specific duties that had been assigned by law to the Commissioner of the U.S. Office of Education was to determine the progress of education in the several states. It was noted that voluminous record-keeping done since the establishment of the Office of Education had been almost entirely in terms of inputs into the educational system, i.e., number of classrooms, teacher-pupil ratios, teacher's salaries, etc. Little had been done to carry out the mandate to check progress toward desired outcomes. While possibly serving as the catalyst for this concern, Commissioner Keppel also was echoing needs identified by others. Many were seeing the urgency of gathering information on educational outcomes, information of a type that had not been collected before.

By the 1960's the educational implications of the many social changes that had taken place in the twentieth century had become evident. Employment patterns had been changed drastically by technological development—employment was high and was changed in composition. Unskilled work previously delegated to the uneducated was being done by computer-controlled machines plus a few individuals who pushed the buttons; automation was in full swing. Increased productivity and social change in the United States brought many families an affluence their immigrant forefathers could not have foreseen. These people wanted their children to achieve a level of education that would put them in more advantaged positions economically, socially, and politically. Recognizing the need for more and better education for their own children, they also were becoming aware of deficiencies in American education. Poor home environments, outmoded attempts to deal with the education of racial and other minority groups, and simple lack of support for education produced too many children who were driven to the education of the streets in the worst sense of the concept. This situation was seen by increasing numbers of people as one that was no longer tolerable.

Added to these factors was the "population explosion." The sheer numbers of U.S. citizens seeking education had reached a staggering figure. And the educational scene had changed in makeup as well as size. Larger and larger proportions of students were attending school beyond the mandatory age, completing high school, and seeking post-high-school education. These changes called for new approaches to education and for serious reconsideration of the bases for financing it.

The 1966 renewal of the Elementary and Secondary Education Act and the increased federal funds for education accompanying it triggered concern about federal control of education. In addition, considerable alarm was expressed on the part of some concerning the lack of effectiveness in the expenditure of the billions of dollars involved. As a result of these concerns, the Act required that evaluation be built into new programs. Within this framework, the public in general (and public officials in particular) became aware of the fact that we did not have comprehensible, dependable data that could be used as a basis for public understanding of educational progress. We did not know the extent to which various goals were being achieved; we did not know the real nature and extent of problems which still existed. It was within this setting that the organization of the Exploratory Committee on Assessing the Progress of Education (ECAPE) took place.

The Exploratory Committee

Following a number of conferences and discussions, John W. Gardner, President of the Carnegie Corporation, asked a distinguished group of Americans to form the Exploratory Committee under the chairmanship of Ralph W. Tyler to consider development of an assessment program that would provide landmarks of educational progress as a basis for meeting the changing educational needs of our society over the years. ECAPE was given three charges: (*a*) to explore with both professional educators and lay people from throughout the country the ways in which a national assessment of educational progress might best be structured to provide needed information while avoiding inadvertent damage to present educational efforts, (*b*) to develop procedures and instruments that might be used to secure information on the progress of education in the country, (*c*) to suggest the makeup of a group that would consider implementation of the plan and procedures developed by this exploratory effort and guide the conduct of successive assessments of the progress of education in the United States.

ECAPE directed its initial attention to a series of conferences on the basic characteristics that might best comprise a periodic report to the public on the progress of education in the nation. Participating in these conferences were school administrators, curriculum specialists, psychometric specialists, and laymen actively interested in education. It became obvious early in these discussions that a new type of communication was needed.

Achievement tests had long been used to help focus on differences in the academic development of individuals. They had provided a description of accomplishments in terms of scores and norms that could be used in working with individual students. Procedures for describing the achievement of large groups of individuals had been on a normative basis also. Procedures for reporting the actual achievements of large groups to the thoughtful adult public had not been developed. It became obvious to the members of ECAPE that the tools and techniques which had been developed were not adequate for reporting educational progress meaningfully.

Procedure Development

Two guidelines for procedure development were established:

1. Reports should be on the basis of age-level groups.
2. For each age group included in a national assessment, there should be an attempt to describe (a) things that almost all persons of that age level have accomplished, (b) things that average persons have achieved, and (c) things that the most advanced persons of that age level have accomplished.

It was recognized that in the initial effort it would not be possible to put together assessment instruments which would tap all important educational objectives. On the other hand it was thought important that more than the three R's be involved in the initial work, that both cognitive and affective outcomes be included, and that the over-all assessment be extended to provide comprehensive coverage of all important educational objectives as soon as feasible.

OBJECTIVES

Three specific criteria were established as a basis for developing instruments and procedures. While no attempt was to be made to assess the outcomes of specific school systems or school programs, it was considered important that the objectives used as a basis for an assessment be objectives which schools reported they were seeking to attain. It was thought important that scholars in each subject matter area consider the achievements that students were asked to demonstrate as authentic to the respective disciplines. Third, it was considered important that the assessment procedures and instrumentation be based on objectives that were thought significant by discerning lay adults. At no time was consideration given to assessing objectives that were specific to only a few institutions.

A basic concern was that the assessments should reflect, rather than restrict, curriculum changes.

With these goals in mind for the development of procedures, the Exploratory Committee decided that the information needed could not be obtained through a conventional testing program at the national level, which would have required all students to take all items. Attention was focused on descriptions of what large groups could do on individual items. Regular achievement tests which provided reports about individual differences in the achievement of students were not only inappropriate but inadequate for this task. Items which described either what practically all or what only the most advanced of a given age level could do were not found in large numbers in standardized achievement tests. Very easy and very difficult items did not contribute to the aim of identifying individual differences.

A decision was made to report to the public in terms of the exercises themselves. This placed a demand for high face validity on each exercise, whereas, when the responses from test items were summed into achievement scores for individuals, the single item did not have to bear scrutiny.

Efficiency also was a consideration. It would be very wasteful of time and effort to have all students take all items, as must be done in a testing program. Adequate descriptions of group achievement could be obtained by having each student in a random sample respond only to a small portion of a large number of exercises.

While many of the general technical considerations mentioned above gave direction to the committee's thinking, they also resulted in procedures that helped to alleviate the fears expressed by those who were concerned with the possible evaluation of schools and/or individual students. Many concerned individuals found it difficult to conceptualize a non-test approach to gathering national achievement data. The need for innovative procedures for accumulating achievement information was obvious to those working directly with the program, but was extremely difficult to communicate to those who held fears of national control of curriculum, invidious comparisons of school systems, or punishment through the withholding of funds from school systems that might not achieve what was expected of them. As the work of ECAPE progressed, it became apparent that technically adequate procedures which would avoid these types of negative outcomes could be developed.

Because ECAPE was asked to break new ground in the obtaining and reporting of achievement information, it would be well to consider separately the development of procedures that might be proposed for the assessment program and the development of instruments to implement those procedures.

Early in the exploratory period, it became obvious that there was need for the counsel and advice of lay people as well as of professional educators and those technically proficient in the fields of psychometry, achievement-testing, and sampling. Two major factors guided the activities of the Exploratory Committee as it pursued the development of procedures that might characterize a national assessment: First, the product must convey meaningful information on the progress of education to the thoughtful lay public as well as to professional educators; second, the design of procedures must be as practical and as efficient as possible in producing and conveying this information. While a large number and a wide variety of groups contributed to the deliberations, one sustaining advisory body was the technical advisory group chaired by John W. Tukey.

ECAPE's work was developmental in every sense of the word. Many suggestions were made, many alternatives considered, and many procedures tested for their viability. Procedures were formulated, shaped, and reshaped in the light of ongoing data-gathering and deliberations. Several characteristics of the procedures that ECAPE recommended in its 1968 report to the Carnegie Corporation and to the Fund for the Advancement of Education should be noted.

PROPOSED CHARACTERISTICS

It was determined early in the deliberations that the assessment should focus initially on four age levels. The age levels chosen were nine, at which age children have been exposed to the basic program of primary education; thirteen, following elementary-school education; seventeen, the last age at which groups are found in school in large numbers; and young adults.

It was decided that the procedures should focus on assessment of *what* American youth had learned—not *where* or *how* it had been learned. Sampling was to include students from public, private, and parochial schools as well as youth not in school at all. Only a small per cent at each age level would need to be involved. The decision to attempt to describe what youth of a given age level could do and the inclusion of a young adult group called for procedures to conduct part of the survey in a non-school setting.

In addition to attempting to describe the achievements of total U.S. populations at various age levels, it was considered important to look also at certain subpopulations in the country. The dimensions selected for subpopulation stratification were sex, region of the country, type of community, and socioeconomic background. The United States was divided into four geographical subdivisions— northeast, southeast, central, and west. Four types of communities were considered important to report on individually—large city, urban fringe, smaller city, and rural small town. It was considered desirable to collect information separately on those who came from an environment that fell below some poverty-level index, and on those whose home environment was above such an index. Thus, with boys and girls considered separately in the four age levels, the stratification design became one of 4 x 4 x 4 x 2 x 2, or 256 subcells created by the five main effects to be given consideration in the sampling.

Early in the deliberations of ECAPE with its technical advisory group, consideration was given to the feasibility of defining sub-objectives with enough specificity that exercises developed at two points in time for successive assessments (perhaps three to five years apart) could be used as a basis for comparing changes over time. It was considered unlikely that such specificity could be obtained, so that a process of chaining items across successive assessments was accepted. While new items would be prepared for each assessment, some exercises from previous assessments would be administered with them.

As the magnitude of the task of collecting this information came into clearer focus, it became evident that it would be unrealistic to organize, every three to five years, a new staff to conduct an assessment of ten subject areas. A cycling approach with a continuing staff was deemed more workable. The plan called for the administration of the exercises from three or four subjects each year and the return to each subject matter field every three to five years. A single staff could then be continuously in operation gathering and reporting the results of assessments. This cycling of assessments in subject fields at the same age levels every few years is somewhat different from either the conventional longitudinal or horizontal designs for gathering data on differences. The major concern was to describe progress in education in terms of changes over the years in what students at given age levels can do.

The design did not call for the involvement of an individual more than once in his lifetime. Thus, the procedure was not longitudinal in the usual sense. The primary basis for comparison was to be the performance of similarly defined age groups at two or more points in time. It was decided that the information could be gathered most efficiently by an unmatched design with each package of exercises administered to a different group of individuals at the age level.

The approach to reporting was envisioned as including exercises themselves in the report as well as presenting the proportions of defined groups which give various classifiable types of responses. Thus, it might be reported that 53 per cent of the nine-year-olds from large cities could solve a given mathematics problem; or that 67 per cent of the thirteen-year-old girls from the central region were able to identify their congressman; or that 37 per cent of the boys from above the poverty-level index in the country were able to set up specified equipment and propose an appropriate procedure for testing a specific scientific hypothesis. The unmatched design was considered best for maximizing the amount of information obtained and minimizing both the amount of student time needed and interference with normal school activities. Since the focus was not on comparisons among individuals, it was not necessary that all examinees take the same exercises. Thirty students, spending forty minutes taking *different* sets of exercises, would provide one response to each of a total set of exercises that would take one student twenty hours to complete. Fifteen thousand students responding to those same exercises would provide five hundred responses to each exercise. It was considered highly unlikely that a student in the sample would be asked to contribute more than forty minutes or an hour, once in a lifetime, to an assessment. The unmatched design and lack of need to reliably assess individuals in specific subject matter removed some practical limitations involved in test development. The need for high content validity along with the attempt to describe the accomplishments of the extreme groups at the various age levels (i.e., what practically all can do and what the most advanced can do) posed new and challenging problems of instrument development.

Instrument Development

The Exploratory Committee recognized very early that it would not be feasible to build its own staff with the skills and capabilities needed to produce the desired instruments. Therefore, it turned to existing organizations for work on instrument development, under contract to ECAPE.

The contractors were The American Institutes for Research, Educational Testing Service, The Psychological Corporation, and Science Research Associates. In line with the proposal of the early conferees that more than the three R's be covered, contracts were let for work in ten areas: reading, writing, literature, art, music, mathematics, science, social studies, citizenship, and vocational education. In the discussions with the contractors, several decisions were made about the subject matter to be covered. It was decided that study skills should be made part of the developmental work within each subject field, and that affective outcomes should be included in the objectives to be covered in each subject field.

Owing to the unusual nature of the project and to the desire to secure the benefit of different points of view, the Exploratory Committee contracted with two agencies to work independently in five of the ten subject areas. The first step was the development of objectives that would serve as the basis for instrument development.

STATEMENTS OF OBJECTIVES

The Exploratory Committee decided that objectives that serve as a basis for instrument development should meet three criteria: They should be objectives (a) that the school currently is seeking to attain, (b) that scholars in the field consider authentic to their discipline, and (c) that thoughtful laymen consider important for American youth to learn. With these criteria in mind, the contractors set to work with subject matter specialists and others to develop initial sets of objectives. Each contractor was given complete freedom to bring together those consultants whom he believed were most competent to assist in developing the sets of objectives. This approach resulted in some lack of uniformity in the structure given to the objectives developed, but it was thought to be the best way to take advantage of the thinking of professionals and to arrive at objectives that do reflect those things considered authentic to the disciplines and which also are current objectives of school programs.

It is not unusual for professionals to interact on such things as objectives and tasks. An unusual aspect of this project, however, was the inclusion of non-professionals in the development of the objectives. This called for securing thoughtful lay persons actively interested in education. To identify such persons, officers of various national and state organizations concerned with education (National School Board Association, National Congress of Parents and Teachers, National Catholic Education Association, U.S. Chamber of Commerce, NAACP, and so forth) were asked to nominate individuals. From these nominations, persons who lived in large cities, suburban communities, and rural–small–town areas throughout the country were selected to attend conferences to review the objectives that had been developed. Eleven panels were organized, each chaired by one of the lay panelists with a member of the ECAPE staff in attendance, and each in possession of the full report from the contractor of the objectives and their development. Each panel went over all the objectives developed, providing eleven independent reviews. Following the panel meetings the eleven chairmen were brought together to pool their recommendations to the Committee. In general, there was a basic unanimity of reaction not only on the part of the lay panels but also with respect to lay and professional judgments.

Except for suggested minor revisions, the lay panelists accepted the contractors' objectives for most subject areas as important goals for American youth. There was general agreement among the lay panelists that the objectives set forth for social studies were not as clear as they might be. Also it was agreed that they were lacking in sufficient specificity to identify what might be done under each particular objective. Therefore, it was recommended that this area be developed further prior to the production of exercises.

A special conference of experts in the social-studies area was held following the lay review meetings. At this conference, teachers of social studies, professors of social-studies education, and experts from the disciplines which contribute to the social studies were brought together to consider the social-studies objectives and to establish guidelines for further work on them. Following this conference, a revised set of objectives for social studies was developed and approved.

A study was made of the objectives developed for the ten national assessment areas and their relationship to other statements of objectives in these areas which had appeared in the professional literature of the twenty-five years preceding the initiation of this project. Since the national assessment objectives were developed for a specific purpose, their wording, phrasing, and organization were somewhat more uniform than that found in other statements of objectives over the years, even within a single subject matter field. However, it was possible to classify those objectives that had appeared in print[1] in terms of how they related to the objectives developed specifically for this project. When the classification was finished, it was clear that national assessment had not produced a set of new objectives for these areas. Rather, its objectives represented a reorganization, restatement, and something of a summarization of objectives which frequently had appeared in print in the last quarter century. Since one criterion for the national assessment objectives was that they be ones for which the schools were teaching, this similarity was a hoped-for and expected outcome.

EXERCISE DEVELOPMENT

The development of exercises was approached with great anticipation that new types of data-gathering devices could be perfected —devices that could lead to improved communication about student achievement with laymen and professionals alike. For the

---

1. These presumably served as the basis for major curriculum development projects in these areas in recent history.

development of the exercises, the Exploratory Committee again turned to contractors that had professional staffs and consultants already available. The same four contractors that had been involved in the development of the objectives were asked to develop the exercises. The contractors were charged with developing exercises that would meet three specific criteria: (a) Each exercise must sample the behavior of one of the objectives. (b) Each exercise must have enough face validity to communicate achievement information meaningfully to laymen. (c) One-third of the exercises should be ones that practically all of the individuals of a given age level could do; one-third, that approximately half could do; and one-third that only the most advanced could do.

Within this framework the contractors were encouraged to ignore practical limitations and to produce the best plan they could evolve for developing exercises that met the criteria. They were not limited to exercises which could provide a reliable measure of an individual. They were not limited to any particular type of items such as, for example, paper-and-pencil exercises. It was hoped that they would be creative in developing procedures which would enable students to exhibit the behaviors set forth in the objectives in a manner that could be reported meaningfully to non-professional adults.

When related to this goal, the first set of exercises received from the contractors was disappointing. While some unusual approaches were developed—observation of behavior, the use of tape recorders for stimulus presentation and the recording of responses, and the imaginative use of some apparatus—a large proportion of the exercises were much like traditional test items both in form and content. The items were largely multiple choice in format and called for responses normally called for on regular achievement tests. Approximately ten thousand items were developed by the contractors.

INITIAL EXERCISE REVIEWS

Even though professional people from the subject matter fields had been involved in the development of the exercises, it was deemed desirable to obtain an independent subject matter review of the exercises. The Exploratory Committee consulted the national organizations of subject matter specialists in each of the areas (National Council of Teachers of Mathematics, the National Council on Social Studies, the American Vocational Association, and so on.) and asked for nominations of members who might review these exercises. Exercises were sent to one or more of the nominees along with several specific questions. The reviewer was asked whether, in his judgment, the exercise sampled the objective for which it had been written. He was asked what, in his judgment, was the desired answer. He was asked to estimate what proportion of the age-level group could respond with the keyed answer. Last, he was asked if he could detect any flaws in the item that would tend to make it in any way ambiguous or otherwise unsatisfactory. These reviewers helped identify a number of problems, made suggestions for improvements, and offered ideas for new items which they were confident would more adequately sample the objectives. While this review by subject matter specialists was going on, another review was being conducted.

It is important not only that questions used in a national assessment program be meaningful to thoughtful American adults but also that they be questions which would not be considered imprudent, an invasion of privacy, or in any other way improper. To evaluate the potential offensiveness of the exercises, a series of conferences were initiated. Lay persons nominated for the earlier reviews of objectives were asked to review exercises from the standpoint of two questions: (a) Is this something that I would want presented to my child? (b) Is there some important group in my community that would find it offensive to have this type of item included in a national assessment? It was considered inappropriate and unnecessary to ask these very busy people to review all exercises (including those in multiplication, addition, etc.) for offensiveness. These reviews led to the deletion of some items and to the revision of others—revision aimed at preserving measurement of an objective by an item while avoiding potentially offensive wording or context.

The reaction to items in citizenship was particularly interesting. The review groups were from different types of communities and different parts of the country. They represented major segments of our society—labor, management, different religious groups, different races, etc.—and brought diverse points of view to the review task. At each conference, it immediately became apparent to the conferees that, to get at the most important concepts and knowledges in the citizenship area, it would be necessary to cover sensitive areas. As one panelist put it, "If we remove everything about politics, sex, religion, race, minority groups, and the police, there isn't much meaningful material left in the area of citizenship." There was little difficulty with items which touched on knowledge in the citizenship area. Similarly, there was little difficulty with items related to generally accepted behavior. However, when the reviewers came to items which attempted to get at actual citizenship practice, a good deal of uneasiness was expressed. A lack of agreement on what constitutes good citizenship led to considerable rewording of exercises in an attempt to secure concensus if not unanimity.

These lay reviewers were asked to do a most challenging task in attempting to present the reactions of various lay groups of their communities. Their contribution to a national assessment program should never be minimized. They gave crucial guidance in a very difficult area at a time when social sensitivities were reaching a new height in American culture.

INITIAL TRYOUT STUDIES

Many items written to tap what practically all of a given age group could do appeared to be more difficult than indicated by this labeling. The difficulty estimate of the item-writer often was at considerable variance from the estimate of the ECAPE staff. As a result, a study of the difficulty of the items labeled as "90%" (presumably items which practically everyone of a given age level could do) was conducted by the ECAPE staff. A random sample of the items labeled as "90%" items by the contractors was selected for study. No attempt was made to sample students randomly at various age levels throughout the country, but a two-way split on both socioeconomic status and geographic area provided a four-cell sampling. The use of this sample provided rough estimates of the difficulty level of the items for a national group.

In spite of the limitations of the sampling involved in this study, it is interesting to note that correct responses to individual "easy"

items were given by as few as 4 and by as many as 100 per cent
of the group tested. These items, one must remember, were intended
by the contractors to be easy enough to be answered correctly by
most of the examinees of a given age level. Only a small number of
the items in any area met this goal and in one subject area the highest percentage of correct responses was in the 50's.

FEASIBILITY

A second study reinforced many of the impressions produced
by the "90% study." In this second study, attempts were made to
identify problems related to stimulus presentation and/or response
procedures and/or scoring schemes of the exercises. Contracts
were let to two organizations to study independently the feasibility
of the administration of each item type to school populations. A
survey-research organization was engaged to study the feasibility
of the administration of the exercises to seventeen-year-olds and
adults in their homes. The survey group, much to its surprise,
discovered that it was no more difficult to get adults and seventeen-
year-olds in the home to respond to achievement exercises than it
was to get them to respond to opinion questions. In fact, many of
those responding found it a most enjoyable task.

The in-school administrations substantiated several of the problems previously considered. It was readily apparent from the
results that the difficulty of items, particularly the "easy" items, had
been grossly underestimated. This was particularly true at the
nine-year-old level. It also became obvious that part of the problem
of item difficulty was caused by the heavy verbal loadings of many
exercises in all areas, not just in the reading areas. In many instances
this verbal factor alone precluded the possibility of obtaining correct responses from anywhere near 90 per cent of the group.

CONFERENCE OF SUBJECT MATTER SPECIALISTS

The results of the initial exercise reviews, the "90% study,"
and the feasibility studies led to a decision to hold a series of item-
review conferences during the summer of 1967. Subject matter
specialists and others working in, or closely allied to, each subject
matter area were brought together to review the exercises. A different panel was assembled to review the exercises for each age

group—nine, thirteen, seventeen, and adult. At least one of the item-writers was present as well as ECAPE staff members.

The tasks of the reviewers were: (*a*) to evaluate each exercise in relation to the objective which it was designed to measure, and (*b*) to suggest editorial changes which they thought would improve an exercise. In addition to these two tasks, the reviewers were asked to make any other comments or suggestions which they believed would improve the exercises. The most common comments coming from the reviewers across the ten areas were as follows:

1. The exercises were too difficult, particularly those designed for nine-year-olds.
2. The exercises were too "textbookish," particularly those designed to assess knowledge.
3. There were gaps in the coverage of the areas and inadequate sampling of some behaviors and some content.

In addition, specific recommendations were received in each subject area—some related to equipment needed; some, to the specific wording of an objective; some, to the type or types of exercises produced.

These summer review conferences set the direction for further work on the exercises. In five of the subject areas, the suggestions were specific enough that they could be implemented within a few months. In the other five areas the problems identified were so serious that considerable additional efforts were required, including the production of new approaches and of many completely new exercises.

At this point, ECAPE asked the help of item-writers other than those used by the original contractors in filling some of the gaps that the reviewers had identified. Although the original plan for exercise development had not included this step, it seemed to be the best way to break out of the mold of traditional paper-and-pencil, multiple-choice item-writing. This step was necessary in six of the ten areas.

By mid-winter of 1967/68, new and revised exercises were ready for another review in five of the areas. These reviews were similar to those of the summer conferences, but, because of the added refinement of the exercises, the reviewers were able to concentrate on final revisions of exercises prior to the final tryouts. Not all problems were solved, but the reviewers were confident that the exercises were sufficiently refined at the conclusion of these conferences to proceed to formal tryouts with them.

Three of the areas required enough additional item production that the pre-tryout review conferences could not be held until the spring of 1968. In two areas the problems were so serious that they required extensive reconsideration and redevelopment into the 1968/69 academic year.

These numerous review conferences have demonstrated clearly that the goals which the Exploratory Committee set itself were not easy to achieve. The development of imaginative exercises that directly measure important educational objectives and that are worded so simply that the task is easily communicated to all American youth is an extremely challenging job.

Bringing reviewers, item writers, and ECAPE staff members together in one place had the distinct advantage of promoting an interchange of ideas. Such an interchange resulted in the resolution of many differences in viewpoint and in the achievement of consensus on most exercises.

DIRECTIONALITY

An issue that was raised at the various subject matter conferences was that of the directionality, or lack of it, of the exercises. The concept of directionality is clarified by the following statements:

1. Each objective must be agreed upon by schools, scholars, and laymen as an important goal for the nation as a whole.
2. The purpose of the national assessment is to determine the extent to which these objectives are being achieved.
3. Therefore, every national assessment exercise must have a "correct" or a "desired" response. Otherwise, changes that take place over time are neither correct nor incorrect, desirable nor undesirable, and tell nothing about the extent to which an objective is being attained.

Another way of stating this point is that the national assessment project was not designed to be a survey of how people feel about things. It was designed to determine whether knowledges or skills improve over time and whether attitudes change in a direction considered desirable by the great majority of our society. This leaves to the pollsters the area of those attitudes which have no generally desired direction.

Not everyone understood or agreed with the concept of directionality in relation to the national assessment exercises. Only one of the four contractors had, in fact, attempted to develop all affective exercises with a desired direction. Thus, many of the attitudinal exercises reviewed at the subject matter conferences did not have directionality. They had to be altered or dropped from the pool of exercises.

The purpose of national assessment is first to "take a reading" of *desired* knowledges, skills, and attitudes and then to reassess the same attributes several years later in order to measure progress over time. It is not the purpose of national assessment simply to survey how respondents feel about things.

FORMAL TRYOUTS

Formal tryouts of the exercises for the areas of citizenship, literature, science, social studies, and writing were made in the spring of 1968. Three contractors shared in the effort. The group-administerable exercises were given to two classrooms, one high SES (socioeconomic status) and one low SES, totaling between fifty and sixty examinees. The individually administered exercises were given to a minimum of six examinees. The results of the tryouts were used primarily to identify special problems in the exercises that had not been eliminated in the many prior reviews and tryouts.

In addition, the tryouts provided information about the time required for each exercise. They also provided much needed experience in the field with the practical problems associated with securing the co-operation of school systems and with the actual administration of packages of exercises. These formal tryouts led to the final revision of exercises for use in an actual national assessment.

SPECIAL STUDIES

The ECAPE project was itself a research effort. But, in order to carry it out most effectively, it was necessary to undertake a number of studies designed to answer specific questions about the exercises and about the best methods of administering them. Studies were aimed at answering practical questions that arose, questions not answered, by and large, in the measurement literature. It was quite surprising to find that many of these questions apparently had been answered previously on an "armchair" basis, without serious attempts to research them. It may well be that the emphasis on the content validity of the exercises was the factor that forced a much closer examination of the exercises and procedures than otherwise would have been made. This great concern with content validity led the Technical Advisory Group to a simple but very powerful principle that guided the exercise development and revisions and much of the research that was done. The principle was simply that everything possible should be done to maximize an examinee's understanding of the task he was being asked to do in each exercise. This led to the need for several special studies.

In-school versus out-of-school administration.—The major problem investigated in this study was whether the physical setting of testing, in school or in the home, would have any effect on results. This factor was investigated for several reasons. Some consideration was given to complete home administration. More important, however, was the need to see whether the results from seventeen-year-olds tested in school might be different from the results of seventeen-year-olds tested outside school.[2]

The Research Triangle Institute (RTI) conducted this study. They tested students in ten schools from three widely divergent socioeconomic levels. Both exercises designed for group administration and those designed for individual administration were used. When used in school, the group exercises were given individually to one sample and in groups to another sample. When used in the home, they were given individually.

The major conclusion of the study was that there were no statistically significant differences between in-school and in-the-home results on either group-administered or individually-administered exercises. It should be noted that the study used only exami-

---

2. It is estimated that somewhere around 25 per cent of seventeen-year-olds are not enrolled in secondary schools.

nees enrolled in school, so that attention could be focused on the setting. In the actual assessment, it may well be that the results of out-of-school youth, seventeen years of age (most of them drop-outs) will be different. This study suggests that, if differences do appear, they are apt to be due to differences in the examinees rather than to differences in the testing setting.

Modes of administration.—An important outcome of the several feasibility studies was to point to the need for an investigation of various modes of administration, to discover ways to maximize understanding and minimize examinee problems with item formats and item directions. The American Institutes for Research (AIR) carried on a study with nine-year-olds involving the following methods of administration:

1. Individual administration: Administrator read all directions and each exercise aloud. He did not read the alternatives for multiple-choice questions, just the stem. Examinee had his own booklet and read along silently. Examinee could ask questions. Examinee gave his response verbally. For reading passages, examinee read the passage to himself.

2. Regular group administration: No questions

   a) No displays. Typical testing situation. Administrator read directions; examinee read and answered exercises. Examinee could not ask questions during administration.

   b) Displays. No printed directions in booklet. Administrator read all directions and used visual displays for all sample exercises. Examinee read and answered exercises. Examinee could not ask questions during administration.

3. Regular group administration: Questions

   a) Same as 2-*a* (no displays) except that examinee could ask questions about directions, about vocabulary, etc., during administration.

   b) Same as 2-*b* (displays) except that examinee could ask questions about vocabulary, etc., during administration.

4. Paced-taped group administration

   a) No displays. Administrator turned on tape recorder. All directions were read on tape. All exercises, including alternatives in choice-type exercises, were read aloud on tape. The tape was paced so that all examinees followed timing of the tape. Examinees read along in their booklets. Questions allowed at end of test. Reading passage read by examinees; not on tape.

b) Display. Same as 4-a except that visual displays were used for explaining directions for each format.

The exercises selected for the study were easy ones; the sample was selected from poor readers. The purpose was to see whether the various methods showed differences among poor readers on easy items. It was assumed that, if differences appeared in this situation, they would be magnified when more difficult items were used. If differences did not appear, a further study using more difficult exercises would be needed. Further, it was assumed that good readers could function satisfactorily under any of the testing conditions.

Each examinee was interviewed individually after the testing for an average of thirty minutes as a posttest, a repeat of the test itself, with the examinee saying aloud what he thought each exercise directed him to do. Frequently, he was asked to pronounce a key word or to define it, and his responses to each exercise were recorded by the interviewer. Each examinee received a total score on the posttest as well as on his original test. The purpose of this procedure was to see what the examinees could do on the exercises with maximum help short of specific cues to the answers.

A comparison between the results of the use of "displays" and the results of the use of "no displays" showed virtually no difference in the performance of the examinees.

There was a slight advantage of paced-tape *over* individual administration, but it came entirely from the multiple-choice questions, for which alternatives were read aloud on tape but not read aloud by the individual examiner. The over-all results for the paced-tape mode of administration were good enough (and the uniformity of administration guaranteed by paced-tape was important enough) that paced-tape was used for all administrations of group-administerable exercises during the formal tryouts of the national assessment exercises. The obvious exception to the use of paced-tape was for the area of reading.

There was a slight advantage of individual administration over the other modes for short-answer exercises. This fact suggested that consideration should be given to having all open-end exercises administered individually with the interviewer recording responses or to taping an examinee's verbal responses to open-end exercises.

Posttest results were very similar across all four modes of administration and were better than the regular test results. This suggests that the method of *working* individually with an examinee when one gives maximum help in understanding each task (as opposed to *testing* him individually) may come closer to getting at his "true" knowledge level.

A major consequence of this study was to indicate the need for a follow-up study designed to attempt to test the conclusions drawn from this one and to seek answers to several questions raised by it.

AIR was commissioned to test a sample of both nine- and thirteen-year-olds using: (*a*) individual administration, (*b*) individual administration of paced-tape, (*c*) self-paced tape, and (*d*) group administration of paced-tape.

Methods (*a*) (individual administration and (*d*) (group administration of paced-tape) were repetitions of 1 and 4 in the previous study. Method (*b*) (individual administration of paced-tape) was added to check on the possibility that, in a group paced-tape administration some examinees might receive cues to answers from more able students who marked their choices immediately following a given response. Method (*c*) (self-paced tape) was different. It was designed so that each examinee, working individually in a carrel, listened to the same tape of directions and exercises used for the paced-tape administrations but started the tape whenever he was ready to hear the directions or to hear a new exercise. The tape shut itself off after each exercise and the examinee could take as long as he wanted to perform a given exercise before proceeding to the next one. Thus, one had self-paced tape administration. Each examinee marked his answers to choice-type questions in his own booklet but responded verbally to open-end exercises. A second tape recorder recorded his verbal response for later scoring. Self-paced tape had the advantage of letting each examinee work at his own rate, an advantage that group-paced tape did not have.

The results were discouraging in relation to the anticipation for the self-paced situation. Method (*d*) (group administration of paced-tape) proved best for both age groups for the multiple-choice exercises. Method (*d*) was not as good as method (*a*) (individual administration) for age nine for the short-answer exercises but method (*d*) was as good as method (*a*) for short-answer exercises for age-thirteen examinees. The self-paced method yielded poorer results than either group-paced or individual administration. The contractor speculated that perhaps the novelty of the individual carrels, with tape recorders and ear phones, may have distracted examinees from the task of answering a set of questions.

It was decided to shelve the idea of self-paced tape in a "trailer" for the first year of the assessment. Further, it was decided to classify most short-answer exercises for age-nine examinees as individually-administered exercises.

Regional voice.—A question of concern that was raised by the original paced-tape study was whether the same voice would be understood equally well by students in different parts of the country. In order to check this question, a study was designed to compare the results obtained using a single voice that is considered to be of national TV or radio quality with those obtained using a voice that reflected a definite regional accent. The study was designed by the ECAPE staff, with field work being done by the Southeastern Regional Laboratory (SEL), AIR, and RTI.

The first part of this study (using a "national" male voice, a regional male voice, and a regional female voice, with classes randomly split for the three methods) showed that examinees hearing either male voice did significantly better than those hearing the female voice. As between the two male, taped voices, girls did significantly better when hearing the regional male voice; boys did not.

The superior results obtained from using male voices were due to large differences on four exercises only. This fact led to some questioning of the results and to two replications of the study, using the two male voices only. In these replications, there were no significant differences between the two taped voices for either boys or girls.

It was decided that a national TV-type male voice would be used for administration of group exercises in the national assessment.

Mathematics study.—A major concern of ECAPE's reviewers regarding the mathematics exercises was their formal wording. Mathematicians insist that wording be precise and accurate; mathematics educators are more inclined to opt for less precise language that is more easily understood by examinees. To investigate the validity of this concern, the ECAPE staff designed and carried out a study that compared the results obtained from the use of a set of exercises that were worded formally with those obtained from the use of the same exercises edited in the direction of simpler language. In addition, the same exercises were presented both in multiple-choice and open-ended versions, and all multiple-choice exercises were tried with and without an "I Don't Know" choice added. The major findings were:

1. The wording of most exercises made little difference. Easy exercises were easy, and difficult ones were difficult regardless of wording.

2. The "I Don't Know" choice made a significant difference. In 25 of 32 exercises the "I Don't Know" choice produced a p-value (item difficulty) closer to that produced by the open-ended version than the p-value produced by the same exercise without that choice. This suggests that guessing is reduced when examinees are given the option of responding that they do not know.

3. The open-ended versions of exercises produced 10-point (or more) lower p-values (were more difficult) than the multiple-choice versions in about forty per cent of the comparisons. Small differences were found for the very easy and the very difficult exercises, but over half of the exercises with p-values between 26 and 74 yielded large differences. This suggests that, when an examinee definitely

has developed an arithmetic or mathematical skill or when he definitely does not have the skill, the item-format is immaterial. In the middle ranges of skill development, the choice-type mathematics question is considerably easier than the open-ended one.

This study contributed significantly to a decision to add the "I Don't Know" alternative to almost all multiple-choice exercises proposed for use in the national assessment.

Choices study.—In order to investigate further the differences between examinee responses that are related to specific alternatives in a multiple-choice exercise, the staff developed a study that compared the results obtained from giving three versions of the same multiple-choice exercises with the same question open-ended. The different versions, using social-studies exercises of the knowledge type, were designed as follows:

1. Contractors original exercise
2. ECAPE revision with alternatives that were designed to make the choice more difficult
3. ECAPE revision with other "logical" choices
4. Open-ended version

The general results and conclusions were as follows:

1. Some exercises were so easy that there were no differences in p-values between the four versions.
2. For almost two-thirds of the exercises, there were large differences in p-values between the various versions. Almost always the open-ended version was the most difficult. Sometimes the three multiple-choice versions showed large differences. Recognition of factual knowledge is much easier than recall.
3. The "I Don't Know" response often was chosen for the multiple-choice questions, but examinees preferred to omit a response to an open-ended exercise rather than write "I Don't Know."

The research done for national assessment was very specific in nature. It was done to provide information useful in achieving the goal of maximizing understanding of each task presented to an examinee. Much of it has implications for testing in other settings, both by the teacher in his classroom and by test publishers.

Summary and Implications

Developmental work for a national assessment of the type designed by ECAPE never can end. Several aspects of the envisioned program dictate this conclusion. Continued adjustments will need to be made in instrumentation to reflect objectives that change over the years. Much as factors involved in the gross national product (GNP) have been altered over the years, educational factors contributing to the description of the progress of education will need to be altered as progress is made. A second factor that necessitates continued development is the use of exercises in reporting. As exercises are revealed in national assessment reports, they will cease to be useful as part of an ongoing assessment program. Thus, new exercises to tap ongoing objectives and new exercises to tap new objectives will be needed at each cycling of a subject field.

The early conferees who met to discuss the project recommended that the assessment program should become more comprehensive as rapidly as possible. Many subject fields—e.g., physical education, speech, listening, and foreign languages—would need to be developed to reach this goal. A most cogent argument for the need for continuing developmental work is found in the pioneering nature of the project. During ECAPE's nearly four years of existence, many problems and complexities were uncovered; many techniques were developed and tried out; many disappointments were experienced in the effort to develop the type of instrumentation needed. The Exploratory Committee made great progress in virgin territory, in spite of much backing and filling and many false starts. A good deal of evidence was gathered which indicated that developing exercises of the type needed was a task to which few, if any, could bring experience. Much has been learned, but it is only a fraction of what must be learned about the nature of a truly effective approach to periodically inventorying the status and progress of education in this country.

Some new tools have been developed by the Committee. The

effectiveness of these tools will remain unknown until an actual assessment is conducted. As this book goes to press, the first results of the first assessment are being accumulated and analyzed. These results will be helpful to the American public. With equal assurance they will point to a need for the design of better instruments and better techniques for ultimate production of even more informative data on the progress of education.

There are several characteristics of the project undertaken by the Exploratory Committee and of the techniques used in its developmental work which in toto, as well as individually, point up the uniqueness of this undertaking. Since this is clearly true, it is well to note some of the more important lessons that have been learned in the process.

The first two decades of the second half of the twentieth century found an increasing amount of concern and involvement of parents and laymen in the activities of the school. Blind acceptance of the judgment of "experts" was becoming passé. By the mid-1960's, by which time there was an increasing dialogue between schools and their publics regarding appropriateness of curriculums, the demonstrated unanimity of educators and laymen on the objectives that should serve as the basis for an initial assessment was most encouraging. It indicated that the scholar from a discipline, the conveyor of that discipline, and the parents of students could communicate meaningfully with one another in regard to the objectives of education.

The Exploratory Committee with a small central staff arranged for the development work to be done through contractual arrangements with established organizations. The contractors were asked to serve a role quite different from that of their other contractual involvements. They were asked to work on pieces of a large project. They were asked to work with each other in a developmental project which involved successive changes in many specifications, changes dictated by the developmental experience. In addition, the project involved the combined efforts of people whose work had been primarily test development, others whose work had been primarily sample design, and still others primarily from the area of survey research. The organizations involved were employed not only for the use of their existing administrative structure, but also for the *expertise* and experience that their existing staffs could bring to the solution of the many interrelated and complex problems of this undertaking. Within this unique framework, a number of experiences deserve note.

ECAPE faced the need to develop a new type of instrumentation to assess educational achievement. This undertaking was closer to the ongoing activities of the organizations that became involved than to any other existing agencies in the country. It may have been too close. People from agencies who worked on exercise development were very good in their special area of test development. They found it difficult to shed basic premises which underlay test development but which were not applicable as limitations on group assessment. Reorientation to the desirable characteristics of instrumentation for describing the achievement of groups proved most difficult for many of these people. With the removal of the need for reliable measures of individuals, many freedoms were granted for development of new stimulus and response mechanisms to describe group achievement. However, in developing "exercises," many of the contractors began by doing what they do so well, by producing stimulus and response mechanisms with a high similarity to items developed to reliably differentiate among individuals.

The exercise-developers were asked to do something else which departs quite drastically from their usual activity. The concept of using exercises to report meaningfully to lay people has an analogy in opinion-polling. The report of opinion polls presents the question asked and summarizes the responses obtained. In general, this type of reporting has always been envisioned as part of the reporting of the national assessment.

In developing achievement tests, we have long been concerned that the total set of items will be perceived by the test-taker as calling for a demonstration of his achievements in the area designated by the title of the test. Beyond this, however, the specific content of individual items often has been ignored in the additive approach of scoring across items to get a reliable index of achievement for an individual. Asking that individual items be meaningful in and of themselves requires a high degree of content validity for each exercise. Exercise-developers found it most difficult to produce exercises which could meet the criterion of being sufficiently meaningful to allow each individual exercise to be used in reporting.

The construction of exercises which could be used to describe what practically all of a given age level could do proved to be a very difficult task. Only somewhat less difficult was the development of exercises to describe what the most advanced could do. Two factors loomed large in the contractors' attempts to develop exercises that would describe what practically everyone of a given age level could do. The sheer verbal loading of large numbers of the exercises indicated a lack of understanding of the very limited verbal skills of many examinees, particularly at the nine-year-old level. In addition, there was a seeming misperception of the simplicity needed in exercises that would indeed present tasks that most nine-year-olds could complete. The contractor was faced with developing difficult exercises which have the type of face validity described above and that are difficult strictly on the basis of behavior set forth in the objectives.

A surprising and positive outcome of the developmental work was the discovery that achievement-type exercises could be administered, with relative ease, in the home to adults and to out-of-school seventeen-year-olds.

The task undertaken by ECAPE was a unique research and developmental project. It has been a national undertaking in every sense of the word. It has drawn together professionals in education and non-professionals. It has brought together teachers, curriculum specialists, psychometricians, and sampling experts. It has involved the best minds that the Exploratory Committee was able to tap in all relevant areas. It is aimed toward a goal that all people value—a public understanding of the progress of education in the United States of America.

CHAPTER XIV

International Impact of Evaluation

TORSTEN HUSÉN

The Need for Cross-national Evaluation

Evaluative judgments have always been passed upon the relative merits of educational systems in different countries. Deans of admissions over the years have tried to evaluate in their way a French *baccalauréat* or an "English General Certificate of Education, A—level," in terms of graduation from different types of high schools in the United States. Much of this rather intuitive evaluation has taken place under the auspices of a booming discipline called comparative education. Bereday distinguishes between different stages in the development of comparative education.[1] In the beginning, comparative educators confined themselves to the collection of descriptive data from one or more countries. In the next stage, they tried to interpret these data in terms of the social sciences. The third stage involved the simultaneous review or juxtaposition of several systems in order to develop a framework within which comparisons could be made. In the fourth and final stage, presumably, comparisons in terms of testing hypotheses are to be made, the criteria of comparability having been established by means of data obtained during the previous stages.

Apart from the results of the more formalized attempts of the educators to make comparisons, quite a lot of folklore has prevailed, particularly concerning the "productivity" or "efficiency" of the various systems. An American admiral some years ago wrote a widely publicized article in which he, without presenting any evidence, flatly stated that one school year in the United States is worth only two-thirds of a school year in Europe.

1. G. Z. F. Bereday, *Comparative Method in Education* (New York: Holt, Rinehart & Winston, 1964).

335

The need for making cross-national or cross-cultural evaluations in education has grown rapidly for various reasons during the last two decades. Some of the reasons for this need for more accurate evaluation of the outcomes of various educational systems should be pointed out.

International student mobility has increased tremendously during the last few decades. Thus, for instance, in the United States in 1967 there were close to 90,000 foreign students, a considerable part of them from developing countries. The number of students in Europe, particularly from Africa and Asia, has recently grown to tens of thousands. Furthermore, a growing number of young people go to school in a country other than their native one because of the movement of their parents. The extramural department of the University of Stockholm recently launched an international program for Swedish upper-secondary students. For two of the three years, these students are taught mainly in English, French, and German during their stay in a country in which the language is spoken. The increase in the exchange of university students has led to a growing demand for an international *baccalauréat* or matriculation examination whereby university entrance requirements can be evaluated cross-nationally.

Technical assistance in the educational field, provided both multilaterally and bilaterally, has created a demand for techniques by which the "quality" of the educational systems in emerging countries can be assessed. There is indeed a strong need for both fruitful theoretical models and international standards by which educational systems can be evaluated. The more interested we have become in education as an investment in human capital and as an instrument for bringing about economic growth and social change, particularly in the developing countries, the stronger the need to develop such models and measuring instruments has become. So far, many of the studies of the relationship between education and economic growth have been limited to the use of very crude "output" variables—for instance, enrolment and graduation figures. No quality measures have been used until recently, because no internationally valid and applicable instruments for measuring outcomes of instruction have existed.

The International Project for the Evaluation
of Educational Achievement (I.E.A.)

There has been a growing awareness that countries can learn from each other with regard to educational structure and practices found within the various systems. Both cognitive and non-cognitive outcomes of schooling can be related to the different patterns of "input" factors, such as per pupil expenditure, teacher competence, number of hours of instruction, grouping practices, and so forth. Within countries, particularly in those with national policy-making and centralized administration in education, many practices are very uniform, whereas the cross-national variations in practice may cover a much larger range. One can therefore take advantage of the cross-national variability of the socioeconomic structure and educational practices to relate them to measures of outcomes. For instance, the long-range effect of the age of school entry upon student performance or the effect of sex differences on science achievement cannot be studied with any prospect of success within a system in which input variables cover a narrow or no range, whereas they can be studied cross-nationally with reasonable expectation of success.

So far, most of the cross-national variables established have been independent ones, most of them pertaining to input of money, physical plant, and personnel. The situation has been much less satisfactory with regard to output variables. In most cases so far, enrolment and graduation figures have been used as evaluative measures.[2] It is obvious that comparability among countries and systems in these respects may be doubted.

Until recently, no cross-nationally valid and applicable criteria whereby school systems or individual students could be evaluated have existed. During the latter part of the 1950's, researchers from ten countries met once a year at the Unesco Institute for Education in Hamburg in order to exchange information and experiences relative to school failures, examinations, and methods of evaluation. The lack of international evaluation instruments was strongly felt, and it was decided that attempts should be made to devise inter-

2. F. Harbison and C. Myers, *Education, Manpower, and Economic Growth* (New York: McGraw-Hill Book Co., 1964), p. 196.

nationally valid criterion measures which would make it possible to evaluate uniformly the educational practices (including "standards") of different countries. A feasibility study comprising judgment samples of over eight thousand thirteen-year-old students was carried out in twelve countries. Apart from forming the basis for advancing hypotheses on the role of education in its sociocultural context, it was expected that the study would show whether or not it was possible to apply in a uniform way the same test instruments and the same coding and punching schemes and to carry out data-processing at one computation center. A 120-item test over the areas of science, geography, reading comprehension, and non-verbal intelligence was devised. The pilot study showed that it was administratively possible to carry out a study of this type and that comparability in various respects could be achieved.[3]

From the pilot project, carried out from 1959 to 1961, the International Project for the Evaluation of Educational Achievement (I.E.A.) was developed. The first phase of this project, which covered mathematics, was reported in 1967.[4] It was not the first attempt to evaluate outcomes of instruction across countries or systems. An earlier study had been made of achievements of students in England, California, and Australia—all English-speaking countries.[5] Another study had attempted to evaluate the performances in elementary-school mathematics of children in Middle Western United States and the Netherlands.[6] But, prior to the I.E.A. study of mathematics in 1961-65, no large-scale international study had been conducted that employed representative national samples and tests devised to be applicable at the international level.

The countries participating in the mathematics phase of the

3. A. W. Foshay, *Educational Achievements of Thirteen-Year-Olds in Twelve Countries* (Hamburg, Germany: UNESCO Institute for Education, 1962).

4. T. Husén *et al.* (eds.), *International Study of Achievement in Mathematics: A Comparison of Twelve Countries* (2 vols; New York: John Wiley & Sons, 1967).

5. D. A. Pidgeon, "A Comparative Study of Basic Attainments," *Educational Research*, I (November, 1958), 50-68.

6. Klaas Kramer, "Arithmetic Achievement in Iowa and the Netherlands," *Elementary School Journal*, LIX (February, 1959), 258-63.

I.E.A. project were Australia, Belgium, England, Finland, France, Israel, Holland, Japan, Scotland, Sweden, the United States, and the Federal Republic of Germany. Since the beginning in 1966 of the second phase (to be described later in this chapter), which deals with six subject areas, another six countries have joined the project—i.e., Chile, India, Iran, Italy, Poland, and Thailand. Co-operative machinery had to be set up. Thus, in each country, a leading research institute referred to as the "National Center" took on the responsibility of conducting the study in that particular country. The institute was represented by its head on the I.E.A. Council, in which final authority on policy decisions was placed. The Council met for at least a week once a year. Between meetings a standing committee acted on its behalf. This committee appointed a technical director who was responsible for the technical decisions, which had to be made within the framework of decisions made by the council and the standing committee. During the mathematics phase, the chairman of the council and the technical director were the same person. Since a loose association of this kind was not a legal entity and was not eligible to receive research grants from governmental or other sources, it was decided to incorporate the organization. The incorporation was completed in 1967, and the International Association for the Evaluation of Educational Achievement is incorporated in Belgium. Its secretariat, including the co-ordinator of the project, is placed at the Unesco Institute in Hamburg. The chairman, the technical director, and one standing committee member constitute the so-called Bureau of I.E.A.

I.E.A. is now an international, non-profit, scientific association, the principal aims of which are:

1. To undertake educational research on an international scale
2. To promote research aimed at examining educational problems common to many countries and thereby devise evaluative procedures which can provide facts which can be useful in the ultimate improvement of educational systems
3. To provide, within the framework of the Association, the means whereby research centers which are members of the Association, can undertake co-operative projects

Membership in I.E.A. is restricted to institutions engaged in educational research—countries are not eligible, only institutions which in a sense may be said to "represent" countries. To be eligible for admission, institutions must be adequately qualified and equipped with resources required to carry out the research projects envisaged, particularly large-scale surveys. Thus, in order to be admitted, an institution must meet certain criteria, such as:

1. To be able to produce national representative samples
2. To be able to insure the co-operation of schools selected
3. To have resources sufficient for survey research
4. To have competent psychometricians and statisticians in their service or have access to them

The I.E.A. group decided at the completion of the pilot study, which involved a few test items from several subject areas, to embark upon a comprehensive cross-national study in one subject area, a study in which several target populations within secondary education would be sampled using random probability techniques, and for which specific testing instruments would have to be devised. The subject chosen for the first phase of the project was mathematics. Two major groups in the school systems were sampled: (*a*) thirteen-year-olds (both age and grade populations), since they represented, at that time, the oldest groups still in full-time schooling in all twelve systems, and (*b*) preuniversity-grade students. In some countries in which there was an important terminal point between these two levels, an intermediate population was sampled.

In addition to taking the mathematics tests, the students responded to a "Student Opinion Booklet" including attitudinal and descriptive measures and to a background questionnaire. Furthermore, background questionnaires were administered to teachers and school principals. Certain data pertaining to the national system as a whole were provided by a case-study correspondent in each country. In all, 133,000 students from 5,450 schools were tested, and questionnaires were completed by 13,500 teachers and 5,400 school principals. Approximately fifty million pieces of information (each individual response from each individual student, teacher, or principal) were recorded and stored on magnetic tape at the University of Chicago Computation Center, where the data-processing and the statistical analyses were carried out, partly at the time that the researchers met in Chicago. From these data it was possible to study the "effectiveness" of different educational practices in school or class organization in relation to both cognitive and non-cognitive outcomes. These outcomes were also related to social, economic, and ecological factors. A data bank has been established at the University of Chicago and is open to all *bona fide* researchers.[7]

Some Technical Problems Associated with Cross-national Evaluations

The establishment of measures of dependent variables, i.e., measures of outcomes, such as has been attempted in the I.E.A. project, implies that (*a*) the measuring instruments should meet certain reasonable criteria of comparability and (*b*) the samples should be comparable, i.e., be entirely representative samples of the target populations agreed upon.

It appears inadvisable at this point to discuss in detail the technical problems related to the construction of international evaluation instruments. The standard procedure in any evaluative process is, of course, to begin with an analysis of the objectives which are to be achieved in the educational systems under consideration. But since the curriculums and syllabuses in most of the participating countries are drawn up at the national level, the objectives vary from country to country, depending not only upon differences in educational traditions but also upon variations in social and economic structure and values which are implicit in the educational policy as stated by central authorities or leading national bodies. It might at the outset seem reasonable to confine a set of international achievement tests to objectives and thereby to contents which are regarded as essential in all the countries or systems under evaluation. But one will soon discover that in many subject areas the common denominator of about equally emphasized topics is small— in some areas extremely small. Furthermore, the topics are introduced at various grade levels and are allotted a widely varying instructional time. Thus, comparability in terms of identical topics, taught at the same age levels with the same instructional emphasis,

7. D. Wolf, *Data Bank Manual* (I.E.A. Study [Stockholm: Almqvist & Wiksell, 1967]).

does not exist. The problem becomes even more difficult when it comes to evaluating non-cognitive outcomes of schooling. The I.E.A. group had to face criticism both before and after the completion of the mathematics study because the tests were considered in almost every country not to "do justice" to the students of that particular country. The procedure adopted in devising the mathematics tests has been described in some detail in the report on Phase One of I.E.A.[8] In each country a committee of mathematicians, mathematics educators, and educational researchers was set up and asked to provide a national analysis of the mathematics curriculum at the relevant grade or age levels. The analysis was carried out in terms of detailed topical areas and broad behavioral categories, such as "operations," "use of symbols," and so forth. The national papers together with illustrative items taken from examinations and tests in the respective countries were submitted to an international committee which consisted of mathematics educators and test experts. Furthermore, the national experts were asked to rate each topic as to what extent it was taught at a given grade level—universally, restrictedly, experimentally, or not at all. The international committee reviewed the material and prepared pretest versions of the test items. These were submitted to the national committees for review and criticism before the final pretesting took place. Each item was pretested in at least three geographical language areas. The mathematics teacher of each student included in the sample was asked in the teacher's questionnaire to rate each item on a three-point scale as to the opportunity that the students in his or her class had had to learn the topic tapped by the particular item. The student's "opportunity to learn" was, by the way, the one of all the independent variables which explained the largest portion of the variance in the criterion. The average correlation between countries on item difficulties turned out to be close to $+.85$ for the thirteen-year-old population.

At this point, it should be noted that in the construction of an evaluation instrument the basic problem is to devise tests that can be administered and scored uniformly in all countries using it. We cannot "do justice" to all those tested with conventional I.Q. tests

8. Husén et al., op. cit.

within a given country because we have not been able to include items which take into account differences among groups with various social and cultural background, i.e., with different levels of opportunity. In many cases, we are therefore missing the point of giving the test. The same holds true for achievement tests. We cannot entirely eliminate test results that arise from differences in "opportunity." The important thing in carrying out cross-national evaluations is to cover the broadest possible spectrum of objectives and contents at a particular age or grade level. The chief aim of carrying out international evaluations is not to make over-all comparisons between countries—we are not engaged in an international contest—but to obtain meaningful comprehensive measures of both cognitive and non-cognitive outcomes and to relate these to a comprehensive set of input variables, including those which measure opportunity. Thereby, provisions are made for a fruitful multivariate analysis of how outcomes are related to inputs. Weighting procedures have been developed for the next phase of the I.E.A. Project whereby cross-national differences in instructional emphasis can be taken into account.

The second comparability problem has to do with the proper definition of target populations to be studied and the drawing of representative samples by means of random sampling methods. Obviously, the easiest way to go about the definition problem is to confine the study to age populations. But these are seldom meaningful cross-nationally in terms of school structure. In the mathematics phase of the I.E.A. Project, the thirteen-year-olds were chosen because this was the oldest age group in full-time schooling in all the participating countries. In the second phase of the I.E.A. Project, two age populations are being studied. The ten-year-olds have been selected because they represent in several European countries the last year before the students are divided into academic and non-academic programs, some being transferred to the academic secondary school at the close of that year. Since compulsory schooling has been generally extended and a growing proportion of students voluntarily stay on in full-time schooling, the second population studied in Phase Two are the fourteen-year-olds.

Difficulties arise in arriving at a definition of a target population in terms of school organization which is communicable across languages and systems. In the mathematics study, one population was defined as "those students who are in the last grade of the pre-university school." In the United States this meant the high-school Seniors, whereas in England it indicated those students who were about to sit for the G.C.E., A—level, and in France those about to complete the *baccalauréat*. Thus, in the last two countries, the students who were in separate vocational schools and who were not in a grade or type of school from which transfer to the university could take place were left out of the mathematics study.

Attempts to carry out international surveys have constantly been hindered by the fact that we have no international terminology in education. The lack of a common "currency" makes it extremely difficult, for instance, to construct international questionnaires or test manuals. "Secondary education" operationally means the high school in the United States, the tripartite system from 11+ in England, or the "*gymnasium* level" covering the age range from sixteen to twenty in Sweden. A "comprehensive" school in England is a school providing all "secondary" programs under one roof to all students of secondary-school age (eleven to eighteen years). In the United States it is mainly a high school with the entire range of academic and non-academic programs. In Sweden it is a school providing education for all the children in a given area from Grade I to Grade IX and in which no "streaming" or "ability grouping" is allowed until after Grade VIII. Thus, in developing international questionnaires, quite a lot of careful preparation has to be devoted to operational definitions, explanations, and accurate coding schemes.

The Concepts of "Standard" and "Yield"

Both educators and laymen often use the term "standard" in evaluating the quality of school education, both nationally and internationally. The word has connotations vague enough to blur the issues. In the first place, standards are thought of as being in one way or another absolute and thus almost metaphysically anchored. It is therefore regarded as a sacrilege to change standards, especially to lower them. Attempts to broaden the opportunities for secondary and higher education have often been met with the objection that they would "lower the standards."

It is therefore of utmost importance to establish meaningful and operational definitions of standards, particularly at the international level. Various statistical descriptions could be attached to "standards," depending upon their relationship to national or international assessments.

As already indicated, the very word "standard" tends to imply that evaluation is in absolute rather than in relative terms. A student or a group of students is evaluated in terms of having either passed or failed, not in terms of position in a distribution of achievements and the norms derived therefrom.

Standards may be expressed in relative terms, i.e., by relating individual or group performances to norms derived from a reference population, which is the usual procedure in national evaluation programs. One finds, for example, that the average performance of American students in mathematics is far below that of their British counterparts in the "last grade of the preuniversity school." To make cross-national assessments of standards in such a way is, however, for various reasons far from satisfying. The major flaw in using average performance as an index of "standard" or "yield" at a certain grade level in the secondary school in various countries derives from the fact that quite different proportions of the corresponding age or grade groups are compared. One should, in

TABLE 1

MEAN MATHEMATICS SCORES AND PER CENTS OF AGE GROUPS ENROLLED
IN MATHEMATICS IN FINAL YEAR OF SECONDARY EDUCATION: BY COUNTRIES

COUNTRY	MEAN MATHEMATICS SCORE	PER CENT OF AGE GROUP ENROLLED IN MATHEMATICS
Israel	36.4	7.0
England	35.2	5.0
Belgium	34.6	4.0
France	33.4	5.0
The Netherlands	31.9	5.0
Japan	31.4	5.0
Germany	28.8	4.7
Sweden	27.3	16.0
Scotland	25.5	5.4
Finland	25.3	7.0
Australia	21.6	14.0
United States	13.8	18.0

Source: Adapted from T. Husén et al. (eds.), International Study of Achievement in Mathematics: A Comparison of Twelve Countries (2 vols.; New York: John Wiley & Sons, 1967), II, 118, Table 3.36.

the first place, take into account the different proportions of students who have been retained in the systems. But, in the second place, it is also important to find out what happened to those who either were not admitted to the system or were screened out of it. Such considerations are especially important when international evaluations on the respective "yield" of the comprehensive versus the selective school structure are carried out, or when broadened educational opportunities are evaluated. In a highly selective system, in which a small intellectual and social elite survives the various screening procedures, the high standard in terms of average performance of the elite has to be weighed against the broadened opportunities for a major proportion of the young people in a more "retentive" system.

In the I.E.A. Project, comparisons have been made in terms of international percentiles.[9] These have been defined by the composite distribution of all the national samples tested at a given grade or age level. The preuniversity students actually taking mathematics and, as a rule, belonging to the mathematics-science track were of special interest. Their proportion varied from 4 to 18 per cent of the corresponding age group (seventeen to nineteen years). As can be seen in Figure 1, the average mathematics score among the American high-school graduates is far below, for instance, sixth-form students in England or *Abiturienten* in the Federal Republic of Germany. But one has to take into account that in the United States about 18 per cent of the seventeen- and eighteen-year-olds are taking mathematics and science in the graduating class, as compared to only about 5 per cent in England or Germany.

A comparison in terms of international percentiles based on the composite distribution of all the mathematics students would not be fair to systems with high "retention" or holding power. Therefore, in the I.E.A. study, we went one step further and calculated the proportions of the *total age group* that reached given percentile scores. In Figure 1 the dotted line gives the mean performance of the preuniversity mathematics students in the twelve countries with Israel and England at the top and Australia and the United States at the bottom. The proportion, 4 per cent of the age group, is

9. *Ibid.*

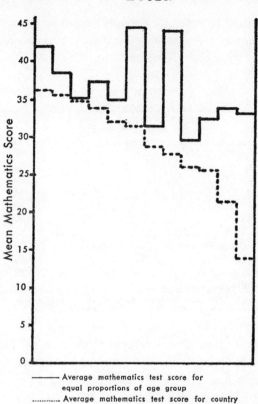

Fig. 1.—Mean mathematics scores or the total sample and for equal proportions (upper 4 per cent) of the age group in each country, at the terminal mathematics level

chosen because it is the lowest proportion of the population eighteen to nineteen years of age in any country who take mathematics at that age. The national mean scores of the top 4 per cent are represented by the solid lines. The range between countries in the elite group is smaller than that for the entire group of terminal mathematicians. The United States' top 4 per cent scored at about the same level as students in most European countries which still have the elitist and selective secondary-school system. On the basis of composite distributions for all the terminal mathematics students, we have been able to establish international percentile scores applicable to the total age groups. In Table 2 we have given the percentage of the total age group within each country which has reached the standard achieved by the upper tenth of all mathematics students. Evidence available indicates that these percentages tend to be higher for the more retentive systems.

TABLE 2

PER CENT OF AGE GROUP IN EACH COUNTRY REACHING 90TH PERCENTILE OF SCORES OF ALL MATHEMATICS STUDENTS ENROLLED IN FINAL YEAR OF SECONDARY SCHOOL

Australia	0.42
Belgium	0.92
England	1.30
Finland	0.24
France	1.10
Germany	0.32
Japan	1.68
The Netherlands	0.25
Scotland	0.32
Sweden	1.28
United States	0.81

Source: Adapted from T. Husén et al. (eds.), International Study of Achievement in Mathematics: A Comparison of Twelve Countries (2 vols.; New York: John Wiley & Sons, 1967), II, 131, Table 3.41.

Thus, the evaluation of the relative "productivity" of various national educational systems has to be carried out in terms of "how many are brought how far." Evaluation cannot be confined to the average quality of the "end products" of the systems. Apart from taking into consideration the price paid in terms of social bias, dropout, grade repeating, and inefficient utilization of talent, one also has to take into account the highly varying "retention" of the systems.

In order to evaluate educational systems in terms of their "total yield" in a particular subject area, one has to test students at *all* major terminal points. This was not done in the I.E.A. mathematics study but is being done in the second phase of the Project. Through the use of the formula ("How many are brought how far?"), Postlethwaite tried to arrive at a methodology that seems to be useful.[10] Students in the thirteen-year-old population were used as a "base line." By using anchoring items employed in the

10. T. N. Postlethwaite, *School Organization and Student Achievement* (Stockholm: Almqvist & Wiksell, 1967).

tests for two adjacent age levels, it was possible to express the scores for the secondary terminal students on the scale for the thirteen-year-olds. Thus, by multiplying the proportion of the students of the total age group by measures of their average performance according to the common scale, one can arrive at an over-all measure of the "yield." Since in most countries the intermediate population (fifteen-to-sixteen-year-olds), in which a major terminal point is located, was not tested, it could not be included in the calculations; this, of course, made the comparisons between the mathematics total "yield" of the various systems less reliable. Attempts to carry out "yield" estimates will be of particular importance in evaluating the quality of educational systems in emerging countries, in which there is often already a high dropout rate at the elementary-school level and a strict selectivity at the secondary level. To evaluate the systems by means of assessing only the quality of the end products would be grossly misleading.

The Future Role of Cross-national Evaluations

For reasons indicated in the introductory part of this chapter, international evaluation methods are bound to gain growing importance in a shrinking world. Increased mobility will make it important to establish international achievement tests at all levels of the educational system, particularly at the secondary level. The increased enrolment of foreign students in most universities calls for international university entrance examination tests. We need techniques whereby achievements in a given subject area can be expressed not only in terms of international norms but also in terms of those of another country. A project directed by A.D.C. Peterson of Oxford University is attempting to establish an international *baccalauréat*, i.e., a matriculation examination, the use of which could be international in scope.

The growing technical assistance and educational planning carried out both at the international and national levels make it imperative to establish methods of assessing the quality of educational systems in terms of international standards. The International Institute of Educational Planning in 1966 organized an international conference of educators, economists, sociologists, statisticians, and planners on the theme of "quality in education." The working paper for the conference consisted of a recent book by Beeby[11] on the quality of education in developing countries.

The I.E.A. Project is, in its second phase, dealing with six subject areas: science, civics, English as a foreign language, French as a foreign language, reading comprehension, and literature. By extending considerably the collection of background information, attempts are being made to account for more of the variance of the "outcomes" of the systems than was possible in the mathematics study.

The world can be regarded as one big laboratory, in which a wide range of structural and pedagogical practices are employed. By relating the outcomes of various systems to different input factors, countries can learn much from each other, provided that adequate international evaluation instruments by means of which output can be measured have been developed.

11. C. H. Beeby, *The Quality of Education in Developing Countries* (Cambridge: Harvard University Press, 1966).

CHAPTER XV

The Impact of Machines
on Educational Measurement

E. F. LINDQUIST

The statement that machines have had a profound impact on educational measurement may now seem a truism. Yet certain facets of the impact may not be obvious at all or may deserve more concern than has been accorded them. Undoubtedly, the most conspicuous effect of machines on measurement has been quantitative in character. That is, machines have facilitated, and thus permitted and even stimulated, more and more testing. This chapter, however, will be concerned mainly with the effect of machines on the *quality* of educational measurement—particularly on the quality of the measuring *instruments* used and the quality of the scores obtained from them.

The past twenty years have been a period of dramatic, even phenomenal, growth in educational testing in this country. During this period the number of tests administered annually has multiplied many times. Many new nationwide and wide-scale testing programs have been initiated and have succeeded beyond expectations. Test-publishers and testing agencies have prospered extraordinarily. The public awareness of the role and importance of tests in the whole educational process has been greatly intensified. There are many factors which together account for this remarkable growth, but that which most of all has made this growth possible has been the rapid technological change taking place during this period—specifically, the development of the electronic computer and the electronic test-scoring machine. These machines have relieved schools, teachers, and school administrators of an almost impossible clerical burden that would otherwise have been imposed upon them by today's comprehensive testing practices, or that might have prevented many schools from giving the tests at all. Machines have also provided the schools with far more adequate, more readily interpretable, and more prompt reports of test results than they would have otherwise obtained, and have thus contributed greatly to the more effective use and better interpretation of test results. Machines have also made possible many kinds of testing and informational services that would otherwise be utterly impracticable, such as, for example, those provided in the American College Testing Program. Finally, machines have made possible large-scale research projects and studies of representative samples of school populations, such as Project TALENT and the study of the equality of educational opportunity recently reported by Coleman,[1] that would otherwise never have been attempted at all. This chapter is a very brief and incomplete summary of the contributions of machines to testing, but it should be enough to support the statement that machines have had a truly tremendous—and on the whole beneficial—impact upon educational measurement during the past twenty years.

This period of rapid expansion in the quantity and scope of testing has witnessed also considerable improvement in the effectiveness with which test results are used. However, there has been relatively little improvement in the *quality* of the tests themselves or of the scores obtained from them. Basically, practically all of the *major* testing instruments used today, those which together account for at least 95 per cent of all standardized testing, have remained fundamentally unchanged in nature and quality of content during this period. During these years, also, there has been little or no experimentation with, or successful development of, new and improved types of tests or tests measuring hitherto unmeasured objectives, and little or no research or development of any consequence that has been concerned with, or has led to, improvements in basic measurement procedures. The machines themselves may have, to a very considerable extent, been responsible for the relative lack of progress along these lines. Indeed, during this period, in order to make test-scoring and test administration easier and

---

1. James S. Coleman *et al.*, *Equality of Educational Opportunity* (2 vols.: Publication of the National Center for Educational Statistics, OE38001 [Washington: Government Printing Office, 1966]), I.

more convenient for the schools, test-builders have made a number of definite sacrifices and compromises in the quality or efficiency of their tests and in the scores obtained from them. At the same time, they have accepted restrictions upon test development that may definitely have prevented the use of, or even the search for, new and possibly improved types of test exercises.

These compromises and restrictions were made so long ago, their effect has been so gradual, and they have come to be taken so much for granted, that the present generation of students of educational measurement and the majority of test-users may be hardly conscious of them at all. It should be worthwhile, therefore, to devote a few paragraphs to a historical review of these developments.

In the early objective tests used during the 1920's and early 30's, the examinee was permitted to record his answers to both recognition-type and free-response-type items in the test booklet itself. Scoring was then accomplished usually by comparing the student's responses with those printed on fanfolded or strip scoring keys, which had to be applied to each printed column in the test booklet. This imposed a heavy clerical burden on the test-users, which itself would have prevented really wide-scale use of the tests. Therefore, in the early 1930's, the practice of having the student mark or record his answers on a separate answer sheet was introduced.

The advantage of more convenient scoring thus gained involved a quite definite sacrifice in either the quality or the efficiency, or both, of the scores obtained. To use this answer sheet, the student had to perform certain operations not previously required of him. That is, for each item, he had to note the item and response numbers, turn to the separate answer sheet, find and mark the correspondingly numbered space, and then find his place again in the test booklet. This required considerable extra time. To allow for this, the time limits of the tests were substantially increased, usually by at least 15 per cent and sometimes by more than 25 per cent. This additional time could otherwise have been spent by the student in responding to more items, and the reliability and validity of the scores could thereby have been improved.

There is no question, then, that the reliability and validity of the scores *per unit of testing time* were significantly reduced with the introduction of the separate answer sheet. Furthermore, students differed in the time required to perform these irrelevant marking operations. The inability of some to complete the test in the allotted time caused a reduction in the number of items that they could attempt, introduced an irrelevant factor into the validity of their scores, and thus further reduced that validity.

The separate answer sheet made possible the scoring machine, and the effect of the machine was to intensify further some of the consequences just noted. More time has been required by examinees in meticulously filling the answer spaces on machine scorable sheets than in marking manually scorable sheets, and there is a greater variability among examinees in rate and accuracy of doing the former than the latter task.

The importance of these particular negative effects, however, should not be exaggerated. They certainly are real; they have reduced by some amount the reliability and validity of the scores per unit of testing time; but undoubtedly they have been more than offset by the advantages gained. If these were the only negative effects, there would be little cause for concern.

The really serious negative effect of the separate answer sheet and of scoring considerations in general has been their restricting influence on test development. In the early days of the hand-scored booklet, the test-designer was relatively free to use any type of test exercise he desired. If he could not find an item-type well adapted to a specific purpose, he was free to exercise his ingenuity to invent and develop new and improved types of test exercises to serve that purpose. In those days, a great deal of interest was shown in, and a great deal of time spent on, devising, experimenting with, and comparing various types of test exercises, and much was written about their relative advantages and disadvantages. The author did a fair amount of this kind of research and writing himself, and, in retrospect, it seems to him that the early thinking about and experimentation with various types of test exercises were even more seriously restricted by scoring considerations than anyone then realized. Our primary attempt then was to rank various types of test exercises in the order of their *general* usefulness. Instead, had scoring considerations permitted, we should have begun with the premise (or perhaps it would be better called the axiom) that every type of test exercise *is superior* to every other type for some specific purpose or purposes. We should then have tried to define more clearly the specific purposes for which each item-type is superior; or conversely, for each type of test content we should have identified or devised the best way of testing that particular type of content. Other factors permitting, we should then have used *all* types of test exercises, each for the purpose, or with the elements of content, to which it was best suited. Furthermore, had we been free to use this approach, we would have been stimulated to the invention of still more effective item-types for a wider variety of specialized purposes.

Unfortunately, we were not permitted to take this approach. We learned very early that some of these otherwise promising item-types were too difficult to score, that some lent themselves more readily than others to marking on separate answer sheets, and particularly, that some could not be scored with the first scoring machine, the IBM 805. We thus very early abandoned the free-response exercise, which for many purposes was far superior to any other, and one after another discontinued the use of other non-machine-scorable types of items. The gradual but inexorable effect of all this was finally to reduce test-designers to the use of the *one* type of test exercise which was most readily machine-scorable, namely, the multiple-choice exercise with only one response to be selected. Today, the term "objective test" is practically synonymous in the minds of most people with "multiple-choice test," accompanied of course by separate machine-scorable answer sheets.

Scoring machines and scoring considerations have imposed still other serious restrictions on test development. Some of these will be pointed out in this chapter. The preceding discussion should indicate that machines have had negative and restrictive influences upon tests and that it is highly desirable that these restrictive influences be eliminated if possible.

For some time the primary objective in scanner construction was to develop more *efficient* means of transcribing educational data of any kind, but particularly test-performance data, directly from an original document to a tabulator or a computer. During recent years, the concern of some machine-designers has focused more and more upon developing *ways of scoring* that will permit and facilitate better *testing*. Effort has been expended upon developing machines that would satisfy the three following criteria.

First, a good scoring machine or procedure should leave the test-designer free to employ any desired type of test exercise in any desired typographical format, with almost total disregard for scoring considerations. Maximum test validity should be his single dominating concern. Accordingly, the ideal machine must be capable of scoring booklets as well as answer sheets. It must also permit the use of free-response items, at least items for which the correct responses are single numbers or words or very short sets of symbols.

Second, the machine must permit the examinee to mark or record his responses in the easiest and least time-consuming way possible, eliminating or rendering negligible, even in booklet-scoring, any effect of the marking factor on the scores obtained.

Third, for practical economic reasons, the machine must permit the use of inexpensive paper and of low-cost printing methods in the manufacture of the booklets to be scored.

How a scanner reads a mark and what kind of mark it reads are of prime importance. Some scanners look for the marks in very precisely located positions on the answer sheet. If a mark is not found in the precise location expected, due either to imprecise printing or to carelessness in marking, the machine misses the mark and a scoring error results. Such a machine demands very precise registration of the printed image on the sheet to the so-called registration edges. Since *perfect* precision cannot be obtained, the examinee has to make a *large* mark, so that some part of his mark at least will cover the precise location. Hence, the test requires that the examinee *fill* a large circle or the space between two parallel lines. This need for high precision in printing as well as the fact that the machines read only one side of the sheet at a time, also renders most scoring machines impracticable for booklet-scoring. Incidentally, in booklet-scoring, one first has to slice off the stapled fold or hinge to divide the booklet into separate sheets which may then be fed consecutively into the machine. Booklets are typically printed in signatures consisting of multiples of four pages and are folded, stapled, and trimmed after printing. With this kind of trimming, uniformity and precision in the relation of the printed image to the trimmed edge are exceedingly difficult to maintain.

It has proved possible to design a scanner that, instead of looking for a mark in a precise location, *searches* for the mark in a relatively large *area* and finds the mark no matter where within this area it is located. Furthermore, it searches for the *densest* rather than for the largest mark, so that a very small mark will suffice. This feature permits the examinee to make his mark in the simplest and quickest way possible—that is, with a single horizontal stroke of his pencil. Also, with this type of scanner, the examinee need not position his mark very precisely, so that special care in marking is not required of him. It would be difficult to conceive of an easier or less time-consuming marking requirement.

A good scanner should be able to read both sides of each sheet simultaneously by reflected light, and to find marks *anywhere* on either side of the sheet. In effect, it should report the page number and the co-ordinates of each mark to an on-line computer. The computer can then assign any desired meaning or weight to each mark and can perform any desired operation on this information. This feature of the scanner makes it particularly adaptable to scoring booklets.

Occasional hand corrections are necessary with any scoring machine, due primarily to damaged sheets and to failure of students to follow instructions for marking. This problem can become very difficult if the edit clerk has to leaf through many booklet pages to find the errors to be corrected. In the ideal scanner-computer combination, the on-line computer edits the data from each individual sheet, notes any clues to sheet damage or to errors, indicates omissions or inconsistencies in marking, directs the scanner to mark and offset neatly in the stack each sheet that needs hand-checking, and prints out instructions telling the edit clerk what possible errors to look for on each offset sheet—all while scanning at the very high pages-per-hour rate required for efficient processing of the very large number of pages involved in booklet-scoring. Finally, the machine should handle documents of varying sizes and weights, from IBM cards up to sheets measuring 8½ by 11 inches, and should be able to read punched holes as well as marks from IBM cards. Such versatility is essential for all kinds of data collection.

A scanner possessing all of these desirable characteristics has already been developed and is in use at Measurement Research Center in Iowa City, Iowa. Hopefully, other machines with these same characteristics will soon become readily and widely available.

The significance of these machine characteristics for test development may be suggested in a brief comment upon the most important general features of a good scoring system. The first has to do with the way in which the mark can be used. The mark will most often be used simply to *underline* a number, a letter, or a symbol, and all that should be required of the examinee is that his mark lie below the character underlined and above the character in the line below it. That is, no printed outline, such as a circle or parallel lines, is needed to contain the mark. The mark can also be used to advantage in many other ways. The mark can be of any length, and the scanner can recognize and attach meaning to its length. Thus the mark may be used to underline not only an entire word, but also an entire phrase. It may similarly be used to strike out a wrong response or to delete a superfluous or incorrect word or phrase in a passage. If the marks may be sensed anywhere on the page, they may be made directly on maps, drawings, pictures, statistical tables, etc.—for instance, to identify a map location, or to locate an incongruous or missing element in a picture or line drawing. The mark may also be used to locate a point on a vertical linear scale or an interval in a frequency distribution, so that by a single mark the examinee may be able to give a close approximation to a multidigit number.

The second major feature of a good scoring system has to do with the meanings which may be assigned to the marks by an on-line computer. Quite literally, the computer can assign any desired objective meaning to or perform any desired logical operation on any particular mark or set of marks. It may assign different scoring weights to different items, or to different responses to the same item, or to different combinations of items or responses. It may give credit to one mark on the condition that (or the extent to which) that mark is accompanied by other marks in specified locations; that is, it may do pattern-scoring. It may also assign different meanings or weights to marks of different lengths. Because of the tremendous capacity of the modern computer, any kind of scoring now becomes feasible.

The third important feature of a good scoring system has to do with the scoring of free-response exercises to which the correct response consists of a single word or number, or of a brief set of symbols. This scoring is made possible by what may be called the virtual *character-recognition* capability of machines of the type just described. Suppose one wants to score a free-response item to which the correct response is a three-digit number. One can print beside or below the question three compact sets of the digits *0* to *9*. If his answer is, say, *365*, the examinee simply underlines the *3* in the first set, the *6* in the second, and the *5* in the third. This underlining procedure actually takes less of the student's time than is required to write out the answer, particularly if he has to block-print the number in the stylized characters that would be demanded by *de facto* character recognition machines. If the correct answer is a word, the examinee need usually be presented only with a single alphabet, in which he is required to underline the first two or three letters of the word. The chances that he will think of a wrong answer beginning with the same letters is usually negligible, or can be made so by item selection. If necessary, however, he can be presented with a sufficient number of successive alphabets to spell out the entire word. Furthermore, there is no problem of legibility; that is, there is no danger of confusing an *8* with a capital *B* or with a *3*, and so on.

One interesting feature is that these sets may contain any characters which the test-designer may desire or any alphabet that he may select or devise. In an algebra-test item, for example, several blocks of characters might successively contain the plus and minus marks, the digits *0-9*, and the characters a, b, a^2, b^2, and the student might be directed to spell out the middle term, for instance, in the square of the quantity $(3a-2b)$. Eventually, machine scoring of free-response items will be made possible also by *de facto* character-recognition machines, but a very long time will probably elapse before such machines will be able to recognize *reliably* and efficiently more than a very limited number of predetermined characters, especially if the characters are hand-formed by untrained examinees.

It should be apparent that, with a system of this versatility and flexibility, the test-designer not only can employ almost any type of objective-test exercise which has ever been suggested in the past but also can devise many new and improved item-types to better serve certain specific requirements. Consider the testing of language skills at the elementary- and secondary-school levels. A major weakness in most current language-skills tests has been that they do for the student (and leave untested) some of the most important things he would have to do for himself in the natural writing situation. Nearly all are proofreading tests. In them, the error situations are usually pointed out to the student. Furthermore, in the associated multiple-choice items, usually only one or two really plausible choices are suggested, so that guessing is made easy. If one were to stand beside the student while he is writing, pointing out specific situations to him, and saying such things as: "Did you make a capitalization error here?", "What different punctuation mark, if any, is needed here?", "Is this word grammatically correct?", etc., one would be giving him the same help he gets, in effect, in these tests. A type of exercise can now be devised that avoids this weakness.

The nature of this exercise is indicated in the following directions to the examinee.

Directions: On each page of this test you will find, to the left, samples of student writing. Across the bottom of each page you will also find a list of about thirty words, selected for that page. The writing contains many errors in punctuation, capitalization, grammar and diction. Part of your task is to find and underline each error. The other is either to classify each error or to indicate the proper correction.

In the right-hand margin of each page, opposite each line of writing, you will find printed any forms of punctuation needed in that line, and the abbreviations "C" for "capitalization," "G" for "grammar," "De" for "delete," "WW" for "wrong word," and "Tr" for "transpose." If you underline a capitalization error, underline also the "C" in the margin in the same line. If you underline a grammar error, underline also the "G" in the margin. If you underline a punctuation error (including a failure to punctuate at all), underline the error and also the *correct* punctuation in the margin. If you find a punctuation mark where none belongs, underline the mark and also the "De" for "delete" in the margin. If you find a word that is definitely inappropriate or in bad taste and that should be replaced by a better word, underline the entire word and also the "WW" for "wrong word" in the margin. In each such case, you should be able to find a better word in the list at the bottom of the page. Find this word and simply underline it in the list. If a word or phrase should simply be deleted without replacement, underline the entire word or phrase and also the "De" in the margin. If you can find a word or phrase that should be moved to another place in the same sentence, underline the entire word or phrase and also the "Tr" for "transpose" in the margin. Then underline the space (between words in the same sentence) to which the word or phrase should be moved.

There are never more than two errors in the same line, and these are never of the same type. For example, there would never be two capitalization or two diction errors in the same line. You will receive no credit for finding an error unless you also make the appropriate associated mark or marks in the margin or in the word list. Study carefully the sample paragraph, in which a number of errors have been correctly marked, and then proceed with the test.

In actual use, the student would, of course, be given a worked example and a practice exercise. Careful consideration of the preceding directions will reveal to the reader that the mechanics of test-taking are really quite simple and the directions easy for high-school and upper-grade students to follow. The most important feature of the test is that, as in natural writing, the student is required to use *all* of his writing skills simultaneously, with *no* artificial clues that will help him find or classify errors. Another is that, because of the very large number of possible combinations in double marking, guessing is practically eliminated.

With the on-line computer it is possible to extract and provide much more information about the test performance of the examinee than would be feasible with hand-scoring or with non-computerized scoring machines. For instance, the computer can readily provide separate scores for each skill category, or for each kind of punctuation mark if desired, or can distinguish between errors of commission and errors of omission, such as overpunctuation and underpunctuation. As measures of group performance, particularly, such diagnostic information could be quite useful in improving instruction or in revising a curriculum.

This example has been presented, not for its own sake, but to suggest the freedom in item design that is now readily possible with machine-scorable booklets and the most versatile scoring machines. What, in general, are some of the major improvements that might be made in the quality of tests by taking advantage of these machine characteristics in test design? In the first place, if one were to take any objective test which was designed for use with a separate answer sheet and simply convert it to a machine-scorable booklet, without introducing any change in test content, one could immediately achieve a significant gain in the validity and reliability of the scores *per unit of testing time*, assuming that the time limits would be reduced in accordance with the time saved by eliminating the answer sheet. At the same time, the influence of any irrelevant marking factor would be essentially eliminated. Finally, the instructions to the examinee and the task of administering the test would be made simpler and more convenient.

These automatic and immediate gains through simple conversion to booklet-scoring, however, are in themselves quite minor in relation to other possible types of improvement. By far the most important is that resulting from the freedom to use, with each particular element, idea, skill, concept, or ability to be tested, the specific type of test exercise which is optimum for that particular element. With many tests, definite improvement will come simply through the reinstatement of the free-response item, particularly in mathematics tests, information tests, verbal analogy tests, number-series completion tests, foreign-language vocabulary tests, and the like. An immediate gain in these instances would be the elimination of the guessing factor.

In general, a more important gain would be the increased *validity* which would result from the fact that the mental processes required from the student in this situation would be more nearly those that we really want to measure than would be the case in the multiple-choice situation. What we very often really want to determine is whether or not, by means of *unaided* recall, or by following a valid line of reasoning, the student is able to *provide* the correct answer (rather than merely to recognize it when it has been provided, or to arrive at it by indirect or inverse processes, such as by eliminating wrong answers, or by working backwards from the right answer). Short-answer items have generally been regarded as most useful in informational and in mathematical-reasoning tests, but there is at least a possibility that, once we put our minds to it, we can develop good ways of using free-response, short-answer items in reasoning and comprehension tests in general.

The reintroduction of short-answer, free-response items is important, but still greater improvements will come from the reintroduction of other hitherto-discarded objective types of exercises, and from the design and use of new item-types. To make the most of this possibility, we must not only use in each individual test whatever single type of test exercise is most appropriate for that test (as in the language-skills example), but must also be prepared to use different types of exercises in the *same* test, each in connection with the elements to which it is best adapted. For testing the understanding of one concept, for example, the item-writer may wish to use a single-response, multiple-choice item but be able to think of only two good distractors or foils. If so, he need use only two. If he can think of seven really functional distractors, he may use all seven. If in the same test he wants to ask which *two* of the suggested responses are correct—that is, if he wants to use a multiple-response, as contrasted to a single-response, multiple-choice item—and give credit only if all correct answers are checked, and no more—he may do so. If he wants to give varying credit to the various multiple-responses independently in accordance with their importance, he may do so. In a given test, items *13* and *14* may be free-response items; item *15* may require the student to indicate in which of a number of categories each of a number of listed things belongs; and item *16* may require him to indicate the *order* in which a number of operational steps should be taken or the order of importance of a number of factors. In some multiple-choice items, the examinee may be asked to mark the responses he feels sure are incorrect; in others, the one response he feels is best.

This full range of heterogeneity is not likely to become a common characteristic of tests, but there is no theoretical reason why it should not occur occasionally. Directions to the student should not be a problem, because the basic marking requirements can be very simple, and each individual item can contain the specific instructions needed to supplement the general marking instructions. Every experienced item-writer knows that in building a test which must be homogeneous as to item-type, he is often forced to set aside many good content ideas which do not fit the particular item-type being employed. Having to do this may not be so serious if the purpose of the test is only to predict an external criterion, but it can be quite serious if the purpose of the test is to *define* an educational objective, and this *is* the case in all achievement-testing. In achievement-testing, items should be written and employed only because they are essential elements in a complete *definition* of the desired outcomes of instruction. Ideally, no important element should be omitted for any extraneous reasons, certainly not just for reasons of convenience in scoring. If with each individual element in an achievement test, we use the item-type which is *best* adapted to that particular element, the result is bound to be a distinct upgrading in the quality of achievement-testing in general.

If one gives up the notion that tests must be homogeneous as to item-type, one must also give up the notion that each item must be given a unit or uniform weight in scoring, since many item-types (such as multiple-response items) naturally involve variable weighting. In any case, variable weighting of both items and responses is definitely desirable for two reasons: First, it should enable us to extract more of the information about the student that is contained in his *total* test performance than can possibly be expressed in a single score in which all items are given the same weight and in which the information contained in his choice of wrong responses is totally ignored, and, second, it will enable us to improve the *definition* of objectives which is implied in the test and in the score obtained from it.

Many will object to these suggestions on the grounds that empirical studies have shown repeatedly that there is no appreciable difference between weighted and unweighted scores in their correlations with any external criterion or concomitant variables. So far as achievement tests are concerned, however, this fact may be quite irrelevant. Perhaps the reason why we have given up so often on item-weighting in the past is that we have judged the results by the wrong standards, i.e., by relying exclusively on statistical or correlational evidence rather than on logic and judgment. The purpose of an achievement test is *not* to predict any external criterion; the test itself *is* the criterion. The author's overriding concern should be with how to provide an *operational definition*, through the individual items *and* through the way of scoring them, of the outcomes to be measured. The *whole* process of achievement-test construction (not only that aspect of the process concerned with item construction and selection, but also that aspect concerned with scoring) is basically an exercise in subjective judgment. *Both* are aspects of *content* validity.

Test-designers do *now* resort to variable-weighting on a subjective basis in test construction. They do so by including more items in categories considered important than in those considered less important. However, the items needed in the more important categories are often more difficult to construct and more time-consuming to test. The result frequently is an inability to include the desired proportion of such items, which, therefore, receive far less weight than they deserve. In building a high-level reading-comprehension test, for example, it is far more difficult to build items calling for comprehension of large units of content, or items requiring the student to relate and draw inferences from ideas drawn from different parts of a long passage, or items requiring him to grasp implied meanings, than it is to build items testing for understanding of detail, such as for direct interpretation of single words and sentences. Surely we could often improve the *content* validity of such tests by adding a larger increment to the student's score when he succeeds on an involved and time-consuming reasoning or comprehension item than is added when he succeeds on a simple and quickly answerable word-meaning item. It makes just as good sense to decide subjectively what weight an item or an individual response deserves as to decide subjectively whether or not an item belongs in the test at all, and we must be willing to trust our judgment in both instances.

Space has not permitted adequate consideration of both the pro's and the con's of the suggestions made here. A warning against certain possible misinterpretations should be added.

First, these remarks certainly are not meant to imply that, because of the restrictions mentioned, the tests in present use are not good tests. On the contrary, test-designers have developed a very high degree of skill in the use of multiple-choice exercises, and have built many very good tests of this type. The important point being made here is that, with these restrictions removed, it would be possible in many instances to build still *better* tests.

Second, it is not implied that we should now dispose of the separate answer sheet and convert all tests to the type in which the responses are recorded in the booklet. Surely we would effect *some* improvement in the validity or efficiency of the score in every instance were we to do this, but in many instances the improvements thus gained would not be sufficient to offset the economic advantages of the separate answer sheet, which makes possible the *re-use* of the booklets and effects other economies as well, such as reductions in transportation costs.

Third, the answers to many item-types not now being used can be as readily recorded on a separate answer sheet as in the booklet itself, such as the answers to multiple-response items or to free-response items. Accordingly, many of the suggested improvements in tests can be made in separate answer-sheet types of tests, granting that the scanner used in scoring the answer sheets is on-line to a computer, or that the detailed item-response information can somehow be transmitted to a computer. Undoubtedly, in the future many tests and test booklets will be of a mixed character in this respect and will consist of two bookets, one of which is consumable and the other of which is re-usable. A part of the consumable booklet will provide for the recording of responses to questions contained in the re-usable booklet, as is the case on present answer sheets. Another part will contain questions and answers based on reading passages and on pictorial and other source material contained in the re-usable booklet, and a third part will consist of tests that are wholly contained in the consumable booklet—tests like the language-skills test described, in which the marking must be done in the test itself.

Finally, the same characteristics of a scanner which allow the tester almost complete freedom in test design also permit many important improvements in the design of questionnaires and other data-collection instruments. It is now possible to design questionnaires in which the task for the respondent is made maximally simple and convenient; in which he never has to note, transfer, mark, record, or even look at a single code number; and in which all he has to do is to underline words or symbols. The questionnaire need not be cluttered by any material (such as code numbers for key punchers) that is of no interest or value to the respondent. The computer assigns all necessary code numbers to the data on the basis of the position of the mark on the page. This feature is important both in educational measurement and in educational research. In the future, we probably will do more and more in our testing programs in the way of collecting information from and about the examinee, information which may be reported to the teacher and to the counselor along with test scores and which may be used by them in better interpretation of the test results. The consumable booklet used in a testing program, then, may frequently contain an important student-information section, as well as sections calling for the recording of test responses.

It should be apparent that this chapter has been concerned almost exclusively with testing instruments intended for widescale use—that is, with published standardized tests that will be printed and used in quantities sufficiently large to justify the relatively heavy developmental and make-ready costs involved. (It is just such tests, of course, that have the greatest total influence upon educational practices.) To score a test in which full advantage has been taken of the possibilities noted—specifically, to score a test that is highly heterogeneous with reference both to item form and to item-scoring procedures—each test page must be specially printed in a form appropriate for machine-scanning, and the computer on-line to the scanner must be specifically programed for each individual item and page. Such scoring can be highly worthwhile and economically feasible in wide-scale testing, but it is obviously impracticable in small-scale testing, such as with the relatively informal tests intended only for individual classrooms, buildings, or school systems. If tests of the latter type are to be machine-scored, they must, for the present at least, continue to be restricted to uniform and simple item-types to which the responses can be recorded on uniform or standardized "preprogramed" answer sheets.

The developmental and make-ready costs just referred to may seem to constitute a serious deterrent factor in experimentation with and development of new test forms. It should be noted, however, that, in nearly all instances, preliminary experimentation and tryout of new item-types and new test forms need be done on a relatively small scale only, with manual scoring of test materials inexpensively prepared by typewriter-duplicator methods. Only after it has been demonstrated that the new test forms have sufficient promise, is it necessary to resort to wide-scale experimentation and tryouts in which the higher make-ready costs are incurred. Many research workers in measurement do not now have ready access to scoring machines with the capabilities here noted. This fact, however, need not deter them from engaging, on a small-scale manual scoring basis, in research and development with new item-types and new test forms. Eventually, highly versatile scoring machines are certain to become widely available, and much significant research leading to the exploitation of such machines can be done in advance of their general availability.

Incidentally, the preceding comments concerning small, informal testing do not imply that the possibilities of qualitative improvements of the kind here noted are denied to all so-called instructional tests in general—i.e., tests intimately and uniquely related to specific instructional materials. In the highly individualized systems of computer-based and computer-monitored instruction of the future, it will be almost impossible to distinguish the testing materials from the teaching materials. In these systems, it will be particularly important to be able to exercise maximum freedom and flexibility in the design and format of the materials. There will surely be a need for devices that will "read" student responses from workbooks and progress tests directly into a central computer, and it will be highly desirable that undue restrictions not be placed upon the design of these materials and that artificialities and irrelevant factors not be introduced into these materials simply to fit the requirements of the scanning device. Most of these instructional systems inevitably will be uniformly employed on a wide scale—including many school districts and thousands of school pupils—since the per pupil cost of developing and administering such systems would otherwise be prohibitively high. Accordingly, the degree of flexibility here suggested in standardized-test construction is equally feasible in the construction of instructional tests and workbook-type materials needed in closed systems of computer-monitored, individualized instruction.

This chapter has been concerned with only one major aspect of the effect of machines on educational measurement—that is, with their qualitative effects on test development. It is this aspect which is least well understood, and with reference to which the possibilities for future improvement are least well recognized and appreciated. There are many other ways, of course, in which machines, especially the computer, now offer significant opportunities to improve the effectiveness and efficiency, as well as the quality, of educational measurement. These improvements will consist primarily of further extensions and elaborations of the general kinds of services briefly reviewed in the second paragraph of this chapter. In the future, machines will make possible still more efficient, more inexpensive, and more prompt test-scoring and data-processing services; will permit the provision of still more convenient, more readily interpretable, and more timely reports of test results; will enable test administrators to integrate, relate, and analyze more thoroughly the results of testing programs; will facilitate the development of more adequate informational services in general; and will render feasible more extensive and more thorough test research. These and other ways in which the computer and electronic data-processing techniques and procedures can contribute to the improvement of educational measurement are so widely and exhaustively discussed elsewhere in the educational literature that there seems little need to review them here. It is to the opportunity, opened by scanners and computers together, to improve the quality of educational measurements that attention most needs to be directed. Whether or not machines and related technology will indeed exercise the possible desirable effects in this direction depends, of course, upon the extent to which individual tests authors, test agencies and publishers, and measurement-research workers in general recognize and take advantage of these opportunities. It is to be hoped that they will do so, and that in the future we will use our amazing machines, not only to do *more* and *more* testing, but to do *better* and *better* testing as well.

CHAPTER XVI

Needed Concepts and Techniques for Utilizing More Fully the Potential of Evaluation

ROBERT E. STAKE
and
TERRY DENNY

Considered broadly, evaluation is the discovery of the nature and worth of something. In relation to education, we may evaluate students, teachers, curriculums, administrators, systems, programs, and nations. The purposes for our evaluation may be many, but always, evaluation attempts to describe something and to indicate its perceived merits and shortcomings.

Evaluation is not a search for cause and effect, an inventory of present status, or a prediction of future success. It is something of all of these but only as they contribute to understanding substance, function, and worth.

Evaluation in education occasionally features normative distributions of student achievement, self-study of curriculums by members of a local school faculty, and experimental comparisons of new and old instructional treatments. But the preponderance of evaluation features informal, intuitive monitoring by teachers, students, and administrators. Evaluation reports, unfortunately, usually tell little more than that the work proposed was completed, that the complaints of the staff were justified, and that there were greater differences within groups of students (or schools or curriculums) than there were between the groups. Most evaluation reports give only the participants some notion of what occurred; the outsider gains little insight. Most formal reports avoid explicit subjective judgments by insiders and outsiders as if they were evil.

Educators and laymen alike cannot now visualize and explain what is happening in our classrooms. Part of the reason for this failing is our inability to share perceptions and measurements. Part is our lack of motivation to share them. What *should* be told? What should be shared? Our needs are not only procedural; we need also a commitment to full and accurate reporting.

Regarding the Recruitment and Training of Evaluators

Before considering the needs for new evaluation methodology, we wish to acknowledge that the successful use of methods depends on the people who use them. We will point out that the specific technical skills suited to educational testing and to educational research are not (to the surprise of some readers) perfectly suited to educational evaluation. Mobilization of the appropriate skills will require recruitment of already-skilled persons from other fields in addition to the training of persons from our own ranks.

As is indicated in the sections that follow, the concepts and techniques that will serve evaluation have roots in philosophy, sociology, anthropology, linguistics, history, and economics as well as in psychology. Men from these disciplines have contributed often to educational practice. Whether the school needs just a consultant or the director of evaluation, these several fields should be regarded as sources of personnel. The responsibility of evaluation usually involves creating a better frame of reference for understanding educational programs. The contributions of men from allied fields are not the answers they have generated but the perspectives they bring. New viewpoints do not automatically solve problems, improve decision-making, and increase satisfactions—but they do enable a teacher, an administrator, or a curriculum-director to see the situation in a new way and lead him to try a remedy that otherwise may not have seemed reasonable.

Few graduate programs aim at training evaluation (as we have defined the term "evaluation") specialists. In contrast, many programs are devoted to the training of testing-and-measurement specialists and of research-design-and-analysis specialists. The demand for research specialists continues to grow. A recent head of the U.S. Office of Education Bureau of Research cited the need for training researchers as one of two outstanding national needs.[1]

1. "Bright Seeks 'Basic' Educational Research" (Report by James Welsh of interview with Richard L. Bright), *Educational Researcher*, Official newsletter of the A.E.R.A., no. 2, 1968.

The plea for training evaluators is much less frequently heard. In spite of the fact that evaluation is a desirable and often mandatory responsibility within funded programs, few schools of education provide explicitly relevant course work and supervised experience.

Evaluation specialists are and will be increasingly needed—but more of the same will not suffice. From what source should they be recruited? How should they be trained and what should they know as a result of their training?

Consideration of the core content of a program to train educational evaluators reveals a variety of needs. Doctoral-level programs must be designed to produce evaluation theorists and consultants with competences to cope with evaluation problems of great intellectual import and administrative size. In addition, less-extensive evaluation training programs are needed to provide a large number of persons who are able to gather useful evaluation information at the local level. Training programs at all levels will have to be created which will provide task-oriented experiences for teams of researchers drawn from a variety of disciplines and specialities, having heterogeneous backgrounds and different future roles. Experiences would be designed to broaden the base from which educational evaluation problems are viewed. A variety of methodological and evaluation strategies might be employed in prototypic evaluation exercises. Training might include experience in working with a social demographer, a mechanical engineer, a philosopher of science, and others in designing strategies to attack school evaluation problems. Such training exercises should include confrontation experiences and work problems drawn from the workaday world of educational evaluators. Prototypic instruments will have to be constructed for use with work problems and for use in simulation exercises.

Some research-oriented professors ignore some important distinctions between educational research and educational evaluation. The researcher is concerned foremost with the discovery and building of principles—lawful relationships with a high degree of generalizability over several instances of a class of problems. He seeks to develop rules (explanatory statements) about processes which govern common educational activities. He seeks to understand the basic forces that interact wherever there is teaching and learning. He seeks the causes of maturity and sophistication, of retardation and alienation. The evaluator shares some of these concerns. He is particularly concerned with deriving principles on which to make decisions about instructional practice. Gagné has observed that the evaluator's and the survey researcher's assessment tasks coalesce when the evaluator centers his attention on the accomplishment of certain performance objectives as the crucial part of a set of comprehensive educational goals.[2] These concerns are important for educational evaluation.

But educational evaluation is more than assessing student performance. It includes the task of gathering information about the nature and worth of educational *programs* in order to improve decisions about the management of those programs. The evaluator must attend to the effects of the program on teacher performance, administrative arrangements, and community attitudes, and to how the program complements and obtrudes upon other parts of the total curriculum. The evaluator has his own collection of concepts and issues. Scriven has spelled out many of them—the distinction between formative and summative evaluation, the distinction between evaluation and process studies, and the distinction between intrinsic and payoff evaluation, for example.[3] All these are central to the training of the evaluation specialist.

Evaluation can be seen as a form of applied research, but one which places special demands on the methods of inquiry. The evaluator is concerned with finding immediately relevant answers for decision-making. He has an obligation to deal directly with personal standards and subjective judgments. The focal point of his work—unlike that of the researcher—is that one curriculum, or that one program, or that one lesson, or that one textbook he is evaluating.

2. Robert M. Gagné, "Instructional Variables and Learning Outcomes," (paper presented at the UCLA Symposium on Problems in the Evaluation of Instruction, Los Angeles, December 1967 [*Proceedings* in press, Holt, Rinehart, and Winston]).

3. Michael Scriven, "Methodology of Evaluation," *American Educational Research Association Monograph Series on Curriculum Evaluation*, 1 (Chicago: Rand McNally, 1967), pp. 39-83.

The distinction between research and evaluation can be over-stated as well as understated. The principal difference is the degree to which the findings are generalizable beyond their application to a given product, program, or locale. Almost always the steps taken by the researcher to attain generalizability tend to make his inquiries artificial or irrelevant in the eyes of the practitioner. The evaluator sacrifices the opportunity to manipulate and control but gains relevance to the immediate situation. Researcher and evaluator work within the same inquiry paradigm but play different management roles and appeal to different audiences.

Some work has been done on field-testing training programs for the preparation of local educational evaluators. Filep reported on the development of a prototypic training program developed for the Educational Products Information Exchange Institute (EPIE) which utilized videotaped feedback procedures, sensitivity-training, simulation exercises, and the exploration of non-reactive measures of teachers' views of educational materials.[4] Many similar programs can be identified in centers and laboratories across the nation. They have yet to draw effectively upon the experience and training materials of each other.

Both the evaluation-theory and local-evaluation training programs, like educational-research training programs, must include skill development in general educational research methodology. Educational evaluators should have some familiarity with alternative social-science research strategies—those found in sociology, anthropology, and ethnology, for example. Their skills in devising techniques and constructing instruments idiosyncratic to the evaluation tasks at hand and in training other professionals and paraprofessionals in the use of such instruments and techniques should be considerable.

Whatever the level of training, we need evaluators who are facile in using unobtrusive measures for data collection as well as in indexing programs through more traditional measures.[5] Educa-

4. Robert T. Filep, "IRA Training Program Has Successful Dress Rehearsal," *EPIE Forum*, I (November, 1967), 10-15.

5. Eugene Webb and Others, *Unobtrusive Measures: Nonreactive Research in the Social Sciences* (Chicago: Rand McNally, 1966).

tional evaluators must understand the fallibility of tests and of less traditional avenues of assessment and be able to conceptualize assessment problems related to process and outcome in a variety of ways. The argument for the use of unobtrusive measurements in educational evaluation rests on the presumption that it is possible to select a group of measures which have compensatory strengths and unshared weaknesses.[6] Traditional educational research measures and unobtrusive measures are complementary to one another and not intersubstitutable in the training of educational researchers.

It seems apparent that the tasks subsumed under the heading of "curriculum evaluation" are sufficiently complex to discourage any expectation of producing a significant number of seasoned curriculum specialists to meet existing and anticipated evaluative needs. A broad recruiting base insofar as undergraduate and previous graduate training are concerned seems well advised for both doctoral and subdoctoral training programs. Which feeder groups will prove to be most helpful, most productive of theory advancement, and most appropriate for local evaluator roles, we have no way of knowing. Each specialist viewing the scene discovers a crying need for more of his particular *expertise*.

One final observation: In the selection and training of educational evaluation trainees, regardless of the depth and breadth of the training program and the academic qualifications of the candidates, consideration should be given to their tolerance for ambiguity and to their ability to persevere in working on unpleasant tasks.

Regarding the Representation of Goals and Priorities

At the present time, evaluation specialists have little ability for reporting what persons and programs and institutions are trying to do. They can, of course, ask them, and report what they say. But there is some distinction between what educators propose to pursue, what they see themselves pursuing, and what they in fact do pursue. It is not a matter of deception. Evaluators, educators, all human beings, have enormous difficulties in reporting the sum and sweep of their objectives. We all have goals, and we con-

6. Lee Sechrest, "The Use of Innocuous and Non-intervening Variables as Evaluative Criteria," (paper presented at Annual Meeting of the American Educational Research Association, Chicago, 1968 [mimeographed]).

sciously and unconsciously give priority to some goals over others. But we have few reliable ways to report them to others, or even to reveal them to ourselves.

An evaluator's technical skill should help the educator convey his purposes, both those that quickly come to mind and those implicit in what he does. What are the present methods for getting him to formulate a statement of philosophy or a rationale; to detail the encounters he wants students to have; to specify the behavioral capabilities he wants students to attain; or to sketch the way the ideal individual, team, or system works? Our methods now are crude, unstandardized, and unvalidated. They should be more evocative, more sensitive than indicated by the bald request, "Please state your objectives in the following space."

To supplement the offered statement of goals, our evaluation methods must tease out the additional concerns and purposes of the educator. Some of our goal-listing methods must rely on something other than the educator's ability to originate goal dimensions. The evaluator must offer choices: "Which is more your hope—outcome A or outcome B?" and as practicable, "Which of these two video-taped sequences most closely represents what you are trying to accomplish?" The evaluator must develop a battery of standard routines for seeking out unique and subtle purposes.

Scriven has proposed representing objectives through test items.[7] Krathwohl helped clarify the problem by discussing the levels of specificity of objectives.[8] Gagné has shown how student achievements can be analyzed to indicate intermediate objectives.[9] Taylor and Maguire offered a model for the transformation of objectives from societal needs to student behaviors.[10] Atkin [11] and

7. Scriven, *op. cit.*, pp. 39-83.

8. David R. Krathwohl, "Stating Objectives Appropriately for Program, for Curriculum, and for Instructional Materials Development," *Journal of Teacher Education*, XII (March, 1965), 83-92.

9. Robert M. Gagné, "The Analysis of Instructional Objectives for the Design for Instruction," *Teaching Machines and Programmed Learning, II: Data and Directions*, ed. Robert M. Glaser (Washington, D.C.: National Education Association, 1965), pp. 21-65.

10. Peter A. Taylor and Thomas O. Maguire, "A Theoretical Evaluation Model," *Manitoba Journal of Educational Research*, I (June, 1966), 12-17.

11. J. Myron Atkin, "Some Evaluation Problems in a Course Content Im-

Eisner,[12] in a different vein, protested against the constraining effects of specified objectives on educators. These writings are a part of a foundation for new methods of representing educational objectives.

Not only must the evaluator report the goals but also he must indicate the relative importance of the goals. Goals are not equally desirable; some have priority over others. Different educators will set different priorities, and the same educator will change his priorities over time. Priorities are complex and elusive, but the evaluation responsibility includes the job of representing them. New conceptualizations and new scaling techniques are needed to take a first step toward discharging this responsibility.

The great weakness in our present representation of goals is that it does not guide the allocation of resources. Goals compete for our support, for our efforts. Relying on some explicit or implicit priority system, those who administer education decide among alternate investments, operational expenditures, and insurances. Evaluation requires an acknowledgment of priorities. But to say only "Goal H ranks higher than Goal D" is trivial, perhaps misleading. It is necessary to show what that priority means operationally. A conceptualization and symbolic language that will permit at least gross representation of what priorities mean (i.e., how hard do we work on what) is needed. Ultimately, an outside evaluator should be able to examine our goal specifications, priority lists, and progress reports and identify objectively the areas of under- and over-allocation of resources.

Later in the life of a program, its impact, as seen and as judged, will serve as a basis for reallocating resources. Until then, the logic of the connections between what is intended and what is provided is a principal focus of evaluation.

provement Project," *Journal of Research in Science Teaching*, 1 (June, 1963), 129-32; "Shortcomings of Behavioral Objectives in Curriculum Development," (paper presented at Annual Meeting of the American Educational Research Association, Chicago, 1968 [mimeographed]).

12. Elliot W. Eisner, "Educational Objectives: Help or Hindrance," *The School Review*, LXXV (Autumn, 1967), 250-60.

Regarding Techniques for Assessing
Instructional Materials and Classroom Instruction

Publishers of instructional materials usually provide the purchaser with information on the nature of the content, on the sort of technological and instructional *expertise* involved in the writing of the materials and on the results of whatever field-testing took place prior to publication. They also indicate the cautionary measures that were employed during the developmental stages. Such information tends to add a measure of credibility to the products, and this is good. But the evaluator's needs range wide—from the structure of the materials to the extent of their coverage. The evaluator needs to know the intentions of the materials' authors or developers insofar as they are known, the reasons which underlie the particular ordering or sequencing of the materials, the instructional settings for which the materials are primarily designed, the assumptions made about the entry behavior of the learner, the kind and extent of teacher control required for effective instructional use, and the outcomes likely to be achieved under acceptable conditions of use.

Presently we have little information about such matters. Only a few of the techniques and instruments needed to get it are available, and there is too little interest in their development. However, some beginnings can be seen in the recent work of the Eastern Regional Institute for Education (ERIE), the Educational Products Information Exchange Institute (EPIE), the Social Science Education Consortium (SSEC), and the UCLA Center for the Study of Evaluation of Instructional Programs (CSEIP).

Louise Tyler's recent report presents workable guidelines for the development of a list of specifications termed "essential," "necessary," and "needed" for published materials of instruction.[13] The organization, format, and spirit of this report are comparable to those of the APA *Standards for Educational and Psychological*

---

13. Louise L. Tyler, "Technical Standards for Curriculum Evaluation" (paper presented at Annual Meeting of the American Educational Research Association, Chicago, 1968 [mimeographed]).

Tests and Manuals,[14] and Lumsdaine's guidelines for programed instruction.[15] Hopefully research institutes, consortia, laboratories, professional groups, and individual researchers will attempt to produce needed analytical techniques to assess the structure and coverage of the content of instructional materials as well as to produce performance criteria for evaluating the behavior of the users of such materials under a variety of specifiable conditions of use. Preliminary work which holds promise of applicability to the tasks of curriculum-material evaluation includes content analysis, content-coverage assessment by subject experts, semantic-differential-technique applications, and structured interviews of users. Hopefully, the impetus provided by Tyler and others for specifications of standards will be sustained and a coherent set of systematic techniques for scrutiny of existing materials will emerge. Given useful specifications and workable analyses, it seems imperative that we integrate information about the use and misuse of the same materials in the context of the formal curriculum—in the transactions of the classroom.

Traditional observation schedules and techniques have not markedly advanced understanding of what happens in a classroom in the name of teaching. The reviews of Medley and Mitzel [16] and more recently those of Meux and Simon and Boyer reveal the strengths and weaknesses of verbal-interaction analysis, observation scales, sign systems, and the like.[17]

Shortcomings of these techniques lie more with our lack of understanding of how widely they may validly be used than with their inherent weaknesses. Microteaching and other techniques util-

---

14. American Psychological Association, *Standards for Educational and Psychological Tests and Manuals* (Washington, D.C.: The Association, 1966).

15. Arthur A. Lumsdaine, "Criteria for Assessing Programed Instructional Materials," *Audiovisual Instruction*, VIII (February, 1963), 84-89.

16. Donald M. Medley and Harold E. Mitzel, "Measuring Classroom Behavior by Systematic Observation," *Handbook of Research on Teaching*, ed. N. L. Gage (Chicago: Rand McNally, 1963), pp. 247-328.

17. Milton O. Meux, "Studies of Learning in the School Setting," *Review of Educational Research*, XXXVII (December, 1967), 539-62; Anita Simon and E. Gil Boyer (eds.), *Mirrors for Behavior: An Anthology of Classroom Observation Instruments* (Philadelphia: Research for Better Schools, Inc., 1968).

izing video-tape playback are potential evaluation tools, particularly when teacher and student judgments are sought.

Needed but not available are reliable classroom-observation techniques and instruments oriented to a variety of subject-matter contents as well as to the verbal interaction of the teacher and learners. For example, evaluators interested in assessing the teaching of elementary reading, science, social studies, foreign languages, and English find few field-tested techniques and instruments for assessing classroom instruction in these instructional areas. There are promising signs of help in the making. Social studies curriculum-evaluators should note the classroom-analysis scheme of Oliver and Shaver.[18] Smith has pointed the way for those interested in charting the logical development of ideas in the classroom.[19] Content specialists need to be involved in the production of schedules and techniques for assaying transactions in content areas.

Still another lack is evident in that the affective component of instruction is almost neglected in the current instructional-assessment schedules. Techniques and controls to check on the reliability of the classroom observer's perceptions of such important transactions as surprise, interest, hostility, eagerness, and boredom are needed. Also needed are indicators of the shifts and consistencies in the climate and general goal orientations of a class as it goes about its tasks. McKeachie studied the effects of classroom organizational structure on an individual's "personalogical" variables;[20] and Lindvall has developed a schedule for use with IPI programs.[21] All of this called-for research and development will have to pay attention to the widely reported phenomenon of experimenter bias and the obtrusiveness of the classroom observer. These represent important

18. Donald W. Oliver and James P. Shaver, *Teaching Public Issues in the High School* (Boston: Houghton Mifflin Co., 1966).

19. B. Othanel Smith and Others, *A Study of the Strategies of Teaching* (Project No. 1640, Office of Education, U.S. Department of Health, Education, and Welfare [Urbana, Ill.: College of Education, University of Illinois, 1967]).

20. Wilbert J. McKeachie, *The Appraisal of Teaching in Large Universities* (Ann Arbor: University of Michigan, 1959).

21. C. M. Lindvall, "IPI Instrument," *Mirrors for Behavior: An Anthology of Classroom Observation Instruments,* eds. Anita Simon and E. Gil Boyer (Philadelphia: Research for Better Schools, Inc., 1968).

research problems for the evaluator who seeks distortion-free assessments of classroom transactions. Should the problem of reactivity be resolved satisfactorily, the perceptual inputs of the observer would remain to be minimized or checked. Some progress has been made in controlling these contaminators of objective assessment.[22]

Regarding the Measurement of Student Performance

There is a great need for simple ways of meaningfully describing to "outsiders" what the students are doing in and after training.

There are those who claim that all evaluation should be centered on what the students have learned—"for if no learning is apparent, what education has there been?" There are those who claim that evaluation should concentrate on providing opportunity for experience rather than on standardized performance—"for only self-directed and individually meaningful learning escapes the limits of indoctrination." People differ in the extent to which they find knowledge of student performances useful. But few contend that knowledge of what students can do before and after training is not a part of the evaluation picture. Yet we have a marked inability to show how students perform.

Some educators are less handicapped than others. Many elementary school teachers, for example, escort parents around the classroom, showing samples of work done by the sons or daughters or other children. Teacher marks, comments, and other judgments are usually available. The parent has an opportunity to contemplate the sophistication and the uniqueness of his child's work.

The school administrator has no corresponding medium for showing a visitor what students as a whole are doing. Obviously the diversity of tasks and undertakings in his many classrooms is great. Conventional test scores are available but total test scores represent a confusing collage of student knowledge and are rendered obscure by technical denotation (e.g., reference-group norms, predictive validity). Outstanding work by a few students cannot satisfy the inquiry about what the students are accomplishing. Work samples, performance, or mastery-test results, drawn from large numbers

22. Simon and Boyer, *op. cit.*

of students, can be carefully chosen to represent both the school's typically intellective and the school's typically non-intellective pursuits.

For effective use in evaluation, these tasks must be meaningful; each must have content validity. Can students of this group write a check a bank would accept? Can students of that group solve a certain type of quadratic equation? Can students of still another group propose and analyze arguments for and against the continuation of the Peace Corps? Obviously, information as to the performance of a specified per cent of the students and randomly chosen examples of the compositions would not indicate the balance or breadth of the curriculum; but they would give evaluators and audiences opportunity to share an important conceptualization of what is happening in the schools.

These mastery items or work samples are what Tyler sought:

> Because current achievement tests seek to measure individual differences among pupils taking the tests, the items are concentrated on those which differentiate among the children. Exercises which all or nearly all can do, as well as those which only a very few can do, are eliminated because these do not give much discrimination. But, for the purposes of assessing the progress of education, we need to know what all, or almost all, of the children are learning and what the most advanced are learning as well as what is being learned by the middle or "average" children. To obtain exercises of this sort is a new venture for most test constructors.[23]

The descriptors he sought are the little-recognized main contribution of the National Assessment Program. The uniqueness and merit of those self-contained descriptors have been obscured by attention to the program's sampling plan and the possible misuse of its findings. Throughout education today, whether evaluation is national or local, new descriptors, new indices, new concepts are needed.

The choice of content is a difficult problem. Many items will not be high-priority tasks for many curriculums. Many tasks will be branded as "irrelevant" and "trivial." But a trial period must not be prevented by these objections. Educators are sometimes unreasonably opposed to having their students measured on tasks not taught

---

23. Ralph W. Tyler, "The Objectives and Plans for a National Assessment of Educational Progress," *Journal of Educational Measurement*, III (Spring, 1966), 1-10.

in the school—perhaps on items they do not even consider important. (Certainly they have an obligation to plead for more relevant tasks.) The value of performance indicators cannot be known until they have had a chance to enrich the communicability of educators and evaluators.

A second major concern regarding the measurement of performances, is the need for better techniques for generating test items. Whether they are to be used to evaluate programs or individual pupils, ways of defining the universe of anticipated outcomes are needed. This need might have been discussed in the section relating to goals. It is not important whether we think of performance as objectives for teaching or as outcomes of learning—the need is for rational, step-by-step procedures for deriving specifications of student behavior from the more general objectives that have been established.

The need for these procedures is not based on a claim that test items or performance tasks are better devised by engineers than artists. As Bormuth pointed out, present practice is intuitive and artistic rather than deliberate and rational.[24] Content-process grids, taxonomies of objectives, item analyses, and other devices of the contemporary psychometrician provide little assurance that the content of education will be suitably represented in any collection of items. It is only a possibility, not a certainty, that a more systematic engineering of items will yield representativeness, that automatically generated items will yield better generalizations about student competence. But it is a possibility to which more attention should be given.

The theoretical foundations for rational item generation rest in several disciplines. From psychology, Gleser, Cronbach, and Rajaratnam have conceptualized the complex of sampling errors that make some items more generalizable for some purposes than others.[25] Decision theory, from mathematics and economics, as

24. John R. Bormuth, "On the Theory of Achievement Test Items" (dittoed; Chicago: University of Chicago, 1968).

25. G. C. Gleser, L. J. Cronbach, and N. Rajaratnam, "Generalizability of Scores Influenced by Multiple Sources of Variance," *Psychometrika*, XXX, (1965), 395-418.

conceived by von Neumann and Morgenstern[26] or Wald[27], has promise. Gagné's 1962 analyses of subject matter and the skills involved in mastering subject matter—though more pragmatic than theoretical—imply a certain philosophy of subject matter.[28] Other epistemological writings deal more explicitly with the problem of *what* is to be learned.[29] Bormuth has found a theoretical paper by Menzel[30] helpful in developing a transformational grammar of test questions.[31] Others who are working on the item-generation problem include Lord,[32] Hively,[33] Osburn.[34]

In calling for task-descriptor language and rational item-generation procedures, we have not intended to imply that conventional achievement tests are without value. They are well conceived. Their reliabilities are high. For their primary purpose (i.e., describing individual student standing) they have merit, and their authors should be encouraged to continue their work. For comparing programs, unfortunately, they are of little value.

26. John von Neumann and Oskar Morgenstern, *Theory of Games and Economic Behavior* (2nd ed.; Princeton: Princeton University Press, 1947).

27. Abraham Wald, *Statistical Decision Functions* (New York: John Wiley & Sons, 1950).

28. Robert M. Gagné, "The Acquisition of Knowledge," *Psychological Review*, LXIX (1962), 355-65.

29. Michael Scriven, "Student Values as Educational Objectives" (Publication No. 124 [Boulder, Colo.: Social Science Education Consortium, 1966]); Stanley E. Elam, ed., *Education and the Structure of Knowledge* (Fifth Annual Phi Delta Kappa Symposium on Educational Research [Chicago: Rand McNally, 1964]).

30. P. Menzel, "The Transformation Count" (Technical Report [Inglewood, Calif.: Southwest Regional Laboratory (SWERL), October 3, 1967]).

31. Bormuth, *op. cit.*

32. Frederic M. Lord, "Item Sampling in Test Theory and in Research Design" (Research Bulletin No. 65-22 [Princeton: Educational Testing Service, June, 1965]).

33. Wells Hively, "Generalizability of Performance by Job Corps Trainees on a Universe-Defined System of Achievement Tests in Elementary Mathematical Calculation," (paper presented at Annual Meeting of the American Educational Research Association, Chicago, 1968).

34. H. G. Osburn, "Item Sampling for Achievement Testing" (Houston: Psychology Department, University of Houston, 1967 [mimeographed]).

Regarding Diagnosis for Purposes of Selecting
from Alternative Instructional Treatments

Diagnostic tests and techniques currently enable us to establish the status or condition of the learner, the teacher, the classroom operation, or, as in the case of large-scale accreditation studies, the institutional milieu. Diagnostic instruments are commonly validated on their ability to predict, from the results of tests of a skill or content area, the future performance level of an individual or group. For example, if current performance on tests of reading or school readiness correlates highly with future performance, these instruments are regarded as having strong diagnostic power. Such tests can yield descriptive statements of the current strengths and weaknesses of individuals or groups and serve well as future performance indicators. For the evaluator who wishes to go beyond status assessment and is less concerned with predictive validity in the usual psychometric sense, such diagnoses are inadequate.

Current diagnostic tools generally do not prescribe which treatments are most appropriate among those available to us. We need a large catalogue of performance indicators which underlie learning strengths and weaknesses within and across subject-matter domains. The important characteristic of such indicators is neither that they correlate highly with terminal performance nor that they are logically integral to that process. Rather, it is critical that they provide bases for selecting from among competing instructional treatments. As things now stand, we are sometimes able to diagnose ills quite well and to make predictions about subsequent learner performance, only to find that we cannot then prescribe treatments likely to deter undesirable behavior or to facilitate change in desirable directions.

The activity of the Pittsburgh Research and Development Center in diagnosing pupil achievement in the Individually Prescribed Instruction project impresses us.[35] Student-performance outcomes and attitudes are compared with teacher attitudes in the context of the teacher's perceived and observed pedagogical

35. Richard C. Cox, "Achievement Testing in a Program of Individualized Instruction: Some Considerations," *Learning Research and Development Center Newsletter,* University of Pittsburgh, Vol. IV, No. 3, February, 1967.

adequacy to ferret out prescriptions for self- or in-service training that are suggested by the results of such analyses. An outcome of Gagné's instructional task-analysis work may be to advance the art of diagnosis.[36] Glaser distinguished between tests which assess student performance and tests which reveal the relative standings of students.[37] Gagné, also, distinguished between tests designed for the purpose of predicting performance and those that measure learning outcomes.

The lack of clear conceptions of the structure and dynamics of the construct being diagnosed makes diagnostic-test development and sampling procedures very difficult. This problem is a persistent one in assaying the instructional needs of a student, class, or full-range curriculum program, and in choosing between alternatives to employ as remedial procedures. Moving diagnosis from an assessment to a prescription will increase the need for specificity in statements of instructional intents. We need a catalogue of statements of curriculum aims which have common meaning to the evaluator and to the practitioner. The question of the optimal degree of specificity of intents is currently *de rigueur* and is most visible in the behavioral objectives "controversy." [38] Unfortunately, the current discussions have not led to the solution of problems involved in developing diagnostic instruments of the sort advocated for educational evaluation.

Instruments are needed to identify deterrents to learning; to reveal the misunderstandings, the poor habits, the debilitative attitudes, the prepotent needs of individuals and of groups which interfere with the achievement of sought-after goals. Clinicians have amassed considerable diagnostic evidence that suggests that current, undesirable behavior can be as important as are personal inadequacies or shortcomings. It is one thing to assess what is lacking for the achievement of an intended educational goal and quite

36. Robert M. Gagné, "Instructional Variables and Learning Outcomes," *op. cit.*

37. Robert Glaser, "Instructional Technology and the Measurement of Learning Outcomes," *American Psychologist*, XVIII (August, 1963), 519–21.

38. W. James Popham and Others, "Instructional Objectives," *American Educational Research Association Monograph Series on Curriculum Evaluation*, 3 (Chicago: Rand McNally, in press).

another matter to identify present factors which may militate against the accomplishment of that goal.

Reconceptualization of diagnosis as a heuristic or as a preventative procedure (as well as a procedure in remediation) is a necessary first step toward assessing the strengths and weaknesses of an instructional program designed to enable optimal selection from among possible subsequent tactics. We need, then, to develop an array of diagnostic strategies which will make more rational the choice of tactics based on instructional intents, on the pool of available tactics, on the contingencies between intents and tactics and between tactics and outcomes, and on the personnel and material resources available. The availability of such diagnostic-decision strategies and techniques could facilitate the needed change of role of the curriculum-evaluation specialist from describer to prescriber, from passive assessor to active interventionist.

Regarding Standards and Judgments of Merit

In preparation for claiming the worth of any component of education, it is necessary to know what is expected of it, both locally and afar. Immediate expectations are likely to be called objectives. More enduring expectations are likely to be called standards. We especially look for standards among the statements of leaders in and outside the field of education.

Different spokesmen and authorities expect different things— their several standards should be known to the evaluator and ultimately by his audience. A complete evaluation report should contain a statement of what experts contend should be provided by every school in the way of instructional materials, classroom settings, and laboratory facilities. The reader should know what these leaders say about what students should be able to do.

Minimum standards are not the only useful ones. It is also useful to know what specialists and authorities consider to be exemplary, commendable, satisfactory, unsatisfactory, and intolerable.

At the present time, an evaluator is faced with a discouraging search for standards. Some are available in check lists and accreditation schedules but most are to be found in the literature, buried in problem-oriented appeals for improvement. With today's automated information storage and retrieval systems, the evaluator can be saved much of the search for them. He should have access to as complete an array of standards as he would like merely by specifying the referent, the context of use, and the authorities he recognizes. The ERIC system should acknowledge an obligation to provide information about standards and should have its entries coded accordingly. The evaluator should get answers to such inquiries as "I want to know what specialists in school libraries say is the minimum librarian-student ratio," or "As far as college admissions officers are concerned, how important is it for students to have at least two years of high-school credit in a foreign language?" or "On what grounds do reading specialists object to teaching reading in preschool programs?" Since these same requests would occur repeatedly, the retrieval system could develop sophisticated inquiry procedures for them.

As to judgments, we need (*a*) to be willing to admit them into our studies and (*b*) to devise instruments for collecting them. Polling is a respectable aspect of social science research, but it has yet to be accepted in educational evaluation. When plans for evaluating one of the federal-aid-to-education programs were being developed, a suggestion that a subcontract be let to an opinion-survey organization was rejected on the grounds that paying for such a survey would not represent a proper use of evaluation funds. Such irrational objection to survey data is likely to continue.

Survey data do need cautious interpretation. *Some* questions are misleading; *some* opinions are "phony." We do not know which ones. Still we must examine opinions. They are an important background to education and part of the foreground in education planning. We cannot ignore the informal traffic in evaluative opinions. Technically competent pollsters provide a flow of much more valid information.

The principal obstacle to using public-opinion (and professional-opinion) data seems to be that a single viewpoint is likely to be given too much credence. The evaluator's obligation is not so much to examine the credibility of opinions. Nor will it often be his obligation to get a precise representation of community feeling (as the Gallup poll people do). It should be his responsibility to assure that the scope and diversity of opinions of the community are known. Values and decisions are not expected to derive directly from popularity—the audience of the evaluation will make up its mind as to how to weight the opinions offered.

We need simple instruments and protocols for gathering opinions. Usually the questions or sortings should be tailored to deal with the local or institutional situation. The specialist in evaluation should be more reluctant than many of them are to use a device built for some other community. Those imports do have value as models, of course. No matter how brief or simple, the polling device should be subjected to professional review and trial runs before being used in the evaluation study.[39]

And Synthesis

But what is to be done after all the information is collected? Have we techniques to fit together the separate pieces? Can we tease out the logical inconsistency, the departure from precedent, the emerging trend, the consensus of opinion? Can we relate the immediate situation to abstract standards? Can we portray the whole as a whole, ignoring the insignificant elements without sacrificing its complexity? Can we use the aggregate as a foundation for planning, for decision-making, for correcting errors, for rewarding the greater successes, for understanding the impact of what we do? Full access to information does not guarantee wise use of it. What can be done to increase wise usage?

One school of thought holds that we should invest in the development of formal procedures for processing evaluation information and drawing inferences. Accordingly, the evaluator needs something akin to the experimentalist's factorial design and analysis of variance. Accordingly, he needs some device for accounting for a multiplicity of variations, for drawing inferences, and for registering his confidence in them. This is the way of operations analysis, the systematic organization and processing of data to improve the operation.[40]

39. Frederick F. Stephan and Philip J. McCarthy, *Sampling Opinions: An Analysis of Survey Procedures* (New York: John Wiley & Sons, 1958).

40. Desmond L. Cook, *Program Evaluation and Review Technique: Applications in Education* (U.S. Office of Education Cooperative Research Monograph, 1966, No. 17, OE-12024; Richard I. Miller (Director), *Catalyst for Change: A National Study of ESEA Title III (PACE)* (Notes and

Another point of view is that we should invest in the development of model evaluation projects. Reports from (more than personal observation of) such projects provide examples for other projects, guiding the collection and analysis of information as well as the reporting of it. This approach would rely more on the intuitive powers of the evaluator to organize and less on his ability to formulate a language to convey his conclusions to others. Both approaches appear to be worth pursuing. There may be no replacement for the evaluator's personal powers of synthesis and composition, but we should try to bring a more objective technology into this critical endeavor.

What resources are needed to produce the necessary concepts and techniques for utilizing more fully the potential of evaluation in education? What agencies will produce the needed theory, the needed measuring scales, the needed representations, and the needed training activities? How should we allocate our resources to overcome these needs? We have many questions, but few answers.

In discussing ways to strengthen evaluation methods, we have alluded to different strategies, different viewpoints and different research findings. Some needs we have merely noted, identifying them as candidates for future attention. We are aware that other authors would have emphasized other needs. How similar has been our assignment here to an evaluation assignment—in the necessity to highlight some dimensions and treat others lightly! We suppose that there is no one right way, no one value, no one Truth. Successful evaluation depends on recognition of many purposes, many outcomes, and many values—and it depends on a methodology that portrays these complexities throughout education.

Working Papers Concerning the Administration of Programs Authorized under Title III of Public Law 89-10, The Elementary and Secondary Education Act of 1965 as Amended by Public Law 89-750, Prepared for the Subcommittee on Education of the Committee on Labor and Public Welfare, United States Senate [Washington, D.C.: U.S. Government Printing Office, April, 1967]).

CHAPTER XVII

Outlook for the Future

RALPH W. TYLER

The preceding chapters have described and explained some of the significant changes that have taken place in educational evaluation. They have also suggested a number of important implications of these developments for educational practice. In some cases, the reader can discern patterns of future movement that appear to be imminent, but predicting what is to come is hazardous. In a world that is rapidly changing, the future is full of surprises. Nevertheless, this chapter attempts to suggest features of the road ahead, as well as to review the current situation.

A Brief Summary

In providing a background against which recent changes can be examined, Merwin in chapter ii emphasizes the fact that neither evaluation practice nor theory has been static since the latter part of the nineteenth century. It was then that self-conscious attention in educational discussions and publications began to be given to the use of standardized evaluation procedures in schools. However, the separation of theoretical and technical work in testing from scholarly work in learning and teaching, in guidance and counseling, and in other aspects of education has prevented until recently a continuing comprehensive development of evaluation theory and practice relevant to and appropriate for the changes taking place in the entire range of educational activities. Hence, new ideas, new procedures, and new instruments of evaluation in earlier periods came and went like fads in fashion because these innovations in evaluation were not deeply rooted in the needs and developments in other educational areas.

Bloom discusses in chapter iii several major issues relating to the construction and use of evaluation instruments. He clearly illustrates the need for resolving evaluation issues in terms of a comprehensive consideration of education in its broadest context rather than examining them solely in terms of psychometric theory or the ease and efficiency of test construction, administration, and scoring.

Berdie in chapter iv describes increasingly sophisticated practices in the field of guidance which have led to several reformulations of the role of educational evaluation both as a tool of guidance and as one means for appraising the effectiveness of particular procedures used in the guidance process. However, theories of educational, vocational, and personal decision-making and what constitutes success in each of these arenas of life have not yet been accompanied by appropriate instruments and procedures for appraising the soundness of these decisions and the later success of individuals in achieving significant educational, vocational, and personal goals. Prediction of subsequent educational performance has reached a dead end so far as traditional instruments and procedures are concerned. The use of biographical data, questionnaires, and interview material is extending the range of information about the individual that is useful in guidance, but more and better instruments are needed. Particularly, the lack of comprehensive procedures that an individual student can use for gaining self-understanding is a serious gap in guidance practice. No less important is the need for a more adequate conception of the nature of the impact guidance can be expected to make on the personal development of the student, and the working out of the means for assessing the impact. Some promising beginnings have been made to fill these gaps, but no great strides have yet been taken.

In chapter v, Whitla reviews the very active situation of research in college admissions, many of the recent findings becoming outdated by the shifts in educational policy and procedures resulting from the social changes in society and the political impact of student unrest. Rank in class and scholastic-aptitude test scores furnish only a portion of the information needed to appraise the probable success of students in college. Furthermore, grades in college furnish only a very limited indication of the extent to which the graduate will utilize his college education effectively in his occupation, his civic life, and his personal self-realization. Personality factors appear to offer additional information of value in college admissions, but the conception of how they operate in a given college and the instruments for appraising them are both inadequate to furnish a satisfactory basis for research. A similar inadequacy exists regarding the influence of demographic factors on success in particular colleges. Social class, the education and income of parents, and rural and urban settings are found to have some relationship to college performance, but the nature of the relations and the way in which these factors operate in different types of colleges have not been worked out, and the procedures that can be used for appropriate appraisals have not yet been devised and tested. Today, the greatest demand is for means that can appraise the potential of students coming from disadvantaged backgrounds. Colleges that continue traditional practices are not likely to provide the most effective educational environment for disadvantaged students. Hence, there is currently increasing interest in the use of instruments designed to evaluate college environments. The recognition that students form peer groups that can profoundly influence the educational development of individuals is creating a need for more adequate theories of peer-group influences and corresponding procedures of measurement.

Stalnaker, in chapter vi, outlines the several purposes and kinds of scholarship programs in operation and indicates the fact that the means of evaluation used in selecting recipients in some programs are often inappropriate or only partly relevant to the purpose. He points out that no major or noteworthy research has been undertaken on the selection techniques used in specific scholarship programs. It seems clear that new evaluation procedures and instruments are needed to serve the variety of purposes of scholarship programs and new ideas are required for a comprehensive appraisal of their success. The National Merit Scholarship Program has conducted the most significant research on the factors involved in successful academic performance, the results of which indicate directions for new evaluation efforts requiring new techniques and devices. Particularly needed are measures of individual idiosyncrasies, means for appraising a diversity of talents, and assessments of success beyond the classroom.

Thelen, in chapter vii, presents a new and fresh view of the dynamics of group instruction and explains the evaluation procedures that are required to furnish feedback, diagnosis, and trouble-shooting in the complex, ongoing social system which is the classroom. For the unstructured class, the calibrated and highly educated human nervous system of teachers and students is the diagnostic tool. Trouble-shooting involves interpretation of the diagnosis, the evaluation of the presumed direction for the instructional group, and suggestion of what ought to be done about it. Thelen outlines a comprehensive theory of group instruction, which is far different from the conceptions on which most work in educational evaluation has been based. The elaboration of the relevant evaluation theory and the refinement of the necessary procedures is a major area of future work in evaluation.

In chapter viii, Lindvall and Cox discuss evaluation both as a procedure for gathering pupil data to use in planning and monitoring individual programs and as a procedure for gathering and analyzing data in such a way that it leads to improvements in materials and in the instructional system. They find that tests of pupil performance which are currently in general use are typically not appropriate for use in individual instruction because they do not indicate clearly what the pupil has now learned and what assignment he is ready to undertake. What is required is the development of tests which provide measures clearly related to the sequences of instructional objectives around which the course is organized.

Placement tests are needed in systems of individualized instruction which will permit the placement of each pupil in a learning continuum commensurate with his performance level. These tests must be broad in scope both with relation to the objectives of the course and with relation to a considerable range of instructional units. Tests of this sort are not now generally available and must be developed. Similarly with preunit and curriculum-embedded examinations, current tests on the market have been based on a wide survey of content focused on the performance of the "average" student. They do not furnish dependable measures of individual performance on sequenced units.

For purposes of monitoring individualized instructional systems, in addition to the other measures, postunit tests are required. Because these, too, are based on the instructional units of the system, the tests now available are not appropriate. New tests must be constructed. Individualized instruction as well as group instruction requires new concepts, procedures, and instruments of evaluation.

In chapter ix, Hemphill discusses the need to differentiate research investigations from evaluation studies and shows by illustration that comprehensive evaluation studies require a considerable expansion of the currently available lists of techniques for data collection and interpretation. Particularly, he points out the present lack of means of appraising the achievement of objectives in the affective domain, in preception, and in the more complex cognitive processes. He also outlines the requirements for evaluation studies in the context of practical educational decisions. Theory formulation and methods of interpreting data for this purpose will need to be developed more fully before systematic evaluation can be of greatest usefulness in making decisions.

Flanagan in chapter x describes very promising possibilities for the use of evaluation procedures in the development of instructional procedures, materials and programs. By the use of pretests and posttests, their effectiveness can be appraised in terms of the specific parts that facilitate learning and those parts that are not achieving the gains in understanding, skills, or attitudes intended. Revisions can then be made and the educational effectiveness increased. This method of development has been demonstrated in several fields, but its wide use is dependent upon further theoretical developments relating to the kinds of roles instructional procedures and materials can serve and the construction of instruments appropriate to these theoretical conceptions. In this chapter, illustrations are given of the efforts under way to develop the needed theories and practical procedures, including the exciting experimental Program for Learning in Accordance with Needs.

In chapter xi, Provus forcefully presents the experiences of educational administrators in seeking to monitor ongoing educational programs in the schools and to make decisions regarding the acceptance or rejection of pilot demonstrations in the schools. He shows the need for a conception of the multiple aspects of the situation ranging from the use of evaluation in assisting the process of developing a "new program," through the identification of those programs in operation which meet the specifications of the "new program to be tested" to the actual test of the new program in operation under varying specified conditions. Evaluation theory that is commonly practiced today is a great oversimplification of the situation faced in the schools. New theories and evaluation procedures are urgently needed to guide administrative decisions in education.

Brickell in Chapter XII analyzes the situation now faced by a typical school in selecting and developing innovative practices that promise to improve educational effectiveness. A school is a complex system serving a variety of human individuals as clients, through the efforts of teachers who are varied in their abilities, interests, and personalities. The several components that comprise the system are interlocking so that changes in objectives or program, or teachers or pupils, have influences upon the others and are in turn influenced by these changes. Hence, it is not a simple matter to predict the probable consequences of a proposed innovation. Yet, choices must be made; either the present practice is to be followed or a change made, and the practice selected among the several possibilities should be the one that, carried on with resources that can be obtained, is predicted to furnish the best educational results. To make these choices evaluation processes can be of great help.

Brickell shows how these processes can aid in predicting the probable consequences of the practices being considered, as well as in ascertaining the results actually obtained when the innovative practice is utilized in the school. The major contribution of this chapter is in presenting outlines for analyzing significant general and specific characteristics of a proposed innovation, for estimating the fit of the innovation to the current system, for assessing the accommodation of the school to the innovation, and for assessing the adaptability of the school for future innovation. The use of these criteria should greatly improve the quality of the choices made by a school in selecting and adopting innovative practices.

In chapter xiii, Merwin and Womer describe the problems involved in using educational evaluation to obtain information about the progress of education in the nation that could serve as a basis for public understanding of educational problems to be faced, of progress being made, and of aspirations not yet fulfilled. For this purpose, it has also been necessary to work out new conceptions, to design new procedures, and to construct new instruments. The achievement testing programs commonly conducted in the schools do not provide the model for national assessments, and the instruments do not furnish information about the progress of students in the lowest third or the highest third of their age group.

Husén, in chapter xiv, discusses the need for cross-national educational evaluations because of (*a*) increasing student mobility, (*b*) the demand for techniques by which the quality of educational systems of the emerging nations can be assessed, and (*c*) the growing awareness that nations can learn from each other with regard to educational structure and practices within the system in relation to its input and its results. In describing the current international project for the evaluation of educational achievement, he explains the need for new appraisal instruments and procedures. The most critical theoretical problem is the definition of comparability in terms of objectives, content, and target populations for any multinational project. This long-range effort should make important contributions to the development of educational evaluation.

In chapter xv, Lindquist discusses the profound changes taking place in the administration and scoring of evaluation instruments and in the analysis, recording, and reporting of results. However, there has been no comparable improvement in the quality of the evaluation instruments. He points out that practically all of the major testing instruments used today in the large-scale testing programs have remained fundamentally unchanged in nature and quality of content during the past twenty years when technological developments have been most dramatic. As a result, the maximum educational benefits of these developments have not been obtained, and the limiting conditions of some machine-scored exercises have reduced the contributions of evaluation. He demonstrates that imaginative efforts to design new evaluation programs and to build new instruments are finding the new machines a great help. They do not need to be an obstacle. Here is an exciting area for further development.

Stake and Denny in chapter xvi remind us that evaluation is not the search for cause and effect, is not the inventory of present status nor the prediction of future success. It is something of all of these, but only as they contribute to understanding substance, function, and worth. But, to accomplish this fundamental purpose, great changes are needed. One is to establish a broader basis for recruiting evaluators to include a wide range of scholars with roots in various disciplines. Their training must also be adequate to a fuller understanding of the purposes and processes of education. More attention needs to be given to the identification of important educational goals and to the priority among them. Particularly, the evaluator must be able to move back and forth from proposed objectives to program and from learning experiences to the significant goals they represent.

The authors explain the great need for more valid techniques for assessing instructional materials and classroom instruction. Particularly, they cite the shortcomings in current appraisals in furnishing meaningful measures of student performance. They point out that, although the concept of educational diagnosis is a very old one, we have not yet worked out valid ways by which teachers may select wisely among alternative instructional treatments. Furthermore, since the worth of any component of education is related to what is expected of it, defensible standards are required. These are not provided by current norms furnished with achievement tests. Evaluators have done little thus far in devising procedures for establishing meaningful and useful standards. Finally, they comment on the need to make a sound and helpful synthesis of evaluation data. This is not simply a matter of comparing results in terms of standard scores but rather an effort to find a comprehensive and unified interpretation that is consistent with the variety of data obtained. We do not yet have an adequate theory of synthesis, and even less the needed procedures.

A Concluding Comment

The authors of this volume have outlined and illustrated many of the great changes that have taken place in educational evaluation since the publication by the Society of the last yearbook on this subject. These changes have been influenced by a variety of factors, including new needs for evaluation, new conditions that must be met, new knowledge that has been gained about education, and new technologies that can be utilized. The interaction among these factors has had striking effects, many of which have been spelled out in the earlier chapters.

In reviewing the progress of the past twenty years and speculating about the future developments in educational evaluation, one is impressed by the dynamic effects of relating more closely the development of evaluation to the particular area in which it is needed and will be used. For a generation prior to World War II, evaluation specialists, with a few notable exceptions, were segregated as a subdivision of psychology seeking general answers to the problems of educational measurement. In this atmosphere, isolated from educational practice, the evaluation specialists developed theories and practices based on older or inadequate conceptions of schooling, of the educational tasks of the school, and of the changing social and educational environment in which learning and teaching are conducted. As a result, the evaluation procedures and devices that were published and generally available served only part of the nearly universal needs for evaluation that exist throughout the educational world.

As these needs became more pressing, persons whose original training and experience were in various fields of educational practice became involved in evaluation, and at the same time, persons trained in the speciality of educational evaluation were employed to work in particular areas of education. Out of the interaction stimulated by arrangements of this sort, the theory and practice of educational evaluation began to develop more rapidly and relevantly. The foundations upon which many of these developments seem to be building are four essential and interrelated operations:

1. Clarifying the particular educational function for which evaluation is needed, that is, for example, studying and formulating the purposes and the steps involved in diagnosing individual learning, or reviewing the current purposes and conditions in connection with which students are admitted or denied admission to college.

2. Formulating a body of theory, including concepts and assumptions relevant to this educational function, that is, outlining the concepts and assumptions involved in diagnosis for individualized instruction, or stating the concepts and assumptions that reflect the best current thinking about college admissions.

3. Selecting and developing evaluation instruments and proce-

dures that are consistent with this body of theory, that is, these concepts and assumptions.

4. Revising on a continuous basis, in the light of information obtained from the use of these instruments and procedures, the statement of function developed in operation 1, above, the formulation of theory developed in 2, above, and the instruments and procedures developed in 3, above.

If these steps can be followed vigorously while communication among various groups working in different areas can be instituted and maintained, there is hope that the past twenty years will have been only a beginning to a much greater development and improvement in educational evaluation during the next two decades.

Index

Abilities, relative stability of, 231

Academic performance: measurement and prediction of, 82-87; measures of independence as predictors of, 91

Achievement motivation, correlation of, with grades, 90-91

Achievement quotient, short life of approval of, 22-23

Achievement tests, use of, in past, 308-9

Actuarial data, use of, in guidance programs, 70-71

Adaptation, strategy of, in collective instruction, 130-31

Admissions (college): new instruments for use in processes of, 99-100; personality factors in, 88-93; summary of problems of, 101; see also College admissions

Ahmann, J. Stanley, 89

Allport, Gordon W., 69

American College Testing Program (ACT), 82, 352

American Educational Research Association, monograph series of, 19

American Institutes for Research, 223, 225, 227, 232, 325, 327, 328

Anderson, Allen R., 194

Answer sheet, see Separate answer sheet

Arbuckle, Dugald S., 51

Astin, Alexander W., 79

Atkin, J. Myron, 376

Atkinson, R. C., 182

Ayres, Leonard P., 8; quoted, 7

Banta, Thomas J., 203

Barnette, W. Leslie, Jr., 76

Barttell, C. J., 71

Bennett, Lloyd M., 67

Ben-Zeev, Saul, 153

Berdie, Ralph F., 52, 73, 87, 392

Bereday, G. Z. F., 335

Bereiter, Carl, 99

Berg, Irwin A., 64

Biological information: use of, as predictor and criterion, 78; use of computers in relation to, 79

Biological Sciences Curriculum Study, 18

Bion, Wilfred, 112

Blocher, Donald H., 79

Bloom, Benjamin S., 96, 280, 391

Bormuth, John R., 383, 384

Boy, Angelo V., 51

Boyer, E. Gil, 379

Brickell, Henry M., 396

Brim, Orville G., Jr., 51; quoted, 52

Brown, B. R., 198

Brown, William F., 88

Bruner, Jerome, 95

Bucknell Continuous Progress Plan, 183-84, 188; nature and use of, 183-85

Burgess, Elva, 90

Burk, Frederic L., 157

Calia, Vincent F., 72

Campbell, Donald T., 75, 197, 281

Campbell, Vincent N., 223

Careers, students lack of information about, 232

Carnegie Corporation, 223, 311

Centralization of concern for evaluation, concepts of evaluation influenced by, 23-24

Chahbazi, Parviz, 90

Change and innovation: characterizing alternatives considered in, 290-91; developing a program of, 288-90; seeking alternatives in, 288-90

Changing concepts of evaluation, content of evaluation in relation to, 14-20

Clark, Kenneth E., 75, 97

Clarke, Robert B., quoted with Gelatt, 58

Classroom instruction, techniques for assessment of, 378-81

Coleman, James S., 3, 17, 231, 352

Collective individual instruction: assignment as strategy in, 129-30; diagnosis and trouble-shooting in, 127-32; teaching strategies in, 128-29; see also Individualized instruction

CONSTITUTION AND BY-LAWS
OF
THE NATIONAL SOCIETY FOR THE
STUDY OF EDUCATION

(As adopted May, 1944, and amended June, 1945, February, 1949, September, 1962 and February, 1968)

ARTICLE I

NAME

The name of this corporation shall be "The National Society for the Study of Education," an Illinois corporation not for profit.

ARTICLE II

PURPOSES

Its purposes are to carry on the investigation of educational problems, to publish the results of same, and to promote their discussion.

The corporation also has such powers as are now, or may hereafter be, granted by the General Not For Profit Corporation Act of the State of Illinois.

ARTICLE III

OFFICES

The corporation shall have and continuously maintain in this state a registered office and a registered agent whose office is identical with such registered office, and may have other offices within or without the State of Illinois as the Board of Directors may from time to time determine.

ARTICLE IV

MEMBERSHIP

Section 1. *Classes.* There shall be two classes of members—active and honorary. The qualifications and rights of the members of such classes shall be as follows:

(*a*) Any person who is desirous of promoting the purposes of this corporation is eligible to active membership and shall become such on payment of dues as prescribed.

(*b*) Active members shall be entitled to vote, to participate in discussion, and, subject to the conditions set forth in Article V, to hold office.

(*c*) Honorary members shall be entitled to all the privileges of active

i

members, with the exception of voting and holding office, and shall be exempt from the payment of dues. A person may be elected to honorary membership by vote of the active members of the corporation on nomination by the Board of Directors.

(*d*) Any active member of the Society may, at any time after reaching the age of sixty, become a life member on payment of the aggregate amount of the regular annual dues for the period of life expectancy, as determined by standard actuarial tables, such membership to entitle the member to receive all yearbooks and to enjoy all other privileges of active membership in the Society for the lifetime of the member.

Section 2. *Termination of Membership.*

(*a*) The Board of Directors by affirmative vote of two-thirds of the members of the Board may suspend or expel a member for cause after appropriate hearing.

(*b*) Termination of membership for nonpayment of dues shall become effective as provided in Article XIV.

Section 3. *Reinstatement.* The Board of Directors may by the affirmation vote of two-thirds of the members of the Board reinstate a former member whose membership was previously terminated for cause other than nonpayment of dues.

Section 4. *Transfer of Membership.* Membership in this corporation is not transferable or assignable.

ARTICLE V

BOARD OF DIRECTORS

Section 1. *General Powers.* The business and affairs of the corporation shall be managed by its Board of Directors. It shall appoint the Chairman and Vice-Chairman of the Board of Directors, the Secretary-Treasurer, and Members of the Council. It may appoint a member to fill any vacancy on the Board until such vacancy shall have been filled by election as provided in Section 3 of this Article.

Section 2. *Number, Tenure, and Qualifications.* The Board of Directors shall consist of seven members, namely, six to be elected by the members of the corporation, and the Secretary-Treasurer to be the seventh member. Only active members who have contributed to the Yearbook shall be eligible for election to serve as directors. A member who has been elected for a full term of three years as director and has not attended at least two-thirds of the meetings duly called and held during that term shall not be eligible for election again before the fifth annual election after the expiration of the term for which he was first elected. No member who has been elected for two full terms as director in immediate succession shall be elected a director for a term next succeeding. This provision shall not apply to the Secretary-Treasurer who is appointed by the Board of Directors. Each director shall hold office for the term for which he is elected or appointed and until his successor shall have been selected and qualified. Directors need not be residents of Illinois.

Section 3. *Election.*

(*a*) The directors named in the Articles of Incorporation shall hold office until their successors shall have been duly selected and shall have qualified. Thereafter, two directors shall be elected annually to serve three years, beginning March first after their election. If, at the time of any annual election, a vacancy exists in the Board of Directors, a director shall be elected at such election to fill such vacancy.

(*b*) Elections of directors shall be held by ballots sent by United States mail as follows: A nominating ballot together with a list of members eligible to be directors shall be mailed by the Secretary-Treasurer to all active members of the corporation in October. From such list, the active members shall nominate on such ballot one eligible member for each of the two regular terms and for any vacancy to be filled and return such ballots to the office of the Secretary-Treasurer within twenty-one days after said date of mailing by the Secretary-Treasurer. The Secretary-Treasurer shall prepare an election ballot and place thereon in alphabetical order the names of persons equal to three times the number of offices to be filled, these persons to be those who received the highest number of votes on the nominating ballot, provided, however, that not more than one person connected with a given institution or agency shall be named on such final ballot, the person so named to be the one receiving the highest vote on the nominating ballot. Such election ballot shall be mailed by the Secretary-Treasurer to all active members in November next succeeding. The active members shall vote thereon for one member for each such office. Election ballots must be in the office of the Secretary-Treasurer within twenty-one days after the said date of mailing by the Secretary-Treasurer. The ballots shall be counted by the Secretary-Treasurer, or by an election committee, if any, appointed by the Board. The two members receiving the highest number of votes shall be declared elected for the regular term and the member or members receiving the next highest number of votes shall be declared elected for any vacancy or vacancies to be filled.

Section 4. *Regular Meetings.* A regular annual meeting of the Board of Directors shall be held, without other notice than this by-law, at the same place and as nearly as possible on the same date as the annual meeting of the corporation. The Board of Directors may provide the time and place, either within or without the State of Illinois, for the holding of additional regular meetings of the Board.

Section 5. *Special Meetings.* Special meetings of the Board of Directors may be called by or at the request of the Chairman or a majority of the directors. Such special meetings shall be held at the office of the corporation unless a majority of the directors agree upon a different place for such meetings.

Section 6. *Notice.* Notice of any special meeting of the Board of Directors shall be given at least fifteen days previously thereto by written notice delivered personally or mailed to each director at his business address, or by telegram. If mailed, such notice shall be deemed to be delivered when deposited in the United States mail in a sealed envelope so addressed, with postage thereon prepaid. If notice be given by telegram, such notice shall be deemed to be delivered when the telegram is delivered to the telegraph company. Any director may waive notice of any meeting. The attendance of a director at any meeting shall constitute a waiver of notice of such meeting, except where a director attends a meeting for the express purpose of objecting to the transaction of any business because the meeting is not lawfully called or convened. Neither the business to be transacted at, nor the purpose of, any regular or special meeting of the Board need be specified in the notice or waiver of notice of such meeting.

Section 7. *Quorum.* A majority of the Board of Directors shall constitute a quorum for the transaction of business at any meeting of the Board, provided, that if less than a majority of the directors are present at said meeting, a majority of the directors present may adjourn the meeting from time to time without further notice.

Section 8. *Manner of Acting.* The act of the majority of the directors present at a meeting at which a quorum is present shall be the act of the Board of Directors, except where otherwise provided by law or by these by-laws.

Article VI

THE COUNCIL

Section 1. *Appointment.* The Council shall consist of the Board of Directors, the Chairmen of the corporation's Yearbook and Research Committees, and such other active members of the corporation as the Board of Directors may appoint.

Section 2. *Duties.* The duties of the Council shall be to further the objects of the corporation by assisting the Board of Directors in planning and carrying forward the educational undertakings of the corporation.

Article VII

OFFICERS

Section 1. *Officers.* The officers of the corporation shall be a Chairman of the Board of Directors, a Vice-Chairman of the Board of Directors, and a Secretary-Treasurer. The Board of Directors, by resolution, may create additional offices. Any two or more offices may be held by the same person, except the offices of Chairman and Secretary-Treasurer.

Section 2. *Election and Term of Office.* The officers of the corporation shall be elected annually by the Board of Directors at the annual regular meeting of the Board of Directors, provided, however, that the Secretary-Treasurer may be elected for a term longer than one year. If the election of officers shall not be held at such meeting, such election shall be held as soon thereafter as conveniently may be. Vacancies may be filled or new offices created and filled at any meeting of the Board of Directors. Each officer shall hold office until his successor shall have been duly elected and shall have qualified or until his death or until he shall resign or shall have been removed in the manner hereinafter provided.

Section 3. *Removal.* Any officer or agent elected or appointed by the Board of Directors may be removed by the Board of Directors whenever in its judgment the best interests of the corporation would be served thereby, but such removal shall be without prejudice to the contract rights, if any, of the person so removed.

Section 4. *Chairman of the Board of Directors.* The Chairman of the Board of Directors shall be the principal officer of the corporation. He shall preside at all meetings of the members of the Board of Directors, shall perform all duties incident to the office of chairman of the Board of Directors and such other duties as may be prescribed by the Board of Directors from time to time.

Section 5. *Vice-Chairman of the Board of Directors.* In the absence of the Chairman of the Board of Directors or in the event of his inability or refusal to act, the Vice-Chairman of the Board of Directors shall perform the duties of the Chairman of the Board of Directors, and when so acting, shall have all the powers of and be subject to all the restrictions upon the Chairman of the Board of Directors. Any Vice-Chairman of the Board of Directors shall perform such other duties as from time to time may be assigned to him by the Board of Directors.

Section 6. *Secretary-Treasurer.* The Secretary-Treasurer shall be the managing executive officer of the corporation. He shall: (*a*) keep the minutes of the meetings of the members and of the Board of Directors in one or more books provided for that purpose; (*b*) see that all notices are duly given in accordance with the provisions of these by-laws or as required by law; (*c*) be custodian of the corporate records and of the seal of the corporation and see that the seal of the corporation is affixed to all documents, the execution of which on behalf of the corporation under its seal is duly authorized in accordance with the provisions of these by-laws; (*d*) keep a register of the postoffice address of each member as furnished to the secretary-treasurer by such member; (*e*) in general perform all duties incident to the office of secretary and such other duties as from time to time may be assigned to him by the Chairman of the Board of Directors or by the Board of Directors. He shall also: (1) have charge and custody of and be responsible for all funds and securities of the corporation; receive and give receipts for moneys due and payable to the corporation from any source whatsoever, and deposit all such moneys in the name of the corporation in such banks, trust companies or other depositories as shall be selected in accordance with the provisions of Article XI of these by-laws; (2) in general perform all the duties incident to the office of Treasurer and such other duties as from time to time may be assigned to him by the Chairman of the Board of Directors or by the Board of Directors. The Secretary-Treasurer shall give a bond for the faithful discharge of his duties in such sum and with such surety or sureties as the Board of Directors shall determine, said bond to be placed in the custody of the Chairman of the Board of Directors.

ARTICLE VIII

COMMITTEES

The Board of Directors, by appropriate resolution duly passed, may create and appoint such committees for such purposes and periods of time as it may deem advisable.

ARTICLE IX

PUBLICATIONS

Section 1. The corporation shall publish *The Yearbook of the National Society for the Study of Education,* such supplements thereto, and such other materials as the Board of Directors may provide for.

Section 2. *Names of Members.* The names of the active and honorary members shall be printed in the Yearbook or, at the direction of the Board of Directors, may be published in a special list.

ARTICLE X

ANNUAL MEETINGS

The corporation shall hold its annual meetings at the time and place of the Annual Meeting of the American Association of School Administrators of the National Education Association. Other meetings may be held when authorized by the corporation or by the Board of Directors.

ARTICLE XI

CONTRACTS, CHECKS, DEPOSITS, AND GIFTS

Section 1. *Contracts.* The Board of Directors may authorize any officer or officers, agent or agents of the corporation, in addition to the officers so authorized by these by-laws to enter into any contract or execute and deliver any instrument in the name of and on behalf of the corporation and such authority may be general or confined to specific instances.

Section 2. *Checks, drafts, etc.* All checks, drafts, or other orders for the payment of money, notes, or other evidences of indebtedness issued in the name of the corporation, shall be signed by such officer or officers, agent or agents of the corporation and in such manner as shall from time to time be determined by resolution of the Board of Directors. In the absence of such determination of the Board of Directors, such instruments shall be signed by the Secretary-Treasurer.

Section 3. *Deposits.* All funds of the corporation shall be deposited from time to time to the credit of the corporation in such banks, trust companies, or other depositories as the Board of Directors may select.

Section 4. *Gifts.* The Board of Directors may accept on behalf of the corporation any contribution, gift, bequest, or device for the general purposes or for any special purpose of the corporation.

Section 5. *Dissolution.* In case of dissolution of the National Society for the Study of Education (incorporated under the GENERAL NOT FOR PROFIT CORPORATION ACT of the State of Illinois), the Board of Directors shall, after paying or making provision for the payment of all liabilities of the Corporation, dispose of all assets of the Corporation to such organization or organizations organized and operated exclusively for charitable, educational, or scientific purposes as shall at the time qualify as an exempt organization or organizations under Section 561 (C) (3) of the Internal Revenue Code of 1954 (or the corresponding provision of any future United States Internal Revenue Law), as the Board of Directors shall determine.

Article XII

BOOKS AND RECORDS

The corporation shall keep correct and complete books and records of account and shall also keep minutes of the proceedings of its members, Board of Directors, and committees having any of the authority of the Board of Directors, and shall keep at the registered or principal office a record giving the names and addresses of the members entitled to vote. All books and records of the corporation may be inspected by any member or his agent or attorney for any proper purpose at any reasonable time.

Article XIII

FISCAL YEAR

The fiscal year of the corporation shall begin on the first day of July in each year and end on the last day of June of the following year.

Article XIV

DUES

Section 1. *Annual Dues.* The annual dues for active members of the Society shall be determined by vote of the Board of Directors at a regular meeting duly called and held.

Section 2. *Election Fee.* An election fee of $1.00 shall be paid in advance by each applicant for active membership.

Section 3. *Payment of Dues.* Dues for each calendar year shall be payable in advance on or before the first day of January of that year. Notice of dues for the ensuing year shall be mailed to members at the time set for mailing the primary ballots.

Section 4. *Default and Termination of Membership.* Annual membership shall terminate automatically for those members whose dues remain unpaid after the first day of January of each year. Members so in default will be reinstated on payment of the annual dues plus a reinstatement fee of fifty cents.

ARTICLE XV

SEAL

The Board of Directors shall provide a corporate seal which shall be in the form of a circle and shall have inscribed thereon the name of the corporation and the words "Corporate Seal, Illinois."

ARTICLE XVI

WAIVER OF NOTICE

Whenever any notice whatever is required to be given under the provision of the General Not For Profit Corporation Act of Illinois or under the provisions of the Articles of Incorporation or the by-laws of the corporation, a waiver thereof in writing signed by the person or persons entitled to such notice, whether before or after the time stated therein, shall be deemed equivalent to the giving of such notice.

ARTICLE XVII

AMENDMENTS

Section 1. *Amendments by Directors.* The constitution and by-laws may be altered or amended at any meeting of the Board of Directors duly called and held, provided that an affirmative vote of at least five directors shall be required for such action.

Section 2. *Amendments by Members.* By petition of twenty-five or more active members duly filed with the Secretary-Treasurer, a proposal to amend the constitution and by-laws shall be submitted to all active members by United States mail together with ballots on which the members shall vote for or against the proposal. Such ballots shall be returned by United States mail to the office of the Secretary-Treasurer within twenty-one days after date of mailing of the proposal and ballots by the Secretary-Treasurer. The Secretary-Treasurer or a committee appointed by the Board of Directors for that purpose shall count the ballots and advise the members of the result. A vote in favor of such proposal by two-thirds of the members voting thereon shall be required for adoption of such amendment.

MINUTES OF THE ANNUAL MEETING OF THE SOCIETY

The 1968 meeting of the Society was held in the American Room of the Traymore Hotel in Atlantic City at 2:30 P.M., Sunday, February 18, with Harold G. Shane presiding and with some four hundred members and friends present.

The annual meeting has been most often devoted to presentations of Parts I and II of the yearbook. However, since Part II, *Innovation and Change in Reading Instruction,* had been scheduled for presentation in Boston on April 25, only Part I, *Metropolitanism: Its Challenge to Education,* was presented.

The programs of both meetings follow:

PROGRAM OF THE ATLANTIC CITY MEETING

Joint Meeting of the National Society for the Study of Education and the American Association of School Administrators

Sunday, February 18, 2:30 P.M.
American Room, Traymore Hotel

Presiding: Harold G. Shane, University Professor of Education, Indiana University, and Chairman of the Board of Directors of the National Society; John H. Harris, Director, Metropolitan Schools, Nashville, Tennessee

Presentation of

Metropolitanism: Its Challenge to Education

(Part I of the Society's Sixty-seventh Yearbook)

Introducing the Yearbook

Robert J. Havighurst, Professor of Education, University of Chicago and Fordham University; Editor of the Yearbook

Critique of the Yearbook

C. Taylor Whittier, Director, Central Atlantic Regional Education Laboratory
Luvern L. Cunningham, Dean, College of Education, Ohio State University

Informal Discussion

Robert A. Dentler, Director, Center for Urban Education (New York), Mr. Shane, Mr. Harris, Mr. Havighurst, Mr. Whittier, Mr. Cunningham, and audience

ix

Joint Meeting of the National Society for the Study
of Education and the International Reading Association

Thursday, April 25, 7:30 P.M.
Grand Ballroom, Sheridan-Boston Hotel

Presiding: Edgar Dale, Professor of Education, Ohio State University

Presentation of

Innovation and Change in Reading Instruction

(Part II of the Society's Sixty-seventh Yearbook)

Presentation of the Yearbook

Helen M. Robinson, William Scott Gray Research Professor of
Education, University of Chicago; Editor of the Yearbook

Critique of the Yearbook

Marion D. Jenkinson, Ontario Institute for Studies in Education

Audience Participation

SYNOPSIS OF THE PROCEEDINGS OF THE BOARD OF DIRECTORS OF THE SOCIETY FOR 1968

I. Meeting of February 18, 1968

The Board of Directors met at 9:00 a.m. on February 18, 1968 in the Dennis Hotel (Atlantic City) with the following members present: Messrs. Harold G. Shane (presiding), Edgar Dale, William C. Kvaraceus, Paul A. Witty, and Herman G. Richey (Secretary).

At the request of the Board, Robert J. Havighurst (Chairman of the Committee on Educational Leadership) and Robert M. McClure (Chairman of the Committee on Curriculum) attended the morning session of the meeting.

1. The Secretary reported that the election of members of the Board of Directors held in November and December of 1967 had resulted in the election of Ruth Strang and Robert J. Havighurst, each for a term of three years beginning March 1, 1967.

2. Officers of the Board of Directors for the year beginning March 1, 1967, were elected as follows: William C. Kvaraceus, Chairman; Ralph W. Tyler, Vice-Chairman; and Herman G. Richey, Secretary.

3. The Secretary-Treasurer reported on membership, finances, and sales for the first six months of the fiscal year, 1967-1968.

4. It was announced that all arrangements had been made for the presentation of Part II, *Innovation and Change in Reading Instruction*, at the annual convention of the International Reading Association on April 25, and that Edgar Dale, a member of the Yearbook Committee, Helen M. Robinson, Editor of the Yearbook and Marion D. Jenkinson of the Ontario Institute for Studies in Education would participate in the meeting.

5. The Board expressed its thanks to the American Association of School Administrators and to the International Reading Association for their co-operation in the presentation of the Society's yearbooks.

6. In order to remove the last possible obstacle to qualifying for tax-exempt status, the Constitution was amended by adding to Article XI the following section:

Section 5. *Dissolution*. In case of dissolution of the National Society for the Study of Education (incorporated under the GENERAL NOT FOR PROFIT CORPORATION ACT of the State of Illinois), the Board of Directors shall, after paying or making provision for the payment of all liabilities of the Corporation, dispose of all assets of the Corporation to such organization or organizations organized and operated exclusively for charitable, educational, or scientific purposes as shall at the time qualify as an exempt organization or organizations under Section 561 (C) (3) of the Internal Revenue Code of 1954 (or the corresponding provision of any future United States Internal Revenue Law), as the Board of Directors shall determine.

The Board voted unanimously in favor of the amendment.

7. Progress reports were presented for the following authorized yearbooks: *The United States and International Education* (Harold G. Shane), *Educational Evaluation: New Roles, New Means* (Ralph W. Tyler), *Language and School Programs* (Albert H. Marckwardt), *Mathematics Educa-*

tion (E. G. Begle), *The Curriculum* (Robert M. McClure), and *Leaders in Education* (Robert J. Havighurst).

8. Two proposals for yearbooks, one on educational philosophy and the other on early learning, were discussed at length and it was agreed that information that would make a final decision possible should be collected before the next meeting.

9. Discussion on several proposals (Creativity, Industrial Education, Social Studies) was deferred to a later meeting.

10. Topics submitted to the Board were as follows: Materials for Children's Learning, Instruction, Change and Innovation, Teacher Education, The Junior College, and Higher Education. Discussion of these topics was deferred to the next meeting of the Board.

II. MEETING OF JULY 18-19, 1968

The Board of Directors met at 7:30 P.M. on July 18, 1968 in the Hilton Hotel (Chicago) with all members present: William C. Kvaraceus (presiding), John I. Goodlad, Robert J. Havighurst, Ruth Strang, Ralph W. Tyler, Paul A. Witty, and Herman G. Richey (Secretary).

1. The Secretary-Treasurer presented the "Report of the Treasurer of the Society, 1967-68." (The report is printed on the following page.)

2. It was agreed that arrangements should be made to present *The United States and International Education* (Part I of the Sixty-eighth Yearbook) at the Atlantic City meeting and *Educational Evaluation: New Roles, New Means* (Part II) at the annual meeting of the American Educational Research Association in Los Angeles.

3. The Secretary reported that the membership had reached an all-time high—about 5600.

4. The Secretary reported that the Internal Revenue Service had approved the Society's application for tax-exempt status under Section 503 (C) of the Internal Revenue Act of 1954.

5. Progress reports on authorized yearbooks were presented.

6. Mr. Havighurst was authorized to continue his efforts to involve Phi Delta Kappa in the establishment of a joint commission on leadership in education.

7. Proposed yearbooks were discussed. In response to the request of the Board made at its February meeting, Mr. Witty presented a tentative outline for a yearbook on early learning. He listed the names of persons heavily involved in the field and recommended next steps to be taken by the Board.

8. The Board approved the proposal for a yearbook on educational philosophy submitted by Laurence Thomas.

9. The Board discussed other proposals on creativity, sociology in education, technology in education, learning experiments, application to theory, media of education, humanities and the arts in education, and social sciences. It was agreed that members of the Board would study these proposals and report on them at the next meeting.

REPORT OF THE TREASURER OF THE SOCIETY

1967-68

RECEIPTS AND DISBURSEMENTS

Receipts:

Membership dues	$ 40,564.53
Sale of yearbooks	65,090.68
Interest and dividends	2,691.17
Miscellaneous	1,551.25
Total	**$109,897.65**

Disbursements:

Yearbooks:

Manufacturing	$ 41,064.89
Reprinting	23,818.39
Preparation	2,319.42
Meetings of Board and Society	1,701.84

Secretary's Office:

Editorial, secretarial, and clerical	23,035.81
Supplies	3,901.86
Equipment	33.17
Telephone and telegraph	276.00

Miscellaneous:

Bank charges	13.68
Refunds and transfer of commercial orders	303.25
Safe deposit box	4.00
Filing and notary fees	19.58
Insurance	208.00
Promotional materials and mailing	797.52
Other	22.50
Total	**$ 97,519.91**

Excess receipts over disbursements	$ 12,377.74
Deficit in checking account, June 30, 1967	$ (3,032.25)
Transfer to interest-bearing accounts	$ 9,000.00
Cash in checking account, June 30, 1968	$ 345.49

STATEMENT OF CASH AND SECURITIES

As of June 30, 1968

Cash:

University National Bank, Chicago, Illinois—
Checking account.................................$ 345.49
Savings account...................................   2,522.79
Hyde Park Savings and Loan Assn...................... 15,000.00
Chicago Federal Savings and Loan Assn................. 10,000.00
Home Federal Savings and Loan Assn................... 10,000.00
Telegraph Savings and Loan Assn...................... 10,000.00
Hyde Park Bank and Trust Co.......................... 15,000.00

Securities:

38 shares First National Bank of Boston, capital stock.....   1,063.97
U.S. Government "H" Bonds, dated March 1, 1967....... 15,000.00
                                                       ————————
Total assets.......................................$78,932.25

Charges against current assets:
Annual dues paid for 1969............................   607.00
Life membership fund................................. 8,000.00
Reprinting (7/1/68-12/31/68)........................ 12,000.00
                                                       ————————
Total..$20,607.00
Net assets...$58,325.25

MEMBERS OF THE NATIONAL SOCIETY FOR THE STUDY OF EDUCATION

[This list includes all persons enrolled November 1, 1968, whether for 1968 or 1969. An asterisk (*) indicates Life Members of the Society.]

Aarestad, Amanda B., 1887 Gilmore Ave., Winona, Minn.
Aaron, Ira Edward, Col. of Educ., University of Georgia, Athens, Ga.
Aaron, Robert L., R and D Center, University of Georgia, Athens, Ga.
Abate, Harry, Board of Education, 607 Walnut Ave., Niagara Falls, N.Y.
Abbott, Frank C., Colorado Comm. on Higher Education, Denver, Colo.
Abbott, Samuel Lee, Jr., Plymouth State College, Plymouth, N.H.
Abbott, Whitt K., Alice Robertson Junior High School, Muskogee, Okla.
Abel, Frederick P., Western Illinois University, Macomb, Ill.
Abel, Harold, Sch. of Educ., University of Oregon, Eugene, Ore.
Abelson, Harold H., Sch. of Educ., City University, New York, N.Y.
Abercrombie, Mrs. Charlotte, 1121 N. Waverly Pl., Milwaukee, Wis.
Ables, Jack B., East Aurora Jr. High School, East Aurora, N.Y.
Abraham, Willard, Arizona State University, Tempe, Ariz.
Abrahamson, Edward, Prin., Flower Hill School, Huntington, N.Y.
Abrahamson, Stephen, Sch. of Med., Univ. of So. Calif., Los Angeles, Calif.
Abramowitz, Mortimer J., 345 Lakeville Rd., Great Neck, N.Y.
Achilles, Charles M., Box 317 B, Rt. # 1, Geneva, N.Y.
Ackerlund, George C., Southern Illinois Univ., Edwardsville, Ill.
Ackerman, Thomas J., Univ. of Florida, Gainesville, Fla.
Ackley, James F., 19320 Springport, Rowland Heights, Calif.
Adair, Mary R., Asst. Prof. of Spec. Educ., University Park, Pa.
Adams, Donald K., Sch. of Educ., Syracuse Univ., Syracuse, N.Y.
Adams, Ernest L., Michigan State University, East Lansing, Mich.
Adams, Fern B., Office of Co. Supt. of Schls., Los Angeles, Calif.
Adams, James A., 1106 S. State St., Tahlequah, Okla.
Adams, Mrs. Ruth R., Sch. of Educ., New York City College, New York, N.Y.
Adatto, Albert, 228—165th Ave., N.E., Bellevue, Wash.
Adelberg, Arthur J., Supt., Schl. Dist. #3, Elmhurst, Ill.
* Adell, James C., 16723 Fernway Rd., Shaker Heights, Ohio
Aden, Robert C., Middle Tennessee St. Univ., Murfreesboro, Tenn.
Adler, Mrs. Leona K., 101 Central Park W., New York, N.Y.
Adler, Manfred, John Carroll University, Cleveland, Ohio
Adler, Norman A., 51 West 52nd St., New York, N.Y.
Adolphsen, Louis J., Hinsdale Senior High School, Hinsdale, Ill.
Ahlers, Shirley, Texas Tech. Univ., Lubbock, Tex.
Ahrendt, Kenneth M., 301—120 W. 19th St., North Vancouver, B.C., Can.
Ahrnsbrak, Henry C., 425 Berwyn Dr., Madison, Wis.
Airasian, Peter W., Cath. Educ. Res. Cent., Boston Col., Chestnut Hill, Mass.
Akemann, Mrs. Rhea, Marion Community Schools, Marion, Ind.
Akins, Harold S., 1300 High St., Wichita, Kan.
Alagna, Agostino A., 478 W. 26th St., Chicago, Ill.
Alberg, Gary L., 1990 Lakeaires Blvd., White Bear Lake, Minn.
Albohm, John C., Supt. of Schools, Alexandria, Va.
Albrecht, Milton C., State Univ. of New York, Buffalo, N.Y.
Albright, Frank S., 37 Yale Terrace, West Orange, N.J.

Alcock, Wayne T., Dillond Univ., New Orleans, La.
Alexander, Burton F., Petersburg High School, Petersburg, Va.
Alexander, Elenora, Rm. 234, 1300 Capitol Ave., Houston, Texas
Alexander, William M., Col. of Educ., Univ. of Florida, Gainesville, Fla.
Algier, Mrs. Ann S., 133 Buckwood Drive, Richmond, Ky.
Alkin, Marvin C., University of California, Los Angeles, Calif.
Allen, David, 8437 Truxton Ave., Los Angeles, Calif.
Allen, Dwight W., Sch. of Educ., Stanford University, Stanford, Calif.
Allen, Edward E., Akron Central Schools, Akron, N.Y.
Allen, Graham, Coburg Teachers College, Coburg, Melbourne, Australia
Allen, Harold D., Grad. Sch. of Educ., Rutgers Univ., New Brunswick, N.J.
Allen, Mrs. Irene A., R.F.D. 1, Swanton, Vt.
Allen, James Robert, 1249 Lake Ave., Fort Wayne, Ind.
Allen, John E., 306 Arbour Dr., Newark, Dela.
Allen, Ross L., State Univ. College, Cortland, N.Y.
Allen, Warren G., State Teachers College, Minot, N.D.
Allison, John J., 200 Bloomfield Ave., West Hartford, Conn.
Allman, Reva White, Alabama State College, Montgomery, Ala.
Alm, Richard S., Dept. of Educ., University of Hawaii, Honolulu, Hawaii
Almcrantz, Mrs. Georgia, 402 Brown Circle, Knox, Ind.
Almen, Rev. Dr. Louis, 231 Madison Ave., New York, N.Y.
Almroth, Frank S., 20 Hilltop Ter., Wayne, N.J.
Alper, Arthur E., University of Florida, Gainesville, Fla.
Alpert, Harvey, 20 Woodland Dr., Old Bethpage, N.Y.
Alprin, Stanley I., Cleveland State University, Cleveland, Ohio
Al-Rubaiy, Abdul Amir, Kent State University, Kent, Ohio
Alt, Pauline M., Central Connecticut State College, New Britain, Conn.
Altman, Harold, 12006 Stanwood Dr., Los Angeles, Calif.
Altman, Herbert H., 832 Ocean Ave., Brooklyn, N.Y.
Amacher, Mrs. Walter, 7471 Mudbrook St., N.W., Massillon, Ohio
Amar, Wesley F., Waller High School, Chicago, Ill.
Ambrose, Edna V., 2124 N.E. 7th Ter., Gainesville, Fla.
Amershek, Kathleen, Col. of Educ., Univ. of Maryland, College Park, Md.
Ames, John L., Queens College, Kissena Blvd., Flushing, N.Y.
Amidon, Edna P., 65—30th Ave., W., Eugene, Ore.
Amioka, Shiro, University of Hawaii, Honolulu, Hawaii
Amsden, Robert L., 17 Parker Ave., Maplewood, N.J.
Anastasiow, Nicholas J., 2948 Friendship Rd., Durham, N.C.
Anders, Mrs. Elizabeth M., 3601 Palm Dr., Riviera Beach, Fla.
Anderson, Bernard, John Spry Elementary School, Chicago, Ill.
Anderson, Donald G., Oakland Public Schls., 1025 Second Ave., Oakland, Calif.
Anderson, Doyle R., 935 Lewis Ave., St. Joseph, Mich.
Anderson, Edmond C., Sequoyah Junior High School, Dallas, Tex.
Anderson, Ernest M., Kansas State Col., Pittsburg, Kan.
Anderson, Floydelh, West Virginia State College, Institute, W.Va.
Anderson, G. Lester, University of New York, Buffalo, N.Y.
Anderson, Harold, 1531 W. Mourilaine, Ft. Collins, Colo.
Anderson, Harold A., North Park College, Chicago, Ill.
Anderson, Howard R., Houghton Mifflin Co., Boston, Mass.
Anderson, Isabel C., Sch. of Educ., Temple University, Philadelphia, Pa.
Anderson, J. Paul, Col. of Educ., Univ. of Maryland, College Park, Md.
Anderson, James W., 742 Ashland Ave., St. Paul Park, Minn.
Anderson, Kenneth E., Sch. of Educ., Univ. of Kansas, Lawrence, Kan.
Anderson, Lester W., Sch. of Educ., Univ. of Michigan, Ann Arbor, Mich.
Anderson, Linnea M., 3409 N. California, Peoria, Ill.
Anderson, Marion A., Ginn & Co., Statler Office Bldg., Boston, Mass.
Anderson, Patricia S. B., 25 Lascelles Blvd., Toronto, Ont., Canada
Anderson, Philip S., Wisconsin State University, River Falls, Wis.
Anderson, Robert Henry, Grad. Sch. of Educ., Harvard Univ., Cambridge, Mass.
Anderson, Roger C., St. Cloud State Col., St. Cloud, Minn.

Anderson, Ruth, 2569—7th Ave., Apt. 24 I, New York, N.Y.
Anderson, Stuart A., Riverside-Brookfield Twp. High School, Riverside, Ill.
Anderson, Thomas, Box 257, Newman, Ill.
Anderson, Vernon E., Col. of Educ., University of Maryland, College Park, Md.
Anderson, W. Harold, 908 W. Main St., Waupun, Wis.
Anderson, William J., P.O. Box 288, Georgetown, Texas
Andree, R. G., Southern Illinois University, Edwardsville, Ill.
Andregg, Neal B., 2553 Richmond Hill Rd., Augusta, Ga.
Andrews, Clay S., Dept. of Educ., San Jose State College, San Jose, Calif.
Andrews, Esther, 1937 N. Wilton Pl., Hollywood, Calif.
Andrews, Richard L., 2436 Edglea Dr., Lafayette, Ind.
Andrews, Sam D., Bowling Green State University, Bowling Green, Ohio
Andrews, Stella F., 544 Washington Ave., Pleasantville, N.Y.
Andrisek, John R., 119 Meadow Dr., Berea, Ohio
Angelini, Arrigo L., University of Sao Paulo, Sao Paulo, Brazil
Angell, George W., State University College, Plattsburg, N.Y.
Angelo, Rev. Mark V., St. Bonaventure Univ., St. Bonaventure, N.Y.
Angelo, Mrs. Sadie R., Sch. of Educ., Univ. of Wis., Milwaukee, Wis.
Angle, Philip H., Central Bucks School, Doylestown, Pa.
*Annis, Helen W., 6711 Conway Ave., Takoma Park, Md.
Ansel, James O., Western Michigan University, Kalamazoo, Mich.
Anselm, Karl R., Ventura Hall, Stanford University, Stanford, Calif.
Anthony, Sally M., San Diego State Col., San Diego, Calif.
Antoine, Tamlin C., P.O. Box 1647, Taipei, Taiwan, Rep. of China
Antonelli, Luiz K., Queens College, Flushing, N.Y.
Apel, J. Dale, Kansas State Univ., Manhattan, Kansas
Apple, Joe A., San Diego State College, San Diego, Calif.
Apple, Michael W., 141–30 84th Rd., Briarwood, L.I., N.Y.
Appleton, David, Supt. of Schools, Pine St., North Conway, N.H.
Arcarese, Lawrence C., State Univ. Col. of Arts & Sci., Plattsburgh, N.Y.
Archer, Marguerite P., 137 Highbrook Ave., Pelham, N.Y.
Archer, N. Sidney, East. Reg. Inst. for Educ., Inc., Syracuse, N.Y.
Arends, Wade B., 439 Wildwood, Park Forest, Ill.
Armistead, Roy B., 9234 Queenston Dr., St. Louis, Mo.
Armogida, Harry, Dept. of Educ., Miami University, Oxford, Ohio
Armstrong, Betty W., Univ. of Cincinnati, Cincinnati, Ohio
Armstrong, Mrs. Carmen L., R.F.D. No. 2, 5 Points Rd., Sycamore, Ill.
Armstrong, Mrs. Jenny R., Univ. of Wisconsin, Madison, Wis.
Armstrong, J. Niel, Sch. of Educ., Agric. & Tech. College, Greensboro, N.C.
Arnaud, E. E., Our Lady of the Lake College, San Antonio, Tex.
*Arnesen, Arthur E., 440 East First South St., Salt Lake City, Utah
Arnoff, Melvin, 4325 Groveland Rd., University Heights, Ohio
Arnold, Gala, 740 "J" Ave., Coronado, Calif.
Arnold, J. E., Box 8540, University Station, Knoxville, Tenn.
Arnold, Marshall, 301 S. Water St., Henderson, Ky.
Arnold, Phyllis D., 628 Patterson Ave., San Antonio, Tex.
Arnold, Shirley L., 54 Kehr St., Buffalo, N.Y.
Arnsdorf, Val E., Sch. of Educ., Univ. of Delaware, Newark, Del.
Arnstein, George E., ACCESS, NEA, 1201—16th St., N.W., Washington, D.C.
Aromi, Eugene J., Univ. of So. Alabama, Mobile, Ala.
Arthur, Douglas C., Petaluma City Schools, Petaluma, Calif.
Arveson, Raymond G., 38060 Logan Dr., Fremont, Calif.
Arvin, Charles L., Crawfordsville Community Schools, Crawfordsville, Ind.
Ashburn, Arnold G., Mississippi Southern College, Hattiesburg, Miss.
Ashe, Robert W., Dept. of Educ., Arizona State University, Tempe, Ariz.
Askins, Billy E., Box 4234, Texas Tech. College, Lubbock, Texas
Aspridy, Chrisoula, 2986 Lyell Rd., Rochester, N.Y.
Atkins, Thurston A., Teachers Col., Columbia Univ., New York, N.Y.
Atkinson, Francis D., Jr., 1100 E. Lemon St., Tempe, Ariz.
Atkinson, William N., Jackson Junior College, Jackson, Mich.
Aubin, Albert E., 3258 Sawtelle Blvd., Los Angeles, Calif.

Auble, Donavon, Western Col. for Women, Oxford, Ohio
Aubry, A. J., L. B. Landry School, New Orleans, La.
Auer, Michael, Col. of Educ., Michigan State Univ., East Lansing, Mich.
Austin, David B., Richmond College, Staten Island, New York
Austin, Martha Lou, Univ. of South Florida, Tampa, Fla.
Austin, Mary C., 2263 Demington Dr., Cleveland, Ohio
Austin, Roy S., State University College, Potsdam, N.Y.
Ausubel, David P., City University of New York, New York, N.Y.
Avegno, T. Sylvia, 907 Castle Pt. Terrace, Hoboken, N.J.
Avinger, W. H., Abilene Christian College, Abilene, Texas
Ayer, Joseph C., 4200 Manchester Road, Middletown, Ohio
Azzarelli, Joseph J., New York University, Washington Sq., New York, N.Y.

Babcock, William E., 131 W. Nittany Ave., State College, Pa.
Bach, Jacob O., Southern Illinois University, Carbondale, Ill.
Bachar, James R., 586 East End Ave., Pittsburgh, Pa.
Bachman, Ralph V., South High School, Salt Lake City, Utah
Backus, Thomas A., 570—115th Ave., Treasure Island, Fla.
Bacon, William P., Sch. of Educ., Univ. of the Pacific, Stockton, Calif.
Bacsalmasi, Stephen, York Cent. Dist. H. S. Brd., Richmond Hill, Ont., Canada
Baer, Campion, Capuchin Sem. of St. Mary, Crown Point, Ind.
Bagott, Nancy, 835 N. Sixth Ave., Tucson, Ariz.
Bahn, Lorene A., 2843 Lomita Circle, Springfield, Mo.
Bahner, Joel H., Frankfurt American Elementary School No. 1, APO, N.Y.
Bahner, John M., 5335 Far Hills Ave., Dayton, Ohio
Bahrenburg, Erma M., 27 Ninth St., Carle Place, L.I., N.Y.
Baich, Henry, University of Portland, Portland, Ore.
Bailer, Joseph R., Dept. of Educ., Western Maryland College, Westminster, Md.
Bailey, Lucile, 119 E. University Dr., Tempe, Arizona
Bajek, Michalina, 1634 Neil Ave., Columbus, Ohio
Bajek, Robert S., 3830 S. Scoville, Berwyn, Ill.
Bajwa, Ranjit Singh, 2235 Georgetown Blvd., Ann Arbor, Mich.
Baker, Arthur F., 10 Ditson Place, Methuen, Mass.
Baker, Charles, Gladwin High School, Gladwin, Mich.
Baker, Charles R., P.O. Box 367, San Andreas, Calif.
Baker, Eugene H., 1848 N. Chestnut Ave., Arlington Heights, Ill.
Baker, Harry J., 19050 Wiltshire, Lathrup Village, Mich.
Baker, I. D., Greenville College, Greenville, Ill.
Baker, John E., Col. of Educ. & Nurs., Univ. of Vermont, Burlington, Vt.
Baker, Lillian Mrs. 20257 Allentown Dr., Woodland Hills, Calif.
Baker, Rebecca, Southern Illinois University, Carbondale, Ill.
Baker, Robert C., Bemidji State College, Bemidji, Minn.
Baker, Robert E., Sch. of Educ., George Washington Univ., Washington, D.C.
Baker, William E., 11247 Dempsey Ave., Granada Hills, Calif.
Baldauf, R., 122 Forest Ave., Oak Park, Ill.
Baldwin, Alan L., Redwood City Sch. Dist., Redwood City, Calif.
Baldwin, Rollin, 924 West End Ave., New York, N.Y.
Balian, Arthur, 6804 W. Dickinson St., Milwaukee, Wis.
Ball, George G., State College of Iowa, Cedar Falls, Iowa
Ballantine, Francis A., San Diego State College, San Diego, Calif.
Ballou, Stephen V., Div. of Educ., Fresno State College, Fresno, Calif.
Balser, Paul, Forest Hills H.S., 67-01—110th St., Forest Hills, N.Y.
Balzer, David M., Col. of Educ., University of Toledo, Toledo, Ohio
Bandy, George R., Northern Montana College, Havre, Mont.
Banks, Marie, State University College, Plattsburgh, N.Y.
Banner, Carolyn, 409 Lafayette, Jefferson City, Mo.
Bany, Mary, 411 N. Third St., Alhambra, Calif.
Baratta, Anthony N., Sch. of Educ., Fordham University, New York, N.Y.
Barbaree, Frank, P.O. Box 547, Jackson, Ala.
Barbe, Richard H., Sch. of Educ., University of Delaware, Newark, Del.

Barbe, Walter B., 803 Church St., Honesdale, Pa.
Barber, Anson B., 4415 Main St., Apt. 18, Snyder, N.Y.
Barber, Grant W., 1251 Shipman St., Birmingham, Mich.
Barber, Richard L., Col. of Arts & Sci., Univ. of Louisville, Louisville, Ky.
Barclay, Doris, 5151 State College Dr., Los Angeles, Calif.
Bardellini, Justin M., 337 Menlo Court, Walnut Creek, Calif.
Barden, Michael W., 42 Crosby Rd., Chestnut Hills, Mass.
Barkan, Maxine L., 3822 Grand Teton Ct., Irving, Texas
Barkley, Margaret V., Arizona State University, Tempe, Ariz.
Barlow, Melvin L., Sch. of Educ., Univ. of California, Los Angeles, Calif.
Barnard, Douglas P., 1633 W. 7th Pl., Mesa, Ariz.
Barnard, J. Darrell, 16 Links Drive, Great Neck, N.Y.
Barnard, W. Robert, Evans Chem. Lab., 88 W. 18th Ave., Columbus, Ohio
Barnes, Cyrus W., Beachlake, Pa.
Barnes, Fred P., Col. of Educ., University of Illinois, Urbana, Ill.
Barney, Angelo T., 818 Black Rd., Joliet, Ill.
Barr, Charlotte A., Chicago State College, Chicago, Ill.
Barr, Dixon A., Sch. of Educ., East. Kentucky State Col., Richmond, Ky.
Barratt, Thomas K., Supt., Warren County Sch. Dist., Warren, Pa.
Barrett, George M., 152 Philcris Dr., Dover, Del.
Barron, Donald, 240 W. 22nd St., Deer Park, N.Y.
Barron, William E., University of Texas, Austin, Tex.
Barros, Raymond, Catholic University of Valparaiso, Valparaiso, Chile
Barry, Florence G., 5956 Race Ave., Chicago, Ill.
Bartel, Fred C., 2921 Richland Ave., Louisville, Ky.
Barter, Alice K., 4675 Booth Rd., Oxford, Ohio
Bartlett, Fernand E., 740 Westcott St., Syracuse, N.Y.
Bartley, Imon D., Southwest Missouri State College, Springfield, Mo.
Barton, Carl L., Superintendent, Community Cons. Sch. Dist. 70, Freeburg, Ill.
Barton, George E., Jr., 1010 Short St., New Orleans, La.
Bastidas, Alfonso, G. R. C., M-214, Bloomington, Ind.
Batha, Robert, Chester Junior-Senior High School, Chester, Calif.
Batinich, Mary Ellen, 9215 S. Troy Ave., Chicago, Ill.
Batten, James W., Box 2455, East. Carolina College, Greenville, N.C.
Battle, J. A., University of South Florida, Tampa, Fla.
Battle, John A., 11 Jones St., New Hyde Park, N.Y.
Battles, John J., 2811 Avenue "D," Brooklyn, N.Y.
Bauer, Edith B., Brigham Young University, Provo, Utah
Bauer, Norman J., Col. of Educ., Wisconsin State Univ., Oshkosh, Wis.
Bauman, Reemt R., Col. of Educ., Univ. of Toledo, Toledo, Ohio
Baumann, Max, 3800 Washington Ave., Baltimore, Md.
Baumgartner, Reuben A., Senior High School, Freeport, Ill.
Baumgartner, Rolla W., Dist. IX-XI, USDESEA, APO, New York
Bauthues, Donald J., 219 5th Ave., N.E. No. 29, Puyallup, Wash.
Baxter, Eugenia, 629 Fourth St., Monongahela, Pa.
Baxter, Marlin B., Moline Public Schools, 1619 Eleventh Ave., Moline, Ill.
Beach, Lowell W., 3606 Univ. H.S., Univ. of Michigan, Ann Arbor, Mich.
Beach, Mary L., 412 Delaware Drive, Westerville, Ohio
Beall, David C., Dir., Pupil Personnel Serv., Mentor, Ohio
Beamer, George C., North Texas State College, Denton, Tex.
Beamer, Rufus W., Virginia Polytechnic Inst., Blacksburg, Va.
Bear, David E., 12 Ramona Pl., Godfrey, Ill.
Beard, Richard L., 1812 Meadowbrook Hgts. Rd., Charlottesville, Va.
Beaton, Daniel W., 425 S. Catalina Ave., Redondo Beach, Calif.
Beattie, George W., P.O. Box 100, Aptos, Calif.
Beatty, Charles J., 13011 Bellevue St., Beltsville, Md.
Beatty, Walcott H., 209 Kensington Way, San Francisco, Calif.
Beaty, Edgar, Middle Tennessee State College, Murfreesboro, Tenn.
Beaubier, Edward W., 19692 Lexington Lane, Huntington Beach, Calif.
Beauchamp, George A., Sch. of Educ., Northwestern University, Evanston, Ill.
Beaumont, Anne E., 68 Eaton Crest Dr., Eatontown, N.J.

Beaumont, Urville J., Tenney High School, Methuen, Mass.
Beaver, Eugene H., Chicago Vocational High School, Chicago, Ill.
Bebb, Randall R., State College of Iowa, Cedar Falls, Iowa
Bebell, Clifford S., Southern Colorado State Col., Pueblo, Colo.
Beck, Hubert Park, Sch. of Educ., City College, 523 W. 121st St., New York, N.Y.
Beck, John M., 5832 Stony Island Ave., Chicago, Ill.
Beck, Norman W., Supt., Monroe County Schls., Waterloo, Ill.
Beck, Robert H., 233 Burton Hall, University of Minnesota, Minneapolis, Minn.
Becken, Elliot D., Supt. of Schools, Medford, Ore.
Becker, Harry A., Superintendent of Schools, Norwalk, Conn.
Becker, Millie A., 7637 S. Loomis Blvd., Chicago, Ill.
Bedell, Ralph, 701 Lewis Hall, Univ. of Missouri, Columbia, Mo.
Beebe, Nelson, Jr., Pennsville Memorial High School, Pennsville, N.J.
Beeching, Robert B., 1461 W. Shaw, Fresno, Calif.
Beery, Cleo C., La Verne College, La Verne, Calif.
Beery, John R., Sch. of Educ., University of Miami, Coral Gables, Fla.
Behal, Rose, 9812 Broadview Rd., Brecksville, Ohio
Behnke, Donald J., 60 Everit Ave., Hewlett, N.Y.
Behrens, Herman D., 811 S. Johnson St., Ada, Ohio
* Behrens, Minnie S., Pomeroy, Iowa
Beighley, Archie F., Dept. of Educ., Winona State Col., Winona, Minn.
Beitler, Roger T., 2676 Walnut Blvd., Ashtabula, Ohio
Belcastro, Frank P., Merrimack College, North Andover, Mass.
Belcher, Eddie W., Louisville Public Schls., 506 W. Hill St., Louisville, Ky.
Belgum, Loretta E., San Francisco State College, San Francisco, Calif.
Bell, Jack, Superintendent of Schools, Overland Park, Kan.
Bell, Keith A., 22906—72 Pl., W., Mountlake Terrace, Wash.
Bell, Mildred, Harding College, Searcy, Ark.
Bell, Robert M., 2819 W. Sherwin Ave., Chicago, Ill.
Bell, Robert W., Wells Lane, Stony Brook, N.Y.
Bell, Wilmer V., 702 Kingston Rd., Baltimore, Md.
Bellack, Arno A., Tchrs. Col., Columbia University, New York, N.Y.
Bemis, James Richard, 5243 Tango Ave., Yorba Linda, Calif.
Benben, John S., 7 Victoria Rd., Ardsley, N. Y.
Benda, Harold, Educ. Dept., West Chester State College, West Chester, Pa.
Bender, Kenneth R., University of Mississippi, University, Miss.
Bender, Martin L., 384 Prospect Ave., Hackensack, N.J.
Bender, Ralph E., Ohio State University, Columbus, Ohio
Benito, Sabado S., Off. of Soc. Sci., Wiley College, Marshall, Texas
Benner, Robert D., Dept. of Elem. Educ., Colorado State Col., Greeley, Colo.
Bennett, Dale E., Col. of Educ., Univ. of Ill., Urbana, Ill.
Bennett, Lloyd M., Texas Woman's University, Denton, Tex.
Bennett, Nancy, 716 Village Drive, Columbus, Ohio
Bennett, Robert N., Greene Central School, Greene, N.Y.
Bennett, Roger V., Univ. of Virginia, Charlottesville, Va.
Bennett, Thomas L., Bowling Green State Univ., Bowling Green, Ohio
Bennett, William R., 335 N. Ashley, Bourbonnais, Ill.
Bennie, William A., Univ. of Texas, Austin, Texas
Bentley, Caryl B., Rt. 1, Co. T, Sun Prairie, Wis.
Bentley, Harold, Northern Essex Community Col., Haverhill, Mass.
Bentley, Mrs. Harriett P., 2085 Wooster Rd., Rocky River, Ohio
Bentley, Robert, 1535 Walton Ave., Bronx, N.Y.
Benvenuto, Arthur, 158 Garden Pkwy., Henrietta, N.Y.
Berg, Arthur D., Music Consult., Dearborn Pub. Schools, Dearborn, Mich.
Berg, Dorothy D., 5924 N. Forest Glen Ave., Chicago, Ill.
Berg, Paul C., Sch. of Educ., Univ. of South Carolina, Columbia, S.C.
Berg, Selmer H., 1216 Running Springs Rd., Walnut Creek, Calif.
Berger, Allen, University of Alberta, Edmonton, Alba., Can.
Bergeson, Clarence O., State University College, Geneseo, N.Y.
Bergeson, John B., 2415 Skyline St., Kalamazoo, Mich.
Berghoefer, Clara M., 1434 Punahou St., Honolulu, Hawaii

Berkihiser, Frances, Evangel College, Springfield, Mo.
Berkowitz, Edward, 2 Loretta Dr., Syosset, L.I., N.Y.
Berkowitz, Howard, State University College, Oneonta, N.Y.
Berlin, Pearl, University of Massachusetts, Amherst, Mass.
Berlin, Robert S., 383 Grand St., New York, N.Y.
Bernard, Donald H., 134 Paulison Ave., Ridgefield Park, N.J.
Bernard, Harold W., 1985 S.W. Warwick Ave., Portland, Ore.
Bernd, John M., 824 Ellis St., Stevens Point, Wis.
Bernert, Roman A., S.J., Marquette Univ., Milwaukee, Wis.
Bernhoft, Otto L., Prin., South H.S., Fargo, N.D.
Berning, Norbert J., 204 W. Sunset Pl., DeKalb, Ill.
Bernstein, Abbot A., 104 Edwards Rd., Clifton, N.J.
Bernstein, Abraham, Dept. of Educ., Brooklyn College, Brooklyn, N.Y.
Bernstein, Mrs. Jean C., 310 Illinois St., Park Forest, Ill.
Berry, Henry W., P.O. Box 266, Normal, Ala.
Berson, Mrs. Minnie, 1909 Locust Grove Rd., Silver Spring, Md.
Bertness, Henry J., 2909 N. 29th St., Tacoma, Wash.
Bertolaet, Frederick W., Univ. of Mich., Ann Arbor, Mich.
Bertolli, Robert L., 44 A St. Paul Street, Brookline, Mass.
Bertrand, John R., Berry College. Mt. Berry, Ga.
Besselsen, Gilbert, 800 Auburn, Dubuque, Iowa
Best, Mrs. Drusilla, 1148—8th Ave., S.W., Faribault, Minn.
Bettelheim, Bruno, 1365 E. 60th St., Chicago, Ill.
Bettina, Al, Eastern New Mexico University, Portales, N.M.
Betts, Emmett A., Sch. of Educ., University of Miami, Coral Gables, Fla.
Bettwy, Leroy J., 827 Fruithurst Dr., Pittsburgh, Pa.
Beyer, Fred C., Superintendent of County Schools, Modesto. Calif.
Beynon, Robert P., Devel. & Resch., Bowling Green Univ., Bowling Green, Ohio
Bickert, Roderick N., Supt. of Schools, Mason City, Iowa
Bidwell, Mrs. Wilma W., 1223 Western Ave., Albany, N.Y.
* Bigelow, M. A., Litchfield, Conn.
Bigelow, Roy G., 404 S. 37th Ave., Hattiesburg, Miss.
Biggs, Sarah Dorothy, 804 Court, Fulton, Mo.
Biggy, Mary Virginia, 16 Park Ln., Concord, Mass.
Billups, Mrs. Clairene B., 2409 Tidewater Dr., Norfolk, Va.
Binford, George H., Central High School, Charlotte Courthouse, Va.
Binford, Linwood T., J. Andrew Bowler School, Richmond, Va.
Bingham, William C., Rutgers University, New Brunswick, N.J.
Binkley, Marvin Edward, 1000 Noelton Ln., Nashville, Tenn.
Bird, Barbara R., 541 Sligh Blvd., N.E., Grand Rapids, Mich.
Bird, Charles A., 23 Fraser Pl., Hastings on Hudson, N.Y.
Birdsell, Don F., Supt. of Schools, Wheaton, Ill.
Birkemeyer, Florence, State College of Arkansas, Box 963, Conway, Ark.
Bishop, Clifford L., State College of Iowa, Cedar Falls, Iowa
Bishop, Martha D., Dept. of Educ., Winthrop College, Rock Hill, S.C.
Bissell, Norman E., 295 Erkenbrecker Ave., Cincinnati, Ohio
Bjork, Alton J., Dept. of Educ., Illinois State University, Normal, Ill.
Black, Hubert P., Lee College, Cleveland, Tenn.
Black, Hugh C., Dept. of Educ., Univ. of California, Davis, Calif.
Black, Leo P., State Dept. of Educ., State Office Bldg., Denver, Colo.
Black, Mrs. Marian W., Sch. of Educ., Florida State Univ., Tallahassee, Fla.
Black, Millard H., 10031 Vecino Lane, La Habra, Calif.
Blackburn, Clifford S., 420 West "D" St., North Little Rock, Ark.
Blackhurst, A. Edward, University of Kentucky, Lexington, Ky.
Blackledge, Mrs. Helen V., Southern Heights Sch., Fort Wayne, Ind.
Blackman, Charles A., Michigan State Univ., East Lansing, Mich.
Blackshear, John S., 3933 Wisteria Ln., S.W., Atlanta, Georgia
Blackwell, Leslie, 5618 20th St., N.E., Seattle, Wash.
Blackwell, Lewis F., Jr., Box 1026, University, Ala.
Blackwell, Sara, N.Y. State Col. of H.E., Cornell Univ., Ithaca, N.Y.
Blaine, Russell K., 1816 Park Ave., S.E., Cedar Rapids, Iowa

Blake, Duane L., Colorado State Univ., Fort Collins, Colo.
Blake, John, 517 E. 87th St., New York, N.Y.
Blakely, Richard F., Iona College, New Rochelle, N.Y.
Blanchard, Robert W., 22 Valley Rd., Montclair, N.J.
Blanchard, Walter J., Rhode Island Col., Warwick, R.I.
Blaney, Mrs. Rose Marie, Shelter Rock School, Manhasset, N.Y.
Blankenship, A. H., Educational Research Council, Cleveland, Ohio
Blanton, Roy R., Jr., Appalachian State Tchrs. College, Boone, N.C.
Blaser, John W., Wahtonka High School, The Dalles, Ore.
Blessington, John P., Whitby School, Greenwich, Conn.
Bleyer, John F., 126 West Point Dr., Greensburg, Pa.
Blezien, Stephen S., 311 Emmerson Ave., Itasca, Ill.
Bliesmer, Emery P., Read. Ctr., Pennsylvania State Univ., University Park, Pa.
Bligh, Harold F., 81 Lincoln Ave., Ardsley, N.Y.
Blocher, R. Banks, So. Shore Academy & Day Sch., South Hanover, Mass.
Block, Elaine C., Hunter College, New York, N.Y.
Blomenberg, Gilbert, 345 North 2nd St., Seward, Neb.
Blomgren, Glen H., Fresno State College, Fresno, Calif.
Blommers, Paul, East Hall, State University of Iowa, Iowa City, Iowa
Bloom, Herbert C., 3481 Sheridan Ave., Miami Beach, Fla.
Blough, John A., 2840 Proctor Drive, Columbus, Ohio
Blum, Mrs. Joanne L., Point Park Junior College. Pittsburgh, Pa.
Blythe, L. Ross, 108 Green Acres, Valparaiso, Ind.
Boario, Dora A., 422 Third St., Leechburg, Pa.
Bock, R. Darrell, Dept. of Educ., Univ. of Chicago, Chicago, Ill.
Bodkin, Raymond C., Box 196, Stanley, Va.
Boeck, Clarence H., 5101 Ewing Ave., So., Minneapolis, Minn.
Boeck, Robert W., 4090 Geddes Rd., Ann Arbor, Mich.
Boenig, Robert W., State Univ. Col., Fredonia, N.Y.
Boerstler, Mrs. Myrtle, 1310 N. Placentia Ave., Fullerton, Calif.
Boger, D. L., Morehouse College, Atlanta, Ga.
Boggess, Violet F., 2445 New Milford Rd., Atwater, Ohio
Bogle, Frank P., Superintendent of Schools. Millville, N.J.
Bogren, Mrs. Nadine, 1702 Wiggins Ave., Saskatoon, Sask., Can.
Boisclair, Cecile, University of Montreal, Montreal, Que., Canada
Boldt, Frederick J., 3704 Duffy Way, Bonita, Calif.
Bolin, Mrs. Phyllis W., 605 N.W. 18th St., W. Lauderdale, Fla.
Bolton, Dale L., Dept. of Educ., Univ. of Washington, Seattle, Wash.
Boltuck, Charles J., St. Cloud State Col., St. Cloud, Minn.
Bonar, Hugh S., Lewis College, Joliet, Ill.
Bond, George W., 3 Julia Ave., New Paltz, N.Y.
Bond, Horace M., Sch. of Educ., Atlanta University, Atlanta, Ga.
Bonk, Edward C., North Texas University, Denton, Tex.
Booker, Ann, 849 E. 215th St., Bronx, N.Y.
*Booker, Ivan A., N.E.A. Mem. Div., 1201 Sixteenth St., N.W., Washington, D.C.
Bookwalter, Karl W., Indiana University, Bloomington, Ind.
Boos, Robert W., 1335 Waukegan Rd., Glenview, Ill.
Booth, Delores C., 6604 Tremont St., Oakland, Calif.
Borden, Miles B., Amityville Pub. Schools, Amityville, N.Y.
Borders, Frances R., 3617 Raymond St., Chevy Chase, Md.
Borg, Robert L., Scott Hall, University of Minnesota, Minneapolis, Minn.
Borg, Walter R., 1 Garden Cir., Hotel Claremont, Berkeley, Calif.
Bortnick, Robert, 1225 N. LaGrange Rd., LaGrange Park, Ill.
Bortz, A. G., Bridgewater Col., Bridgewater, Va.
Bosch, Albert C., 500 W. 235th St., New York, N.Y.
Bosch, Gerald, 228 Ellen Ave., State College, Pa.
Bosco, J. Anthony, SUNY, 1400 Western Ave., Albany, N.Y.
Bosco, James, Western Michigan University, Kalamazoo, Mich.
Bossard, Grace, Route 3, Box 6, Seaford, Del.
Bossier, Antonia M., 1661 No. Roman St., New Orleans, La.
Bossing, Nelson L., Col. of Educ., Southern Ill. Univ., Carbondale, Ill.

Bothell, John E., Colorado State College, Greeley, Colo.
Bouchard, John B., State Univ. Col., Fredonia, N.Y.
Boula, James A., 316 S. 2nd St., Springfield, Ill.
Boulac, Brian Michael, University of Notre Dame, Notre Dame, Ind.
Bouseman, John W., Cent. Y.M.C.A. Comm. Col., Chicago, Ill.
Bower, Robert K., 1905 E. Loma Alta Dr., Altadena, Calif.
Bowers, A. Eugene, Fayette County Schools, Fayetteville, Ga.
Bowers, Norman D., Sch. of Educ., Northwestern Univ., Evanston, Ill.
Bowers, Victor L., Southwest Texas State College, San Marcos, Tex.
Bowman, Howard A., Box 3307, Terminal Annex, Los Angeles, Calif.
Bowman, Orrin H., 66 Creekview Drive, Rochester, N.Y.
Box, Russell C., Univ. of the Americas, Mexico City, Mexico
Boyajy, Robert J., 10 North Drive, Livingston, N.J.
Boyd, Laurence E., Sch. of Educ., Atlanta University, Atlanta, Ga.
Boyd, Robert D., Dept. of Educ., Univ. of Wisconsin, Madison, Wis.
Boyd, Robert M., Col. of Educ., Ohio University, Athens, Ohio
Boyer, Francis J., Northern Illinois University, DeKalb, Ill.
Boykin, Leander L., Florida A. & M. University, Tallahassee, Fla.
Boyle, Patrick J., Campion College High School, Regina, Sask., Canada
Boyle, William J., 620 W. Clairemont Ave., Eau Claire, Wis.
Boynton, Paul M., Connecticut State Dept. of Educ., Hartford, Conn.
Braam, L. S., Sch. of Educ., Syracuse University, Syracuse, N.Y.
Bracewell, George, Southern Illinois University, Carbondale, Ill.
Brackbill, A. L., Jr., Millersville State College, Millersville, Pa.
Bradford, James L., 1692 Northwest Blvd., Columbus, Ohio
Bradley, Mrs. George W., East Tenn. State Univ., Johnson City, Tenn.
Bradley, Mrs. Howard R., 2147 Blue Hills Road, Manhattan, Kan.
Bradtmueller, Weldon G., Northern Ill. Univ., De Kalb, Ill.
Brady, Florence A., 186 Oakland Rd., Maplewood, N.J.
Brady, Francis X., Elmira College, Elmira, N.Y.
Brady, John C., Bemidji State College, Bemidji, Minn.
Brain, George B., Col. of Educ., Washington State Univ., Pullman, Wash.
Brainard, Lois, San Jose State College, San Jose, Calif.
Bramwell, John R., Univ. of Oregon, Eugene, Ore.
Brandinger, Mrs. Alice, 19 Carnation Pl., Trenton, N.J.
Brandt, Willard J., University of Wisconsin-Milwaukee, Milwaukee, Wis.
Branom, Wayne T., Superintendent of Schools, Hillside, N.J.
Brantley, Mabel, 623 N. First St., DeKalb, Ill.
Brantley, Mrs. Sybil, 108 Lomaland Dr., West Monroe, La.
Braswell, Robert H., Box 652, Orangeburg, S.C.
Brauer, Walter L., Washington H.S., Milwaukee, Wis.
Braun, Frank R., Col. of Educ., University of Minnesota, Minneapolis, Minn.
Braun, Frederick G., Col. of Educ., Univ. of Hawaii, Honolulu, Hawaii
Braun, Gertrude E., West Conn. State Col., Danbury, Conn.
Braun, Irma D., 228 Ocean Blvd., Atlantic Highlands, N.J.
Braun, Mrs. Mary Ann, 821 N. Second St., Effingham, Ill.
Braun, Ray H., 101 N. McCullough St., Urbana, Ill.
Bravo, Anna, 32 Beach Hill St., Ft. Salonga, N.Y.
Bredesen, Dorothy A., 644 "D" St., N.E., Washington, D.C.
Breeding, Clifford C., 2708 Bridal Wreath Ln., Dallas, Texas
Breen, John F., 124 Smith St., Freeport, N.Y.
Bregman, Sydell, 17 Bodnarik Dr., Edison, N.J.
Breihan, Edna, 1512 Briggs St., Lockport, Ill.
Brenner, Anton, Merrill-Palmer School, 71 Ferry E., Detroit, Mich.
Brereton, Matthew J., 22 Oakland Ter., Newark, N.J.
Bresina, Bertha M., 8308 E. Highland Ave., Scottsdale, Arizona
Breslin, Frederick D., Glassboro State College, Glassboro, N.J.
Bretsch, Howard S., Sch. of Educ., University of Michigan, Ann Arbor, Mich.
Bretz, Frank H., 1909 Arlington Ave., Columbus, Ohio
Brewster, Maurice A., Jr., Memorial Univ., St. John's, Newfoundland
Brewton, Raymond E., Supt. of County Schools, Palo Pinto, Texas

Brick, Michael, Tchrs. Col., Columbia University, New York, N.Y.
Brickman, Benjamin, Dept. of Educ., Brooklyn College, Brooklyn, N.Y.
Brickman, William W., University of Pennsylvania, Philadelphia, Pa.
Bridgers, Raymond B., R.D. 2, Broadway Rd., Oswego, N.Y.
Bridges, C. M., Col. of Educ., University of Florida, Gainesville, Fla.
Bridges, Lonnie H., Box 10194, Southern University, Baton Rouge, La.
Bridges, Raymond H., Box 10194, Southern University, Baton Rouge, La.
Briggs, Albert A., Dunbar Vocational High School, Chicago, Ill.
Briggs, Joseph M., 1710½ Cherry St., Fremont, Ohio
Bright, John H., 628 Cuesta Ave., San Mateo, Calif.
*Bright, Orville T., 516½ Prospect Ave., Lake Bluff, Ill.
Brill, Donald M., 5420 Maher Ave., Madison, Wis.
Brim, Burl, West Texas State University, Canyon, Tex.
Brimhall, Mrs. Alice, 111 Monticello Ave., Piedmont, Calif.
Briner, Conrad, 1221 Cambridge Ave., Claremont, Calif.
Brink, William G., Sch. of Educ., Northwestern University, Evanston, Ill.
Brinkman, A. John, 5529 S. Blackstone Ave., Chicago, Ill.
Brinkman, J. Warren, Kansas State Tchrs. College, Emporia, Kan.
Brinkmann, E. H., So. Illinois Univ., Edwardsville, Ill.
Brinkmeier, Oria A., 2203 Carter Ave., St. Paul, Minn.
Briscoe, Laurel A., 1520 Cedar Ridge Dr., N.E., Albuquerque, N.M.
Brish, William M., Supt., Washington Co. Schools, Hagerstown, Md.
Brislawn, J., 28th & Lilac St., Longview, Wash.
Bristol, Stanley I., Joseph Sears School, Kenilworth, Ill.
*Bristow, William H., 70 Exeter St., Forest Hills, N.Y.
Britt, Laurence V., S.J., John Carroll Univ., Cleveland, Ohio
Brittain, Clay V., 1810 Panda Ln., McLean, Va.
Britton, Edward C., Sacramento State Col., Sacramento, Calif.
Britton, Ernest R., Superintendent of Schools, Midland, Mich.
Broadbent, Frank W., 6401 Allison Ave., Des Moines, Iowa
Broderick, Catherine M., City Sch. Dist., South Rochester, N.Y.
Brody, Erness B., Rutgers University, New Brunswick, N.J.
Broening, Angela M., 3700 N. Charles St., Baltimore, Md.
Bromwich, Rose M., 13507 Hart St., Van Nuys, Calif.
Bronson, Homer D., Chico State College, Chico, Calif.
Bronson, Moses L., 290 Ninth Ave., New York, N.Y.
Brookins, Jack E., 1323 Bayview, North Bend, Ore.
Brooks, B. Marian, City College, 135th and Convent, New York, N.Y
Brostoff, Theodore M., 10474 Santa Monica Blvd., Los Angeles, Calif.
Brother Adelbert James, Manhattan College, New York, N.Y.
Brother Cosmas Herlihy, St. Francis College, Brooklyn, N.Y.
Brother Francis Wray, St. Mary's Col., Winona, Minn.
Brother Joseph Brusnahan, 5900 Walnut Grove, Memphis, Tenn.
Brother Leo Gilskey, 414 N. Forest Ave., Oak Park, Ill.
Brother Stephen Walsh, St. Edward's University, Austin, Tex.
Brother U. Cassian, St. Mary's Col., St. Mary's, Calif.
Brottman, Marvin A., 8926 Bellefort, Morton Grove, Ill.
Brougher, John F., Shippensburg State College, Shippensburg, Pa.
Brousseau, Sandy E., 43 Carlos Ct., Walnut Creek, Calif.
Brown, Aaron, 1468 President St., Brooklyn, N.Y.
Brown, Camille, University of California, Los Angeles, Calif.
Brown, Carol L., 40 E. 18th St., Columbus, Ohio
Brown, Mrs. Carol S., 853 S. High St., Columbus, Ohio
Brown, Chester J., Col. of Educ., University of Arizona, Tucson, Ariz.
Brown, Cynthiana Ellen, 6644 Wildlife Rd., Malibu, Calif.
Brown, Douglas H., Pine Wood Dr., Contoocook, N.H.
Brown, Douglas M., Superintendent of Schools, Shorewood, Wis.
Brown, Mrs. Edith F., 2821 N. 2nd St., Harrisburg, Pa.
Brown, Francis A., 2821 N. 2nd St., Harrisburg, Pa.
Brown, George W., Superintendent of Schools, Webster Groves, Mo.
Brown, Gerald W., California State College, Hayward, Calif.

Brown, Gertrude E., 2835 Milan St., New Orleans, La.
Brown, Howard L., Schl. Admin. Center, 49 E. College Ave., Springfield, Ohio
Brown, Jeannette A., 2020 Minor Rd., Charlottesville, Va.
Brown, Jeremy, Castleton State Col., Castleton, Vt.
Brown, Kenneth B., University of Missouri, Columbia, Mo.
Brown, Kenneth R., California Tchrs. Assn., 1705 Murchison Dr., Burlingame, Calif.
Brown, Lawrence D., Sch. of Educ., Indiana University, Bloomington, Ind.
Brown, Marion R., 404 Riverside Dr., New York, N.Y.
Brown, Mrs. Marjorie D., 4455 West 64th St., Los Angeles, Calif.
Brown, Marjorie M., University of Minnesota, St. Paul, Minn.
Brown, Pauline, 25800 Hillary St., Hayward, Calif.
Brown, Perry, Lock Haven State College, Lock Haven, Pa.
Brown, Robert S., 702 N. Grandview, Stillwater, Okla.
Brown, Roy A., Asst. Supt., Bethlehem Area Schools, Bethlehem, Pa.
Brown, Sara M., So. Connecticut State Col., New Haven, Conn.
Brown, Susan C., Box 155, Fall River Mills, Calif.
Brown, Rev. Syl, St. Mary's Col., Winona, Minn.
Brown, Thomas J., Hofstra Univ., Hempstead, N.Y.
Brown, Virginia H., 1 Lafayette Plaisance, Detroit, Mich.
Brown, Warren M., Supt. of Schools, Ferguson, Mo.
Brown, Woodrow W., Superintendent of Schools, York, Pa.
Brownell, Samuel M., Yale Univ. & Univ. of Conn., New Haven, Conn.
Brownell, William A., 701 Spruce St., Berkeley, Calif.
Browning, Mrs. Linda, 5335 Far Hills Ave., Dayton, Ohio
Browning, Roy W., Topeka Public Schools, Topeka, Kan.
Brownlee, Geraldine D., 6937 S. Crandon Ave., Chicago, Ill.
Brownstein, Jewell, Dept. of Educ., Univ. of Louisville, Louisville, Ky.
Browy, Marjorie J., California State College, Los Angeles, Calif.
Broz, Joseph R., 3402 Clarendon Rd., Cleveland, Ohio
Brubaker, Leonard A., 409 Marian Ave., Normal, Ill.
Bruce, William C., Bruce Publishing Co., Milwaukee, Wis.
Brumbaugh, W. Donald, University of Utah, Salt Lake City, Utah
Brunnelle, Paul E., Prin., Winthrop High School, Winthrop, Me.
Brunetti, Frank A., 36 C. Escondido Village, Stanford, Calif.
Bruning, Charles R., University of Minnesota, Minneapolis, Minn.
Brunk, Jason W., State University College, Buffalo, N.Y.
Brunner, Edward F., 316 S. Fletcher, Ferandina Beach, Fla.
Bruno, Gordon A., Darien H.S., Darien, Conn.
Brunson, Mrs. Dewitt, P.O. Box 484, Orangeburg, S.C.
Bryan, Ray J., 220 Curtiss Hall, Iowa State Univ., Ames, Iowa
Bryant, B. Carleton, 810 Clear Lake Ave., West Palm Beach, Fla.
Bryant, Ira B., Kashmere Gardens High Sch., Houston, Tex.
Bryant, Merle L., University of Minnesota, Duluth, Minn.
Bryant, R. A., Box 268, Cedartown, Ga.
Bryner, James R., 185 Salisbury Dr., Saskatoon, Sask., Canada
Buchanan, Alfred K., 80 Grove St., Plantsville, Conn.
Buchanan, Paul G., 61 Rosemary St., Buffalo, N.Y.
Buck, James E., Oregon College of Educ., Monmouth, Ore.
Buckley, J. L., Superintendent of Schools, Lockhart, Tex.
Buckley, Richard Dale, Sch. of Educ., Wisconsin State University, Oshkosh, Wis.
Buckner, John D., 4246 W. North Market St., St. Louis, Mo.
Buckner, William N., 2643—15th St., N.W., Washington, D.C.
Budd, Mrs. Edith M., 3227 Parker Ave., West Palm Beach, Fla.
Bueker, Armin H., Superintendent of Schools, Marshall, Mo.
Buelke, John A., Western Michigan University, Kalamazoo, Mich.
Bulla, Helen M., Asst. Prin., Waterford Twsp. H.S., Pontiac, Mich.
Bullock, Portia C., 408 Tea St.,N.W., Washington, D.C.
Bullock, William J., Superintendent of Schools, Kannapolis, N.C.
Bunger, Marianne, Alaska Methodist University, Anchorage, Alaska
Bunker, James G., Supt., Novato Unified Sch. Dist., Novato, Calif.

Bunnell, Mrs. Constance O., Mamaroneck High School, Mamaroneck, N.Y.
Bunnell, Robert A., Ford Foundation, 320 E. 43rd St., New York, N.Y.
Buntrock, Richard M., West Bend Pub. Schools, West Bend, Wis.
Buol, Mary Steudler, 91 Ten Acre Rd., New Britain, Conn.
Burch, Charles H., 1803 McDonald Dr., Champaign, Ill.
Burch, Mary J., 1123 Old Hillsborough Rd., RFD 4, Chapel Hill, N.C.
Burchell, Helen R., Univ. of Pennsylvania, Philadelphia, Pa.
Burdick, A. E., Arkansas State Teachers College, Conway, Ark.
Burdick, Richard L., Educ. Dept., Carroll College, Waukesha, Wis.
Burg, Mrs. Mary, 2259 Wolfangle Rd., Cincinnati, Ohio
Burgdorf, Otto P., 36-12—210th St., Bayside, N.Y.
Burke, Carolyn L., 52 Portage, Highland Park, Mich.
Burke, Doyle K., Newport Spec. Sch. Dist., Newport, Ark.
Burke, Eileen M., 48 Bayberry Rd., Trenton, N.J.
* Burke, Gladys, 244 Outlook, Youngstown, Ohio
Burke, Henry R., 197 Ridgewood Ave., Glen Ridge, N.J.
Burke, Paul J., 1 Lookout Pl., Ardsley, N.Y.
Burke, Thomas O., 424 Bayberry Dr., Plantation, Fla.
Burke, Thomas S., 3171 W. 83rd St., Chicago, Ill.
Burkett, Lowell A., 1025 15th St., N.W., Washington, D.C.
Burks, Herbert M., Jr., 134 Mimosa Dr., Charlottesville, Va.
Burks, John B., Jersey City State College, Jersey City, N.J.
Burnett, Joe R., University of Illinois, Urbana, Ill.
Burnham, Robert A., 107-D Escondido Village, Stanford, Calif.
Burns, Constance M., University of Bridgeport, Bridgeport, Conn.
Burns, Cranford H., Box 1549, Mobile, Ala.
Burns, Mrs. Doris, 115 W. 86th St., Apt. 6F, New York, N.Y.
Burns, Hobert W., San Jose State Col., San Jose, Calif.
Burns, James W., 2115 Waite Ave., Kalamazoo, Mich.
Burr, Elbert W., Monsanto Chemical Co., Lindbergh and Olive, St. Louis, Mo.
Burrell, E. William, Salve Regina Col., Newport, R.I.
Burrough, Rudolph V., 526 Kirby, Shreveport, La.
Burrows, Alvina Treut, 117 Nassau Ave., Manhasset, N.Y.
Burt, Lucile, Lincoln School, 338 Forest Ave., Fond du Lac, Wis.
Bushnell, Allan C., 309 South St., New Providence, N.J.
Buswell, Guy T., 1836 Thousand Oaks Blvd., Berkeley, Calif.
Butler, Mrs. B. LaConyea, Spelman College, Atlanta, Ga.
Butler, E. Frank, Contra Costa College, San Pablo, Calif.
Butler, Laurence, 630 Leonard St., Ashland, Ore.
Butler, Lester G., 468 E. Lincoln Ave., Columbus, Ohio
Butler, Thomas M., 1166 W. North St., Decatur, Ill.
Butts, David P., University of Texas, Austin, Tex.
Butts, Franklin A., 54 N. Hamilton St., Poughkeepsie, N.Y.
Butts, Gordon K., Southern Illinois University, Carbondale, Ill.
Butts, R. Freeman, Tchrs. Col., Columbia University, New York, N.Y.
Buyse, R., Sch. of Educ., University of Louvain, Tournai, Belgium
Buzard, Judith, 52 E. 14th Ave., Columbus, Ohio
Buzash, G. A., 65 Colonial Ave., Pitman, N.J.
Byerly, Carl L., 5057 Woodward Ave., Detroit, Mich.
Byers, Joe L., Michigan State Univ., East Lansing, Mich.
Byram, Harold M., Sch. of Educ., Michigan State Univ., East Lansing, Mich.
Byrne, John, Dist. Supt., Chicago Board of Education, Chicago, Ill.
Byrne, Richard Hill, Col. of Educ., Univ. of Maryland, College Park, Md.

Caccavo, Emil, 123 Willow St., Roslyn Heights, N.Y.
Cadd, Ayrles W., Box 17, Shandon, Calif.
Cady, Henry L., Ohio State University, Columbus, Ohio
Cafiero, Albert J., Supt., Oradell Pub. Schools, Oradell, N.J.
Cafone, Harold C., Dept. of Educ., Oakland Univ., Rochester, Mich.
Cahan, Mrs. Ruth, 1916 Overland Ave., Los Angeles, Calif.
Cahraman, Thomas P., 35550 Bella Vista Dr., Yucaipa, Calif.

Cain, E. J., University of Nevada, Reno, Nev.
Cain, Lee C., Georgia Southern Branch, Statesboro, Ga.
Cain, Ralph W., Sutton Hall, University of Texas, Austin, Tex.
Caird, Florence B., Joyce Kilmer School, Chicago, Ill.
Caldwell, Cleon C., 2917 Noble Ave., Bakersfield, Calif.
Caldwell, Herbert M., 21908 De La Osa St., Woodland Hills, Calif.
Caldwell, O. K., Fostoria High School, Fostoria, Ohio
Califf, Stanley N., Chapman College, Orange, Calif.
Calip, Rev. Osmundo A., St. John's University, Jamaica, N.Y.
Call, Mrs. Ardell, Utah Education Association, Salt Lake City, Utah
Callahan, William T., 131 Jericho Turnpike, Jericho, N.Y.
Callan, John H., McQuaid Hall, Seton Hall Univ., South Orange, N.J.
Callas, Eliza E., 7080 Oregon Ave., N.W., Washington, D.C.
Callaway, A. Byron, Col. of Educ., Univ. of Georgia, Athens, Ga.
Calmes, Robert E., 5216 Mission Hill Dr., Tucson, Ariz.
Calvert, Lloyd, Supt. of Schools, Windsor, Conn.
Calvin, Thomas H., State Educ. Dept., State Univ. of N.Y., Albany, N.Y.
Cameron, Don C., 350 E. 700 S., St. George, Utah
Campbell, A. Leedy, Dir., Urban Educ., Brd. of Educ., Kansas City, Mo.
Campbell, Clyde M., Michigan State University, East Lansing, Mich.
Campbell, E. G., Col. of Educ., Univ. of Maryland, College Park, Md.
Campbell, Roald F., Sch. of Educ., University of Chicago, Chicago, Ill.
Campbell, Ronald T., 23644 Edward, Dearborn, Mich.
Campos, Mrs. M. A. Pourchet, Caixa Postal 30.F86, Sao Paulo, S. P., Brazil
Canar, Donald A., Central YMCA Schls., 211 W. Wacker Dr., Chicago, Ill.
Candoli, Italo C., 315 Bryant Ave., Worthington, Ohio
Canfield, John M., Superintendent of Schools, West Plains, Mo.
Cannon, Frances O., Alabama College, Montevallo, Ala.
Cannon, Wendell, Univ. of So. California, Los Angeles, Calif.
Cantlon, R. Jerry, Illinois State University, Normal, Ill.
Capehart, Bertis E., 120 Squire Hill Rd., Upper Montclair, N.J.
Capocy, John S., 4628 Seeley St., Downers Grove, Ill.
Cappa, Dan, California State Col., Los Angeles, Calif.
Cappelluzzo, Emma M., University of Massachusetts, Amherst, Mass.
Capps, Lelon R., Bailey Hall, University of Kansas, Lawrence, Kan.
Capps, Mrs. Marian P., Virginia State College, Norfolk, Va.
Capri, Walter P., 2339 Chateau Way, Livermore, Calif.
Carder, W. Ray, Hillsboro High School, Hillsboro, Ore.
Cardina, Philip J., Box 269, R.D. 2, Farmingdale, N.J.
Cardinale, Anthony, Dir., Dependents Educ., Dept. of Defense, Washington, D.C.
Cardozo, Joseph A., Box 9958, Baton Rouge, La.
Cardwell, Robert H., Tyson Junior High School, Knoxville, Tenn.
Carey, Clarence B., Dir., Jones Commercial H.S., Chicago, Ill.
Carey, Jess Wendell, Park College, Parkville, Mo.
Carey, Justin P., 105 Lyncroft Rd., New Rochelle, N.Y.
Carlin, James B., University of Mississippi, University, Miss.
Carline, Donald E., 365 Seminole, Boulder, Colo.
Carlisle, John C., Col. of Educ., Utah State Univ., Logan, Utah
Carlson, Mrs. Evelyn F., 6899 N. Wildwood, Chicago, Ill.
Carlson, F. Roy, Mt. Ida Junior College, Newton Centre, Mass.
Carlson, Robert A., No. 901—640 Main St., Saskatoon, Sask., Canada
Carlson, Mrs. Ruth K., 1718 LeRoy Ave., Berkeley, Calif.
Carlson, Thorston R., 415 Monte Vista Lane, Santa Rosa, Calif.
Carlson, Waymann, Southern California College, Costa Mesa, Calif.
Carlson, Wesley H., 4th St. & Bayard Ave., Wilmington, Del.
Carman, Beatrice D., 223 Chapel Dr., Tallahassee, Fla.
Carmichael, John H., 913 Cherry Ln., East Lansing, Mich.
Carne, Vernon E., 1383 Dorothy Dr., Decatur, Ga.
Carnochan, John L., Jr., Route 5, Frederick, Md.
Carpenter, Aaron C., P.O. Box 387, Grambling, La.
Carpenter, James L., 206 S. 19th Ave., Maywood, Ill.

Carpenter, N. H., Superintendent, City Schools, Elkin, N.C.
Carr, Carolyn Jane, 1409 N. Walnut Grove Ave., Rosemead, Calif.
Carr, Julian W., 795 Kinderkamack Rd., River Edge, N.J.
Carriere, Robert H., 57 Theroux Dr., Chicopee, Mass.
Carrington, Joel A., Univ. of Maryland, College Park, Md.
Carroll, Clifford, Gonzaga University, Spokane, Wash.
Carroll, Emma C., Milwaukee Technical College, Milwaukee, Wis.
Carroll, John B., Educational Testing Service, Princeton, N.J.
Carroll, Margaret L., 208 Fairmont Rd., DeKalb, Ill.
Carruth, Edwin Ronald, University of Southern Mississippi, McComb, Miss.
Carsello, Carmen J., University of Illinois Circle Campus, Chicago, Ill.
Carstater, Eugene D., Bur. of Naval Personnel, Washington, D.C.
Carter, Burdellis L., 6437 Lupine Dr., Indianapolis, Ind.
Carter, Harold D., Sch. of Educ., University of California, Berkeley, Calif.
Carter, James S., North High School, Phoenix, Ariz.
Carter, Dr. Lamore J., Grambling Col., Grambling, La.
Carter, Margaret Ann, Wayne State University, Detroit, Mich.
Carter, Richard C., Supt. of Schools, Palmer, Alaska
Carter, Sims, 214 Spalding Dr., Beverly Hills, Calif.
Carter, Susan C., 10634 Eggleston Ave., Chicago, Ill.
Carter, Thomas D., Alamo Hgts. Indep. Sch. Dist., San Antonio, Texas
Carter, Vincent, San Jose State College, San Jose, Calif.
Cartwright, William H., Duke University, Durham, N.C.
Case, Charles W., 236 Charing Road, Rochester, N.Y.
Caselli, Robert E., 1614 S. Phillips Ave., Sioux Falls, S.D.
Casey, Barbara A., 700 Seventh St., Apt. 220, Washington, D.C.
Casey, John J., 674 Academy St., New York, N.Y.
Casey, Neal E., 7607 Kirwin Lane, San Jose, Calif.
Cash, Christine B., Jarvis Christian College, Marshall, Tex.
Caskey, Helen C., Tchrs. Col., University of Cincinnati, Cincinnati, Ohio
Casper, T. A., Suite 14, 2707 Seventh St., E., Saskatoon, Sask., Canada
Cassidy, Rosalind, University of California, 405 Hilgard Ave., Los Angeles, Calif.
Castaneda, Alberta M., Wooldridge Hall, Univ. of Texas, Austin, Tex.
Castrale, Remo, Supt. of Schools, Johnston City, Ill.
Catlin, Dorothy M., 440 S. Beverly Lane, Arlington Heights, Calif.
Catrambone, A. R., Superintendent of Schools, Camden, N.J.
Caughran, Alex M., 93 N. Main St., Orono, Me.
Caulfield, Patrick J., Dept. of Educ., St. Peter's College, Jersey City, N.J.
Cawein, Paul E., 2032 Belmont Rd., N.W., Apt. 600, Washington, D.C.
Cawrse, Robert C., 26927 Osborn Rd., Bayvillage, Ohio
Cayco, Florentino, President, Arellano University, Manila, Philippines
Cecco, Mrs. Josephine L., Springfield College, Springfield, Mass.
Cecil, Eddie D., Div. of Educ., Benedict College, Columbia, S.C.
Center, Benjamin, 1653 Roseview Drive, Columbus, Ohio
Center, William R., University of South Alabama, Mobile, Ala.
Chall, Jeanne, Grad. Sch. of Educ., Harvard University, Cambridge, Mass.
Chambers, William M., 2113 Chambers, N.W., Albuquerque, N.M.
Champagne, R. P., Holy Savior Central High School, Lockport, La.
Champoux, Mrs. Ellen M., 301 Mendenhall St., Apt. 2, Greenboro, N.C.
Chandler, H. F., 1320 Haskell Ave., Lawrence, Kan.
Chang, Alvin K., 3642 S. Court St., Palo Alto, Calif.
* Chang, Jen-chi, Florida Normal and Ind. Mem. College, St. Augustine, Fla.
Chang, Mrs. Lynette Y.C., Univ. of Victoria, Victoria, B.C., Can.
Channell, W. R., Argentine High School, Kansas City, Kan.
Chansky, Norman M., Temple University, Philadelphia, Pa.
Chao, Sankey C., 154 Redwood Ave., Wayne, N.J.
Chaplin, Charles C., 265 Hawthorne St., Brooklyn, N.Y.
Chapline, Elaine Burns, Queens Col., Flushing, N.Y.
Chapman, Richard F., Supt. of Schools, Groton, Conn.
Charles, Ramon L., 327 Nickell Rd., Topeka, Kan.
Charlton, Huey E., 3785 Wisteria Lane, S.W., Atlanta, Ga.

Charters, Alexander N., Syracuse University, Syracuse, N.Y.
Chase, Francis S., Dept. of Educ., Univ. of Chicago, Chicago, Ill.
Chase, Naomi C., University of Minnesota, Minneapolis, Minn.
Chasnoff, Robert, Newark State College, Union, N.J.
Chatwin, Jerry M., P. O. Box 276, Borrego Springs, Calif.
Chay, Josephine S., 2534 W. Charleston Ave., Chicago, Ill.
Cheatham, Alflorence, Dist. Supt., Dist. 19, Chicago, Ill.
Cheeks, L. E., 213 McFarland St., Kerrville, Tex.
Cheers, Arlynne Lake, Grambling College, Grambling, La.
Chern, Mrs. Nona E., 492 Concord Rd., Broomall, Pa.
Chiavaro, John, Newfane Cent. Sch., Newfane, N.Y.
Chidekel, Samuel J., Prin., James Madison Sch., Skokie, Ill.
Chidester, Charles B., 8646 Linden St., Munster, Ind.
Chievitz, Gene L., Bldg. 12, University of New Mexico, Albuquerque, N.M.
Childs, James N., 300 Sixth St., S.W., Little Falls, Minn.
Childs, Vernon C., 1514 South 14th St., Manitowoc, Wis.
Christenson, Bernice M., 5045 Alta Canyada Rd., La Canada, Calif.
Christina, Robert J., 122 Smalley Rd., Syracuse, N.Y.
Christine, Ray O., Arizona State University, Tempe, Ariz.
Christoplos, Florence, 6410 Sandy Street, Laurel, Md.
Chronister, G. M., Univ. of B.C., Vancouver, B.C., Canada
Chuck, Harry C., 265 Kanoelani Dr., Hilo, Hawaii
Chudler, Albert A., Intern. Sch. of Kuala Lumpur, Kuala Lumpur, Malaysia
Chung, Yong Hwan, Dept. of Educ., Wiley College, Marshall, Texas
Church, John, Dept. of Educ., 721 Capitol Mall, Sacramento, Calif.
Churchill, Donald W., Bemidji State College, Bemidji, Minn.
Cianciolo, Patricia J., Michigan State University, East Lansing, Mich.
Cicchelli, Jerry J., Prin., Oradell Public School, Oradell, N.J.
Ciccoricco, Edward A., 48 Clark St., Brockport, N.Y.
Ciklamini, Joseph, 921 Carnegie Ave., Plainfield, N.J.
Ciminillo, Lewis, Col. of Educ., Indiana University, Bloomington, Ind.
Cioffi, Joseph M., 652 Doriskill Ct., River Vale, N.J.
Clabaugh, R. E., Superintendent of Schools, Arlington Heights, Ill.
Clague, W. Donald, La Verne Col., La Verne, Calif.
Clanin, Edgar E., 309 Highland Dr., West Lafayette, Ind.
Clare, Mrs. Elizabeth Rae, 949 N. Alfred St., Los Angeles, Calif.
Clark, Angeline, 583 Harley Drive, Apt. 7, Columbus, Ohio
Clark, Barbara B., 3520 Meadow Lane, Minnetonka, Minn.
Clark, Charles S., 5760 A Millbank Road, Columbus, Ohio
Clark, David L., 3105 Brown Cliff Rd., Bloomington, Ind.
Clark, Elmer J., Col. of Educ., Southern Illinois Univ., Carbondale, Ill.
Clark, Franklin B., Dist. Supt. of Schools, Athens, N.Y.
Clark, John F., 507 Marview Lane, Solana Beach, Calif.
Clark, Leonard H., 240 Van Nostrand Ave., Jersey City, N.J.
Clark, Lewis E., Supt., Coquille Sch. Dist. # 8, Coquille, Ore.
Clark, Maurice P., Supt. of Schools, Western Springs, Ill.
Clark, Max R., Supt. of Schools, 142 Main St., Calmar, Iowa
Clark, Moses, Alabama State College, Montgomery, Ala.
Clark, Raymond M., Michigan State University, East Lansing, Mich.
Clark, Richard M., State University of N.Y., Albany, N.Y.
Clark, Sidney L., 855 Bronson Rd., Fairfield, Conn.
Clark, Stephen C., OSD/ARPA, RDFV-V, APO, San Francisco, Calif.
Clark, Thomas H., 4402½ Worth St., Dallas, Tex.
Clark, Woodrow Wilson, 101 W. Leake St., Clinton, Miss.
Clarke, Juno-Ann, San Francisco State Col., San Francisco, Calif.
Clarke, Stanley C. T., 11615—78th Ave., Edmonton, Alba., Canada
Clarkston, Emmerine A., 8216 Eberhart Ave., Chicago, Ill.
Classon, Miss Marion E., 19 Nantes Rd., Parsippany, N.J.
Clayton, Thomas E., 7 Kelly Dr., Manlius, N.Y.
Clegg, Ambrose A., Sch. of Educ., Univ. of Massachusetts, Amherst, Mass.
Cleland, Donald L., Sch. of Educ., Univ. of Pittsburgh, Pittsburgh, Pa.

Clifford, Mrs. Miriam, 920 Monmouth Ave., Durham, N.C.
Clifford, Paul I., Sch. of Educ., Atlanta University, Atlanta, Ga.
Clift, Virgil A., Sch. of Educ., New York University, New York, N.Y.
Cline, Marion, Jr., Univ. of Texas, El Paso, Texas
Clinton, Robert, Jr., 3002 McElroy, Austin, Texas
Clouser, John J., 901 Graceland St., Des Plaines, Ill.
Clouthier, Raymond P., St. Norbert College, West DePere, Wis.
Clymer, Theodore W., 4325 Via Presada, Santa Barbara, Calif.
Cobb, Beatrice M., Cambell Shore Rd., Gray, Me.
Cobb, Jacob E., Indiana State Univ., Terre Haute, Ind.
Cobb, Joseph L., 2706 Baynard Blvd., Wilmington, Del.
Cobban, Margaret R., 424 Victoria St., Glassboro, N.J.
Coblentz, Dwight O., 615 N. School St., Normal, Ill.
Cobley, Herbert F., Superintendent of Schools, Nazareth, Pa.
Cobun, Frank E., State University College, New Paltz, N.Y.
Cochi, Oscar R., 471 Manse Ln., Rochester, N.Y.
Cochran, Alton W., Supt. of Schools, Charlestown, Ind.
Cochran, John R., Kalamazoo Public Schools, 1220 Howard St., Kalamazoo, Mich.
Cochran, Russell T., Woodrow Wilson Jr. H.S., Hanford, Calif.
Code, Allen L., 208 S. Third St., Seneca, S.C.
Coen, Alban Wasson, II, Central Michigan University, Mt. Pleasant, Mich.
Cofell, William L., St. John's University, Collegeville, Minn.
Coffee, James M., 5903 Woodside Drive, Jacksonville, Fla.
Coffey, Thomas F., 5900 N. Glenwood Ave., Chicago, Ill.
Coffey, Warren C., 7416 East Parkway, Sacramento, Calif.
Cogswell, Mark E., Northern State College, Aberdeen, S.D.
Cohen, George, 8 Etheride Pl., Park Ridge, N.J.
Cohen, Hyman Z., 744 Henry Rd., Far Rockaway, N.Y.
Cohen, Jerome, Miami-Dade Jr. Col., Miami, Fla.
Cohen, Robert I., Roosevelt University, Chicago, Ill.
Cohen, Samuel J., 9 Coventry Rd., Syosset, N.Y.
Cohler, Milton J., 3450 N. Lake Shore Drive, Chicago, Ill.
Cohodes, Aaron, 1050 Merchandise Mart, Chicago, Ill.
Colbath, Edwin H., 97-16 118th St., Richmond Hill, N.Y.
Colburn, A. B., Cascade Senior High School, Everett, Wash.
Cole, Glenn A., University of Arkansas, Fayetteville, Ark.
Cole, James C., 1946 Mira Flores, Turlock, Calif.
Cole, James E., University of Utah, Salt Lake City, Utah
Cole, Mary I., Western Kentucky State College, Bowling Green, Ky.
Coleman, Alwin B., Sch. of Educ., West. Mich. Univ., Kalamazoo, Mich.
Coleman, Mary E., 3122 Valley Lane, Falls Church, Va.
Coleman, Mary Elisabeth, University of Pennsylvania, Philadelphia, Pa.
Colestock, Hazelmae, 1517 S. Theresa, St. Louis, Mo.
Colla, Frances S., 49 Regina St., Trumbull, Conn.
Collier, Mrs. Anna K., 903 Fourth St., Liverpool, N.Y.
Collier, Calhoun C., Michigan State University, East Lansing, Mich.
Collier, Richard E., 4822 Eades St., Rockville, Md.
Collings, Miller R., 9201 W. Outer Dr., Detroit, Mich.
Collins, F. Ethel, Box 138, R.D. 2, Altamont, N.Y.
Collins, Helen C., 1203 Gilpin Ave., Wilmington, Del.
Collins, Kathleen M., Catholic University of America, Washington, D.C.
Collins, Mary Lucille, Beaubien Sch., 5025 N. Laramie Ave., Chicago, Ill.
Collins, Paul W. R. No. 5, Box 221C, Ocala, Fla.
Collins, Mrs. Ray, 3101 W. Carson, Torrance, Calif.
Collins, Robert E., State Dept. of Education, St. Paul, Minn.
Collins, Ted, 1023 Oakdale St., West Covina, Calif.
Collison, Sidney B., 410 New London Road, Newark, Del.
Colman, John E., C.M., Sch. of Educ., St. John's University, Jamaica, N.Y.
Combs, Lawrence, 1595 Yearling Drive, Florissant, Md.
Combs, W. E., Florida A. & M. University, Tallahassee, Fla.
Comer, J. M., Box 820, Rt. 2, Collinsville, Ill.

Conan, Mrs. Beatrice, 2063—74th St., Brooklyn, N.Y.
Conaway, John O., 431 S. Brown, Terre Haute, Ind.
Condra, James B., Birmingham-Southern College, Birmingham, Ala.
Congreve, Willard J., Lab. Schls., University of Chicago, Chicago, Ill.
Conley, Jack, Prin., Elementary School, Culver City, Calif.
Conley, William H., Sacred Heart University, Bridgeport, Conn.
Connelly, John C., San Francisco State College, San Francisco, Calif.
Conner, John W., University High School, Univ. of Iowa, Iowa City, Ia.
Connor, E. Faye, Huntington College Library, Huntington, Ind.
Connor, William H., Washington Univ. Grad. Inst. of Education, St. Louis, Mo.
Conry, Rev. Thomas P., S.J., John Carroll Univ., Cleveland, Ohio
Converse, David T., State Univ. Col., Buffalo, N.Y.
Conway, Marie M., Jefferson Court No. 31, 4925 Saul St., Philadelphia, Pa.
Cook, Frances Colwell, Lincoln Cons. Lab. School, Ypsilanti, Mich.
Cooke, Dorothy E., 11 S. Lake Ave., Albany, N.Y.
Cookingham, Frank, Michigan State University, East Lansing, Mich.
Cool, Dwight W., 827 E. Oakwood, Glendora, Calif.
Cooley, Robert L., Supt., Dunkirk Public Schools, Dunkirk, N.Y.
Cooling, Elizabeth, 600 Mt. Pleasant Ave., Providence, R.I.
Coon, Herbert L., Sch. of Educ., Ohio State University, Columbus, Ohio
Cooper, Bernice L., Baldwin Hall, Univ. of Georgia, Athens, Ga.
Cooper, Dian Annise, 500 E. 33rd St., Chicago, Ill.
Cooper, George H., 2913 Washington Blvd., Chicago, Ill.
Cooper, J. David, 1610 Dorchester Dr., Bloomington, Ind.
Cooper, John H., 63 Lucero St., Thousand Oaks, Calif.
Cooper, Joyce, University of Florida, Gainesville, Fla.
Copeland, Harlan G., University of Wisconsin, Madison, Wis.
Corbin, Joseph W., 2700 Warwick Lane, Modesto, Calif.
Cordasco, Frank M., Montclair State Col., Upper Montclair, N.J.
Corey, Stephen M., University of Miami, Coral Gables, Fla.
Corley, Clifford L., Oregon College of Education, Monmouth, Ore.
Corman, Bernard R., 705-11025—82nd Ave., Edmonton, Alba., Canada
Cornell, Francis G., 7 Holland Ave., White Plains, N.Y.
Cornish, Robert L., Arkansas University, Fayetteville, Ark.
Corona, Bert C., 426 Locust St., Modesto, Calif.
Cortage, Cecelia, 2053 Illinois Ave., Santa Rosa, Calif.
Cortner, Frederick D., Pembroke State College, Pembroke, N.C.
Cory, N. Durward, 908 W. North St., Muncie, Ind.
Cosby, Joseph H., Hargrave Military Academy. Chatham, Va.
Cosentino, Bruno, 6 Glenside Dr., New City, N.Y.
Cosper, Cecil, Western Carolina College, Culowhee, N.C.
Coster, John K., North Carolina State University, Raleigh, N.C.
Cotner, Janet, Scott, Foresman & Co., Collingswood, N.J.
Cotter, Katharine C., Boston Col., Chestnut Hill, Mass.
Cotton, Henry F., Lynnfield High School, Lynnfield, Mass.
Cottone, Sebastian Charles, School Planning Dept., Philadelphia, Pa.
Couch, Paul E., Arkansas State College, State College, Ark.
Couche, Martha E., Rust College, Holly Springs, Miss.
Coughlan, Robert J., Sch. of Educ., Northwestern Univ., Evanston, Ill.
Coulter, Myron L., Sch. of Educ., West. Michigan Univ., Kalamazoo, Mich.
* Courtis, S. A., 22445 Cupertino Rd., Cupertino, Calif.
Courtney, Robert W., Box 198, Middlebush, N.J.
Covert, Warren O., Western Illinois University, Macomb, Ill.
Cowan, Persis H., 1612 Fair Oaks Ave., South Pasadena, Calif.
Coward, Gertrude O., Charlotte-Mecklenburg Bd. of Educ., Charlotte, N.C.
Cowles, Clifton V., Jr., Arkansas State College, State College, Ark.
Cowles, James D., T-112-A Northington, Tuscaloosa, Ala.
Cowles, Milly, Sch. of Educ., Univ. of South Carolina, Columbia, S.C.
Cox, Edwin A., Superintendent of Schools, North Parade, Stratford, Conn.

Cox, Hugh F., Rt. 1, Box 478, Gridley, Calif.
Cox, John A., 735 N. Allen St., State College, Pa.
Cox, Robert A., University of Pittsburgh, Pittsburgh, Pa.
Cozine, June E., Col. of Educ., Kansas State Univ., Manhattan, Kan.
* Craig, Gerald S., Tchrs. Col., Columbia University, New York, N.Y.
Craig, James C., 9403 Crosby Rd., Silver Spring, Md.
Craig, Jimmie M., 11512 Fuerte Farms Rd., El Cajon, Calif.
Craig, Robert C., Michigan State University, East Lansing, Mich.
Cramer, Ronald L., Oakland Univ., Box 710, Rochester, Mich.
Crane, Donald C., 67 Payson Lane, Piscataway, N.J.
Crarey, Hugh W., 751 E. 84th Pl., 3E, Chicago, Ill.
Craton, Edward J., 1777 Glenwood Ct., Bakersfield, Calif.
Craver, Samuel M., 3 Hilltop Ct., Rt. 2, Chapel Hill, N.C.
Crawford, Dorothy M., 212 W. Washington St., Ottawa, Ill.
Crawford, Leslie W., Univ. of Victoria, Victoria, B.C., Can.
Crawford, T. James, Sch. of Business, Indiana University, Bloomington, Ind.
Crawshaw, Stanley M., Hampton, Nebr.
Creason, M. Frank, 9101 Grant Lane, Overland Park, Kan.
Cresci, Gerald D., 1171 Los Molinos Way, Sacramento, Calif.
Crescimbeni, Joseph, Jacksonville University, Jacksonville, Fla.
Crespy, H. Victor, 94 Broad St., Freehold, N.J.
Creswell, Mrs. Rowena C., 305 Montclair Ave., So., College Station, Tex.
Crews, Alton C., Superintendent of Schools, Huntsville, Ala.
Crews, Roy L., Aurora College, Aurora, Ill.
Crim, Kenneth, 15 N. Main St., Dayton, Ohio
Criscuolo, Nicholas P., Read. Spec., Pub. Schools, New Haven, Conn.
Crocker, Richard F., Jr., Superintendent of Schools, Caribou, Me.
Croft, Harry E., 518 N. Everett Dr., Palatine, Ill.
Crohn, Burrill L., 944 Third Ave., New York, N.Y.
Cromartie, Sue W., Col. of Educ., University of Georgia, Athens, Ga.
Crombe, William A., 1087 Webster Rd., Webster, N.Y.
Cron, Celeste Maia, 801 Gull Ave., San Mateo, Calif.
Cronin, Rev. Robert E., 3245 Rio St., Apt. 811, Falls Church, Va.
Crook, Robert B., Queens Col., Flushing, N.Y.
Crosley, Mrs. Alice J., 411 Washington Ave., Defiance, Ohio
Cross, Donald A., Bathurst Tchrs. Col., Bathurst, N.S.W., Australia
Crossland, Mrs. Kathryn M., 3326 Pinafore Drive, Durham, N.C.
Crosson, Robert Henry, 2747 West 35th Ave., Denver, Colo.
*Crow, Lester D., 5300 Washington St., Hollywood, Fla.
Crowell, R. A., Col. of Educ., University of Arizona, Tucson, Ariz.
Crowley, Mary C., 7 Boone Lane, Dearborn, Mich.
Crowley, Robert J., 545 S. Fifth Ave., Ann Arbor, Mich.
Croy, Hazel, California State College, Fullerton, Calif.
Cruckson, Fred A., 72 S. Portland St., Fond du Lac, Wis.
Crum, Clyde E., Div. of Educ., San Diego State College, San Diego, Calif.
Culbertson, Jack A., Ohio State University, Columbus, Ohio
Cumbee, Carroll F., Apt. D-4, Trojan Arms Apt., Troy, Ala.
Cummings, C. Thomas, Canajoharie Central Schools, Canajoharie, N.Y.
Cummings, Mabel Anna, 6044 Linden St., Brooklyn, N.Y.
Cummings, Reta Gines, 190 S. Prospect St., Orange, Calif.
Cummings, Susan N., Arizona State University, Tempe, Ariz.
Cummins, L. Ross, Dept. of Educ. & Psych., Bates Col., Lewiston, Me.
Cummins, Lester L., 3512 S. 263rd St., Kent, Wash.
Cunningham, George S., 4 Glenwood St., Orono, Me.
Cunningham, Luvern L., Dean of Educ., Ohio State Univ., Columbus, Ohio
Cunningham, Myron, Col. of Educ., University of Florida, Gainesville, Fla.
Cupp, Gene R., 1704 N. Park Ave., Canton, Ohio
Currey, Ralph B., State Dept. of Education, Charleston, W.Va.
Currie, Robert J., Col. of Educ., University of Idaho, Moscow, Idaho
Currier, Mrs. Lynor O., 1925 Harwood Rd., Annapolis, Md.

Curry, John F., Box 6765, North Texas State College, Denton, Tex.
Curry, Laura J., 19121 S.W. 97th Ave., Miami, Fla.
Curtin, James R., Col. of Educ., University of Minnesota, Minneapolis, Minn.
Curtin, James T., 4140 Lindell Blvd., St. Louis, Mo.
Curtin, John T., 21761 Mauer Dr., St. Clair Shores, Mich.
Curtis, Delores M., University of Hawaii, Honolulu, Hawaii
Curtis, E. Louise, Macalester College, St. Paul, Minn.
Curtis, Francis H., Univ. of Scranton, Scranton, Pa.
Curtis, James E., 325 Conifer Ln., Santa Cruz, Calif.
Curtis, James P., University of Alabama, University, Ala.
Cusick, Ralph J., 6443 N. Wayne Ave., Chicago, Ill.

Daddazio, Arthur H., 41 Brady Ave., Newburgh, N.Y.
Daeufer, Carl J., Trust Ter. of Pacific Islands, Marianas Isls.
D'Agostino, Nicholas E., Wolcott High School, Wolcott, Conn.
Dahl, John A., California State College, Los Angeles, Calif.
Daines, Mrs. Delva, 615 E. 700 North, Provo, Utah
Dale, Arbie Myron, Sch. of Commerce, New York University, New York, N.Y.
Dale, Edgar, Sch. of Educ., Ohio State University, Columbus, Ohio
D'Alessio, Theodore, 10 Gaston St., W. Orange, N.J.
Dal Santo, John, 917 Washington St., Mendota, Ill.
Daly, Edmund B., 1839 N. Richmond St., Chicago, Ill.
Daly, Francis M., Jr., Eastern Michigan University, Ypsilanti, Mich.
D'Amico, Michael F., 144-29 Thirty-seventh St., Flushing, L.I., N.Y.
Dandoy, Maxine A., Fresno State College, Fresno, Calif.
Daniel, George T., N. 319 Locust Rd., Spokane, Wash.
Daniel, Dr. Kathryn B., 83 Nob Hill, Columbia, S.C.
Daniel, Sheldon C., 3805 Hibiscus, Sarasota, Fla.
Daniel, Walter G., Dept. of Educ., Howard University, Washington, D.C.
Daniels, Paul R., 4300 N. Charles St., Baltimore, Md.
Danielson, Paul J., Col. of Educ., University of Arizona, Tucson, Ariz.
Darcy, Natalie T., Dept. of Educ., Brooklyn College, Brooklyn, N.Y.
Darling, Dennis E., 501 N. Clarendon, Kalamazoo, Mich.
Darr, George F., 155 Rodeo Rd., Glendora, Calif.
Darrow, Helen F., 162 N. Carmelina Ave., Los Angeles, Calif.
D'Ascoli, Louis N., 5 Hughes Ter., Yonkers, N.Y.
Daubek, Gerald G., Univ. of Kentucky Ext., Fort Knox, Ky.
Dave, Vidya Deodatta, Ranchhod Bhuvan, Ambawadi, Ahmedabad, India
Davenport, William R., University of Michigan at Flint, Flint, Mich.
Davern, Francis E., 308 E. Jackson, Macomb, Ill.
Davey, Mrs. Elizabeth P., 5748 Harper Ave., Chicago, Ill.
Davidson, Mrs. Evelyn K., Dept. of Educ., Kent State University, Kent, Ohio
Davidson, Jack L., Superintendent of Schools, Oak Ridge, Tenn.
Davidson, Terrence R., University of Michigan, Ann Arbor, Mich.
Davies, Daniel R., Croft Consult. Serv., Tucson, Ariz.
Davies, Don, NCTEPS (NEA), 1201—16th St., N.W., Washington, D.C.
Davies, J. Leonard, Bur. of Educ. Resch., Univ. of Iowa, Iowa City, Iowa
Davies, Lillian S., Illinois State University, Normal, Ill.
Davis, Alice Taylor, 3800 Williams Ln., Chevy Chase, Md.
Davis, Ann E., 525 N.W. Armstrong Way, Corvallis, Ore.
Davis, David Carson, 1045 E St., Apt. 4, Lincoln, Nebr.
Davis, David E., Supr., Tyrrell Co. Public Schools, Columbia, N.C.
Davis, Donald E., University of Minnesota, Minneapolis, Minn.
Davis, Donald Jack, Texas Technological College, Lubbock, Tex.
Davis, Dwight E., 6726 S. Washington Ave., Lansing, Mich.
Davis, Dwight M., 505 Glenview Dr., Des Moines, Iowa
Davis, Mrs. Eldred D., Knoxville College, Knoxville, Tenn.
Davis, Frederick B., 3700 Walnut St., Philadelphia, Pa.
Davis, Guy C., Trinidad State Junior College, Trinidad, Colo.

Davis, H. Curtis, 1605 Park Ave., San Jose, Calif.
Davis, Harold S., Educ. Res. Council, Rockefeller Bldg., Cleveland, Ohio
Davis, Hazel Grubbs, Queens Col., City Univ. of N.Y., Flushing, N.Y.
Davis, Howard, 1142 Medway Rd., Philadelphia, Pa.
Davis, J. Clark, Col. of Educ., University of Nevada, Reno, Nev.
Davis, J. Sanford, Box 646, Madison, Conn.
Davis, Joseph H., 8300 Jackson St., St. Louis, Mo.
Davis, Marianna W., Claflin College, Orangeburg, S.C.
Davis, Milton J., 725 West 18th St., North Chicago, Ill.
Davis, O. L., Jr., Col. of Educ., Univ. of Texas, Austin, Tex.
Davis, Paul Ford, Morehead State Univ., Morehead, Ky.
Davis, Ron W., 223 Hillcrest Cir., Chapel Hill, N.C.
Davis, Warren C., 65 S. Plymouth Ave., Rochester, N.Y.
Davoren, David, Superintendent of Schools, Milford, Mass.
Dawkins, M. B., 1110 Izard St., Little Rock, Ark.
Dawkins, Sue, 17 E. 14th Ave., Columbus, Ohio
Dawson, Kenneth E., 3804 Evans Rd., Atlanta, Ga.
Dawson, W. Read, Baylor University, Waco, Tex.
Day, H. I., Ontario Institute for Studies in Educ., Toronto, Ont., Can.
Day, James F., Dept. of Educ., Univ. of Texas, El Paso, Texas
Deady, John E., Supt. of Schools, Springfield, Mass.
Deam, Calvin W., Sch. of Educ., Boston University, Boston, Mass.
Dease, E. Richard, 413 Lorraine Rd., Wheaton, Ill.
DeBernardis, Amo, 6049 S. W. Luradel, Portland, Ore.
Debin, Louis, 83-37—247th St., Bellerose, N.Y.
DeBoer, Dorothy L., 3930 W. Southport Ave., Chicago, Ill.
DeBoer, John J., 6910 Oglesby, Chicago, Ill.
Debus, Raymond L., 7 Brooks St., Lane Cove, New South Wales, Australia
Deep, Donald, 124 Longmount Drive, Pittsburgh, Pa.
Deever, Merwin, Col. of Educ., Arizona State University, Tempe, Ariz.
DeGrow, Gerald S., 509 Stanton St., Port Huron, Mich.
Dejnozka, Edward L., 49 Rockleigh Drive, Trenton, N.J.
DeKock, Henry C., Col. of Educ., State Univ. of Iowa, Iowa City, Iowa
Delaney, Eleanor C., Sch. of Educ., Rutgers Univ., New Brunswick, N.J.
Della Penta, A. H., Superintendent of Schools, Lodi, N.J.
Deller, W. McGregor, Superintendent of Schools, Fairport, N.Y.
Delmonaco, Thomas M., 44 Lanewood Ave., Framingham Centre, Mass.
Delon, Floyd G., 302 Natl. Old Line Bldg., Little Rock, Ark.
DeLong, Arthur R., Grand Valley State College, Allendale, Mich.
Demerio, William D., 56 W. Mohawk St., Oswego, N.Y.
Demming, John A., Bldg. S-502, 6th St., N., West Palm Beach, Fla.
DeMoraes, Maria P. Tito, WHO Reg. Off., 8 Scherfigsvej, Copenhagen, Denmark
Dempsey, Richard A., P.O. Box 1167, Darien, Conn.
Denemark, George W., University of Kentucky, Lexington, Ky.
Denham, Lynne S., 2111 E. Broadway, Logansport, Ind.
Denning, Mrs. Bernadine, 5057 Woodward, Rm. 1338, Detroit, Mich.
Dennis, Donald A., 14540 Greenleaf St., Sherman Oaks, Calif.
Dennis, Ronald T., Northwestern State College, Natchitoches, La.
Deno, Stanley L., Col. of Educ., Univ. of Delaware, Newark, Del.
Denova, Charles C., Hughes Tool Co., Culver City, Calif.
Denson, Lucille D., Braemar House, Hollywood Pk., Liverpool, N.Y.
De Ortega, Eneida Santizo, Calle Real 6101, Betania-Panama, Rep. of Panama
DePaul, Frank J., 2727 North Long Ave., Chicago, Ill.
Derby, Orlo Lee, State Univ. Col., Brockport, N.Y.
DeRidder, Lawrence M., Col. of Educ., Univ. of Tennessee, Knoxville, Tenn.
DeRoche, Edward F., Marquette Univ., Milwaukee, Wis.
DeSantis, Joseph P., 430 Buffalo Ave., Niagara Falls, N.Y.
Desimowich, Donald M., Route 3, Box 30, Hartland, Wis.
Desjarlais, Lionel P., 1684 Rhodes Ct., Ottawa 8, Ont., Canada
Desoe, Hollis L., Board of Educ., 51 Route 100, Briarcliff Manor, N.Y.
DeStefano, Anthony J., 48 Lenox Ave., Hicksville, N.Y.

Detrick, Frederick M., 10 Sheldon Rd., Pemberton, N.J.
Deutschman, Mrs. Marilyn L., 201 St. Pauls Ave., Jersey City, N.J.
De Vane, M. L., Dir. of Instrn., Lenoir City Schools, Lenoir, S.C.
DeVault, M. Vere, University of Wisconsin, Madison, Wis.
Devenport, Claude N., 2810 Leeway Drive, Apt. 3, Columbia, Mo.
Devens, John S., Columbia College, Columbia, S.C.
Devine, Florence E., 4822 Central Ave., Western Springs, Ill.
Devine, Thomas G., Sch. of Educ., Boston University, Boston, Mass.
Devor, J. W., 6309 E. Holbert Rd., Bethesda, Md.
DeVries, Ted, Ball State University, Muncie, Ind.
DeWalt, Homer C., Supt. of Schools, Diocese of Erie, Erie, Pa.
Deyell, J. Douglas, Provincial Teachers College, North Bay, Ont., Canada
Dickey, Otis M., Superintendent of Schools, Oak Park, Mich.
Dickmeyer, Mrs. K. H., 200 8th Ave., S.E., Fairfax, Minn.
*Diederich, A. F., St. Norbert College, West DePere, Wis.
Diedrich, Richard C., 155 Knox Dr., West Lafayette, Ind.
Diefenderfer, Omie T., 828 Third St., Fullerton, Pa.
Diehl, T. Handley, Miami University, Oxford, Ohio
Diener, Russell E., 1034 Novara St., San Diego, Calif.
Dierzen, Mrs. Verda, Comm. Consol. Sch. Dist., Woodstock, Ill.
Dieterle, Louise E., 10700 S. Avenue F, Chicago, Ill.
Dietz, Elisabeth H., 1093 Northern Blvd., Baldwin, N.Y.
Diffley, Jerome, St. Bernard College, St. Bernard, Ala.
Diggs, Eugene A., Supt., Sch. Dist. No. 110, Overland Park, Kansas
DiGiacento, Mrs. Rose, 68 Pilgrim Ave., Yonkers, N.Y.
DiGiammarino, Frank, Lexington Public Schools, Lexington, Mass.
DiLeonarde, Joseph H., 6309 N. Cicero Ave., Chicago, Ill.
DiLieto, Ray Marie, 4 Bayberry Lane, Westport, Conn.
Dillehay, James A., Bowling Green State Univ., Bowling Green, Ohio
Dillman, Duane H., 77 Chatham Rd., Columbus, Ohio
Dillon, Frances H., Moorhead State Col., Moorhead, Minn.
Dillon, Jesse D., Jr., David W. Harlan School, Wilmington, Del.
DiLuglio, Domenic R., 1849 Warwick Ave., Warwick, R.I.
Dimitroff, Lillian, 1525 Brummel St., Evanston, Ill.
Dimond, Ray A., Jr., 4034 E. Cambridge, Phoenix, Ariz.
Dimond, Stanley E., 2012 Shadford Rd., Ann Arbor, Mich.
DiNardo, V. James, Massachusetts State College, Bridgewater, Mass.
DiPasquale, Vincent C., Moorhead State Col., Moorhead, Minn.
Disberger, Jay, Box 268, Haven, Kan.
Disko, Michael, 16 Briarwood Dr., Athens, Ohio
Distin, Mr. Leslie, Connetquot High School, Bohemia, N.Y.
Dittemore, Ron, 707 W. Market St., Savannah, Mo.
Dittmer, Daniel G., 1647 Francis Hammond Pkwy., Alexandria, Va.
Dittmer, Jane E., Kouts High School, Kouts, Ind.
Dixon, Glendora, Talmadge Jr. H.S., Independence, Ore.
Dixon, James T., 13 Lake Rd., Huntington Station, L.I., N.Y.
Dixon, W. Robert, University of Michigan, Ann Arbor, Mich.
Dobbs, Edith, Fort Hays Kansas State College, Hays, Kan.
Dodd, John M., State Univ. Col., Buffalo, N.Y.
Dodds, A. Gordon, Superintendent of Schools, Edwardsville, Ill.
Dodge, Norman B., 523 S. Oneida Way, Denver, Colo.
Dodson, Dan W., New York University, Washington Sq., New York, N.Y.
Dodson, Edwin S., Col. of Educ., University of Nevada, Reno, Nev.
Dohemann, H. Warren, San Francisco State Col., San Francisco, Calif.
Doherty, Benton H., 403 Washington, Park Ridge, Ill.
Dohmann, C. William, 640 Main St., El Segundo, Calif.
Dolan, Francis, LaSalle-Peru Twp. High School, LaSalle, Ill.
Doll, Ronald C., 17 Rossmore Ter., Livingston, N.J.
Domian, E. O., 1595 Northrop, St. Paul, Minn.
Dommer, Carolyn, Michigan State Univ., East Lansing, Mich.
Donahoe, Thomas J., 74 Fallston St., Springfield, Mass.

Donatelli, Rosemary V., Loyola University, Chicago, Ill.
Donner, Arvin N., Col. of Educ., University of Houston, Houston, Tex.
Donnersberger, Mrs. Anne, 8030 S. Paxton, Chicago, Ill.
Donoghue, Mildred R., California State College, Fullerton, Calif.
Donovan, Charles F., Sch. of Educ., Boston College, Chestnut Hill, Mass.
Donovan, Daniel E., C.M., St. John's Prep. Sch., Brooklyn, N.Y.
Donovan, David, 119 S. Highland, Ossining, N.Y.
Doody, Louise E., 191 Dedham St., Newton Highlands, Mass.
Dooley, Bobby J., 118 Fain Hall, University of Georgia, Athens, Ga.
Dorricott, H. J., Western State College, Gunnison, Colo.
Doss, Jesse Paul, 12631 Fletcher Dr., Garden Grove, Calif.
Dotson, John M., 154 Jones Dr., Pocatello, Idaho
Douglas, L. M., Westminster College, New Wilmington, Pa.
Douglass, Harl R., Col. of Educ., University of Colorado, Boulder, Colo.
Douglass, Malcolm P., Claremont Grad. Sch., Claremont, Calif.
Dow, John A., 2597 W. Calimyrna, Fresno, Calif.
Dowling, Thomas I., Superintendent, Dist. No. 50, Greenwood, S.C.
Downing, Carl, Central State Col., Edmond, Okla.
Doyle, Andrew McCormick, 1106 Bellerive Blvd., St. Louis, Mo.
Doyle, Rev. E. A., 255 N. Eighth St., Ponchatoula, La.
Doyle, James F., 2930 Forrest Hills Dr., S.W., Atlanta, Ga.
Doyle, Jean, 511 E. High St., Lexington, Ky.
Doyle, Walter, University of Notre Dame, Notre Dame, Ind.
Drag, Francis L., California Western Univ., San Diego, Calif.
Dragositz, Anna, Educational Testing Service, Princeton, N.J.
Drake, Thelbert L., Univ. of Connecticut, Storrs, Conn.
Draves, David D., University of New Hampshire, Durham, N.H.
Drechsel, Lionel C., 2009 Fillmore, Ogden, Utah
*Dreikurs, Rudolph, 6 N. Michigan Ave., Chicago, Ill.
Dreisbach, Dodson E., Gibraltar, Pa.
Dressel, Paul L., Michigan State University, East Lansing, Mich.
Drew, Alfred S., Purdue University, Lafayette, Ind.
Drew, Robert E., Community Unit School Dist. 303, St. Charles, Ill.
Driver, Cecil E., Vandenberg Elem. School, APO, New York, N.Y.
Dropkin, Stanley, Queens College, Flushing, N.Y.
Drucker, Howard, 1423 Galleon Way, San Luis Obispo, Calif.
Drummond, Harold D., Univ. of New Mexico, Albuquerque, N.M.
Drummond, William H., 623 S. Decatur, Olympia, Wash.
DuBois, Helen, Medical Center, Maple Ave. Ext., Glen Cove, N.Y.
Ducanis, Alex J., 230 N. Craig, Apt. 703, Pittsburgh, Pa.
Duckers, Ronald L., 320 Jon Court, Des Plaines, Ill.
Duckworth, Alice, 100 Reef Rd., Fairfield, Conn.
Dudley, James, Col. of Educ., Univ. of Maryland, College Park, Md.
Duff, Franklin L., Bur. of Instr. Res., Univ. of Illinois, Urbana, Ill.
Duffett, John W., 341 Bellefield Ave., Pittsburgh, Pa.
Duffey, Robert V., 9225 Limestone Pl., College Park, Md.
Dufford, William E., Box 651, Orangeburg, S.C.
Duffy, Bernard A., Seton Hall University, South Orange, N.J.
DuFour, Stuart, Hartnell College, Salinas, Calif.
Duggan, John M., College Entrance Examination Board, New York, N.Y.
Duke, Ralph L., Sch. of Educ., University of Delaware, Newark, Del.
Duke, Reese D., Dept. of Educ., Rice Univ., Houston, Texas
Dumler, Marvin J., Concordia Teachers College, River Forest, Ill.
Dunbar, Donald A., Mt. Lebanon Sch. Dist., Pittsburgh, Pa.
Duncan, Ernest R., Sch. of Educ., Rutgers Univ., New Brunswick, N.J.
Duncan, J. A., Agric. Hall, University of Wisconsin, Madison, Wis.
Duncan, William B., Miami Edison Senior High School, Miami, Fla.
Dunham, Ralph E., 2117 Popkins Ln., Alexandria, Va.
Dunkel, Harold B., Dept. of Educ., University of Chicago, Chicago, Ill.
Dunkeld, Colin G., 414 W. Ells, Champaign, Ill.
Dunkle, Maurice Albert, Superintendent, Calver Co. Schls., Prince Frederick, Md.

Dunn, Mary S., Chicago State College, Chicago, Ill.
Dunnell, John P., 1004 Wenonah, Oak Park, Ill.
Dunning, Frances E., 125 Owre Hall, Univ. of Minnesota, Minneapolis, Minn.
Durant, Adrian J., Jr., 1115 Holiday Park Dr., Champaign, Ill.
Durante, Spencer E., 1615 Van Buren Ave., Charlotte, N.C.
Durflinger, Glenn W., 5665 Cielo Ave., Goleta, Calif.
Durkee, Frank M., Box 911, Harrisburg, Pa.
Durost, Walter N., RFD # 2, Box 120, Dover, N.H.
Durr, William K., Col. of Educ., Michigan State Univ., East Lansing, Mich.
Durrell, Donald D., Boston University, 332 Bay State Rd., Boston, Mass.
Dutton, Wilbur H., 1913 Greenfield Ave., Los Angeles, Calif.
Dutro, Richard F., Lakewood Public Schools, Lakewood, Ohio
DuVall, Lloyd A., 583 Harley Dr., Apt. 6, Columbus, Ohio
Dwyer, John E., Superintendent of Schools, Elizabeth, N.J.
Dwyer, Roy E., P.O. Box 343, Thonotasassa, Fla.
Dyer, Frank E., Supt., Delano Jt. Union High School, Delano, Calif.
Dyke, Elwood E., Southport Elem. Sch., 723—76th St., Kenosha, Wis.
Dykes, Mrs. Alma, 9755 Cincinnati-Columbus Rd., Cincinnati, Ohio
Dyson, R. E., 202 Northlawn Ave., East Lansing, Mich.
Dziak, Susanne S., 3436 S. 112th St., Omaha, Neb.
Dziuban, Charles D., 3460 Buford Hgwy., Atlanta, Ga.

Eaddy, Edward Allen, Superintendent of Schools, Georgetown, S.C.
Earles, Lucius C., Jr., 123 Peabody St., N.W., Washington, D.C.
Early, Margaret J., Read. Lab., Syracuse Univ., Syracuse, N.Y.
Eash, Maurice J., Hunter College, 695 Park Ave., New York, N.Y.
Easterly, Ambrose, 510 W. Elk Grove Blvd., Elk Grove Village, Ill.
Eaton, Albert G., Saybrook School, Ashtabula, Ohio
Eaton, Edward J., 4042 N.W. 35th Ave., Fort Lauderdale, Fla.
Ebel, Robert L., Michigan State University, East Lansing, Mich.
Eberle, August William, Indiana Univ., Bloomington, Ind.
Eberman, Paul W., 1801 John F. Kennedy Blvd., Philadelphia, Pa.
Eboch, Sidney C., Dept. of Educ., Ohio State Univ., Columbus, Ohio
Echevarris, Major Ramon L., Inter. Amer. University, APO, New York
Eckert, Edwin K., Supt., Lutheran Schools, Chicago, Ill.
Eckert, Ruth E., Col. of Educ., University of Minnesota, Minneapolis, Minn.
Eckhardt, John W., 13 Panorama Gardens, Bakersfield, Calif.
Eddins, William N., P.O. Box 9036, Crestline Heights Br., Birmingham, Ala.
Edelmann, Anne M., 7614 Garden Rd., Cheltenham, Pa.
Edelstein, David S., Connecticut State College, Yonkers, N.Y.
Eden, Donald F., Adams State College, Alamosa, Colo.
Edick, Helen M., 125 Terry Rd., Hartford, Conn.
Edinger, Lois V., University of North Carolina, Greensboro, N.C.
Edmundson, W. Dean, Detroit Public Schls., 12021 Evanston, Detroit, Mich.
Edson, William H., 206 Burton Hall, Univ. of Minnesota, Minneapolis, Minn.
Edstrom, A. E., Senior High School, 1001 State Hwy., Hopkins, Minn.
Edwards, Andrew S., Georgia Southern College, Statesboro, Ga.
Edwards, Arthur U., Eastern Illinois University, Charleston, Ill.
Edwards, Carlos R., Boys High School, Brooklyn, N.Y.
Edwards, Derwin W., Miami University, Oxford, Ohio
Edwards, Gerald F., Rt. 2, Box 406, Edgerton, Wis.
Edwards, Joseph O., Jr., 42 Eastridge Circle, Pacifica, Calif.
Edwards, Marcia, Burton Hall, University of Minnesota, Minneapolis, Minn.
Edwards, T. Bentley, Sch. of Educ., Univ. of California, Berkeley, Calif.
Egan, Gerard V., 79 Ward Pl., South Orange, N.J.
Egelston, Elwood, Jr., Illinois State University, Normal, Ill.
Egge, Donald E., 325 N.E. 10th St., Newport, Ore.
Eggerding, Roland F., Lutheran High School, South, St. Louis, Mo.
Eherenman, William C., Wisconsin State University, Platteville, Wis.
Ehlers, Henry J., Duluth Branch, University of Minnesota, Duluth, Minn.
Eibler, Herbert J., University of Michigan, Ann Arbor, Mich.

Eicher, Charles E., 718 Tulip Tree, Bloomington, Ind.
Eichholz, G. C., Educ. Research, Inc., Tampa, Fla.
Eidell, Terry L., CAESA, Univ. of Oregon, Eugene, Ore.
Eikaas, Alf T., Kjolsdalen, Nordfjord, Norway
Einolf, W. L., Birchrunville, Pa.
Eisenstein, Herbert S., Pennsylvania State University, Middletown, Pa.
Eiserer, Paul E., Tchrs. Col., Columbia University, New York, N.Y.
Eisner, Elliot W., Stanford University, Stanford, Calif.
Eke, Verne M., 954 S. Carondelet St., Los Angeles, Calif.
Elder, Rachel A., Tolman Hall, University of California, Berkeley, Calif.
Elder, Richard D., Child Study Cent., Kent State Univ., Kent, Ohio
Eldridge, M. L., Spring Branch Elem. Sch., Houston, Tex.
Elkins, Keith, 7330 Pershing Blvd., University City, Mo.
Elland, A. H., Hutchinson Junior College, 1300 Plum, Hutchinson, Kan.
Elle, Martin J., Southern Oregon College, Ashland, Ore.
Ellenburg, Fred C., Rt. No. 1, Grove Lakes, Statesboro, Ga.
Ellerbrook, Louis William, Box 4628, S.F.A. Sta., Nacogdoches, Tex.
Ellery, Marilynne, Ohio Northern University, Ada, Ohio
Ellingson, Mark, Rochester Institute of Technology, Rochester, N.Y.
Elliott, Arthur H., Simon Fraser University, Burnaby 2, B.C., Canada
Elliott, David L., Sch. of Educ., Univ. of California, Berkeley, Calif.
Ellis, Mrs. Celia Diamond, 1125 S. LaJolla Ave., Los Angeles, Calif.
Ellis, Frederick E., Western Washington State Col., Bellingham, Wash.
Ellis, G. W., Drew Junior High School, 1055 N.W. 52nd St., Miami, Fla.
Ellis, John F., Simon Fraser University, Burnaby, B.C., Canada
Ellis, Joseph R., Northern Illinois University, DeKalb, Ill.
Ellis, Robert L., 1125 S. LaJolla Ave., Los Angeles, Calif.
Ellison, Alfred, New York University, Washington Sq., New York, N.Y.
Ellison, F. Robert, 1354 Laurel St., Casper, Wyo.
Ellison, Jack L., Francis W. Parker Sch., Chicago, Ill.
Ellner, Carolyn L., Univ. of California at L.A., Los Angeles, Calif.
Ellson, Douglas G., Indiana University, Bloomington, Ind.
Ellwein, Mrs. Ileane, 2905 S. Jefferson St., Sioux Falls, S.D.
Emanuel, Joseph, 617 E. Wayne St., Fort Wayne, Ind.
Emeson, David L., 411 N. Dubuque St., Iowa City, Iowa
Emmet, Thomas A., 5440 Cass Ave., Suite 412, Detroit, Mich.
Emmons, Jean F., Col. of Educ., Ohio State University, Columbus, Ohio
Ende, Russell S., Northern Illinois University, DeKalb, Ill.
Endres, Mary P., Purdue University, Lafayette, Ind.
Endres, Richard J., 707 Salisbury Rd., Columbus, Ohio
Engelhardt, Jack E., 1500 Maywood Ave., Ann Arbor, Mich.
Engelhardt, Nickolaus L., Jr., Purdy Station, N.Y.
Engle, Shirley H., Sch. of Educ., Indiana University, Bloomington, Ind.
Engler, David, McGraw-Hill Book Co., New York, N.Y.
English, John W., Superintendent of Schools, Southfield, Mich.
English, Marvin D., National College of Education, Evanston, Ill.
Enoch, June E., Manchester College, North Manchester, Ind.
Entwisle, Doris, Johns Hopkins University, Baltimore, Md.
Eraut, Michael R., University of Sussex, Brighton, Sussex, England
Erbe, Wesley A., Col. of Educ., Univ. of Iowa, Iowa City, Iowa
Erdman, Robert L., Univ. of Utah, Salt Lake City, Utah
Erickson, Harley E., University of North Iowa, Cedar Falls, Iowa
Erickson, L. W., Sch. of Educ., Univ. of California, Los Angeles, Calif.
Erickson, Ralph J., Virginia Union University, Richmond, Va.
Erickson, Ralph W., 105 Third Ave., Columbus, Miss.
Erickson, Wayne C., 266 Orrin St., Winona, Minn.
Ersted, Ruth, State Department of Education, St. Paul, Minn.
Ervin, John B., 5933 Enright St., St. Louis, Mo.
Ervin, William B., 1 Midland Pl., Newark, N.J.
Erxleben, Arnold C., 157 Bemis Dr., Seward, Neb.
Erzen, Richard, Bradley Univ., Peoria, Ill.

Eson, Morris E., State University of New York, Albany, N.Y.
Essig, Lester Clay, Jr., Utah State University, Logan, Utah
Estes, Kenneth A., 1722 Woodhurst Ave., Bowling Green, Ky.
Estes, Sidney H., Urban Lab. in Educ., Atlanta, Ga.
Estle, Glen L., 1000 Pfingsten Rd., Northbrook, Ill.
Estvan, Frank J., Col. of Educ., Wayne State Univ., Detroit, Mich.
Etheridge, Robert F., Miami University, Oxford, Ohio
Etscovitz, Lionel, 5 Shaw Pl., Lexington, Mass.
Ettinger, Mrs. Bernadette C., 474 Brooklyn Blvd., Brightwaters, L.I., N.Y.
Eurich, Alvin C., P.O. Box 219, Aspen, Colo.
Evans, Edgar Ernest, Alabama State College, Montgomery, Ala.
Evans, Harley, Jr., 35952 Matoma Dr., Eastlake, Ohio
Evans, J. Bernard, 3163 Warrington Rd., Shaker Heights, Ohio
Evans, Mary Beth, Dir., Tchr. Educ., Graceland Col., Lamoni, Iowa
Evans, Orlynn R., F-15 So. Campus Court, Lafayette, Ind.
Evans, Ralph F., Fresno State College, Fresno, Calif.
Evans, Rupert N., Col. of Educ., Univ. of Illinois, Urbana, Ill.
Evans, Warren D., 34 E. Winding Rd., Mechanicsburg, Pa.
Eve, Arthur W., 99 Virginia Ave., Centerville, Ohio
Evenson, Warren L., 1528 S. Douglas St., Springfield, Ill.
Evertts, Eldonna L., N.C.T.E., 1415 S. Western Ave., Champaign, Ill.
Ewart, Mrs. Annie G., Shorewood Public Schools, Shorewood, Wis.
* Ewigleben, Mrs. Muriel, 3727 Weisser Park Ave., Ft. Wayne, Ind.
Ewing, Parmer L., Dept. of Educ. Admin., So. Ill. Univ., Carbondale, Ill.
Eyster, Elvin S., Dept. of Bus. Educ., Indiana Univ., Bloomington, Ind.

Fadden, Joseph A., Marywood College, Scranton, Pa.
Faddis, Mrs. Gabrielle J., Col. of Educ., Temple University, Philadelphia, Pa.
Failor, Harvey A., 13800 Ford Road, Dearborn, Mich.
Fair, Jean E., Wayne State University, Detroit, Mich.
Fairbanks, Gar, Supt. of Schools, Rocky Hill, Conn.
Falk, Alma M., 1330 New Hampshire Ave., N.W., Washington, D.C.
Falk, Philip H., 3721 Council Crest, Madison, Wis.
Fallon, Berlie J., Dept. of Educ., Texas Technological Col., Lubbock, Tex.
Fanslow, W. V., R.F.D. 3, Amherst, Mass.
Farber, Bernard E., Brady Elementary School, Detroit, Mich.
Fargen, J. Jerome, Catherine Spalding College, Louisville, Ky.
Farley, Gilbert J., Belmont Abbey Col., Belmont, N.C.
Farmer, Geraldine, University of Alberta, Edmonton, Alba., Canada
Farmer, James E., American Embassy (AID) APO New York
Farrell, Joseph I., 109 Cornell Ave., Hawthorne, N.J.
Farrell, Mathew C., University of Scranton, Scranton, Pa.
Fasan, Walter R., 3401 West 65th Pl., Chicago, Ill.
Faust, Claire Edward, 206 Floral Ave., Mankato, Minn.
Fawcett, Claude W., Sch. of Educ., Univ. of California, Los Angeles, Calif.
Fawley, Paul C., Dept. of Educ., University of Utah, Salt Lake City, Utah
Fay, Leo C., Sch. of Educ., Indiana University, Bloomington, Ind.
Faycock, John, Teachers College, Columbia University, New York, N.Y.
Fea, Henry Robert, University of Washington, Seattle, Wash.
Fecheck, Theresa A., 1330 Presidential Drive, Columbus, Ohio
Fee, Edward M., Bok Technical High School, Philadelphia, Pa.
Feely, Robert W., 10117 Albany Ave., Evergreen Park, Ill.
Feingold, S. Norman, 1640 Rhode Island Ave., N.W., Washington, D.C.
Feley, Ruth A., North Main St., East Granby, Conn.
Feller, Dan, 9951-B Robbins Dr., Beverly Hills, Calif.
Felsenthal, Mrs. Norman, 1434 Grand Ave., Iowa City, Iowa
Feltner, Bill D., Inst. of Higher Educ., Univ. of Georgia, Athens, Ga.
Fenderson, Julia K., Culver City Unified Schools, Culver City, Calif.
Fennema, Elizabeth H., 121 N. Allen, Madison, Wis.
Fenollosa, George M., Houghton Mifflin Co., 110 Tremont St., Boston, Mass.

Fenske, Arthur S., 106 Highland Ave., Hartland, Wis.
Ferguson, Arthur L., 311 Green St., Chenoa, Ill.
Feringer, F. R., Western Washington State College, Bellingham, Wash.
Ferris, Donald, 1316 N. Salisbury St., West Lafayette, Ind.
Ferris, Francis X, Spencerport, N.Y.
Ferry, Richard E., 236 Delmar, Decatur, Ill.
Fesperman, Mrs. Kathleen C., Newberry College, Newberry, S.C.
Feuerbach, F. Kenneth, Hammond High School, Hammond, Ind.
Feuers, Mrs. Stelle, Pierce College, Woodland Hills, Calif.
Ficek, Daniel E., 315 Arno, S.E., Albuquerque, N.M.
Fiedler, E. L., Superintendent of Schools, Abilene, Kan.
Field, Robert L., 1506 Jackson St., Oshkosh, Wis.
Fields, Ralph R., Tchrs. Col., Columbia University, New York, N.Y.
Fielstra, Clarence, Sch. of Educ., Univ. of California, Los Angeles, Calif.
Fielstra, Helen, San Fernando Valley State College, Northridge, Calif.
Fieman, Marvin E., 307 S. Arnaz Dr., Los Angeles, Calif.
Figurel, J. Allen, Indiana University, N.W. Campus, Gary, Ind.
Filbeck, Orval, Abilene Christian College, Abilene, Tex.
Filbeck, Robert W., Lincoln Job Corps Center, Lincoln, Neb.
Fillmer, Henry T., University of Florida, Gainesville, Fla.
Filosa, Mary G., 32 Ross Hall Blvd., No., Piscataway, N.J.
Fina, Robert P., 522 Fourth St., Catasauqua, Pa.
Finch, F. H., Col. of Educ., Univ. of Illinois, Urbana, Ill.
Finder, Morris, State University of N.Y., Albany, N.Y.
Findlay, Stephen W., Delbarton School, Morristown, N.J.
Findley, Dale, 1639 S. Sixth St., Terre Haute, Ind.
Findley, Warren G., Col. of Educ., University of Georgia, Athens, Ga.
Findley, William H., Jr., 111 Curtiss Pkwy., Miami Springs, Fla.
Fink, Abel K., State University College, 1300 Elmwood Ave., Buffalo, N.Y.
Fink, Herbert J., Tuley High School, 1313 N. Claremont Ave., Chicago, Ill.
Fink, Martin B., 3713 Merridan Dr., Concord, Calif.
Fink, Stuart D., Northern Illinois University, DeKalb, Ill.
Finster, Virginia, 2203 Mocking Bird Drive, Baytown, Texas
Finucan, J. Thomas, Assumption High School, Wisconsin Rapids, Wis.
Firth, Gerald R., University of Alabama, Tuscaloosa, Ala.
Fischer, John H., Tchrs. Col., Columbia University, New York, N.Y.
Fischer, Louis, San Fernando Valley State College, Northridge, Calif.
Fischler, Abraham S., 5000 Taylor St., Ft. Lauderdale, Fla.
Fischoff, Ephraim, 15 Riverview Pl., Lynchburg, Va.
Fish, Lawrence D., NWREL, 710 S.W. 2nd Ave., Portland, Ore.
Fishback, Woodson W., Southern Illinois University, Carbondale, Ill.
Fishell, Kenneth N., Syracuse University, Syracuse, N.Y.
Fisher, Carol M., R.R. No. 2, 5747 Detrick-Jordan Rd., Springfield, Ohio
Fisher, George, Ohio State University, Columbus, Ohio
Fisher, Ijourie Stocks, Miami-Dade Junior College, Miami, Fla.
Fisher, Lawrence A., Col. of Medicine, Univ. of Illinois, Chicago, Ill.
* Fisher, Mrs. Welthy H., Literacy Village, P.O. Singar Nagar, Lucknow, U.P.,
    India
Fisher, Welthy H., 50 W. 67th St., New York, N.Y.
Fishler, Edward, 72 Hedgerow Lane, Commack, L.I., N.Y.
Fisk, Robert S., State University of New York, Buffalo, N.Y.
Fitz, John Allen, 2923 West 235th St., Torrance, Calif.
Fitzgerald, William F., 5835 Kimbark Ave., Chicago, Ill.
Fitzpatrick, E. D., Illinois State University, Normal, Ill.
Fitzpatrick, Evelyn, Radford College, Radford, Va.
Flagg, E. Alma, 44 Stengel Ave., Newark, N.J.
Flamand, Ruth K., 72 Goldenridge Dr., Levittown, Pa.
Flanagan, John C., P.O. Box 1113, Palo Alto, Calif.
Flanagan, William F., 100 Tanner Ave., Warwick, R.I.
Flanders, Ned A., Sch. of Educ., Univ. of Mich., Ann Arbor, Mich.

Fleck, Henrietta, H.E. Dept., New York Univ., Washington Sq., New York, N.Y.
Fleming, Elyse S., Western Reserve University, Cleveland, Ohio
Fleming, Harold D., 2020 Birchmont Dr., Bemidji, Minn.
Fleming, Robert S., 311 W. Franklin St., Richmond, Va.
Fletcher, Ruby J., University of Utah, Salt Lake City, Utah
Fliegel, Norris E., 98 Riverside Dr., New York, N.Y.
Fliegler, Louis A., Dept. of Spec. Educ., Kent State Univ., Kent, Ohio
Fligor, R. J., Southern Illinois University, Carbondale, Ill.
Flint, Jack M., Kansas City Community Junior College, Kansas City, Kan.
Flores, Vetal, Drawer M, Bronte, Tex.
Flower, George E., Ontario Inst. for Studies in Educ., Toronto, Ont., Canada
Flowers, Anne, 509 N. Hamilton St., Richmond, Va.
Flug, Eugene R. F., Stout State University, Menomonie, Wis.
Fluitt, John L., Col. of Educ., Louisiana State Univ., New Orleans, La.
Flusche, Ernest A., P.O. Box 506, Oklahoma City, Okla.
Fochs, John S., 1732 Wauwatosa Ave., Wauwatosa, Wis.
Focht, James R., Educ. Dept., Salisbury State Col., Salisbury, Md.
Fogg, William E., Long Beach State College, Long Beach, Calif.
Foglia, Guido F., Queens College, Huntington Sta., L. I., N.Y.
Foley, Robert L., 2901 S. Parkway, Chicago, Ill.
Fonacier, Andres M., Laoag, Ilocos Norte, Philippines
Foord, James, University of Manchester, Manchester, England
Foran, Mary Ellen, 6301 N. Sheridan Rd., Chicago, Ill.
Foran, William L., 1007 Alberta, Oceanside, Calif.
Forbing, Shirley E., California State College, Long Beach, Calif.
Force, Dewey G., Jr., Pattee Hall, Univ. of Minnesota, Minneapolis, Minn.
Force, William R., 3754 Broomfield Rd., Mt. Pleasant, Mich.
Ford, Gervais W., San Jose State College, San Jose, Calif.
Ford, Roxana R., Sch. of Home Econ., Univ. of Minnesota, St. Paul, Minn.
Fordell, Pat, Dearborn Board of Educ., Dearborn, Mich.
Forer, Ruth K., 6013 Greenbush Ave., Van Nuys, Calif.
Forese, Joseph, Jr., Amherst, Mass.
Forrester, Carl M., Lake Park H.S., 6 N. 600 Medina Rd., Roselle, Ill.
Fortess, Lillian, 96 Bay State Rd., Boston, Mass.
Fortin, John E., Murray State University, Murray, Ky.
Fosback, Alta B., P.O. Box 443, Carlton, Ore.
Foshay, Arthur W., Tchrs. Col., Columbia University, New York, N.Y.
Fossieck, Theodore H., The Milne Sch., State Univ. of New York, Albany, N.Y.
Foster, E. M., Fresno State Col., 4021 Mt. Vernon Ave., Bakersfield, Calif.
Foster, Gordon, Merrick Hall, Univ. of Miami, Coral Gables, Fla.
Foster, Richard S., 324 Grace Ave., Newark, N.Y.
Fournier, Rev. Edmond A., 241 Pearson Ave., Ferndale, Mich.
Fowler, William, Ontario Inst. for Stud. in Educ., Toronto, Ont., Canada
Fowlkes, John Guy, 204 Educ. Bldg., Univ. of Wisconsin, Madison, Wis.
Fox, David J., 609 W. 114th St., New York, N.Y.
Fox, Marion W., 3200 Atlantic Ave., Atlantic City, N.J.
Fox, Robert S., 102 Univ. Sch., University of Michigan, Ann Arbor, Mich.
Frain, Thomas J., 1931 Brunswick Ave., Trenton, N.J.
Francis, Ida L., Public Schools, Somerville, N.J.
Frandsen, Arden N., Utah State University, Logan, Utah
Frank, Charlotte, 2005 Yates Ave., Bronx, N.Y.
Frankland, Elizabeth M., 512 Algoma Blvd., Oshkosh, Wis.
Franklin, Arthur J., Univ. of So. Louisiana, Lafayette, La.
Franklin, David L., 5742 S. Laurel, LaGrange, Ill.
Franklin, Ruby Holden, Roosevelt University, 430 S. Michigan Ave., Chicago, Ill.
Franks, Gene, Miami University, Oxford, Ohio
Franson, Arthur H., 50 N. Spring, LaGrange, Ill.
Franz, Evelyn B., Dept. of Educ., Trenton State College, Trenton, N.J.
Franzen, William L., Col. of Educ., Univ. of Toledo, Toledo, Ohio
Frase, H. Weldon, 1635 Hutchinson, S.E., Grand Rapids, Mich.

Fraser, Dorothy McClure, Hunter College, New York, N.Y.
Fraser, Hugh W., 32 Beckwith Ter., Rochester, N.Y.
Fraser, Rosemary, Miami University, Oxford, Ohio
Frasier, Vance C., 1921 Harrison Ave., Evanston, Ill.
Frazier, Melvin E., Indiana State University, Terre Haute, Ind.
Fred, Bernhart G., 108 McCormick Dr., DeKalb, Ill.
Frederick, William C., Shoreline School District, Seattle, Wash.
Fredman, Norman, 76-07 168th St., Flushing, N.Y.
Fredrick, James R., Arizona State College, Flagstaff, Ariz.
Freeberg, Howard, 207 Sixth Ave. East, West Fargo, N.D.
Freedman, Albert M., Pacific Univ., Forest Grove, Ore.
Freeman, Daniel M., R.D. 1, W. Springfield, Pa.
Freeman, Donald, 831 Crown Blvd., East Lansing, Mich.
Freeman, Kenneth H., RFD 1, Peru, Ill.
Freeman, Robert P., 406 Hollywood Ave., Hampton, Va.
Freeman, Ruges Richmond, Jr., 8027 Bennett Ave., St. Louis, Mo.
Fremont, Herbert, Queens College, Flushing, N.Y.
French, Henry P., 2 Bedford Way, Pittsford, N.Y.
French, William M., Muhlenberg College, Allentown, Pa.
Frerichs, Allen H., Northern Illinois University, DeKalb, Ill.
Fretwell, Elbert K., Jr., Pres., State Univ. Col., Buffalo, N.Y.
Freund, Evelyn, 5954 Guilford, Detroit, Mich.
Frey, Loraine, 1115 N. Hayes, Pocatello, Ida.
Frick, Herman L., Florida State University, Talahassee, Fla.
Frick, Ralph, 142 N. Harvey, Oak Park, Ill.
Fridlund, John V., 414 N. Elm St., Itasca, Ill.
Frieberg, Carter N., Loyola University, 820 N. Michigan Ave., Chicago, Ill.
Friedhoff, Walter H., Illinois State University, Normal, Ill.
Friedrich, Kurt, San Diego State College, San Diego, Calif.
Frisbie, Mrs. Babette, Gloversville Public Schools, Gloversville, N.Y.
Frisk, Jack L., Supt. of Schools, Yakima, Wash.
Froehlich, Gustave J., Bur. of Inst. Res., Univ. of Illinois, Urbana, Ill.
Frohnhoefer, Joseph J., Jr., State Univ. Col. at Buffalo, Buffalo, N.Y.
Froling, Raymond S., Nether Providence Sch. Dist., Wallingford, Pa.
Frost, Ralph J., Jr., Maine Twp. High School East, Park Ridge, Ill.
Frutchey, Fred P., U.S. Department of Agriculrure, Washington, D.C.
Frye, Richard M., Purdue University, Lafayette, Ind.
Fryer, Thomas W., Jr., Miami-Dade Junior College, Miami, Fla.
Fuglaar, Ollie B., Louisiana State University, Baton Rouge, La.
Full, Harold, 870 United Nations Plaza, New York, N.Y.
Fullagar, William A., Col. of Educ., Univ. of Rochester, Rochester. N.Y.
Fuller, R. Buckminster, Southern Illinois University, Carbondale, Ill.
Fullerton, Craig K., 2712 North 52nd St., Omaha, Neb.
Fulton, Helen L., 955 Campbell Rd., Houston, Texas
Fultz, Mrs. Jane N., Col. of Educ., Univ. of Hawaii, Honolulu, Hawaii
Funderburk, Earl C., Fairfax County Schools, Fairfax, Va.
Furey, Mary Z., 7926 Jackson Rd., Alexandria, Va.
Furlow, Mrs. Florine D., 2968 Collier Dr., N.W., Atlanta, Ga.
Furst, Philip W., 790 Riverside Dr., New York, N.Y.
Futch, Olivia, Woman's College, Furman University, Greenville, S.C.

Gabler, June, Mt. Clemens Sch. Dist., 167 Cass Ave., Mt. Clemens, Mich.
Gadbury, Mrs. Nada M., 2401 New York Ave., Muncie, Ind.
Gaetano, Mary Ann, Col. of Educ., Ohio University, Athens, Ohio
Gage, N. L., Sch. of Educ., Stanford University, Stanford, Calif.
Gaines, Berthera E., 4208 S. Galvez St., New Orleans, La.
Gaines, John C., State University of Tennessee, Nashville, Tenn.
Gaiter, Worrell G., Florida A. & M. University, Tallahassee, Fla.
Galbreath, Dorothy J., 3001 South Parkway, Chicago, Ill.
Gale, Ann V., 403 Jackson Ave., Glencoe, Ill.

Gale, Frederick, 20820 River Rd., Haney, B.C., Canada
Gallicchio, Francis A., 325 College Ave., Mt. Pleasant, Pa.
Gallington, Ralph O., Florida State University, Tallahassee, Fla.
Galloway, Geraldine, 111 Northwest Tenth St., Fairfield, Ill.
Galtere, Gordon R., Rt. 206, Red Lion, Vincentown, N.J.
Gambert, Charles A., 606 Sixth St., Niagara Falls, N.Y.
Gambino, Vincent, Dept. of Educ., Roosevelt University, Chicago, Ill.
Gamelin, Francis C., Augustana College, Rock Island, Ill.
Gandy, Frances C., 2597 Avery Ave., Memphis, Tenn.
Gannon, John T., Supt. of Schools, Eagle Grove, Iowa
Gans, Leo, 4300 West 62nd St., Indianapolis, Ind.
Gansberg, Lucille, 2255-C Goodrich St., Sacramento, Calif.
Gantz, Ralph M., Superintendent of Schools, New Britain, Conn.
Garbe, Lester, 2110 W. Marne Ave., Milwaukee, Wis.
Garbee, Frederick E., State Dept. of Educ., Los Angeles, Calif.
Garbel, Marianne, 6732 Crandon Ave., Chicago, Ill.
Garber, M. Delott, Central Connecticut State College, New Britain, Conn.
Gardiner, Robert J., Asst. Prin., Bakersfield H.S., Bakersfield, Calif.
Gardner, Harrison, 1007 Ravinia, West Lafayette, Ind.
Gardner, James E., 24450 Hatteras St., Woodland Hills, Calif.
Garetto, Lawrence A., 5162 Walnut Ave., Chino, Calif.
Garfinkel, Alan, 4946 Arbor Village Dr., Columbus, Ohio
Garinger, Elmer H., 2625 Briarcliff Pl., Charlotte, N.C.
Garland, Colden G., 223 Varinna Dr., Rochester, N.Y.
Garlich, Marvin O., 8901 McVicker Ave., Morton Grove, Ill.
Garoutte, Bill Charles, Univ. of California Medical Center, San Francisco, Calif.
Garrett, Charles G., 837 N. Cline St., Griffith, Ind.
Garrison, C. B., Supt. of Schools, Pine Bluff, Ark.
Garrison, Harry L., 4802 E. Mercer Way, Mercer Island, Wash.
Garrison, Martin B., Supt. of Schools, University City, Mo.
Garrity, William J., Jr., 45 Gaynos Dr., Bridgeport, Conn.
Gartrell, Callie, P.O. Box 33, Cheboygan, Mich.
Garvey, Reba, Allegheny College, Meadville, Pa.
Gaston, Don, Couns., New Rochelle High School, New Rochelle, N.Y.
*Gates, Arthur I., Tchrs. Col., Columbia University, New York, N.Y.
Gates, James O., Jr., East Cent. State Col., Ada, Okla.
Gathercole, F. J., Superintendent of Schools, Saskatoon, Sask., Canada
Gatti, Ora J., 20 Irving St., Worcester, Mass.
Gauerke, Warren E., 316 Merriweather Rd., Grosse Pointe Farms, Mich.
Gaunt, W. F., Sch. Dist. of Affton, 8309 Mackenzie Rd., Affton, Mo.
Gauvey, Ralph E., Roger Williams Jr. Col., Providence, R.I.
Gavin, Ann M., State College of Boston, Boston, Mass.
Gaynor, Alan K., 220 Sullivan St., Apt. 3-F, New York, N.Y.
Gazelle, Hazel N., 60 N. Auburn Ave., Sierra Madre, Calif.
Geckler, Jack W., Asst. Supt., Oak Ridge Schools, Oak Ridge, Tenn.
Geer, Owen C., Box 625, Tema, Ghana, West Africa
Geeslin, Robert H., Florida State Univ., Tallahassee, Fla.
Geigle, Ralph C., Superintendent of Schools, Reading, Pa.
Geiken, Lloyd A., Prin., Shorewood High School, Shorewood, Wis.
Geiss, Doris T., 117 Southern Blvd., Albany, N.Y.
Geitgey, Richard, Box 26, 797 N. Portage Rd., Doylestown, Ohio
Gelerinter, Alfred, Sch. Psych., Rochester City Schools, Rochester, N.Y.
Gellman, William, Jewish Vocational Service Library, Chicago, Ill.
Geng, George, Glassboro State College, Glassboro, N.J.
Gentry, George H., P.O. Box 30, Baytown, Tex.
George, Howard A., Northwest Missouri State College, Maryville, Mo.
George, John E., Sch. of Educ., Univ. of South Carolina, Columbia, S.C.
Georgiades, William, Univ. of Southern California, Los Angeles, Calif.
Georgiady, Nicholas P., 110 W. Bull Run Dr., Oxford, Ohio
Gephart, Woodrow W., Supt. of Schools, Jefferson, Ohio
Geraty, T. S., 7422 Hancock Ave., Takoma Park, Md.

Gerber, Wayne J., Bethel College, Mishawaka, Ind.
Gerhardt, Frank, 2355 S. Overlook Rd., Cleveland Heights, Ohio
Gerlach, Vernon S., Arizona State University, Tempe, Ariz.
Gerletti, John D., 1901 Mission St., South Pasadena, Calif.
Gerlock, D. E., Dept. of Educ., Valdosta State College, Valdosta, Ga.
Gernet, Herbert F., 414 Park Ave., Leonia., N.J.
Gesler, Harriet L., 70 Agnes Dr., Manchester, Conn.
Gest, Mrs. Viola S., P.O. Box 254, Seguin, Tex.
Getz, Howard G., Tulip Tree House No. 916, Bloomington, Ind.
Getzels, J. W., Dept. of Educ., University of Chicago, Chicago, Ill.
Geyer, John J., Sch. of Educ., Rutgers Univ., New Brunswick, N.J.
Ghalib, Hanna, P. O. Box 4638, Beirut, Lebanon
Gialas, George J., 1150 Wayland Ave., Cornwells Heights, Pa.
Gibbons, Constance M., 74 Franklin Ave., Oakville, Conn.
Gibbs, Edward Delmar, Univ. of Puget Sound, Tacoma, Wash.
Gibbs, Edward. III, 1145 Clinton Ter., South Plainfield, N.J.
Gibbs, Gloria Stanley, 501 East 32nd St., Chicago, Ill.
Gibbs, John Donald, 1147 S. Ash St., Moses Lake, Wash.
Gibbs, Wesley, Superintendent, Dist. No. 68, 9300 N. Kenton, Skokie, Ill.
Gibert, James M., Randolph-Macon Woman's College, Lynchburg, Va.
Gibson, Mrs. Kathryn Snell, Prairie View A & M College, Prairie View, Tex.
Gibson, R. Oliver, State University of New York, Buffalo, N.Y.
Giesecke, G. Ernst, Provost, University of Toledo, Toledo, Ohio
Giesy, John P., 1017 Blanchard, Flint, Mich.
Gilbert, Daniel, 8446 Major, Morton Grove, Ill.
Gilbert, Mrs. Doris Wilcox, 1044 Euclid Ave., Berkeley, Calif.
Gilbert, Floyd O., Minnesota State College, St. Cloud, Minn.
Gilbert, Harry B., Dept. of Educ., Fordham University, Bronx, N.Y.
Gilbert, Jerome H., 815 Ashbury, El Cerrito, Calif.
Gilbert, John H., Dept. of Educ., Monmouth College, West Long Branch, N.J.
Gilbert, William B., Onondaga Central School, Nedrow, N.Y.
Giles, LeRoy H., University of Dubuque, Dubuque, Iowa
Gili, Joe D., West Washington High School, Campbellsburg, Ind.
Gilk, Edwin John, P.O. Box 642, Columbia Falls, Mont.
Gilkey, Richard W., 5516 S.W. Seymour St., Portland, Ore.
Gill, Margaret, Mills College, Oakland, Calif.
Gilland, Thomas M., 504 S. Washington St., Greencastle, Pa.
Gillespie, Paul R., Miami-Dade Junior College, Miami, Fla.
Gillette, B. Frank. Superintendent of Schools, Los Gatos, Calif.
Gillham, Mrs. Lillie G., 3814 W. Rovey Ave., Phoenix, Ariz.
Gillis, Ruby, 6300 Grand River Ave., Detroit, Mich.
Gilmore, Douglas M., Central Michigan University, Mt. Pleasant, Mich.
Gimberndt, Ruth B., 380 Broadway, Jericho, N.Y.
Gimble, Mrs. Vernon S., 707 N. Main St., Cheboygan, Mich.
Gingerich, Julia B., 1408 Lewis, Des Moines, Iowa
Gjerstad, Olive, 653 Park Ave. W., Highland Park, Ill.
Glaess, Herman L., Concordia Teachers College. Seward. Neb.
Glaser, Robert, Res. & Dev. Cent., Univ. of Pittsburgh, Pittsburgh, Pa.
Glasman, Naftaly S., 412 North St., Oakland, Calif.
Glasow, Ogden L., P.O. Box 143, Macomb, Ill.
Glass, Olive Jewell, 3910 Latimer St., Dallas, Tex.
Glassman, Milton R., Kent State University, Kent, Ohio
Glatt, Charles A., Sch. of Educ., Ohio State Univ., Columbus, Ohio
Glaza, Stephen M., Superintendent of Schools, Marshall. Mich.
Glazer, Mrs. Carol J., 43-70 Kissena Blvd., Apt. 14E, Flushing, N.Y.
Glendenning, Donald E., 201 Rachael Ave., Ottawa 8, Ont., Canada
Glenn, J. Curtis, 1531 West 103rd St., Chicago, Ill.
Glicken, Irwin J., 2135 W. Walters, Northbrook, Ill.
Glock, Marvin D., Stone Hall, Cornell University, Ithaca, N.Y.
Glogau, Arthur H., Oregon College of Education, Monmouth, Ore.
Gobetz, Wallace, 540 East 22nd St., Brooklyn, N.Y.

Goble, Robert I., McGuffey No. 301, Miami University, Oxford, Ohio
Godfrey, Mary E., Pennsylvania State University, University Park, Pa.
Goebel, E. J., Supt., Archdiocese of Milwaukee, Milwaukee, Wis.
Goff, Howard J., P.O. Box 174, Moline, Ill.
Goff, Robert J., Univ. of Massachusetts, Amherst, Mass.
Gold, Charles E., 1418 E. Colton Ave., Redlands, Calif.
Gold, Louis L., 1030 Washington St., Indiana, Pa.
Gold, Milton J., Hunter College, 695 Park Ave., New York, N.Y.
Goldberg, Miriam L., Tchrs. Col., Columbia University, New York, N.Y.
Goldberg, Nathan, 75-47—196th St., Flushing, N.Y.
Goldhammer, Keith, 2929 Highland Way, Corvallis, Ore.
Goldman, Bert A., Sch. of Educ., Univ. of North Carolina, Greensboro, N.C.
Goldman, Harvey, University of Wisconsin, Milwaukee, Wis.
Goldman, Samuel, Sch. of Educ., Syracuse University, Syracuse, N.Y.
Goldner, Ralph H., Sch. of Educ., New York University, New York, N.Y.
Goldstein, Herbert, Yeshiva University, 55 Fifth Ave., New York, N.Y.
Goldstein, Sanford G., 115 Woodgate Terr., Rochester, N.Y.
Goltry, Keith, Dept. of Educ., Parsons College, Fairfield, Iowa
Gomberg, Adeline W., Beaver College, Glenside, Pa.
Gomes, Lawrence A., Jr., 4 Vincent Ave., Belmont, Mass.
Gonzalez, Alice M., University of Puerto Rico, Rio Piedras, Puerto Rico
Goo, Frederick J. K., c/o Bur. of Indian Affairs Sch., Barrow, Alaska
Good, Richard M., 12521 Eastbourne Dr., Silver Spring, Md.
Good, Warren R., 1604 Stony Run Dr., Northwood, Wilmington, Del.
Goodlad, John I., Sch. of Educ., Univ. of California, Los Angeles, Calif.
Goodman, John O., University of Connecticut, Storrs, Conn.
Goodman, Kenneth S., Wayne State Univ., Detroit, Mich.
Goodpaster, Robert L., University of Kentucky-Ashland Center, Ashland, Ky.
Goodside, Samuel, 504 Beach 139th St., Belle Harbor, L.I., N.Y.
Goodwin, William L., 136 Pine St., Lewisburg, Pa.
Googins, Duane G., 2964—116th Ave., N.W., Coon Rapids, Minn.
Goolsby, Thomas M., Florida State Univ., Tallahassee, Fla.
Goossen, Carl V., 108 Burton Hall, Univ. of Minnesota, Minneapolis, Minn.
Gordon, Alice S., 6532 N. Newgard Ave., Chicago, Ill.
Gordon, Mrs. Catherine J., 326 Wellesley Rd., Philadelphia, Pa.
Gordon, Irving, 5859 Beacon St., Pittsburgh, Pa.
Gordon, Ted E., 317 N. Lucerne, Los Angeles, Calif.
Gordon, William M., Sch. of Educ., Miami University, Oxford, Ohio
Gore, Jeffrey B., 5795-A N. Meadows Blvd., Columbus, Ohio
Gorham, Marion, Elem. Prin., Emerson School, Concord, Mass.
Gorman, Anna M., Col. of Educ., University of Kentucky, Lexington, Ky.
Gorman, William J., 219-40—93rd Ave., Queens Village, N.Y.
Gormley, Charles L., Dept. of Educ., Alabama College, Montevallo, Ala.
Gorn, Mrs. Janice L., New York University, Washington Sq., New York, N.Y.
Gorth, William P., P.O. Box 2337, Stanford, Calif.
Gorton, Harry B., L57 Alexander Dr., R.D. 2, Irwin, Pa.
Gotsch, Richard E., 8701 Mackenzie Rd., St. Louis, Mo.
Gottenid, Allan J., Comm. on Educ., ELCT, P.O. Box 412, Arusha, Tanzania
Gough, Jessie P., LaGrange College, LaGrange, Ga.
Gould, Norman M., Supt., Madera County Schools, Madera, Calif.
Gow, James S., 4519 Middle Rd., Allison Park, Pa.
Gowan, John Curtis, San Fernando Valley State Col., Northridge, Calif.
Gowin, D. Bob, Dept. of Educ., Stanford University, Stanford, Calif.
Graber, Eldon W., Dept. of Educ., Bluffton College, Bluffton, Ohio
Grabowski, A. A., 2512 Southport Ave., Chicago, Ill.
Graff, Orin B., Col. of Educ., University of Tennessee, Knoxville, Tenn.
Grahm, Milton L., Cambridge School of Business, Boston, Mass.
Grant, Eugene B., Northern Illinois University, DeKalb, Ill.
Grant, Wayman R. F., Booker T. Washington Junior High School, Mobile, Ala.

Grau, R. T., Clinton Public Schls., Box 110, Clinton, Iowa
Graven, John P., 7337-B South Shore Dr., Chicago, Ill.
Graves, Jack A., 6693 Burgundy St., San Diego, Calif.
Graves, Linwood D., 115 Leathers Circle, N.W., Atlanta, Ga.
Gray, C. William, Ohio University, Lancaster, Ohio
Gray, Dorothy, Dept. of Educ., Queens College, Flushing, N.Y.
Gray, Mary Jane, Loyola University, 820 N. Michigan, Chicago, Ill.
Gray, Ronald F., Canadian Nazarene Col., Winnipeg, Manitoba, Canada
Graybeal, William S., 1330 Massachusetts Ave., N.W., Washington, D.C.
Graye, Mytrolene L., 25 W. 132nd St., New York, N.Y.
Grayson, William H., Jr., 21-71—34th Ave., Long Island City, N.Y.
Green, C. M., 310 Hunting Hill Ave., Middletown, Conn.
Green, Donald Ross, 680 Dry Creek Rd., Monterey, Calif.
Green, Gertrude B., 100 W. Hickory Grove Rd., Bloomfield Hills, Mich.
Green, John A., Col. of Educ., Univ. of Idaho, Moscow, Idaho
Greenberg, Gilda M., University of Tennessee, Nashville, Tenn.
Greenberg, Mrs. Judith W., Sch. of Educ., City College, New York, N.Y.
Greenblatt, Edward L., 211 Calle de Arboles, Redondo Beach, Calif.
Greene, Bert I., 1111 Grant St., Ypsilanti, Mich.
Greene, Charles E., P.O. Box 185, East Side Sta., Santa Cruz, Calif.
Greene, Frank P., 707 Sumner Ave., Syracuse, N.Y.
Greene, John G., 1717 Flamingo Drive, Orlando, Fla.
Greene, Mrs. Maxine, 1080—5th Ave., New York, N.Y.
Greene, Mrs. Minnie S., 1121 Chestnut St., San Marcos, Tex.
Greenfield, Curtis O., 345 W. Windsor Ave., Phoenix, Ariz.
Greenman, Margaret H., P.O. Box 56, Goreville, Ill.
Greenwood, Edward D., Menninger Clinic, Box 829, Topeka, Kan.
Greenwood, Mrs. JoAnn, 403 Newdale Court, North Vancouver, B.C., Canada
Greer, Evelyn, Fayette County Schls., 400 Lafayette Dr., Lexington, Ky.
Greer, Mrs. Shirley J., 8441 E. Hubbell St., Scottsdale, Arizona
Gregg, Russell T., Sch. of Educ., University of Wisconsin, Madison, Wis.
Greif, Ivo P., Illinois State University, Normal, Ill.
Grein, Mary O., Dept. of Educ., Lock Haven St. Col., Lock Haven, Pa.
Greivell, Richard, Waukesha Public Schls., South Campus, Waukesha, Wis.
Grenda, Ted T., Box 189, Stone Ridge, N.Y.
Grennell, Robert L., State University College, Fredonia, N.Y.
Griffin, Gary A., 11915 Kiowa Ave., Los Angeles, Calif.
Griffing, Barry L., State Office Bldg., 217 W. First St., Los Angeles, Calif.
Griffith, Maurice F., Superintendent of Schools, Casper, Wyo.
Griffith, William S., Dept. of Educ., Univ. of Chicago, Chicago, Ill.
Griffiths, Daniel E., 54 Clarendon Rd., Scarsdale, N.Y.
Griffiths, John A., Superintendent of Schools, Monongahela, Pa.
Griffiths, Ruth, Massachusetts State College, Worcester, Mass.
Grimes, Wellington V., 4 Liberty Sq., Boston, Mass.
Grimsley, Mrs. Edith E., Danville, Ga.
* Grizzell, E. Duncan, 640 Maxwelton Ct., Lexington, Ky.
Groff, Frank E., New Hope-Solebury Joint School Dist., New Hope, Pa.
Groff, Warren H., 721 Highland Ave., Jenkintown, Pa.
Gromacki, Chester P., 1000 N. Lemon St., Fullerton, Calif.
Gronlund, Norman E., Col. of Educ., University of Illinois, Urbana, Ill.
Grose, Robert F., Amherst College, Amherst, Mass.
Gross, Neal, Grad. Sch. of Educ., Harvard University, Cambridge, Mass.
Gross, Robert D., 123 Ninth Ave., Iron River, Mich.
Grossman, Ruth H., Sch. of Educ., City College of N.Y., New York, N.Y.
Grossnickle, Foster E., 1116 Melbourne Ave., Melbourne, Fla.
Grotberg, Edith H., Dept. of Educ., American University, Washington, D.C.
Grover, Burton L., 706 N. 8th St., Manitowoc, Wis.
Groves, Vernon T., Olivet Nazarene College, Kankakee, Ill.
Gruber, Frederick C., Grad. Sch. of Educ., Univ. of Pa., Philadelphia, Pa.
Grudell, Regina C., 45 Chadwick Rd., Teaneck, N.J.

Guba, Egon G., NISEC, Indiana Univ., Bloomington, Ind.
Guckenheimer, S. N., Heath Area Vocational School, Heath, Ohio
Guditus, C. W., Dept. of Educ., Lehigh University, Bethlehem, Pa.
Guilford, Jerome O., 705 Searles Rd., Toledo, Ohio
Gulutsan, Metro, University of Alberta, Edmonton, Alba., Canada
Gunn, Jack G., 2828 Fifth Ave., Laurel, Miss.
Gunther, John F., 3 Cek Ct., Sayville, L.I., N.Y.
Gurr, Rev. John E., 1316 Peger Rd., Fairbanks, Alaska
Guss, Carolyn, R.R. 2, Box 139, Bloomington, Ind.
Gussner, William S., Superintendent of Schools, Jamestown, N.D.
Gustafson, A. M., Alice Vail Junior High Sch., 5350 E. 16th St., Tucson, Ariz.
Gustafson, Alma L., 1211 North 5th St., East Grand Forks, Minn.
Guszak, Frank J., Sutton Hall 432, University of Texas, Austin, Tex.
Guttchen, Robert S., 137-16 231st St., Jamaica, N.Y.
Gwynn, J. Minor, 514 North St., Chapel Hill, N.C.

Haage, Catherine M., College of New Rochelle, New Rochelle, N.Y.
Haas, Richard J., Jr., 119 Stubbs Dr., Trotwood, Ohio
Haberman, Martin, Dept. of Educ., Rutgers Univ., New Brunswick, N.J.
Hack, Walter G., Ohio State University, Columbus, Ohio
Hacking, Eleanor, 34 Hamlet St., Fairhaven, Mass.
Hackmann, Jane, 38 Signal Hill Blvd., East St. Louis, Ill.
Hackney, Ben H., Jr., 4618 Walker Rd., Charlotte, N.C.
Hadden, John F., 61 Rochester St., Bergen, N.Y.
Haddock, Thomas T., 7232 N. 12th Ave., Phoenix, Ariz.
Haffner, Hyman, 6229 Nicholson St., Pittsburgh, Pa.
Hagen, Donald E., 13028 Root Rd., Columbia Station, Ohio
Hagen, Elizabeth, Tchrs. Col., Columbia University, New York, N.Y.
Hager, Walter E., 4625 S. Chelsea Ln., Bethesda, Md.
Haggerson, Nelson L., 132 W. Balboa Dr., Tempe, Ariz.
Hagglund, Oliver C., Gustavus Adolphus College, St. Peter, Minn.
Hagstrom, Ellis A., 1330 Christmas Lane, N.E., Atlanta, Ga.
Hahn, Albert R., Veterans' Administration Hospital, Phoenix, Ariz.
Hahn, L. Donald, Western Illinois University, Macomb, Ill.
Haight, Wilbur T., 314 S. DuPont Blvd., Milford, Del.
Haimowitz, Clement, Box 134, Hillsboro Rd., Belle Mead, N.Y.
Halbert, Bernice, 204 Whaley, Marshall, Texas
Hale, Gifford G., Sch. of Educ., Florida State University, Tallahassee, Fla.
Hale, R. Nelson, State Teachers College, Slippery Rock, Pa.
Hales, Russell G., University of Utah, Salt Lake City, Utah
Haley, Charles F., Col. of Educ., Northeastern University, Boston, Mass.
Haley, Elizabeth, 1938 Channing Ave., Palo Alto, Calif.
Haley, Gerald J., 5625 N. Natoma Ave., Chicago, Ill.
Halfter, Mrs. Irma Theobald, 222 N. Grove Ave., Oak Park, Ill.
Hall, Barbara C., 2 Knollcrest Court, Normal, Ill.
Hall, Clarence L., Pacific Grove Unified Schl. Dist., Pacific Grove, Calif.
Hall, J. Floyd, 301 S. Harvey, Oak Park, Ill.
Hall, James A., Superintendent of Schools, Port Washington, N.Y.
Hall, John E., Jackson State College, Jackson, Miss.
Hall, John W., 7½ University Ave., Canton, N.Y.
Hall, Joseph I., 3333 Elston Ave., Chicago, Ill.
Hall, Keith A., Pennsylvania State Univ., University Park, Pa.
Hall, Morris E., Stephen F. Austin State Col., Nacogdoches, Texas
Hall, Robert H., Gulf Coast Junior College, Panama City, Fla.
Hall, Walter J., Jr., Haverford Senior High School, Havertown, Pa.
Hall, William Frank, 125 E. Lincoln St., Phoenix, Ariz.
Hall, William H., 291 E. 1st St., Corning, N.Y.
Hall, William P., Gaithersburg Senior High School, Gaithersburg, Md.
Hallenbeck, Edwin F., Roger Williams Junior College, Providence, R.I.
Hallgren, Ragnar F., Box 297, R.D. 1, Mount Joy, Pa.
Halligan, W. W., Jr., Converse College, Spartanburg, S.C.

Halliwell, Joseph W., 17 Mary Drive, Woodcliff Lake, N.J.
Halpern, Aaron, Clifton Senior High School, Clifton, N.J.
Hamada, Kiyoshi, Gakuin Univ., Chofu, Tokyo, Japan
Hamblen, Charles P., The Norwich Free Academy, Norwich, Conn.
Hamilton, Gene E., Edgewood Elementary School, Minneapolis, Minn.
Hamilton, Herbert M., Sch. of Bus. Adm., Miami Univ., Oxford, Ohio
Hamilton, Lester L., Box 5285, North Charleston, S.C.
Hammel, John A., 1275 Cook Rd., Grosse Pointe Woods, Mich.
Hammer, Eugene L., Dept. of Educ., Wilkes College, Wilkes-Barre, Pa.
Hammer, Viola, Redwood City Schools, Redwood City, Calif.
Hammock, Robert C., Col. of Educ., University of S. Alabama, Mobile, Ala.
Hammond, Granville S., 8321 Ashwood Dr., Alexandria, Va.
Hancock, Barbara, Consult. in Educ., Sacramento Co. Schools, Sacramento, Calif.
Hancock, Emily, Florida Southern College, Lakeland, Fla.
Handley, W. Harold, Granite School District, Salt Lake City, Utah
Hanigan, Levin B., Superintendent, Echobrook School, Mountainside, N.J.
Hanisits, Richard M., 8623 S. Kilpatrick Ave., Chicago, Ill.
Hanitchak, John J., Sch. of Educ., Indiana Univ., Bloomington, Ind.
Hanna, Alvis N., Prin., John Tyler School, Tyler, Tex.
Hanna, Paul R., Stanford University, Stanford, Calif.
Hannemann, Charles E., 931 E. 5th Ave., Lancaster, Ohio
Hannifin, Mrs. Blanche B., 5259 Strohm Ave., North Hollywood, Calif.
Hannon, Elizabeth F., 1432 S. Crescent Ave., Park Ridge, Ill.
Hannon, Joseph P., 108 I Escondido Village, Stanford, Calif.
Hansen, Calvin G., 550 Mountain View, Moab, Utah
Hansen, Dorothy Gregg, 722 Ivanhoe Rd., Tallahassee, Fla.
Hansen, G. G., Superintendent of County Schools, Aurora, Neb.
Hansen, Helge E., 15735 Andover Dr., Dearborn, Mich.
Hansen, Henry R., Sacramento State College, Sacramento, Calif.
Hansen, Maxine Mann, 1036 W. Shaw Ct., Whitewater, Wis.
Hansen, R. G., 2075 St. Johns Ave., Highland Park, Ill.
Hansen, Robert E., Cherry Hill High School, Cherry Hill, N.J.
Hansen, Stewart R., St. John's University, Collegeville, Minn.
Hanson, Donald L., 1709 Cherry Lane, Cedar Falls, Iowa
Hanson, Earl H., 3243 Ninth Ave., Rock Island, Ill.
Hanson, Eddie, Jr., Rt. No. 1, Box 1432, Auburn, Calif.
Hanson, Ellis G., 3810 Bel Aire Rd., Des Moines, Iowa
Hanson, Frances F., Sch. of Educ., Portland State Col., Portland, Ore.
Hanson, Gordon C., Wichita State Univ., Wichita, Kansas
Hanson, Ralph A., 5835 Kimbark Ave., Chicago, Ill.
Hanson, Wesley L., 3021 Washburn Pl., Minneapolis, Minn.
Hanuska, Julius P., 550 Edith Ave., Johnstown, Pa.
Happy, Kenneth F., State University College, Plattsburgh, N.Y.
Hardesty, Cecil D., 6401 Linda Vista Rd., San Diego, Calif.
Harding, James, Prin., Dunbar Elementary School, Dickinson, Tex.
Harding, Lowry W., Arps Hall, Ohio State University, Columbus, Ohio
Harding, Merle D., 421 Irving St., Beatrice, Neb.
Hardy, J. Garrick, Alabama State College, Montgomery, Ala.
Hargett, Earl F., 2124 Terrace Ave., Knoxville, Tenn.
Harlow, James G., Pres., West Virginia Univ., Morgantown, W.Va.
Harmon, Ruth E., 1720 Commonwealth Ave., West Newton, Mass.
Harnack, Robert S., Sch. of Educ., State Univ. Col., Buffalo, N.Y.
Harney, Paul J., University of San Francisco, San Francisco, Calif.
Harootunian, Berj, Sch. of Educ., Syracuse Univ., Syracuse, N.Y.
Harper, Ray G., Michigan State Univ., East Lansing, Mich.
Harrington, Edmund Ross, 309 Ave. E., Redondo Beach, Calif.
Harrington, Johns H., 1515 Greenbriar Rd., Glendale, Calif.
Harris, Albert J., 345 E. Grand St., Mt. Vernon, N.Y.
Harris, Ben M., 325 Sutton Hall, University of Texas, Austin, Texas
Harris, C. W., P.O. Box 1510, Deland, Fla.
Harris, Charles R., Box 4163, Midland, Texas

Harris, Claude C., 501 S. 30th St., Muskogee, Okla.
Harris, Dale B., Burrowes Bldg., Pennsylvania State Univ., University Park, Pa.
Harris, Eugene, Capitol Area Vocational School, Baton Rouge, La.
Harris, Fred E., Baldwin-Wallace College, Berea, Ohio
Harris, Janet D., 130 Boylston St., Chestnut Hill, Mass.
Harris, John W., Niles Township Comm. High School, Skokie, Ill.
Harris, Larry A., Col. of Educ., Indiana University, Bloomington, Ind.
Harris, Lewis E., 3752 N. Hight St., Columbus, Ohio
Harris, Mary Jo, Educ. Dept., Univ. of South. Alabama, Mobile, Ala.
Harris, Nelson H., Fayetteville College, Fayetteville, N.C.
Harris, Raymond P., Mt. Vernon Public Schools, Mt. Vernon, N.Y.
Harris, Robert B., Bryan Adams High School, Dallas, Tex.
Harris, Ruby Dean, Univ. Hall, University of California, Berkeley, Calif.
Harris, Theodore L., Dept. of Educ., Univ. of Puget Sound, Tacoma, Wash.
Harrison, C. Barker, 6143 Haddington St., Memphis, Tenn.
Harrison, Edward N., Park Terrace Apts., Jefferson City, Tenn.
Harrison, James P., 200 S. Providence Rd., Wallingford, Pa.
Harry, David P., Jr., 1659 Compton Rd., Cleveland Heights, Ohio
Harsanyi, Mrs. Audrey, Pennsylvania State University, University Park, Pa.
Harshbarger, Lawrence H., Educ. Dept., Ball State Univ., Muncie, Ind.
Hart, Mrs. Lawrence W., P.O. Box 14, Rock Falls, Ill.
Hart, Mary A., 28 McKesson Hill Rd., Chappaqua, N.Y.
Hart, Ruth M. R., 1100 Douglas Ave., Minneapolis, Minn.
Harting, Roger D., 4711 Orchard Ln., Columbia, Mo.
Hartley, Harold V., Jr., Clarion State Col., Clarion, Pa.
Hartley, James R., Univ. Extn., University of California, Riverside, Calif.
Hartsell, Horace C., Univ. of Texas, Dental Branch, Houston, Texas
Hartsig, Barbara A., California State College, Fullerton, Calif.
Hartstein, Jacob I., Kingsborough Community College, Brooklyn, N.Y.
Hartung, Maurice L., Dept. of Educ., University of Chicago, Chicago, Ill.
Hartwell, Mrs. Lois, Northern State Col., Aberdeen, S.D.
Hartzog, Ernest E., 5283 Chollas Pkwy., San Diego, Calif.
Harvey, Jasper, University of Alabama, University, Ala.
Harvey, Leonard, 258 Riverside Drive, New York, N.Y.
Harvey, Valerien, Univ. Laval, Quebec, Canada
Harwell, John Earl, Nicholls State Col., Thibodaux, La.
Hasenpflug, Thomas R., 600 Hunt Rd., Jamestown, N.Y.
Hash, Mrs. Virginia, State College of Iowa, Cedar Falls, Iowa
Haskew, Laurence D., Col. of Educ., University of Texas, Austin, Tex.
Haskins, Esther N., Box 4798, Carmel, Calif.
Hasman, Richard H., 61 Oakwood Ave., Farmingdale, N.Y.
Hastie, Reid, University of Minnesota, Minneapolis, Minn.
Hastings, Glen R., Dept. of Educ., State Col. of Iowa, Cedar Falls, Iowa
Hastings, Howard H., 255 W. Vermont, Villa Park, Ill.
Hastings, J. Thomas, Educ. Bldg., University of Illinois, Urbana, Ill.
Hatalsan, John W., 4184 Palisades Rd., San Diego, Calif.
Hatashita, Elizabeth S., 6510 Cielo Drive, San Diego, Calif.
Hatch, J. Cordell, Pennsylvania State University, University Park, Pa.
Hatch, Terrance E., Col. of Educ., Utah State University, Logan, Utah
Hatfield, Donald M., Dept. of Educ., University of California, Berkeley, Calif.
Haubrich, Vernon F., Sch. of Educ., Univ. of Wisconsin, Madison, Wis.
Hauer, Nelson A., Louisiana State University, Baton Rouge, La.
Haupt, Leonard R., 2801 Glenview Rd., Glenview, Ill.
Hauptfuehrer, Helen, 159 Norris Gym, Univ. of Minn., Minneapolis, Minn.
Hauschild, Mrs. J. R., 20528 Rhoda St., Woodland Hills, Calif.
* Havighurst, Robert J., Dept. of Educ., University of Chicago, Chicago, Ill.
Haweeli, Norman, Glenbrook H.S., 2300 Sherman, Northbrook, Ill.
Hawk, Travis L., University of Tennessee, Knoxville, Tenn.
Hawkins, Edwin L., Horace Mann High School, Little Rock, Ark.
Hawkinson, Mabel J., 11 Gregory St., Oswego, N.Y.
Hawley, Leslie R., 94 Walden Dr., RFD No. 1, Lakeview, Erie Co., N.Y.

Hawley, Ray C., Superintendent of County Schools, Ottawa, Ill.
Hayden, Alice H., Miller Hall, University of Washington, Seattle, Wash.
Hayden, James R., 166 William St., New Bedford, Mass.
Hayes, Allen P., 757 McKinley Ave., Auburn, Ala.
Hayes, Glenn E., California State College, Long Beach, Calif.
Hayes, Gordon M., Consult., State Dept. of Educ., Sacramento, Calif.
Hayes, Paul C., Supt. of Schools, 457 Sawyer Ct., Grove City, Ohio
Hayes, Robert B., Dept. of Pub. Instr., Harrisburg, Pa.
Haynes, Hubert Ray, 108 E. Tilden Dr., Brownsburg, Ind.
Hays, Albert Z., Abilene Christian College, Abilene, Tex.
Hays, Harry N., Supv. Prin., West Branch Area Sch. Dist., Morrisdale, Pa.
Hays, Warren S., 3218 N. Reno Ave., Tucson, Ariz.
Hayward, W. George, 27 Grant Ave., East Orange, N.J.
Hazell, Joseph W., 866 Gooding Dr., Albany, Calif.
Hazleton, Edward W., Bogan High School, Chicago, Ill.
Headd, Pearl Walker, Box 362, Tuskegee Institute, Ala.
Headley, Quentin, 130 N. Union, Bloomington, Ind.
Headley, Ross A., 80 Hauppauge Dr., Commack, N.Y.
Heagney, Genevieve, Towson State Col., Baltimore, Md.
Heald, James E., 4277 Tacoma Blvd., Okemos, Mich.
Heathers, Glen, University of Pittsburgh, Pittsburgh, Pa.
Heavenridge, Glen G., 5844 Gilman St., Garden City, Mich.
Hebeler, Jean R., University of Maryland, College Park, Md.
Heck, Theodore, St. Meinrad Seminary, St. Meinrad, Ind.
Hedden, George W., 1435 Twinridge Rd., Santa Barbara, Calif.
Hedges, William D., 529 Purdue, St. Louis, Mo.
Heding, Howard W., Col. of Educ., Univ. of Missouri, Columbia, Mo.
Heffernan, Helen, 3416 Land Park Dr., Sacramento, Calif.
Heger, Herbert K., 3020 Oaklawn St., Columbus, Ohio
Hegman, M. Marian, 332 South Ave., Medina, N.Y.
Heimann, Therese M., 2330 W. Lapham St., Milwaukee, Wis.
Heimberger, Mary J., Falk Lab Sch., Univ. of Pittsburgh, Pittsburgh, Pa.
Hein, William J., Mills College, Oakland, Calif.
Heinz, John A., California State Polytechnic College, San Luis Obispo, Calif.
Heise, Margaret A., 5361 Princeton Ave., Westminster, Calif.
Heisler, Florence, Dept. of Educ., Brooklyn College, Brooklyn, N.Y.
Heisner, H. Fred, Redlands Unified Sch. Dist., Redlands, Calif.
Heist, Paul H., 4606 Tolman Hall, Univ. of California, Berkeley, Calif.
Held, John T., 426 College Ave., Gettysburg, Pa.
Helge, Erich E., 1118 Sunrise Dr., Seward, Neb.
Heller, Melvin P., Dept. of Educ., Loyola University, Chicago, Ill.
Hellerich, Mahlon H., Wartburg College, Waverly, Iowa
Helmer, Robert D., Superintendent of Schools, Canandaigua, N.Y.
* Helms, W. T., 1109 Roosevelt Ave., Richmond, Calif.
Heltibridle, Mary E., 39 Sullivan St., Mansfield, Pa.
Heming, Hilton P., 12 Leonard Ave., Plattsburgh, N.Y.
Hemink, Lyle H., 4134 Trailing Dr., Williamsville, N.Y.
Hencley, Stephen P., 1505 Indian Hills Dr., Salt Lake City, Utah
Henderson, Edward, New York University, Washington Sq., New York, N.Y.
Henderson, Robert A., Col. of Educ., University of Illinois, Urbana, Ill.
Hendrick, Irving G., University of California, Riverside, Calif.
Hendrickson, Gordon, University of Cincinnati, Cincinnati, Ohio
Hendrix, Holbert H., Nevada Southern Univ., Las Vegas, Nev.
Hengesbach, Robert W., 7886 Munson Rd., Mentor, Ohio
Hengoed, James, Boston University, Boston, Mass.
Henion, Ethel S., 435 N. Central Ave., Ramsey, N.J.
Henjum, Arnold, University of Minnesota, Minneapolis, Minn.
Henle, R. J., 221 N. Grand Blvd., St. Louis, Mo.
Henry, Bailey Ray, Supt. of Schools, Farmington, Mo.
Henry, George H., Alison Hall, Univ. of Delaware, Newark, Del.
* Henry, Nelson B., 2665 Alta Glen Dr., Birmingham, Ala.

Hensarling, Paul R., Texas A. & M., University, College Station, Tex.
Hephner, Thomas A., Ohio State University, Columbus, Ohio
Herbst, Leonard A., 3550 Crestmoor Dr., San Bruno, Calif.
Herge, Henry C., USAID/Jamaica, Dept. of State, Washington, D.C.
Herget, George H., 2619 N.W. 11th Ave., Gainesville, Fla.
Herman, James A., 4325 Virgusell Circle, Carmichael, Calif.
Herman, Wayne L., Jr., Col. of Educ., Univ. of Maryland, College Park, Md.
Hermanowicz, Henry J., Illinois State University, Normal, Ill.
Herr, Ross, 3452 W. Drummond Pl., Chicago, Ill.
Herr, William A., 536 W. Maple St., Hazleton, Pa.
Herrington, Mrs. Evelyn F., Texas A. & I. Univ., Kingsville, Texas
Herrmann, D. J., College of William and Mary, Williamsburg, Va.
Hershberger, James K., 7 Grinnel Drive, Camp Hill, Pa.
Hershey, Gerald L., Sch. of Bus., Indiana University, Bloomington, Ind.
Hertling, James E., 921 Tulip Tree House, Bloomington, Ind.
* Hertzler, Silas, 1618 So. 8th St., Goshen, Ind.
Herz, Mort, 1864 Pattiz Ave., Long Beach, Calif.
Hesla, Arden E., Mankato State College, Mankato, Minn.
Heslep, Thomas R., Superintendent of Schools, Altoona, Pa.
Hess, Clarke F., Marshall College, Huntington, W.Va.
Hess, Glenn C., 44 W. Wheeling St., Washington, Pa.
Hesse, Alexander N., 90 Salisbury Ave., Garden City, L.I., N.Y.
Hetrick, Dr. J. B., Dept. of Educ., Edinboro State Col., Edinboro, Pa.
Hetzel, Walter L., Superintendent of Schools, Ames, Iowa
Heuer, Josephine C., 8444 Edna St., St. Louis, Mo.
Heusner, William W., Michigan State University, East Lansing, Mich.
Hickey, Bernard, 7 Digren Rd., Natick, Mass.
Hickey, Howard, Michigan State University, East Lansing, Mich.
Hickman, Lauren C., Nation's Schools, Chicago, Ill.
Hickner, Marybelle R., 1515½ Main St., Menomonie, Wis.
Hicks, Mrs. Aline Black, 812 Lexington St., Norfolk, Va.
Hicks, Samuel I., Inst. of Educ., Ahmadu Bello Univ., Zaria, Nigeria
Hicks, William R., Southern University, Baton Rouge, La.
Hidy, Mrs. Elizabeth Willson, Box 287, Gila Bend, Ariz.
Hiebert, Noble C., 504 Madison Ave., Plainfield, N.J.
Hieronymus, Albert N., East Hall, State Univ. of Iowa, Iowa City, Iowa
Hiers, Mrs. Turner M., 2951 S. Bayshore Dr., Coconut Grove, Fla.
Higdon, Claude J., 1106 S. Harvard Blvd., Los Angeles, Calif.
Higgins, F. Edward, 9524 S. Keeler Ave., Oak Lawn, Ill.
Highbarger, Mrs. Claire, 1045 N. Quentin Rd., Palatine, Ill.
Hightower, Emory A., 14 W. 64th St., New York, N.Y.
Hilgard, Ernest R., Dept. of Psych., Stanford University, Stanford, Calif.
Hill, Alberta D., Dept. of H. Econ., Iowa State University, Ames, Iowa
Hill, Charles E., 529 Fifth St., S.W., Rochester, Minn.
Hill, George E., Dept. of Educ., Ohio University, Athens, Ohio
Hill, Joe C., 3170 S.W. 8th St., E 505, Miami, Fla.
Hill, Joseph K., Downstate Medical Center, Brooklyn, N.Y.
Hill, Katherine E., Press 23, New York Univ., Washington Sq., New York, N.Y.
Hill, Norman J., 49 S. Lake Ave., Bergen, N.Y.
Hill, Richard, 2206 Haddington Road, St. Paul, Minn.
Hill, Suzanne D., Louisiana State University, New Orleans, La.
Hillerich, Robert L., 950 Huber Lane, Glenview, Ill.
Hillesheim, Rev. Francis E., 1130 W. Bridge St., Wausau, Wis.
Hillson, Maurie, 1208 Emerson Ave., Teaneck, N.J.
Hinds, Charles F., Murray State University Library, Murray, Ky.
Hinds, Jean, 3401 S. 39th St., Milwaukee, Wis.
Hinds, Lillian Ruth, 13855 Superior Rd., Cleveland, Ohio
Hindsman, Edwin, S.W. Educ. Dev. Corp., Commodore Perry Hotel, Austin, Tex.
Hineline, Edna C., Fac. of Educ., Macdonald College, Quebec, Canada
Hines, Vynce A., 1220 S.W. Ninth Rd., Gainesville, Fla.
Hinkle, Michael C., R.R. 6, Evergreen Dr., Crawfordsville, Ind.

Hintz, Edward R., Westwood Heights Schools, Flint, Mich.
Hipkins, Wendell C., 1311 Delaware Ave., S.W., Washington, D.C.
Hirsch, Mrs. Gloria T., 13121 Addison St., Sherman Oaks, Calif.
Hirst, Wilma E., 3458 Green Valley Rd., Cheyenne, Wyo.
Hitchcock, Catharine, 1837 E. Erie Ave., Lorain, Ohio
Hites, Christopher, 302 Portola Rd., Portola Valley, Calif.
Hitt, Harold H., 802 Lawson St., Midland, Tex.
Hittinger, Martha S., 12417 E. Beverly Dr., Whittier, Calif.
Ho, Thomas C. K., 72 Distler Ave., West Caldwell, N.J.
Hoagland, Robert M., 627 Houseman, La Canada, Calif.
Hoak, Duane C., 1031 Newbury St., Toledo, Ohio
Hobbie, Katherine E., State University College, Oneonta, N.Y.
Hobbs, Billy S., White House High School, White House, Tenn.
Hobbs, Earl W., Renton Sch. Dist., 1525 Fourth Ave., N., Renton, Wash.
Hobbs, Walter R., Roger Williams College, Providence, R.I.
Hochstetler, Ruth, 225 S. Nichols, Muncie, Ind.
Hock, Louise E., Sch. of Educ., New York Univ., New York, N.Y.
Hockwalt, Ronald W., 109 Los Feliz St., Oxnard, Calif.
Hodge, Harry F., P.O. Box 940, State University, Ark.
Hodge, William Carey, McKendree College, Lebanon, Ill.
Hodges, James G., 3856 Kenard Court, Columbus, Ohio
Hodges, Lawrence W., University of Montana, Missoula, Mont.
Hodges, Richard E., Grad. Sch. of Educ., Univ. of Chicago, Chicago, Ill.
Hodges, Ruth Hall, Morris Brown College, Atlanta, Ga.
Hodgins, George W., Paramus High School, Paramus, N.J.
Hodnett, Ruth Germann, Scott, Foresman & Co., Chicago, Ill.
Hoeffner, Karl, Prin., Wm. Hawley Atwell Junior High School, Dallas, Tex.
Hoekstra, S. Robert, 2215 Sylvan Ave., S.E., Grand Rapids, Mich.
Hoerauf, William E., 19990 Beaufait, Harper Woods, Mich.
Hoerning, Duane L., R.R. No. 1, Brussells, Wis.
Hoffman, Carl B., Abington Sch. Dist., Abington, Pa.
Hoffman, Matthew R., 180 Ridgeway Ave., Rochester, N.Y.
Hofstrand, John M., USAID/HR, Santo Domingo, Dominican Rep.
Hohl, George W., Superintendent of Schools, Waterloo, Iowa
Holda, Frederick W., 26 Hampden Rd., Monson, Mass.
Holden, A. John, Jr., 19-A Charlesbank Rd., Newton, Mass.
Holland, Benjamin F., Sutton Hall, University of Texas, Austin, Tex.
Holland, Donald F., 7251 N. Bell Ave., Chicago, Ill.
Holliday, Jay N., 10224 N. Wellen Ln., Spokane, Wash.
Hollis, Loye Y., Col. of Educ., University of Houston, Houston, Tex.
Holloway, George E., Jr., State Univ. of New York, Buffalo, N.Y.
Holm, Joy A., 104 Eisenhower Dr., Bloomington, Ill.
Holman, W. Earl, Jackson High School, 544 Wildwood Ave., Jackson, Mich.
Holmes, Daniel L., Willett School, Attleboro, Mass.
Holmes, Emma E., California State Col., Fullerton, Calif.
Holmes, Robert W., Windham College, Putney, Vt.
Holmquist, Emily, Indiana Univ. School of Nursing, Indianapolis, Ind.
Holt, Charles C., 228 S. St. Joseph St., South Bend, Ind.
Holton, Samuel M., University of North Carolina, Chapel Hill, N.C.
Homer, Francis R., 4800 Conshohocken Ave., Philadelphia, Pa.
Honeychuck, Joseph M., 2808 Parker Ave., Silver Spring, Md.
Hood, Edwin M., 19 Seneca Ave., White Plains, N.Y.
Hood, Evans C., Superintendent of Schools, Palestine, Tex.
Hood, W. R., 2627–29th St., S.W., Calgary, Alba., Canada
Hooker, Clifford P., University of Minnesota, Minneapolis, Minn.
Hooper, George J., 3631 S. Yorktown, Tulsa, Okla.
Hoops, Robert C., 76 Branch Ave., Red Bank, N.J.
Hoover, Erna B., Tennessee A. & I. State Univ., Nashville, Tenn.
Hoover, Louis H., 2304 Tenth Ave. So., Broadview, Ill.
Hopkins, Everett P., 1520 Pinecrest Rd., Durham, N.C.
Hopkins, Theresa, Educ'l. Spec., ERIC Clearinghouse, Urbana, Ill.

Hopmann, Robert P., Concordia Teachers College, River Forest, Ill.
Hoppock, Anne, State Department of Education, Trenton, N.J.
Horn, Ernest W., Indiana University, Bloomington, Ind.
Horn, Margaret, Concordia College, St. Paul, Minn.
Horn, Thomas D., Sutton Hall, University of Texas, Austin, Texas
Hornback, Mrs. May, Rt. 1, Old Sauk Rd., Middleton, Wis.
Hornburg, Mabel C., 118 Champlain Ave., Ticonderoga, N.Y.
Hornick, Sandra Jo, Dept. of Educ., Ohio State Univ., Columbus, Ohio
Horning, Leora N., University of Nebraska, Lincoln, Neb.
Horns, Mrs. Virginia, P.O. Box 2525, University, Ala.
Horrocks, John E., Ohio State University, Columbus, Ohio
Horsman, Ralph D., Supt., Mt. Lebanon Public Schools, Pittsburgh, Pa.
Horvat, John J., 825 East 8th Ave., Bloomington, Ind.
Horwich, Frances R., 400 E. Randolph St., Chicago, Ill.
Hosford, Marion H., Trenton State College, Trenton, N.J.
Hoskins, Charles W., 503 Sioux Lane, San Jose, Calif.
Hoskins, Glen C., Dept. of Educ., Southern Methodist Univ., Dallas, Texas
Hotaling, Mrs. Muriel P., 140 Jensen Rd. So., Vestal, N.Y.
Hotchkiss, James M., Sch. of Educ., Universty of Oregon, Eugene, Ore.
Hough, John M., Jr., Mars Hill College, Mars Hill, N.C.
Hough, Robert E., Arthur L. Johnson Regional High School, Clark, N.J.
Houghton, Charles J., 7401 S.W. 72nd Court, Miami, Fla.
Houghton, John J., Superintendent of Schools, Ferndale, Mich.
Houlahan, F. J., Catholic University of America, Washington, D.C.
Houle, Cyril O., Dept. of Educ., University of Chicago, Chicago, Ill.
Hounshell, Paul B., Univ. of North Carolina, Chapel Hill, N.C.
Householder, Daniel L., Sch. of Tech., Purdue University, Lafayette, Ind.
Houston, James J., Jr., Patterson State Col., Wayne, N.J.
Houston, John, Superintendent of Schools, Medford, Mass.
Houston, W. Robert, Col. of Educ., Mich. State University, East Lansing, Mich.
Houts, Earl, Westminster College, New Wilmington, Pa.
Hovet, Kenneth O., University of Maryland, College Park, Md.
Howard, Alexander H., Jr., Central Washington State Col., Ellensburg, Wash.
Howard, Daniel D., Pestalozzi-Froebel Tchrs. College, Chicago, Ill.
Howard, Elizabeth Z., Col. of Educ., Univ. of Rochester, Rochester, N.Y.
Howard, Glenn W., Queens College, Flushing, N.Y.
Howard, Harry, Box 765, Hillsborough, N.C.
Howard, Herbert, Prin., R. B. Walter Elem. School, Tioga, Pa.
Howd, M. Curtis, 200 Winthrop Rd., Muncie, Ind.
Howe, Robert W., Assoc. Prof., Ohio State University, Columbus, Ohio
Howe, Walter A., 6840 Eastern Ave., N.W., Washington, D.C.
Howell, Mrs. Mary N., Home Ec. Dept., Mars Hill College, Mars Hill, N.C.
Howell, Wallace J., Penfield Senior High School, Penfield, N.Y.
Howlett, Dorn, R.D. 1, Edinboro, Pa.
Howsam, Robert B., University of Houston, Houston, Tex.
Hoyle, Anne M., 3900 Hamilton St., L-103, Hyattsville, Md.
Hoyle, Dorothy, Temple University, Philadelphia, Pa.
Hoyt, Cyril J., Burton Hall, Univ. of Minnesota, Minneapolis, Minn.
Hrabi, James S., Dept. of Educ., 10820—98th Ave., Edmonton, Alba., Canada
Hrynyk, Nicholas P., 11010—142nd St., Edmonton, Alba., Canada
Hubbard, Ben, Illinois State University, Normal, Ill.
Huber, H. Ronald, 315 W. State St., Doylestown, Pa.
Hubert, Frank W. R., Texas A. & M. Univ., College Station, Texas
Huck, Charlotte S., Ohio State University, Columbus, Ohio
Huckins, Wesley, 2309 Randy Drive, Kettering, Ohio
Hudson, Bruce M., 11020 Cranston Ave., Livonia, Mich.
Hudson, Douglas, 3981 Greenmont Drive, Warren, Ohio
Hudson, L. P., 1225 Oakwood St., Bedford, Va.
Hudson, Robert I., University of Manitoba, Winnipeg, Manitoba, Canada
Hudson, Wilburn, Cordova High School, Cordova, Ala.

Huebner, Dwayne E., Tchrs. Col., Columbia University, New York, N.Y.
Huebner, Mildred H., So. Connecticut State Col., New Haven, Conn.
Huehn, Kermith S., Superintendent of County Schools, Eldora, Iowa
Huelsman, Charles B., Jr., 203 Selby Blvd., West, Worthington, Ohio
Huff, Jack F., 9030 Glorieta Ct., Elk Grove, Calif.
Hufford, G. N., 116 Seesen St., Joliet, Ill.
Hug, John W., 2090 Frank Rd., Columbus, Ohio
Hughes, John, 534 Michigan Ave., Evanston, Ill.
Hughes, Larry W., 4046 Towanda Trail, Knoxville, Tenn.
Hughes, McDonald, 1732—32nd Ave., Tuscaloosa, Ala.
Hughes, Thomas G., Ventura College, Ventura, Calif.
Hughes, Thomas M., 990 Brower Rd., Memphis, Tenn.
Hughes, Vergil H., San Jose State College, San Jose, Calif.
Hughes, Msgr. William A., Supt., Diocese of Youngstown, Youngstown, Ohio
Hughson, Arthur, 131 East 21st St., Brooklyn, N.Y.
Hulbert, Dolores S., 16301 Lassen St., Sepulveda, Calif.
Hull, J. H., Supt. of Schools, Torrance, Calif.
Hult, Esther M., Dept. of Educ., State College of Iowa, Cedar Falls, Iowa
Hulteen, Curtis D., Box 20-D, R.R. 2, Richmond, Ky.
Hultgren, Robert B., 708 Tana Lane, Joliet, Ill.
Humelsine, Martha, Roberts Wesleyan College, North Chili, N.Y.
Hummel, Mrs. Leonore B., Paterson State College, Wayne, N.J.
Humphrey, Charles F., 6001 Berkeley Dr., Berkeley, Mo.
Humphrey, G. C., 316 Fraser Dr. East, Mesa, Ariz.
Hunkins, Francis P., University of Washington, Seattle, Wash.
Hunsicker, C. L., Mansfield State College, Mansfield, Pa.
Hunt, Dorothy D., 2000 East 46th St., N., Kansas City, Mo.
Hunt, Herold C., Grad. Sch. of Educ., Harvard University, Cambridge, Mass.
Hunt, William A., Dept. of Psych., Loyola University, Chicago, Ill.
Hunter, Eugenia, Woman's Col., Univ. of North Carolina, Greensboro, N.C.
Hunter, James J., Jr., USAID, Rio de Janeiro, SDS, APO New York
Hunter, Richard D., Prin., Washington Jr. High School, Olympia, Wash.
Hunter, Robert W., Grambling College, Grambling, La.
* Huntington, Albert H., 736 Fairview Ave., Webster Groves, Mo.
Huntington, John F., Miami Univ., Oxford, Ohio
Hupper, Richard D., 509—18th St., Apt. 135, Greeley, Colo.
Hurd, Blair E., 4900 Heatherdale Lane, Carmichael, Calif.
Hurd, Paul DeH., Sch. of Educ., Stanford University, Stanford, Calif.
Hurlburt, Lydia Delpha, 311 Richmond, S.E., Salem, Ore.
Hurt, E. L., Jr., Gragg Junior High School, Memphis, Tenn.
Hurt, Mary Lee, U.S. Bureau of Research, Washington, D.C.
Huser, Mary K., 104 Eisenhower Dr., Bloomington, Ill.
Husk, William L., Dept. of Educ., Univ. of Louisville, Louisville, Ky.
Husmann, John L., 256 Ash St., Crystal Lake, Ill.
Huss, Francis C., 4655 Parker Rd., Florissant, Mo.
Husson, Chesley H., Husson College, 157 Park St., Bangor, Me.
Husted, Inez M., P.O. Box 1165, Kingston, Pa.
Husted, Vernon L., Supt., Armstrong Twp. High School, Armstrong, Ill.
Hutchison, James M., 26904 Grayslake Rd., Palos Verdes Peninsula, Calif.
Hutson, Percival W., University of Pittsburgh, Pittsburgh, Pa.
Hutto, Jerome A., Los Angeles State College, Los Angeles, Calif.
Hutton, Duane E., Sch. of Educ., Syracuse University, Syracuse, N.Y.
Hutton, Harry K., Pennsylvania State University, University Park, Pa.
Hyer, Anna L., 7613 Wiley Dr., Lorton, Va.
Hyman, Ronald, Rutgers University, New Brunswick, N.J.
Hyram, George H., 4092 Fieldstone Dr., Florissant, Mo.

Iannacone, George, Supt. of Schools, Palisades Park, N.J.
Iannaccone, Laurence, 10 Donnybrook Dr., Demarest, N.J.
Iglesias-Borges, Ramon, P.O. Box 226, San Lorenzo, Puerto Rico
Igo, Robert V., Pennsylvania State University, University Park, Pa.

Ihrman, Donald L., Superintendent of Schools, Holland, Mich.
Ilowit, Roy, C. W. Post College, Greenvale, L.I., N.Y.
Imbriano, Louis A., Revere Public Schools, Revere, Mass.
Imes, Orley B., 3985 La Cresenta Rd., El Sobrante, Calif.
Imhoff, Myrtle M., California State College, Fullerton, Calif.
Imura, Harry S., University of California, Berkeley, Calif.
Inabnit, Darrell J., Sacramento State College, Sacramento, Calif.
Incardona, Joseph S., 325 Busti Ave., Buffalo, N.Y.
Ingebritson, Kasper I., 2790 Sunny Grove Ave., Arcata, Calif.
Ingle, Robert, 5321 N. Hollywood, Whitefish Bay, Wis.
Ingram, Margaret H., East Carolina College, Greenville, N.C.
Ingrelli, Anthony V., University of Wisconsin-Milwaukee, Milwaukee, Wis.
Inlow, Gail M., Sch. of Educ., Northwestern University, Evanston, Ill.
Inskeep, James E., Jr., San Diego State College, San Diego, Calif.
Ireland, Robert S., 141 Breckenridge, Oakbrook, Ill.
Irsfeld, H. L., Superintendent of Schools, Mineral Wells, Tex.
Irving, James Lee, 5713 Ogontz Ave., Philadelphia, Pa.
Irwin, Alice M., Dept. of Spec. Classes, Public Schls., New Bedford, Mass.
Irwin, Mrs. Norma J., 404 H Educ. Bldg., Kent State University, Kent, Ohio
Irzarry, Casandra Rivera de, 1628 Ave., Central Capara Terrace, Puerto Rico
Isaacs, Ann F., Natl. Assn. Gifted Children, Cincinnati, Ohio
Isacksen, Roy O., Hazel Pk. Jr. H.S., 1140 White Bear Ave., St. Paul, Minn.
Isenberg, Robert M., 3117 Helsel Dr., Silver Spring, Md.
Ishimatsu, Tomiye, Col. of Nursing, Univ. of Utah, Salt Lake City, Utah
Israel, Benjamin L., 2560 Linden Blvd., Brooklyn, N.Y.
Ives, Josephine Piekarz, New York University, New York, N.Y.
Ivie, Claude M., Div. of Curric., State Dept. of Educ., Atlanta, Ga.
Ivins, George H., Roosevelt Univ., 430 S. Michigan Ave., Chicago, Ill.
Ivins, Wilson H., Col. of Educ., Univ. of New Mexico, Albuquerque, N.M.
Izzo, Raymond J., 12 Girard Rd., Winchester, Mass.

Jacklin, William, 411 E. 17th St., Lombard, Ill.
Jackson, Bryant H., Illinois State University, Normal, Ill.
Jackson, Philip W., Dept. of Educ., Univ. of Chicago, Chicago, Ill.
Jackson, Ronald B., 5 Gibson Rd., Lexington, Mass.
Jackson, Thomas A., Florida A. & M. Univ., Tallahassee, Fla.
Jacobs, J., 26141 Schoolcraft Rd., Detroit, Mich.
Jacobs, John F., 12299 Univ. Stat., Gainesville, Fla.
Jacobs, Robert, American Embassy, APO San Francisco, Calif.
Jaeckel, Solomon P., University of Hawaii, Honolulu, Hawaii
Jaeger, Alan Warren, 10220 Dale Dr., San Jose, Calif.
Jaeger, Eloise M., 158 Morris Gym, Univ. of Minnesota, Minneapolis, Minn.
Jaeger, Herman F., Box 10, Grandview, Wash.
Jaffarian, Sara, 251 Waltham St., Lexington, Mass.
Jahns, Irwin R., Florida State Univ., Tallahassee, Fla.
James, C. Rodney, 1687 Guilford Rd., Columbus, Ohio
James, Carl A., Superintendent of Schools, Emporia, Kan.
James, Jo Nell, University of S. Mississippi, Hattiesburg, Miss.
James, Louise, 4015 Lemon St., Riverside, Calif.
* James, Preston E., Dept. of Geog., Syracuse University, Syracuse, N.Y.
James, W. Raymond, 9 Bugbee Rd., Oneonta, N.Y.
Jameson, Sanford C., Reg. Dir., Col. Entr. Exam. Brd., Evanston, Ill.
Jansen, Udo H., Tchrs. Col., Univ. of Nebraska, Lincoln, Neb.
*Jansen, William, 900 Palmer Rd., Bronxville, N.Y.
Jansic, Anthony F., Educ. Clinic, City College of New York, New York, N.Y.
Jardine, Alex, 2105—19th Ave., Greeley, Colo.
Jarrell, George R., P.O. Box 3283, Charleston, S.C.
Jarvie, Lawrence L., Pres., Fashion Inst. of Tech., New York, N.Y.
Jarvis, Mrs. Elizabeth O., Bayview House, R.R. 2, Hamilton, Ont., Canada
Jarvis, Galen M., 9040 Kostner Rd., Skokie, Ill.

Jason, Hilliard, Col. of Med., Michigan State Univ., East Lansing, Mich.
Jaspen, Nathan, New York University, New York, N.Y.
Jeffers, Jay W., 931 Franklin Ave., Las Vegas, Nev.
Jefferson, Henry E., 4511 Don Tomaso Drive, Los Angeles, Calif.
Jefferson, James L., 866 Lincoln St., S.W., Birmingham, Ala
Jeffries, Thomas S., Sch. of Educ., Univ. of Louisville, Louisville, Ky.
Jelinek, James J., Col. of Educ., Arizona State University, Tempe, Ariz.
Jellins, Miriam H., 2849 Dale Creek Dr., N.W., Atlanta, Ga.
Jenkins, Clara Barnes, St. Paul's College, Lawrenceville, Va.
Jenkins, David S., Supt., Anne Arundel County Schools, Annapolis, Md.
Jenkins, Ernest W., Box 70, Fullerton, Neb.
Jenkins, James J., University of Minnesota, Minneapolis, Minn.
Jenkins, Jerry Allen, Sch. of Educ., Indiana State Univ., Terre Haute, Ind.
Jenkins, Offa Lou, Marshall University, Huntington, W.Va.
Jenkins, Walter D., 712 Cactus Lane, Las Vegas, Nev.
Jenks, William F., Holy Redeemer College, Washington, D.C.
Jenness, L. S., Forest View High School, Arlington Heights, Ill.
Jensen, Arthur M., Tuttle School, 1042—18th Ave., Minneapolis, Minn.
Jensen, Arthur R., University of California, Berkeley, Calif.
Jensen, Esther M., University of Wisconsin, Milwaukee, Wis.
Jensen, Gale E., 3055 Lakewood Dr., Ann Arbor, Mich.
Jensen, Grant W., Kern Jt. Union H.S. Dist., Bakersfield, Calif.
Jenson, Dean, Bowling Green State University, Bowling Green, Ohio
Jenson, T. J., 1024 Lyn Rd., Bowling Green, Ohio
Jeremiah, James T., Pres., Cedarville Col., Cedarville, Ohio
Jess, C. Donald, Superintendent of Schools, Bergenfield, N.J.
Jetton, Clyde T., 720 Amherst, Abilene, Tex.
Jewell, R. Ewart, Superintendent of Schools, 547 Wall St., Bend, Ore.
Jewett, Mary Jane, 9 Lincoln Place, New Platz, N.Y.
Jex, Frank B., Dept. of Educ. Psych., Univ. of Utah, Salt Lake City, Utah
Jinks, Elsie H., 1597 Lochmoor Blvd., Grosse Pointe Woods, Mich.
Jobe, Mrs. Mildred, Moffat County High School, Craig, Colo.
John, Martha A., Sch. of Educ., Boston Univ., Boston, Mass.
Johns, Edward B., Dept. of P.E., University of California, Los Angeles, Calif.
Johns, O. D., Col. of Educ., Univ. of Oklahoma, Norman, Okla.
Johns, Mrs. Thomas L., 9000 Breezewood Ter., Greenbelt, Md.
Johnsen, E. Peter, Col. of Educ., Univ. of Rochester, Rochester, N.Y.
Johnson, Mrs. Andrew L., 101 E. 14th Ave., Apt. L, Columbus, Ohio
Johnson, B. Lamar, Sch. of Educ., Univ. of California, Los Angeles, Calif.
Johnson, Calvin T., Mt. Baker Junior-Senior High School, Deming, Wash.
Johnson, Claudine, 112-39—175th St., Jamaica, N.Y.
Johnson, Dale A., 1318 Gibbs Ave., St. Paul Minn.
Johnson, Dale L., Dept. of Psych., University of Houston, Houston, Tex.
Johnson, Mrs. Dorothea N., 317 Whitman Blvd., Elyria, Ohio
Johnson, Dorothy E., Ball State University, Muncie, Ind.
Johnson, Mrs. Dorothy K., 7 Dalston Circle, Lynbrook, N.Y.
Johnson, Douglas, Jr., 707 E. 14th St., Panama City, Fla.
Johnson, Douglas A., 3750 Esperanzo Dr., Sacramento, Calif.
Johnson, Eleanor M., Box 360, Middletown, Conn.
Johnson, Forbes R., 122 Evans St., Iowa City, Ia.
Johnson, Frances Joan, 390 Fifth St., Prairie Du Sac, Wis.
Johnson, G. Orville, Col. of Educ., Ohio State University, Columbus, Ohio
Johnson, George L., Lincoln University of Missouri, Jefferson City, Mo.
Johnson, Gladys V., 3229—4th Ave., South, Great Falls, Mont.
Johnson, Harry C., Duluth Branch, Univ. of Minnesota, Duluth, Minn.
Johnson, Homer M., Dept. of Educ. Admin., Utah State Univ., Logan, Utah
Johnson, Irwin T., Col. of Educ., Univ. of Wyoming, Laramie, Wyo.
Johnson, J. O., Central Jr. H.S., Rochester, Minn.
Johnson, Jasper H., Whitworth College, Spokane, Wash.
Johnson, John L., 805 S. Crouse Ave., Syracuse, N.Y.
Johnson, Leonard E., Prin., Bugbee Sch., West Hartford, Conn.

Johnson, Lois V., California State Col., Los Angeles, Calif.
Johnson, Loren W., 37 Eglantine, Pennington, N.C.
Johnson, Margaret E., Alpine School District, American Fork, Utah
Johnson, Mrs. Marjorie Seddon, 61 Grove Ave., Flourtown, Pa.
Johnson, Mrs. Mary Jane, 275 Clinton Ave., Brooklyn, N.Y.
Johnson, Olive Lucille, 1925 Thornwood Ave., Wilmette, Ill.
Johnson, Paul E., Livonia Public Schools, Livonia, Mich.
Johnson, Paul O., Salem H.S., Geremonty Dr., Salem, N.H.
Johnson, Philip E., 53 Front St., Bath, Me.
Johnson, Robert Leonard, 2500 South 118th St., West Allis, Wis.
Johnson, Roger E., 218 Park Ridge Ave., Temple Terrace, Fla.
* Johnson, Roy Ivan, 2333 Southwest Eighth Dr., Gainesville, Fla.
Johnson, Theodore D., 5236 N. Bernard St., Chicago, Ill.
Johnson, Valdimar K., University of Victoria, Victoria, B.C., Canada
Johnson, Walter F., Col. of Educ., Michigan State Univ., East Lansing, Mich.
Johnson, Walter R., Libertyville High School, Libertyville, Ill.
Johnston, Aaron M., Col. of Educ., Univ. of Tennessee, Knoxville, Tenn.
Johnston, Edgar G., 2301 Vinewood Ave., Ann Arbor, Mich.
Johnston, Lillian B., 538 W. Vernon Ave., Phoenix, Ariz.
Johnston, William R., 1241 Satinwood Lane, Whitewater, Wis.
Jones, Annie Lee, University of North Carolina, Chapel Hill, N.C.
Jones, Clyde A., University of Connecticut, Storrs, Conn.
Jones, Daisy M., Sch. of Educ., Arizona State University, Tempe, Ariz.
Jones, Dilys M., 316 S. Fayette St., Shippensburg, Pa.
Jones, Donald W., 508 W. North St., Muncie, Ind.
Jones, Earl, Texas A and M University, Bldg. C, Bryan, Tex.
Jones, Elvet Glyn, Western Washington State Col., Bellingham, Wash.
Jones, Harvey E., 104 Lee Avenue, Tahlequah, Okla.
Jones, Henry W., Western Washington State College, Bellingham, Wash.
Jones, Howard Robert, State University of Iowa, Iowa City, Iowa
Jones, Jack J., Supt. of Schools, Borrego Springs, Calif.
Jones, John E., University of Oregon, Eugene, Ore.
Jones, Kenneth G., State University College, Oswego, N.Y.
Jones, Lloyd Meredith, State University of New York, Farmingdale, N.Y.
Jones, Mildred L., Box 272, Macdonald College, Quebec, Canada
Jones, Nevin, Prin., Model School, Box 67, Shannon, Ga.
Jones, Olwen M., Fox Run Lane, Greenwich, Conn.
Jones, Richard N., Carroll Rd., Monkton, Md.
Jones, Richard V., Jr., Stanislaus State College, Turlock, Calif.
Jones, Robert William, Lincoln Community High School, Lincoln, Ill.
Jones, Ruth G., 3938 Walnut Ave., Lynwood, Calif.
Jones, Vyron Lloyd, R. 7, Box 346, Terre Haute, Ind.
Jones, Wendell P., Sch. of Educ., Univ. of California, Los Angeles, Calif.
Jones, William E., California State College, Hayward, Calif.
Joneson, Della, 1040 State St., Ottawa, Ill.
Jongsma, Eugene A., 913 Jefferson St., Valparaiso, Ind.
Jonsson, Harold, Div. of Educ., San Francisco State Col., San Francisco, Calif.
Jordan, A. B., 5811 Riverview Blvd., St. Louis, Mo.
Jordan, Benjamin W., Educ. Bldg., Wayne State Univ., Detroit, Mich.
Jordan, Beth C., Virginia Polytechnic Institute, Blacksburg, Va.
Jordan, Lawrence V., West Virginia State College, Institute, W.Va.
Jordan, Ralph, State University College, Brockport, N.Y.
Joselyn, Edwin G., 4068 Hampshire Ave., N., Minneapolis, Minn.
Joy, Donald M., Light & Life Press, Winona, Ind.
Joyner, Judith R., University of South Carolina, Columbia, S.C.
Joynt, Denis, University of Papua and New Guinea, Boroko, Papua
Juan, K. C., Fisk University, Nashville, Tenn.
Judenfriend, Harold, 363 Beech Spring Rd., South Orange, N.J.
Judy, Mrs. Earleen W., 307 Deer Trail Rd., Reynoldsburg, Ohio
Julstrom, Eva, 7647 Colfax Ave., Chicago, Ill.
June, Elmer D., 619 Bamford Rd., Cherry Hill, N.J.

Junge, Charlotte W., Col. of Educ., Wayne University, Detroit, Mich.
Junker, Margaret, 9138 S. Claremont Ave., Chicago, Ill.
Jurjevich, J. C., Jr., 1844 74th Ave., Elmwood Park, Ill.
Justman, Joseph, Sch. of Educ., Fordham Univ., New York, N.Y.
Juvancic, William A., Eli Whitney Elem. Sch., Chicago, Ill.

Kaar, Mrs. Galeta M., 7050 Ridge Ave., Chicago, Ill.
* Kaback, Goldie Ruth, 375 Riverside Dr., New York, N.Y.
Kabrud, Margaret J., Univ. of North Dakota, Ellendale Cent., Ellendale, N.D.
Kacik, Terrence D., Rt. 18, Cedar Hill Rd., Pottstown, Pa.
Kaffer, Roger L., St. Charles Borromeo Seminary, Lockport, Ill.
Kahn, Albert S., Sch. of Educ., Boston University, Boston, Mass.
Kahnk, Donald L., 720 East Ninth St., Fremont, Neb.
Kahrs, Mary V., Mankato State College, Mankato, Minn.
Kairies, Eugene B., P.O. Box 354, Garrett Park, Md.
Kaiser, Eldor, 543 Iles Park Pl., Springfield, Ill.
Kalfas, Henry J., 8423 Richmond Ave., Niagara Falls, N.Y.
Kalina, David L., 288 Bay 38 St., Brooklyn, N.Y.
Kalish, Thomas F., 140 Trailsway, Madison, Wis.
Kallenbach, W. Warren, San Jose State College, San Jose, Calif.
Kalme, Albert P., West Virginia State Col., Institute, W.Va.
Kamil, Irving, 885 Bolton Ave., Bronx, N.Y.
Kandyba, Bernard S., 9403 N. Parkside Dr., Des Plaines, Ill.
Kane, Dermott P., 1300 West 97 Pl., Chicago, Ill.
Kane, Elmer R., 7530 Maryland Ave., Clayton, Mo.
Kane, Ewald, 6451 Columbia Rd., Olmsted Falls, Ohio
Kane, James L., Stratford School, Garden City, L.I., N.Y.
Kantor, Bernard R., 117 S. Poinsettia Pl., Los Angeles, Calif.
Kaplan, Lawrence, 65 Clover Ln., Lido Beach, N.Y.
Kaplan, Louis, 111 Via Monte de Oro, Redondo Beach, Calif.
Kaplan, Sandra N., 310 S. Almont Dr., Apt. 309, Los Angeles, Calif.
Karlin, Robert, Dept. of Educ., Queens College, Flushing, N.Y.
Karlsen, Bjorn, Sonoma State Col., Rohnert Park, Calif.
Karr, Johnston T., Dept. of Pub. Instr., State House, Indianapolis, Ind.
Kasdon, Lawrence M., 13 W. 13th St., New York, N.Y.
Kashuba, Michael, 920 Corbett Ave., Scranton, Pa.
Kass, Corrine E., 1216 E. Helen, Tucson, Ariz.
Kata, Joseph J., Redbank Valley Joint Schools, New Bethlehem, Pa.
Katenkamp, Theodore W., Jr., 9128 Bengal Rd., Randallstown, Md.
Katz, Mrs. Florine, Educ. Clinic, City College, New York, N.Y.
Katz, Joseph, University of British Columbia, Vancouver, B.C., Canada
Kauffman, Merle M., Col. of Educ., Bradley University, Peoria, Ill.
Kaufman, Jennie M., 21 N. Fourth St., Grand Haven, Mich.
Kaulfers, Walter V., University of Illinois, Urbana, Ill.
Kavanaugh, J. Keith, 1639 So. Maple Ave., Berwyn, Ill.
Kaya, Esin, New York University, Washington Sq., New York, N.Y.
Kean, John M., Box 7, George Peabody College, Nashville, Tenn.
Keane, John M., 4148 W. 82nd Pl., Chicago, Ill.
Kearl, Jennie W., State Department of Education, Salt Lake City, Utah
Kearney, George G., Rt. No. 1, Box 1108, Morgan Hill, Calif.
Keck, Winston B., Westfield State College, Westfield, Mass.
Keefer, Daryle E., Southern Illinois University, Carbondale, Ill.
Keesling, James W., 5721 S. Kimbark Ave., Chicago, Ill.
Kehas, Chris D., Claremont Graduate School, Claremont, Calif.
Keislar, Evan R., University of California, Los Angeles, Calif.
Keithley, Perry G., 2202 Deane Dr., Pullman, Wash,
Keleher, Gregory C., St. Bernard College, St. Bernard, Ala.
* Keliher, Alice V., Wheelock College, Boston, Mass.
Kelleher, William J., Hirsch High School, Chicago, Ill.
* Keller, Franklin J., 333 E. Mosholu Pkwy., New York, N.Y.

Kingsley, Iva Marie, Box 157, Bellmont Rur. Sta., Flagstaff, Arizona
Kinlin, J. F., 44 Eglinton Ave., W., Toronto, Ont., Canada
Kinsellar, Frances M., Rye St., Broad Brook, Conn.
* Kinsman, Kephas Albert, 2009 Appleton St., Long Beach, Calif.
Kintzer, Frederick C., University of California, Los Angeles, Calif.
Kinyon, Charles W., Wheatland-Chili Central High School, Henrietta, N.Y.
Kinzer, John R., 5756 East 6th St., Tucson, Arizona
Kinzer, Suzanne M., 3 S. Main St., Pittsford, N.Y.
Kirby, Inabell T., 2002 E. Main St., Decatur, Ill.
Kirchhaefer, Esther, Illinois State University, Normal, Ill.
Kirchman, Mrs. Rose, Jamaica High School, Jamaica, N.Y.
Kirk, Samuel A., Col. of Educ., Univ. of Arizona, Tucson, Arizona
Kirkland, Eleanor R., 8707 Mohawk Way, Fair Oaks, Calif.
Kirkland, J. Bryant, North Carolina State College, Raleigh, N.C.
Kirkman, Ralph E., Middle Tennessee State University, Murfreesboro, Tenn.
Kirkpatrick, James E., Black Hills State College, Spearfish, S.D.
Kirsch, Victor, Commack Public Schools, Commack, N.Y.
Kise, Leonard, Northern Illinois Univ., DeKalb, Ill.
Kiser, Chester, State University of New York, Buffalo, N.Y.
Kissinger, Doris C., 34 Roosevelt St., Glen Head, L.I., N.Y.
Kitch, Donald E., 520 Messina Hall, Sacramento, Calif.
Kitson, Elizabeth W. P., 9411 Jamaica Dr., Miami, Fla.
Kittell, Jack E., Col. of Educ., University of Washington, Seattle, Wash.
Kitts, Harry W., Dept. of Agric. Educ., Univ. of Minn., St. Paul, Minn.
Kizer, George A., Iowa State Univ., Ames, Iowa
Kjarsgaard, Donald R., Western Washington State Col., Bellingham, Wash.
Klahn, Richard P., Des Moines Indep. Comm. Sch. Dist., Des Moines, Iowa
Klaus, Catherine R., Box 337, Clermont, Iowa
Klausmeier, Herbert J., Sch. of Educ., University of Wisconsin, Madison, Wis.
Kleffner, John H., Assoc. Supt. of Cath. Schools, Oklahoma City, Okla.
Klein, Howard A., Col. of Educ., Univ. of Sask., Saskatoon, Sask.
Klein, Philip, 1520 Spruce St., Philadelphia, Pa.
Klein, Richard K., Department of Public Instruction, Bismarck, N.D.
Klein, Russel, 4975 Whiteaker St., Eugene, Ore.
Kleis, Russell J., Michigan State University, East Lansing, Mich.
Klevan, Albert, 45 W. Bayberry Rd., Clemont, N.Y.
Kleyensteuber, Carl J., Northland College, Ashland, Wis.
Klinckmann, Evelyn, San Francisco Col. for Women, San Francisco, Calif.
Kline, Charles E., Purdue University, Lafayette, Ind.
Kline, Francis F., 1643 Elmwood Ct., Oshkosh, Wis.
Kling, Martin, Grad. Sch. of Educ., Rutgers State Univ., New Brunswick, N.J.
Klohr, Paul R., 420 Walhalla Rd., Columbus, Ohio
Klopf, Gordon J., Bank Street Col. of Educ., New York, N.Y.
Klopfer, Leopold E., University of Pittsburgh, Pittsburgh, Pa.
Kluwe, Mary Jean, Lang. Educ. Dept., Public Schools, Detroit, Mich.
Knape, Clifford S., 1024 North 18-A St., Waco, Tex.
Knapp, Frederick C., 272 Rochelle Park, Tonawanda, N.Y.
Knapp, William D., 6800 Schoolway, Greendale, Wis.
Knepp, A. Christine, Route 4, Jonesboro, Tenn.
Knight, Octavia B., North Carolina College, Durham, N.C.
Knight, Reginald R., 4338 Heather Rd., Long Beach, Calif.
Knirk, Frederick G., 161 Brookside Lane, Fayetteville, N.Y.
Knoblock, Peter, 805 S. Crouse Ave., Syracuse, N.Y.
Knolle, Lawrence M., Chatham College, Pittsburgh, Pa.
Knope, Mrs. Perle, Madison Public Schools, Madison, Wis.
Knorr, Amy Jean, University of Arizona, Tucson, Ariz.
Knowlden, Gayle E., 3003 Laurel Ave., Manhattan Beach, Calif.
Knox, Carl S., 2017 Louisiana St., Lawrence, Kan.
Knox, Stanley C., St. Cloud State College, St. Cloud, Minn.
Koch, Mrs. Sylvia L., 539 N. Highland Ave., Los Angeles, Calif.
Koehler, Everette E., The King's College, Briarcliff Manor, N.Y.

Koehring, Dorothy, State College of Iowa, Cedar Falls, Iowa
Koenig, Vernon H., 11878 Ridgecrest Dr., Riverside, Calif.
Koeppe, Richard P., Asst. Supt., Denver Public Schools, Denver, Colo.
Koerber, Walter F., Scarborough Board of Education, Scarborough, Ont., Canada
Koerner, Warren A., 4608 West 106th St., Oak Lawn, Ill.
Koester, George A., San Diego State College, San Diego, Calif.
Koff, Robert H., 652 Glenbrook Dr., Palo Alto, Calif.
Kohler, Lewis T., 7659 Whitsett Ave., N. Hollywood, Calif.
Kohlmann, Eleanor L., 169 MacKay Hall, Iowa State University, Ames, Iowa
Kohn, Martin, 35 West 92nd St., New York, N.Y.
Kohrs, E. V., Gillette, Wyoming
Kokras, Nocolaos, Elia-Gonnon, Parissa, Greece
Kollar, Theodore H., Paterson Cath. Reg. H.S., Paterson, N.J.
Konecny, Frank J., 101 S. Rita St., Waco, Tex.
Konishi, Walter K., San Jose State College, San Jose, Calif.
Konkel, Dorothy A., Shorewood Public Schools, Shorewood, Wis.
Konrad, Abram G., Tabor College, Hillsboro, Kan.
Konsh, Adeline, 7 East 14th St., New York, N.Y.
Konstantinos, K. K., Lenape Regional High School, Medford, N.J.
Kontos, George, Jr., 351 N.E. Chambers Ct., Newport, Ore.
Koontz, David, West Virginia State College, Institute, W. Va.
Koos, Leonard V., Route 2, Newago, Mich.
Kopan, Andrew T., 5401 S. Hyde Park Blvd., Chicago, Ill.
Kopfstein, Kurt A., 6230 N. Avers, Chicago, Ill.
Koppenhaver, Albert H., Lowell Jt. School Dist., Whittier, Calif.
Korey, Harold, 5026 Jarlath, Skokie, Ill.
Korntheuer, Gerhard A., St. Johns College, Winfield, Kan.
Kotoshirodo, Milton, 2063 Aamanu St., Pearl City, Hawaii
Kovach, Gaza, Pocahontas High School, Pocahontas, Va.
Kowitz, George T., Dept. of Educ. Psych., Univ. of Oklahoma, Norman, Okla.
Koyanagi, Elliot Y., 2630 Dekist St., Bloomington, Ind.
Kozma, Ernest J., 8081 Worthington Park Dr., Strongsville, Ohio
Krafft, Larry J., 739 Roslyn St., Glenside, Pa.
Kraft, Milton Edward, Earlham College, Richmond, Ind.
Kramer, William A., 3558 S. Jefferson Ave., St. Louis, Mo.
Kratz, Gerald B., Huron Valley Schools, Milford, Mich.
Kraus, Howard F., 512 Alameda de las Pulgas, Belmont, Calif.
Kraus, Philip E., Hunter College, New York, N.Y.
Krause, Frank, 5120 Southgreen Dr., Indianapolis, Ind.
Krause, Victor C., Concord Teachers College, River Forest, Ill.
Kravetz, Nathan, 555 Kappock St., Riverdale, N.Y.
Kravetz, Sol, 11545 Duque Dr., Studio City, Calif.
Kravitz, Bernard, 4098 Union Bay Circle, N.E., Seattle, Wash.
Kravitz, Jerry, 986 Van Buren St., Baldwin, N.Y.
Krawitz, E. Harris, 6503 N. Le Mal, Lincolnwood, Ill.
Kreinheder, Adeline E., Muhlenberg Col., Allentown, Pa.
Kreismer, Clifford R., Clara E. Coleman Sch., 100 Pinelynn Rd., Glen Rock, N.J.
Kreitlow, Burton W., Dept. of Educ., University of Wisconsin, Madison, Wis.
Kress, Roy A., 800 Moredon Rd., Meadowbrook, Pa.
Krich, Percy, Dept. of Educ., Queens College, Flushing, N.Y.
Krippner, Stanley C., Dept. of Psychiatry, Maimonides Hosp., Brooklyn, N.Y.
Kroenke, Richard G., Valparaiso University, Valparaiso, Ind.
Krolikowski, W. P., Loyola University, Chicago, Ill.
Kroman, Nathan, University of Saskatchewan, Saskatoon, Sask., Canada
Kropp, John P., 12455 Russell Ave., Chino, Calif.
Kropp, Russell P., Florida State University, Tallahassee, Fla.
Krueger, Louise W., 1520 Laburnum Ave., Chico, Calif.
Krug, Edward, Dept. of Educ., University of Wisconsin, Madison, Wis.
Kruppa, Richard A., Ohio State University, Columbus, Ohio
Kruszynski, Eugene S., San Francisco State College, San Francisco, Calif.
Krzesinski, Daniel J., R.D. 1, Attica, N.Y.

Kubalek, Josef, Karlinske nam. 6, Praha 8 Karlin, CSSR, Czech.
Kubik, Edmund J., 9741 S. Leavitt St., Chicago, Ill.
Kuhn, Donald K., 8520 Mackenzie Rd., St. Louis, Mo.
Kuhn, Doris Young, Dept. of Eng., Univ. of Nebraska, Lincoln, Neb.
Kuhn, Joseph A., 99 Buffalo Ave., Long Beach, N.Y.
Kuhnen, Mrs. Mildred, 2106 Park Ave., Chico, Calif.
Kulberg, Janet M., 24 Peters St., Orono, Me.
Kullman, N. E., Jr., 153 Murray Ave., Delmar, N.Y.
Kumpf, Carl H., Superintendent of Schools, Clark, N.J.
Kunimoto, Mrs. Tadako, 734—16th Ave., Honolulu, Hawaii
Kuntz, Allen H., 72 Lombardy St., Lancaster, N.Y.
Kunzler, William J., 34 Overbrook Dr., Kirksville, Mo.
Kurtz, John J., Inst. for Child Study, Univ. of Maryland, College Park, Md.
Kusmik, Cornell J., 7400 Augusta St., River Forest, Ill.
Kutz, Frederick B., Newark High School, Newark, Del.
Kvaraceus, William C., Clark University, Worcester, Mass.
Kyle, Helen F., Rhode Island College, Providence, R.I.
Kynard, Alfred T., Prairie View A. & M. College, Prairie View, Tex.

Labatte, Henry, 40 College St., Toronto, Ontario, Canada
LaBay, Michael J., Col. of Educ., University of Toledo, Toledo, Ohio
Lacey, Archie L., Hunter Col., City University of N.Y., New York, N.Y.
Lache, Sheldon, University of Connecticut, Storrs, Conn.
Lacivita, James, 1206 A. Boxwood Dr., Mt. Prospect, Ill.
Lackey, Kenneth E., 809 Lockett Rd., St. Louis, Mo.
Ladd, Edward T., Emory University, Atlanta, Ga.
Ladd, Eleanor M., Col. of Educ., University of Georgia, Athens, Ga.
Ladd, Paul, Wooster High School, Wooster, Ohio
LaDue, Donald C., Elem. Educ. Dept., Temple University, Philadelphia, Pa.
LaFauci, Horatio M., 871 Commonwealth Ave., Boston, Mass.
Lafferty, Charles W., Supt. of Schools, Fairbanks, Alaska
Lafferty, Henry M., East Texas State Univ., Commerce, Texas
LaForce, Charles L., 426 Malden Ave., LaGrange Park, Ill.
Lafranchi, W. E., Stabley Library, State College, Indiana, Pa.
LaGrone, Herbert F., Sch. of Educ., Texas Christian Univ., Fort Worth, Tex.
Lahaderne, Henrietta M., IDEA, 1100 Glendon Ave., Los Angeles, Calif.
Laird, A. W., Western Kentucky State College, Bowling Green, Ky.
Lake, Doris S., State Univ. Col., Oneonta, N.Y.
Lamb, Howard E., Sch. of Educ., University of Delaware, Newark, Del.
Lambert, Philip, Educ. Psych. Dept., Univ. of Wisconsin, Madison, Wis.
Lambert, Pierre D., Sch. of Educ., Boston College, Chestnut Hill, Mass.
Lambert, Ronald T., University of Minnesota, Minneapolis, Minn.
Lambert, Sam M., N.E.A., 1201 Sixteenth St., N.W., Washington, D.C.
Lampard, Dorothy M., Univ. of Letherbridge, Letherbridge, Alba., Canada
Lampshire, Richard H., Drake University, Des Moines, Iowa
Lamson, William E., 4850 E. Melissa St., Tucson, Ariz.
Landskov, Norvin L., Univ. of Southern Mississippi, Hattiesburg, Miss.
Lane, Frank T., USAID, Rio de Janiero/SUN, APO New York, NY.
Lane, Mrs. Mary B., 10 Lundy's Lane, San Mateo, Calif.
Lang, Mrs. Pauline R., Southern Connecticut State Col., New Haven, Conn.
Lange, Lorraine, State Univ. of New York, Buffalo, N.Y.
Lange, Paul W., 2304 Linden Dr., Valparaiso, Ind.
Lange, Phil C., Tchrs. Col., Columbia University, New York, N.Y.
Langeveld, M. J., Prins Hendriklaan 6, Bilthoven, Holland
Langland, Lois E., 4021 Olive Hill Dr., Claremont, Calif.
Langley, Elizabeth M., 4937 W. Wellington Ave., Chicago, Ill.
Langman, Muriel Potter, 913 Congress St., Ypsilanti, Mich.
Langston, Genevieve R., Eureka College, Eureka, Ill.
Langston, Roderick G., 1451 S. Loma Verde St., Monterey Park, Calif.
Lanham, Frank W., 3212 Charing Cross, Ann Arbor, Mich.
Lanier, Ruby, Route No. 2, Box 619, Hickory, N.C.

Lanning, Frank W., Northern Illinois University, DeKalb, Ill.
Lano, Richard L., University of California, Los Angeles, Calif.
Lansing, Marvin G., 122 Mappa St., Eau Claire, Wis.
Lansu, Walter J., 6036 Metropolitan Plaza, Los Angeles, Calif.
Lantz, James S., 330 Washington St., Tekonsha, Mich.
Lantz, Ralph G., Pennsylvania State University, University Park, Pa.
Laramy, William J., Haverford Junior High School, Havertown, Pa.
Larkin, Lewis B., 15818 Westbrook, Detroit, Mich.
Larkins, William J., 32000 Chagrin Blvd., Cleveland, Ohio
Larmee, Roy A., Cntr. for Educ. Admn., Ohio State Univ., Columbus, Ohio
Larsen, Arthur Hoff, Illinois State University, Normal, Ill.
Larson, Mrs. Anna Marie, 5605 Wexford Rd., Baltimore, Md.
Larson, Eleanore E., Col. of Educ., Univ. of Rochester, Rochester, N.Y.
Larson, L. C., Audio-Visual Center, Indiana University, Bloomington, Ind.
Larson, Vera M., 13601 N.E. Fremont St., Portland, Ore.
Lashinger, Donald R., State University of New York, Albany, N.Y.
Laska, John, Sutton Hall, Univ. of Texas, Austin, Texas
Lassanske, Paul A., 4389 Hodgson Rd., St. Paul, Minn.
Lathrop, Irvin T., California State College, Long Beach, Calif.
Lattimer, Everett C., Magee Rd., Glenmont, N.Y.
Laudico, Minerva G., Centro Escolar University, Manila, Philippines
Lauria, Joseph L., 6401 Shoup Ave., Canoga Park, Calif.
Laurier, Blaise V., Les Clercs de Saint-Viateur, Montreal, Quebec, Canada
Lavenburg, F. M., Public Schls., 155 Broad St., Bloomfield, N.J.
Lavenburg, Jack, 2185 Seventeenth Ct., W., Eugene, Ore.
Laverty, John A., 5944 S. Washtenaw Ave., Chicago, Ill.
Lawhead, Victor B., Ball State University, Muncie, Ind.
Lawler, Marcella R., Tchrs. Col., Columbia University, New York, N.Y.
Lawrence, Clayton G., Marion College, Marion, Ind.
Lawrence, Richard E., Univ. of New Mexico, Albuquerque, N.M.
Lawrence, Ruth E., 627 Grove St., Denton, Tex.
Lawrie, Jack D., Superintendent of Schools, Washington, N.C.
Lawski, A. J., Edsel Ford High School, 20601 Rotunda Dr., Dearborn, Mich.
Layton, Donald H., University of California, Los Angeles, Calif.
Lazar, Alfred L., California State College, Long Beach, Calif.
Lazow, Alfred, 2631 W. Berwyn Ave., Chicago, Ill.
Leavitt, Jerome E., Col. of Educ., Univ. of Arizona, Tucson, Arizona
Lebofsky, Arthur, 485 E. Lincoln Ave., Mt. Vernon, N.Y.
Lechiara, Francis J., 1400 Miller Rd., Coral Gables, Fla.
Lee, Annabel, Univ. of Puget Sound, Tacoma, Wash.
Lee, Della, Asst. Prin., Public School, Bronx, N.Y.
Lee, Ernest C., Prin., Beaufort H.S., Beaufort, Victoria, Australia
Lee, Harold Fletcher, Box 38, Lincoln University, Jefferson City, Mo.
Lee, Howard D., Atwater School, Shorewood, Wis.
Lee, J. Murray, Southern Illinois University, Carbondale, Ill.
Lee, James Michael, University of Notre Dame, Notre Dame, Ind.
Lee, John J., Col. of Educ., Wayne State University, Detroit, Mich.
Lee, William B., U.S.D.E.S.E.A., APO New York, N.Y.
Lee, William C., Fairleigh Dickinson University, Rutherford, N.J.
Leeds, Donald S., Northeastern University, Boston, Mass.
Leeds, Willard L., Ford Foundation, Caracas, Venezuela, S.A.
Leese, Joseph, State Univ. Col., Albany, N.Y.
Lefever, David Welty, Sch. of Educ., Univ. of California, Los Angeles, Calif.
* Lefforge, Roxy, 1945 Fruit St., Huntington, Ind.
Lehman, Lloyd W., Benjamin C. Willis Educ'l Serv., Chicago, Ill.
Lehmann, Irvin J., Michigan State University, East Lansing, Mich.
Lehmkuhl, Carlton B., 4 Wilogreen Rd., Natick, Mass.
Lehsten, Nelson G., Sch. of Educ., Univ. of Michigan, Ann Arbor, Mich.
Leib, Joseph A., 240 Sinclair Pl., Westfield, N.J.
Leibert, Robert E., 1005 W. Gregory Ave., Kansas City, Mo.

Leibik, Leon J., 204 Dodge Ave., Evanston, Ill.
Leigh, Robert K., Florida State Univ., Tallahassee, Fla.
Leinster, Carolyn J., 3 S. Main St., Pittsford, N.Y.
Leitch, John J., Jr., Admin. Off., Wheeler Rd., Central Islip, N.Y.
Lembo, John M., 77 N. Duke St., Millersville, Pa.
Lemin, Paul C., Superintendent of Schools, Cheboygan, Mich.
Lennon, Joseph L., Providence College, Providence, R.I.
Lennon, Lawrence J., 310 N. Webster Ave., Scranton, Pa.
Leonard, Lloyd L., Dept. of Educ., Northern Illinois Univ., DeKalb, Ill.
Leonard, William P., Univ. of Pittsburgh, Pittsburgh, Pa.
Lepera, Alfred G., 254 Franklin St., Newton, Mass.
LePere, Jean M., Michigan State University, East Lansing, Mich.
Lepore, Albert R., 2614 Lancaster Rd., Hayward, Calif.
Lester, J. William, Superintendent, Diocesan Schls., Fort Wayne, Ind.
Leverson, Leonard O., 201 W. Newhall Ave., Waukesha, Wis.
Levin, Alvin I., 12336 Addison St., North Hollywood, Calif.
Levin, J. Joseph, 221 N. Cuyler Ave., Oak Park, Ill.
Levine, Daniel U., Sch. of Educ., Univ. of Missouri, Kansas City, Mo.
Levine, Murray, Dept. of Psych., Yale University, New Haven, Conn.
Levine, Stanley L., 1627 Anita Ln., Newport Beach, Calif.
Levinson, Leo, Clarkston Sch. Dist. No. 1, New City, N.Y.
Levit, Martin, Sch. of Educ., University of Missouri, Kansas City, Mo.
Levy, Nathalie, 506 Mississippi Ave., Bogalusa, La.
Lewis, Arthur J., Tchrs. Col., Columbia University, New York, N.Y.
Lewis, Edward R., 5293 Greenridge Rd., Castro Valley, Calif.
Lewis, Elizabeth V., P.O. Box 1833, University, Ala.
Lewis, Mrs. J. R., Blue Mountain College, Blue Mountain, Miss.
Lewis, Maurice S., Col. of Educ., Arizona State University, Tempe, Ariz.
Lewis, P. Helen, 1634 Neil Ave., Box 84, Columbus, Ohio
Lewis, Philip, 6900 S. Crandon Ave., Chicago, Ill.
Lewis, Robert, 915 N. Union St., Natchez, Miss.
Lewis, Roland B., Eastern Washington State College, Cheney, Wash.
Lewis, William, Millikin Univ. Library, Decatur, Ill.
Leyton-Soto, Mario, Univ. de Chile, Castro 441, Santiago, Chile
Liberman, Norman J., 343 E. 30th St., New York, N.Y.
Licata, William, State Univ. Col., Buffalo, N.Y.
Licthy, E. A., Illinois State University, Normal, Ill.
Lieb, L. V., Dept. of Educ., State University College, Oswego, N.Y.
Lieberman, Ann, 13040 Hartland St., North Hollywood, Calif.
Lieberman, Marcus, 5835 Kimbark Ave., Chicago, Ill.
Lien, Ronald L., Mankato State College, Mankato, Minn.
Lifton, Eli, Winthrop Junior High School, Brooklyn, N.Y.
Liggett, Donald R., Grinnell College, Grinnell, Ia.
Liggitt, William A., 703 St. Marks Ave. ,Westfield, N.J.
Light, Alfred B., 93 Bailey Ave., Plattsburgh, N.Y.
Lighthall, Frederick, Dept. of Educ., Univ. of Chicago, Chicago, Ill.
Lightwine, Louise M., University of Portland, Portland, Ore.
Ligon, Mary Gilbert, Hofstra College, Hempstead, N.Y.
Liljeblad, Maynard T., P.O. Box 1067, Hanford, Calif.
* Lincoln, Edward A., Thompson St., Halifax, Mass.
Lind, Arthur E., 1422 Johnston Ave., Richland, Wash.
Lindberg, Lucile, Queens College, Flushing, N.Y.
Lindeman, Richard H., Tchrs. Col., Columbia University, New York, N.Y.
Lindemer, George Charles, Seton Hall University, South Orange, N.J.
Lindgren, Henry C., Psych. Dept., Amer. Univ. of Beirut, Beirut, Lebanon
Lindman, Mrs. Margaret R., Prin., College Hill School, Skokie, Ill.
Lindvall, C. Mauritz, Sch. of Educ., University of Pittsburgh, Pittsburgh, Pa.
Linehan, Mrs. Louise W., 4 Bolton Pl., Fair Lawn, N.J.
Linn, Frank J., S.E. Mo. State College, Cape Girardeau, Mo.
Linson, Marvin G., 933 Fulton St., Aurora, Colo.
Lipham, James M., Dept. of Educ., University of Wisconsin, Madison, Wis.

Lipscomb, William A., 107 Yellowstone Dr., Jerome, Idaho
Lissovoy, Vladimir de, Pennsylvania State Univ., University Park, Pa.
Litherland, Bennett H., 541—21st St., Rock Island, Ill.
Litin, Mrs. Annette, 5302 N. Granite Reef Rd., Scottsdale, Ariz.
Litsinger, Dolores A., San Fernando Valley State College, Northridge, Calif.
Little, J. Kenneth, Bascom Hall, University of Wisconsin, Madison, Wis.
Little, Sara, Presbyterian Sch. of Christian Education, Richmond, Va.
Littlefield, Roy S., Superintendent of Schools, Dell, Ark.
Litwin, Mrs. Zelda, Responsive Environment Program, Brooklyn, N.Y.
Litzky, Leo, 11 Pomona Ave., Newark, N.J.
Livingston, Thomas B., Box 4060, Texas Tech. Station, Lubbock, Tex.
Livo, Mrs. Norma J., 11960 W. 22nd Pl., Denver, Colo.
Llewellyn, Ardelle A., San Francisco State College, San Francisco, Calif.
Lloyd, Francis V., Jr., 5834 Stony Island Ave., Chicago, Ill.
Lloyd-Jones, Esther M., 430 West 116th St., New York, N.Y.
Lobdell, Lawrence O., Union Free School Dist. 30, Valley Stream, N.Y.
Locke, William W., 1317 Pine St., Kingsport, Tenn.
Lockett, B. T., 1848 Tiger Flowers Dr., N.W., Atlanta, Ga.
Lockwood, William L., 215 Harbor St., Glencoe, Ill.
Lofgren, Marie Luise S., 5068 Cocoa Palm Way, Fair Oaks, Calif.
Logan, Lillian May, Brandon Univ., Brandon, Manitoba, Canada
Logdeser, Mrs. Thomas, 11616 Woodview Blvd., Parma Heights, Ohio
Lohman, Maurice A., Tchrs. Col., Columbia University, New York, N.Y.
Lohmann, Victor L., State Teachers College, St. Cloud, Minn.
Lola, Justita O., Bicol Teachers College, Legaspi, Albay, Philippines
Lomax, James L., Lomax Junior High School, Valdosta, Ga.
London, Jack, 2328 Derby St., Berkeley, Calif.
Long, Isabelle, 4343 Harriet Ave., S., Minneapolis, Minn.
Longsdorf, Homer, 413 Leslie, Lansing, Mich.
Longstreet, Wilma S., 4103 W. 10th Ave., Gary, Ind.
Lonsdale, Mrs. Maxine deLappe, 1405 Campbell Lane, Sacramento, Calif.
Lonsdale, Richard C., 220 Palmer Ave., North Tarrytown, N.Y.
Lonsway, Rev. Francis A., O.F.M., Bellarmine Col., Louisville, Ky.
Looby, Thomas F., 241 S. Ocean Ave., Patchogue, N.Y.
Loomis, Arthur K., 917 W. Bonita Ave., Claremont, Calif.
Loomis, William G., 684 Illinois Ave., N.E., Salem, Ore.
Looney, William F., Pres., State Col. at Boston, Boston, Mass.
Loop, Alfred B., 2619 Franklin St., Bellingham, Wash.
Loree, M. Ray, Box 742, University of Alabama, University, Ala.
Lorenz, Donald W., Lutheran High School East, Harper Woods, Mich.
Lorenzen, R. W., Div. of Voc. Educ., Univ. of California, Los Angeles, **Calif.**
Loudon, Mrs. Mary Lou, 1408 Stephens Ave., Baton Rouge, La.
Loughlin, Leo J., 257 Rolfe Rd., DeKalb, Ill.
Loughrea, Mildred K., 659 City Hall, St. Paul, Minn.
Love, Virginia H., 709 N. Grand Ave., Sherman, Tex.
Lovette, Joanne P., 88 Rt. 119 South, Indiana, Pa.
Lowe, A. J., University of South Florida, Tampa, Fla.
Lowe, Alberta L., Col. of Educ., University of Tennessee, Knoxville, Tenn.
Lowe, Mary G., Dept. of H.E., University of Utah, Salt Lake City, Utah
Lowe, R. N., Sch. of Educ., University of Oregon, Eugene, Ore.
Lowe, Viola C., 1512 S. Gamon Rd., Wheaton, Ill.
Lowe, William T., 328 Hopeman, University of Rochester, Rochester, N.Y.
Lowery, Zeb A., Rutherford County Schools, Rutherford, N.C.
Lowes, Ruth, 2004 Seventh Ave., Canyon, Tex.
Lowey, Warren G., Box 64, Setauket, L.I., N.Y.
Lowther, Jesse R., 15425 Kercheval, Grosse Pointe, Mich.
Lowther, Malcolm A., Sch. of Educ., Univ. of Michigan, **Ann Arbor, Mich.**
Lowther, William L., Supt. of Schools, Boonton, N.J.
Lubell, Richard M., 2 Stoddard Pl., Brooklyn, N.Y.
Lubin, Harry, Supt. of Schools, Bellmawr, N.J.
Lucas, J. H., 2006 Fayetteville St., Durham, N.C.

Lucas, Robert E., Fort Morgan High School, Fort Morgan, Colo.
Lucash, Benjamin, 9801 Montour St., Philadelphia, Pa.
Lucietto, Lena, 5835 Kimbark Ave., Chicago, Ill.
Lucio, William H., Sch. of Educ., University of California, Los Angeles, Calif.
Lucito, Leonard J., Apt. 704, 700 Seventh St., S.W., Washington, D.C.
Ludeman, Ruth, Augsburg College, Minneapolis, Minn.
Luebke, Martin F., 1704 W. Jackson St., Springfield, Ill.
Luetkemeyer, Joseph F., 7002 St. Annes Ave., Lanham, Md.
Luhmann, Philip, 1407 E. 54th St., Chicago, Ill.
Lukens, Mrs. Eunice T., 12421 South 69th Ave., Palos Heights, Ill.
Luker, Arno Henry, Colorado State College, Greeley, Colo.
Lund, S. E. Torsten, 45-B Tolman Hall, Univ. of California, Berkeley, Calif.
Lunde, Mrs. Josephine, 505 Oxford, Grand Forks, N.D.
Lunney, Gerald H., Educ'l Research Council of America, Cleveland, Ohio
Lunt, Robert B., Supt. of Schools, Town Hall, Cape Elizabeth, Me.
LuPone, O. J., 4520 Culbertson, LaMesa, Calif.
Lutz, Frank W., New York University, New York, N.Y.
Lutz, Jack, Plymouth-Whitemarsh Jt. High School, Plymouth Meeting, Pa.
Lynch, Florence M., 8338 S. Kedvale Ave., Chicago, Ill.
Lynch, James M., Superintendent of Schools, Rt. No. 9, East Brunswick, N.J.
Lynch, John C., DePaul University, Chicago, Ill.
Lynch, Patrick D., Col. of Educ., Univ. of New Mexico, Albuquerque, N.M.
Lyon, Bruce W., Wright State Univ., Dayton, Ohio
Lyons, Mrs. Cora E., P.O. Box 133, Amboy, Ill.
Lyons, John H., 17 Colton Rd., Somers, Conn.
Lyons, Paul R., 300-11 Diamond Village, Gainesville, Fla.

Maag, Raymond E., 122 W. Franklin Ave., Minneapolis, Minn.
Maccia, George S., Dept. of Educ., Ohio State University, Columbus, Ohio
MacConnell, John C., Muhlenberg College, Allentown, Pa.
MacDonald, Donald V., University of Scranton, Scranton, Pa.
Macdonald, Leland S., 5609—19th St., N., Arlington, Va.
MacDonald, M. Gertrude, 78 Sheffield Rd., Melrose, Mass.
MacGown, Paul C., 3128 N. Ash St., Spokane, Wash.
Mack, Esther, San Jose State College, San Jose, Calif.
* MacKay, James L., 3737 Fredericksburg Rd., San Antonio, Tex.
MacKay, Vera A., Col. of Educ., Univ. of British Columbia, Vancouver, B.C.
MacKay, William R., 124 Underhill Rd., Bellingham, Wash.
Mackenzie, Donald M., White House, Park College, Parkville, Mo.
MacKenzie, Elbridge G., Anderson College, Anderson, Ind.
Mackenzie, Gordon N., Tchrs. Col., Columbia University, New York, N.Y.
Mackintosh, Helen K., 215 Wolfe St., Alexandria, Va.
MacLean, Effie, Saskatoon Pub. Sch. Brd., Saskatoon, Sask., Canada
MacLeay, Ian A., P.O. Box 560, Lennoxville, Quebec, Canada
MacLeod, James J., 6300 Grand River, Detroit, Mich.
MacNaughton, Elizabeth A., 2990 Richmond Ave., Houston, Texas
MacRae, Douglas G., Fulton County Board of Educ., Atlanta, Ga.
Madden, George R., Col. of Educ., University of Kentucky, Lexington, Ky.
Maddox, Mrs. Clifford R., 525 Enid Ave., Dayton, Ohio
Madeja, Stanley S., 9917 Nolmhurst Rd., Bethesda, Md.
Madonna, Mrs. Shirley M., 47-27—215th St., Bayside, N.Y.
Madore, Normand William, Illinois State University, Normal, Ill.
Maehara, Oei, 3535 Pinao St., Honolulu, Hawaii
Magary, James F., Sch. of Educ., Univ. of So. California, Los Angeles, Calif.
Maginnis, Maria, 20522 Parthenia St., Canoga Park, Calif.
Magoon, Thomas M., 1316 Canyon Rd., Silver Spring, Md.
Magram, P. Theodore, 34 Park Drive E., Syosset, N.Y.
Mahaffey, James P., State Dept. of Educ., Columbia, S.C.
Mahar, Robert J., Col. of Educ., Temple University, Philadelphia, Pa.
Maher, Alan E., Unqua School, Massapequa, N.Y.
Maher, Trafford P., St. Louis University, 15 N. Grand Blvd., St. Louis, Mo.

Mahon, Bruce R., Mount Royal Junior College, Calgary 2, Alba., Canada
Mailey, James H., Supt. of Schools, Midland, Tex.
Mailliard, Mrs. Margaret E., 221 E. 49th St., Chicago, Ill.
Mains, Mrs. Susie T., 29 West St., Barre, Vt.
Malan, Russell, Superintendent of Schools, Harrisburg, Ill.
Mallett, Jerry J., 3912 Garrison, Toledo, Ohio
Maloof, Mitchell, 63 Main St., Williamstown, Mass.
Manchester, Frank S., Radnor School Dist., Wayne, Pa.
Mandel, E. Jules, 20918 Calimali Rd., Woodland Hills, Calif.
Mangan, John C., Dept. of Educ., Temple University, Philadelphia, Pa.
Mangum, G. C., P.O. Box 494, Darlington, S.C.
Manion, Richard T., Prin., Noah Wallace School, Farmington, Conn.
Manker, Charles C., Jr., University of South Florida, Tampa, Fla.
Manley, Francis J., Frontier Central Sch., Bay View Rd., Hamburg, N.Y.
Mann, James W., Roosevelt University, Chicago, Ill.
Mann, Jesse A., Georgetown Univ., Washington, D.C.
Mann, Sidney J., Syracuse City Schools, Syracuse, N.Y.
Mann, Mrs. Thelma T., 949 Hunakai St., Honolulu, Hawaii
Mann, Vernal S., Box 266, State College, Miss.
Manning, Doris E., University of Arizona, Tucson, Ariz.
Mannos, Nicholas T., Niles Twp. High School West, Skokie, Ill.
Manoil, Adolph, Sch. of Educ., Boston University, Boston, Mass.
Manolakes, Theodore, Col. of Educ., University of Illinois, Urbana, Ill.
Manone, Carl, 34 Kirkline Ave., Hellertown, Pa.
Manuel, Herschel T., University of Texas, Austin, Tex.
Mapel, Seldon B., Jr., 1919 Mercedes Rd., Denton, Tex.
Marburger, Carl L., Dept. of Educ., 225 W. State St., Trenton, N.J.
Marc-Aurele, Paul, 455, 80 Rue Est, Charlesbourg, Quebec 7, Canada
Marchie, Howard E., 26 Norman St., Springfield, Mass.
Marcus, Marie, Louisiana State University, New Orleans, La.
Margarones, John J., 210 College St., Lewiston, Me.
Margolis, Henry, 2030 S. Taylor Rd., Cleveland Heights, Ohio
Mark, Arthur, 6 Cross Brook Ln., Westport, Conn.
Markarian, Robert E., Springfield College, Springfield, Mass.
Marker, Robert W., State University of Iowa, Iowa City, Iowa
Marks, Dorothy M., 7428 San Jose, Dallas, Tex.
Marks, Merle B., University of So. California, Los Angeles, Calif.
Marks, Ralph M., 402 Patterson St., Ogdensburg, N.Y.
Marksberry, Mary Lee, Sch. of Educ., Univ. of Missouri, Kansas City, Mo.
Marksheffel, Ned D., Oregon State University, Corvallis, Ore.
Markus, Frank W., Mid-Continent Reg. Educ. Lab., Kansas City, Mo.
Marquand, Richard L., Michigan State Univ., East Lansing, Mich.
Marquardt, Robert L., Thiokol Chemical Corp., Ogden, Utah
Marquis, Francis N., Wright State Campus, Dayton, Ohio
Marquis, R. L., Jr., Box 5282, North Texas Sta., Denton, Tex.
Marsden, W. Ware, 2217 West 5th St., Stillwater, Okla.
Marsh, Mrs. Augusta B., 252 Bronner St., Prichard, Ala.
Marshall, Beth, 1325 S. Orange, Fullerton, Calif.
Marshall, Daniel W., Filene Center, Tufts University, Medford, Mass.
Marshall, Thomas O., 17 Mill Rd., Durham, N.H.
Marshall, Wayne P., 704 East 36th St., Kearney, Neb.
Marso, Ronald N., Bowling Green State Univ., Bowling Green, Ohio
Marston, Mrs. Marjorie, 860 Lake Shore Dr., Chicago, Ill.
Martin, C. Keith, Col. of Educ., Univ. of Md., College Park, Md.
Martin, Edwin D., 2341 Quenby, Houston, Tex.
Martin, F. Gerald, Sacred Heart Seminary, Detroit, Mich.
Martin, Frieda, 2428½ Wabash, Terre Haute, Ind.
Martin, Jackson J., 661 Grace St., Livermore, Calif.
Martin, Kathryn J., 2208 Fairhill Ave., Glenside, Pa.
Martin, Mavis D., SWCEL, 117 Richmond, N.E., Albuquerque, N.M.

Martin, R. Lee, State Univ. Col., Oswego, N.Y.
Martin, Robert M., University of Hawaii, Honolulu, Hawaii
Martin, William R., 320 N.W. 19th Ave., Fort Lauderdale, Fla.
Martini, Miss Angiolina A., 1555 Oxford St., Berkeley, Calif.
Martinson, John S., 7 Rustic Lane, S.W., Tacoma, Wash.
Martire, Harriette A., St. Joseph College, West Hartford, Conn.
Martorana, Sabastian V., State University of New York, Albany, N.Y.
Marx, George L., Col. of Educ., University of Maryland, College Park, Md.
Marzolf, Stanley S., Illinois State University, Normal, Ill.
Marzullo, Santo P., Manpower Training Center, Rochester, N.Y.
Masem, Paul W., University of South Carolina, Columbia, S.C.
Masia, Bertram B., Dept. of Educ., Western Reserve Univ., Cleveland, Ohio
Masiko, Peter, Miami-Dade Junior College, Miami, Fla.
Mason, George E., 235 Pine Forest Dr., Athens, Ga.
Mason, John M., Michigan State University, East Lansing, Mich.
Masoner, Paul H., University of Pittsburgh, Pittsburgh, Pa.
Massey, William J., 4906 Roland Ave., Baltimore, Md.
Massialas, Byron G., University of Michigan, Ann Arbor, Mich.
Massingill, Richard A., 15905 Harrison, Livonia, Mich.
Mathiott, James E., 3165 Ramona, Palo Alto, Calif.
Mathis, Claude, Sch. of Educ., Northwestern University, Evanston, Ill.
Matthew, Eunice Sophia, 340 Riverside Dr., New York, N.Y.
Matthews, James W., Star Rt. 3, McGrath Rd., Fairbanks, Alaska
Matthews, William P., 1114 N. Centennial, High Point, N.C.
Mattila, Ruth Hughes, P.O. Box 872, Las Vegas, N.M.
Mattke, W. J., Centennial School Dist. No. 12, Circle Pines, Minn.
Mattox, Daniel V., Jr., Pennsylvania State Univ., State College, Pa.
Matwijcow, Peter, Roger Williams Jr. Col., Providence, R.I.
Matzner, G. C., Eastern Illinois University, Charleston, Ill.
Maucker, James William, State College of Iowa, Cedar Falls, Iowa
Mauk, Gertrude, Box 312, Garden City, Mich.
Maurer, Marion V., 148 Ann St., Apt. 23, Clarendon Hills, Ill.
Maurer, Robert L., California State Polytechnic College, Pomona, Calif.
Mauth, Leslie J., Ball State University, Muncie, Ind.
Maw, Wallace H., Sch. of Educ., University of Delaware, Newark, Del.
Maxcy, Horace P., Michigan State University, East Lansing, Mich.
Maxwell, Ida E., 9 Chester Creek Rd., Cheyney, Pa.
May, Charles R., 2312 Foxcroft Circle, Denton, Tex.
May, John B., State Teachers College, Salisbury, Md.
May, Robert E., Emerson Vocational High School, Buffalo, N.Y.
Mayer, Lewis F., 4275 W. 196th St., Fairview Park, Ohio
Mayer, Ronald W., 275 Vernon St., San Francisco, Calif.
Mayhew, Lewis B., 945 Valdez Pl., Stanford, Calif.
Mayhew, Thomas H., Superintendent of Schools, Maywood, N.J.
Maynard, Glenn, Kent State University, Kent, Ohio
Mayo, Samuel T., Sch. of Educ., Loyola University, Chicago, Ill.
Mayor, John R., AAAS, 1515 Massachusetts Ave., N.W., Washington, D.C.
Mazyck, Harold E., Jr., 2007 Chelsea Lane, Greensboro, N.C.
McAllister, David, Kathmandu, State Dept., Washington, D.C.
McArthur, L. C., Jr., Drawer 1180, Sumter, S.C.
McAuliffe, M. Eileen, 5649 N. Kolmar Ave., Chicago, Ill.
McBirney, Ruth, Boise Junior College, Boise, Idaho
McBride, James H., 1246 Riverside Drive, Huron, Ohio
McBride, Ralph, Supt., Buckley-Loda Unit No. 8, Loda, Ill.
McBride, William B., Ohio State University, Columbus, Ohio
McBrine, Joseph, Superintendent of Schools, Lincoln, Me.
McBurney, Mrs. Doris, 1641 West 105th St., Chicago, Ill.
McCaffery, James F., Asst. Prin., Abington H.S., Abington, Pa.
McCaffrey, Austin J., Amer. Textbook Pub. Inst., 432 Park Ave., New York, N.Y.
McCahon, David M., 2307 Tilbury Ave., Pittsburgh, Pa.

McCaig, Thomas E., 3447 W. Pierce Ave., Chicago, Ill.
McCain, Paul M., Arkansas College, Batesville, Ark.
McCann, Lewis E., 18637 San Fernando Mission Blvd., Northridge, Calif.
McCann, Thomas W., 19 Jeffery Pl., Trumbull, Conn.
McCarthy, Joseph F. X., 641 Forest Ave., Larchmont, N.Y.
McCarthy, Joseph J., 9531 S. Kostner, Oak Lawn, Ill.
McCartney, Hilda, 2916 Redwood Ave., Costa Mesa, Calif.
McCarty, Henry R., San Diego County Bd. of Educ., San Diego, Calif.
McCaslin, James J., 5916 N. Crittenden, Indianapolis, Ind.
McCaul, Robert L., Col. of Educ., University of Chicago, Chicago, Ill.
McClanahan, L. D., 5820 Woolman Ct., Parma, Ohio
McClard, Donavon, San Diego State College, San Diego, Calif.
McCleary, Lloyd E., University of Illinois, Urbana, Ill.
McClellan, James E., 70 Greentree Dr., Doylestown, Pa.
McClelland, Denis A., 275 Broadview Ave., Toronto 8, Ont., Canada
McClendon, Patricia R., Winthrop College, Rock Hill, S.C.
McClintock, Eugene, Kaskaskia College, Shattuc Rd., Centralia, Ill.
McClintock, James A., Drew University, Madison, N.J.
McClure, Donald E., Eureka College, Eureka, Ill.
McClure, L. Morris, Col. of Educ., Univ. of Maryland, College Park, Md.
McClure, Nancy, Col. of Educ., Univ. of Kentucky, Lexington. Ky.
McClure, Robert M., 3314 Tennyson St., N.W., Washington, D.C.
McClurkin, W. D., Peabody College, Nashville, Tenn.
McClusky, Howard Yale, Elem. Sch., University of Michigan, Ann Arbor, Mich.
McCollum, Elinor C., 619 Ridge Ave., Evanston, Ill.
McCollum, Robert E., Col. of Educ., Temple Univ., Philadelphia, Pa.
McConnell, Emma, Vassar College, Poughkeepsie, N.Y.
McConnell, Gaither, Cen. for Tchr. Educ., Tulane Univ., New Orleans, La.
McConnell, Thomas R., Center for Study of Higher Educ., Berkeley, Calif.
McCook, T. Joseph, Supt., Brevard County Schools, Titusville, Fla.
McCormick, Ethel M., Lehigh Univ., Bethlehem, Pa.
McCormick, Felix J., Tchrs. Col., Columbia University, New York, N.Y.
McCormick, Robert W., Ohio State University, Columbus, Ohio
McCracken, Oliver, Jr., Superintendent of Schools, Skokie, Ill.
McCuaig, Susannah, 8830 Piney Branch Rd., 310 Silver Spring, Md.
McCue, L. H., Jr., E. C. Glass High School, Lynchburg, Va.
McCue, Robert E., 2308 N. Hazelwood Ave., Davenport, Iowa
McCuen, John T., 1340 Loretta Dr., Glendale, Calif.
McCullough, Constance M., 80 Vincente Rd., Berkeley, Calif.
McCully, Clyde C., 1415 W. Twain, Fresno, Calif.
McCuskey, Dorothy, Western Michigan University, Kalamazoo, Mich.
McCutcheon, Nancy Sue, Sch. of Educ., Univ. of South Carolina, Columbia, S.C.
McDaniel, Ernest D., Educ. Resch. Cent., Purdue Univ., Lafayette, Ind.
McDaniel, Marjorie C., Indiana State University, Terre Haute, Ind.
McDaniels, Garry L., 1310 Harbrooke, Ann Arbor, Mich.
McDavit, H. W., South Orange-Maplewood Public Schools, South Orange, N.J.
McDiarmid, Garnet Leo, 102 Bloor St. West, Toronto, Ont., Canada
McDonald, Donald, Texas Technological College, Lubbock, Tex.
McDonald, L. R., Woodruff Senior High School, Peoria, Ill.
McDowell, John B., 11 Blvd. of Allies, Pittsburgh, Pa.
McElhinney, James, 3816 Brook Dr., Muncie, Ind.
McElroy, Louis A., Technical-Vocational School, Gary, Ind.
McEwen, Gordon B., 13602 E. Walnut, Whittier, Calif.
McFarland, John W., Sch. of Educ., Univ. of Texas, El Paso, Texas
McFarren, G. Allen, 11 Willow Lane Ct., Tonawanda, N.Y.
McFeaters, Margaret M., 608 Brown's Lane, Pittsburgh, Pa.
McGary, Carroll R., 125 Stroudwater St., Westbrook, Me.
McGavern, John H., University of Hartford, Hartford, Conn.
McGee, Ralph G., 1526 Washington Ave., Wilmette, Ill.
McGee, Robert T., Asst. Supt. Pennsbury School Dist., Fallsington, Pa.

McGeoch, Dorothy M., Tchrs. Col., Columbia University, New York, N.Y.
McGinnis, Frederick A., Wilberforce University, P.O. Box 22, Wilberforce, Ohio
McGinnis, James H., Knoxville College, Knoxville, Tenn.
McGlasson, Maurice A., Sch. of Educ., Indiana University, Bloomington, Ind.
McGowan, Richard, 2466 W. Oakfield Dr., Grand Island, N.Y.
McGrath, Earl J., 525 West 120th St., New York, N.Y.
McGrath, G. D., Col. of Educ., Arizona State University, Tempe, Ariz.
McGrath, J. H., Dept. of Ed. Admin., Illinois State Univ., Normal, Ill.
McGrath, John W., Superintendent of Schools, Belmont, Mass.
McGraw, Mrs. Robert, 108 Grannis Rd., Orange, Conn.
McGregor, Louis, Wayland Baptist College, Plainview, Texas
McGroarty, Rosemary, Queens College Teacher Corps, Flushing, N.Y.
McGuire, George K., 7211 Merrill Ave., Chicago, Ill.
McGuire, J. Carson, Col. of Educ., University of Texas, Austin, Tex.
McHugh, Walter J., California State College, Hayward, Calif.
McInerney, George K., 88-42—210th St., Jamaica, N.Y.
McIntyre, John V., Wyckoff Public Schools, Wyckoff, N.J.
McIntyre, Margaret, George Washington Univ., Washington, D.C.
McIntyre, Richard E., 422 Richmond Ave., Burlington, N.C.
McIsaac, John S., 2829 Fourth Ave., Beaver Falls, Pa.
McKay, Jean W., Board of Education, Manassas, Va.
McKean, Robert C., Col. of Educ., University of Colorado, Boulder, Colo.
McKee, Frances, Div. of Educ., Bemidji State College, Bemidji, Minn.
McKelpin, Joseph P., 620 Peachtree St., N.E., Atlanta, Ga.
McKenna, John J., Jr., Brd. of Educ., Greenvillage Rd., Madison, N.J.
McKenney, James L., Grad. Sch. of Business, Harvard Univ., Boston, Mass.
McKercher, Mrs. Berneth N., 1600 Dryden Rd., Metamora, Mich.
McKinney, Antha, 733 W. Wayne St., Fort Wayne, Ind.
* McKinney, James, 505 Aragon Blvd., San Mateo, Calif.
McKinney, Lorella A., State Univ. Col., New Paltz, N.Y.
McKnight, Eloise, Dept. of Educ., St. Univ. Col., New Paltz, N.Y.
McKown, George W., 2603 S. Forest Ave., Palatine, Ill.
McKoy, Judith B., Hunter College, New York, N.Y.
McKune, Esther J., State Univ. Col., Oneonta, N.Y.
McLain, William T., P.O. Box 86, Newark, Del.
McLaren, Dallas C., 3240 Manoa Rd., Honolulu, Hawaii
McLaughlin, Eleanor T., Albion College, Albion, Mich.
McLaughlin, Kenneth F., 871 N. Madison, Arlington, Va.
McLaughlin, Rita E., 242 Marlborough St., Boston, Mass.
McLees, Mrs. Martha P., Univ. of South Carolina, Columbia, S.C.
McLellan, Keith A., 113 Heaslip St., Wollongong 2500, N.S.W., Australia
McLendon, Jonathan C., Col. of Educ., Univ. of Georgia, Athens, Ga.
McLennan, John A., Farmingdale Senior High School, Farmingdale, L.I., N.Y.
McMahan, John Julia, Keene State College, Keene, New Hampshire
McMahon, Charles W., 22218 Gregory, Dearborn, Mich.
McMahon, Frances E., University of Missouri, Columbia, Mo.
McManamon, James, O.F.M., Supt., P.O. Box 644, Columbus, Neb.
McManus, William E., Supt. Catholic Schls, 430 N. Michigan, Chicago, Ill.
McMaster, Blanche E., 102 Hull St., Bristol, Conn.
McMillan, Ann, Box 356, Blue Mountain Col., Blue Mountain, Miss.
McNally, Harold J., 7132 N. Crossway Rd., Fox Point, Wis.
McNeil, Don C., Dept. of Spec. Educ., University of Texas, Austin, Tex.
McNeill, Charles A., Sch. of Educ., University of S.C., Columbia, S.C.
McNutt, C. R., 116 Ridge Rd., Woodbridge, Va.
McPhee, Roderick F., Superintendent of Schools, Glencoe, Ill.
McPherson, Virgil L., Adams State College, Alamosa, Colo.
* **McPherson, W. N., Darke County Superintendent of Schools, Greenville, Ohio**
McSwain, E. T., University of North Carolina, Greensboro, N.C.
McSweeney, Maryellen, Mich. St. Univ., E. Lansing, Mich.
McTeer, Blanche R., 803 Lafayette St., Beaufort, S.C.

McWilliams, Elma A., William Carey College, Hattiesburg, Miss.
* Mead, Arthur R., 1719 N.W. 6th Ave., Gainesville, Fla.
Meade, David W., Red Wing High School, Red Wing, Minn.
Meaders, O. Donald, Col. of Educ., Michigan State Univ., East Lansing, Mich.
Mease, Clyde D., Superintendent of Schools, Humboldt, Iowa
Medeiros, Edward J., State Dept. of Education, Providence, R.I.
Medeiros, Joseph V., Superintendent of Schools, New London, Conn.
Medler, Byron W., Ball State Univ., Muncie, Ind.
Mednick, Martha T., 4101 Cathedral Ave., N.W., Apt. 806, Washington, D.C.
Medsker, Leland L., Ctr., Study of Higher Educ., Univ. of Calif., Berkeley, Calif.
Medsker, Nancy D., 611 Jerome St., Marshalltown, Ia.
Medved, A. A., Cherry Lawn School, Darien, Conn.
Meeks, Heber J., 12931 Morene St., Poway, Calif.
Meer, Samuel J., 631 Lafayette Ave., Mt. Vernon, N.Y.
Megiveron, Gene Erwin, 3170 Angelus Dr., Pontiac, Mich.
Megonegal, E. Russell, 464 Granite Ter., Springfield, Pa.
Mehrens, William, Michigan State Univ., East Lansing, Mich.
Meier, Frederick A., State Col. at Salem, Salem, Mass.
Meier, Mrs. Paralee B., 13 Woodside Ln., Chico, Calif.
Meier, Willard H., Dept. of Educ., La Sierra Col., Riverside, Calif.
Meinberg, Shirley, McGraw-Hill Book Co., Manchester, Mo.
Meinke, Dean L., Col. of Educ., University of Toledo, Toledo, Ohio
Meiselman, Max S., 87-56 Francis Lewis Blvd., Queens Village, N.Y.
Meissner, Harley W., 13 Devonshire, Pleasant Ridge, Mich.
Melberg, Merritt E., 1222 W. 22nd St., Cedar Falls, Iowa
Melbo, Irving R., University of Southern California, Los Angeles, Calif.
Melby, Ernest O., Michigan State University, East Lansing, Mich.
Mellott, Malcolm E., Col. of Educ., Temple University, Philadelphia, Pa.
Melnick, Curtis C., Supt., Dist. 14, Chicago Public Schls., Chicago, Ill.
Melnik, Amelia, Col. of Educ., University of Arizona, Tucson, Ariz.
Melnyk, Maria, 4432 S. Christiana Ave., Chicago, Ill.
Melrose, Ezra, Weaver High School, Hartford, Conn.
Melton, Arthur W., Dept. of Psychol., Univ. of Michigan, Ann Arbor, Mich.
Melvin, Keith L., Peru State College, Peru, Neb.
Mendel, Mrs. Dolores M., Paterson State College, Wayne, N.J.
* Mendoza, Romulo Y., 17 Iba, Sta. Mesa Heights, Quezon City, Philippines
Menge, Carleton P., University of New Hampshire, Durham, N.H.
Menge, Joseph W., Wayne University, Detroit, Mich.
Merchant, Vasant V., 308 W. Forest Ave., Flagstaff, Ariz.
Meredith, Cameron W., Southern Illinois Univ., Edwardsville, Ill.
Meredith, Thomas R., Prentice-Hall, Inc., Englewood Cliffs, N.J.
Merenda, Peter F., 258 Negansett Ave., Warwick, R.I.
Merideth, Howard V., Central Sch. Dist. No. 2, Syosset, L.I., N.Y.
Merigis, Harry, Eastern Illinois University, Charleston, Ill.
Merkhofer, Beatrice E., Chicago State College, Chicago, Ill.
Merryman, John E., Col. of Educ., Indiana University, Indiana, Pa.
Mersand, Joseph, Jamaica High Sch., 168th St. and Gothic Dr., Jamaica, N.Y.
Merwin, Jack C., Col. of Educ., Univ. of Minn., Minneapolis, Minn.
Messersmith, E. B., Loyola University, Los Angeles, Calif.
Messick, Rosemary, 111 N. Dunn, Bloomington, Ind.
Mestdagh, William A., 1640 Vernier Rd., Grosse Pointe Woods, Mich.
Metcalfe, William W., 68 Blue Hills Rd., Amherst, Mass.
Metfessel, Newton S., Univ. of Southern California, Los Angeles, Calif.
Metzner, William, 1121 Welsh Rd., Philadelphia, Pa.
Meyer, Ammon B., Route 1, Fredericksburg, Pa.
Meyer, Goldye W., Univ. of Bridgeport, Bridgeport, Conn.
Meyer, Lorraine V., 4501 N. 41st St., Milwaukee, Wis.
Meyer, Mrs. Marie, Douglass Col., Rutgers Univ., New Brunswick, N.J.
Meyer, Richard C., East. Texas State University, Commerce, Tex.
Meyer, Warren G., 5829 Portland Ave., So., Minneapolis, Minn.

Meyer, William T., Adams State College, Alamosa, Colo.
Meyerhoff, Herman, 5400 E. Pomona Blvd., Los Angeles, Calif.
Meyers, Howard E., Peru State Col., Peru, Neb.
Meyers, Max B., 324 E. 59th St., Brooklyn, N.Y.
Meyers, Robert E., Middlebury High School, Middlebury, Ind.
Meyers, Russell W., 5835 Kimbark Ave., Chicago, Ill.
Michael, Calvin B., Col. of Educ., East. Mich., Univ., Ypsilanti, Mich.
Michael, Lloyd S., Evanston Township High School, Evanston, Ill.
Michael, William B., Sch. of Educ., Univ. of So. California, Los Angeles, Calif.
Michaelis, John U., Sch. of Educ., Univ. of California, Berkeley, Calif.
Michaels, Melvin L., Highland Park High School, Highland Park, N.J.
Michalak, Daniel A., 13941 Minock Ave., Detroit, Mich.
Micheels, William J., Stout State University, Menomonie, Wis.
Michie, James K., Superintendent of Schools, St. Cloud, Minn.
Mickelsen, John K., 106 Jackson Dr., Liverpool, N.Y.
Mickelson, John M., Sch. of Educ., Temple University, Philadelphia, Pa.
Middledorf, Carl W., St. Peter's Lutheran School, East Detroit, Mich.
Middleton, C. A., State College of Iowa, Cedar Falls, Iowa
Miles, F. Mike, 424 Oakland Ave., Iowa City, Iowa
Mikulak, Michael N., 620 Sunset St., Iowa City, Iowa
Milchus, Norman J., 20504 Williamsburg Rd., Dearborn Heights, Mich.
Milheim, Robert P., Wright State Univ., Dayton, Ohio
Milhollan, Frank E., 6003—85th Pl., Hyattsville, Md.
Millar, Allen R., Southern State Tchrs. College, Springfield, S.D.
Miller, Arthur L., 5625 Rosa Ave., St. Louis, Mo.
Miller, Benjamin, 251 Ft. Washington Ave., New York, N.Y.
Miller, C. Earl, Jr., 157 Eldridge Ave., Mill Valley, Calif.
Miller, Carroll H., Dept. of Educ., Northern Illinois Univ., DeKalb, Ill.
Miller, Carroll L., Howard University, Washington, D.C.
Miller, Mrs. Daisy Lee, 7106 Farralone Ave., Canoga Pk., Calif.
Miller, Eliza Beth, Catskill High School, Catskill, N.Y.
Miller, Ethel B., 133 Joanne Ln., DeKalb, Ill.
Miller, G. Dean, State Dept. of Educ., St. Paul, Minn.
Miller, G. Harold, Gastonia City Schools, Gastonia, N.C.
Miller, George E., Univ. of Illinois Col. of Medicine, Chicago, Ill.
Miller, George R., University of Pittsburgh, Pittsburgh, Pa.
Miller, Mrs. Helen H., 1471 Westhaven Rd., San Marino, Calif.
Miller, Henry, Sch. of Educ., City College of New York, New York, N.Y.
Miller, Herbert R., 1229 Larrabee St., Los Angeles, Calif.
Miller, Howard G., North Carolina State College, Raleigh, N.C.
Miller, Ingrid O., Edina-Morningside Senior High School, Edina, Minn.
Miller, Ira E., Eastern Mennonite College, Harrisonburg, Va.
Miller, Jack W., Box 35, Peabody College, Nashville, Tenn.
Miller, Jacob W., Brooke Rd., Savbrooke Park, Pottstown, Pa.
Miller, John L., Supt. of Schools, Great Neck, N.Y.
Miller, Leon F., Northwest Missouri State College, Maryville, Mo.
Miller, Lyle L., Col. of Educ., University of Wyoming, Laramie, Wyo.
Miller, Mrs. Marian B., Dept. of Pub. Instr., Dover, Del.
Miller, Mrs. Mildred T., Box 215, Mooresville, N.C.
Miller, N. A., Jr., Watauga High School, Boone, N.C.
Miller, Norman N., Superintendent of Schools, Tyrone, Pa.
Miller, Paul A., 608 E. McMillan St., Cincinnati, Ohio
Miller, Richard I., Col. of Educ., University of Kentucky, Lexington, Ky.
Miller, Ross, West Georgia College, Carrollton, Ga.
Miller, Texton R., North Carolina State University, Raleigh, N.C.
Milling, Euleas, 231 Spring St., N.W., Concord, N.C.
Mills, Boyd C., Eastern Washington State Col., Cheney, Wash.
Mills, Donna M., 530 Taft Place, Gary, Ind.
Mills, Forrest L., Racine Public Library, Racine, Wis.
Mills, Henry C., Provost, St. John's Univ., Jamaica, N.Y.
Mills, Patricia, Miami University, Oxford, Ohio

Mills, Ruth I., Concord College, Athens, W.Va.
Mills, William H., Sch. of Educ., Univ. of Michigan, Ann Arbor, Mich.
Milner, Ernest J., Sch. of Educ., Syracuse University, Syracuse, N.Y.
Mimaki, James M., 11224 Huston St., North Hollywood, Calif.
Mims, Samuel, Bethany Bible College, Santa Cruz, Calif.
Mincy, Homer F., Superintendent of Schools, Greeneville, Tenn.
Miniclier, Gordon E., 1965 Laurel Ave., St. Paul, Minn.
Mininberg, Elliot I., 7-13 Washington Square, New York, N.Y.
Minkler, F. W., 15 Oakburn Crest, Willowdale, Ont., Canada
Minkoff, Sol., 601 N. Eastwood, Mt. Prospect, Ill.
Minnis, Roy B., 7889 E. Kenyon Ave., Denver, Colo.
Minock, Mrs. Daniel F., 5520 Donna Ave, Tarzana, Calif.
Minogue, Mildred M., 612 Ridge Ave., Evanston, Ill.
Minor, Pearle Estelle, 1716 Allison St., N.W., Washington, D.C.
Misner, Paul J., Western Michigan Univ., Kalamazoo, Mich.
Mitby, Norman P., 211 N. Carroll St., Madison, Wis.
Mitchell, Addie S., Dept. of Eng., Morehouse College, Atlanta, Ga.
Mitchell, Donald P., 5166 Tilden St., N.W., Washington, D.C.
Mitchell, Guy Clifford, Sch. of Educ., Baylor University, Waco, Tex.
Mitra, Gopal C., 5120 S. Hyde Park Blvd., Chicago, Ill.
Mitzel, Harold E., 928 S. Sparks St., State College, Pa.
Miyasato, Albert H., 297 Puiwa Rd., Honolulu, Hawaii
Mobley, Frank, Dept. of Educ., Louisiana College, Pineville, La.
Moe, Alden J., Dept. of Educ., Clarke College, Dubuque, Iowa
Moffatt, Maurice P., 210 Valencia Blvd., Largo, Fla.
Mohr, Raymond E., 2050 S. 108th St., Milwaukee, Wis.
Molenkamp, Alice, 5 Homeside Lane, White Plains, N.Y.
Moll, Boniface E., St. Benedict's College, Atchison, Kan.
Molloy, Eugene J., Superintendent, Catholic Schools, Brooklyn, N.Y.
Monell, Ira H., 2714 Augusta Blvd., Chicago, Ill.
Monfort, Jay B., 3150 Maranja Dr., Walnut Creek, Calif.
Monke, Mrs. Edgar W., High Point High School, Beltsville, Md.
Monnin, Lloyd N., 4733 W. National Rd., Springfield, Ohio
Monroe, Bruce Perry, 640 Sea Breeze Dr., Seal Beach, Calif.
Monroe, Charles R., Wilson Junior College, 7047 S. Stewart Ave., Chicago, Ill.
Monroe, Mrs. Helen V., 1253 Lake Breeze, Oshkosh, Wis.
Monsanto, David, P.O. Box 672, Charlotte Amalie, Virgin Islands
Montor, Karel, 732 Cottonwood Dr., Severna Park, Md.
Monts, Elizabeth A., Home Ec. Dept., Univ. of Wisconsin, Madison, Wis.
Moody, Lamar, 1100 Bridle Park Rd., Rt. 3, Box 303, Starkville, Miss.
Moore, Alexander M., Crispus Attucks High School, Indianapolis, Ind.
Moore, Arnold J., Col. of Educ., Kansas State Univ., Manhattan, Kan.
Moore, Barry E., 103 William Dr., Normal, Ill.
Moore, C. Fletcher, Box 186, Elon College, N.C.
Moore, Harold E., Col. of Educ., Arizona State University, Tempe, Ariz.
Moore, Robert Ezra, 20 Tapia Dr., San Francisco, Calif.
Moore, Wilhelmina E., C. D. Hine Library, State Office Bldg., Hartford, Conn.
Moore, William J., 372 High St., Richmond, Ky.
Moorefield, Thomas E., Off. of Educ., 400 Maryland Ave., Washington, D.C.
Moorhead, Sylvester A., Sch. of Educ., Univ. of Mississippi, University, Miss.
Moray, Joseph, San Francisco State College, San Francisco, Calif.
Morden, Frederick P., Dept. of Educ., Univ. of Mich., Ann Arbor, Mich.
Morehouse, Charles O., 601 S. Howard St., Kimball, Neb.
Moreland, Kenneth O., 107 William Dr., Normal, Ill.
Moretz, Elmo E., Grad. Sch. of Educ., Eastern Kentucky Univ., Richmond, Ky.
Morford, John A., John Carroll University, Cleveland, Ohio
Morgan, Donald L., 20 Graham Ave., Brookeville, Pa.
Morgan, Lorraine Lee, 6909 Meade St., Pittsburgh, Pa.
Morgan, Muriel, Newark State College, Union, N.J.
Morgan, Roland R., Superintendent, Mooresville City Schls., Mooresville, N.C.
Morgenroth, Edwin C., 714 W. California Blvd., Pasadena, Calif.

Morgenstern, Anne, 2037 Oliver Way, Merrick, L.I., N.Y.
Moriarty, Thomas E., 112 Independence, Kingston, R.I.
Moriconi, R. J., 2107 Celeste Dr., Modesto, Calif.
Morley, Franklin P., 101 Arthur Ave., Webster Groves, Mo.
Morris, Earl W., Rt. 5, East Lake Drive, Edwardsville, Ill.
Morris, George L., Kearney State Col., Kearney, Neb.
Morris, Gregory A., 811 Maple St., West Mifflin, Pa.
Morris, James D., Col. of Educ., Univ. of Hawaii, Honolulu,, Hawaii
Morris, James L., 675 Omar Circle, Yellow Springs, Ohio
Morris, James V., P.O. Box 2702, Wilmington, Del.
Morris, Rev. John E., Diocesean Schls., Paterson, N.J.
Morris, John K., 6906 Lincoln Oaks Dr., Fair Oaks, Calif.
Morris, M. B., 1133 Westridge, Abilene, Tex.
Morris, Mrs. Marjorie S., 16225 Moorpark, Encino, Calif.
Morrison, D. A., East York Bd. of Educ., 670 Cosburn Ave., Toronto, Ont.
* Morrison, J. Cayce, 580 North Bank Ln., Lake Forest, Ill.
Morrison, Leger R., 16 Brown St., Warren, R.I.
Morrissey, Madeline M., 110 Livingston St., Brooklyn, N.Y.
Morrow, Richard G., 502 State St., Madison, Wis.
Morrow, Robert O., Dept. of Psych., State College of Ark., Conway, Ark.
Morse, Richard N., 2109 Lemmon Way, Hanford, Calif.
Morse, William C., 2010 Penncraft Ct., Ann Arbor, Mich.
Morton, R. Clark, 210 Drummond St., Warrensburg, Mo.
Mosbo, Alvin O., Colorado State College, Greeley, Colo.
Moseley, S. Meredith, 424 N.W. 15th Way, Fort Lauderdale, Fla.
Moser, Robert P., 316 Master Hall, Univ. of Wis., Madison, Wis.
Moser, William G., 95 Concord Rd., Chester, Pa.
Moses, Elizabeth, 7483 Countrybrook Dr., Indianapolis, Ind.
Mosher, Frank K., Utica Col. of Syracuse University, Utica, N.Y.
Moss, Theodore C., 88 Sixth Ave., Oswego, N.Y.
Mother A. Husson, Convent of the Sacred Heart, Portsmouth, R.I.
Mother C. Welch, San Francisco College for Women, San Francisco, Calif.
Mother Margaret Burke, Barat Col. of the Sacred Heart, Lake Forest, Ill.
Mother Mary Aimee Rossi, San Diego Col. for Women, San Diego, Calif.
Mother Mary Dennis, Rosemont College, Rosemont, Pa.
Mother M. Gonzaga, Blessed Sacrament College, Cornwells Heights, Pa.
Mother Miriam Regina, Sacred Heart School, Vineland, N.J.
Mother Rose Alice, 2675 Larpenteur Ave. East, St. Paul, Minn.
Mott, Edward B., R.F.D., Richmondville, N.Y.
Motyka, Agnes L., 6311 Utah Ave., N.W., Washington, D.C.
Mour, Stanley I., University of Louisville, Louisville, Ky.
Mouton, R. von Phul, P.O. Drawer E, Lafayette, La.
Muck, Mrs. Ruth E. S., 1091 Stony Point Rd., Grand Island, N.Y.
Muck, Webster C., Bethel Col., St. Paul, Minn.
Muckenhirn, Erma F., Dept. of Educ., East. Mich. Univ., Ypsilanti, Mich.
Muellen, T. K., 3666 Spruell Dr., Silver Spring, Md.
Mueller, Richard J., Northern Illinois University, DeKalb, Ill.
Mueller, Siegfried G., 5429 Sawyer, Chicago, Ill.
Mueller, Van D., Col. of Educ., Univ. of Minn., Minneapolis, Minn.
Mullen, Norman, Superintendent of Schools, Woodsville, N.H.
Muller, Philippe H., University of Neuchatel, Neuchatel, Switzerland
Mulliner, John H., 1509 Topp Lane, Glenview, Ill.
Mullins, Martin M., 501 Claremont Dr., Morgan Hill, Calif.
Mulrooney, Thomas W., Board of Public Education, Wilmington, Del.
Mumford, Kennedy A., 14845 Robinson St., Miami, Fla.
Munro, James J. R., Sch. of Educ., Univ. of Mont., Missoula, Mont.
Muns, Arthur C., Northern Illinois Univ., DeKalb, Ill.
Munshaw, Carroll, 555 Byron St., Plymouth, Mich.
Muntyan, Milosh, Michigan State University, East Lansing, Mich.
Munves, Elizabeth D., New York University, 37 Washington Sq., New York, N.Y.
Murdick, Olin J., Superintendent, Diocesan Schools, Saginaw, Mich.

Murdock, Mrs. Ruth, Andrews University, Berrien Springs, Mich.
Murfin, Don L., Prin., South H.S., Bakersfield, Calif.
Murphy, Anne P., 480 S. Jersey St., Denver, Colo.
Murphy, Daniel A., Seton Hall University, South Orange, N.J.
Murphy, Dennis K., Grinnell College, Grinnell, Iowa
Murphy, Forrest W., 201 S. Hickory St., Aberdeen, Miss.
Murphy, Kenneth B., Jersey City State Col., Jersey City, N.J.
Murphy, Loretta M., 415 Larkin Ave., Joliet, Ill.
Murphy, William F., 37 High St., Milford, Mass.
Murray, Joseph A., Jr., Cranston School Dept., Cranston, R.I.
Murray, William J., 1 Bay View Pl., South Boston, Mass.
Murthy, Vincent, Prin., Mt. Tabor Train. Col., Kerala State, South India
Musgrave, Ray S., Univ. of Southern Mississippi, Hattiesburg, Miss.
Musick, James E., University of California, Los Angeles, Calif.
Muskal, Fred, 1517 East 54th St., Chicago, Ill.
Myer, Marshall E., Col. of Educ., Univ. of Tenn., Knoxville, Tenn.
Myers, Donald A., 1100 Glendon Ave., Los Angeles, Calif.
Myers, G. T., Superintendent of Schools, Lancaster, S.C.
Myers, Garry C., Ed., *Highlights for Children*, Honesdale, Pa.

Nacke, Phil L., Carl Hayden High School, Phoenix, Ariz.
Nadler, Leonard, Col. of Educ., Univ. of Md., College Park, Md.
Nafziger, Mary K., Goshen College, Goshen, Ind.
Nagel, Wilma I., Dept. of Educ., Univ. of Rhode Island, Kingston, R.I.
Nagy, Richard, North Junior High School, Bloomfield, N.J.
Nahm, Helen, Dean, Sch. of Nurs., Univ. of California, San Francisco, Calif.
Nahshon, Samuel, Hebrew Teachers College, Brookline, Mass.
Nair, Ralph K., University of California, Santa Barbara, Calif.
Nakashima, Mitsugi, P.O. Box 155, Kaumakani, Kanai, Hawaii
Nally, Thomas P., University of Rhode Island, Kingston, R.I.
Nance, Mrs. Afton Dill, State Educ. Bldg., 721 Capitol Ave., Sacramento, Calif.
Nance, Helen M., Illinois State University, Normal, Ill.
Narkis, William F., 1046 S. 22nd Ave., Bellwood, Ill.
Nash, Philip C., Rt. 1, 21 Sycamore Pl., Carmel, Calif.
Naslund, Robert A., Sch. of Educ., Univ. of So. California, Los Angeles, Calif.
Nason, Doris E., University of Connecticut, Storrs, Conn.
Nasser, Sheffield T., 6801 Pennywell Dr., Nashville, Tenn.
Nasstrom, Roy R., Jr., 6212 Antioch St., Oakland, Calif.
Nations, Jimmy E., 9806 Georgia Ave., No. 201, Silver Spring, Md.
Nattress, LeRoy W., 430 N. Mich. Ave., Chicago, Ill.
Nault, William H., Field Enterprises Educational Corp., Chicago, Ill.
Naus, Grant H., 374 "D" Ave., Coronado, Calif.
Naylor, Marilyn, 233 W. Cascade, River Falls, Wis.
Neal, Ellis H., Superintendent of Schools, Pendleton, Ore.
Neale, Daniel C., Col. of Educ., University of Minnesota, Minneapolis, Minn.
Nearhoff, Orrin, 2745 Bennett Ave., Des Moines, Iowa
Nearing, Mrs. Jewell, 9050 S. Parnell, Chicago, Ill.
Nebel, Dale, Colorado State College, Greeley, Colo.
Nelson, Carl B., New York State University College, Cortland, N.Y.
Nelson, Clifford L., Dept. of Ag. Ed., Univ. of Minnesota, St. Paul, Minn.
Nelson, Edith I., 380 Claremont Ave., Montclair, N.J.
Nelson, Ethel C., 692 Des Plaines Ave., Des Plaines, Ill.
Nelson, Florence A., Univ. of South Carolina, 825 Sumter St., Columbia, S.C.
Nelson, Frank G., R. 2, Box 169-0, Pullman, Wash.
Nelson, Jack L., State Univ. Col., Buffalo, N.Y.
Nelson, Janice Ann, 8350 Olentangy River Rd., Worthington, Ohio
Nelson, Joan B., University of Pittsburgh, Pittsburgh, Pa.
Nelson, John M., Dept. of Educ., Purdue University, Lafayette, Ind.
Nelson, Kenneth G., Shore Acres, Dunkirk, N.Y.
Nelson, Lois Ney, 7 Lakeview Dr., Daly City, Calif.
Nelson, Margaret B., State College of Iowa, Cedar Falls, Iowa

Nelson, Norbert J., 2103 Indiana Trail Dr., West Lafayette, Ind.
Nelson, Orville W., Stout State College, Menomonie, Wis.
Nelson, Pearl Astrid, Boston University, 332 Bay State Rd., Boston, Mass.
Nelson, Quentin D., 5101 N. Francisco Ave., Chicago, Ill.
Nelson, Sylvia, 415 W. 8th St., Topeka, Kans.
Nelson, Torlef, University of Hawaii, Honolulu, Hawaii
Nelum, J. Nathaniel, Div. of Educ., Bishop College, Dallas, Tex.
Nemzek, Claude L., Educ. Dept., Univ. of Detroit, Detroit, Mich.
Nerbovig, Marcella, Northern Illinois University, DeKalb, Ill.
Nesbitt, Hyacinth P., Box 712, Frederiksted, St. Croix, U.S. Virgin Is.
Nesbitt, William O., University of Houston, Houston, Tex.
Nesi, Carmella, 906 Peace St., Pelham Manor, N.Y.
Netsky, Martin G., Dept. of Path., University of Virginia, Charlottesville, Va.
Neuner, Elsie Flint, 2 Atlas Place, Mt. Vernon, N.Y.
Neville, Donald, Child Study Center, Peabody College, Nashville, Tenn.
Neville, Richard F., Col. of Educ., University of Maryland, College Park, Md.
Nevin, Mrs. Virginia L., 418 Franklin St., Fayetteville, N.Y.
Newburn, H. K., Col. of Educ., Arizona State University, Tempe, Ariz.
Newbury, David N., 22929 John Rd., Hazel Park, Mich.
Newcomer, Charles A., Lock Haven State Col., Lock Haven, Pa.
Newman, David, Sch. Psych., Oceanside, N.Y.
Newman, Herbert M., Educ. Dept., Brooklyn College, Brooklyn, N.Y.
Newman, Wilfred, West High School, Rochester, N.Y.
Newsom, Herman A., P.O. Box 5243, North Texas Station, Denton, Tex.
Newton, Kathryn L., 52 Fourteenth Ave., Columbus, Ohio
Newton, W. L., Florida State University, Tallahassee, Fla.
Nicholas, William T., 1019 Caldwell Ave., Modesto, Calif.
Nichols, David L., University of Maine, Orono, Me.
Nichols, Richard H., 1703 S.W. 16th Ct., Gainesville, Fla.
Nichols, Richard J., Newark State College, Newark, N.J.
Nicholson, Jon M., Carleton College, Northfield, Minn.
Nicholson, Lawrence E., Psych. Dept., Harris Tchrs. Col., St. Louis, Mo.
Nicholson, Omega, Texas Wesleyan Col., Ft. Worth, Texas
Nicholson, Sarah Alice, 1009 E. Hatton St., Pensacola, Fla.
Nickerson, Donald R., Beaver Country Day School, Chestnut Hill, Mass.
Nickles, Martin, Jefferson Junior High School, Pittsburgh, Pa.
Niehaus, Philip C., Sch. of Educ., Duquesne University, Pittsburgh, Pa.
Niemeyer, John H., Bank Street College of Education, New York, N.Y.
Nigg, William J., Superintendent of Schools, Mankato, Minn.
Niland, William P., 417 Candleberry Rd., Walnut Creek, Calif.
Nimroth, William T., 1011 Wood Bridge, Ann Arbor, Mich.
Nixon, Clifford L., Penbrooke State College, Penbrooke, N.C.
Nixon, John Erskine, Sch. of Educ., Stanford University, Stanford, Calif.
Noar, Gertrude, 500 E. 77th St., New York, N.Y.
Noe, Samuel V., 506 West Hill St., Louisville, Ky.
Nolan, William J., Superintendent of Schools, Falls Village, Conn.
Noll, Frances E., 1810 Taylor St., N.W., Washington, D.C.
Noll, Victor H., Col. of Educ., Michigan State Univ., East Lansing, Mich.
Noon, Elizabeth F., F. A. Owen Publishing Co., Dansville, N.Y.
Norcross, Claude E., 301 E. Lucard, Taft, Calif.
Nord, Larry R., Supt., Southington Local Schools, Southington, Ohio
Nordberg, H. Orville, Sacramento State College, Sacramento, Calif.
Norman, Ralph Paul, 18395 Clemison Ave., Saratoga, Calif.
Norman, Robert H., 315—4th Ave., N.W., Faribault, Minn.
Norris, Mrs. Dorothy G., 1907 Dumaine St., New Orleans, La.
Norris, Ralph C., 112-116—11th St., Des Moines, Iowa
North, Stewart D., 502 State St., Madison, Wis.
Northey, Ethel May, 224 Iowa Ave., Muscatine, Iowa
Northrup, Sunbeam Ann, 1816 Queens Lane, Arlington, Va.
Norton, Chauncey E., 31 Decker Rd., R.D. 1, Newfield, N.J.
Norton, Frank Edgar, Jr., 225 Fairway Dr., Wharton, Texas

Novak, Benjamin J., Frankford High School, Philadelphia, Pa.
Novotney, Jerrold M., 1100 Glendon Ave., Los Angeles, Calif.
Now, Herbert O., State Dept. of Educ., Findlay, Ohio
Nowak, Arlene T., Educ. Dept., Univ. of Detroit, Detroit, Mich.
Nowicki, Ervin E., 2967 N. Prospect Ave., Milwaukee, Wis.
Noyes, M. Elliot, Great Neck No. Senior High School, Great Neck, N.Y.
Nunnally, Nancy, 5916 Monticello Ave., Cincinnati, Ohio
Nussel, Edward J., Col. of Educ., Univ. of Toledo, Toledo, Ohio
Nutter, H. E., Norman Hall, University of Florida, Gainesville, Fla.
* Nutterville, Catherine, 1701—16th St., N.W., Washington, D.C.
Nutting, William C., 4653 Fortuna Way, Salt Lake City, Utah
Nuzum, Lawrence H., Marshall University, Huntington, W.Va.
Nye, Robert E., Sch. of Music, University of Oregon, Eugene, Ore.
Nygaard, Joseph M., Butler University, Indianapolis, Ind.
Nystrand, Raphael O., Ohio State Univ., Columbus, Ohio

Oakland, Thomas D., 2702 Greenlawn Pkwy., Austin, Tex.
Oaks, Ruth E., B-104 Haverford Villa, Haverford, Pa.
Oberholtzer, Kenneth E., Superintendent of Schools, Denver, Colo.
Obourn, L. C., Superintendent of Schools, East Rochester, N.Y.
O'Brien, Cyril C., P.O. Box 666, Edmonton, Alba., Canada
O'Connor, John D., Maple Park, Ill.
O'Connor, Mrs. Marguerite O., Maple Park. Ill.
O'Connor, P. D., 17 Pacific St., Manly, N.S.W., Australia
O'Donnell, Lewis B., State University of New York, Oswego, N.Y.
Oehring, Esther A., Southern Oregon College, Ashland, Ore.
Oen, Urban T., Michigan State Univ., East Lansing, Mich.
O'Fallon, O. K., Sch. of Educ., Kansas State University, Manhattan, Kan.
O'Farrell, John J., Loyola University, 7101 W. 80th St., Los Angeles, Calif.
O'Hare, Mary Rita, 212 Hollywood Ave., Tuckahoe, N.Y.
O'Hearn, George T., 576 Park Lane, Madison, Wis.
Ohlsen, Merle M., Col. of Educ., University of Illinois, Urbana, Ill.
Ojeman, Ralph H., Educ. Research Council, Rockefeller Bldg., Cleveland, Ohio
O'Kane, Robert M., 306 Nut Bush Circle, Jamestown, N.C.
O'Keefe, Kathleen, 5441 Sanger Ave., Alexandria, Va.
Okula, Frederick S., 90 Mattatuck Rd., Bristol, Conn.
Olander, Herbert T., University of Pittsburgh, Pittsburgh, Pa.
* Oldham, Mrs. Birdie V., 621 W. 2nd St., Lakeland, Fla.
Olds, Victoria M., CSWE, 345 E. 46th St., New York, N.Y.
O'Leary, Francis V., 5480 S. Cornell Ave., Chicago, Ill.
Olicker, Isidore I., 85-17—143rd St., Jamaica, N.Y.
Oliver, George J., Richmond Professional Institute, Richmond, Va.
Oliver, T. S., N .M. Highlands University, Las Vegas, N.M.
Ollenburger, Alvin, 2613 Jean Duluth Rd., Duluth, Minn.
Olmsted, M. D., State University College, Oneonta, N.Y.
Olphert, Warwick B., Univ. of New England, Armidale, N.S.W., Australia
Olsen, Eugene A., Purdue University, Lafayette, Ind.
Olsen, Hans C., Jr., University of Missouri, St. Louis, Mo.
Olson, Boyd E., P.O. Box 226, Singapore, Rep. of Singapore
Olson, Gerald Victor, 8610 W. 19th St., Phoenix, Ariz.
Olson, LeRoy C., 329 Nichols Ave., McDaniels Crest, Wilmington, Del.
Olson, Manley E., Col. of Educ., Univ. of Minnesota, Minneapolis, Minn.
Olson, R. A., Ball State University, Muncie, Ind.
Olson, Richard F., Western Pub. Educ. Co., Ossining, N.Y.
* Olson, Willard C., Sch. of Educ., University of Michigan, Ann Arbor, Mich.
Olson, William L., 1945 Sharondale Ave., St. Paul, Minn.
O'Malley, Mrs. Martha R., 44 Glenview Dr., Belleville, Ill.
O'Mara, J. Francis, 29 Snowling Rd., Uxbridge, Mass.
O'Neill, John H., 1039 W. Vine St., Springfield, Ill.
O'Neill, John J., Boston State College, Boston, Mass.

O'Neill, Leo W., Jr., Col. of Educ., University of Maryland, College Park, Md.
O'Neill, Patrick J., Superintendent, Diocesan Schools, Fall River, Mass.
Onkle, Paul, 8309 Mackenzie Rd., St. Louis, Mo.
Oole, Eugenia M., 6012 Drew Ave. So., Minneapolis, Minn.
O'Piela, Joan M., Res. & Dev., Detroit Pub. Schools, Detroit, Mich.
Oppenheimer, J. J., Belknap Campus, University of Louisville, Louisville, Ky.
Oppleman, Dan L., P.O. Box 182, Cedar Falls, Iowa
Ore, Malvern L., 903 East 52nd St., Chicago, Ill.
Ore, Stanley H., Jr., 2221 Emmers Dr., Appleton, Wis.
O'Reilly, Robert C., University of Nebraska at Omaha, Omaha, Neb.
Orlovich, Joseph Jr., 206 S. Reed St., Joliet, Ill.
O'Rourke, Joseph, 3197 Gerbert Rd., Columbus, Ohio
Orr, Beryl, 609 Gladys Dr., Middletown, Ohio
Orr, Charles W., 137 Oakmont Circle, Durham, N.C.
Orr, Louise, 925 Crockett St., Amarillo, Tex.
Orton, Don A., Lesley College, Cambridge, Mass.
Orton, Kenneth D., Tchrs. Col., University of Nebraska, Lincoln, Neb.
Osborn, Wayland W., 2701 Hickman Rd., Des Moines, Iowa
O'Shields, Eva W., 6600 Arcadia Woods Rd., Columbia, S.C.
Osibov, Henry, University of Oregon, Eugene, Ore.
Ostler, Ruth-Ellen, 318 State St., Albany, N.Y.
Ostrander, Raymond H., 15 Winter St., Weston, Mass.
Ostwalt, Jay H., P.O. Box 387, Davidson, N.C.
Osuch, A. E., 6636 N. Odell, Chicago, Ill.
Osuna, Pedro, Sch. of Educ., Univ. of the Pacific, Stockton, Calif.
Oswalt, Howard C., 1518 N. McAllister Ave., Tempe, Ariz.
Oswalt, William W., Jr., 9 Berger St., Emmaus, Pa.
Otomo, Aiko, 3085 Felix St., Honolulu, Hawaii
O'Toole, James J., Valley Central Jr. H.S., Middletown, N.Y.
Otto, Henry J., University of Texas, Austin, Tex.
Otts, John, University of South Carolina, Columbia, S.C.
Ouellette, Helen C., College of St. Rose, Albany, N.Y.
Overfield, Ruth, State Educ. Bldg., 721 Capitol Ave., Sacramento, Calif.
*Overstreet, George Thomas, 811 S. Frances St., Terrell, Tex.
Owen, John M., Psych. Dept., State University College, Potsdam, N.Y.
Owings, Ralph S., Univ. of Southern Mississippi, Hattiesburg, Miss.

Pace, C. Robert, Sch. of Educ., University of California, Los Angeles, Calif.
Packer, C. Kyle, 629 Deerfield Dr., North Tonawanda, N.Y.
Page, Ellis B., Bur. of Educ. Res., Univ. of Connecticut, Storrs, Conn.
Pagel, Betty Lou, 304 E. 5th Ave., Cheyenne, Wyo.
Painter, Fred B., Superintendent, Brighton School Dist. No. 1, Rochester, N.Y.
Palisi, Anthony T., Seton Hall Univ., 181 Stanton, Rahway, N.J.
Palisi, Marino A., 300 Woodland Ave., Point Pleasant Beach, N.J.
Palladino, Joseph R., State College, Framingham, Mass.
Pallesen, Lorraine Sysel, 2727 Royal Ct., Lincoln, Neb.
Palliser, Guy C., P.O. Box 30-632, Lower Hutt, New Zealand
Palmer, Albert, San Joaquin Delta College, Stockton, Calif.
Palmer, Anne M. H., 22277 Cass Ave., Woodland Hills, Calif.
Palmer, Dale H., Univ. of Washington, Seattle, Wash.
Palmer, Frank J., 208 Church St., North Syracuse, N.Y.
Palmer, James Bey, Illinois State University, Normal, Ill.
Palmer, John C., Tufts University, Medford, Mass.
Palmer, Lulu, State Department of Education, Montgomery, Ala.
Paltridge, James G., 2632 Tamalipas Ave., El Cerrito, Calif.
Panos, Robert J., 12903 Crookston Lane, Rockville, Md.
Papanek, Ernst, 1 West 64th St., New York, N.Y.
Papke, Ross R., Wisconsin State Univ., Richland Center, Wis.
Paradis, Edward E., Univ. of Minn., Minneapolis, Minn.
Parelius, Allen M., St. Louis University, St. Louis, Mo.
Parisho, Eugenia B., Lab. School, Univ. of North. Iowa, Cedar Falls, Ia.

Park, Mary Frances, Educ. Dept., Sam Houston State Col., Huntsville, Texas
Park, Maxwell G., 44 Clayton Ave., Cortland, N.Y.
Parker, Don H., Emlimar, Big Sur, Calif.
Parker, Emma C., Catholic University of America, Washington, D.C.
Parker, Glenn C., Harrisburg Schools, Harrisburg, Pa.
Parker, Jack F., University of Oklahoma, Norman, Okla.
Parker, James R., 210 Thornbrook Rd., DeKalb, Ill.
Parker, Jesse J., Louisiana State University, Baton Rouge, La.
Parker, Mrs. Lilla C., Box 464-A, Donnan Road, Macon, Ga.
Parker, Virjean, 765 Commonwealth Ave., Boston, Mass.
Parker, Wilfred G., 322 Eagle Dr., Placentia, Calif.
Parkinson, Daniel S., 409 W. Vine St., Oxford, Ohio
Parr, Kenneth E., Box 1348, c/o Tapline, Beirut, Lebanon
Parrett, Betty J., Marion County Interm. Educ. Dist., Salem, Ore.
Parry, O. Meredith, William Penn Senior High School, York, Pa.
Parsey, John M., 305 Droste Circle, East Lansing, Mich.
Parsley, Kenneth B., 214 St. Ives Dr., Severna Park, Md.
Parsons, Brooks A., Superintendent of Schools, Norwood, Ohio
Parsons, David R., Alexander Mackie Col., Paddington, N.S.W., Australia
Pascoe, David D., LaMesa Spring Valley Sch. Dist., LaMesa, Calif.
Passow, Aaron Harry, Teachers College, Columbia University, New York, N.Y.
Paster, Julius, 867 Barbara Dr., Teaneck, N.J.
Patch, Robert B., 4 Carleton Dr., Glens Falls, N.Y.
Pate, Mildred, 1806 East 6th St., Greenville, N.C.
Paterson, John J., 377 Lawnview Dr., Morgantown, W.Va.
Paton, Maurice, 936 N. Ashland Ave., Chicago, Ill.
Paton, William, Superintendent of Schools, Oconomowoc, Wis.
Patrick, Edward M., Jr., 77 Belchertown Rd., Amherst, Mass.
Patrick, Robert B., 433 W. Park Ave., State College, Pa.
Patten, W. George, 602 Eagle Heights, Madison, Wis.
Patteson, Charles, Lynchburg College, Lynchburg, Va.
Patterson, Gordon E., New Mexico Highlands Univ., Las Vegas, N.M.
Patterson, Harold D., 3736 Crestbrook Rd., Birmingham, Ala.
* Patterson, Herbert, 406 S. Stallard Ave., Stillwater, Okla.
Patterson, Walter G., 1330 Highland Ave., Needham, Mass.
Patton, Earl D., Superintendent of Schools, Culver City, Calif.
Patty, Delbert L., 9103 Lincolnshire W., DeKalb, Ill.
Paul, Marvin S., 4750 W. Glenlake Ave., Chicago, Ill.
Paul, Warren I., 2203 Indiana Ave., Columbus, Ohio
Paulsen, Gaige B., 36 Fairview Ave., Athens, Ohio
Paulson, Alice T., 113½ N. Main St., Blue Earth, Minn.
Paulson, Casper F., Jr., Oregon College of Education, Monmouth, Ore.
Paulston, Rolland G., University of Pittsburgh, Pittsburgh, Pa.
Pautz, Wilmer A., Wisconsin State University, Eau Claire, Wis.
Paxson, Robert C., Troy State College, Troy, Ala.
Paxton, Mrs. J. Hall, 1405 Pine St., Apt. 606, St. Louis, Mo.
Payne, David L., Box 310, MSCW, Columbus, Miss.
Payne, LaVeta M., P.O. Box 591, Pierson and Suhrie Dr., Collegedale, Tenn.
Payne, William V., Tuskegee Institute, Tuskegee Institute, Ala.
Paynovitch, Nicholas, 921 W. Las Lomitas, Tucson, Ariz.
Payzant, Thomas W., 2011 Shalett St., New Orleans, La.
Paziotopoulos, James A., St. Constantine School, Oak Park, Ill.
Pearson, James R., Dade Co. Public Schools, Miami, Fla.
Pearson, Lois, State University College, Buffalo, N.Y.
Pebley, Wilson A., 310 Lincoln Way East. McConnellsburg, Pa.
Peccolo, Charles M., 2840 Nevada St., Manhattan, Kan.
Peckenpaugh, Donald H., Rt. 1, West Bend, Wis.
Pederson, Arne K., Pacific Lutheran University, Tacoma, Wash.
Pederson. Clara A., Dept. of Educ., Univ. of North Dakota, Grand Forks, N.D.
Pedvin, Ruth E., 9150 Roberds St., Alta Loma, Calif.
Peiffer, Paul D., 5902 Jonestown Rd., Harrisburg, Pa.

Peirce, Leonard D., Olympia Public Schools, Olympia, Wash.
Pella, Milton O., Wisconsin High School, Univ. of Wisconsin, Madison, Wis.
Pellegrin, Lionel, 945 E. River Oaks Dr., Baton Rouge, La.
Pellett, Vernon L., 1103 Catalpa Cir., Madison, Wis.
Pelton, Frank M., Dept. of Educ., Univ. of Rhode Island, Kingston, R.I.
Pelty, Michael A., 4906 S. Greenwood, Chicago, Ill.
Peltz, Seamen, 6650 S. Ellis Ave., Chicago, Ill.
Pendarvis, S. T., McNeese State College, Lake Charles, La.
Penn, Floy L., Mt. Lebanon Public Schls., Bower Hill Rd., Pittsburgh, Pa.
Penniman, Blanche L., Bergenfield High School, Bergenfield, N.J.
Pentecost, Percy M., 540 Coconut St., Satellite Beach, Fla.
Perdew, Philip W., Sch. of Educ., University of Denver, Denver, Colo.
Perkins, Frederick D., Alto High School, Alto, La.
Perry, Arthur V., Superintendent of Schools, Batavia, Ill.
Perry, Clarence R., Shady Lane, Dover, Mass.
Perry, Harold J., 1040 Park Ave., West Highland Park, Ill.
Perry, James Olden, 3602 S. MacGregor Way, Houston, Tex.
Perry, T. Edward, Chagrin River Rd., Gates Mills, Ohio
Perryman, Lucile C., 330 Third Ave., New York, N.Y.
Pescosolido, John R., Central Connecticut State College, New Britain, Conn.
Peters, J. L., Sr., 3505 Rangeley Dr., Flint, Mich.
Peters, Jon S., California State College, Hillary Rd., Hayward, Calif.
Peters, Mary Magdalene, 1366 Lafayette Rd., Claremont, Calif.
Petersen, Clarence E., 10 Fulton St., Redwood City, Calif.
Petersen, Dorothy G., Trenton State College, Trenton, N.J.
Petersen, Dwain F., 323 Emerson Ln., Mankato, Minn.
Peterson, Bernadine H., University of Wisconsin, Madison, Wis.
Peterson, Donald W., 4708—25th Ave., Rock Island, Ill.
Peterson, Donovan, Amer. Embassy, Tegucigueka, Honduras, Central Amer.
Peterson, Douglas W., Dept. of Educ., Kalamazoo College, Kalamazoo, Mich.
Peterson, Mrs. Leona, 341 Poplar Ave., Elmhurst, Ill.
Peterson, Miriam E., 5422 Wayne Ave., Chicago, Ill.
Pethick, Wayne M., 6136 Northwest Hwy., Chicago, Ill.
Petor, Andrew P., 661 Catalpa St., New Kensington, Pa.
Petrequin, Gaynor, 3905 S.E. 91st Ave., Portland, Ore.
Pettersch, Carl A., 200 Southern Blvd., Danbury, Conn.
Petterson, Mrs. Muriel, County Schls. Serv. Center, San Luis Obispo, Calif.
Pettigrew, Julia R., 14622 N.W. 13th Rd., Miami, Fla.
Pettiss, J. O., Dept. of Educ., Louisiana State University, Baton Rouge, La.
Petty, Mary Clare, Col. of Educ., University of Oklahoma, Norman, Okla.
Petty, Olan L., Box 6906, Col. Sta., Duke University, Durham, N.C.
Petty, Walter T., Sch. of Educ., State Univ. of New York, Buffalo, N.Y.
Pewitt, Edith M., North Texas State Univ., Denton, Texas
Pezzullo, Thomas J., 268 Greenville Ave., Johnston, R.I.
Pfost, H. Philip, University of South Florida, Tampa, Fla.
Phay, John E., Bur. of Educ. Res., University of Mississippi, University, Miss.
Phelan, William F., 201 Sunrise Hwy., Patchogue, N.Y.
Phelps, H. Vaughn, 8727 Shamrock Rd., Omaha, Neb.
Phelps, Harold R., Illinois State University, Normal, Ill.
Phelps, Roger P., 718 Barnes Ave., Baldwin, L.I., N.Y.
Phillips, Cecil K., State College of Iowa, Cedar Falls, Iowa
Phillips, Don O., 1158 S. Harris Ave., Columbus, Ohio
Phillips, James A., Jr., Col. of Educ., Kent State University, Kent, Ohio
Phillips, James E., 1446 E. Maryland Ave., St. Paul, Minn.
Phillips, Leonard W., Nevada Southern Univ., Las Vegas, Nev.
Phillips, Paul, Supt. of Schools, 520 W. Palmer St., Morrisville, Pa.
Phillips, Richard C., Univ. of North Carolina, Chapel Hill, N.C.
Phillips, Thomas Arthur, 1536 S. Sixth St., Terre Haute, Ind.
Phillips, Thomas P., 7814 Elba Rd., Alexandria, Va.
Philp, William A., 440 Williams Ave., Natchitoches, La.
Phleger, John V., Superintendent of Schools, Geneseo, Ill.

Phoenix, William D., 8561 Holmes Rd., Kansas City, Mo.
Piche, Gene L., Univ. of Minnesota, Minneapolis, Minn.
Pickett, Louis L., County Supt. of Schools, Court House, Davenport, Iowa
Pickett, Paul C., Upper Iowa University, Fayette, Iowa
Pickett, Vernon R., 2411 Brookland Ave., N.E., Cedar Rapids, Ia.
Pickrel, Glenn E., Supt. of Schools, Dists. 58 and 99, Downers Grove, Ill.
Pierce, Arthur N., Supt. of Schools, Hanover, N.H.
Pierce, Raymond K., 81 Thimbleberry Lane, Levittown, Pa.
Pierce, Truman M., Sch. of Educ., Auburn University, Auburn, Ala.
Pierleoni, Robert G., 21 Nova Ln., Rochester, N.Y.
Pierson, John T., Niagara Co. Community College, Niagara Falls, N.Y.
Piggush, Kenneth J., 324 Sauganash, Park Forest, Ill.
Pikunas, Justin, Psych. Dept., University of Detroit, Detroit, Mich.
Piland, Joseph C., 1117 W. Market St., Normal, Ill.
Pilch, Mrs. Mary M., State Dept. of Education, Centennial Bldg., St. Paul, Minn.
Pilon, A. Barbara, 4055 N. Riverside Dr., Columbus, Ind.
Ping, Charles J., Tusculum College, Greeneville, Tenn.
Pinkham, Mrs. Rossalie G., Southern Connecticut State College, New Haven, Conn.
Pino, Charles E., 74 Eastern Ave., Revere, Mass.
Pins, Arnulf M., 345 E. 46th St., New York, N.Y.
Pirtle, Mrs. Ivyl, Palm Beach Curric. Lab., West Palm Beach, Fla.
Pitkin, Royce, Goddard College, Plainfield, Vt.
Pitman, John C., 88 Chestnut St., Camden, Me.
Pittman, Dewitt Kennieth, 6700 Monroe Rd., Charlotte, N.C.
Piucci, Virginio, Rhode Island Col., Providence, R.I.
Pletcher, James D., Niagara County Community College, Niagara Falls, N.Y.
Pletcher, Paul R., Jr., 3001 Floravista Ct., Riverside, Calif.
Pletsch, Douglas H., University of Guelf, Guelf, Ont., Canada
Plimpton, Blair, Superintendent of Schools, 400 S. Western Ave., Park Ridge, Ill.
Pliska, Stanley Robert, 1041 S. Lexan Cr., Norfolk, Va.
Plucker, Orvin L., Supt. of Schools, Kansas City, Kan.
Plumb, Valworth R., University of Minnesota, Duluth Branch, Duluth, Minn.
Pochini, Renzo, 556 W. 31st St., San Mateo, Calif.
Pockat, Delmar B., 6614 Arcadia Woods Rd., Columbia, S.C.
Poehler, W. A., Concordia College, St. Paul, Minn.
Poelker, Msgr. Gerard L., Supt., Diocesan Schls., Jefferson City, Mo.
Pogue, E. Graham, Ball State University, Muncie, Ind.
Pohek, Marguerite V., 13 Coolidge Ave., Glen Head, N.Y.
Pohlmann, Neil A., Bowling Green State University, Bowling Green, Ohio
Poindexter, Robert C., 1013 N. Frink St., Peoria, Ill.
Pole, E. John, Ball State University, Muncie, Ind.
Polglase, Robert J., 10 Amy Dr., Westfield, N.J.
Pollach, Samuel, California State College, Long Beach, Calif.
Pollack, Alan, 3010 Duncan St., Apt. 1, Columbia, S.C.
Polley, Warren P., Antioch Community High School, Antioch, Ill.
Polmantier, Paul C., University of Missouri, Columbia, Mo.
Pond, Millard Z., Superintendent of Schools, Dist. No. 4, Eugene, Ore.
Pool, Harbison, 509 W. 121st St., New York, N.Y.
Poole, Albert E., 214 N. Washington Cir., Lake Forest, Ill.
Pooley, Robert C., University of Wisconsin, Madison, Wis.
Pope, Madaline, Rt. 3, Box 544, Courtland, Ohio
Popper, Samuel H., Burton Hall, University of Minnesota, Minneapolis, Minn.
Portee, Richard C., 4939 Dorchester Ave., Chicago, Ill.
Porter, Donald A., Edmonton Public Schools, Edmonton, Alba., Canada
Porter, LeRoy E., 770 E. Meadow Dr., Palo Alto, Calif.
Porter, M. Roseamonde, MTEC, Ponape, East. Caroline Islands
Porter, R. H., The Steck Co., P.O. Box 2028, Austin, Tex.
Porter, William E., Pulaski High School, Pulaski, Va.
Porter, Willis P., Sch. of Educ., Indiana University, Bloomington, Ind.
Potell, Herbert, New Utrecht High School, Brooklyn, N.Y.
Potts, Alfred M., ERIC, New Mexico State University, La Cruces, N.M.

Potts, John F., Voorhees Junior College, Denmark, S.C.
Poulos, Chris G., 2935 Stanford Ave., Iowa City, Iowa
Poulos, Thomas H., Michigan School for the Deaf, Flint, Mich.
Poulter, James R., Superintendent of Schools, Anamosa, Iowa
Pound, Miss G., 1911 Kenwood St., Prince George, B.C., Canada
Pounds, Ralph L., Tchrs. Col., University of Cincinnati, Cincinnati, Ohio
Powell, O. Bert, Winthrop College, Rock Hill, S.C.
Powell, Mrs. Ruth Marie, 1601 Lock Rd., Nashville, Tenn.
Powell, W. Conrad, University of North Carolina, Chapel Hill, N.C.
Powers, Francis P., State College, Fitchburg, Mass.
Powers, Fred R., 619 Cleveland Ave., Amherst, Ohio
Powers, Philander, Ventura College, 4667 Telegraph Rd., Ventura, Calif.
Prasch, John, 8224 S. Hazelwood Dr., Lincoln, Neb.
Pratt, Anna M., 105 Colton Ave., San Carlos, Calif.
Prentice, Justus A., Board of Coop. Educ'l Serv., Buffalo, N.Y.
Preseren, Herman J., Wake Forest College, Winston-Salem, N.C.
Pressman, Florence, 3080 Broadway, New York, N.Y.
Preston, Albert P., Prin., Washington High School, Norfolk, Va.
Preston, Ralph C., Sch. of Educ., University of Pennsylvania, Philadelphia, Pa.
Prestwood, Elwood L., 426 Righters Mill Rd., Gladwyne, Pa.
Pricco, Ernest, Melrose Park School, Melrose Park, Ill.
Price, John, Lyman Hall High School, Wellingford, Conn.
Price, Louis E., University of New Mexico, Albuquerque, N.M.
Price, Randel K., University of Missouri, Columbia, Mo.
Price, Robert Diddams, 7819 Pinemeadow Lane, Cincinnati, Ohio
Price, Robert R., Agric. Hall, Oklahoma State Univ., Stillwater, Okla.
Price, Uberto, Appalachian State College, Boone, N.C.
Pridgen, Mrs. Ennie Mae, 1507 Russell St., Charlotte, N.C.
Priestley, Mabel, 4129 Marlton Dr., Los Angeles, Calif.
Prince, Mrs. Virginia Faye, P.O. Box 4015, St. Louis, Mo.
Pritchett, John P., Trenton Junior College, 101 W. State St., Trenton, N.J.
Pritchett, Karen, 2402 Woodmere Dr., Cleveland Heights, Ohio
Probst, Glen W., 650 Stark Ct., Columbus, Ohio
Procunier, Robert W., 999 Kedzie Ave., Flossmoor, Ill.
Prokop, Polly, Rt. 1, Archer Ave., Lemont, Ill.
Propeck, G. E., California State College, Long Beach, Calif.
Propsting, Mrs. M., 44 Henrietta St., Waverley, N.S.W., Australia
Protheroe, Donald W., 154 Chambers Bldg., University Park, Pa.
Pruitt, Robert E., Superintendent of Schools, Quincy, Mass.
Prutzman, Stuart E., 135 Alum St., Lehighton, Pa.
Pryor, Guy C., Our Lady of the Lake Col., San Antonio, Texas
Przewlocki, Lester E., Supt. of Schools, Dist. No. 4, Addison, Ill.
Puffer, Richard J., 4401—6th St., S.W., P.O. Box 1689, Cedar Rapids, Iowa
Pugmire, Dorothy Jean, 468 E. Fourth St. No., Logan, Utah
Purdy, Ralph D., Century House, Lincoln, Neb.
Puryear, Royal W., Florida Normal and Ind. Mem. College, St. Augustine, Fla.
Putnam, John F., Office of Education, Dept. of H.E.W., Washington, D.C.
Putzkau, Philo T., University of Connecticut, Storrs, Conn.
Pyfer, Jean L., 503 Fess, Bloomington, Ind.

Quall, Alvin B., Whitworth College, Spokane, Wash.
Quanbeck, Martin, Augsburg College, Minneapolis, Minn.
Quaranta, Joseph L., 3534 Maxwell Rd., Toledo, Ohio
Quatraro, John A., 25 Harrison Ave., Delmar, N.Y.
Queen, Bernard, Marshall University, Huntington, W.Va.
Queensland, Kenneth, Supt. of Schools, Blue Earth, Minn.
Quick, Henry E., 293 Main St., Box 279, Oswego, Tioga County, N.Y.
Quick, Otho J., Northern Illinos University, DeKalb, Ill.
Quilling, Joan I., Owen Hall, Michigan State Univ., East Lansing, Mich.
Quinn, Villa H., State Department of Education, Augusta, Me.
Quintero, Angel G., Secretary of Education, Rio Piedras, Puerto Rico

Quish, Bernard A., 4343 W. Wrightwood Ave., Chicago, Ill.

Raack, Mrs. Marilyn L., San Francisco State College, San Francisco, Calif.
Rabin, Bernard, Bowling Green State University, Bowling Green, Ohio
Rachford, George R., Col. of Grad. Studies, Univ. of Omaha, Omaha, Neb.
Rackauskas, John A., 6558 S. Rockwell St., Chicago, Ill.
Racky, Donald J., Lane Technical High School, Chicago, Ill.
Radcliffe, David H., 516 N. Jackson St., Danville, Ill.
Radebaugh, Byron F., Northern Illinois University, DeKalb, Ill.
Rademaker, Dean B., Superintendent of Schools, Virginia, Ill.
Rader, William D., 240 Laurel Ave., Wilmette, Ill.
Rafalides, Madeline B., Jersey City State College, Jersey City, N.J.
Raffone, Alexander M., Woodbridge Public Schools, Woodbridge, Conn.
Ragan, William Burk, University of Oklahoma, Norman, Okla.
Ragouzis, Perry, 401 Scott Ave., Fort Collins, Colo.
Ragsdale, Ted R., 301 W. College St., Carbondale, Ill.
Rahn, James E., Concordia Academy, St. Paul, Minn.
Railton, Esther P., California State Col., Hayward, Calif.
Raine, Douglas, Rt. 6, Box 296, Tucson, Ariz.
Rains, S. L., 1827 Swan Dr., Dallas, Texas
Ramer, Earl M., University of Tennessee, Knoxville, Tenn.
Ramey, Mrs. Beatrix B., Dept. of Educ., Appalachian State Univ., Boone, N.C.
Ramig, Clifford L., 11859 Canfield Ct., Cincinnati, Ohio
Ramos, John P., Jr., 117 Green Ave., Madison, N.J.
Ramos, Rafael E., 164 A Hook Rd., APO New York, N.Y. 09845
Ramseyer, Lloyd L., Blufften College, Blufften, Ohio
Randall, Edwin H., Western State College, Gunnison. Colo.
Randall, Robert S., S.W. Educ'l Devel. Lab., Austin, Tex.
Randall, William M., Wilmington College, 1220 Market St., Wilmington, N.C.
Randolph, Helen, Fresno State College, Fresno, Calif.
Rankin, Earl F., Jr., 3921 Lynncrest Dr., Fort Worth, Tex.
Rankin, Paul T., 16823 Plainview Rd., Detroit, Mich.
Rankine, Fred C., 5573 Toronto Rd., Vancouver, B.C., Canada
Rappaport, David, 2747 Coyle Ave., Chicago, Ill.
Rasmussen, Elmer M., Dana College, Blair, Neb.
Rasmussen, H. L., 427 S.W. Bade Ave., College Place, Wash.
Rasmussen, L. V., Superintendent of Schools, Duluth, Minn.
Rast, Lawrence R., Ohio State University, Columbus, Ohio
Rausch, Richard G., "Rescue," 120 Main St., Danbury, Conn.
Rawson, Kenneth O., Superintendent of Schools, Clintonville, Wis.
Ray, Helen, Nelson and Wright Schools, Rockford, Ill.
Ray, Rolland, State University of Iowa, Iowa City, Iowa
Razik, Taher A., State University of New York, Buffalo, N.Y.
Rea, Robert E., 8001 National Bridge St., St. Louis, Mo.
Reavis, Margaret, 14601 Firmona, Lawndale, Calif.
Reavis, Peyton, 125 E. Prince Rd., Tucson, Ariz.
Red, S. B., University of Houston, 3801 Cullen Blvd., Houston, Tex.
Reddin, Estoy, Dept. of Educ., Lehigh University, Bethlehem, Pa.
* Reddy, Anne L., P.O. Box 64, Runnymede, Bluffton, S.C.
Rediger, Milo A., Taylor University, Upland, Ind.
Reed, Harold J., Office of Educ., Dept. of HEW, Washington, D.C.
Reed, John L., 122 White St., Saratoga Springs, N.Y.
Reed, Marilyn D., 735 Highland Dr., Columbus, Ohio
Reed, Ted B., Stroman High School, Victoria, Tex.
Reed, Zollie C., 3636 Kingshill Rd., Birmingham, Ala.
Reese, Clyde, State College of Arkansas, Conway, Ark.
Reeves, Emily D., Centre College of Kentucky, Danville, Ky.
Reeves, Glenn D., Saginaw Public Schools, Saginaw, Tex.
Reeves, Louis H., 905 Thorndale Drive, Ottawa, Ont., Canada
Regier, Margaret, Roosevelt Univ., 430 S. Michigan Ave., Chicago, Ill.
Regner, Olga W., 116 South 4th St., Darby, Pa.

Rehage, Kenneth J., Dept. of Educ., University of Chicago, Chicago, Ill.
Reid, Clarence E., Jr., 8740 Skyview, Beaumont, Texas
Reid, Leon L., Rt. 2, Box 221, McDonald, Pa.
Reilley, Albert G., 28 Long Ave., Framingham, Mass.
Reiner, Kenneth, 3191 S. Evelyn Way, Denver, Colo.
Reiner, William B., Hunter College, 695 Park Ave., New York, N.Y.
* Reinhardt, Emma, Pittsfield, Ill.
Reinstein, Barry J., Univ. of South Carolina, Columbia, S.C.
Reisboard, Richard J., 5500 S.W., 77th Ct., Miami, Fla.
Reisen, Seymour, 120 E. 184th St., Bronx, N.Y.
Reisman, Diana J., 223 N. Highland Ave., Merion Station, Pa.
Reisman, Morton, Anshe Emet Day Sch., 3760 N. Pine Grove Ave., Chicago, Ill.
Reiter, Anne, 155 West 68th St., New York, N.Y.
Reitz, Donald J., Loyola College, 4501 N. Charles St., Baltimore, Md.
Reitz, Louis M., St. Thomas Seminary, 7101 Brownsboro Rd., Louisville, Ky.
Reller, Theodore L., Sch. of Educ., Univ. of California, Berkeley, Calif.
Rempel, P. J., 495 Mariposa Dr., Ventura, Calif.
Renard, John N., Oxnard Evening High School, Oxnard, Calif.
Renfrow, O. W., Thornton Township High School, Harvey, Ill.
Rennels, Max R., 506 N. Cotton Ave., Bloomington, Ind.
Renouf, Edna M., 116 Yale Square, Swarthmore. Pa.
Replogle, V. L., Metcalf School, Normal, Ill.
Reuter, George S., Jr., Sioux Empire College, Hawarden, Iowa
Reuwsaat, Emily A., Bloomsburg State College, Bloomsburg, Pa.
Revie, Virgil A., California State Col., Long Beach, Calif.
Rex, Ronald G., Michigan State University, East Lansing, Mich.
Reyna, L. J., 227 Beacon St., Boston, Mass.
Reynolds, Mrs. Dorothy S., 640 Hudson St., Denver, Colo.
Reynolds, James Walton, Box 7998, University of Texas, Austin, Tex.
Reynolds, Lee, 113 Woodland Dr., Boone, N.C.
Reynolds, M. C., University of Minnesota, Minneapolis, Minn.
Rhodes, Gladys L., State University College, Geneseo. N.Y.
Rhodes, Patricia Hertert, Rt. 2, Box 343, Sonora, Calif.
Ricciardi, Richard S., Dept. of Education, 100 Reef Rd., Fairfield, Conn.
Rice, Arthur H., R.R. 3, 3705 Cameron, Bloomington, Ind.
Rice, David, Indiana State University, Evansville, Ind.
Rice, Dick C., 120 Houck Ave., Centerbury, Ohio
Rice, Eric D., Rt. 2, Box 200 A, El Centro, Calif.
Rice, James A., University of Houston, Houston, Tex.
Rice, John E., Jenkintown High School, Jenkintown, Pa.
Rice, Robert K., 4820 Campanile Dr., San Diego, Calif.
Rice, Roy C., Arizona State University, Tempe. Ariz.
Rice, Theodore D., 33963 N. Hampshire, Livonia, Mich.
Richards, Eugene R., 131 Robin Rd., Bowling Green, Ky.
Richards, H. L., P.O. Box 326, Grambling, La.
Richardson, Canute M., Paine College, Augusta, Ga.
Richardson, John S., Sch. of Educ., Ohio State Univ., Columbus, Ohio
Richardson, Orvin T., Ball State University, Muncie, Ind.
Richardson, Thomas H., 852 Valley Rd., Upper Montclair, N.J.
Richardson, William R., University of North Carolina, Chapel Hill, N.C.
Richey, Herman G., Dept. of Educ., University of Chicago, Chicago, Ill.
Richey, Robert W., Sch. of Educ., Indiana University, Bloomington, Ind.
Richey, Ruth, P.O. Box 41, Alpena, Mich.
Richmond, George S., 507½ E. Locust, Normal, Ill.
Richter, Charles O., Public Schools, 7 Whiting Lane, West Hartford, Conn.
Riedel, Mark T., 210 S. Edgewood, LaGrange, Ill.
Riederer, L. A., 2160 Cameron St., Regina, Sask., Canada
Riehm, Carl L., 1300 Fisherman Dr., Norfolk, Va.
Riese, Harlan C., 511 North Ave., East, Missoula, Mont.
*Riethmiller, M. Gorton, Olivet College, Olivet, Mich.

Riggle, Earl L., 180 Highland Dr., New Concord, Ohio
Riggs, William J., 716 Clover Ct., Cheney, Wash
Rigney, Mrs. Margaret G., Hunter College, Park Ave. and 68th St., New York,N.Y.
Rigney, Raymond P., 31 East 50th St., New York, N.Y.
Rikkola, V. John, Dept. of Educ., Massachusetts State Col., Salem, Mass.
Riley, Garland G., 910 Colby Ct., DeKalb, Ill.
Rinehart, Alice D., Lehigh University, Bethlehem, Pa.
Ringler, Leonore, New York Univ., New York, N.Y.
Ringler, Mrs. Norma, 3721 Lytle Rd., Shaker Heights, Ohio
Rinsland, Roland Del, 100 W. 73rd St., New York, N.Y.
Riordan, Eugene, Queen of Apostles College, Dedham, Mass.
Ripper, Eleanor S., Geneva College, Beaver Falls, Pa.
Rippey, Robert M., 18845 Hood Ave., Homewood, Ill.
Ripple, Richard E., Stone Hall, Cornell University, Ithaca, N.Y.
Risinger, Robert G., Col. of Educ., University of Maryland, College Park, Md.
Risinger, Mrs. Rosalie C., Essex County Voc. & Tech. H.S., Newark, N.J.
Risk, Thomas M., 319 Elm St., Vermillion, S.D.
Ritchie, Harold L., Superintendent of Schools, West Paterson, N.J.
Ritscher, Richard C., 116 N. Josephine Ave., Madison, S.D.
Ritter, William E., 2910 E. State St., Sharon, Pa.
Rittschoff, Louis W., 240 Kenwood Dr., Thiensville, Wis.
Rivard, Thomas L., Superintendent of Schools, Chelmsford, Mass.
Rivlin, Harry N., 302 Broadway, New York, N.Y.
Roaden, Arliss, Dept. of Education, Ohio State University, Columbus, Ohio
Roark, Bill, 314 W. Earl Way, Hanford, Calif.
Robarts, James R., Florida State University, Tallahassee, Fla.
Robbins, Edward T., 235 East Oakview Pl., San Antonio, Texas
Robbins, Jerry H., Sch. of Educ., Univ. of Miss., Oxford, Miss.
Robbins, Melvyn P., Ontario Inst. for Stud. in Educ., Toronto, Ont., Canada
Robeck, Mildred C., 452 Venado Dr., Santa Barbara, Calif.
Roberson, James A., Jefferson County Schools, Mt. Vernon, Ill.
Roberts, Dodd Edward, University of Maine, Orono, Me.
Roberts, Jack D., Dept. of Educ., Queens College, Flushing, N.Y.
Roberts, James B., Dept. of Educ., West Texas State Col., Canyon, Tex.
Roberts, James P., I.D.E.A., Los Angeles, Calif.
Roberts, R. Ray, 3309 Rocky Mount Rd., Fairfax, Va.
Robertson, Anne McK., Tchrs. Col., Columbia University, New York, N.Y.
Robertson, Jean E., University of Alberta, Edmonton, Alba., Canada
Robertson, Robert L., 315 East Main St., Springfield, Ky.
Robinson, Alice, Board of Educ., 115 E. Church St., Frederick, Md.
Robinson, Cliff, Chico State College, Chico, Calif.
Robinson, H. Alan, Hofstra Univ., Hempstead, L.I., N.Y.
Robinson, Helen M., Rochester, N.Y.
Robinson, Herbert B., California State Col., Long Beach, Calif.
Robinson, John D., 106 S. Overhill Dr., Bloomington, Ind.
Robinson, Lucille T., 603 Buena Vista, Redlands, Calif.
Robinson, Phil C., 1367 Joliet Pl., Detroit, Mich.
Robinson, Robert S., Jr., Eastern Michigan Univ., Ypsilanti, Mich.
Robinson, Virginia H., Arizona State University, Phoenix, Ariz.
Robinson, Walter J., Northwestern State College, Natchitoches, La.
Robinson, Walter K., New England College, Henniker, N.H.
Robison, W. L., Norfolk City Schools, Norfolk, Va.
Roche, Lawrence A., Duquesne University, Pittsburgh, Pa.
Rockfort, George B., Jr., Northeastern University, Boston, Mass.
Rockwell, Perry J., Jr., Wisconsin State Univ., Platteville, Wis.
Roden, Aubrey H., State Univ. of New York, Buffalo, N.Y.
Rodgers, John O., 4115 Honeycomb Cir., Austin, Texas
Rodgers, Margaret, Lamar State College of Technology, Beaumont, Tex.
Rodgers, Paul R., 255 W. Vermont St., Villa Park, Ill.
Rodney, Clare, Long Beach State College, Long Beach, Calif.
Rodriguez-Dias, Manolo, Alfred Univ., Alfred, N.Y.

Roe, Anne, 5151 E. Holmes St., Tucson, Arizona
Roenigk, Elsie Mae, 121 Oak Ridge Dr., Butler, Pa.
Roeper, George A., City and Country School, Bloomfield Hills, Mich.
Roff, Mrs. Rosella Zuber, 4410 S. 148th St., Seattle, Wash.
Rogers, Martha E., Div. of Nurse Educ., N.Y.U., New York, N.Y.
Rogers, Virgil M., 3810 Birchwood Rd., Falls Church, Va.
Rohan, William, E. G. Foreman High School, Chicago, Ill.
Roletta, Vincent M., 35 Clearview Dr., Spencerport, N.Y.
Rolfe, Howard C., 5160 Atherton, Long Beach, Calif.
Roller, Lawrence W., King George County Public Schls., King George, Va.
Rollins, William B., Jr., 7772 Otto St., Downey, Calif.
Rolloff, John A., University of Arkansas, Fayetteville, Ark.
Romano, Louis, Michigan State University, East Lansing, Mich.
Romano, Louis A., 227—65th St., West New York, N.J.
Rome, Samuel, 9852 Cerritos Ave., Anaheim, Calif.
Romoser, Richard C., Clarion State College, Clarion, Pa.
Rondinella, Orestes R., 48 Sheridan Ave., West Orange, N.J.
Roosa, Jack L., Greenville Central School, Greenville, N.Y.
Rorison, Margaret L., University of S.C., Columbia, S.C.
Rosamilia, M. T., 183 Union Ave., Belleville, N.J.
Roschy, Bertha B., 204 Greenwell Dr., Hampton, Va.
Rose, Gale W., New York University, New York, N.Y.
Rose, Mrs. Ruth R., 908 S.W. 18th Ct., Fort Lauderdale, Fla.
Rosebrock, Allan F., State Dept. of Educ., 175 W. State St., Trenton, N.J.
Rosecrance, Francis C., Florida Atlantic University, Boca Raton, Fla.
Rosen, Carl L., 500 Satellite Dr., El Paso, Texas
Rosen, Sidney, Col. of Educ., University of Illinois, Urbana, Ill.
Rosenbaum, Wyatt I., 2645 Chesapeake Lane, Northbrook, Ill.
Rosenberg, Donald A., Supt., Lutheran Schools, Wausau, Wis.
Rosenberg, Max, 5057 Woodward Ave., Detroit, Mich.
Rosenberger, Russell S., Dept. of Educ., Gettysburg Col., Gettysburg, Pa.
Rosenbluh, Benjamin J., Central High School, Bridgeport, Conn.
Rosenblum, Beth W., 45 East 40th St., Paterson, N.J.
Rosenstein, Pearl, 5 Tanglewood Circle, Cheshire, Conn.
Rosenthal, Alan G., 18 Homeside Lane. White Plains, N.Y.
Rosenthal, Alice M., SUNY, Buffalo, N.Y.
Rosenthal, Lester, 94 Stirling Ave., Freeport, N.Y.
Rosenthal, Samuel, 5213 N. Moody Ave., Chicago, Ill.
Rosenzweig, Celia, 6239 N. Leavitt St., Chicago, Ill.
Rosewell, Paul T., MacMurray College, Jacksonville, Ill.
Rosin, Bill, Box 2096, Eastern New Mexico Univ., Portales, N.M.
Ross, Mrs. Alice M., 1446 Wilbraham Rd., Springfield, Mass.
Ross, John G., 6457 Hagan Blvd., El Cerrito, Calif.
Ross, Richard H., P.O. Box 197, Menomonie, Mich.
Ross, Robert D., Auburn Community College, Auburn, N.Y.
Rossi, Mary Jean, University of Miami, Miami, Fla.
Rossien, Saul Antioch-Putney Grad. School, Philadelphia, Pa.
Rossmiller, Richard A., 1212 S.W. Fifth Ave., Gainesville, Fla.
Roth, Mrs. Frances, 21598 Ellacott Pkwy., Cleveland, Ohio
Roth, Lois H., State Dept. of Education, Denver, Colo.
Rothenberg, William, Jr., 1 S. Broadway, Hastings-on-Hudson, N.Y.
Rothenberger, Otis J., 1517 Pennsylvania St., Allentown, Pa.
Rothstein, Jerome H., San Francisco State College, San Francisco, Calif.
Rothwell, Angus B., Coord. Council for Higher Educ., Madison, Wis.
Rousseve, Numa Joseph, Xavier University, New Orleans, La.
Row, Howard E., State Dept. of Pub. Instr., Dover, Del.
Rowley, Judge Kernan, Morris Brown College, Atlanta, Ga.
Rozendaal, Julia, University of North. Iowa, Cedar Falls, Iowa
Rozran, Andrea Rice, 1255 N. Sandberg Terrace, Chicago, Ill.
Rubadeau, Duane O., State University College, Geneseo, N.Y.
Ruby, Eula, 685 Benson Way, Thousand Oaks, Calif.

Ruch, Mary A. R., R.F.D. No. 1, Tower City, Pa.
Rucinski, Philip R., Wisconsin State Univ., Oshkosh, Wis.
Rucker, Chauncy N., Rockridge Apts., Baxter Rd., Storrs, Conn.
Rucker, W. Ray, 8655 Pomerado Rd., San Diego, Calif.
Rudman, Herbert C., Col. of Educ., Michigan State Univ., East Lansing, Mich.
Rudolf, Kathleen Brady, 53 Cook St., Rochester, N.Y.
Rueff, Charles M., Jr., 626 S. Sixth St., McComb, Miss.
Rugen, Mabel E., Sch. of Pub. Health, Univ. of Michigan, Ann Arbor, Mich.
Rugen, Myrtle L., 2240 Pfingsten Rd., Northbrook, Ill.
Ruggles, Stanford D., 3095 Kellner Pl., Columbus, Ohio
Rule, Philip, East Otero School Dist., Rt. 1, LaJunta, Colo.
Rummel, J. Francis, Sch. of Educ., Univ. of Montana, Missoula, Mont.
Rumpf, Edwin L., 1805 Rupert St., McLean, Va.
Runbeck, Junet E., Bethel College, St. Paul, Minn.
Runyan, Charles S., Marshall University, Huntington, W.Va.
Rusch, Reuben R., State University of New York, Albany, N.Y.
Russel, John H., Col. of Educ., Univ. of Toledo, Toledo, Ohio
Russell, Mrs. Audrey B., Admin. Bldg., 228 W. Franklin St., Elkhart, Ind.
Russell, David L., Dept. of Psych., Ohio University, Athens, Ohio
Russell, Elder H., P.O. Box 4313, Phoenix, Ariz.
Russell, Irene, Lock Haven State College, Lock Haven, Pa.
* Russell, John Dale, R.R. 10, Russell Rd., Bloomington, Ind.
Russell, William J., Pelham Memorial High School, Pelham, N.Y.
Russo, Anthony J., Dept. of Public Schools, 211 Veazie St., Providence, R.I.
Russum, Elizabeth H., 925 Rockford Rd., Birmingham, Ala.
Ruter, Charles, Jefferson Co. Schools, Louisville, Ky.
Rutherford, William L., 1607 Rabb Rd., Austin, Tex.
Rutledge, James A., Univ. High School, Univ. of Nebraska, Lincoln, Neb.
Ruud, Josephine B., North Dakota State Univ., Fargo, N.D.
Ryan, Carl J., 220 W. Liberty St., Cincinnati, Ohio
Ryan, Kelvin, University of Chicago, Chicago, Ill.
Rzepka, Louis, DePaul University, Chicago, Ill.

Sack, Saul, Grad. Sch. of Educ., Univ. of Pennsylvania, Philadelphia, Pa.
Safford, George R., 3640 Scenic Dr., Redding, Calif.
Sage, Daniel D., Syracuse University, Syracuse, N.Y.
Sager, Kenneth, Lawrence University, Appleton, Wis.
Sahlin, Clarence J., North Park College, Chicago, Ill.
Salatino, A. P., State University of New York, Geneseo, N.Y.
Sales, M. Vance, Arkansas State University, State University, Ark.
Salett, Stanley J., 225 W. State St., Trenton, N.J.
Salinger, Herbert E., 26036 Adamor Rd., Calabasas, Calif.
Salisbury, Arnold W., Superintendent of Schools, Cedar Rapids, Iowa
Salisbury, C. Jackson, 410 Conshohocken St. Rd., Narberth, Pa.
Sallee, Mrs. Mozelle T., 4401 North Ave., Richmond, Va.
Salmon, Hanford A., 310 Stratford St., Syracuse, N.Y.
Salmons, George B., State College, Plymouth, N.H.
* Salser, G. Alden, 516 E. Estelle, Wichita, Kan.
Salten, David G., 41 Park Ave., New York, N.Y.
Saltzman, Irving J., Dept. of Psych., Indiana Univ., Bloomington, Ind.
Sam, Norman H., Lehigh University, Bethlehem, Pa.
Samlin, John R., Illinois Valley Comm. Col., LaSalle, Ill.
Sample, William J., 33 Chestnut Ave., Vineland, N.J.
Samson, Gordon E., Cleveland State University, Cleveland, Ohio
Sand, Ole, Natl. Educ. Assn., 1201 Sixteenth St., N.W., Washington, D.C.
Sander, Paul J., 3139 E. Monterosa, Phoenix, Ariz.
Sanders, Leslie A., Superintendent, Coweta County Schls., Turin, Ga.
Sanders, Mrs. Ruby, P.O. Box 1956, Waco, Tex.
Sandilos, Peter C., Superintendent of Schools, West Long Branch, N.J.
Sands, Miss Billie L., Michigan State Univ., East Lansing, Mich.
Sangster, Cecil Henry, 1248 Cross Cres. S.W., Calgary, Alba., Canada

Santigian, M. Marty, 4596 E. Fredora, Fresno, Calif.
Sapir, Selma, 60 Bretmore Ave., Yonkers, N.Y.
Sartain, Harry W., Falk Lab. Schls., Univ. of Pittsburgh, Pittsburgh, Pa.
Sarver, Cyril C., Hillsdale Jr. H.S., Box 49, Hillsdale, Ill.
Saterlie, Mary E., Board of Educ., Baltimore Co., Towson, Md.
Sather, Verlie, Winona State College, Winona, Minn.
Satterlee, O. Ward, State University College, Potsdam, N.Y.
Saunders, Margaret C., 701 Wheeling Ave., Muncie, Ind.
Sauter, Joyce C., 444 Duarte Rd., Arcadia, Calif.
Sauvain, Walter H., Dept. of Educ., Bucknell Univ., Lewisburg, Pa.
Savage, Kent B., Fairview Senior High School, Berkeley, Mo.
Savage, Mary E., 114 Middleton Pl., Bronxville, N.Y.
Saville, Anthony, Sch. of Educ., Nevada Southern Univ., Las Vegas, Nev.
Sax, Gilbert, University of Washington, Seattle, Wash.
Saxe, Richard W., Univ. of Toledo, Toledo, Ohio
Saylor, Charles F., 535 Kathryn St., New Wilmington, Pa.
Saylor, Galen, Tchrs. Col., University of Nebraska, Lincoln, Neb.
Scales, Eldridge E., 795 Peachtree St., Atlanta, Ga.
Scanlan, William J., Highland Park Sr. High School, St. Paul, Minn.
Scanlon, Kathryn L., Sch. of Educ., Fordham University, New York, N.Y.
Scarborough, C. C., North Carolina State University, Raleigh, N.C.
Scarbrough, Paul, Univ. of Texas at El Paso, Texas
Scarnato, Samuel A., Asst. Supt., Morgantown, W. Va.
Schaadt, Mrs. Lucy G., Cedar Crest College, Allentown, Pa.
Schaefer, Alan E., 900 Crestfield Ave., Libertyville, Ill.
Schaefer, Wilbert S., 194 Hillside Ave., Mineola, L.I., N.Y.
Schaeffer, Norma C., 10700 S. Hamlin, Chicago, Ill.
Schaffer, Phyllis J., Room 922, Eigenmann Center, Bloomington, Ind.
Schaibly, Colon L., Waukegan Township High School, Waukegan, Ill.
Schall, William E., 734 S. Pugh St., State College, Pa.
Schalm, Philip, 1317-14 St., East, Saskatoon, Sask., Canada
Scharf, Louis, 350 Sterling St., Brooklyn, N.Y.
Schasteen, Joyce W., 2500 Spruce St., Bakersfield, Calif.
Schauerman, Sam, Jr., 22806 Eriel Ave., Torrance, Calif.
Schectman, Aaron H., Monmouth College, Monmouth, N.J.
Schell, Leo M., Col. of Educ., Kansas State Univ., Manhattan, Kansas
Schell, Very Rev. Joseph O., John Carroll Univ., Cleveland, Ohio
Schenke, Lahron H., 301 Chamberlin Dr., Charleston, Ill.
Schenkman, Jerome G., 255 E. Houston St., New York, N.Y.
Scherer, Frank H., Rutgers University, New Brunswick, N.J.
Schifreen, Edward B., 314 Iris Rd., Cherry Hill, N.J.
Schiller, Clarke E., 73F, Escondido Village, Stanford, Calif.
Schiller, Leroy, Mankato State College, Mankato, Minn.
Schilling, Paul M., Superintendent of Schools, LaGrange Park, Ill.
Schleif, Mabel, 1908 Hennepin Ave., Minneapolis, Minn.
Schlenker, Alma H., 1450 Westgate Dr., Bethlehem, Pa.
Schlessinger, Fred R., 1399 LaRochelle Dr., Columbus, Ohio
Schmidt, David F., 401 E. 11th Ave., Columbus, Ohio
Schmidt, Florence M., 5925 Canterbury Dr., Culver City, Calif.
Schmidt, L. G. H., J. J. Cahill Mem. Sch., Mascot, N.S.W., Australia
Schmidt, Lyle D., 3320 Edgemere Ave., N.E., Minneapolis, Minn.
Schmidt, Ralph L. W., 568 Magnolia Wood Dr., Baton Rouge, La.
Schmidt, William S., County Superintendent of Schools, Upper Marlboro, Md.
Schminke, Clarence W., Sch. of Educ., Univ. of Oregon, Eugene, Ore.
Schnabel, Robert V., 6902 S. Calhoun St., Fort Wayne, Ind.
Schneider, Albert A., Superintendent of Schools, Albuquerque, N.M.
Schneider, Arthur J., Webster Cent. School, Webster, N.Y.
Schneider, Byron J., 4800 Chicago Beach Drive, Chicago, Ill.
Schneider, Erwin H., Sch. of Music, Ohio State University, Columbus, Ohio
Schneider, Raymond C., University of Washington, Seattle, Wash.

Schneider, Samuel, 315 West 70th St., New York, N.Y.
Schnell, Fred, 2724 Highland Terrace, Sheboygan, Wis.
Schnell, Rodolph L., Univ. of Calgary, Calgary, Alba., Canada
Schnepf, Virginia, 1117 Bryan, Normal, Ill.
Schneyer, J. Wesley, 7454 Ruskin Rd., Philadelphia, Pa.
Schnitzen, Joseph P., University of Houston, Houston, Tex.
Schoch, Norman J., Newark Sr. H.S., East Delaware Ave., Newark, Del.
Schoeller, Arthur W., 8626 W. Lawrence Ave., Milwaukee, Wis.
Scholl, Margaret, 1206 Marshall Lane, Austin, Tex.
Scholl, Paul A., Univ. of Connecticut, Storrs, Conn.
Schollmeyer, Fred C., Dade County Public Schools, Miami, Fla.
Schomer, John T., Jr., 45 Pleasant St., Natick, Mass.
Schooler, Virgil E., 209 S. Hillsdale Dr., Bloomington, Ind.
Schooling, Herbert W., Col. of Educ., Univ. of Missouri, Columbia, Mo.
Schor, Theodore, 149 N. Fifth Ave., Highland Park, N.J.
Schorow, Mitchell, 806 Milburn, Evanston, Ill.
Schott, Marion S., Central Missouri State College, Warrensburg, Mo.
Schowe, Ben M., Jr., 500 Morse Rd., Columbus, Ohio
Schreiber, Daniel, 7 Peter Cooper Rd., New York, N.Y.
Schreiber, Herman, 80 Clarkson Ave., Brooklyn, N.Y.
Schroeder, Carl N., 39 Othoridge Rd., Lutherville, Md.
Schroeder, Marie L., 3125 N. Spangler St., Philadelphia, Pa.
Schroeder, W. P., State Polytechnic College, San Luis Obispo, Calif.
Schuller, Charles F., Michigan State University, East Lansing, Mich.
Schulman, Milton, 660 Locust St., Mt. Vernon, N.Y.
Schumann, Victor, 1537 Cedar Lane, Waukesha, Wis.
Schumer, Harry, University of Wisconsin, Madison, Wis.
Schuster, Rev. James F., Supt., Altoona-Johnstown Cath. Schools, Altoona, Pa.
Schwanholt, Dana B., Valparaiso University, Valparaiso, Ind.
Schwartz, Alfred, Drake University, Des Moines, Iowa
Schwartz, Fred R., Michigan State Univ., East Lansing, Mich.
Schwartz, Judy Iris, 28 Illinois Ave., Long Beach, N.Y.
Schwartz, William P., 273 Ave. P., Brooklyn, N.Y.
Schwarz, Peggy M., 25 Cornell St., Scarsdale, N.Y.
Schwarzenberger, Alfred J., Sault Sainte Marie, Mich.
Schwebel, Milton, Sch. of Educ., New York University, New York, N.Y.
Schwyhart, Keith, Earlham College, Richmond, Ind.
Sciranka, Paul G., 323 Monte Vista Ave., Oakland, Calif.
Scobey, Mary-Margaret, San Francisco State College, San Francisco, Calif.
Scofield, Alice Gill, San Jose State College, San Jose, Calif.
Scofield, J. Woodleigh, 17169 Hawthorne Ave., Fontana, Calif.
Scott, Guy, 1521 N. Webster, Liberal, Kan.
Scott, Loren L., Idaho State University, Pocatello, Idaho
Scott, Thomas B., University of Tennessee, Knoxville, Tenn.
Scott, Waldo L., Soundview Gardens, Port Washington, N.Y.
Scribner, Jay D., University of California, Los Angeles, Calif.
Scritchfield, Floyd C., Nevada Southern Univ., Las Vegas, Nev.
Seagoe, May V., Sch. of Educ., University of California, Los Angeles, Calif.
Searles, Warren B., Queens Col., Flushing, N.Y.
Sears, Jesse B., 40 Tevis Pl., Palo Alto, Calif.
Seaton, Donald F., Superintendent of Schools, Boone, Iowa
Seay, Maurice F., W. Michigan University, Kalamazoo, Mich.
Sebaly, A. L., Western Michigan Universty, Kalamazoo, Mich.
Sechler, Hazel B., Western New Mexico Univ., Silver City, N.M.
See, Harold W., Col. of Educ., Univ. of Bridgeport, Bridgeport, Conn.
Seelye, Margaret R., 335 W. Drummond, Bourbonnais, Ill.
Segal, Marilyn, The Pre-School, Hollywood, Fla.
Sehmann, Henry R., 1171 Bryant Rd., Long Beach, Calif.
Seidman, Eric, University of Maryland, College Park, Md.
Seifert, George G., Bowling Green State Univ., Bowling Green, Ohio
Seifert, Leland B., Haverstraw-Stony Point School Dist., Stony Point, N.Y.

Seitz, Robert, 1603 N. Denver Dr., Marion, Ind.
Seitzer, Robert H., Superintendent of Schools, East Orange, N.J.
Sekerak, Martha M., Box G-1067, Hanford, Calif.
Selden, Edward H., Dept. of Psych., Wisconsin State Univ., River Falls, Wis.
Self, David W., Univ. of Alabama, University, Alabama
Sellery, Austin R., 344 Sunset Way, Palm Springs, Calif.
Seltzer, Richard W., 639 Redlion Rd., Huntingdon Valley, Pa.
Seltzer, Ronald, 4004 Bleckley Rd., Lincoln, Neb.
Selzer, Edwin, 168-06 Jewel Ave., Flushing, N.Y.
Semmel, Melvyn I., University of Michigan, Ann Arbor, Mich.
Semrow, Joseph J., North Central Association, Chicago, Ill.
Sentman, Everett E., United Educators, Inc., Lake Bluff, Ill.
Severino, D. Alexander, Alisal H.S., Salinas, Calif.
Severson, John E., 11 Chalon Cir., Salinas, Calif.
Seyfert, Warren C., 5607 Gloster Rd., Washington, D.C.
Shaddick, Bryan A., 1023 Lincoln St., Hobart, Ind.
Shafer, Robert E., Arizona State University, Tempe, Ariz.
Shafer, William C., 25 Bar Beach Rd., Port Washington, N.Y.
Shafran, Lillian, 711 E. 11th St., New York, N.Y.
Shallcross, Mrs. Margaret, 4803 Oakridge, Toledo, Ohio
Shane, Harold G., Sch. of Educ., Indiana University, Bloomington, Ind.
Shank, Lloyd L., Superintendent of Schools, Arkansas City, Kan.
Shankman, Florence, Temple University, Philadelphia, Pa.
Shapiro, Benjamin, Grad. Sch. of Educ., Rutgers Univ., New Brunswick, N.J.
Shapiro, Lillian L., 82-30—210th St., Hollis Hills, N.Y.
Shaplin, Judson T., Washington University, St. Louis, Mo.
Sharp, George M., Lakewood Terr., New Milford, Conn.
Shaw, Frances, 4717 Central Ave., Indianapolis, Ind.
Shaw, M. Luelle, 1126 N.W. Eighth Ave., Miami, Fla.
Shaw, Robert C., Superintendent of Schools, Columbia, Mo.
Shea, James, 59 Old Farm Road, Levittown, N.Y.
Shea, Warren D., New Mexico Inst. of Mining and Tech., Socorro, N.M.
Shear, Twyla M., Michigan State Univ., East Lansing, Mich.
Shedd, Mark R., Supt. of Schools, Philadelphia, Pa.
Sheeley, Vernon, Box 3585, University Sta., Laramie, Wyo.
Sheely, Richard L., Lancaster City Schools, Lancaster, Ohio
Sheerin, James S., Eliz. Carter Brooks School, New Bedford, Mass.
Sheldon, John M., San Diego State College, San Diego, Calif.
Sheldon, Muriel Inez, Los Angeles City Board of Educ., Los Angeles, Calif.
Sheldon, William Denley, 508 University Pl., Syracuse, N.Y.
Shelton, Nollie W., 328 Blowing Rock Rd., Boone, N.C.
Shepard, Loraine V., Antioch Col., Yellow Springs, Ohio
Shepard, Samuel, Jr., 4633 Moffitt Ave., St. Louis, Mo.
Sheppard, Lawrence E., Daly City Schools, Daly City, Calif.
Sherer, Harry, 2158 Fielding Rd., Riverside, Calif.
Sheridan, Alton, NEA, 1201 Sixteenth St., N.W., Washington, D.C.
Sheridan, William C., 333 Washington St., Brookline, Mass.
Sherk, John K., Jr., 6112 Summit St., Kansas City, Mo.
Sherman, Mrs. Helene, 350 Central Park West, New York, N.Y.
Sherman, Mrs. Twyla, Col. of Educ., Wichita State Univ., Wichita, Kansas
Shermis, S. Samuel, R. 1, West Lafayette, Ind.
Sherwood, Virgil, Radford College, Radford, Va.
Sherwyn, Fred, State Dept. of Educ., Cupertino, Calif.
Shier, John B., 200 Elm High Dr., Edgerton, Wis.
Shimel, W. A., Univ. Ext., Univ. of Wis., Rhinelander, Wis.
Shinol, Julian W., Edinboro State College, Edinboro, Pa.
Shnayer, Sidney W., Chico State College, Chico, Calif.
Shoemaker, Marjorie P., Bowling Green State Univ., Bowling Green, Ohio
Shohen, Samuel S., 229 Friends Lane, Westbury, L.I., N.Y.
Sholund, Milford, Gospel Light Press, 725 E. Colorado, Glendale, Calif.
Shope, Nathaniel H., Appalachian State Univ., Boone, N.C.

Shores, J. Harlan, University of Illinois, Urbana, Ill.
Short, Edmund C., University of Toledo, Toledo, Ohio
Short, Robert Allen, 15510—112th St., Bothell, Wash.
Short, William T., 2368 Walnut Grove Ave., San Jose, Calif.
Showalter, Miriam R., Roosevelt University, Chicago, Ill.
Showkeir, James R., 1909 Penbrook Lane, Flint, Mich.
Shroff, Piroja, California Col. of Arts & Crafts, Oakland, Calif.
Shulman, Lee S., Col. of Educ., Michigan State Univ., East Lansing, Mich.
Shultz, Kenneth M., Kettering, Ohio
* Shuman, Elsie, 805 S. Florence St., Kirksville, Mo.
Siard, Gladys M., Ligonier, Pa.
* Sias, A. B., Route 3, Box 459B, Orlando, Fla.
Sidden, Curtis A., 357 Lake Forest Dr., Spartanburg, S.C.
Siders, Stanford K., R.D. #2, West Salem, Ohio
Siegel, Martin, 1472 Dalton Dr., Schenectady, N.Y.
Siegner, C. Vernon, Peru State College, Box 75, Peru, Neb.
Siemons, Alice E., San Francisco State College, San Francisco, Calif.
Sieving, Eldor C., Concordia Teachers College, River Forest, Ill.
Siewers, Karl, 2301 Estes Ave., Chicago, Ill.
Sigwalt, J. Q., Box 351, Republic, Pa.
Silberman, Charles E., 342 Madison Ave., New York, N.Y.
Silva, J. Winston, California State Dept. of Educ., Sacramento, Calif.
Silvaroli, Nicholas J., Arizona State University, Tempe, Ariz.
Silver, Albert W., 1341 Nicolet Pl., Detroit, Mich.
Silvern, Leonard C., Educ. & Trng. Consults. Co., Los Angeles, Calif.
Simmons, Eleanor L., Fall River Elem. School, McArthur, Calif.
Simmons, Muriel H., 304—22nd Ave. North, Nashville, Tenn.
Simmons, Virginia Lee, Indianapolis Public Schools, Indianapolis, Ind.
Simms, Naomi, 333 College Ct., Kent, Ohio
Simon, Dan, Superintendent of Schools, East Chicago, Ind.
Simon, Herman, 3410 Palisades Ave., Union City, N.J.
Simons, Henrietta, 8830 Rayford Dr., Los Angeles, Calif.
Simons, Herbert D., 46 Shepard St., Cambridge, Mass.
Simpkins, Katherine W., P.O. Box 88, Chesapeake, Ohio
Simpson, Mrs. Anne E., Bethel Park Senior High School, Bethel Park, Pa.
Simpson, Mrs. Elizabeth A., 5627 Blackstone Ave., Chicago, Ill.
Simpson, Frederick W., University of Tulsa, Tulsa, Okla.
Simpson, Mrs. Hazel D., Col. of Educ., University of Georgia, Athens, Ga.
Simpson, Raymond J., San Francisco State College, San Francisco, Calif.
Sims, Harold W., 9423 Harvard Ave., Chicago, Ill.
Sims, Stephen B., Leonia Public Schools, Leonia, N.J.
Sincock, William R., Allegheny College, Meadville, Pa.
Sinderson, Louise, Chicago State Col., Chicago, Ill.
Singe, Anthony L., 772 Lansing St., Utica, N.Y.
Singer, H. Halleck, University of Pennsylvania, Philadelphia, Pa.
Singer, Harry, Div. of Soc. Sci., Univ. of California, Riverside, Calif.
Singletary, James Daniel, USAID/Education, APO San Francisco, Calif. 96243
Singleton, Edward M., 2804 Wilmot Ave., Columbia, S.C.
Singleton, Ira C., Silver Burdett Co., Morristown, N.J.
Singleton, John, University of Pittsburgh, Pittsburgh, Pa.
Singleton, Stanton J., Col. of Educ., University of Georgia, Athens, Ga.
Sipay, Edward R., State University of New York, Albany, N.Y.
Sipe, H. Craig, State Univ. of New York, Albany, N.Y.
Sires, Ely, 5018 LaCrosse Lane, Madison, Wis.
Sister Angelita, O.S.F., St. John Grade Sch., Bancroft, Iowa
Sister Ann Augusta, 400 The Fenway, Boston, Mass.
Sister Ann Mary Gullan, Mount Senario College, Ladysmith, Wis.
Sister Anna Marie (Weinreis), Presentation College, Aberdeen, S.D.
Sister Anne Martina (Ganser), St. Joseph's Col., Crookston, Minn.
Sister Charles Marie, Col. of St. Francis, Joliet, Ill.
Sister Dorothy Marie Riordan, College of St. Elizabeth, Convent Station, N.J.

Sister Fides Huber, College of St. Catherine, St. Paul, Minn.
Sister Helen Thompson, Clarke College, Dubuque, Iowa
Sister Irene Rita Fontaine, Holy Union Convent, 1 Main St., Groton, Mass.
Sister James, S.Sp.S., St. Rose de Lima H.S., Bay St. Louis, Miss.
Sister James Claudia, Siena Heights College, Adrian, Mich.
Sister James Edward, Brescia College, Owensboro, Ky.
Sister John Vianney Coyle, St. Francis Convent, Graymoor, Garrison, N.Y.
Sister Josephine Concannon, Boston College, Chestnut Hill, Mass.
Sister Margaret Mary, R.S.M., Gwynedd-Mercy College, Gwynedd Valley, Pa.
Sister Margaret Mary, Gwynedd-Mercy College, Gwynedd-Valley, Pa.
Sister Margaret Mary, Monsignor O'Brien High School, Kalamazoo, Mich.
Sister Margaret Mary O'Connell, College of Notre Dame of Md., Baltimore, Md.
Sister Marie Claudia, Barry College, Miami Shores, Fla.
Sister Marie Gabrielle, Diocesan Sisters College, Woodstock, Conn.
Sister Mary Agnello, Regis College, Framingham Campus, Framingham, Mass.
Sister Mary Agnes Hennessey, Mount Mercy College, Cedar Rapids, Iowa
Sister Mary Albertus, Mt. St. Vincent College, Halifax, Nova Scotia, Canada
Sister Mary Alice Huber, Mt. St. Joseph College, Buffalo, N.Y.
Sister Mary Alma, St. Mary's College, Notre Dame, Ind.
Sister Mary Basil, Good Counsel College, White Plains, N.Y.
Sister Mary Benedict Phelan, Clarke College, Dubuque, Iowa
Sister Mary Bernice, Our Lady of the Elms, Akron, Ohio
Sister Mary Bonnita, Felician College, Chicago, Ill.
Sister M. Brideen Long, Holy Family College, Manitowoc, Wis.
Sister Mary Camilla, St. Francis Convent, Jerseyville, Ill.
Sister M. Camille Kliebhan, Cardinal Stritch College, Milwaukee, Wis.
Sister Mary Charles, Molloy Catholic College for Women, Rockville Centre, N.Y.
Sister Mary Chrysostom, College of Our Lady of the Elms, Chicopee, Mass.
Sister Mary Clarissa, Dominican College of Blauvelt, Blauvelt, N.Y.
Sister Mary David, College of St. Benedict, St. Joseph, Minn.
Sister Mary de Lourdes, Saint Joseph College, West Hartford, Conn.
Sister Mary Dolores, College of St. Francis, Joliet, Ill.
Sister Mary Dorothy, Queen of Apostles Col. Library, Harrimon, N.Y.
Sister Mary Edward, 1229 Mt. Loretto Ave., Dubuque, Iowa
Sister Mary Edwina, 5286 South Park Ave., Hamburg, N.Y.
Sister Mary Fidelia, Immaculata College, Bartlett, Ill.
Sister Mary Fidelma, Marylhurst College, Marylhurst, Ore.
Sister M. Fleurette, St. Willibrord Convent, Chicago, Ill.
Sister M. Francis Regis, 444 Centre St., Milton, Mass.
Sister Mary Fridian, Dept. of Educ., St. Francis College, Fort Wayne, Ind.
Sister Mary Gabrieline, Marygrove College, Detroit, Mich.
Sister Mary Gabrielle, Nazareth College, Nazareth, Mich.
Sister Mary Giles, Mariam College, Indianapolis, Ind.
Sister M. Gregory, Marymount Col., Palo Verdes Estates, Calif.
Sister M. Harriet Sanborn, Aquinas College, Grand Rapids, Mich.
Sister Mary Helen, Dominican Col., Racine, Wis.
Sister Mary Hugh, Fontbonne College, St. Louis, Mo.
Sister Mary Irmina Saelinger, Villa Madonna College, Covington, Ky.
Sister Mary Jeanne, St. Mary's Academy, South Bend, Ind.
Sister Mary Joanne, Marycrest College, Davenport, Iowa
Sister Mary John Francis, Mount Mercy Col., Milwaukee, Wis.
Sister M. Judith, Villa Madonna Academy, Covington, Ky.
Sister Mary Judith, Dept. of Educ., Briar Cliff College, Sioux City, Iowa
Sister Mary Kathleen, Mt. St. Agnes College, Mt. Washington, Baltimore, Md.
Sister M. Laurina, Mount Mary College, Yankton, S.D.
Sister Mary Lawrence, Mary Manse College, Toledo, Ohio
Sister Mary Leo, Immaculata College, Immaculata, Pa.
Sister Mary Liguori, Mercyhurst College, Erie, Pa.
Sister Mary Madeleine, Col. of Our Lady of Mercy, Burlingame, Calif.
Sister M. Margarita, Rosary College, River Forest, Ill.

Sister M. Matthew, Sacred Heart Dominican College, Houston, Tex.
Sister Mary Mercita, St. Mary College, Xavier, Kan.
Sister M. Merici, Educ. Dept., Ursuline College, Louisville, Ky.
Sister M. Merle, St. Matthia School, Chicago, Ill.
Sister Mary Paul, Mt. Mercy College, Pittsburgh, Pa.
Sister M. Pierre, Marian College of Fond du Lac, Fond du Lac, Wis.
Sister Mary Priscilla, Notre Dame College, Cleveland, Ohio
Sister Mary Rachel, 345 Belden Hill Rd., Wilton, Conn.
Sister Mary Raymial, 10216 South Vernon Ave., Chicago, Ill.
Sister Mary Rose Agnes, Our Lady of Cincinnati College, Cincinnati, Ohio
Sister Mary of St. Michael, College of the Holy Names, Oakland, Calif.
Sister Mary Stephanie, Mt. St. Mary College, Hooksett, N.Y.
Sister Mary Theodine Sebold, Viterbo College, La Crosse, Wis.
Sister M. Veronice Engelhardt, Maria Regina College, Syracuse, N.Y.
Sister Mary Vianney, St. Xavier College, 103rd and Central Park, Chicago, Ill.
Sister Mary Vincent Therese Tuohy, 245 Clinton Ave., Brooklyn, N.Y.
Sister Mary Warin, Notre Dame of Dallas, Irving, Tex.
Sister Mary Zeno, Notre Dame College, 320 E. Ripa Ave., St. Louis, Mo.
Sister Maryl Hofer, Marian College, Indianapolis, Ind.
Sister Mildred Clare, Nazareth College, Nazareth, Ky.
Sister Miriam Richard, St. James Convent, Elkins Park, Pa.
Sister Muriel Hogan, Ottumwa Heights College, Ottumwa, Iowa
Sister Patrick Mary, 501 E. 163rd St., Calumet City, Ill.
Sister Regina Clare, Mt. St. Mary's College, Los Angeles, Calif.
Sister Rita Donahue, Notre Dame College, Staten Island, N.Y.
Sister Rose Matthew, Marygrove College, Detroit, Mich.
Sister Rosemarie Julie, Educ. Dept., College of Notre Dame, Belmont, Calif.
Skaggs, Darcy A., 3699 N. Holly Ave., Baldwin Park, Calif.
Skalski, John M., Sch. of Educ., Fordham University, New York, N.Y.
Skatzes, D. H., Box 125, Old Washington, Ohio
Skinner, Halver M., Montana State College, Bozeman, Montana
Skinner, Richard C., Clarion State College, Clarion, Pa.
Skinner, William S., Arizona State University, Scottsdale, Ariz.
Skipper, Mrs. Dora Sikes, Florida State University, Tallahassee, Fla.
Skogsberg, Alfred H., Bloomfield Junior High School, Bloomfield, N.J.
Skrocki, Patricia M., 409 Espanola Ave., Parchment, Mich.
Slater, J. Marlowe, Dept. of Educ. Psych., Univ. of Illinois, Urbana, Ill.
Sletten, Vernon, Sch. of Educ., Univ. of Montana, Missoula, Mont.
Sliepcevich, Elena M., 1425 "N" St., N. W., Washington, D.C.
Sligo, Joseph R., 102 N. Lancaster St., Athens, Ohio
Slobetz, Frank, St. Cloud State College, St. Cloud, Minn.
Slocum, Helen M., Norris Gym, Univ. of Minnesota, Minneapolis, Minn.
Slocum, Thomas J., 11 S. Cagwin, Joliet, Ill.
Smallenburg, Harry W., Supt. of Schools, Los Angeles Co., Los Angeles, Calif.
Smart, Barbara C., Public Schools, Palmer, Alaska
Smedstad, Alton O., Superintendent, Elem. Schools, Hillsboro, Ore.
Smelser, Rex H., 501 Broad St., Lake Charles, La.
Smiley, Marjorie B., Hunter College, 695 Park Ave., New York, N.Y.
Smith, Adean M., 1409 N. 67th St., Wauwatosa, Wis.
Smith, Alvin H., St. Andrews Presbyterian College, Laurinburg, N.C.
Smith, Anne M., 1720 Ellencourt, South Pasadena, Calif.
Smith, Ara K., 609 Lafayette St., Michigan City, Ind.
Smith, B. Othanel, Col. of Educ., University of Illinois, Urbana, Ill.
Smith, Calvert C., YMCA High School, Chicago, Ill.
Smith, Cleovis C., 4801 Tremont St., Dallas, Tex.
Smith, Clodus R., 9203 St. Andrews Pl., College Park, Md.
Smith, David C., Michigan State University, East Lansing, Mich.
Smith, E. Brooks, Wayne State University, Detroit, Mich.
Smith, Emmitt D., Box 745, West Texas Station, Canyon, Tex.
Smith, Frank A., 531-A West Ninth Pl., Mesa, Arizona

Smith, Garmon, W. Piedmont Community College, Morgantown, N.C.
Smith, Gary F., 400 E. Market St., Salem, Ind.
Smith, Gary R., Wayne State University, Detroit, Mich.
Smith, Gerald R., 4325 Etter Dr., Bloomington, Ind.
Smith, Hannis S., State Office Annex, 117 University Ave., St. Paul, Minn.
Smith, Harry E., The Grier School, Tyrone, Pa.
Smith, Henry P., Sch. of Educ., University of Kansas, Lawrence, Kan.
Smith, Herbert A., Colorado State University, Fort Collins, Colo.
Smith, Hester M., 26 Holmes Rd., Rochester, N.Y.
Smith, Hilda C., Dept. of Educ., Loyola University, New Orleans, La.
Smith, James B., 221 S. Missouri, Belleville, Ill.
Smith, James J., Jr., New York Urban League, Albany, N.Y.
Smith, James O., 504 Roosevelt Dr., Shelbyville, Ind.
Smith, John W., 10001 Princeton Ave., Chicago, Ill.
Smith, Joseph M., 172 Charter Rd., Wethersfield, Conn.
Smith, Kenneth E., Grad. Sch. of Educ., Univ. of Chicago, Chicago, Ill.
Smith, Kenneth J., University of Miami, Coral Gables, Fla.
Smith, Lawrence J., Central Michigan University, Mt. Pleasant, Mich.
Smith, Leslie F., 705 N. Killingsworth, Portland, Ore.
Smith, Lewis B., University of Idaho, Moscow, Ida.
Smith, Lloyd N., Dept. of Educ., Indiana State University, Terre Haute, Ind.
Smith, Mary Alice, State College, Lock Haven, Pa.
Smith, Mrs. Maxine, 172 W. Third St., San Bernardino, Calif.
Smith, Menrie M., Rte. 4, Hamilton, Ala.
Smith, Nila Blanton, 9712 Sylvia Ave., Northridge, Calif.
Smith, Paul E., 156 N. Columbus Dr., Mt. Vernon, N.Y.
Smith, Paul M., 1001 Maple, Wasco, Calif.
Smith, Philip John, Box 13, P.O. Cottesloe, Western Australia
Smith, Priscilla R., Western State Col., Gunnison, Colo.
Smith, Robert M., Pennsylvania State Univ., University Park, Pa.
Smith, Russell F. W., 9 Bursley Pl., White Plains, N.Y.
Smith, Sisera, 115 South 54th St., Philadelphia, Pa.
* Smith, Stephen E., East Texas Baptist College, Marshall, Tex.
Smith, W. Holmes, El Camino Col., Torrance, Calif.
Smith, Walter, Public Schools, Los Alamos, N.M.
Smolens, Richard, 69 Wooleys, Great Neck, N.Y.
Snapper, Marion, Calvin College, Grand Rapids, Mich.
Snead, William E., 1021 Farnway Ln., St. Louis, Mo.
Snearline, Paul A., 815 Market St., Lewisburg, Pa.
Snider, Donald A., 2680 Fayette, Mountain View, Calif.
Snider, Glenn R., Col. of Educ., University of Oklahoma, Norman, Okla.
Snider, Hervon Leroy, Sch. of Educ., University of Idaho, Moscow, Idaho
Sniderman, S. M., Highland Park Pub. Schools, Highland Park, Mich.
Snowden, Terrence J., Campus Sch., Wisconsin State Col., Stevens Point, Wis.
Snyder, Agnes, 50 Central Ter., Clifton Park, Wilmington, Del.
Snyder, Darl E., 424 S. Sixth Ave., La Grange, Ill.
Snyder, Harvey B., Pasadena College, 1539 E. Howard St., Pasadena, Calif.
Snyder, Helen I., 1020 W. Beaver Ave., State College, Pa.
Snyder, Jack, Encyclopaedia Britannica Educ. Corp., Chicago, Ill.
Snyder, Jerome R., 1114 Mogford St., Midland, Tex.
Snyder, Marjorie Sims, Child Study Cntr., Kent State Univ., Kent, Ohio
Snyder, Robert D., Superintendent of Schools, Wayzata, Minn.
Snyder, Ruth C., 110 Laurelton Rd., Rochester, N.Y.
Soares, Anthony T., 290 Lawrence Rd., Trumbull, Conn.
Sobin, Gloria A., 370 Seymour Ave., Derby, Conn.
Soeberg, Mrs. Dorothy, 106 Ridge Rd., Whittier, Calif.
Sokol, John, Tchrs. Col., Columbia University, New York, N.Y.
Soles, Stanley, San Francisco State College, San Francisco, Calif.
Solomon, Benjamin, Indust. Rela. Cntr., Univ. of Chicago, Chicago, Ill.
Solomon, Ruth H., 91 N. Allen St., Albany, N.Y.

Somers, Mary Louise, Sch. of SSA, Univ. of Chicago, Chicago, Ill.
Sommer, Maynard E., 1032 Sueno Ct., Camarillo, Calif.
Sommers, George, 950 Federal Reserve Bank Bldg., Minneapolis, Minn.
Sommers, Mildred, Board of Educ., 290 W. Michigan Ave., Jackson, Mich.
Sommers, Wesley S., 820 Sixth St., Menomonie, Wis.
Sonntag, Ida May, 5101 Norwich Rd., Toledo, Ohio
Sonstegard, Manford A., Southern Illinois Univ., Edwardsville, Ill.
Sorbo, Paul J., Jr., Board of Education, Windsor, Conn.
Sorensen, Edwin, P.O. Box 210, Northport, N.Y.
Sorenson, A. Garth, Moore Hall, University of California, Los Angeles, Calif.
Sorenson, Helmer E., Oklahoma A. & M. Univ., Stilwater, Okla.
Sorenson, Mrs. Virginia, 105 N. Division Ave., Grand Rapids, Mich.
Sorenson, Wayne L., Hayward Unified Sch. Dist., Hayward, Calif.
Sosulski, Michael C., Dutchess Comm. Col., Poughkeepsie, N.Y.
Soucy, Leo A., Dist. Supt. of Schools, Auburn, N.Y.
Southall, Maycie K., Box 867, Peabody Col., Nashville, Tenn.
Sowards, G. Wesley, Sch. of Educ., Stanford University, Stanford, Calif.
Spalke, E. Pauline, P.O. Box 405, Salem Depot. N.H.
Sparling, Joseph J., Old Oxford Rd., Chapel Hill, N.C.
Spaulding, Robert L., Duke University, Durham, N.C.
Spaulding, Seth, Sch. of Educ., Univ. of Pittsburgh, Pittsburgh, Pa.
Spear, William G., 7233 W. Lunt Ave., Chicago, Ill.
Spears, Sol, El Marino School, Culver City, Calif.
Speciale, Anna G., 83 Rockledge Ave., White Plains, N.Y.
Speer, Hugh W., University of Missouri, Kansas City, Mo.
Speicher, A. Dean, 8008 Kennedy Ave., Highland, Ind.
Speights, Mrs. R. M., Limestone College, Gaffney, S.C.
Spence, Joseph R., Clarion State College, Clarion, Pa.
Spence, Ralph B., 355 Beechwood Dr., Athens, Ga.
Spencer, Doris U., Johnson State College, Johnson, Vt.
Spencer, Edward M., Fresno State College, Fresno, Calif.
Spencer, Elizabeth F., Ball State University, Muncie, Ind.
Spencer, James E., P.O. Box 813, Danville, Calif.
Sperber, Robert I., 21 Lowell Rd., Brookline, Mass.
Sperger, Zelma M., Board of Education, Salt Lake City, Utah
Spigle, Irving S., Park Forest Pub. Schools, Park Forest, Ill.
Spinner, Arnold, New York University, New York, N.Y.
Spinola, A. R., Superintendent, Denville School Dist. No. 1, Denville, N.J.
Spitzer, Herbert F., Col. of Educ., State University of Iowa, Iowa City, Iowa
Spitzer, Lillian K., IDEA, 1100 Glendon Ave., Los Angeles, Calif.
Sporing, W. Dwight, High School, 8th and Walnut Sts., Dayton, Ky.
Springman, John H., 1215 Waukegan Rd., Glenview, Ill.
Squire, James R., Ginn & Co., Boston, Mass.
Stabler, Ernest, Wesleyan University, Middletown, Conn.
Stafford, H. D., P.O. Box 21, Murrayville, B.C., Canada
Staggs, Jack, Sam Houston State Col., Huntsville, Texas
Stahl, Albert F., Bloomfield Hills, Mich.
Stahlecker, Lotar V., Kent State University, Kent, Ohio
Stahly, Harold L., 8343 Manchester Dr., Grand Blanc, Mich.
Staidl, Doris J., 1 East Gilman, Madison, Wis.
Staiger, Ralph C., 701 Dallam Rd., Newark, Del.
Staiger, Roger P., Dept. of Chem., Ursinus College, Collegeville, Pa.
Stalnaker, John M., 569 Briar Lane, Northfield, Ill.
Stanard, David C., Cubberly H.S., 4000 Middlefield Rd., Palo Alto, Calif.
Stang, Genevieve E., 730 First St., Apt. H, Bowling Green, Ohio
Stanley, Calvin, Texas Southern University, Houston, Tex.
Stanton, William A., Purdue University, Lafeyette, Ind.
Starner, Norman Dean, Wyalusing Valley Joint High School, Wyalusing, Pa.
Starner, William S., Rutgers Univ., Newark, N.J.

Starnes, Thomas A., Atlanta Public Schools, Atlanta, Ga.
Starr, Fay H., M. W. Regional Educ. Lab., St. Ann, Ill.
Stathopulos, Peter H., 320 Second Ave., Phoenixville, Pa.
Statler, Charles R., Univ. of South Carolina, Columbia, S.C.
Stauffer, Arthur L., Jr., State Univ. Col., Fredonia, N.Y.
Stauffer, Russell G., University of Delaware, Newark, Del.
Staven, LaVier L., 1304 MacArthur Rd., Hays, Kan.
Steadman, E. R., 277 Columbia, Elmhurst, Ill.
Stedje, Raynard L., 3146 Minnehaha Ave., So., Minneapolis, Minn.
Steele, Joe Milan, 304 Hollywood Ct., Wilmette, Ill.
Steele, Lysle H., P.O. Box 66, Beloit, Wis.
Steen, Mrs. Peggy, 133 Mission St., Santa Cruz, Calif.
Steer, Donald R., University of Michigan, Ann Arbor, Mich.
Steeves, Frank L., University of Vermont, Burlington, Vt.
Steg, Doreen E., 1616 Hepburn Dr., Villanova, Pa.
Stegall, Alma Lirline, Virginia State College, Petersburg, Va.
Steger, Robert I., 530 S. Tenth Ave., LaGrange, Ill.
Steigelman, Vivian R., 1440 Navallier, El Cerrito, Calif.
Stein, Michael W., Western Jr. H.S., Greenwich, Conn.
Steinberg, Paul M., Hebrew Union Col., New York, N.Y.
Steinberg, Warren L., 2737 Dunleer Pl., Los Angeles, Calif.
Steiner, Harry, 5 Belaire Dr., Roseland, N.J.
Steinhagen, Margaret J., 107 McKendree Ave., Annapolis, Md.
Steinhauer, Charlotte H., 1560—75th St., Downers Grove, Ill.
Steininger, Earl W., 535 West 5th St., Dubuque, Iowa
Steinkellner, Robert H., Southern Illinois University, Edwardsville, Ill.
Stell, Samuel C., Robeson County Bd. of Educ., Lumberton, N.C.
Stephens, Bertha L., 121 E. Evans Ave., Pueblo, Colo.
Stephens, E. R., Univ. of Iowa, Iowa City, Iowa
Stephens, John M., Box 70, Shawnigan Lake, B.C., Canada
Stephens, Kenton, Oak Park Schools, Oak Park, Ill.
Stephenson, Alan R., 11227 Plymouth Ave., Cleveland, Ohio
Sterling, A. M., 1017 Garner Ave., Schenectady, N.Y.
Sternberg, William N., Public Sch. 114, 1155 Cromwell Ave., New York, N.Y.
Sterner, William S., Rutgers Univ., Newark, N.J.
Stetson, Ethel A., 47 Westchester Ave., North Babylon, N.Y.
Stevens, J. H., 916 Carter Hill Rd., Montgomery, Ala.
Stevens, Paul C., Rapid City Public Schools, Rapid City, S.D.
Stewart, Frederick H., 600 E. St. Rd., Trevose, Pa.
Stewart, James T., Delgado Institute, New Orleans, La.
Stewart, Lawrence H., University of California, Berkeley, Calif.
Stickler, W. Hugh, Florida State University, Tallahassee, Fla.
Stickley, William T., 2107 Adelbert Rd., Cleveland, Ohio
Stiemke, Eugenia A., Valparaiso University, Valparaiso, Ind.
Stier, Lealand D., P.O. Box 247, Saratoga, Calif.
Stiles, Grace Ellen, 10 Fortin Rd., Kingston, R.I.
Stirzaker, Norbert A., 766 Palmetto, Spartanburg, S.C.
Stitt, J. Howard, Northern Arizona University, Flagstaff, Ariz.
Stitt, Sam C., Superintendent of Schools, Ellinwood, Kan.
Stivers, Stephen N., Idaho State University, Pocatello, Idaho
Stockman, Verne, Eastern Illinois University, Charleston, Ill.
Stoddard, George D., 434 E. 87th St., New York, N.Y.
Stofega, Michael E., 271 State St., Perth Amboy, N.J.
Stoffler, James A., Colorado State College, Greeley, Colo.
Stoia, George, 234 Conover Rd., Pittsburgh, Pa.
Stokes, Maurice S., Savannah State College, Savannah, Ga.
Stolee, Michael J., 6618 San Vincente Ave., Coral Gables, Fla.
Stolurow, Lawrence M., 110 Pleasant St., Lexington, Mass.
Stone, Curtis C., Kent State University, Kent, Ohio
Stone, Franklin D., Univ. of Iowa, Iowa City, Iowa
Stone, George P., Union College, Lincoln, Neb.

Stone, Howard L., 1732 Wauwatosa Ave., Wauwatosa, Wis.
Stone, James C., University of California, Berkeley, Calif.
Stone, Paul T., Huntingdon College, Montgomery, Ala.
Stonehocker, D. Doyle, 1515 Oakdale St., Burlington, Iowa
Stoneking, Lewis W., Parsons College, Fairfield, Iowa
Stoner, Lee H., Sch. of Educ., Indiana Univ., Bloomington, Ind.
Stoops, John A., Dept. of Educ., Lehigh University, Bethlehem, Pa.
Stordahl, Kalmer E., Northern Michigan Univ., Marquette, Mich.
Storen, Helen F., 114 Morningside Dr., New York, N.Y.
Storlie, Theodore R., 1400 W. Maple Ave., Downers Grove, Ill.
Storm, Jerome F., 432 S. 21st St., Richmond, Ind.
Stormer, Donald L., Rt. # 1, Waunakee, Wis.
Stottler, Richard H., University of Maryland, College Park, Md.
Stoughton, Robert W., State Department of Education, Hartford, Conn.
Stoumbis, George C., Col. of Educ., Univ. of Utah, Salt Lake City, Utah
Strahler, Violet R., 5340 Brendonwood Ln., Dayton, Ohio
Strain, John Paul, Dept. of Educ., Tufts University, Medford, Mass.
Strain, Mrs. Sibyl M., 2236 Los Lunas St., Pasadena, Calif.
Strand, Helen A., Luther College, Decorah, Iowa
Strand, William H., Sch. of Educ., Stanford University, Stanford, Calif.
Strang, Ruth M., 102 Bloor St., W., Toronto, Ont., Canada
Strathairn, Pamela L., Women's Phy. Ed. Dept., Stanford Univ., Stanford, Calif.
Straub, Raymond R., Jr., 1120 S. Gay St., Phoenixville, Pa.
Strauss, John F., Jr., Darien High School, Delavan, Wis.
Strawn, Aimee W., Chicago State Col., South, Chicago, Ill.
Strayer, George D., Jr. Col. of Educ., University of Washington, Seattle, Wash.
Strebel, Jane D., Bd. of Educ., 807 N.E. Broadway, Minneapolis, Minn.
Street, William Paul, Univ. of Kentucky, Lexington, Ky.
Streich, William H., Farmington Pub. Schools, Farmington, Conn.
Streitmatter, Kenneth D., Saipan, Marianas Islands
Strem, Bruce E., 109 Marykay Rd., Timonium, Md.
Streng, Alice, University of Wisconsin-Milwaukee, Milwaukee, Wis.
Strickland, C. G., Sch. of Educ., Baylor University, Waco, Tex.
Strickland, J. D., 3302 Conner Dr., Canyon, Tex.
Stringfellow, Mrs. Jackie R., 1833 Second St., S.E., Moultrie, Ga.
Strohbehn, Earl F., 12151 Mellowood Dr., Saratoga, Calif.
Strole, Lois E., R.R. No. 2, West Terre Haute, Ind.
Stromberg, Francis I., Oklahoma State University, Stillwater, Okla.
Strowbridge, Edwin D., Oregon State University, Corvallis, Ore.
Stuardi, J. Edwin, 550 Dauphin St., Mobile, Ala.
Stuart, Alden T., St. Andrews Rd., Southampton, N.Y.
Stuart, Chester J., Canisius Hall, Fairfield University, Fairfield, Conn.
Stuber, George, Clayton School Dist., 7530 Maryland Ave., Clayton, Mo.
Studer, Harold R., Harrisburg Public Schools, Harrisburg, Pa.
Stuenkel, Walter W., Concordia College, Milwaukee, Wis.
Stutzman, Carl R., 2130 Aaron Way, Sacramento, Calif.
Sudyk, James Edward, 830 Williams Way, Mountain View, Calif.
Suehr, John H., Michigan State University, East Lansing, Mich.
Suess, Alan R., M. Golden Labs., Purdue Univ., Lafayette, Ind.
Sugarman, Alan, Ramapo Cent. Sch. Dist. No. 2, Spring Valley, N.Y.
Sugden, W. E., Superintendent of Schools, 7776 Lake St., River Forest, Ill.
Suhd, Melvin, 8501 Tampa, Northridge, Calif.
Suhr, Virtus W., Northern Illinois University, DeKalb, Ill.
Suiter, Phil E., Chesapeake High School, Chesapeake, Ohio
Sullivan, Dorothy D., University of Maryland, College Park, Md.
Sullivan, Edmund V., 102 Bloor St., W., Toronto, Ont., Canada
Sullivan, Floyd W., 1015 Lena St., N.W., Atlanta, Ga.
Sullivan, John J., Roosevelt Sch. Dist., Phoenix, Arizona
Sullivan, Mona Lee R., 3511 Donaldson Dr., Atlanta, Ga.
Sullivan, Robert E., Notre Dame Col., Cotabato City, Philippines
Sullivan, Ruth E., 306 Bayswater, Salem Harbour, Andalusia, Pa.

Sullivan, Stephen P., 3532 Herschel View, Cincinnati, Ohio
Sulzer, Edward Stanton, Southern Illinois University, Carbondale, Ill.
Summerer, Kenneth, Michigan State Univ., East Lansing, Mich.
Summerton, Rev. O., S.J., P.O. Sitagarha, DT. Hazaribagh, Bihar, India
Sundquist, Ralph R., Jr., Hartford Seminary Foundation, Hartford, Conn.
Sunzeri, Adeline V., 6142 Afton Pl., Hollywood, Calif.
Supworth, Flora D., Miami-Dade Jr. Col., Coral Gables, Fla.
Susskind, Edwin C., 405 Fountain St., New Haven, Conn.
Sutherland, Angus W., Public Schools, Detroit, Mich.
Sutherland, Jack W., San Jose State College, San Jose, Calif.
Sutherland, Margaret, Col. of Educ., University of California, Davis, Calif.
Sutton, Elizabeth W., 800 Fourth St., S.W., Washington, D.C.
Swann, Mrs. A. Ruth, 2713 Mapleton Ave., Norfolk, Va.
Swanson, Gordon I., Dept. of Agric. Educ., Univ. of Minnesota, St. Paul, Minn.
Swanson, Herbert L., El Camino Col., Torrance, Calif.
Swanson, J. Chester, Sch. of Educ., University of California, Berkeley, Calif.
Swanson, Reynold A., Board of Education, 100 N. Jefferson, Green Bay, Wis.
Swarr, Philip C., State University College, Courtland, N.Y.
Swartout, Sherwin G., State Univ. Col., Brockport, N.Y.
Swartzmiller, Jean, 90 Ridge Ave., North Plainfield, N.J.
Sweany, H. Paul, Michigan State University, East Lansing, Mich.
Swenson, Esther J., Box 1942, University, Ala.
Swertfeger, Floyd F., Route 3, Box 16, Farmville, Va.
Swindall, Wellington, Palmdale School, 3000 E. Wier Ave., Phoenix, Ariz.
Swindel, Mrs. Mabel A., Three Rivers Jr. Col., Poplar Bluff, Mo.
Syvinski, Henry B., Villanova University, Villanova, Pa.

Tadena, Tomas P., Univ. of the Philippines, Quezon City, Philippines
Tag, Herbert G., University of Connecticut, Storrs, Conn.
Tajima, Yuri, 1918 N. Bissell, Chicago, Ill.
* Tallman, Russell W., 2024 Avalon Rd., Des Moines, Iowa
Tamashunas, Edward, 2220 Park Ave., Bridgeport, Conn.
Tambe, Naren, Box 1393, Durham, N.C.
Tannenbaum, Bernard M., 3600 N. Lake Shore Dr., Chicago, Ill.
Tanner, B. William, 650 S. Detroit Ave., Toledo, Ohio
Tanner, Daniel, Rutgers University, New Brunswick, N.J.
Tanner, Wilbur H., Northwestern State University, Alva, Okla.
Tanruther, Edgar M., Indiana State Univ., Terre Haute, Ind.
Tant, Norman, Morehead State College, Morehead, Ky.
Taplette, Owinda W., N. O. Public Schools, New Orleans, La.
Tarver, K. E., John P. Odom School, 3445 Fannett Rd., Beaumont, Tex.
Tashow, Horst, P.O. Box 268, Bend, Ore.
Tate, Virginia, 2228 Eighth St. Cr., Charleston, Ill.
Taylor, Azella, 18 Vista Rd., Ellensburg, Wash.
Taylor, Mrs. Emily C., Mayo Elementary School, Edgewater, Md.
Taylor, Faith, 10427 Montrose Ave., Bethesda, Md.
Taylor, George E., Gateway Sch. Dist., Monroeville, Pa.
Taylor, James I., Miami-Dade Jr. Col., Coral Gables, Fla.
Taylor, John M., 9905 S.W. 196th St., Miami, Fla.
Taylor, Kenneth I., Madison Public Schools, Madison, Wis.
Taylor, M. Ruth, Hillcrest School, Drexel Hill, Pa.
Taylor, Marvin, Div. of Educ., Queens College, Flushing, N.Y.
Taylor, Marvin J., St. Paul School of Theology, Kansas City, Mo.
Taylor, Mrs. Mary C., Box 164, Rt. No. 1, New Lenox, Ill.
Taylor, Peter A., Fac. of Educ., Univ. of Manitoba, Winnepeg, Man., Canada
Taylor, Robert E., 1835 Riverhill Rd., Columbus, Ohio
Taylor, Wayne, 160 Kenberry, East Lansing, Mich.
Taylor, Zina Lee, 407 Waltham, Hammond, Ind.
Teague, Carroll, Pasadena Ind. School District, Pasadena, Tex.
Teare, Benjamin R., Jr., Carnegie-Mellon Univ., Schenley Park, Pa.
Telego, Gene, Ashland College, Ashland, Ohio

Telfer, Richard G., Shorewood Public Schools, Shorewood, Wis.
Telford, Charles W., San Jose State College, San Jose, Calif.
Temp, George E., Educ. Test. Service, Berkeley, Calif.
Tempero, Howard E., Teachers Col., University of Nebraska, Lincoln, Neb.
Temple, F. L., Box 2185, University, Ala.
Templin, Mildred C., Inst. of Child Welfare, Univ. of Minnesota, Minneapolis,
    Minn.
TenEyck, Adelaide L. C., 3601 N. St. Francis, Wichita, Kan.
Tenny, John W., Wayne State University, Detroit, Mich.
Terlaje, Shirley A., P.O. Box 1719, Agana, Guam
Terrill, Maymie I., 2477 Overlook Rd., Cleveland Heights, Ohio
Tetz, Henry E., Oregon College of Education, Monmouth, Ore.
Thatcher, Alfred W., State Univ. Col., Potsdam, N.Y.
Thelen, L. J., University of Massachusetts, Amherst, Mass.
Theus, Robert, Southern Illinois University, Carbondale, Ill.
Thevaos, Deno G., 575 Westview Ave., State College, Pa.
Thomann, Don F., Dept. of Educ., Ripon College, Ripon, Wis.
Thomas, A. M., Can. Assn. for Adult Educ., Toronto, Ont., Canada
Thomas, David C., University of Victoria, Victoria, B.C., Canada
Thomas, Granville S., Superintendent of Schools, Salem, N.J.
Thomas, J. Alan, University of Chicago, Chicago, Ill.
Thomas, James E., Supt. of Schools, Bristol, Tenn.
Thomas, John, 2250 Missouri, Las Cruces, N.M.
Thomas, T. M., 45 Potter Pl., Springfield, Mass.
Thomas, Virginia F., Iowa State Univ., Ames, Iowa
Thomas, Wade F., Santa Monica City College, Santa Monica, Calif.
Thompson, Mrs. Alberta S., Dept. of H.E., Kent State Univ., Kent, Ohio
Thompson, Anton, Long Beach Public Schls., 715 Locust Ave., Long Beach,
    Calif.
Thompson, Barry B., Waco Independent School Dist., Waco, Tex.
Thompson, Bertha Boya, Western Col. for Women, Oxford, Ohio
Thompson, Charles H., Grad. Sch., Howard University, Washington, D.C.
Thompson, Evelyn S., University of Houston, Houston, Tex.
Thompson, Franklin J., South Pasadena High School, South Pasadena, Calif.
Thompson, Fred R., Col. of Educ., Univ. of Maryland, College Park, Md.
Thompson, Gary, 821 Harley Dr., Columbus, Ohio
Thompson, Helen M., Thompson Reading Clinic, Orange, Calif.
Thompson, James H., 4 Wallace Dr., Athens, Ohio
Thompson, John D., P.O. Drawer 877, Seminole Public Schools, Seminole, Tex.
Thompson, John F., 1483 Carver St., Madison, Wis.
Thompson, O. E., University of California, Davis, Calif.
Thompson, Olive L., 1541 Iroquois Ave., Long Beach, Calif.
Thompson, Ralph H., Western Washington State Col., Bellingham, Wash.
Thompson, Ray, North Carolina College, Durham, N.C.
Thompson, Mrs. Sheilah, 930 Whitchurch St., North Vancouver, B.C., Canada
Thoms, Denis, Campus View # 124, Bloomington, Ind.
Thomsen, Ronald W., Box 361, Sidney, Iowa
Thomson, Procter, Pitzer Hall, Claremont Men's College, Claremont, Calif.
Thorn, Elizabeth, Provincial Teachers College, North Bay, Ont., Canada
Thorndike, Robert L., Tchrs. Col., Columbia University, New York, N.Y.
Thornsley, Jerome R., 764 Laurel Ave., Pomona, Calif.
Thornton, James W., Jr., San Jose State College, San Jose, Calif.
Throne, Elsie M., 306 Lincoln Ave., Avon-by-the-Sea, N.J.
Thursby, Mrs. Ruth E., 3628 Taft St., Riverside, Calif.
Thursly, Marilyn, 3435 Mogadore Rd., Mogadore, Ohio
Thyberg, Clifford S., 1717 W. Merced Ave., West Covina, Calif.
Tidrow, Joe, Dept. of Educ. and Phil., Texas Tech. College, Lubbock, Tex.
Tidwell, Robert E., 1602 Alaca Pl., Tuscaloosa, Ala.
Tiedeman, Herman R., Illinois State University, Normal, Ill.
Tiffany, Betty Jane, 305 E. Church St., Ridgecrest, Calif.
Tiffany, Burton C., Supt. of Schools, Chula Vista, Calif.

Tillan, Lynn, 417 Hillsboro Pkwy., Syracuse, N.Y.
Tillman, Rodney, George Washington University, Washington, D.C.
Timberlake, Walter B., 319 W. Dayton, Yellow Springs Rd., Fairborn, Ohio
Timmons, F. Alan, 1700 Octavia St., San Francisco, Calif.
Tinari, Charles, Shackamaxon School, Scotch Plains, N.J.
Tingle, Mary J., Col. of Educ., University of Georgia, Athens, Ga.
Tink, Albert K., 18 Wendall Pl., DeKalb, Ill.
Tinker, Miles A., P.O. Box 3193, Santa Barbara, Calif.
Tinney, James J., Supt. of Schools, Rutland, Vt.
Tins, Mildred A., Mark Twain School, Wheeling, Ill.
Tipton, Elis M., Box 502, Mariposa, Calif.
Tisdall, William J., University of Kentucky, Lexington, Ky.
Tittle, Carol K., 133 W. 94th St., New York, N.Y.
Todd, G. Raymond, R.D. No. 3, Bethlehem, Pa.
Todd, Neal F., 128 Main St., Ware, Mass.
Todd, Thomas W., 311 Belmont Ave., Elyria, Ill.
Toepfer, Conrad F., Jr., State Univ. Col., Buffalo, N.Y.
Toles, Caesar F., Bishop Junior College, 4527 Crozier St., Dallas, Tex.
Tolleson, Sherwell K., Box 182A, Tenn. Polytech. Inst., Cookeville, Tenn.
Tollinger, William P., Superintendent, Wilson Borough Schls., Easton, Pa.
Tom, Chow Loy, 47 W. Brighton Rd., Columbus, Ohio
Tomacek, Carolyn L., 747 N. Wabash, Chicago, Ill.
Tomaszewski, Raymond J., 333 Richard Ter., S.E., Grand Rapids, Mich.
Toops, Herbert A., 1430 Cambridge Blvd., Columbus, Ohio
Toporowski, Theodore T., Danbury State College, Danbury, Conn.
Topp, Robert F., Col. of Educ., Northern Illinois University, DeKalb, Ill.
Torchia, Joseph, Millersville State Col., Millersville, Pa.
Torkelson, Gerald M., 408 Miller, Univ. of Washington, Seattle, Wash.
Torrance, E. Paul, University of Georgia, Athens, Ga.
Tothill, Herbert, Eastern Michigan University, Ypsilanti, Mich.
Totten, W. Fred, Mott Sci. Bldg., 1401 E. Court St., Flint, Mich.
Toussaint, Isabella H., 1670 River Rd., Beaver, Pa.
Towers, Richard L., Sch. of Educ., Univ. of South Carolina, Columbia, S.C.
Townsend, Richard G., 2553 E. 76th St., Chicago, Ill.
Trachtman, Gilbert M., Sch. of Educ., New York Univ., New York, N.Y.
Tracy, Elaine M., St. Olaf College, Northfield, Minn.
Tracy, Neal H., University of North Carolina, Chapel Hill, N.C.
Traeger, Carl, 375 N. Eagle St., Oshkosh, Wis.
Traiber, Frank, USAID Mission, Guatemala, State Dept., Washington, D.C.
Trail, Orval L., Superintendent of Schools, Galesburg, Ill.
Trakas, Georgia, 4667 E. Main St., Columbus, Ohio
Tramondo, Anthony, White Plains High School, White Plains, N.Y.
Trauger, Ruth, Kutztown State College, Kutztown, Pa.
Travelstead, Chester C., Col. of Educ., Univ. of New Mexico, Albuquerque, N.M.
Travers, John F., Boston College, Chestnut Hill, Mass.
Travis, Vaud A., Dept. of Educ., Northeastern State College, Tahlequa, Okla.
Traxler, Arthur E., 6825 S.W. 59th St., Miami, Fla.
Treece, Marion B., Southern Illinois University, Carbondale, Ill.
Treffinger, Donald J., 1010 N. Salisbury, W. Lafayette, Ind.
Tremont, Joseph J., 22 Fletcher St., Ayer, Mass.
Trice, J. A., Superintendent of Schools, Pine Bluff, Ark.
Trigg, Harold L., State Board of Educ., Greensboro, N.C.
Triggs, Frances, Mountain Home, N.C.
Trippe, Matthew J., University of Michigan, Ann Arbor, Mich.
Trout, Douglas G., Tusculum College, Greenville, Tenn.
Trout, Len L., 2000 Royal Dr., Reno, Nev.
Trow, William Clark, Sch. of Educ., University of Michigan, Ann Arbor, Mich.
Truher, Helen Burke, 245 Hillside Rd., South Pasadena, Calif.
Trumble, Verna J., 42 West St., Johnson City, N.Y.
Trump, J. Lloyd, National Educ. Assn., 1201 Sixteenth St., N.W., Washington,
    D.C.

Trump, Paul L., American Col. Test. Program, Box 168, Iowa City, Iowa
Truncellito, Louis, Georgetown Univ., Washington, D.C.
Trusty, Francis M., University of Rochester, Rochester, N.Y.
Tucker, Jan L., 407 N. Roosevelt, Bloomington, Ind.
Tucker, Sylvia B., 30929 Rue Langlois, Palos Verdes, Pen., Calif.
Tudyman, Al, 4470 Hillsborough Dr., Castro Valley, Calif.
Tully, Glover E., Board of Regents, Tallahassee, Fla.
Tupper, Frank B., 389 Congress St., Portland, Me.
Turansky, Isadore, Western Michigan University, Kalamazoo, Mich.
Turchan, Donald G., 1026 White Dr., New Castle, Ind.
Turck, Merton J., Jr., Tennessee Polytechnic Inst., Cookeville, Tenn.
Turner, Delia F., 3310 Edgemont, Tucson, Ariz.
Turner, Howard, Col. of Educ., Univ. of S.W. Louisiana, Lafayette, La.
Turner, Mrs. Nell B., 3431 Sangamon Ave., Dayton, Ohio
Turney, David T., Sch. of Educ., Indiana State Univ., Terre Haute, Ind.
Turnquist, Carl H., Detroit Pub. Schls., 5057 Woodward Ave., Detroit, Mich.
Tuseth, Alice A., 6410—37th Ave. No., Minneapolis, Minn.
Tuttle, Edwin A., Jr., State Univ. Col., New Paltz, N.Y.
Twombly, John J., Sch. of Educ., State Univ. of N.Y., Albany, N.Y.
Tydings, R. N., Hobbs Municipal Schools, Hobbs, N.M.
Tyler, Fred T., University of Victoria, Victoria, B.C., Canada
Tyler, I. Keith, Ohio State University, Columbus, Ohio
Tyler, Louise L., University of California, Los Angeles, Calif.
Tyler, Priscilla, Univ. of Missouri, Kansas City, Mo.
Tyler, Ralph W., 5825 Dorchester Ave., Chicago, Ill.
Tyler, Robert, Educ. Dept., Southwestern State College, Weatherford, Okla.
Tyree, Marshall J., New York University, New York, N.Y.
Tyrrell, Francis M., Immaculate Conception Seminary, Huntington, N.Y.
Tystad, Edna, Thoreau Public Schools, Thoreau, N.M.

Ubben, Gerald, University of Tennessee, Knoxville, Tenn.
Uhl, Norman P., 1106 Lullwater Rd., N.E., Atlanta, Ga.
Uhlir, Richard F., 800½ W. White St., Champaign, Ill.
Umansky, Harlan L., Emerson High School, Union City, N.J.
Umbarger, Helen D., East Chicago Public Schools, East Chicago, Ind.
Umholtz, Mrs. Anne K., 292 N. Fifth Ave., Highland Park, N.J.
Umstattd, James G., Sutton Hall, University of Texas, Austin, Tex.
Underwood, Mrs. Anna, Box 72, Southard, Okla.
Underwood, Mrs. Frances A., 5900 Hilltop Rd., Pensacola, Fla.
Underwood, Frederic, St. Paul's Schools, Garden City, N.Y.
Underwood, Helen B., School of Voc. Nurs., Napa, Calif.
Underwood, Mary Hope, R. 2, Chapel Dr. 29, Whitewater, Wis.
Underwood, William J., 304 Lakeview, Lee's Summit, Mo.
Unger, Mrs. Dorothy Holberg, 99 Lawton Rd., Riverside, Ill.
Unruh, Adolph, Univ. of Missouri, 8001 Natural Bridge Rd., St. Louis, Mo.
Urbach, Floyd, Univ. of Nebraska, Waverly, Neb.
Urdang, Miriam E., Queens College, Flushing, N.Y.
Usdan, Michael D., Teachers Col., Columbia University, New York, N.Y.
Usitalo, Richard J., 2015 Clairemont Cir., Olympia, Wash.
Utley, Quentin, 136 E.S. Temple, Salt Lake City, Utah

Vail, Edward O., Los Angeles City Schools, Los Angeles, Calif.
* Vakil, K. S., 119, Marzbanabad, Andheri, Bombay, India
Valentine, Mrs. M., 138 Highland, Highland Park, Mich.
Valone, Katherine G., 6638 S. Marshfield, Chicago, Ill.
Van Auken, Robert A., Superintendent of Schools, North Olmsted, Ohio
Van Bruggen, John A., 1590 Innes St., N.E., Grand Rapids, Mich.
Vance, Douglas S., Mesa Public Schools, Mesa, Ariz.
Van Every, Donald F., 535 Reid Rd., Grand Blanc, Mich.
Vanderhoof, C. David, Superintendent of Schools, Little Silver, N.J.
Vander Horck, Karl J., 1892 N. Pascal, St. Paul, Minn.
Vander Linde, Louis F., 3344 Pall Dr., Warren, Mich.

Vander Meer, A. W., 627 W. Hamilton, State College, Pa.
Van de Roovaart, Elizabeth G., 203 East 113th St., Chicago, Ill.
Vanderpool, J. Alden, 1736 Escalante Way, Burlingame, Calif.
Vander Werf, Lester S., Long Island Univ., Brookville, N.Y.
Van Istendal, Theodore G., Spartan Village, East Lansing, Mich.
Van Loo, Eleanor, South Macomb Com. College, Detroit, Mich.
Van Pelt, Jacob J., 721 N. Juanita St., LaHabra, Calif.
Van Wagenen, Marvin J., 1729 Irving Ave., South, Minneapolis, Minn.
Van Zanten, Mrs. Hazel, 4754 Curwood, S.E., Grand Rapids, Mich.
Van Zwoll, James A., Col. of Educ., University of Maryland, College Park, Md.
Varn, Guy L., Supt. of Schools, 1616 Richland St., Columbia, S.C.
Varner, Charles S., Supt. of Schools, Runnells, Iowa
Varner, Leo P., Bakersfield Cntr., Fresno State Col., Bakersfield, Calif.
Varty, Jonathan W., 149 Brixton Rd., Garden City, N.Y.
Vasey, Hamilton G., 346 Second Ave., S.W., Cedar Rapids, Iowa
Vaughan, W. Donald, R. D., Pipersville, Pa.
Vaughn, C. A., Jr., Howey Academy, Howey-in-the-Hills, Fla.
Vaught, Maxine H., 1415 Crestwood Dr., Fayetteville, Ark.
Vayhinger, Harold P., Ohio Northern Univ., Ada, Ohio
Veltman, Peter, 600 College Ave., Wheaton, Ill.
Venatta, Janet R., Ball State Univ., Muncie, Ind.
Verill, John E., University of Minnesota, Duluth, Minn.
Verseput, Robert Frank, 8 South St., Dover, N.J.
Versteegh, Madge, 3407 Grand Ave., Des Moines, Iowa
Vial, Lynda W., 6522 Pennsylvania Ave., Kansas City, Mo.
Vigilante, Nicholas J., 2046 N.W. 18th Lane, Gainesville, Fla.
Vikner, Carl F., Gustavus Adolphus College, St. Peter, Minn.
Vinicombe, Harry W., Jr., 2445 Lyttonsville Rd., Silver Spring, Md.
Vint, Virginia H., 910 Snyder Drive, Bloomington, Ill.
Vislay, Patricia Jean, 1937 Greenfield Ave., Los Angeles, Calif.
Vlahakos, Irene J., Cent. Connecticut State Col., New Britain, Conn.
Vlcek, Charles, Central Washington State College, Ellensburg, Wash.
Voelker, Paul Henry, 552 N. Neville St., Pittsburgh, Pa.
Vogel, Francis X., Col. of Educ., Florida State Univ., Tallahassee, Fla.
Voigt, Harry R., St. Paul's College, Concordia, Mo.
Voigt, Virginia E., 9 East Clark Pl., South Orange, N.J.
Volante, William, 220 W. Jersey St., Elizabeth, N.J.
Vonk, Paul K., 5355 Timber Trail, N.E., Atlanta, Ga.
Voris, George A., R.D. No. 1, Goodyear Lake, Oneonta, N.Y.
Voss, Burton E., Univ. High Sch., University of Michigan, Ann Arbor, Mich.
Votaw, M. JoAnne, 1634 Neil Ave., Columbus, Ohio
Vroon, John W., 937 Woodland Ave., Knoxville, Tenn.

Wade, D. E., Col. of Educ., Univ. of Houston, Houston, Texas
Wagner, Robert W., Ohio State University, Columbus, Ohio
Wagstaff, Lonnie H., Oklahoma University, Norman, Okla.
Wagstaff, Robert F., Box 541, LeClaire, Iowa
Waimon, Morton D., Illinois State University, Normal, Ill.
Waine, Sidney I., 34 Thomas Dr., Hauppauge, N.Y.
Wainscott, Carlton O., 3607 Fleetwood, Austin, Tex.
Waldron, Margaret L., Ayrshire, Iowa
Walker, Charles Lynn, San Jose State College, San Jose, Calif.
Walker, John S., 906 N. Bittersweet Ln., Muncie, Ind.
Walker, K. P., Superintendent of Schools, Jackson, Miss.
Walker, Mary Louise, 502 Rio Vista Dr., Daytona Beach, Fla.
Walker, Robert N., 2629 Pocomoke St., North, Arlington, Va.
Walker, W. Del, Superintendent Jefferson County Schls., Lakewood, Colo.
Wall, G. S., Stout State University, Menomonie, Wis.
Wall, Harry V., 17013 Alwood St., West Covina, Calif.
Wall, Jessie S., Box 194, Univ. of So. Mississippi, Hattiesburg, Miss.
Wallace, Donald G., Col. of Educ., Drake University, Des Moines, Iowa

Wallace, Mrs. Helen, 5765 S.W. 35th St., Miami, Fla.
Wallace, James O., 1300 San Pedro Ave., San Antonio, Tex.
Wallace, Marjorie E., Wise State University, Richland, Wis.
Wallace, Morris S., Dept. of Educ., Texas Tech. College, Lubbock, Tex.
Wallace, Richard C., Holliston Public Schools, Holliston, Mass.
Wallen, Norman E., San Francisco State Col., San Francisco, Calif.
Waller, Virginia P., Henderson City Schools, Henderson, N.C.
Wallin, William H., 1765 Santa Anita, Las Vegas, Nev.
Walsh, J. Hartt, Col. of Educ., Butler University, Indianapolis, Ind.
Walsh, John E., International Textbook Co., Scranton, Pa.
Walter, Raymond L., Box 265, Millbrook, Ala.
Walter, Robert B., 434 N. DelMar Ave., San Gabriel, Calif.
Walthew, John K., 4 Larkspur Lane, Trenton, N.J.
Walz, Edgar, Concordia Senior College, Fort Wayne, Ind.
Walz, Garry R., 1718 Arbordale, Ann Arbor, Mich.
Wampler, W. Norman, Superintendent of Schools, Bellflower, Calif.
Wantoch, Mrs. Ardell H., McNeal Hall, University of Minnesota, St. Paul, Minn.
Ward, Cecil M., 112 Williams Court, Mobile, Ala.
Ward, Ted, Michigan State University, East Lansing, Mich.
Ward, Virgil S., Sch. of Educ., University of Virginia, Charlottesville, Va.
Wardeberg, Helen L., Cornell University, Ithaca, New York
Ware, Mrs. Dorothy, 109 Touraine Rd., Grosse Pointe Farms, Mich.
Warren, Alex M., 101 Eddy St., Ithaca, N.Y.
Warren, John H., 1000 Clove Rd., Staten Island, New York, N.Y.
Warren, Mary Lou, 1334 Division St., Port Huron, Mich.
Warren, Robert A., 1057 S. 9th St., East, Salt Lake City, Utah
Warshavsky, Mrs. Belle, 35 Cooper Dr., Great Neck, N.Y.
Warshavsky, Bernard, 910 West End Ave., New York, N.Y.
Warwick, Raymond, Box 73, Delmont, N.J.
Warwick, Ronald P., 5055 Jamieson, Toledo, Ohio
Washington, B. T., Williston School, 401 South 10th St., Wilmington, N.C.
Washington, Mrs. Justine W., 1228 Kent St., Augusta, Ga.
Washington, Walter, Utica Junior College, Utica, Miss.
Wasserman, Mrs. Lillian, 1684 Meadow Lane, East Meadow, N.Y.
Wasserstrom, Arthur H., 26 S. Hampton, Apt. D, Columbus, Ohio
Wasson, Margaret, 3705 University Blvd., Dallas, Tex.
Waterman, David C., Indiana State University, Terre Haute, Ind.
Waterman, Floyd T., University of Omaha, Omaha, Neb.
Waters, E. Worthington, Morgan State College, Baltimore, Md.
Waters, Mrs. Emma B., 228 E. Valley Ave., Holly Springs, Miss.
Watkins, Ralph K., 702 Ingleside Dr., Columbia, Mo.
Watkins, Ray H., Dallas Baptist College, Dallas, Tex.
Watkins, Thomas W., Supt., Wissahickon Sch. Dist., Ambler, Pa.
Watkins, W. O., Eastern New Mexico University, Portales, N.M.
Watson, Carlos M., Indiana State College, Terre Haute, Ind.
Watson, D. Gene, 5835 Kimbark Ave., Chicago, Ill.
Watson, David R., Highland Park, Ill.
Watson, John E., N. Z. Council for Educ. Res., Wellington, New Zealand
Watson, Mrs. Marie, 22 Burlington St., Bordentown, N.J.
Watson, Norman E., Orange Coast College, Costa Mesa, Calif.
Watson, Paul E., Univ. of Pittsburgh, Pittsburgh, Pa.
Watson, William Crawford, 29 Woodstock Rd., Mt. Waverly, Victoria, Australia
Watt, Ralph W., 1206 Parker Ave., Hyattsville, Md.
Wattenberg, William W., 20220 Murray Hill, Detroit, Mich.
Watters, Velma V., 1365 Mozley Pl., S.W., Atlanta, Ga.
Watts, Mrs. Helen S., University of Dubuque, Dubuque, Iowa
Wawrzyniak, Alex S., 2329 Desmond Dr., Decatur, Ga.
Waxwood, Howard B., Jr., Witherspoon School, Princeton, N.J.
Way, Gail W., 1232 Henderson St., Chicago, Ill.
Wayson, William W., 832 Westmoreland Ave., Syracuse, N.Y.
Weakley, Mrs. Mary L., 1426 Center St., Geneva, Ill.

Weaver, Gladys C., 4708 Tecumseh St., College Park, Md.
Webb, Anne K., 1402 W. Main St., Shelbyville, Ky.
Webb, E. Sue, 216 West 5th St., Shawano, Wis.
Webb, Holmes, Dept. of Educ., Texas Tech. College, Lubbock, Tex.
Webber, Warren L., Music Dept., Cedarville College, Cedarville, Ohio
Weber, Clarence A., N. Eagleville Rd., Storrs, Conn.
Weber, Martha Gesling, Bowling Green State University, Bowling Green, Ohio
Weber, Wilford A., Syracuse University, Syracuse, N.Y.
Webster, Jerome O., Superintendent of Schools, Windom, Minn.
Weddington, Rachel T., Queens College, 65-30 Kissena Blvd., Flushing, N.Y.
Weeks, Shirley, University of Hawaii, Honolulu, Hawaii
Weele, Jan C. Ter, Hanover Supv. Union # 22, Hanover, N.H.
Wees, Wilfred, Ont. Inst. for Studies in Educ., Toronto, Ont., Canada
Weesner, Gary L., 619 Hendricks Court, Marion, Ind.
Wegrzyn, Helen A., 5240 W. Newport Ave., Chicago, Ill.
Wehner, Freda, Wisconsin State College, Oshkosh, Wis.
Wehrer, Charles S., Jr., Sioux Empire Col., Hawarden, Iowa
Weicker, Jack E., South Side High School, Ft. Wayne, Ind.
Weigert, Barbara, Mercyhurst College, Erie, Pa.
Weiland, Mrs. Harry, 67-14 168th St., Flushing, N.Y.
Weilbaker, Charles R., Tchrs. Col., University of Cincinnati, Cincinnati, Ohio
Weinhold, John D., 1637 Meadow Lane, Seward, Neb.
Weintraub, Samuel, Indiana University, Bloomington, Ind.
Weis, Harold P., 437—23rd Ave., Moline, Ill.
Weisbender, Leo F., 12792 Topaz St., Garden Grove, Calif.
Weisberg, Patricia H., 9411 S. Pleasant Ave., Chicago, Ill.
Weisiger, Louise P., 2722 Hillcrest Rd., Richmond, Va.
Weiss, George D., Kutztown State College, Kutztown, Pa.
Weiss, Joel, 16 Rosedale Rd., Toronto, Ont., Canada
Weiss, M. Jerry, Jersey City State College, Jersey City, N.J.
Weissleder, Claudette P., 135 Belmont Ave., Jersey City, N.J.
Welcenbach, Frank J., Trombly School, Grosse Pointe, Mich.
Welch, Rev. Cornelius A., Siena Col., Loudonville, N.Y.
Welch, Ronald C., Sch. of Educ., Indiana University, Bloomington, Ind.
Welker, Latney C., Jr., Univ. of So. Mississippi, Hattiesburg, Miss.
Welling, Helen F., 64 E. Arndt St., Fond du Lac, Wis.
Welliver, Paul W., 715 Lenox Dr., Jackson, Miss.
Wells, Carl S., Box 485, Col. Sta., Hammond, La.
Wells, Robert S., Superintendent of Schools, Reading, Mass.
Weltner, William H., 500 Riley Rd., Muncie, Ind.
Welton, William B., Prospect Public Schools, Prospect, Conn.
Wendt, Paul R., Southern Illinois University, Carbondale, Ill.
Wenger, Roy E., Kent State University, Kent, Ohio
Wenner, Harry W., 40 Mills St., Morristown, N.J.
Wenrich, Ralph C., Sch. of Educ., University of Michigan, Ann Arbor, Mich.
Wentz, Robert E., 364 Calumet Blvd., Harvey, Ill.
Werley, Harriet H., University of Utah, Salt Lake City, Utah
Werstler, Richard E., Adrian College, Adrian, Mich.
Werth, Trostel G., 18549 S.E. Tibbetts Ct., Gresham, Ore.
Wertheim, Edward G., 13720 Shaker Blvd., Cleveland, Ohio
Wesley, Emory J., Henderson State Tchrs. Col., Arkadelphia, Ark.
Wesner, Max E., Batavia High School, Batavia, Ill.
West, Mrs. B. Bradley, 4563 Nakoma Dr., Okemos, Mich.
West, Charles K., 1005 S. Mattis Ave., Champaign, Ill.
West, Edna, 648 Sunset Blvd., Baton Rouge, La.
West, Helene, Beverly Hills H.S., 310 S. Altmont Dr., Los Angeles, Calif.
West, Lorraine W., Fresno State College, Fresno, Calif.
West, William H., Supt., County Union Schls., Elizabeth, N.J.
Westbrooks, Sadye Wylena, 1433 Sharon St., N.W., Atlanta, Ga.
Westby-Gibson, Dorothy, San Francisco State College, San Francisco, Calif.
Westlund, Hildur L., 920 North 22nd St., Superior, Wis.

Westlund, Ruth E., Northern Illinois University, DeKalb, Ill.
Westover, Frederick L., University of Alabama, University, Ala.
Wetmore, Joseph N., Dept. of Educ., Ohio Wesleyan Univ., Delaware, Ohio
Wetzel, Rev. Chester M., 55 Elizabeth St., Hartford, Conn.
Wewer, William P., 638 Buttonwood St., Anaheim, Calif.
Weyer, F. E., Dept. of Educ., Campbell College, Buies Creek, N.C.
Whalen, Barbara, Concordia Theological Seminary, Springfield, Ill.
Whalen, Thomas J., 232 Pearl St., Stoughton, Mass.
Whaley, Charles, Kentucky Educ. Assn., 101 W. Walnut St., Louisville, Ky.
Whang, H. Henry, 2620 West Prospect, Milwaukee, Wis.
Wharton, William P., Allegheny College, Meadville, Pa.
Whayland, Charles W., Glen Burnie High School, Glen Burnie, Md.
Wheat, Leonard B., Southern Illinois University, Edwardsville, Ill.
Wheeler, Elizabeth, University of Wisconsin-Milwaukee, Milwaukee, Wis.
Wheelock, Warren H., Reading Clinic, Univ. of Missouri, Kansas City, Mo.
Whelan, Gerald J., 7822 Dobson, Chicago, Ill.
Whelan, William J., Andersen EVGC, 1359 Harding Ave., Des Plaines, Ill.
Whetton, Mrs. Betty B., 1810 N. Mitchell St., Phoenix, Ariz.
Whilt, Selma E., Spring Valley, N.Y.
Whitaker, Prevo L., Indiana University, Bloomington, Ind.
White, Andrew W., Col. of Santa Fe, Cerrillos Rd., Santa Fe, N.M.
White, George L., Harcourt, Brace & World, Inc., New York, N.Y.
White, Jack, 501 Cheryl Drive, Muncie, Ind.
White, John C., Edison School, Mesa, Ariz.
White, Joseph Benton, Col. of Educ., Univ. of Florida, Gainesville, Fla.
White, Kenneth E., Dept. of Educ., Hamline Univ., St. Paul, Minn.
White, Mary Lou, 15 Park St., Orono, Me.
White, Theodore, Carver High School, Montgomery, Ala.
White, Verna, California Test Bureau, Los Angeles, Calif.
Whited, Frances M., 29 South Ave., Brockport, N.Y.
Whiteford, Emma B., 740 River Dr., St. Paul, Minn.
Whitehead, Willis A., 23351 Chagrin Blvd., Beachwood, Ohio
Whiteside, Helen, University of New Mexico, Albuquerque, N.M.
Whitmer, Dana P., Superintendent of Schools, Pontiac, Mich.
Whitmore, Keith E., 396 Oakridge Drive, Rochester, N.Y.
Whitt, Robert L., Drake Univ., Des Moines, Iowa
Whittier, C. Taylor, APA Bldg., 1200—17th St., N.W., Washington, D.C.
Wicklund, Lee A., University of Oregon, Eugene, Ore.
Wiebe, Elias H., Pacific College, Fresno, Calif.
Wiebe, Joel A., 315 S. Wilson Ave., Hillsboro, Kan.
*Wieden, Clifford O., 181 Main St., Presque Isle, Me.
Wiegand, Regis B., 182 Shenandoah Dr., Pittsburgh, Pa.
Wiggin, Gladys A., Col. of Educ., Univ. of Maryland, College Park, Md.
Wiggin, Richard G., 4151 North 25th St., Arlington, Va.
Wiggins, Thomas W., 1206 Oklahoma, Norman, Okla.
Wilber, Lora Ann, Stony Brook, L.I., N.Y.
Wilburn, D. Banks, Glenville State College, Glenville, W.Va.
Wilcox, John, State University College, Oneonta, N.Y.
Wildebush, Sarah W., 3927 Meridian Ave., Miami, Fla.
Wiley, Walter E., 620 E. Tenth Pl., Gary, Ind.
Wilhelm, Chester E., Hawthorne High School, Hawthorne, N.J.
Wilinson, Harold A., Station ACC, Abilene, Texas
Wilkerson, Doxey A., Yeshiva Univ., New York, N.Y.
Willard, Robert L., Utica College, Utica, N.Y.
Willey, Laurence V., Jr., 3001 Veazey Terrace, N.W., Washington, D.C.
Williams, Alfred H., 9712 Nova St., Pico Rivera, Calif.
Williams, Arloff L., 316½ W. Koenig St., Grand Island, Neb.
Williams, Arthur E., Dillard Comprehensive High School, Fort Lauderdale, Fla.
Williams, Mrs. B. E., Spelman College, Atlanta, Ga.
Williams, Buford W., Southwest Texas State College, San Marcos, Tex.
Williams, Byron B., University of Rochester, Rochester, N.Y.

Williams, Catharine M., Ohio State University, Columbus, Ohio
Williams, Charles C., North Texas State College, Denton, Tex.
Williams, Chester Spring, Indiana State University, Terre Haute, Ind.
Williams, Clarence M., Col. of Educ., Univ. of Rochester, Rochester, N.Y.
Williams, Donald F., Crozer Theological Seminary, Chester, Pa.
*Williams, Fannie C., 3108 Tours St., New Orleans, La.
Williams, Fountie N., 505 Pennsylvania Ave., Clarksburg, W.Va.
Williams, Frances I., Lab. Sch., Indiana State Univ., Terre Haute, Ind.
Williams, Gloria M., Univ. of Minnesota, St. Paul, Minn.
Williams, Harold A., Flat Top, W.Va.
Williams, Herman, 40 Elmwood St., Tiffin, Ohio
Williams, Howard Y., Jr., 3464 Siems Ct., St. Paul, Minn.
Williams, Mrs. Lois, 200 North 18th St., Montebello, Calif.
Williams, Malcolm, Sch. of Educ., Tennessee A. & I. University, Nashville, Tenn.
Williams, Nat, Superintendent of Schools, Lubbock, Tex.
Williams, Paul E., Danbury State College, Danbury, Conn.
Williams, Richard H., 380 Moseley Rd., Hillsborough, Calif.
Williams, Robert Alan, San Jose State Col., San Jose, Calif.
Williams, W. Morris, USAID, Philippines, APO 96528, San Francisco, Calif.
Williams, Wilbur A., Eastern Michigan University, Ypsilanti, Mich.
Williams, William K., 2342 S. Glen Ave., Decatur, Ill.
Williamson, James L., Arlington Public Schools, Arlington, Tex.
Williamson, Jane, Pacific Lutheran University, Tacoma, Wash.
Wills, Benjamin G., 1550 Bellamy St., Santa Clara, Calif.
Willsey, Alan D., SUNY College, Courtland, N.Y.
Wilshusen, John G., Jr., A. V. Center, Indiana Univ., Bloomington, Ind.
Wilson, Alan S., Hillyer Col., University of Hartford, Hartford, Conn.
Wilson, Alan T., Faircrest Sch., St. Francis, Wis.
Wilson, David A., 9125 Gross Pt. Rd., Skokie, Ill.
Wilson, David H., Seneca St., Interlaken, N.Y.
Wilson, Dustin W., Jr., 945 Forrest St., Dover, Del.
Wilson, Earl H., Sandia Labs., Albuquerque, N.M.
Wilson, Elizabeth, 3148 Que St., N.W., Washington, D.C.
Wilson, Frederick R., 336 S. Division, Ann Arbor, Mich.
Wilson, Harold M., 3006 N. Trinidad St., Arlington, Va.
Wilson, Harry T., Faulk Elementary School, West Chester, Pa.
Wilson, Herbert B., University of Arizona, Tucson, Ariz.
Wilson, James W., Rochester Institute of Technology, Rochester, N.Y.
Wilson, Jean Alice, 715 Tidball Ave., Grove City, Pa.
Wilson, John A. R., 2519 Chapala St., Santa Barbara, Calif.
Wilson, John Leod, Florida Mem. Col., St. Augustine, Fla.
Wilson, Lois, N.Y. State Teachers Assn., Albany, N.Y
Wilson, Merle A., 2800—62nd St., Des Moines, Iowa
Wilson, Robert D., Univ. of California, Los Angeles, Calif.
Wilson, Roy K., N.E.A., 1201—16th St., N.W., Washington, D.C.
Wilson, Yolande M., Sch. of Educ., Univ. of Chicago, Chicago, Ill.
Wilstach, Mrs. Ilah M., 2127 N. Eastern Ave., Los Angeles, Calif.
Wilton, K. M., Univ. of Alberta, Edmonton, Alba., Canada
Wiltse, Earl W., Northern Illinois Univ., DeKalb, Ill.
Winchell, L. R., Jr., Granville Ave. School, Margate City, N.J.
Windoes, Frederic C., Okemus, Michigan
Windsor, John G., 4354 West 9th Ave., Vancouver, B.C., Canada
Winfield, Kenneth, East Stroudsburg State Col., Stroudsburg, Pa.
Wing, Richard L., 845 Fox Meadow Rd., Yorktown Heights, N.Y.
Wing, Sherman W., Superintendent of Schools, Provo, Utah
Wingerd, Harold H., Superintendent of Schools, West Chester, Pa.
Wingren, Raef, Vought Aeronautics, Dallas, Tex.
Winkley, Carol K., 125 Forsythe Ln., DeKalb, Ill.
Winnen, Josephine, University of Wisconsin, Milwaukee, Wis.
Winsor, George E., Wilmington College, Wilmington, Ohio
Winston, Bertha H., 5942 South Parkway, Chicago, Ill.

Winter, Nathan B., 3206 Sunnyside Drive, Rockford, Ill.
Wise, Harold L., 7 Delisio Lane, Woodstock, N.Y.
Wise, Pauline, 928 Larchmont Crescent, Norfolk, Va.
Wishart, James S., 1638 Ridge Rd., West, Rochester, N.Y.
Wisniewski, Richard, Wayne State University, Detroit, Mich.
Wisniewski, Virginia, 4623 Ostrom, Lakewood, Calif.
Witchel, Barbara, 110 Ridge Ave., Passaic, N.J.
Witherspoon, W. H., P.O. Box 527, Rockhill, S.C.
Witt, Marquis G., 195-A Wing Rd., APO New York 09845
Witt, Paul W. F., Tchrs. Col., Columbia University, New York, N.Y.
Witte, Cyril M., R. 2, Box 264, Mt. Airy, Md.
Witten, Charles H., University of South Carolina, Columbia, S.C.
Witter, Sanford C., 1900 W. County Rd., St. Paul, Minn.
Wittick, Mildred Letton, 300 Pompton Rd., Wayne, N.J.
Wittmer, Arthur E., 315 Park Ave. S., Rm. 1920, New York, N.Y.
Witty, Paul A., 5555 N. Sheridan Rd., Chicago, Ill.
Wixon, John L., 29080 Oxford Ave., The Knolls, Richmond, Calif.
Wixted, William G., Marymount College, Boca Raton, Fla.
Wochner, Raymond E., Arizona State University, Tempe, Ariz.
Woerdehoff, Frank J., Dept. of Educ., Purdue University, Lafayette, Ind.
Woestehoff, Orville W., Oak Park Elementary Schls., 122 Forest Ave., Oak Park,
    Ill.
Wohlers, A. E., Ohio State University, Columbus, Ohio
Wolbrecht, Walter F., 316 Parkwood, Kirkwood, Mo.
Wold, Stanley G., 1924 Orchard Pl., Fort Collins, Colo.
Wolf, Dan B., Indiana Univ., Indianapolis, Ind.
Wolf, Helen S., 2035 Heather Terrace, Northfield, Ill.
Wolf, Ray O., Portland State College, Portland, Ore.
Wolf, Vivian C., 2020 W. Atkinson, Milwaukee, Wis.
Wolf, Willavene, Ohio State University, Columbus, Ohio
Wolf, William C., Jr., University of Massachusetts, Amherst, Mass.
Wolfe, Deborah P., Queens College, Flushing, N.Y.
Wolfe, Josephine B., Beaver Hill Apts., Jenkintown, Pa.
Wolfe, William G., Sutton Hall, University of Texas, Austin, Tex.
Wolfson, Bernice J., Schl. of Educ., Univ. of Chicago, Chicago, Ill.
Wolinsky, Gloria F., 69-52 Groton St., Forest Hills, N.Y.
Womack, James, Board of Coop. Educ'l Serv., Huntington, N.Y.
Wong, William T. S., 1640 Paula Dr., Honolulu, Hawaii
Wood, Dan, Center for Urban Educ., 33 W. 42nd St., New York, N.Y.
Wood, Donald I., Dept. of Educ., Rice University, Houston, Tex.
Wood, Joseph E., 18 Duryea Rd., Upper Montclair, N.J.
Wood, Marion C., Hanson RFD, 725 Crescent St., East Bridgewater, Mass.
Wood, Mary Margaret Andrews, University of Georgia, Athens, Ga.
Wood, Roi S., Superintendent of Schools, Joplin, Mo.
Wood, W. Clement, Fort Hays Kansas State College, Hays, Kan.
Wood, Wilma W., Supv., Elem. Educ., Washington, D.C.
Woodard, Prince B., St. Coun. of Higher Educ., Richmond, Va.
Woodburn, A. C., Alamogordo Public Schools, Alamogordo, N.M.
Woodburn, John H., Charles E. Woodward H.S., Rockville, Md.
Woodbury, Tom, Livonia Pub. Schools, Livonia, Mich.
Wooden, Maurice L., West Covina High School, West Covina, Calif.
Woods, Joanne, Univ. of Southern Calif., Los Angeles, Calif.
Woods, Robert K., Div. of Elem. Jr. H.S. Educ., Platteville, Wis.
Woodson, C. C., 435 S. Liberty St., Spartanburg, S.C.
Woodworth, Denny, Col. of Educ., Drake University, Des Moines, Iowa
Woodworth, William O., 999 Kedzie Ave., Flossmoor, Ill.
Woofter, James Andrew, 530 N. Simon St., Ada, Ohio
Woolley, Joan, 4615 Via Corona, Torrance, Calif.
Woolson, Edith L., Box 203, Imperial, Calif.
Wootton, John W., Glen Rock Public Schools, Glen Rock, N.J.

Worden, Allen J., Wise State University, Oshkosh, Wis.
Workman, Stanley, 149-07 Sanford Ave., Flushing, N.Y.
Wozencraft, Marian, State Univ. Col., Geneseo, N.Y.
Wray, Mabel Elizabeth, 224 Mower St., Worcester, Mass.
Wrenn, Michael P., 6544 Greenview Ave., Chicago, Ill.
Wright, Adele J., 275 Glencoe St., Denver, Colo.
Wright, Floyd K., 1432 Price Dr., Cape Girardeau, Mo.
Wright, John R., San Jose State College, San Jose, Calif.
Wright, Samuel Lee, 8919—91st Pl., Lanham, Md.
Wright, William H., Jr., 13542 E. Starbuck St., Whittier, Calif.
Wright, William J., 5835 Kimbark Ave., Chicago, Ill.
Wrightstone, J. Wayne, 21 Hickory Rd., Summit, N.J.
Wronski, Stanley P., Col. of Educ., Michigan State Univ., East Lansing, Mich.
Wu, Julia Tu, Hunter Col., New York, N.Y.
Wuerthner, Robert H., 353 Warren Rd., Ithaca, N.Y.
Wuolle, Mrs. Ethel, P.O. Box 173, Pine City, Minn.
Wyckoff, D. Campbell, Princeton Theological Seminary, Princeton, N.J.
Wyeth, E. R., 18111 Nordhoff St., Northridge, Calif.
Wyllie, Eugene D., Sch. of Bus., Indiana University, Bloomington, Ind.
Wynn, Willa T., 1122 N. St. Clair St., Pittsburgh, Pa.

Yamamoto, Kaoru, Col. of Educ., Penn. State Univ., University Park, Pa.
Yamashiro, Margaret, 3350 Sierra Drive, Honolulu, Hawaii
Yanis, Martin 4239-D, King George Drive, Harrisburg, Pa.
Yates, J. W., 223 Wham, Southern Illinois University, Carbondale, Ill.
Yauch, Wilbur A., Northern Illinois University, DeKalb, Ill.
Yeager, Paul M., Sheridan School, Second and Liberty Sts., Allentown, Pa.
Yee, Albert H., Univ. of Wisconsin, Madison, Wis.
Yelvington, James A., University of California, Los Angeles, Calif.
Yff, Joost, Sch. of Educ., Morehead St. Univ., Morehead, Ky.
Ylinen, Gerald A., Gustavus Adolphus College, St. Peter, Minn.
Ylisto, Ingrid P., Eastern Michigan University, Ypsilanti, Mich.
Yochim, Louise Dunn, 9545 Drake, Evanston, Ill.
York, William, Bowling Green University, Bowling Green, Ohio
Young, Carol A., Doane College, Crete, Neb.
Young, Harold L., Central Missouri State College, Warrensburg, Mo.
Young, J. E. M., Macdonald College Post Office, Quebec
Young, Jean A., Sonoma State College, Rohnert Park, Calif.
Young, John A., 35 Vincent Rd., Dedham, Mass.
Young, Michael Arthur, Univ. of North Carolina, Chapel Hill, N.C.
Young, Paul A., Judson College, Elgin, Ill.
Young, Robert W., 1 Dellwood Dr., RD 2, Long Valley, N.J.
* Young, William E., State Education Department, Albany, N.Y.
Young, William Howard, 1460 Tampa Ave., Dayton, Ohio
Youngblood, Chester E., P.O. Box 413, College, Alaska
Younie, William J., Tchrs. Col., Columbia University, New York, N.Y.
Yourd, John L., Bemidji State Col., Bemidji, Minn.
Yuhas, Theodore Frank, Educ. Dept., Ball State University, Muncie, Ind.
Yunghans, Ernest E., Wartburg College, Waverly, Iowa

Zackmeier, William, Box 710, Diamond Springs, Calif.
Zahn, D. Willard, 7118 McCallum St., Philadelphia, Pa.
Zahorsky, Mrs. Metta, San Francisco State College, San Francisco, Calif.
Zak, Eugene, 7205 Beresford Ave., Parma, Ohio
Zakrzewski, Aurelia R., 4806 Chovin St., Dearborn, Mich.
Zambito, Stephen Charles, Eastern Michigan University, Ypsilanti, Mich.
Zari, Rosalie V., Sch. of Educ., Univ. of California, Berkeley, Calif.
Zavorella, Victor, 388 W. Maple, Canton, Ill.
Zbornik, Joseph J., 3219 Clarence Ave., Berwyn, Ill.
Zdanowicz, Paul John, Supt. of Schools, Lee, Mass.
Zeiler, Edward J., 5340 N. Santa Monica Blvd., Milwaukee, Wis.

Zeldin, David, Oriel Cottage, St. Mary's Rd., Mortimer, Berkshire, England
Zeller, William D., Dept. of Educ., Illinois State Univ., Normal, Ill.
Zelmer, A. C. Lynn, 3604—26th Ave., Calgary, Alba., Canada
Zelnick, Joseph, 386 Livingston Ave., New Brunswick, N.J.
Zepper, John T., Educ. Bldg., University of New Mexico, Albuquerque, N.M.
Ziebold, Edna B., 6401 Linda Vista Rd., San Diego, Calif.
Zieman, Orlyn A., Appleton Public Schools, Appleton, Wis.
Ziemba, Walter J., St. Mary's College, Orchard Lake, Mich.
Zierman, Raymond T., 606 Virginia St., Joliet, Ill.
Zim, Herbert Spencer, Box 34, Vacation Village, Fla.
Zimmerman, Gary E., State University College, Buffalo, N.Y.
Zimmerman, Herbert M., Roosevelt High School, Chicago, Ill.
Zimmerman, William G., Jr., 26 Winthrop Rd., Hingham, Mass.
Zimnoch, W. Tresper Clarke H.S., Edgewood Dr., Westbury, L.I., N.Y.
Zintz, Miles V., 3028 Marble Ave., N.E., Albuquerque, N.M.
Ziobrowski, Stasia M., Sch. of Educ., New York Univ., New York, N.Y.
Zipper, Joseph H., 1569 West 41st St., Erie, Pa.
Zunigha, Bennie Jean, Box 354, Ft. Wingate, N.M.
Zweig, Richard L., 20800 Beach Blvd., Huntington Beach, Calif.

INFORMATION CONCERNING THE NATIONAL SOCIETY FOR
THE STUDY OF EDUCATION

1. PURPOSE. The purpose of the National Society is to promote the investigation and discussion of educational questions. To this end it holds an annual meeting and publishes a series of yearbooks.

2. ELIGIBILITY TO MEMBERSHIP. Any person who is interested in receiving its publications may become a member by sending to the Secretary-Treasurer information concerning name, title, and address, and a check for $8.00 (see Item 5), except that graduate students, on the recommendation of a faculty member, may become members by paying $6.00 for the first year of their membership. Dues for all subsequent years are the same as for other members (see Item 4).

Membership is not transferable; it is limited to individuals, and may not be held by libraries, schools, or other institutions, either directly or indirectly.

3. PERIOD OF MEMBERSHIP. Applicants for membership may not date their entrance back of the current calendar year, and all memberships terminate automatically on December 31, unless the dues for the ensuing year are paid as indicated in Item 6.

4. DUTIES AND PRIVILEGES OF MEMBERS. Members pay dues of $7.00 annually, receive a cloth-bound copy of each publication, are entitled to vote, to participate in discussion, and (under certain conditions) to hold office. The names of members are printed in the yearbooks.

Persons who are sixty years of age or above may become life members on payment of fee based on average life-expectancy of their age group. For information, apply to Secretary-Treasurer.

5. ENTRANCE FEE. New members are required the first year to pay, in addition to the dues, an entrance fee of one dollar.

6. PAYMENT OF DUES. Statements of dues are rendered in October for the following calendar year. Any member so notified whose dues remain unpaid on January 1, thereby loses his membership and can be reinstated only by paying a reinstatement fee of fifty cents.

School warrants and vouchers from institutions must be accompanied by definite information concerning the name and address of the person for whom membership fee is being paid. Statements of dues are rendered on our own form only. The Secretary's office cannot undertake to fill out special invoice forms of any sort or to affix notary's affidavit to statements or receipts.

Cancelled checks serve as receipts. Members desiring an additional receipt must enclose a stamped and addressed envelope therefor.

7. DISTRIBUTION OF YEARBOOKS TO MEMBERS. The yearbooks, ready prior to each February meeting, will be mailed from the office of the distributor, only to members whose dues for that year have been paid. Members who desire yearbooks prior to the current year must purchase them directly from the distributor (see Item 8).

8. COMMERCIAL SALES. The distribution of all yearbooks prior to the current year, and also of those of the current year not regularly mailed to members in exchange for their dues, is in the hands of the distributor, not of the Secretary. For such commercial sales, communicate directly with the University of Chicago Press, Chicago, Illinois 60637, which will gladly send a price list covering all the publications of this Society. This list is also printed in the yearbook.

9. YEARBOOKS. The yearbooks are issued about one month before the February meeting. They comprise from 600 to 800 pages annually. Unusual effort has been made to make them, on the one hand, of immediate practical value, and, on the other hand, representative of sound scholarship and scientific investigation.

10. MEETINGS. The annual meeting, at which the yearbooks are discussed, is held in February at the same time and place as the meeting of the American Association of School Administrators. Members will be notified of other meetings.

Applications for membership will be handled promptly at any time on receipt of name and address, together with check for $8.00 (or $7.50 for reinstatement). Applications entitle the new members to the yearbook slated for discussion during the calendar year the application is made.

5835 Kimbark Ave. HERMAN G. RICHEY, *Secretary-Treasurer*
Chicago, Illinois 60637

PUBLICATIONS OF THE NATIONAL SOCIETY FOR THE STUDY OF EDUCATION

NOTICE: Many of the early Yearbooks of this series are now out of print. In the following list, those titles to which an asterisk is prefixed are not available for purchase.

POSTPAID
PRICE

Distributed by
THE UNIVERSITY OF CHICAGO PRESS, CHICAGO, ILLINOIS 60637
1969